Business & Professional Ethics for Directors, Executives, & Accountants

Business & Professional Ethics for Directors, Executives, & Accountants

Leonard J. Brooks

Professor of Business Ethics & Accounting
Executive Director, Clarkson Centre for Business Ethics
Joseph L. Rotman School of Management
University of Toronto

THOMSON

SOUTH-WESTERN

THOMSON

SOUTH-WESTERN

Business & Professional Ethics for Directors, Executives, & Accountants, 3e

Leonard J. Brooks

VP/Editorial Director:
Jack W. Calhoun

VP/Editor-in-Chief:
George Werthman

Acquisitions Editor:
Julie Lindsay

Developmental Editor:
Sara E. Wilson

Marketing Manager:
Keith Chassé

Production Editor:
Chris Sears

Manufacturing Coordinator:
Doug Wilke

Media Production Editor:
Kelly Reid

Design Project Manager:
Bethany Casey

Production House:
GEX Publishing Services

Cover Designer:
Bethany Casey

Cover Images:
© Digital Vision, Ltd.

Internal Designer:
Roslyn M. Stendahl/Dapper Design,
Bethany Casey

Printer:
Thomson-West
Eagan, MN

For more information
contact South-Western,
5191 Natorp Boulevard,
Mason, Ohio 45040.
Or you can visit our Internet site at:
http://www.swlearning.com

For permission to use material from this
text or product, contact us by
Tel (800) 730-2214
Fax (800) 730-2215
http://www.thomsonrights.com

Library of Congress Control Number:
2003107630

Dedication

Business & Professional Ethics for Directors, Executives & Accountants is dedicated to deepening the understanding of how best to anticipate and respond to the ever-changing stakeholder expectations. Only by maintaining the support of their key stakeholders can an organization, profession, or individual achieve strategic objectives optimally and on a sustained basis. Engendering trust and respect will prove instrumental in building relationships and shaping the future.

I will be very pleased if I can pass along a little of what I have learned on these matters from my father and mother, Max Clarkson, Ross Skinner, Bill Brace, David Selley, Lee Preston, Tom Donaldson, W.E. Gordon, David Olive, David Nitkin, and Ed Waitzer.

I also wish to thank, with all my heart, my wife Jean and our growing family for their love, encouragement and support.

Leonard J. Brooks, Jr.
Toronto, Canada
June 2003

About the Author

Leonard J. Brooks is Professor of Business Ethics & Accounting at the Rotman School of Management of the University of Toronto. He is the Executive Director of the Rotman School's Clarkson Centre for Business Ethics & Board Effectiveness, Director of its Master of Management & Professional Accounting Program, and Director of its Diploma in Investigative & Forensic Accounting Program.

Professor Brooks is the Founding Editor of the *Corporate Ethics Monitor*, a pioneering bi-monthly publication, and is on the Editorial Board of the *Journal of Business Ethics*. He has published articles on ethics issues in journals such as the *Journal of Business Ethics*, *Accounting Organizations and Society*, *Business and Society*, and has authored or co-authored/edited the research monograph *Canadian Corporate Social Performance* and books or publications entitled *Business & Professional Ethics for Accountants (2e)*, *Principles of Stakeholder Management: The Clarkson Principles*, and *Developing and Maintaining an Ethical Corporate Culture*.

Prior to joining the University of Toronto, Professor Brooks obtained his C.A. designation (in 1970) and subsequently became an audit manager and Director of Manpower for Touche Ross & Co. (now Deloitte & Touche) in Toronto. He has served as a member, then Chairman, of the Chartered Accountants' national Board of Examiners, and Chairman of their national Syllabus Committee. Professor Brooks was made a Fellow of the Institute of Chartered Accountants of Ontario in 1982.

Professor Brooks consults to individuals, corporations, governmental and non-governmental organizations, and serves as an expert witness and frequent media-commentator. He is also a former Director of the Canadian Centre for Ethics & Corporate Policy, and a former President of the Canadian Academic Accounting Association.

June 2003

The disasters at Enron, Arthur Andersen, and WorldCom have fundamentally changed expectations for the behavior of directors, executives, and professional accountants. Good risk management practices must now incorporate ethics risk management, accountability, and governance practices that ensure the reputation of individuals, corporations, and accounting firms is protected, and that the support of stakeholders is strong enough to facilitate success. Leaving the development of ethical boundaries to trial and error—risking bad practice—is no longer acceptable.

Corporations and business professionals are now part of a new post *Sarbanes-Oxley Act* era of broadened stakeholder-oriented accountability and governance. Directors, executives, and certainly professional accountants, will soon realize this means considering the impacts and risks of their decisions on the public interest—certainly on more than the traditional short-term set of shareholder interests. Some businesspeople and professionals will want to go beyond developing a good defensive accountability and governance system to develop a competitive advantage where customers, employees, and others will be attracted by distinctly higher levels of trust based on commonly respected values such as: honesty, fairness, compassion, integrity, predictability, and responsibility.

Unless directors, executives, and professional accountants develop effective accountability, governance, and risk management processes that incorporate ethics:

- Directors will be unable to fulfil their due diligence requirements.
- Executives will be unable to develop sound competitive business models and protect their emerging legal liability.
- Professional accountants will be unable to fulfil their role as fiduciaries and as leaders in the development of accountability and governance systems.
- Corporations and the accounting profession as we know them will be further discredited and regulated.

Business & Professional Ethics provides an understanding of why ethics has become a critical success factor, the role of the Enron/Sarbanes-Oxley developments, what the implications are, how ethical behavior can be guided, how ethical decision making can be improved and made defensible, and how special problems facing directors, executives, and the accounting profession can be dealt with. This information is covered as follows:

Part I	**The Ethics Environment**
Ch. 1	Ethics Expectations
Ch. 2	Governance, Accounting, and Auditing, Post Enron
Part II	**Ethical Governance and Accountability**
Ch. 3	Corporate Ethical Governance and Accountability
Ch. 4	Professional Accounting in the Public Interest, Post Enron
Part III	**Significant Issues Facing Business & the Accounting Profession**
Ch. 5	Approaches to Ethical Decision Making
Ch. 6	Managing Risks and Opportunities Ethically

Contents

PART II   **Ethical Governance and Accountability   127**

CHAPTER 4

PART III   **Significant Issues Facing Business and the Accounting Profession 309**

CHAPTER 5   *Approaches to Ethical Decision Making* *310*

CHAPTER 6

Challenges and Opportunities

Expectations for appropriate business and professional accounting behavior have changed dramatically. The demise of Enron, Arthur Andersen, and WorldCom triggered the U.S. *Sarbanes-Oxley Act of 2002*, and galvanized reforms in the accountability and governance of both corporations and professional accounting. Ultimately, these reforms will influence business and professional ethics around the world, and bring new challenges and opportunities for directors, executives, and professional accountants.

The reforms in accountability and governance frameworks have recognized that corporations and professional accountants are more broadly accountable than recent tradition has evidenced. The crisis of corporate reporting credibility that Enron began, Arthur Andersen fostered, WorldCom capped, and the *Sarbanes-Oxley Act* (SOX) sought to remedy, heightened the awareness that corporations and the accounting profession must have the support of many stakeholder groups to achieve their strategic objectives.

That support requires trust—trust based upon the expectation that the corporation and professional accountant will do the right thing; that their actions will respect the interests of the stakeholder group. Earning and maintaining that trust will require changing the strategy, risk management, planning, operations, and decision making of the corporation to take account of the interests and expectations of stakeholder groups in addition to shareholders. It will require a new accountability framework focusing on indicators of performance related to stakeholder expectations for both internal and external reporting.

Governance will have to focus on this new, broader accountability framework in order to ensure that stakeholder trust objectives are met. Such a change will not happen by itself, and directors will be in danger of not fulfilling their risk management, due diligence expectations to shareholders if they ignore this duty. Some directors have understood the value of an excellent reputation, and have been including risks to reputation in their risk management programs. Now that the linkage between ethics, reputation, and trust has been clearly and dramatically drawn, it is timely for corporations to upgrade their accountability and governance frameworks to ensure continued support.

Professional accountants can and should provide a critical element in the trust-oriented accountability and governance system. First, professional accountants can be important agents for ensuring trust. They are expected to serve in the public interest, and must do so to preserve the trust placed in them by society that expects them to behave as a professional. This expectation, which applies to professional accountants in public practice as well as those employed by corporations, will require a rededication to their role as a trusted fiduciary. Second, professional accountants are well placed to understand the role of trust in internal control and accountability frameworks, as well as in the governance frameworks that provide direction and oversight to corporate activities.

Understanding the new trust expectations will resolve challenges and present opportunities for directors, executives, and professional accountants, and provide the essential foundation for ensuring their support in the future.

Purpose of the Book

The crisis of corporate reporting credibility became so severe in mid-2002 that drastic measures were required to restore that credibility and relieve the gridlock that froze capital markets and dampened economies around the world. In fact, pressures for enhanced corporate accountability and a supportive governance framework had been growing for years, and the financial disasters in 2002 accelerated and crystalized their impact.

Telling the story of ongoing pressures for more trusted governance, and of the contributions of the disasters at Enron, Arthur Andersen, and WorldCom, is important to the development of an appropriate understanding of the new SOX world on the part of directors, executives, and accountants. Just as sound governance has recently incorporated the need for a risk management process, now the risk management process must be broadened to involve awareness of factors that can erode the support of stakeholder groups.

The reputation of corporations is recognized as being connected with the degree to which stakeholders trust that corporations will do the right thing. In other words, there is now a concern for both what a corporation does and how it is done. At certain times in the past, the emphasis was so strongly on achieving profit that little attention was given to how the profit was earned. Now that the support of stakeholders is recognized as critical to success, understanding how to build their expectations into corporate behavior, accountability, and governance is an important second objective of the book. Extending this discussion to the new era for professional accountants, and reviewing their potential roles, is a third objective.

Directors, executives, and accountants need to understand how to make ethical decisions that are defensible to stakeholders. Codes of conduct can not cover all situations, so cultures need to be developed and decision processes utilized that are based upon sound ethical decision making frameworks. *Business & Professional Ethics* covers these topics and the development of an ethics risk management process, as well as strategies for dealing with and reporting to stakeholders, and for ensuring ethical behavior in the workplace and during the management of crises.

In a nutshell, *Business & Professional Ethics* examines the background and nature of the new stakeholder-support era of corporate and professional accountability and governance, and provides insights into the development of sound patterns of behavior on the part of directors, executives, and accountants. Successful management of ethical risks and the development of ethical competitive advantages depend upon the mastery of the subjects discussed. Professional accountants must understand the issues covered as a foundation for the fulfilment of their role as fiduciaries and experts in accountability and governance.

Applicability

Business & Professional Ethics is intended as a sourcebook for directors, executives, and professional accountants on post-Enron/SOX accountability and governance, and on appropriate decision making, behavior, and ethics risk management in the new era. Blending text, readings, and cases, it can be used as a stand-alone book in courses in business and/or professional ethics, or in governance. It is also very useful for independent study, or as an adjunct to traditional strategy, governance or accounting texts to provide access to interesting, real-world dilemmas. The material in the book has been used very successfully with MBA and Executive MBA students as well as with accounting students.

The book has been organized into relatively free-standing chapters to facilitate custom publishing of a selection of chapters and/or cases. For example, Chapter 2, which covers the Enron, Arthur Andersen, WorldCom, and Sarbanes-Oxley developments, has been well used to start off Executive MBA Programs. Similarly, directors and executives or MBA students wishing to focus on conflict of interests could benefit from Chapters 2 and 3, plus cases from other chapters. Professional accounting students should be familiar with all chapters.

The coverage provided is largely North American in orientation. Examples, readings, and cases are drawn with that perspective in mind. Basic ethical problems and principles are the same throughout North America, since they are shaped by the same concerns. Where points of difference are noteworthy, they are dealt with specifically.

Because of the prominence of North American (N.A.) capital markets, and the significant impact of the N.A. practices of the Big Four professional accounting firms, the N.A. governance frameworks for both business and professional accountants will serve as a benchmark for developments in other jurisdictions around the world. In addition, domestic and foreign expectations for behavior will be increasingly intertwined since the practices of multinational corporations or firms will be scrutinized increasingly by stakeholders active in major consumer and capital markets and in regulatory arenas around the world. Ethical behavior in international operations and international accountability are specifically explored, however, because differing cultures call for somewhat different ethical behavior.

Author's Approach

To the greatest extent possible, *Business & Professional Ethics* focuses on the development of a practical understanding of the ethical issues driving the development of emerging accountability and governance frameworks, and of the practical skills required to deal with them effectively. Of necessity, this means providing a learning experience embedded with real-life cases and examples. At the same time, these real-life problems are interpreted through exposure to classical positions and articles which have had a lasting impact on business ethics in general, and the accounting ethics in particular. The author's experience as a director, executive, and professional accountant, plus his substantial experience in the teaching of and consulting on business and accounting ethics, management control, and similar governance-related subjects, contributes significantly to the development of the issues and discussions offered.

Organization of the Book

To facilitate the purpose of the book, it is presented in three parts, each with two chapters that include a total of 46 cases, and 17 seminal readings and appendices, as follows:

		CASES	READINGS
PART I	**THE ETHICS ENVIRONMENT**		
Ch. 1	Ethics Expectations	6	3
Ch. 2	Governance, Accounting, and Auditing, Post Enron	5	-
PART II	**ETHICAL GOVERNANCE AND ACCOUNTABILITY**		
Ch. 3	Corporate Ethical Governance and Accountability	8	1
Ch. 4	Professional Accounting in the Public Interest, Post Enron	16	6
PART III	**SIGNIFICANT ISSUES FACING BUSINESS AND THE ACCOUNTING PROFESSION**		
Ch. 5	Approaches to Ethical Decision Making	4	2
Ch. 6	Managing Risks and Opportunities Ethically	7	5
		46	17

Part I provides an understanding of concerns that have been driving the development of ethics expectations both pre- and post-Enron. Chapter 1 deals with concerns traditionally felt by a range of stakeholder groups, and how these concerns produced a broadened stakeholder-oriented accountability expectation. Chapter 2 tells the story of how the Enron, Arthur Andersen, and WorldCom fiascoes precipitated the corporate reporting credibility crisis that led to the *Sarbanes-Oxley Act*, which crystallized ethics expectations into new frameworks for accountability and governance for corporations and professional accounting. Both provide a useful foundation for later chapters.

Part II examines how corporations and professional accountants can develop sound ethical accountability and governance systems that respond to the new ethics expectations. Chapter 3 covers those issues, expectations, and ethics culture promoting systems that directors and executives should understand in order to discharge their duties successfully in the modern era. Chapter 4 deals with the roles and functions of professional accountants in the new accountability system for corporations, both as agents of ethical accountability, and as experts in the development of ethical accountability and governance mechanisms. Both Chapters 3 and 4 cover conflicts of interest assessment and management, and other key elements of a modern ethics-oriented governance system.

Part III offers insights, particularly in Chapter 5, into the increasingly important area of making defensible ethical decisions when codes of conduct do not precisely fit the circumstances. Chapter 6 deals with the super critical areas of ethics risk management, stakeholder management, workplace ethics, corporate social responsibility reporting and audit, ethics for international operations, and ethical crisis management.

Each chapter presents an interesting selection of cases, a selection of very significant readings, and a useful list of references. The combination of text, 46 cases and 17 readings, provides a much richer learning experience than books that present just cases or a limited subset.

http://brooks. swlearning.com

In addition, numerous references are made in the margin where a Website link/reference or a downloadable file is available on the *Business & Professional Ethics* Website at *http://www.brooks.swlearning.com/*. This *BPE* Website is updated continuously with new information, notes, and Website links of interest.

Improvements to the Third Edition

The third edition differs substantially from the second, due to the following general and specific changes and enhancements:

- In general, the focus of the book is broadened to explore the roles and responsibilities of directors, executives, *and* professional accountants from the perspective that each must rise to the expectations that are inherent in the new stakeholder-oriented frameworks of corporate accountability and governance. Previous editions of the book dealt primarily with professional accountants and earlier expectations models.

- The Enron, Arthur Andersen, WorldCom and other recent fiascos that triggered the corporate reporting credibility crisis are analyzed. Key background reports from the Senate and Powers Committees, as well as the *Sarbanes-Oxley Act*, are downloadable from the text's Website.

- The *Sarbanes-Oxley Act of 2002*, and the accountability and governance frameworks it introduces and crystallizes are reviewed and projected for both corporations and the accounting profession.

- The emerging broadened stakeholder-oriented accountability and governance framework for corporations and professional accounting are examined providing insights into the roles and responsibilities expected of directors, executives, and professional accountants.

- Throughout the book, discussions are within a risk management framework reflecting new governance requirements promulgated by stock exchanges and regulators.

- Traditional risk management frameworks are extended to integrate new thinking on the linkages between ethics, values, reputation, and the continued support of stakeholders that is necessary for success.

- A new section is included on Threats to Good Governance and Accountability, within which is an expanded treatment of conflict of interests situations and their management.

- Enhanced coverage is provided of why and how to develop and manage an ethics-oriented culture, and how to utilize public accountability benchmarks to assist in evaluating performance.

- New internationally generated IFAC and IASB frameworks are discussed that apply to ethics codes, accounting standards, and conflict of interests for the accounting profession.

- Recent research into ethical decision making methods is included.

- A new concept—ethics risk management—is explored, as are approaches to stakeholder analysis and management. These techniques are of special significance to proper governance within the new broader stakeholder-accountability framework.

- A total of nine new cases are introduced, bringing the total to 46. New cases cover current incidents involving Martha Stewart's alleged insider trading, Ford/Firestone tire recalls, Enron, Arthur Andersen, World-Com, Elliot Sptizer straightening out the conflicts of interest on Wall Street, and AIDS in South Africa.

Acknowledgements

I have been fortunate to receive excellent suggestions for improving this and earlier versions of *Business & Professional Ethics* from Graham Tucker, Alex Milburn, Bill Langdon, Peter Jackson, and Michael Deck. But I specifically want to acknowledge the searching and insightful contributions by David Selley and particularly Ross Skinner. To my former colleague, Max Clarkson, I owe a debt of gratitude for providing the platform and encouragement for development and exercise of my ideas in the classroom and as a consultant, and the stimulation to search for new ideas to contribute to our discipline. These contributors should rest easy, however, since I did not accept all their suggestions and therefore take responsibility for any errors or omissions.

To my wife, Jean, for her continued support, and for their forbearance my children, Catherine, Len, Heather and John, their spouses Christina and Gabe, and to my granddaughter Bianca, I owe my love and respect.

The End of the Beginning

Amid the tragedy created by the Enron, Arthur Andersen, and WorldCom fiascos, there is a silver lining—the acceleration and crystalization of stakeholder-oriented accountability and governance frameworks for corporations and professional accountants. Awareness of these developments, and what they require to generate and maintain stakeholder support, provides the foundation for the roles, responsibilities, and future success of directors, executives, and professional accountants. We have entered an era wherein appropriate values held and applied hold the key to ethical behavior, reputation and sustained success. *Business & Professional Ethics* provides an orderly development of the issues and skills involved and the understanding necessary to use them effectively—hopefully for the benefit of the business community, the accounting profession, and society as a whole.

Leonard J. Brooks
Professor of Business Ethics & Accounting
Executive Director, The Clarkson Centre for Business Ethics & Board Effectiveness
Joseph L. Rotman School of Management
University of Toronto

Part One

The Ethics Environment

Introduction

Given the increasing complexity of business and professional ethics problems, unless an individual has developed a rather extraordinary interest in business and professional ethics, and has been able to pursue it daily, it is probable that he or she has not developed an adequate awareness of ethical issues. Remedying that deficiency is the purpose of Part 1.

Chapter 1 provides a guide to the rest of the book. It begins with a summary of the forces responsible for the changes in the public's expectations for corporate ethical behavior, and in turn in the public's expectations of accountants who audit those corporations as well as those who serve in the management of the corporations. Responses to these forces and related developments are reviewed, including the new mandate, governance and stakeholder accountability frameworks, new techniques for the management of reputation and ethics risks, and new perspectives on accountability and business ethics.

Chapter 2 examines the profound changes brought by the Enron, Arthur Andersen, and WorldCom debacles, including the Sarbanes-Oxley Act recommendations and related U.S. Securities and Exchange Commission pronouncements, all of which will ultimately inform change in corporate governance and the accounting profession around the world. These two chapters are intended to provide an up-to-date perspective on the changing expectations for ethical behavior for directors, executives, managers, and professional accountants.

Chapter One

Ethics Expectations

Purpose of the Chapter

Business and the professions function within a framework created by the expectations of the public. Enron and the subsequent Arthur Andersen and WorldCom fiascoes have triggered a "sea change" of new expectations for business governance and the accounting profession in the United States and Canada, and are in the process of informing expectations around the world. These new behavioral expectations are based on an acceleration of business and professional ethics trends that have been long in the making. Business and professional ethics have, in effect, entered a time warp.

This chapter explores the changes that the ethics trends have brought to the expectations framework, as well as the developments that have arisen in response to those changes. It also begins to consider what the changes in expectations mean for the professional accountant. As such, this chapter provides an introduction and overview for the book.

The Ethics Environment for Business:
The Battle for Credibility, Reputation, and Competitive Advantage

During the last two decades, there has been an increasing expectation that business exists to serve the needs of both shareholders and society. Many people have a "stake" or interest in a business, its activities, and impacts. If the interests of these stakeholders are not respected, then action that is often painful to shareholders, officers, and directors usually occurs. *In fact, it is unlikely that businesses or professions can achieve their long-run strategic objectives without the support of key stakeholders such as shareholders, employees, customers, creditors, suppliers, governments, host communities, and activists.*

The support for a business, and business in general, depends upon the credibility that stakeholders place in corporate commitments, the company's reputation, and the strength of its competitive advantage. All of these depend upon the trust that stakeholders place in a company's activities, and trust, in turn, depends upon the values underlying corporate activities.

Stakeholders increasingly expect that a company's activities will respect their values and interests. To a large extent, this respect for stakeholder values and interests determines the ethical standing and success of a corporation. Consequently, corporate directors are now expected to govern their company ethically, which means that they are to see that their executives, employees, and agents act ethically. Moreover, the corporation is increasingly expected to be accountable to stakeholders in a transparent or ethical manner. Performance assessment now extends beyond what is achieved to encompass how ethically those results were achieved.

As a result, the emerging governance and accountability regime for business and the professions has become far more concerned with stakeholder interests and ethical matters than has been the case in the past. Directors, executives, and professional accountants, who serve the often conflicting interests of shareholders directly and the public indirectly, must be aware of the public's new expectations for business and other similar organizations, and must manage their risks accordingly. More than just to serve intellectual curiosity, this awareness must be combined with traditional values and incorporated into a framework for ethical decision making and action. Otherwise, as was the case with the Enron and Arthur Andersen debacles, the credibility, reputation, and competitive advantage of capital markets, as well as the organization, management, and the profession will suffer.

What has produced this change in public expectations for business governance, behavior, and accountability? Several factors appear to share causal responsibility as indicated in Table 1.1.

TABLE 1.1

FACTORS AFFECTING PUBLIC
EXPECTATIONS FOR
BUSINESS BEHAVIOR

Physical	Quality of air and water, safety
Moral	Desire for fairness and equity at home and abroad
Bad Judgments	Operating mistakes, executive compensation
Activist stakeholders	Ethical investors, consumers, environmentalists
Economic	Weakness, pressure to survive, to falsify
Competition	Global pressures
Financial malfeasance	Numerous scandals, victims, greed
Governance failures	Recognition that good governance and ethics risk assessment matter
Accountability	Desire for transparency
Synergy	Publicity, successful changes
Institutional reinforcement	New laws—environment, whistle-blowing, recalls, U.S. Sentencing Guidelines, OECD anti-bribery regime, Sarbanes-Oxley Act (SOX) reforms, professional accounting reform

ENVIRONMENTAL CONCERNS

Nothing has galvanized public opinion about the nature of good corporate behavior more than the realization that the public's physical well-being, and the well-being of some workers, was being threatened by corporate activity. Initially, concern about air pollution centered on smokestack and exhaust pipe smog, which caused respiratory irritation and disorders. These problems were, however, relatively localized, so that when the neighboring population became sufficiently irate, local politicians were able and generally willing to draft controlling regulation, although effective enforcement was by no means assured.

Two other problems associated with air pollution, which were slower to be recognized, were acid rain, which neutered lakes and defoliated trees, and the dissipation of the earth's ozone layer. In the first case, the sulphur in exhaust gases combined with rain and fell to the ground far away from the source, often in other legal jurisdictions. Consequently, the reaction by politicians in the source jurisdiction was predictably slow, and many arguments were raised about who was responsible and whether the damage was real or not. Ultimately, however, the level of awareness of the problem became sufficiently widespread to support international treaties and more stringent local regulations.

The dissipation of the earth's ozone layer has been more recently recognized as a serious threat to our physical well-being. The release into the atmosphere of CFCs, once the most common residential and industrial refrigerant, allows CFC molecules to use up molecules of ozone. At the same time, the cutting down of the rain forests in Brazil, which were a main source for replenishing ozone, has contributed further to the depletion of the ozone layer around our planet. This layer is our major barrier from the sun's ultraviolet rays, which produce skin cancer and damage our eyes.

The timing of the recognition of water pollution as a problem worthy of action has paralleled the concern about our depleted ozone layer, partly because of our limited ability to measure minute concentrations of toxins and our inability to understand the precise nature of the risk of water-borne metals and dioxins. Corporations also asserted that they did not have the technical solutions to the elimination of air and water pollution at reasonable cost and therefore could not do so and remain competitive. However, once the short- and long-term threats to personal safety were understood, the public, led by special interest groups, began to pressure companies and governments directly to improve safety standards for corporate emissions.

Government reaction, often prompted by disasters, has been significant at all levels. Locally, no-smoking regulations have been enacted and local ordinances tightened. Environmental regulation has been the subject of international treaties. In both the United States and Canada, environmental protection acts have been enacted that feature significant fines of up to $1–$2 million per day for the corporation convicted of environmental malfeasance. In addition, personal fines and/or jail terms for officers and directors have focused the attention of executives on programs to ensure compliance with environmental standards. Nothing has energized executives in the United States and Canada more than the statement of a judge in regard to the promulgation of the U.S. Sentencing Guidelines on November 1, 1991. He said that the "demonstrated presence of an effective program of environmental protection would constitute an adequate 'due diligence' defence which could reduce the level of fine from $2 million/day to $50,000/day." While this reaction may be viewed as defensive, the "due diligence" movement should be viewed as only one phase, the codification phase, of the movement toward corporate environmental responsibility.

MORAL SENSITIVITY

During the 1980s and 1990s, there was a significant increase in the sensitivity to the lack of fairness and to discrepancies in equitable treatment normally afforded to individuals and groups in society. Several groups were responsible for this heightened social conscience, including the feminist movement and spokespeople for the mentally and physically challenged, for native people, and for minorities. To some degree, the public was prepared to entertain the concerns of these groups because unfortunate events had brought the realization that some special interest groups were worth listening to, as environmentalists, consumer advocates, and anti-apartheid supporters had shown. Also, for most of the period from 1960 onward, disposable incomes and leisure time have been sufficiently high to allow members of the public to focus on issues beyond earning their livelihood. In addition, due to the advances in satellite communications that have allowed virtually "live" coverage of worldwide problems, the thinking of the North American public has become less inner directed and parochial, and more sensitive to problems featured by wide-ranging investigative reporters.

Evidence of public pressure for more fairness and equity is readily available. The desire for equity in employment has resulted in laws, regulations, compliance conditions in contracts, and affirmative action programs in corporations. Pay equity programs have begun to appear to readjust the discrepancy between the pay scales for men and women. Consumer protection legislation has been tightened to the point that the old philosophy of "buyer beware," which tended to protect the large corporation, has been transformed to "vendor beware," which favors the individual consumer. Drug tests for employees have been handled more carefully to minimize the prospect of false findings. All of these are examples in which public pressure has brought about institutional changes through legislatures or courts for more fairness and equity and less discrimination, and therefore will be virtually impossible to reverse. The trend is unmistakable.

Moral sensitivity is also evident in international issues. The campaign to boycott buying from corporations that engage in child or sweatshop labor in foreign countries provides ample testimony to this, and has resulted in the creation of codes of ethical practice for suppliers, as well as compliance mechanisms to ensure they are followed. Organizations such as Social Accountability International and AccountAbility are developing workplace policies, standards, workplace auditor training programs, and reporting frameworks.

http://brooks.
swlearning.com

BAD JUDGMENTS AND ACTIVIST STAKEHOLDERS

Directors, executives, and managers are human, and they make mistakes. Sometimes the public, or specific groups, take offense at these instances of bad judgment and take action to make the directors and management aware that they do not approve. For example, the decision by Shell UK to scuttle the Brent Spar Oil Storage Vessel in a deep part of the ocean rather than take it apart on shore led to demonstrations in support of Greenpeace, which tried to stop the scuttling, and to the boycott of Shell gas stations in Europe. Nestle products were boycotted in North America and Europe to stop the free distribution of baby formula powder to African mothers who were mixing it with contaminated water, thereby killing their babies. Nike and other companies' products were boycotted through the efforts of concerned individuals and groups to stop the use of sweatshop and child labor, particularly in foreign countries. The recall of Firestone tires was ignited by the media, beginning with a television show in Houston, Texas. North American corporations were extravagantly overpaying their executives—including several above $50 million per year—or not reducing executive pay when profits declined, so CalPERS, the California Public Employees Pension Fund, called for the establishment of compensation committees consisting of a majority of independent directors. Activist stakeholders were clearly able to make a difference—one most people thought was for the best.

Two other kinds of activist also made their appearance in the late 1980s and early 1990s: ethical consumers and ethical investors. Ethical consumers were interested in buying products and services that were made in an ethically acceptable manner. Consequently, books such as *Shopping for a Better World, The Ethical Shopper's Guide*, and *Conscious Consumption* were published in the United States, Canada, and in the United Kingdom. They provided ratings of companies, their affiliates, and their suppliers on different performance dimensions such as the hiring and treatment of women, environmental management and performance, charity, progressive staff policies, labor relations, consumer relations, and candor at answering questions. Ethical consumers were then able to "vote with their checkbook."

Ethical investors took the view that their investments should not only make a reasonable return, but should do so in an ethical manner. Originally pioneered by large pension funds such as CalPERS and The New York City Employees Pension Fund, as well as several church investment funds, the movement has been augmented since the early 1990s by several ethical mutual funds. These ethical mutual funds employ screens that are intended to eliminate companies from consideration that are involved in so-called harmful activities such as producing tobacco products, armaments, or atomic energy or misusing animals for testing. Alternatively, individuals or mutual funds can invest in companies that have been screened by an ethical consulting service. A Boston firm, KLD Research & Analytics, provides such a screening service and has created the Domini Social Index (DSI), made up of 400 ethically screened companies. A similar service, the MJI, is available in Canada from Michael Jantzi Research, and in the United Kingdom, FSTE4Good has been created on the London Stock Exchange. The performance of these indices compares well to those for non-screened stocks in each country. A current list of ethical mutual funds and an update on socially responsible investing (SRI) can be found at the Websites of SRI in the United States and the Social Investment Organization (SIO) in Canada. Many consultants offer screening services to investors on a fee-for-service basis. The entire field of ethically screened investing has continued to grow.

http://brooks.
swlearning.com

These developments signal that business decisions are being judged against different standards than before, by groups that have billions at their disposal. For additional information, contact the Investor Responsibility Research Centre (IRRC) and similar Websites.

ECONOMIC AND COMPETITIVE PRESSURES

While the public's expectations have been affected directly by the factors already discussed, a number of underlying or secondary factors are also at work. For instance, in general, the pace of economic activity slowed during the late 1980s, early 1990s, and just before and after the millennium. This placed corporations and the individuals in them in the position of having to wrestle with "no growth" or shrinking volume scenarios instead of the expansion that had been the norm. In the 1990s, growing pressure from global competitors and the drive for improved, costly technology shrank profit margins. Absence of growth and shrinking margins led to downsizing to maintain overall profitability and desirability to capital markets. Whether to maintain jobs, volume-incentive-based earnings, or their companies, some people have resorted to questionable ethical practices, including falsification of transactions and other records, and the exploitation of the environment or workers. The result has been part of the reason for triggering the cases of environmental or financial malfeasance.

The development of global markets has led to the manufacture and sourcing of products throughout the world. The accompanying restructuring has been viewed as enabling greater productivity and lower costs with lower rates of domestic employment. Therefore, the pressure on employed individuals to maintain their jobs may not abate as production increases. Nor, given greater competition, will greater volume necessarily increase profit, so the pressure on corporations probably will not return to levels experienced in the past. As a consequence, corporations will be unable to rely on a return to profitability to restore the risk of unethical behavior to former levels. It would appear that a return to former risk levels will depend on the institution of new regimes of ethical-behavior management and governance.

FINANCIAL SCANDALS: THE EXPECTATIONS GAP AND THE CREDIBILITY GAP

There is no doubt that the public has been surprised, stunned, dismayed, and devastated by financial fiascos. The list of recent classic examples includes Enron, WorldCom, Waste Management, Sunbeam, Adelphia, Tyco, Barings Bank, Livent, Philips Services, and Bre-X, as well as the slightly older U.S. Savings and Loan bankruptcies and bailout and the bankruptcies of several real estate companies.

As a result of these repeated shocks, the public has become cynical about the financial integrity of corporations, so much so that the term *expectations gap* has been coined to describe the difference between what the public thinks it is getting in audited financial statements and what it is actually getting. The public outrage over repeated financial fiascos has led, in both the United States and Canada, to tighter regulation; higher fines; and investigations into the integrity, independence, and role of the accounting and auditing profession, and more recently of executives and directors.

On a broader basis, continuing financial malfeasance has led to a crisis of confidence over corporate reporting and governance. This lack of credibility has spread from financial stewardship to encompass the other spheres of corporate activity, and has become known as the *credibility gap*. Audit committees and ethics committees, both peopled by a majority of outside directors; the widespread creation of corporate codes of conduct; and the increase of corporate reporting designed to promote the integrity of the corporation all testify to the importance being assigned to this crisis.

No longer is it presumed that "whatever company 'X' does is in the best interests of the country." Fiascos related to the environment or to dealings with employees, customers, shareholders, or creditors have put the onus on corporations to manage their affairs more ethically and to demonstrate that they have done so.

Devastated by the sequence of U.S. disasters in 2001 and 2002 involving Enron, Arthur Andersen, and WorldCom, public confidence evaporated in the business community, its financial reporting, and in the accounting profession. Capital markets were reeling. President Bush and other business leaders strove to restore lost confidence, but their efforts were largely in vain. Finally, in record time, the U.S. Congress and Senate passed the Sarbanes-Oxley Act of 2002 (SOX) on July 30. That Act provides for the reform of both corporate governance and the accounting profession, first in the United States, then indirectly in Canada and around the world. Further details are provided in the next chapter.

GOVERNANCE FAILURES AND RISK ASSESSMENT

The Enron, Arthur Andersen, and WorldCom series of disasters made clear that existing modes of governing companies and reporting on their activities were not sufficient to protect investors' interests and, more broadly, the public interest in orderly markets and corporate activities.

Corporate directors have been expected to ensure that their corporations have been acting in the interests of investors within the range of activity deemed suitable by the societies in which they operated. But in the Enron, WorldCom, and other cases, the oversight by company directors failed to contain the greed of executives, managers, and other employees. These and other companies were out of control, and unacceptable practices resulted. To quote the U.S. Senate's report on the *Role of the Board of Directors in the Collapse of Enron*:

> (1) **Fiduciary Failure**. The Enron Board of Directors failed to safeguard Enron shareholders and contributed to the collapse of the seventh largest public company in the United States, by allowing Enron to engage in high risk accounting, inappropriate conflict of interest transactions, extensive undisclosed off-the-books activities, and excessive executive compensation. The Board witnessed numerous indications of questionable practices by Enron management over several years, but chose to ignore them to the detriment of Enron shareholders, employees and business associates.
>
> *Role of the Board of Directors in the Collapse of Enron,*
> U.S. Senate's Permanent Subcommittee on Investigations, 2002, 3.

Clearly, the public was fed up with directors, executives, and others enriching themselves at the public's expense. It was evident that directors and executives were not identifying, assessing, and managing ethics risks in the same manner or depth that they were for other business risks. But the Enron, Arthur Andersen, and WorldCom cases resulted in the bankruptcy of two of the world's largest companies and the disappearance of one of the world's most respected professional accounting firms within a year. This sudden reversal of fortunes, due to the failure to govern ethics risks, changed the calculus of risk management profoundly. The probability of catastrophic failure due to unmanaged ethics risks was undeniably real, and much higher than anyone expected.

Governance reform was perceived as necessary to protect the public interest; where directors had been expected to assess and make sure that the risks faced by their corporation were properly managed, ethics risks were now seen to be a key aspect of the process. Governance reform to ensure this would happen was overdue.

INCREASED ACCOUNTABILITY DESIRED

The lack of trust in corporate processes and activities also spawned the desire for increased accountability on the part of investors and particularly by other stakeholders. Companies around the world have responded by publishing more information on their Websites as well as free-standing reports on their corporate social responsibility performance, including such subjects as environmental, health and safety, philanthropic, and other social impacts. While some information in these reports is skewed toward management objectives, the advent of external verification and the reaction to misinformation are gradually improving the information content involved. The trend is definitely toward increased nonfinancial reporting to match the public's growing expectations.

SYNERGY AMONG FACTORS AND INSTITUTIONAL REINFORCEMENT

Linkages among the factors affecting public expectations for ethical performance have already been identified, but not the extent to which these linkages reinforce each other and add to the public's desire for action. Few days go by where the daily newspapers, radio, and television do not feature a financial fiasco, a product safety issue, an environmental problem, or an article on gender equity or discrimination. In aggregate, the result is a cumulative heightening of the public's awareness of the need for controls on unethical corporate behavior. In addition, many examples are emerging where business executives did not make the right decision and ethical consumers or investors acted and were successful in making companies change their practices or improve their governance structures to ensure that future decision processes were more wholesome. The entire ethical consumer and SRI movement has been strengthened by the knowledge that acting on their concerns can make companies and society better, not poorer.

In turn, the public's awareness impacts on politicians, who react by preparing new laws or the tightening of regulations. In effect, the many issues reaching the public's consciousness result in institutional reinforcement and codification in the laws of the land. The multiplicity of ethical problems receiving exposure is focusing thought on the need for more ethical action, much like a snowball gathering speed as it goes downhill.

One of the most important examples of new legislation is the U.S. Sentencing Guidelines of 1991. As noted previously, it spawned a significant interest by directors and executives everywhere in North America as to whether their companies were providing enough guidance to their personnel about proper behavior. The consequences for not doing so in the past had been minor since directors and senior officers had rarely been held personally accountable for the actions of their employees, and their companies had been able to escape significant fines.

A second example is the new anti-bribery regime spawned by Transparency International's influence upon the OECD, some 30 of whose member countries have signed a protocol declaring that they will enact anti-bribery legislation similar to that of the U.S. Foreign Corrupt Practices Act, which bans bribery of foreign officials. The new anti-bribery regime is more advanced in that it seeks to facilitate extra-territorial legal action.

Another example is the Sarbanes-Oxley Act of 2002, which is driving the reform of corporate governance and professional accounting.

OUTCOMES

Broadly speaking, public expectations have been changed to exhibit less tolerance, heightened moral consciousness, and higher expectations of business behavior. In response to this heightening of expectations, a number of watchdogs and advisors have emerged to help or harry the public and business. Organizations such as Greenpeace, Pollution Probe, and CERES (formerly the Sierra Club) now maintain a watching brief on the business-environment interface. Consultants are available to advise corporations and so-called "ethical" investors on how to screen activities and investments for both profitability and ethical integrity. Mutual funds that specialize in ethical investments have sprung up to serve the needs of small investors. Large investor activity has also become evident as many public-sector and not-for-profit pension funds have taken active interest in the governance of their investee corporations and have presented shareholder resolutions designed to cover their concerns. In the face of all of this interest, politicians have responded by increasing regulations and the fines and penalties (both personal and corporate) involved for malfeasance. The credibility gap has not favored business organizations. Lack of credibility has brought increasing regulation and profound changes in governance and management practices.

New Expectations for Business

NEW MANDATE FOR BUSINESS

The changes in public expectations have triggered, in turn, an evolution in the mandate for business: the laissez-faire, profit-only world of Milton Friedman has given way to the view that business exists to serve society, not the other way around. For some, this may be stating the degree of change too strongly; but even they would concede that the relationship of business to society is one of interdependence where the long-run health of one determines that of the other.

In many forums, Milton Friedman made the following case:

> In a free-enterprise, private property system a corporate executive...has [the] responsibility to make as much money as possible while conforming to the basic rules of society, both...in law and in ethical custom.

> [This is] the appropriate way to determine the allocation of scarce resources to alternative uses.

Friedman, 1970

While there are many arguments for and against this position (see Mulligan, 1986), there are three critical issues that deserve mention. They are (1) the deviation from a profit-only focus does not mean that profit will fall—in fact, profit may rise; (2) profit is now recognized as an incomplete measure of corporate performance and therefore a inaccurate measure for resource allocation; and (3) Friedman explicitly expected that performance would be within the law and ethical custom.

First, there is the myth that business could not afford to be ethical because too many opportunities would be given up for profit to be maximized, or that executives could not afford to divert their attention from profit or else profit would fall. In fact, research studies exist that show short-term profits increasing as well as decreasing when social objectives are taken into account by executives.[1] However, two long-term perspectives also strengthen the case that social and profit goals can mix profitably. The first is a study by Max Clarkson (1988), which ranked the social performance of more than sixty companies on a modified Wartick and Cochran (1985) scale and found that above-average social performance is positively correlated with profits. The second is that the performance of some ethical mutual funds, such as the Parnassus Fund (U.S.) and the Investors Summa Fund (Canada), have surpassed that of the New York Stock Exchange as measured by the Standard & Poor's (S&P) Index or the Toronto Stock Exchange Indices, and a weighted index of 400 ethically screened U.S. stocks—the Domini Social Index—often outperforms the S&P 500. These perspectives are neither conclusive nor exhaustive, nor do they clarify causality. They should, however, give some comfort to executives who hear the theoretical argument that the health of society and the business in it are interdependent, but who are wavering on the implementing a multiple-objective structure.

The second aspect of the Friedman argument, which has eroded since it was first proposed, is the accuracy with which profit guides the allocation of resources to their best use for society. In 1970, when Friedman began to articulate the profit-resource linkage, there was virtually no cost ascribed to the air and water used in the manufacturing process, nor was a significant cost ascribed to the disposal or treatment of wastes. Since the 1980s, the costs of these so-called "externalities" have skyrocketed, yet they still are not fully included in calculating the profit for the year for the polluting company under generally accepted accounting principles. Often, pollution costs are borne by and charged against the profits of other companies, towns, or governments, so the profit-maximization: best-allocation-of-resources linkage is far less direct than Friedman originally envisaged. As the cost associated with these and other externalities rises, the profit: best-resource-use linkage promises to become less and less useful unless the framework of traditional profit computations is modified or supplemented. Perhaps environmental accounting or schemes by which companies buy pollution credits will yield some relief from this dilemma in the future.

Finally, Milton Friedman himself expressed the view that profit was to be sought within the laws and ethical customs of society. This is not appreciated by many who argue for profit-only in its strongest, laissez-faire, bare-knuckled form. Obviously, chaos would result if business was carried out in a no-holds-barred environment. A minimum framework of rules is essential for the effective, low-cost, credible working of our markets and the protection of all participants. Increased regulation is one response to outrageous behavior, or to the increasing ethical needs of society. What most profit-only advocates fail to see is that the alternative to increasing regulation by government is an increasing self-emphasis on better ethical governance and behavior.

---

[1]See, for example, the study by Curtis Verschoor, 1998.

For these reasons, the profit-only mandate of corporations is evolving to one recognizing the interdependence of business and society. Future success will depend on the degree to which business can balance both profit and the interests of other stakeholders. This, in turn, will be impossible to manage unless new governance and reporting structures emerge. If ethical and economic objectives cannot be integrated or balanced successfully, and the interests of shareholders continue to unreasonably dominate those of stakeholders, the tension between business and society's stakeholders will continue to grow. Fortunately, the mandate for business is changing so the focus is shifting from a narrow shareholder-oriented view of what business should be achieving to include a broader stakeholder-oriented set of objectives. *Judgments of the future success of corporations will be made within the broader stakeholder-oriented framework, including both what is achieved and how it is achieved.*

NEW GOVERNANCE AND ACCOUNTABILITY FRAMEWORKS

Based upon this analysis, successful corporations would be best served by governance and accountability mechanisms that focus on a different and broader set of fiduciary relationships than in the past. The allegiances of directors and executives must reflect stakeholder interests in terms of goals, processes and outcomes. Governance objectives and processes must direct attention to these new perspectives, and modern accountability frameworks should include reports that focus on them. If not, the public's expectations will not be met, and regulations may be created to ensure such attention and focus.

REINFORCED FIDUCIARY ROLE FOR PROFESSIONAL ACCOUNTANTS

The public's expectations for trustworthy reports on corporate performance cannot be met unless the professional accountants that prepare or audit those reports focus their primary loyalty on the public interest and adopt principles such as independence of judgment, objectivity, and integrity that protect the public interest. Loyalty to management and/or directors can be misguided because they have frequently proven to be so self-interested that they are untrustworthy. Directors who are supposed to govern management often rely extensively upon professional accountants to fulfill their fiduciary responsibilities. Consequently, the primary fiduciary responsibility of professional accountants should be to the public, or to the public interest. Otherwise, the expectations of stakeholders in society will not be met, and the credibility of corporations will erode, as will the credibility and reputation of the accounting profession.

This is not a new assignment. However, as shown in the Enron, Arthur Andersen, and WorldCom cases, professional accountants have lost track of whom they should ultimately be responsible to. Failure to understand this expectation, and the underpinning values of independence, integrity, and objective judgment and reporting, caused the failure of the entire Arthur Andersen firm.

In addition, these corporate failures have brought the realization that loyalty to the public means more than just loyalty to current investors. Future investors rely upon financial reports, and their interests need to be protected as well as those of other stakeholders in the corporation's broadened fiduciary model.

Reform of the accounting profession is underway in order to reinforce these expectations of the public.

EMERGING GOVERNANCE AND STAKEHOLDER ACCOUNTABILITY MODELS

The reaction by business to the evolution from a profit-only mandate to one recognizing the interdependence of business and society became more readily observable as the 1980s progressed. In addition, several other important trends developed as a result of economic and competitive pressures that had and continue to have an effect on the ethics of business and therefore on the professional accountant. These trends included

- expanding legal liability for corporate directors, and
- management assertions to shareholders on the adequacy of internal controls,

even though significant changes were also occurring in how organizations operate, including

- delayering, employee empowerment, and the use of electronic data interfaces, and
- increased reliance by management on nonfinancial performance indicators used on a real-time basis.

As a result of these trends and changes, corporations began to take a much greater interest in how ethical their activities were, and how to ensure that ethical problems did not arise. It became evident that the traditional command and control (top down) approach was not sufficient, and that organizations needed to create an environment favorable to ethical behavior to foster it, not to impose it. Boards and management were becoming more interested in ethical issues—and partly because—the larger size, quicker pace, and complexity of business entities and dealings were decreasing the ability to check and inspect the decisions of others. The factors have reinforced the need for each employee have a personal code of behavior that is compatible with that of the employer.

The initial corporate reaction to a more demanding ethical environment was the desire to know how ethical its activities have been, then to attempt to manage employees' actions by developing a code of ethics/conduct. After implementing the code, the desire was to monitor activities in relation to it and to report on that behavior, first internally and then externally.

The desire to know about the appropriateness of their activities led many corporations to undertake an inventory of significant impacts on various aspects of society. Often organized by program and by stakeholder group, these listings could be used to identify specific issues, policies, products, or programs that were the most problematic and which therefore needed earliest remedial attention.

It quickly became clear that the "inventory and fix" approach led to a "patched-up" system for governing employee behavior: one that was incomplete and did not offer ethical guidance on all or even most issues to be faced. Employees who had committed a malfeasance, whether voluntarily or not, could still frequently claim that "nobody told me not to do it." In order to reduce this vulnerability and provide adequate guidance, corporations began to develop and implement comprehensive codes of conduct/ethics.

Neither easy to develop nor universally accepted, codes usually had to be refined through a number of revisions. Implementation processes also had to be improved. Even today some executives are uncertain of their role and how to play it most successfully to facilitate strong commitment by employees to the ethical principles involved. More detailed information on the role, nature, content, and monitoring of performance relative to codes is provided in Chapter 3. It is evident that codes of conduct will continue to be the touchstone for the ethical guidance of employees for the foreseeable future.

Although codes of conduct offer an essential framework for employee decision making and control, those corporations in highly vulnerable positions due to their products or productive processes found it in their interest to develop early warning information systems to facilitate fast remedial action in the event of a problem. For instance, Occidental Petroleum recognized its capacity to damage the environment and created a three-tier, notification-to-head-office requirement to provide timely information to senior management and experts in cleanup procedures. Depending on the seriousness of the environmental problem, a "significant matter" had to be reported by computer immediately, an "excursion" within twelve hours (the next business day in New York), and a "reportable incident" within the next reporting cycle (Friedman, 1988). This type of notification system is essential to facilitate crisis management activities and to mobilize response resources on a worldwide basis in an effort to reduce the impact of the problem on the environment and the corporation.

Not content to encourage the use of ethics just through a code of conduct, leading-edge corporations sought ways to inculcate ethics into their corporate culture to foster specific consideration of ethical conduct in operating decisions, in strategic decision making, and in crisis management practices. Mechanisms were developed to ensure that ethical principles were understood, reinforced, and not lost sight of, including general training and training to instill decision frameworks designed to produce sound ethical decisions; compliance check-off lists; the encouragement of internal whistle-blowing to ombudspersons; mind-focusing scorecards and categorizations for operations and strategies; inclusion of ethical performance as a factor in the determination of remuneration and in continuing internal and external reports; the creation of specific ethical operating goals such as for equity employment levels; and the creation of executive positions such as vice president for environmental affairs, and of specific sub-committees of the board of directors to oversee the ethical performance of the corporation.

Although the commitment to these mechanisms grew during the 1980s and early 1990s, nothing galvanized the corporate community more than (1) the promulgation of the U.S. Sentencing Guidelines for environmental offences on November 1, 1991, which led to widespread concern about "due diligence" procedures, and (2) the realization in the summer of 1992 that GE had been sued under the False Claims Act in the United States for $70 million by a whistle-blower too fearful of retribution to report internally to the company (Singer, 1992, p.19). The fact that the whistle-blower could receive up to 25 percent of the outcome was considered shocking, just as the size of the fines in the Sentencing Guidelines had been a year earlier. In combination, these events matured the realization that corporations ought to create an ethical operating environment in order to protect their interests and those of others with a stake in the activities of the corporation.

As a result of the U.S. Sentencing Guidelines, many U.S. directors and executives suddenly became very interested in the governance mechanism that was to convey appropriate guidance to their personnel. U.S.-owned foreign subsidiaries were also involved, as were foreign-owned multinational companies operating in the United States. Consequently, and with the additional stiffening of penalties for environmental malfeasance in Canada, the governance structures of major companies that had been primarily focused on making a profit now began to include a serious focus on how that profit was made.

Early in 1994, Lynn Sharp Paine published a seminal article in the *Harvard Business Review* entitled "Managing for Integrity" in which she made the case for integrating ethics and management. It is reproduced as a reading at the end of the chapter. At about the same time, pronouncements from the Toronto Stock Exchange[2] (1994) and the Canadian Institute of Chartered Accountants[3] (1995) specified that directors were to provide the "social conscience" of their companies and that they were responsible for developing and maintaining an ethical culture at their companies sufficient to support an adequate system of internal control. Without adequate ethical grounds for systems of internal control, the financial statements of the enterprise would be of varying accuracy, and the actions of employees might or might not correspond with what the directors and senior executives hoped. Many examples are available that attest to the fact that without adequate ethical underpinning, companies can get into difficulty.

Later, in 1996, the Caremark National case,[4] which was decided in the Chancery Court of Delaware, added to directors' responsibilities the requirement of proactively seeking out ethical problems. Until this case was decided, directors could claim "hear no evil, see no evil" to avoid prosecution for some corporate wrongdoing, so there were times that directors "didn't want to hear about…" for their own protection. Unfortunately, that left the corporation rudderless. The bottom line is that the expectations for proper corporate governance have changed, and directors are responding—some more quickly than others.

Also during the 1990s, it became understood that management approaches must reflect accountability to stakeholders, not just shareholders. Companies have a wide range of stakeholders—employees, customers, shareholders, suppliers, lenders, environmentalists, governments, and so on—who have a stake in the activities or impacts of the corporation. Even though these stakeholders may not have a legal claim on the corporation, they can influence its fortunes in the short and long runs. Consequently, if a corporation wants to achieve its strategic objectives optimally, the interests of its stakeholders should be taken into account when management make decisions. The best way to do this is to build the recognition of stakeholder interests into the strategic planning exercise. Further insight into the principles of stakeholder management can be found at the *Redefining the Corporation Project* Website (see the text's Website for a link to this site). Schematically, the emerging stakeholder accountability and governance frameworks are represented in Figures 1.1 and 1.2.

http://brooks.swlearning.com

---

[2]See paragraphs 4.3 and 4.4 on page 17 of the *Report of the Toronto Stock Exchange Committee on Corporate Governance in Canada,* December 1994.

[3]See page 2, paragraph 8 of *Guidance for Directors—Governance Processes for Control,* December 1995, published by the Canadian Institute of Chartered Accountants, Toronto, Canada. See also pages 8 and 9 for a discussion of approving and monitoring the organization's ethical values.

[4]See law case summary: Caremark National Inc., in the Readings section of this chapter.

FIGURE 1.1

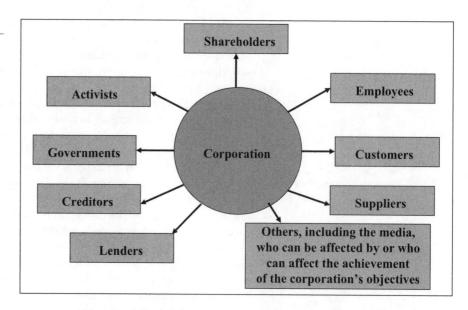

FIGURE 1.2

CORPORATE GOVERNANCE
FRAMEWORK

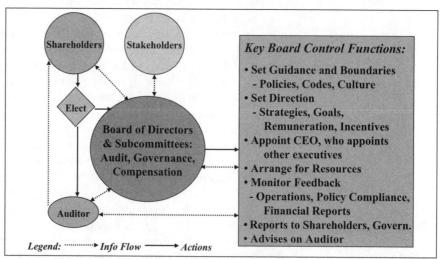

MANAGEMENT BASED ON VALUES, REPUTATION, AND RISKS

In order to incorporate the interests of stakeholders into the policies, strategies, and operations of their corporation, directors, executives, managers, and other employees must understand the nature of their stakeholders' interests and the values that underpin them. The reputation of the company and the degree of support garnered from stakeholders will depend on this understanding and upon the ability of the company to manage the risks facing the company directly as well as those impacting its stakeholders.

Numerous approaches have been developed for examining the interests of stakeholders, including surveys, focus groups, and mapping according to stereotypes. These will be developed more extensively in Chapter 4.

In addition, investigation is underway on the values that lie behind stakeholder interests so that a corporation's policies, strategies, and procedures can take them into account. These values differ somewhat depending on the stakeholder group, as well as regional differences. However, progress has been made toward a set of *hypernorms*—values that are respected by most groups or cultures around the world. According to researchers, the six values known to come closest to universal application around the world are those noted in Table 1.2.

Importance

A *hypernorm* is a value that is almost universally respected by stakeholder groups. Therefore, if a company's activities respect a hypernorm, the company is likely to be respected by stakeholder groups and will encourage stakeholder support for company activities.

Hypernorms involve the demonstration of the following basic values
Honesty, Fairness, Compassion, Integrity, Predictability, Responsibility

Source: R. Berenbeim, The Conference Board, Inc., 1999.[5]

The relevance of these six hypernorms is significant to the future success of corporations. Consequently, they should be built into a corporation's code of conduct, policies, strategies, and activities in an attempt to make sure that the interests of many stakeholder groups are respected, and that the corporation's reputation will generate maximum support.

Reputation has also been a subject of considerable recent study. Not surprisingly, the factors seen as important determinants of reputation are closely aligned with the hypernorms previously identified. Charles Fombrun, of the Reputation Institute, has specified four determinants as identified in Figure 1.3.

Both management and auditors have become increasingly risk management oriented since the mid-1990s. Risk management techniques have been developing as directors, executives, and professional accountants recognize the value in identifying risks early and in planning to avoid or mitigate the unfortunate consequences inherent in the risks. Professional accountants

FIGURE 1.3

DETERMINANTS OF
REPUTATION

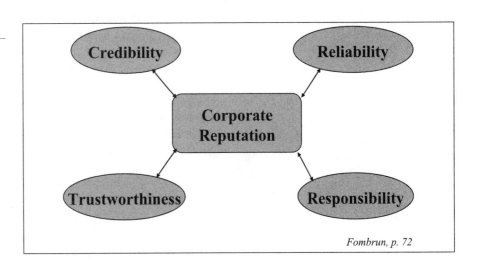

Fombrun, p. 72

---

[5]Ronald E. Berenbeim, The Conference Board, Director, Working Group on Global Business Ethics Principles.

have also shifted their audit approach to the examination of the risks facing a corporation, how the corporation has provided for these risks operationally, and how they have been accounted for in the records and financial reports.

An early study by Mercer Management Consulting identifies some of the risks that were important in companies that experienced large stock price drops between 1993 and 1998. The findings are shown in Table 1.3.

TABLE 1.3

RISK EVENTS CAUSING DROPS OF OVER 25% SHARE VALUE, PERCENTAGE OF *FORTUNE 1000* COMPANIES, 1993–1998

Strategic (58%)	Customer demand shortfall (24%)
	Competitive pressure (12%)
	M & A Integration problems (7%)
	Misaligned products (6%)
	Others (9%)
Operational (31%)	Cost overruns (11%)
	Accounting irregularities (7%)
	Management ineffectiveness (7%)
	Supply chain pressures (6%)
Financial (6%)	Foreign, macro-economic, interest rates
Hazard and other (5%)	Lawsuits, natural disasters

Source: Mercer Management Consulting/Institute of Internal Auditors, 2001.

Companies had not looking systematically for such risks, but as the 1990s came to a conclusion, risk identification and assessment was becoming an important part of strategic and operational management processes, and the oversight of the risk management process was becoming an important part of directors' due diligence activities. Several studies have been published that provide insights on the subject, including those by the Institute of Internal Auditors (2001), the American Institute of Certified Public Accountants (AICPA) and the Canadian Institute of Chartered Accountants (CICA), (2001). Important risk management terms are reproduced in Table 1.4.

Several approaches to the identification and classification of risks exist. The choice of the most appropriate depends upon the nature and scope of the enterprise being assessed, and a full study of the factors involved in that choice is beyond the scope of this book.

TABLE 1.4

IMPORTANT RISK MANAGEMENT TERMS

Risk is the chance of something happening that will have an impact on objectives.

Risk Management includes the culture, processes, and structures that are directed towards the effective management of potential opportunities and adverse effects.

Risk Management Process includes the systematic application of management policies, procedures, and practices to the tasks of establishing the context, identifying, analyzing, assessing, managing, monitoring, and communicating risk.

Source: *Managing Risk in the New Economy*, AICPA & CICA, 2001, p. 4

However, *the risks of failing to meet the expectations of stakeholders* have proven to be so important in the Martha Stewart, Firestone tire recall, Enron, Arthur Andersen, WorldCom, and other similar cases that it would be a serious mistake not to include them in the risk management process. These risks can be referred to as *ethics risks*. A representative list is provided in Table 1.5.

STAKEHOLDER EXPECTATIONS NOT MET	ETHICS RISK
Shareholders	
Stealing, misuse of funds or assets	Honesty, integrity
Conflict of interests with officers	Predictability, responsibility
Performance level	Responsibility, honesty
Reporting transparency, accuracy	Honesty, integrity
Employees	
Safety	Fairness
Diversity	Fairness
Child and/or sweatshop labor	Compassion, fairness
Customers	
Safety	Fairness
Performance	Fairness, integrity
Environmentalists	
Pollution	Integrity, responsibility

In summary, particularly in view of the Enron, Arthur Andersen, WorldCom, and other cases, directors, executives, and professional accountants will find that meeting the expectations of stakeholders is increasingly important. This will involve delving into the values that determine a corporation's reputation, and managing those values so that potential risks are avoided and/or effectively mitigated. To ignore these ethics risks is to risk the fates evident in earlier corporate debacles.

ACCOUNTABILITY

The rise of stakeholder interest and accountability, and the stunning financial debacles of Enron, Arthur Andersen, and WorldCom, has raised the desire for reports that are more relevant to the various interests of stakeholders, more transparent, and more accurate than in the past. In general, it is recognized that corporate reports frequently lack integrity because they do not cover some issues, nor is there always a clear, balanced presentation of how the interests of stakeholders will be affected. Sometimes issues will be mentioned, but in such an obtuse or unclear manner that the lack of transparency will cloud the understanding of the reader. Accuracy, or faithful representation is, of course, fundamental to an understanding of the underlying facts.

The needed improvement in integrity, transparency, and accuracy has motivated the discussion among accountants about the nature of the guidelines they should use for preparation of financial reports—rules or principles. Enron's financial reports clearly lacked integrity, transparency, and accuracy, but they may have been in accord with a very narrow, rules-based interpretation of generally accepted accounting standards and legal definitions. Chapter 2 identifies how accounting rules and legal interpretations with regard to special purpose entities allowed Enron's board and executives to mislead the public, and professional accountants to rationalize their participation in the process and even provide a clean audit certification of the misleading reports. Even though Enron's reports were probably technically compliant with existing U.S. rules was taken as satisfactory, even though they did not show the whole story transparently or accurately, and many people were misled. The misuse of rules allowed fraud-intent Enron executives to take advantage of the reporting system. Principles, however, based upon integrity, transparency, and accuracy are considered by many to provide more robust guidance than rules against such misuse.

The desire for relevancy has spawned many reports that are principally nonfinancial in nature, and tailored to the needs of specific stakeholders. These stakeholder reports, which are discussed more fully in Chapter 6, cover topics such as those identified in Table 1.6. They appear in hard copy and on corporate Websites. Broadly applicable reporting frameworks are being developed to guide corporations – by Global Reporting Initiative (GRI) for comprehensive reports and by AccountAbility for sustainability reports.

TABLE 1.6

STAKEHOLDER REPORT TOPICS

Health and safety	Environmental performance/impact
Sustainability	Corporate social responsibility
Philanthropy	Workplace responsibility

DEVELOPMENTS IN BUSINESS ETHICS

Concepts and Terms

In response to the changes previously described, several concepts and terms have been developed that facilitate an understanding of the evolution taking place in the accountability of business and in the making of ethical decisions. Two of these developments are particularly useful in understanding business ethics, and how business and the professions can benefit from its application. They are the stakeholder concept and the concept of a corporate social contract.

As the ethical environment for business changed, observers and executives realized that many more people than just shareholders had an interest in the corporation or its activities. As previously noted, although some of these had no statutory claim on the corporation, they had a capacity to influence the corporation favorably or unfavorably. Moreover, as time went by, the claims of some of these interested parties became codified through statute or regulation. It became evident that the interests of this set of people with a stake in the business or its impacts—who are affected by or can affect the achievement of the organization's objectives[6]—ought to be considered in corporate plans and decisions. For ease of reference, these people have come to be known as *stakeholders* and their interests as *stakeholder's rights*. Examples of stakeholder

---

[6]R.E. Freeman, *Strategic Management: A Stakeholder Approach*, Pitman, Boston, 1984.

groups include employees, customers, suppliers, lenders, borrowers, host communities, governments, environmentalists, and, of course, shareholders. A corporation's normal set of stakeholders was shown in Figure 1.1.

The relationship between a corporation and its stakeholders has slowly but steadily broadened over the years. Initially, the corporation was established as a means of gathering large amounts of capital from shareholders. It was accountable only to those shareholders and its goal was to generate profits. Later, when larger factories appeared, times were such that child labor was prevalent and no cost was ascribed to environmental practices, which today would not be condoned. As previously described, corporate accountability has broadened to go beyond just shareholders to embrace the reality of stakeholders, and the corporate mandate has evolved to respect stakeholder's interests and thereby engender their support. Profits are to be generated, but not at any cost to society and preferably in a way that supports society. This evolving relationship between corporations and society has come to be known, in concept, as the *corporate social contract*.

Approaches To Ethical Decision Making Through Stakeholder Impact Analysis

The increasing accountability to stakeholders within the newer versions of the corporate social contract has made it incumbent on executives to ensure that their decisions reflect the ethical values established for the corporation and do not leave out of consideration any significant stakeholder's rights. This has led to the development of a form of comprehensive ethical decision making known as *stakeholder impact analysis*. A number of approaches have emerged, several of which are expanded upon in Chapter 5.

All approaches begin with the identification of significant stakeholders, an investigation of their interests, and a ranking of those interests to ensure that the most important are given adequate attention during the remaining analysis, and greater consideration at the decision stage. Chapter 5 provides insights into the saliency of the various stakeholder interests, which are important to the making of ethical decisions.

The first analytical approach, known as the *Five Question Approach*, involves challenging any proposed policy or action with five questions designed to rate the proposal on the following scales: profitability, legality, fairness, impact on the rights of each individual stakeholder, and impact on the environment. The questions are asked and options for action are discarded depending on the degree to which corporate ethical values and stakeholder interests are offended. Often, action options can be modified to be made more ethical as a result of these challenges (Tucker, 1990).

The *Moral Standards Approach*, developed by Professor Manuel Velasquez (1992), focuses on three dimensions of the impact of the proposed action: (1) whether it provides a net benefit to society, (2) whether it is fair to all stakeholders, and (3) whether it is right. Although there is some overlap with the first approach, Velasquez's focus is less company-centered and is therefore better suited to the evaluation of decisions where the impact on stakeholders outside the corporation is likely to be severe. Longer-term impacts are also more readily incorporated.

The last approach to stakeholder impact analysis to be presented in Chapter 5 is the *Pastin Approach*, created by Professor Mark Pastin (1986), who extends the Moral Standards Approach by taking specific account of the culture within the corporation and of so-called "commons problems." Pastin suggests that any proposed decision be evaluated in comparison to the company's ground rules (he calls this "ground rule ethics"), the net benefit it produces (end-point ethics), whether it impinges on any stakeholder's rights and requires rules to resolve the conflict (rule ethics), and, finally, whether it abuses rights apparently belonging to everyone (problems of the commons). Pastin's approach is quite practical and is best suited to decisions with impacts primarily on stakeholders directly attached to the corporation, such as employees or customers.

Chapter 5 also provides frameworks for the management of issues using the stakeholder impact analysis.

The use of stakeholder impact analysis in management decision making, and in the management of contentious issues, will contribute significantly to the development of defensible positions that are necessary to the development and maintenance of stakeholder support for corporate activities.

The Ethics Environment for Professional Accountants

ROLE AND CONDUCT

The aftermath of the Enron, Arthur Andersen, and WorldCom debacles will bring fundamental changes in the role and conduct of those professional accountants who have forgotten where their primary duty is owed. Professional accountants owe their primary loyalty to the public interest, not just to their own financial interests, company directors or management, or to current shareholders at the expense of future shareholders. The reasons for these changes are made clear in Chapters 2 and 3 but, just as in the case of corporate governance, cracks that had been apparent for some time in the governance framework for professional accountants became so serious in early 2002 that the public credibility of the profession was virtually destroyed. Reforms, through new regulations and supervisory structures, and revised codes of conduct that rededicate the accounting profession to its original fiduciary roots have become a necessary restorative that will influence professional accounting behavior around the world.

The need for additional changes in the role and conduct of professional accountants predates the recent debacles. Whether they are involved in the audit or assurance service functions, in management, in consulting, or as directors, professional accountants have been looked upon historically as the arbiters of organizational accountability and experts in the science of decision making. Since we are witnessing a "sea change" in corporate accountability with a broadening beyond just shareholders to stakeholders, it is incumbent on accountants to understand this evolution and how it can impact upon their function. If they do not do so, substandard advice may be given, and the legal and non-legal consequences for ethical shortfalls can be severe.

There is also a very real possibility that the expectations gap between what users of audits and financial statements thought they had been getting and what they actually are receiving will be exacerbated if accountants are seen to be out of step with emerging standards of ethical behavior. Studies have been undertaken, such as those by the Treadway Commission in the United States and the Macdonald Commission in Canada, which have called for a recognition of new levels of ethical behavior in revisions to professional codes of conduct. Some professional codes were revised in response, but the Enron and other debacles will put the spotlight on further revisions. A thorough understanding of the reasons for these revisions and the underlying principles involved are essential for their proper application and the protection of professionals, the profession, and the public.

An appreciation of the sea change underway in the ethics environment for business is essential to an informed understanding of how professional accountants ought to interpret their profession's code as employees of corporations. Although the public expects all professional accountants to respect the professional values of objectivity, integrity, and confidentiality, which are designed to protect the fundamental rights of the public, an employee-accountant must respond to the direction of management and the needs of current shareholders. Trade-offs are difficult. In the future, there will be less escape from the glare of public scrutiny, and greater danger in greeting problems with a wink and a nod or by sweeping them under the rug. Professional accountants will have to ensure their ethical values are current, and that they are prepared to act upon them to best exercise their role and to maintain the credibility of and support for the profession.

GOVERNANCE

Globalization and internationalization have come to the corporate world, the capital markets, and corporate accountability. Stakeholders are global in their reach, and events that were kept secret in far-off jungles are now shown worldwide each evening on CNN. Corporations with far-flung activities are conscious that they are accountable for each of their operations and are looking for effective ways to manage, account for, and disclose activities around the world.

In the accounting profession, there is a desire to develop a globally harmonized set of generally accepted accounting principles (GAAP) to provide analytical efficiencies for the providers of capital to the world's markets and computational and audit efficiencies around the world. Consequently, there has is a plan to gradually harmonize the set of GAAP developed by the International Accounting Standards Board (IASB) in London, England, and those developed by the U.S. Financial Accounting Standards Board (FASB) into a common set that will apply in all countries.

Concurrently, the IASB is developing an international code of conduct for accountants, and all member countries of the IASB have agreed to standardize their country's code on the same or similar basis to the new international code. The details of this international code are reviewed in Chapter 4.

The principles inherent in the new international code will become the basis for future behavior and education of professional accountants. Difficult areas of professional behavior, such as the identification and management of conflicts of interest, will receive a fresh set of guidelines. These are also discussed in Chapter 4.

Globalization has also come to audit firms. They are developing global audit standards to serve their major clients and supportive behavior standards to ensure their judgments are independent, objective, and accurate. The new rulings of the U.S. Securities and Exchange Commission, motivated by the Sarbanes-Oxley Act and the Enron, Arthur Andersen, and WorldCom fiascoes, will inform these global standards. Consequently, the SOX-SEC intention to reinforce the professional accountant's focus on the public interest will be extended worldwide.

SERVICES OFFERRED

In this recently redefined global environment, the offering of nonaudit service to audit clients, which was a contentious issue for Arthur Andersen in the Enron debacle, will be curtailed so that tighter conflict of interest expectations can be met. The advent and growth of multidisciplinary firms in the late 1990s, which included professionals such as lawyers and engineers to provide a broader range of assurance and other services, may continue to reverse itself as major audit firms sell off part of their consulting units. If not, professional accountants should be particularly alert to conflicts where the values and codes of other professionals in their employ differ from those of the accounting profession. Chapter 3 provides insights into these conflicts of interest.

The next chapter, *Governance, Accounting, and Auditing, Post-Enron*, examines the debacles that triggered the new era of governance and accountability for corporations and the accounting profession.

QUESTIONS FOR DISCUSSION

1. Why have concerns over pollution become so important for management and directors?

2. Why are we more concerned now than our parents were about fair treatment of employees?

3. What could professional accountants have done to prevent the development of the credibility gap and the expectations gap?

4. Why are each of integrity, transparency, and accuracy vital to good corporate disclosure?

5. Why might ethical corporate behavior lead to higher profitability?

6. Why is it important for the clients of professional accountants to be ethical?

7. How can corporations ensure that their employees behave ethically?

8. Should executives and directors be sent to jail for the acts of their corporation's employees?

9. Why are the expectations of a corporation's stakeholders important to the reputation of the corporation and to its profitability?

10. How can a corporation show respect for its stakeholders?

11. How can conflicts between the interests of stakeholders be resolved by a corporation's management?

12. What are the common elements of the three approaches to ethical decision making that are briefly outlined in the chapter?

13. Is a professional accountant a businessperson pursuing profit or a fiduciary that is to act in the public interest?

14. Why is it important for a professional accountant to understand the ethical trends discussed in this chapter?

15. Why should a professional accountant be aware of the Ethics Code of the International Federation of Accountants?

CASES

The cases that follow are designed to stimulate an awareness of ethical issues currently facing business and accountants. Specifically, the scenarios covered are as follows:

■ *Martha Stewart's Lost Reputation* offers an opportunity to see how Martha lost her reputation and, with investors, a lot of money, based on allegations of selling a personal investment after receiving a tip from the CEO, who was a personal friend. What constitutes reputation? How do stakeholders fit into reputation and brand image development? What constitutes insider trading, and why is it a conflict of interest situation? Should insider trading be encouraged or banned? These are issues raised by the case.

■ *Bhopal—Union Carbide* is intended to raise the reader's awareness of ethical issues facing modern corporations. It presents the reader with an event which, while improbable, happens repeatedly in different scenarios, and offers the reader an opportunity to explore what they and others believe to be appropriate levels of corporate responsibility and ethical behavior.

■ *The Betaseron® Decision (A)* discusses the dilemmas faced by a pharmaceutical management team when making difficult choices affecting customers' quality of life. The ethical implications of such decisions can be ignored, but not without cost.

■ *Texaco: The Ecuador Issue* outlines the environmental difficulties Texaco faced in its oil operations in Ecuador. Even after leaving the country, Texaco was sued in U.S. courts by South Americans. Did Texaco act responsibly? Could this have been prevented?

■ *Where Were the Accountants?* presents a brief series of scandals and ethical problems upon which management accountants, academic accountants, and auditors could have commented on in time to significantly mitigate the outcome. Why didn't they? Should they have?

■ *To Resign or Serve?* introduces the problem of balancing ethical trade-offs in a modern, creative economic world. How far should an auditor go to protect a fellow professional, the profession, or the public?

READINGS

The selection of readings that follows has been chosen to provide background material to enrich the understanding of the issues identified in the chapter. Lynn Sharp Paine's classic article provides the most compelling arguments for incorporating integrity into corporate decision making and operations, and provides insights into how to make this happen. The article by Andrew Singer reveals the significance of whistle-blowing and the impact it may have on corporations. This impact is one of the catalysts that will lead companies to want to develop ethical corporate cultures in the future. The Caremark National law case dramatically altered directors' responsibilities for overseeing corporations to require them to search out ethical problems rather than wait until they were informed.

REFERENCES

Achar, R., Nitkin, D., Otto, K., Pellizzari, P., and EthicScan Canada, *Shopping with a Conscience*, John Wiley & Sons, Toronto, 1996.

American Institute of Certified Public Accountants (AICPA) and The Canadian Institute of Chartered Accountants (CICA), *Managing Risk in the New Economy*, 2001, p. 4.

Canadian Institute of Chartered Accountants, *Guidance for Directors— Governance Processes for Control*, Toronto, Canada, December 1995. See page 2, paragraph 8 and also pages 8 and 9 for a discussion of approving and monitoring the organization's ethical values.

Clarkson, Max.B.E., "Corporate Social Performance in Canada, 1976–86," *Research in Social Performance and Policy*, JAI Press, Inc., Vol. 10, 1988, pp. 241–265.

Domini Social Index, a market capitalized-weighted common stock index, consisting of 400 U.S. corporations that have passed multiple, broad-based social screens. Maintained by Kinder, Lydenberg, Domini & Co., Cambridge, MA 01238.

Fombrun, C.J., *Reputation: Realizing Value from the Corporate Image*, Harvard Business School Press, Boston, 1996.

Freeman, R.E., *Strategic management: A stakeholder approach*, Pitman, Boston, 1984.

Friedman, F.B., *Practical Guide to Environmental Management*, Environmental Law Institute, Washington, D.C., 1988, p. 34.

Friedman, M., "The Social Responsibility of Business to Increase Profits," *The New York Times Magazine*, September 13, 1970.

Helson, J. et al, Green, K., Nitkin, D., Stein, A., *The Ethical Shoppers Guide to Canadian Supermarket Products*, Broadview Press, Toronto, 1992.

The Institute of Internal Auditors Research Foundation, *Enterprise Risk Management: Trends and Emerging Practices*, 2001.

Macdonald Commission, see *The Report of the Commission to Study the Public's Expectations of Audits*, Canadian Institute of Chartered Accountants, June 1988.

Mulligan, T., "A Critique of Milton Friedman's Essay 'The Social Responsibility of Business Is to Increase Its Profits,'" *Journal of Business Ethics*, 1986, pp. 265–269.

OECD (Organization for Economic Cooperation and Development), http://www.oecd.org.

Paine, L.S., "Managing for Integrity," *Harvard Business Review*, March–April, 1994, pp. 106–117.

Pastin, M., *The Hard Problems of Management: Gaining the Ethics Edge*, Jossey-Bass Publishers, San Francisco, 1986.

Pellizzari, P., *Conscious Consumption: Corporate Social Responsibility and Canada's Grocery Giants*, EthicScan Canada, 2002.

Placenti, F.M., "Caremark National Case," *The National Law Journal*, June 23, 1997, pp. B5, B6.

Report of the Toronto Stock Exchange Committee on Corporate Governance in Canada, Toronto Stock Exchange, Toronto, December 1994, paragraphs 4.3 and 4.4, p. 17.

Sarbanes-Oxley Act of 2002, (see *http://brooks.swlearning.com*).

Singer, A. W., "The Whistle-Blower: Patriot or Bounty Hunter?," *Across The Board*, November 1992, pp. 16–22.

The Role of the Board of Directors in Enron's Collapse, U.S. Senate's Permanent Subcommittee on Investigations, July 8, 2002, (see *http://brooks.swlearning.com*).

Treadway Commission, see the *Report of the National Commission on Fraudulent Public Reporting*, AICPA, 1987.

Tucker, G., "Ethical Analysis for Environmental Problem Solving," *Agenda for Action Conference Proceedings*, The Canadian Centre for Ethics & Corporate Policy 1990, pp. 53–57.

U.S. Sentencing Guidelines of 1991, November 1, 1991.

Velasquez, M.G., *Business Ethics: Concepts and Cases*, Prentice Hall, New Jersey, 1992.

Verschoor, Curtis, C., "A Study of the Link between a Corporation's Financial Performance and Its Commitment to Ethics," *Journal of Business Ethics*, Vol. 17, No. 13, 1998 pp. 1509–1516.

Wartick, S.L. and Cochran, P.L., "The Evolution of the Corporate Social Performance Model," *Academy of Management Review*, Vol. 10, No. 4, 1985, pp. 758–769.

Ethics case

Martha Stewart's Lost Reputation

In June 2002, Martha Stewart began to wrestle with allegations that she had improperly used inside information to sell a stock investment to an unsuspecting investing public. That was when her personal friend, Sam Waksal, was defending himself against Securities and Exchange Commission (SEC) allegations that he had tipped off his family members so they could sell their shares of ImClone Systems Inc. (ImClone) just before other investors learned that ImClone's fortunes were about to take a dive. Observers presumed that Martha was also tipped off and, even though she proclaimed her innocence, the rumors would not go away.

On TV daily, as the reigning guru of homemaking, Martha is the multi-millionaire proprietor, president, and driving force of Martha Stewart Living Omnimedia Inc. (MSO), of which, on March 18, 2002, she owned 30,713,475 (62.6 percent[1]) shares of the class A 30,619,375 (100 percent) shares of the class B stock. On December 27, 2001, Martha's Class A and shares were worth approximately

$17 each, so on paper Martha's MSO class A shares alone were worth over $500 million. Class B shares are convertible into class A shares on a one-to-one basis.

Martha's personal life became public. The world did not know that Martha Stewart had sold 3,928 shares of ImClone for $58 each on December 27, 2001,[2] until June 2002.[3] The sale

1. Proxy Statement for 2002 Annual Meeting of Stockholders of Martha Stewart Living Omnimedia, Inc., held May 9, 2002, SEC Edgar Filing, (see *http://brooks. swlearning.com*).

2. "Martha Scrutiny Heats Up: Shares of Decorator's Company End Tough Week as Martha Stewart's ImClone Links Prove Troubling," *CNN/Money*, June 14, 2002.

3. "Martha Stewart Resigns From NYSE Board," *Reuters* per *FOXNews.com*, October 5, 2002.

—Continued

Continued

generated only $227,824 for Martha, and she avoided losing $45,673 when the stock price dropped the next day,[4] but it has caused her endless personal grief and humiliation, and the loss of reputation as well as a significant drop to $5.26 in the MSO share price.

What Happened?

Martha had made an investment in ImClone, a company that was trying to get the approval of the U.S. Food and Drug Administration (FDA) to bring to market an anti-colon cancer drug called Erbitux. Samuel Waksal, then the CEO of ImClone and a personal friend of Martha's, was apparently warned on or close to December 25, 2001, that the FDA was going to refuse[5] to review Erbitux.[6] According to SEC allegations, Sam relayed the information to his family so they could dump their ImClone shares on an unsuspecting public before the official announcement. Martha claims that she didn't get any inside information early from Sam, but

regulators believe that she may have received information from her broker or her broker's aide. The activities of several of Sam's friends, including Martha, are under investigation by the SEC.

Sam was arrested on June 12, 2002, and charged with "nine criminal counts of conspiracy, securities fraud and perjury, and then freed on $10 million bail."[7] In a related civil compliant, the SEC alleged that Sam "tried to sell ImClone stock and tipped family members before ImClone's official FDA announcement on Dec. 28."[8]

According to the SEC, two unidentified members of Sam's family sold about $10 million worth of ImClone stock in a two-day interval just before the announcement. Moreover, Sam also tried for two days to sell nearly 80,000 ImClone shares for about $5 million, but two different brokers refused to process the trades.[9]

Martha has denied any wrongdoing. She was quoted as saying: "In placing my trade I had no improper information… My transaction was entirely lawful."[10] She admitted calling Sam after selling her shares, but claimed: "I did not reach Mr. Waksal, and he did not return my call."[11] She

maintained that she had an agreement with her broker to sell her remaining ImClone shares "if the stock dropped below $60 per share."[12]

Martha's public, however, was skeptical. She was asked embarrassing questions when she appeared on TV for a cooking segment, and she declined to answer, saying: "I am here to make my salad." Martha's interactions with her broker, Peter Bacanovic, and his assistant, Douglas Faneuil, are also being scrutinized. Merrill Lynch & Co. suspended Bacanovic (who was also Sam Waksal's broker)[13] and Faneuil, with pay, in late June. Later, since all phone calls to brokerages are taped and emails kept, it appeared to be damning when Bacanovic initially refused to provide his cell phone records to the House Energy and Commerce Commission for their investigation.[14] Moreover, on October 4, 2001, Faneuil "pleaded guilty to a charge that he accepted gifts from his superior in return for keeping quiet about circumstances surrounding Stewart's controversial stock sale."[15]

—Continued

4. "Broker's Aide Pleads Guilty in Martha Stewart Matter," *The Washington Post*, October 2, 2002.

5. "ImClone Ex-CEO Takes the 5th: Sam Waksal Declines to Testify; His Brother Harlan Says His Sales Were Not Improper," *CNN/Money*, June 13, 2001.

6. Ibid. Later it became known that the application for review had "multiple deficiencies" and provided insufficient information that the drug would work on its own.

7. Ibid.

8. Ibid.

9. Ibid.

10. "Martha scrutiny heats up."

11. Ibid.

12. Ibid.

13. "Aide to Martha Stewart's Broker Admits He Withheld Information From Investigators," *CBCNEWS*. (see *http://brooks.swlearning.com*), October 2, 2002.

14. "Martha's Broker Under Microscope," *CBSNews.com*, July 9, 2001.

15. "Martha Stewart Resigns."

Continued

Faneuil admitted that he received extra vacation time, including a free airline ticket from a Merrill Lynch employee in exchange for withholding information from SEC and FBI investigators.[16]

According to the *Washington Post* report of Faneuil's appearance in court:

> On the morning of Dec. 27, Faneuil received a telephone call from a Waksal family member who asked to sell 39472 shares for almost $2.5 million, according to court records. Waksal's accountant also called Faneuil in an unsuccessful attempt to sell a large bloc of shares, the records show.
>
> Prosecutors allege that those orders "constituted material non-public information." But

they alleged that Faneuil violated his duty to Merrill Lynch by calling a "tippee" to relate that Waksal family members were attempting to liquidate their holdings in ImClone.

That person then sold "all the Tippee's shares of ImClone stock, approximately 3,928 shares, yielding proceeds of approximately $228,000" the court papers said.[17]

One day later, on October 5, it was announced that Martha resigned from her post as a director of the New York Stock Exchange—a post she held only four months—and the price of MSO shares declined more than 7 percent to $6.32 in afternoon trading.[18] From June 12 to October 12, the share price of MSO had

declined by approximately 61 percent.[19]

Martha's future took a further interesting turn on October 15, when Sam Waksal plead guilty to six counts of his indictment, including bank fraud, securities fraud, conspiracy to obstruct justice, and perjury. But he did not agree to cooperate with prosecutors, and did not incriminate Martha.[20] Waksal's sentencing was postponed until early March 2003 as his lawyers exchange information with U.S. District Judge William Pauley concerning Waksal's financial records.

After October 15, the price of MSO shares rose, perhaps as the prospect of Martha's going to jail appeared to become more remote, and/or people began to consider MSO to be more than just Martha and her reputation. The gain from the low point of the MSO share price in October to December 9, 2002, was about 40 percent.[21]

Martha still has a lot to think about, however. Apparently the SEC gave Martha notice in September of its intent to file civil securities fraud charges

---

16. "Broker's Aide Pleads Guilty."

17. Ibid.
18. Ibid.

19. Assuming a value per share of $13.50 on June 12, the decline to a low of $5.26 in early October amounted to a decline of 61 percent.
20. "ImClone Founder Pleads Guilty," *CBSNews.com*, October 15, 2002.
21. "Market Betting Martha Won't Go to Jail: Shares Up 40 Percent in 6 Weeks," *Financial Post*, December 10, 2001, IN1, 3.

2000–2002 STOCK CHART OF MARTHA STEWART LIVING OMNIMEDIA INC.

Reprinted Courtesy of NAQ, Inc.

—Continued

Continued

against her. Martha's lawyers responded and the SEC is deliberating. Even if Martha gets off with a fine, prosecutors can still bring a criminal case against her in the future. It is an interesting legal question, how, if Martha pleads guilty to the civil charges, she could avoid criminal liability.[22]

Impact on Reputation

Time may tell if Martha did act on inside information. But there is little doubt that the allegations of insider trading have had a major impact on Martha personally, and on the fortunes of MSO and the other shareholders that had faith in her and her company. Assuming a value per share of $13.50 on June 12, the decline to a low of $5.26 in early October represents a loss of market capitalization (i.e., reputation capital as defined by Charles Fombrun)[23] of

approximately $250 million, or 61 percent.

Questions

1. What was the basis of Martha Stewart's reputation?

2. Why did MSO's stock price decline due to Martha Stewart's loss of reputation?

3. Who is Martha Stewart's target market?

4. What qualities were associated with the Martha Stewart brand before the controversy? Which of these were affected by the accusations of insider trading, and how? How would you find out for sure?

5. What level of sales and profits would MSO have reached if Martha's reputation had not been harmed? Refer to the SEC or MSO Websites for information on financial trends.

6. What range would the stock price have been in at the end of 2002 based on your estimates?

7. Martha's overall net worth was huge relative to her investment in ImClone. Assuming she did not have inside information, was there any way she could have avoided the appearance of having it?

8. How could Martha have handled this crisis better?

9. Why is insider trading considered harmful? Should insider trading be banned if it assists in moving a stock price to new a equilibrium quickly, so that non-insiders are trading at appropriate prices sooner?

10. If you wished to sell an investment in a company where one of your friends is an insider, or even a significant employee, should you call your friend to advise him you are about to sell? Why or why not?

---

22. "SEC Knocking On Martha's Door," *CBSNEWS.com*, October 22, 2002.

23. Charles J. Fombrun, *Reputation: Realizing Value from the Corporate Image*, Harvard Business School Press, 1996.

Ethics case

Bhopal—Union Carbide*

On April 24, 1985, Warren M. Anderson, the sixty-three-year-old chairman of Union Carbide Corporation, had to make a disappointing announcement to angry stockholders at their annual meeting in Danbury, Connecticut. Anderson, who had been jailed briefly by the government of India on charges of "negligence and criminal corporate liability," had been devoting all his attention to the company's mushrooming problems. His announcement concerned the complete breakdown of negotiations with officials in the Indian government: they had rejected as inadequate an estimated $200 million in compensation for the deaths of 2,000 people and the injuries of 200,000 others, which had been caused in December 1984 by a poisonous leak of methyl isocyanate gas from a Union Carbide pesticide plant located in Bhopal, India.[1] In the wake of more than $35 billion in suits filed against the company's liability coverage, reported to total only about $200 million, the company's stock tumbled. Angry stockholders filed suit, charging that they had suffered losses of more than $1 billion because the company's managers had failed to warn them of the risks at the Indian plant. Analysts predicted the company would be forced into bankruptcy. Ironically, the Union Carbide plant in Bhopal had been losing money for several years and Anderson had considered closing it.

The deadly methyl isocyanate gas that leaked from the Union Carbide plant is a volatile and highly toxic chemical used to make pesticides. It is 500 times more poisonous than cyanide, and it reacts explosively with almost any substance, including water. Late on the night of December 2, 1984, the methyl isocyanate stored in a tank at the Bhopal factory started boiling violently when water or some other agent accidentally entered the tank. A cooling unit that should have switched on automatically had been disabled for at least a year. Shakil Qureshi, a manager on duty at the time, and Suman Dey, the senior operator on duty, both distrusted the initial readings on their gauges in the control room. "Instruments often didn't work," Qureshi said later. "They got corroded, and crystals would form on them."

By 11:30 p.m. the plant workers' eyes were burning. But the workers remained unconcerned because, as they later reported, minor leaks were common at the plant and were often first detected in this way. Many of the illiterate workers were unaware of the deadly properties of the chemical. Not until 12:40 a.m., as workers began choking on the fumes, did they realize something was drastically wrong. Five minutes later, emergency valves on the storage tank exploded and white toxic gas began shooting out of a pipestack and drifting toward the shantytowns downwind from the plant. An alarm sounded as manager Dey shouted into the factory loudspeaker that a massive leak had erupted and the workers should flee the area. Meanwhile, Qureshi ordered company fire trucks to spray the escaping gas with water to neutralize the chemical. But water pressure was too low to reach the top of the 120-foot-high pipestack. Dey then rushed to turn on a vent scrubber that should have neutralized the escaping gas with caustic soda. Unfortunately, the scrubber had been shut down for maintenance fifteen days earlier. As white clouds continued to pour out of the pipestack, Qureshi shouted to workers to turn on a nearby flare tower to burn off the gas. The flare, however, would not go on because its pipes had corroded and were still being repaired.

Panicked workers poured out of the plant, and the lethal

—Continued

---

*This case has been adapted from Velasquesz, Manuel, *Business Ethics: Concepts and Cases*, 3/e, © 1992, pp. 3–5. Reprinted by permission of Prentice-Hall, Inc., Englewood Cliffs, N.J.

1. All material concerning Union Carbide and the Bhopal plant, including all quotations and all allegations, is drawn directly from the following sources: *The New York Times:* December 9, 1984, p. 1E; December 16, 1984, pp. 1, 8; January 28, 1985, pp. 6, 7; January 30, 1985, p. 6; April 25, 1985, p. 34; *San Jose Mercury News:* December 6, 1984, p. 16A; December 12, 1984, pp. 1, 1H; December 13, 1984, p. 1; *Time:* December 17, 1985, pp. 22–31.

Continued

cloud settled over the neighboring shantytowns of Jaipraksh and Chola. Hundreds died in their beds, choking helplessly in violent spasms as their burning lungs filled with fluid. Thousands were blinded by the caustic gas, and thousands of others suffered burns and lesions in their nasal and bronchial passages. When it was over, at least 2,000 lay dead and 200,000 were injured. The majority of the dead were squatters who had illegally built huts next to the factory. Surviving residents of the slums, most of them illiterate, declared afterward that they had built their shacks there because they did not understand the danger and thought the factory made healthy "medicine for plants."

Union Carbide managers from the United States built the Bhopal plant in 1969 with the blessing of the Indian government, which was anxious to increase production of the pesticides it desperately needed to raise food for India's huge population. Over the next fifteen years, pesticides enabled India to cut its annual grain losses from 25 percent to 15 percent, a saving of 15 million tons of grain, or enough to feed 70 million people for a full year. Indian officials willingly accepted the technology, skills, and equipment that Union Carbide provided, and Indian workers were thankful for the company jobs, without which they would have had to beg or starve, as India has no welfare system. In return, India offered the company cheap labor, low taxes, and few laws requiring expensive environmental equipment or costly workplace protections. In comparison with other factories in India, the Union Carbide plant was considered a model, law-abiding citizen with a good safety record. Said a government official: "They never refused to install what we asked."

At the time of the disaster, the pesticide plant in Bhopal was operated by Union Carbide India Ltd., a subsidiary of the Union Carbide Corporation of Danbury, Connecticut, which had a controlling interest of 50.9 percent in the Indian company. The board of directors of Union Carbide India Ltd. included one top manager from the parent Union Carbide Corporation in the United States and four managers from another Union Carbide subsidiary, based in Hong Kong. Reports from the Indian company were regularly reviewed by the managers in Danbury, who had the authority to exercise financial and technical control over Union Carbide India Ltd. Although day-to-day details were left to the Indian managers, the American managers controlled budgets, set major policies, and issued technical directives for operating and maintaining the plant.

Before the tragedy, the Indian subsidiary had been doing poorly. In an effort to contain annual losses of $4 million from the unprofitable plant, local company managers had initiated several cost-cutting programs. Only a year before, the number of equipment operators on each shift had been reduced from twelve to five; morale dropped and many of the best operators quit and were replaced with workers whose education was below that required by company manuals. Although Warren Anderson and other Union Carbide Corporation (U.S.) managers insisted that responsibility for the plant's operations rested with the local Indian managers, they hastened to say that all cost-cutting measures had been justified.

Two years before the disaster, the American managers had sent three engineers from the United States to survey the plant and, as a result, had told the Indian managers to remedy ten major flaws in safety equipment and procedures. The Indian managers had written back that the problems were corrected. "We have no reason to believe that what was represented to us by Union Carbide India Ltd. did not in fact occur," said the U.S. managers. The U.S. managers

—Continued

Continued

had considered closing the failing plant a year earlier, but Indian city and state officials had asked that the company remain open to preserve the jobs of thousands of workers in the plant and in dependent local industries.

Questions

1. What are the ethical issues raised by this case?

2. Did the legal doctrine of "limited liability" apply to protect the shareholders of Union Carbide Corporation (U.S.)?

3. Were the Indian operations, which were being overseen by the managers of Union Carbide Corporation (U.S.), in compliance with legal or moral or ethical standards?

The Betaseron® Decision (A)

On July 23, 1993, the United States Food and Drug Administration (FDA) approved interferon beta-1b (brand name Betaseron), making it the first treatment for multiple sclerosis to get FDA approval in twenty-five years. Betaseron was developed by Berlex Laboratories, a United States unit of Schering AG, the German pharmaceutical company. Berlex handled the clinical development, trials, and marketing of the drug, while Chiron, a biotechnology firm based in California, manufactured it. The groundbreaking approval of Betaseron represented not only a great opportunity for Berlex but also a difficult dilemma. Available supplies were insufficient to meet initial demand, and shortages were forecasted until 1996. With insufficient supplies and staggering development costs, how would Berlex allocate and price the drug?

The Challenge of Multiple Sclerosis

Multiple sclerosis (MS) is a disease of the central nervous system that interferes with the brain's ability to control such functions as seeing, walking, and talking. The nerve fibers within the brain and spinal cord are surrounded by myelin, a fatty substance that protects the nerve fibers in the same way that insulation protects electrical wires. When the myelin insulation becomes damaged, the ability of the central nervous system to transmit nerve impulses to and from the brain becomes impaired. With multiple sclerosis, there are *sclerosed* (i.e., scarred or hardened) areas in *multiple* parts of the brain and spinal cord when the immune system mistakenly attacks the myelin sheath.

The symptoms of MS depend to some extent on the location and size of the sclerosis. Symptoms include numbness, slurred speech, blurred vision, poor coordination, muscle weakness, bladder dysfunction, extreme fatigue, and paralysis. There is no way to know how the disease will progress for any individual because the nature of the course it takes can change over time. Some people will have a relatively benign course of MS, with only one or two mild attacks, nearly complete remission, and no permanent disability. Others will have a chronic, progressive course resulting in severe disability. A third group displays the most typical pattern, with periods of *exacerbations*, when the disease is active, and periods of *remission*, when

—Continued

Continued

the symptoms recede while generally leaving some damage. People with MS live with an exceptionally high degree of uncertainty because the course of their disease can change from one day to the next. Dramatic downturns as well as dramatic recoveries are not uncommon.

The Promise of Betaseron

Interferon beta is a protein that occurs naturally and regulates the body's immune system. Betaseron is composed of interferon beta-1b that has been genetically engineered and laboratory manufactured as a recombinant product. Although other interferons (i.e., alpha and gamma) had been tested, only beta interferon had been shown, through large-scale trials, to affect MS. Because it is an immunoregulatory agent, it was believed to combat the immune problems that make MS worse. However, the exact way in which it works was yet to be determined.

In clinical studies, Betaseron was shown to reduce the frequency and severity of exacerbations in ambulatory MS patients with a relapsing-remitting form of the disease. It did not reverse damage already done, nor did it completely prevent exacerbations from occurring. However, Betaseron could dramatically improve the quality of life for the person with MS; for example, people taking Betaseron were shown to have fewer and shorter hospitalizations. Betaseron represented the first and only drug to have an effect on the frequency of exacerbations.

Betaseron is administered subcutaneously (under the skin) every other day by self-injection. In order to derive the most benefits from the therapy, it was important that the MS patient maintain a regular schedule of the injections. Some flu-like side effects, as well as swelling and irritation around the injection, had been noted; however, they tended to decrease with time on treatment. In addition, one person who received Betaseron committed suicide, while three others attempted to kill themselves. Because MS often leads to depression, there was no way to know whether the administration of Betaseron was a factor. Lastly, Betaseron was not recommended for use during pregnancy.

The Betaseron Dilemma

In July of 1993, the FDA approval for Betaseron allowed physicians to prescribe the drug to MS patients who were ambulatory and had a relapsing-remitting course of MS. An estimated one-third of the 300,000 people with MS in the United States fell into that category, resulting in a potential client base of 100,000. However, the expedited FDA approval process took only one year instead of the customary three years taken to review new drug applications. As a result, Berlex was unprepared for its manufacture and distribution in the anticipated amount needed. Chiron Corporation had been making the drug in small quantities for experimental use and did not have the manufacturing facilities to handle the expected explosion in demand. Chiron estimated that it would have enough of the drug for about 12,000 to 20,000 people by the end of 1993. By the end of 1994, Chiron expected to be able to provide the drug to 40,000 patients. Depending on demand, it might take until about 1996 to provide the drug to all patients who requested it. Chiron's expanded manufacturing represented the only option for Berlex because the process required for another company to get FDA approval to manufacture the drug would take even longer.

In addition to availability, price was a concern because successes must fund the failures that precede them. Betaseron represented the results of years of expensive, risky research by highly trained scientists in modern research facilities. Furthermore, genetically engineered drugs were extremely expensive to manufacture. In the case of Betaseron, a human interferon

—Continued

Continued

gene was inserted into bacteria, resulting in a genetically engineered molecule. The stringent quality controls on the procedure take time and are expensive. As a result, the price of Betaseron was expected to be about $10,000 per year for each patient.

Betaseron brought great hope to people with MS and a great quandary to Berlex. How should Berlex handle the supply limitations, the distribution, and the price of this drug?

SOURCE: By Ann K. Buchholtz, University of Georgia. This case was written from public sources, solely for the purpose of stimulating class discussion. All events are real. The author thanks Dr. Stephen Reingold, vice president, Research and Medical Programs of the National Multiple Sclerosis Society and Avery Rockwell, chapter services associate of the Greater Connecticut Chapter of the Multiple Sclerosis Society, and two anonymous reviewers for their helpful comments.

Ethics case

Texaco: The Ecuador Issue[1]

In 1964, at the invitation of the Ecuadorian government, Texaco Inc. began operations through a subsidiary, TexPet, in the Amazon region of Ecuador. The purpose of the project was to "develop Ecuador's natural resources and encourage the *colonization* of the area."[2] TexPet was a minority owner of the project and its partner was PetroEcuador, the government-owned oil company. Over the years from 1968 to 1992, the consortium extracted 1.4 billion barrels of oil from the Ecuadorian operations.

Ecuador benefited greatly during this period. Ecuador received approximately 98 percent of all moneys generated by the consortium in the form of royalties, taxes, and revenues. Altogether, this amount represented more than 50 percent of Ecuador's gross national product during that period. TexPet's operations over the years provided jobs for 840 employees and approximately 2,000 contract workers, thereby benefiting almost 3,000 Ecuadorian families directly, in addition to the thousands of Ecuadorian nationals who supplied the company's needs for goods and services. Also, TexPet made substantial contributions to the Quito, Guayaquil, and Loja Polytechnics and other institutions of higher education. Oil is Ecuador's lifeblood—a $1 billion per year industry that accounts for 50 percent of the export earnings and 62 percent of its fiscal budget.

Unfortunately, problems also arose. Although Petroecuador acquired 100 percent of the ownership of the Transecuadorian pipeline in 1986, TexPet still accounted for 88 percent of all oil production and operated the pipeline in 1987 when it ruptured and was buried by a landslide. A spill of 16.8 million gallons (4.4 million barrels) occurred, which Texaco attributed to a major earthquake that devastated Ecuador.

Other spills apparently occurred as well. Although Texaco pulled out of the consortium in 1992 entirely (having retreated to be a silent minority partner in 1990), three lawsuits were filed against it in the United States— the Aquinda (November 1993), the Sequihua (August 1993), and the Jota (in 1994). The indigenous people who launched the lawsuits charged that, during two decades of oil drilling in the Amazon, Texaco dumped more

—Continued

1. By Professor Timothy Rowley of the Rotman School of Management.

2. Sources: Texaco and other Websites: www.texaco.com; see Ecuador pages.

Continued

than 3,000 gallons of crude oil a day—millions of gallons in total—into the environment. The indigenous people say their rivers, streams, and lakes are now contaminated, and the fish and wild game that once made up their food supply are now decimated. They asked in the lawsuit that Texaco compensate them and clean up their land and waters.

Maria Aquinda, for whom the suit is named, says that contaminated water from nearby oil wells drilled by the Texaco subsidiary caused her to suffer chronic stomach ailments and rashes and that she lost scores of pigs and chickens. Aquinda and 76 other Amazonian residents filed a $1.5 billion lawsuit in New York against Texaco. The class action suit, representing 30,000 people, further alleges that Texaco acted "with callous disregard for the health, wellbeing, and safety of the plaintiffs" and that "large-scale disposal of inadequately treated hazardous wastes and destruction of tropical rain forest habitats, caused harm to indigenous peoples and their property." According to the Ecuadorian environmental group Ecological Action, Texaco destroyed more than 1 million hectares of tropical forest, spilled 74 million liters of oil, and used obsolete technology that led to the dumping of 18 million liters of toxic waste. Rainforest Action Network, a San Francisco-based organization, says effects include

poor crop production in the affected areas, invasion of tribal lands, sexual assaults committed by oil workers, and loss of game animals (which would be food supply for the indigenous peoples).

Audits were conducted to address the impact of operations on the soil, water, and air and to assess compliance with environmental laws, regulations, and generally accepted operating practices. Two internationally recognized and independent consulting firms, AGRA Earth & Environmental Ltd. and Fugro-McClelland, conducted audits in Ecuador. Each independently concluded that TexPet acted responsibly and that there is no lasting or significant environmental impact from its former operations. Nonetheless, TexPet agreed to remedy the limited and localized impacts attributable to its operations. On May 4, 1995, Ecuador's Minister of Energy and Mines, the president of Petroecuador, and TexPet signed the Contract for Implementing of Environmental Remedial Work and Release from Obligations, Liability, and Claims following negotiations with Ecuadorian government officials representing the interests of indigenous groups in the Oriente. In this remediation effort, producing wells and pits formerly utilized by TexPet were closed, producing water systems were modified, cleared lands were replanted, and

contaminated soil was remediated. All actions taken were inspected and certified by the Ecuadorian government. Additionally, TexPet funded social and health programs throughout the region of operations, such as medical dispensaries and sewage and potable water systems. That contract settled all claims by Petroecuador and the Republic of Ecuador against TexPet, Texaco, and their affiliates for all matters arising out of the consortium's operations.

In the summer of 1998, the $40 million remediation project was completed. On September 30, 1998, Ecuador's Minister of Energy and Mines, the president of Petroecuador, and the general manager of Petroproduccion signed the Final Release of Claims and Delivery of Equipment. This document finalized the government of Ecuador's approval of TexPet's environmental remediation work and further stated that TexPet fully complied with all obligations established in the remediation agreement signed in 1995.

Meanwhile, in the United States, Texaco made the following arguments against the three lawsuits:

- Activities were in compliance with Ecuadorian laws, and international oil industry standards.

—Continued

Continued

- Activities were undertaken by a largely Ecuadorian workforce —which Texaco believe would always act in the interest of its community/country.
- All investments/operations were approved and monitored by the Ecuadorian government and Petroecuador.
- All activities were conducted with the oversight and approval of the Ecuadorian government.
- Environmentally friendly measures were used, such as helicopters instead of roads.
- The health of Ecuadorians increased during the years Texaco was in Ecuador.
- Ninety-eight percent of the money generated stayed in Ecuador—50 percent of GDP during that period.
- Jobs were provided for 2,800.
- Money was provided for schools.
- Independent engineering firms found no lasting damage.
- A $40 million remediation program was started per an agreement with the Ecuadorian government.
- U.S. courts should not govern activities in a foreign country.

The three lawsuits were dismissed for similar reasons— the Sequihua in 1994, the Aquinda in 1996, and the Jota in 1997. The Aquinda lawsuit, for example, was launched in New York (where Texaco has its corporate headquarters) because Texaco no longer had business in Ecuador and could not be sued there. The case was dismissed by a New York court in November 1996 on the basis that it should be heard in Ecuador. Failing that, the Ecuadorian government should have been involved in the case as well, or that the case should have been filed against the government and the state-owned Petroecuador as well as Texaco. At that point, the Ecuadorian government did get involved and filed an appeal of the decision. This was the first time a foreign government had sued a U.S. oil company in the United States for environmental damage. In addition, in 1997, the plaintiffs in the Aquinda and Jota cases also appealed the district court's decisions.

On October 5, 1998, a U.S. court of appeals remanded both cases to the district court for further consideration as to whether they should proceed in Ecuador or the United States. Written submissions were filed on February 1, 1999. Texaco has long argued that the appropriate venue for these cases is Ecuador because the oil-producing operations took place in Ecuador under the control and supervision of Ecuador's government, and the Ecuadorian courts have heard similar cases against other companies. It is Texaco's position that U.S. courts should not govern the activities of a sovereign foreign nation, just as foreign courts should not govern the activities of the United States. In fact, Texaco claimed the Ambassador of Ecuador, the official representative of the government of Ecuador, noted in a letter to the district court that Ecuador would not waive its sovereign immunity.

Notwithstanding Texaco's arguments, the case was sent back to the court that threw it out, on the basis that the government of Ecuador does have the right to intervene. The question of whether the case can be tried in the United States or Ecuador under these circumstances will now be decided. Texaco claims that it has done enough to repair any damage and disputes the scientific validity of the claims— the Amazonians (or their supporters) seem to have the resources to continue fighting this suit in the U.S. courts.

Questions

1. Should Ecuadorians be able to sue Texaco in U.S. courts?
2. If an oil spill was caused by an act of God, an earthquake, should Texaco be held responsible?
3. Do you find Texaco's arguments against the lawsuits convincing? Why and why not?

SOURCE: Texaco Website: www.texaco.com; see Ecuador pages; various other Websites.

Where Were the Accountants?

"Sam, I'm really in trouble. I've always wanted to be an accountant. But here I am just about to apply to the accounting firms for a job after graduation from the university, and I'm not sure I want to be an accountant after all."

"Why, Norm? In all those accounting courses we took together, you worked super hard because you were really interested. What's your problem now?"

"Well, I've been reading the business newspapers, reports, and accounting journals lately, and things just don't add up. For instance, you know how we have always been told that accountants have expertise in measurement and disclosure, that they are supposed to prepare reports with integrity, and that they ought to root out fraud if they suspect it? Well, it doesn't look like they have been doing a good job. At least, they haven't been doing what I would have expected."

"Remember, Norm, we're still students with a lot to learn. Maybe you are missing something. What have you been reading about?"

"OK, Sam, here are a few stories for you to think about:

1. In this article, "Accountants and the S & L Crisis," which was in *Management Accounting* in February 1993, I found the argument that the $200 million fiasco was due to the regulators and to a downturn in the real estate market, not to accounting fraud . . . but I don't buy it entirely. According to this article, rising interest rates and fixed lending rates resulted in negative cash flow at the same time as a decline in value of the real estate market reduced the value underlying S & L loan assets. As a result, the net worth of many S & Ls fell, and regulators decided to change some accounting practices to make it appear that the S & Ls were still above the minimum capital requirements mandated to protect depositors' funds. Just look at this list of the seven accounting practices or problems that were cited:

- write-off of losses on loans sold over the life of the loan rather than when the loss occurred,

- use of government-issued *Net Worth Certificates* to be counted as S & L capital,

- use of deals involving up-front money and near-term cash flow, which would bolster current earnings at the expense of later,

- inadequate loan loss provisions due to poor loan monitoring,

- write-off of goodwill created on the merger of sound S & Ls with bankrupt S & Ls over a forty-year period,

- write-ups of owned property based on appraisal values, and

- lack of market-based reporting to reflect economic reality.

The problem, for me, is that many of these practices are not in accord with generally accepted accounting principles [GAAP] and yet the accountants went along—at least they didn't object or improve their practices enough to change the outcome. Why not? Where were the accountants?"

2. "I am also concerned about the expertise the accounting profession claims to have in terms of measurement and disclosure. For example, recently there have been many articles on the health costs created by smoking, yet there are no accountants involved. For instance, a May 1994 Report by the Center on Addiction and Substance Abuse at Columbia University estimates that "in 1994 dollars, substance abuse will cost Medicare $20 billion in inpatient hospital costs alone" and that tobacco accounts for 80 percent of those hospitalizations. Over the next twenty years, substance abuse will cost the Medicare program $1 trillion. No wonder the trustees of the Medicare Trust Fund released a report on April 21 "predicting that the Fund would run out of

—Continued

Continued

money in seven years." These are important issues. Why do we have to wait for economists and special interest groups to make these calculations? Shouldn't accountants be able to make them and lend credibility and balance in the process? Wouldn't society benefit? Where were the accountants?

3. "What about the finding of fraud? Are auditors doing enough to prevent and catch fraudulent behavior? I know what our professors say: auditors can't be expected to catch everything; their job is not to search for fraud unless suspicions are aroused during other activities; and their primary task is to audit the financial statements. But aren't the auditors just reacting to discovered problems, when they could be proactive? Couldn't they stress the importance of using codes of conduct and the encouragement of employees to bring forward their concerns over unethical acts? Why is proactive management appropriate in some other areas, such as ironing out personnel problems, but reactive behavior is appropriate when dealing with fraud? Reactive behavior will just close the barn door after the horse has been stolen. In the case of the Bank of Credit & Commerce International (BCCI), for example, at least $1.7 billion was missing."

"I guess I'm having second thoughts about becoming a professional accountant. Can you help me out, Sam?"

Question

1. What would you tell Norm?

To Resign or Serve?

The Prairieland Bank was a medium-sized, Midwestern financial institution. The management had a good reputation for backing successful deals, but the CEO (and significant shareholder) had recently moved to San Francisco to be "close to the big-bank center of activity." He commuted into the Prairieland head office for two or three days each week to oversee major deals.

Lately the bank's profitability had decreased, and the management had begun to renegotiate many loans on which payments had fallen behind. By doing so, the bank was able to disclose to them as current, rather than nonperforming, as the unpaid interest was simply added to the principal to arrive at the new principal amount. Discussions were also under way on changing some accounting policies to make them less conservative.

Ben Hunt, the audit partner on the Prairieland Bank account, was becoming concerned about the risk associated with giving an opinion on the fairness of the financial statements. During the early days of the audit, it became evident that the provision for doubtful loans was far too low, and he made an appointment to discuss the problem with the CEO and his vice president of finance. At the interview, Ben was told that the executives knew the provision was too low, but they didn't want to increase it because that would decrease their reported profits. Instead, they had approached a company that provided insurance to protect leased equipment, such as earth movers, against damage during

—Continued

Continued

the lease, and arranged for insurance against nonpayment on the maturity of their loans. As a result, they said, any defaults on their loans would be made up from the insurance company, so they didn't see any point to increasing the provision for loan losses or disclosing the insurance arrangement.

When he heard of this, Ben expressed concern to the Prairieland management, but they were adamant. Because

Prairieland was such a large account, he sought the counsel of James London, the senior partner in his firm who was in charge of assessing such accounting treatments and the related risk to the auditing firm. James flew out to confer with Ben, and they decided that the best course of action was to visit the client and indicate their intent to resign, which they did.

After dinner, James was waiting at the airport for his

plane home. By coincidence, he met Jack Lane, who held responsibilities similar to his own at one of the competing firms. Jack was returning home as well and was in good spirits. On the flight, Jack let it slip that he had just picked up an old client of James's firm, Prairieland Bank.

Questions

1. Which decision was right: to resign or to serve?
2. What should James do?

Managing for Organizational Integrity

Lynn Sharp Paine

Many managers think of ethics as a question of personal scruples, a confidential matter between individuals and their consciences. These executives are quick to describe any wrongdoing as an isolated incident, the work of a rogue employee. The thought that the company could bear any responsibility for an individual's misdeeds never enters their minds. Ethics, after all, has nothing to do with management.

In fact, ethics has *everything* to do with management. Rarely do the character flaws of a lone actor fully explain corporate misconduct. More typically, unethical business practice involves the tacit, if not explicit, cooperation of others and reflects the values, attitudes, beliefs, language, and behavioral patterns that define an organization's operating culture. Ethics, then, is as much an organizational as a personal issue. Managers who fail to provide proper leadership and to institute systems that facilitate ethical

conduct share responsibility with those who conceive, execute, and knowingly benefit from corporate misdeeds.

Managers must acknowledge their role in shaping organizational ethics and seize this opportunity to create a climate that can strengthen the relationships and reputations on which their companies' success depends. Executives who ignore ethics run the risk of personal and corporate liability in today's increasingly tough legal environment. In addition, they deprive their organizations of the benefits available under new federal guidelines for sentencing organizations convicted of wrongdoing. These sentencing guidelines recognize for the first time the organizational and managerial roots of unlawful conduct and base fines partly on the extent to which companies have taken steps to prevent that misconduct.

Prompted by the prospect of leniency, many companies are rushing to implement compliance-based ethics programs. Designed by corporate counsel, the goal of these programs is to prevent, detect, and punish legal violations. But organizational ethics means more than avoiding illegal practice; and providing employees with a rule book will do little to address

—Continued

Continued

the problems underlying unlawful conduct. To foster a climate that encourages exemplary behavior, corporations need a comprehensive approach that goes beyond the often punitive legal compliance stance.

An integrity-based approach to ethics management combines a concern for the law with an emphasis on managerial responsibility for ethical behavior. Though integrity strategies may vary in design and scope, all strive to define companies' guiding values, aspirations, and patterns of thought and conduct. When integrated into the day-to-day operations of an organization, such strategies can help prevent damaging ethical lapses while tapping into powerful human impulses for moral thought and action. Then an ethical framework becomes no longer a burdensome constraint within which companies must operate, but the governing ethos of an organization.

HOW ORGANIZATIONS SHAPE INDIVIDUALS' BEHAVIOR

The once familiar picture of ethics as individualistic, unchanging, and impervious to organizational influences has not stood up to scrutiny in recent years. Sears Auto Centers' and Beech-Nut Nutrition Corporation's experiences illustrate the role organizations play in shaping individuals' behavior—and how even sound moral fiber can fray when stretched too thin.

In 1992, Sears, Roebuck & Company was inundated with complaints about its automotive service business. Consumers and attorneys general in more than 40 states had accused the company of misleading customers and selling them unnecessary parts and services, from brake jobs to front-end alignments. It would be a mistake, however, to see this situation exclusively in terms of any one individual's moral failings. Nor did management set out to defraud Sears customers. Instead, a number of organizational factors contributed to the problematic sales practices.

In the face of declining revenues, shrinking market share, and an increasingly competitive market for undercar services, Sears management attempted to spur the performance of its auto centers by introducing new goals and incentives for employees. The company increased minimum work quotas and introduced productivity incentives for mechanics. The automotive service advisers were given product-specific sales quotas—sell so many springs, shock absorbers, alignments, or brake jobs per shift—and paid a commission based on sales. According to advisers, failure to meet quotas could lead to a transfer or a reduction in work hours. Some employees spoke of the "pressure, pressure, pressure" to bring in sales.

Under this new set of organizational pressures and incentives, with few options for meeting their sales goals legitimately, some employees' judgment understandably suffered. Management's failure to clarify the line between unnecessary service and legitimate preventive maintenance, coupled with consumer ignorance, left employees to chart their own courses through a vast gray area, subject to a wide range of interpretations. Without active management support for ethical practice and mechanisms to detect and check questionable sales methods and poor work, it is not surprising that some employees may have reacted to contextual forces by resorting to exaggeration, carelessness, or even misrepresentation.

Shortly after the allegations against Sears became public, CEO Edward Brennan acknowledged management's responsibility for putting in place compensation and goal-setting systems that "created an environment in which mistakes did occur." Although the company denied any intent to deceive consumers, senior executives eliminated commissions for service advisers and discontinued sales quotas for specific parts. They also instituted a system of unannounced shopping audits and made plans to expand the internal monitoring of service. In settling the pending lawsuits, Sears offered coupons to customers who had bought certain auto services between 1990 and 1992. The total cost of the settlement, including potential customer refunds, was an estimated $60 million.

Contextual forces can also influence the behavior of top management, as a former CEO of Beech-Nut Nutrition Corporation discovered. In the early 1980s, only two years after joining the company, the CEO found evidence suggesting that the apple juice concentrate, supplied by the company's vendors for use in Beech-Nut's "100% pure" apple juice, contained nothing more than sugar water and chemicals. The CEO could have destroyed the bogus inventory and withdrawn the juice from grocers' shelves, but he was under extraordinary pressure to turn the ailing company around. Eliminating the inventory would have killed any hope of turning even the meager $700,000 profit promised to Beech-Nut's then parent, Nestlé.

A number of people in the corporation, it turned out, had doubted the purity of the juice for several years before the CEO arrived. But the 25 percent price advantage offered by the supplier of the bogus concentrate allowed the operations head to meet cost-control goals. Furthermore, the company lacked an effective quality-control system, and a conclusive lab test for juice purity did not yet exist. When a member of the research department voiced concerns about the juice to operating management, he was accused of not being a team player and of acting like "Chicken Little." His judgment, his supervisor wrote in an annual performance review, was "colored by naiveté and impractical ideals." No one else seemed to have considered the company's obligations to its customers or to have thought about the potential harm of disclosure. No one considered the fact that the sale of adultered or misbranded juice is a legal offense, putting the company and its top management at risk of criminal liability.

—Continued

Continued

An FDA investigation taught Beech-Nut the hard way. In 1987, the company pleaded guilty to selling adultered and misbranded juice. Two years and two criminal trials later, the CEO pleaded guilty to ten counts of mislabeling. The total cost to the company—including fines, legal expenses, and lost sales—was an estimated $25 million.

Such errors of judgment rarely reflect an organizational culture and management philosophy that sets out to harm or deceive. More often, they reveal a culture that is insensitive or indifferent to ethical considerations or one that lacks effective organizational systems. By the same token, exemplary conduct usually reflects an organizational culture and philosophy that is infused with a sense of responsibility.

For example, Johnson & Johnson's handling of the Tylenol crisis is sometimes attributed to the singular personality of then-CEO James Burke. However, the decision to do a nationwide recall of Tylenol capsules in order to avoid further loss of life from product tampering was in reality not one decision but thousands of decisions made by individuals at all levels of the organization. The "Tylenol decision," then, is best understood not as an isolated incident, the achievement of a lone individual, but as the reflection of an organization's culture. Without a shared set of values and guiding principles deeply ingrained throughout the organization, it is doubtful that Johnson & Johnson's response would have been as rapid, cohesive, and ethically sound.

Many people resist acknowledging the influence of organizational factors on individual behavior—especially on misconduct—for fear of diluting people's sense of personal moral responsibility. But this fear is based on a false dichotomy between holding individual transgressors accountable and holding "the system" accountable. Acknowledging the importance of organizational context need not imply exculpating individual wrongdoers. To understand all is not to forgive all.

THE LIMITS OF A LEGAL COMPLIANCE PROGRAM

The consequences of an ethical lapse can be serious and far-reaching. Organizations can quickly become entangled in an all-consuming web of legal proceedings. The risk of litigation and liability has increased in the past decade as lawmakers have legislated new civil and criminal offenses, stepped up penalties, and improved support for law enforcement. Equally—if not more—important is the damage an ethical lapse can do to an organization's reputation and relationships. Both Sears and Beech-Nut, for instance, struggled to regain consumer trust and market share long after legal proceedings had ended.

As more managers have become alerted to the importance of organizational ethics, many have asked their lawyers to develop corporate ethics programs to detect and prevent violations of the law. The 1991 Federal Sentencing Guidelines offer a compelling rationale. Sanctions such as fines and probation for organizations convicted of wrongdoing can vary dramatically depending both on the degree of management cooperation in reporting and investigating corporate misdeeds and on whether or not the company has implemented a legal compliance program. (See the insert "Corporate Fines Under the Federal Sentencing Guidelines.")

Such programs tend to emphasize the prevention of unlawful conduct, primarily by increasing surveillance and control and by imposing penalties for wrongdoers. While plans vary, the basic framework is outlined in the sentencing guidelines. Managers must establish compliance standards and procedures; designate high-level personnel to oversee compliance; avoid delegating discretionary authority to those likely to act unlawfully; effectively communicate the company's standards and procedures through training or publications; take reasonable steps to achieve compliance through audits, monitoring processes, and a system for employees to report criminal misconduct without fear of retribution; consistently enforce standards through appropriate disciplinary measures; respond appropriately when offenses are detected; and, finally take reasonable steps to prevent the occurrence of similar offenses in the future.

There is no question of the necessity of a sound, well-articulated strategy for legal compliance in an organization. After all, employees can be frustrated and frightened by the complexity of today's legal environment. And even managers who claim to use the law as a guide to ethical behavior often lack more than a rudimentary understanding of complex legal issues.

Managers would be mistaken, however, to regard legal compliance as an adequate means for addressing the full range of ethical issues that arise every day. "If it's legal, it's ethical," is a frequently heard slogan. but conduct that is lawful may be highly problematic from an ethical point of view. Consider the sale in some countries of hazardous products without appropriate warnings or the purchase of goods from suppliers who operate inhumane sweatshops in developing countries. Companies engaged in international business often discover that conduct that infringes on recognized standards of human rights and decency is legally permissible in some jurisdictions.

Legal clearance does not certify the absence of ethical problems in the United States either, as a 1991 case at Salomon Brothers illustrates. Four top-level executives failed to take appropriate action when learning of unlawful activities on the government trading desk. Company lawyers found no law obligating the executives to disclose the improprieties. Nevertheless, the executives' delay in disclosing and failure to reveal their prior knowledge prompted a serious crisis of confidence among employees, creditors, shareholders, and customers.

—Continued

Continued

CORPORATE FINES UNDER THE FEDERAL SENTENCING GUIDELINES

What size fine is a corporation likely to pay if convicted of a crime? It depends on a number of factors, some of which are beyond a CEO's control, such as the existence of a prior record of similar misconduct. But it also depends on more controllable factors. The most important of these are reporting and accepting responsibility for the crime, cooperating with authorities, and having an effective program in place to prevent and detect unlawful behavior.

The following example, based on a case studied by the United States Sentencing Commission, shows how the 1991 Federal Sentencing Guidelines have affected overall fine levels and how managers' actions influence organizational fines.

Acme Corporation was charged and convicted of mail fraud. The company systematically charged customers who damaged rented automobiles more than the actual cost of repairs. Acme also billed some customers for the cost of repairs to vehicles for which they were not responsible. Prior to the criminal adjudication, Acme paid $13.7 million in restitution to the customers who had been overcharged.

Deciding before the enactment of the sentencing guidelines, the judge in the criminal case imposed a fine of $6.85 million, roughly half of the pecuniary loss suffered by Acme's customers. Under the sentencing guidelines, however, the results could have been dramatically different. Acme could have been fined from 5 percent to 200 percent the loss suffered by customers, depending on whether or not it had an effective program to prevent and detect violations of law and on whether or not it reported the crime, cooperated with authorities, and accepted responsibility for the unlawful conduct. If a high ranking official at Acme were found to have been involved, the maximum fine could have been as large as $54,800,000 or four times the loss to Acme customers. The following chart shows a possible range of fines for each situation:

WHAT FINE CAN ACME EXPECT?

	Maximum	Minimum
Program, reporting, cooperation, responsibility	$ 2,740,000	$ 685,000
Program only	10,960.000	5,480,000
No program, no reporting no cooperation, no responsibility	27,400,000	13,700,000
No program, no reporting no cooperation, no responsibility, involvement of high-level personnel	54,800,000	27,400,000

Based on Case No.: 88-266, United States Sentencing Commission, *Supplementary Report on Sentencing Guidelines for Organizations*.

The executives were forced to resign, having lost the moral authority to lead. Their ethical lapse compounded the trading desk's legal offenses, and the company ended up suffering losses—including legal costs, increased funding costs, and lost business—estimated at nearly $1 billion.

A compliance approach to ethics also overemphasizes the threat of detection and punishment in order to channel behavior in lawful directions. The underlying model for this approach is deterrence theory, which envisions people as rational maximizers of self-interest, responsive to the personal costs and benefits of their choices, yet indifferent to the moral legitimacy of those choices. But a recent study reported in *Why People Obey the Law* by Tom R. Tyler shows that obedience to the law is strongly influenced by a belief in its legitimacy and its moral correctness. People generally feel that they have a strong obligation to obey the law. Education about the legal standards and a supportive environment may be all that's required to insure compliance.

Discipline is, of course, a necessary part of any ethical system. Justified penalties for the infringement of legitimate norms are fair and appropriate. Some people do need the threat of sanctions. However, an overemphasis on potential sanctions can be superfluous and even counterproductive. Employees may rebel against programs that stress penalties, particularly if they are designed and imposed without employee involvement or if the standards are vague or unrealistic. Management may talk of mutual trust when unveiling a compliance plan, but employees often receive the message as a warning from on high. Indeed, the more skeptical among them may view compliance programs as nothing more than liability insurance for senior management. This is not an unreasonable conclusion, considering that compliance programs rarely address the root causes of misconduct.

Even in the best cases, legal compliance is unlikely to unleash much moral imagination or commitment. The law does not generally seek to inspire human excellence or distinction. It is no

—Continued

Continued

guide for exemplary behavior—or even good practice. Those managers who define ethics as legal compliance are implicitly endorsing a code of moral mediocrity for their organizations. As Richard Breeden, former chairman of the Securities and Exchange Commission, noted, "It is not an adequate ethical standard to aspire to get through the day without being indicted."

INTEGRITY AS A GOVERNING ETHIC

A strategy based on integrity holds organizations to a more robust standard. While compliance is rooted in avoiding legal sanctions, organizational integrity is based on the concept of self-governance in accordance with a set of guiding principles. From the perspective of integrity, the task of ethics management is to define and give life to an organization's guiding values, to create an environment that supports ethically sound behavior, and to instill a sense of shared accountability among employees. The need to obey the law is viewed as a positive aspect of organizational life, rather than an unwelcome constraint imposed by external authorities.

An integrity strategy is characterized by a conception of ethics as a driving force of an enterprise. Ethical values shape the search for opportunities, the design of organizational systems, and the decision-making process used by individuals and groups. They provide a common frame of reference and serve as a unifying force across different functions, lines of business, and employee groups. Organizational ethics helps define what a company is and what it stands for.

Many integrity initiatives have structural features common to compliance-based initiatives: a code of conduct, training in relevant areas of law, mechanisms for reporting and investigating potential misconduct, and audits and controls to insure that laws and company standards are being met. In addition, if suitably designed, an integrity-based initiative can establish a foundation for seeking the legal benefits that are available under the sentencing guidelines, should criminal wrongdoing occur. (See the insert "The Hallmarks of an Effective Integrity Strategy." p. 45)

But an integrity strategy is broader, deeper, and more demanding than a legal compliance initiative. Broader in that it seeks to enable responsible conduct. Deeper in that it cuts to the ethos and operating systems of the organization and its members, their guiding values and patterns of thought and action. And more demanding in that it requires an active effort to define the responsibilities and aspirations that constitute an organization's ethical compass. Above all, organizational ethics is seen as the work of management. Corporate counsel may play a role in the design and implementation of integrity strategies, but managers at all levels and across all functions are involved in the process. (See the chart, "Strategies for Ethics Management." p. 46)

During the past decade, a number of companies have undertaken integrity initiatives. They vary according to the ethical values focused on and the implementation approaches used. Some companies focus on the core values of integrity that reflect basic social obligations, such as respect for the rights of others, honesty, fair dealing, and obedience to the law. Other companies emphasize aspirations—values that are ethically desirable but no necessarily morally obligatory—such as good service to customers, a commitment to diversity, and involvement in the community.

When it comes to implementation, some companies begin with behavior. Following Aristotle's view that one becomes courageous by acting as a courageous person, such companies develop codes of conduct specifying appropriate behavior, along with a system of incentives, audits, and controls. Other companies focus less on specific actions and more on developing attitudes, decision-making processes, and ways of thinking that reflect their values. The assumption is that personal commitment and appropriate decision processes will lead to right action.

Martin Marietta, NovaCare, and Wetherill Associates have implemented and lived with quite different integrity strategies. In each case, management has found that the initiative has made important and often unexpected contributions to competitiveness, work environment, and key relationships on which the company depends.

MARTIN MARIETTA: EMPHASIZING CORE VALUES

Martin Marietta Corporation, the U.S. aerospace and defense contractor, opted for an integrity-based ethics program in 1985. At the time, the defense industry was under attack for fraud and mismanagement, and Martin Marietta was under investigation for improper travel billings. Managers knew they needed a better form of self-governance but were skeptical that an ethics program could influence behavior. "Back then people asked, 'Do you really need an ethics program to be ethical?'" recalls current President Thomas Young. "Ethics was something personal. Either you had it, or you didn't."

The corporate general counsel played a pivotal role in promoting the program, and legal compliance was a critical objective. But it was conceived of and implemented from the start as a companywide management initiative aimed at creating and maintaining a "do-it-right" climate. In its original conception, the program emphasized core values, such as honesty and fair play. Over time, it expanded to encompass quality and environmental responsibility as well.

Today the initiative consists of a code of conduct, an ethics training program, and procedures for reporting and investigating ethical concerns within the company. It also includes a system for disclosing violations of federal procurement law to the

—*Continued*

Continued

THE HALLMARKS OF AN EFFECTIVE INTEGRITY STRATEGY

There is no one right integrity strategy. Factors such as management personality, company history, culture, lines of business, and industry regulations must be taken into account when shaping an appropriate set of values and designing an implementation program. Still, several features are common to efforts that have achieved some success:

☐ *The guiding values and commitments make sense and are clearly communicated.* They reflect important organizational obligations and widely shared aspirations that appeal to the organization's members. Employees at all levels take them seriously, feel comfortable discussing them, and have a concrete understanding of their practical importance. This does not signal the absence of ambiguity and conflict but a willingness to seek solutions compatible with the framework of values.

☐ *Company leaders are personally committed, credible, and willing to take action on the values they espouse.* They are not mere mouthpieces. They are willing to scrutinize their own decisions. Consistency on the part of leadership is key. Waffling on values will lead to employee cynicism and a rejection of the program. At the same time, managers must assume responsibility for making tough calls when ethical obligations conflict.

☐ *The espoused values are integrated into the normal channels of management decision making and are reflected in the organization's critical activities:* the development of plans, the setting of goals, the search for opportunities, the allocation of resources, the gathering and communication of information, the measurement of performance, and the promotion and advancement of personnel.

☐ *The company's systems and structures support and reinforce its values.* Information systems, for example, are designed to provide timely and accurate information. Reporting relationships are structured to build in checks and balances to promote objective judgment. Performance appraisal is sensitive to means as well as ends.

☐ *Managers throughout the company have the decision-making skills, knowledge, and competencies needed to make ethically sound decisions on a day-to-day basis.* Ethical thinking and awareness must be part of every manager's mental equipment. Ethics education is usually part of the process.

Success in creating a climate for responsible and ethically sound behavior requires continuing effort and a considerable investment of time and resources. A glossy code of conduct, a high-ranking ethics officer, a training program, an annual ethics audit—these trappings of an ethics program do not necessarily add up to a responsible, law-abiding organization whose espoused values match its actions. A formal ethics program can serve as a catalyst and a support system, but organizational integrity depends on the integration of the company's values into its driving systems.

---

government. A corporate ethics office manages the program, and ethics representatives are stationed at major facilities. An ethics steering committee, made up of Martin Marietta's president, senior executives, and two rotating members selected from field operations, oversees the ethics office. The audit and ethics committee of the board of directors oversees the steering committee.

The ethics office is responsible for responding to questions and concerns from the company's employees. Its network of representatives serves as a sounding board, a source of guidance, and a channel for raising a range of issues, from allegations of wrongdoing to complaints about poor management, unfair supervision, and company policies and practices. Martin Marietta's ethics network, which accepts anonymous complaints, logged over 9,000 calls in 1991, when the company had about 60,000 employees. In 1992, it investigated 684 cases. The ethics office also works closely with the human resources, legal, audit, communications, and security functions to respond to employee concerns.

Shortly after establishing the program, the company began its first round of ethics training for the entire workforce, starting with the CEO and senior executives. Now in its third round, training for senior executives focuses on decision making, the challenges of balancing multiple responsibilities, and compliance with laws and regulations critical to the company. The incentive compensation plan for executives makes responsibility for promoting ethical conduct an explicit requirement for reward eligibility and requires that business and personal goals be achieved in accordance with the company's policy on ethics. Ethical conduct and support for the ethics program are also criteria in regular performance reviews.

Today top-level managers say the ethics program has helped the company avoid serious problems and become more responsive to its more than 90,000 employees. The ethics network, which tracks the number and types of cases and complaints, has served as an early warning system for poor management, quality and safety defects, racial and gender discrimination, environmental concerns, inaccurate and false records, and personnel grievances regarding salaries, promotions, and lay-offs.

—Continued

Continued

STRATEGIES FOR ETHICS MANAGEMENT

Characteristics of Compliance Strategy

Ethos	Conformity with externally imposed standards
Objective	Prevent criminal misconduct
Leadership	Lawyer-driven
Methods	Education, reduced discretion, auditing and controls, penalties
Behavioral assumptions	Autonomous beings guided by material self-interest

Characteristics of Integrity Strategy

Ethos	Self-governance according to chosen standards
Objective	Enable responsible conduct
Leadership	Management-driven, with aid of lawyers, HR, others
Methods	Education, leadership, accountability, organizational systems and decision processes, auditing and controls, penalties
Behavioral assumptions	Social beings guided by material self-interest, values, ideals, peers

Implementation of Compliance Strategy

Standards	Criminal and regulatory law
Staffing	Lawyers
Activities	Develop compliance standards, train and communicate, handle reports of misconduct, conduct investigations, oversee compliance audits, enforce standards
Education	Compliance standards and system

Implementation of Integrity Strategy

Standards	Company values and aspirations; social obligations, including law
Staffing	Executives and managers with lawyers, others
Activities	Lead development of company values and standards, train and communicate, integrate into company systems, provide guidance and consultation, assess values performance, identify and resolve problems, oversee compliance activities
Education	Decision making and values compliance standards and system

—Continued

Continued

By providing an alternative channel for raising such concerns, Martin Marietta is able to take corrective action more quickly and with a lot less pain. In many cases, potentially embarrassing problems have been identified and dealt with before becoming a management crisis, a lawsuit, or a criminal investigation. Among employees who brought complaints in 1993, 75 percent were satisfied with the results.

Company executives are also convinced that program has helped reduce the incidence of misconduct. When allegations of misconduct do surface, the company says it deals with them openly. On several occasions, for instance, Martin Marietta has voluntarily disclosed and made restitution to the government for misconduct involving potential violations of federal procurement law in addition, when an employee alleged that the company had retaliated against him for voicing said concerns about his plant on CBS news, top management commissioned an investigation by an outside law firm. Although failing to support the allegations, the investigation found that employees at the plant feared retaliation when raising health, safety, or environmental complaints. The company redoubled its efforts to identify and discipline those employees taking retaliatory action and stressed the desirability of an open work environment in its ethics training and company communications.

Although the ethics program helps Martin Marietta avoid certain types of litigation, it has occasionally led to other kinds of legal action. In a few cases, employees dismissed for violating the code of ethics sued Martin Marietta, arguing that the company had violated its own code by imposing unfair and excessive discipline.

Still, the company believes that its attention to ethics has been worth it. The ethics program has led to better relationships with the government, as well as to new business opportunities. Along with prices and technology, Martin Marietta's record of integrity, quality, and reliability of estimates plays a role in the awarding of defense contracts, which account for some 75 percent of the company's revenues. Executives believe that the reputation they've earned through their ethics program has helped them build trust with government auditors, as well. By opening up communications, the company has reduced the time spent on redundant audits.

The program has also helped change employees' perceptions and priorities. Some managers compare their new ways of thinking about ethics to the way they understand quality. They consider more carefully how situations will be perceived by others, the possible long-term, consequences of short-term thinking, and the need for continuous improvement. CEO Norman Augustine notes, "Ten years ago, people would have said that there were no ethical issues in business. Today employees think their number-one objective is to be thought of as decent people doing quality work."

NOVACARE: BUILDING SHARED ASPIRATIONS

NovaCare Inc., one of the largest providers of rehabilitation services to nursing homes and hospitals in the United States, has oriented its ethics effort toward building a common core of shared aspirations. But in 1988, when the company was called InSpeech, the only sentiment shared was mutual mistrust.

Senior executives built the company from a series of aggressive acquisitions over a brief period of time to take advantage of the expanding market for therapeutic services. However, in 1988, the viability of the company was in question. Turnover among its frontline employees—the clinicians and therapists who care for patients in nursing homes and hospitals—escalated to 57 percent per year. The company's inability to retain therapists caused customers to defect and the stock price to languish in an extended slump.

After months of soul-searching, InSpeech executives realized that the turnover rate was a symptom of a more basic problem: the lack of a common set of values and aspirations. There was, as one executive put it, a "huge disconnect" between the values of the therapists and clinicians and those of the managers who ran the company. The therapists and clinicians evaluated the company's success in terms of its delivery of high-quality health care. InSpeech management, led by executives with financial services and venture capital backgrounds, measured the company's worth exclusively in terms of financial success. Management's single-minded emphasis on increasing hours of reimbursable care turned clinicians off. They took management's performance orientation for indifference to patient care and left the company in droves.

CEO John Foster recognized the need for a common frame of references and a common language to unify the diverse groups. So he brought in consultants to conduct interviews and focus groups with the company's health care professionals, managers, and customers. Based on the results, an employee task force drafted a proposed vision statement for the company, and another 250 employees suggested revisions. Then Foster and several senior managers developed a succinct statement of the company's guiding purpose and fundamental beliefs that could be used as a framework for making decisions and setting goals, policies, and practices.

Unlike a code of conduct, which articulates specific behavioral standards, the statement of vision, purposes, and beliefs lays out in very simple terms the company's central purpose and core values. The purpose—meeting the rehabilitation needs of patients through clinical leadership—is supported by four key beliefs: respect for the individual, service to the customer, pursuit of excellence, and commitment to personal integrity. Each value is discussed with examples of how it is manifested in the day-to-day activities and policies of the company, such as how to measure the quality of care.

—Continued

Continued

To support the newly defined values, the company changed its name to NovaCare and introduced a number of structural and operational changes. Field managers and clinicians were given greater decision-making authority; clinicians were provided with additional resources to assist in the delivery of effective therapy; and a new management structure integrated the various therapies offered by the company. The hiring of new corporate personnel with health care backgrounds reinforced the company's new clinical focus.

The introduction of the vision, purpose, and beliefs met with varied reactions from employees, ranging from cool skepticism to open enthusiasm. One employee remembered thinking the talk about values "much ado about nothing." Another recalled, "It was really wonderful. It gave us a goal that everyone aspired to, no matter what their place in the company." At first, some were baffled about how the vision, purpose, and beliefs were to be used. But, over time, managers became more adept at explaining and using them as a guide. When a customer tried to hire away a valued employee, for example, managers considered raiding the customer's company for employees. After reviewing the beliefs, the managers abandoned the idea.

NovaCare managers acknowledge and company surveys indicate that there is plenty of room for improvement. While the values are used as a firm reference point for decision making and evaluation in some areas of the company, they are still viewed with reservation in others. Some managers do not "walk the talk," employees complain. And recently acquired companies have yet to be fully integrated into the program. Nevertheless, many NovaCare employees say the values initiative played a critical role in the company's 1990 turnaround.

The values reorientation also helped the company deal with its most serious problem: turnover among health care providers. In 1990, the turnover rate stood at 32 percent, still above target but a significant improvement over the 1988 rate of 57 percent. By 1993, turnover had dropped to 27 percent. Moreover, recruiting new clinicians became easier. Barely able to hire 25 new clinicians each month in 1988, the company added 776 in 1990 and 2,546 in 1993. Indeed, one employee who left during the 1988 turmoil said that her decision to return in 1990 hinged on the company's adoption of the vision, purpose, and beliefs.

WETHERILL ASSOCIATES: DEFINING RIGHT ACTION

Wetherill Associates, Inc.—a small, privately held supplier of electrical parts to the automotive market—has neither a conventional code of conduct nor a statement of values. Instead, WAI has a *Quality Assurance Manual*—a combination of philosophy text, conduct guide, technical manual, and company profile—that describes the company's commitment to honesty and its guiding principle of right action.

WAI doesn't have a corporate ethics officer who reports to top management, because at WAI, the company's corporate ethics officer *is* top management. Marie Bothe, WAI's chief executive officer, sees her main function as keeping the 350-employee company on the path of right action and looking for opportunities to help the community. She delegates the "technical" aspects of the business–marketing, finance, personnel, operations–to other members of the organization.

Right action, the basis for all of WAI's decisions, is a well-developed approach that challenges most conventional management thinking. The company explicitly rejects the usual conceptual boundaries that separate morality and self-interest. Instead, they define right behavior as logically, expediently, and morally right. Managers teach employees to look at the needs of the customers, suppliers, and the community—in addition to those of the company and its employees—when making decisions.

WAI also has a unique approach to competition. One employee explains, "We are not 'in competition' with anybody. We just do what we have to do to serve the customer." Indeed, when occasionally unable to fill orders, WAI salespeople refer customers to competitors. Artificial incentives, such as sales contests, are never used to spur individual performance. Nor are sales results used in determining compensation. Instead, the focus is on teamwork and customer service. Managers tell all new recruits that absolute honesty, mutual courtesy, and respect are standard operating procedure.

Newcomers generally react positively to company philosophy, but not all are prepared for such a radical departure from the practices they have known elsewhere. Recalling her initial interview one recruit described her response to being told that lying was not allowed, "What do you mean? No lying? I'm a buyer. I lie for a living!" Today she is persuaded that the policy makes sound business sense. WAI is known for informing suppliers of overshipments as well as undershipments and for scrupulous honesty in the sale of parts, even when deception cannot be readily detected.

Since its entry into the distribution business 13 years ago, WAI has seen its revenues climb steadily from just under $1 million to nearly $98 million in 1993, and this in an industry with little growth. Once seen as an upstart beset by naysayers and industry skeptics, WAI is now credited with entering and professionalizing an industry in which kickbacks, bribes, and "gratuities" were commonplace. Employees—equal numbers of men and women ranging in age from 17 to 92—praise the work environment as both productive and supportive.

WAI's approach could be difficult to introduce in a larger, more traditional organization. WAI is a small company founded

—Continued

Continued

by 34 people who shared a belief in right action; its ethical values were naturally built into the organization from the start. Those values are so deeply ingrained in the company's culture and operating systems that they have been largely self-sustaining. Still, the company has developed its own training program and takes special care to hire people willing to support right action. Ethics and job skills are considered equally important in determining an individual's competence and suitability for employment. For WAI, the challenge will be to sustain its vision as the company grows and taps into markets overseas.

At WAI, as at Martin Marietta and NovaCare, a management-led commitment to ethical values has contributed to competitiveness, positive workforce morale, as well as solid sustainable relationships with the company's key constituencies. In the end, creating a climate that encourages exemplary conduct may be the best way to discourage damaging misconduct. Only in such an environment do rogues really act alone.

SOURCE: Lynn Sharp Paine is a John G. McLean professor at the Harvard Business School, specializing in management ethics. Her current research focuses on leadership and organizational integrity in a global environment. Reprinted by permission of *Harvard Business Review.* From "Managing for Organizational Integrity" by Lynn Sharp Paine, March/April, 1994. Copyright © 1994 by the Harvard Business School Publishing Corporation; all rights reserved.

The Whistle-Blower: Patriot or Bounty Hunter?

Andrew W. Singer
Across the Board, November 1992

The False Claims Act provides financial incentives for employees to report their companies' transgressions to the government. Does that debase their motives?

While serving in Vietnam, Emil Stache had the misfortune to stumble onto a booby-trapped Viet Cong bomb. The explosion killed several of his fellow soldiers, and Stache himself suffered severe shrapnel wounds to his left arm and shoulder. He later learned that the trap had been made from a defective U.S. bomb—one that never exploded.

Years later, Stache was manager of quality engineering and reliability at Teledyne Relays, a subsidiary of Teledyne, Inc. He suspected that Teledyne Relays falsified tests on the electromagnetic relays (electronic components used in missiles, planes, rockets and other military hardware) the company manufactured for the U.S. government.

Stache felt it his ethical duty to report the matter: He knew only too well the price of defective hardware. "It was the only thing he could do," explains his lawyer, John R. Phillips. "He complained about it. He got fired."

Stache brought a lawsuit against Teledyne Relays under the federal False Claims Act: he was later joined in the action by the Department of Justice. The suit claims that Teledyne Relays' failure to properly test the relay components defrauded the government of as much as $250 million. If found guilty, the Los Angeles–based company could be liable for as much as $750 million in damages, treble the amount that the government claims it was defrauded.

Who is Emil Stache? A patriot who just did his duty? That certainly is how Phillips and others see him. But if Stache's lawsuit succeeds, he stands to become a very rich patriot, indeed. According to provisions of the amended False Claims Act. Stache and his co-plaintiffs in the suit—another Teledyne Relays employee named Almon Muehlhausen and Taxpayers Against Fraud, a nonprofit organization founded by Phillips—could get 15 percent to 25 percent of any money recovered by the government. Stache himself theoretically could receive as much as $62 million.

(Contacted for comment on the case, Teledyne spokesperson Berkley Baker said, "We have no comment to make. It's in the legal system now.")

CREATING MARKET INCENTIVES

The amended False Claims Act grew out of public outrage in the mid-1980s over reports of fraud and abuse on the part of military contractors—of $600 toilet seats and country-club memberships billed to the government. Congress decided to put some teeth into its efforts to reduce contracting fraud. In 1986, it passed the False Claims Act amendments, whose *qui tam* provisions allow employees who bring forward information about contractor fraud to share with the government in any financial recovery realized by their efforts. (*Qui tam* is Latin shorthand for, "He who sues for the king as well as himself.")

Those market incentives are now bearing fruit. In July, the government recovered $50 million in a case brought by a whistle-blower against a former division of Singer Co. And a week later, the government recovered the largest amount

—Continued

Continued

ever in such an action: a $59.5 million settlement with General Electric Co. (GE). That case, a scandal involving the sale of military-jet engines in Israel, was brought initially by the manager of a GE unit.

U.S. Rep. Howard L. Berman of California, a cosponsor of the 1986 amendment, expects recoveries from *qui tam* actions, most of which are against defense contractors, to reach $1 billion in the next two to three years. The Teledyne Relays suit looms as one of the largest cases, but Phillips speaks of two others in the pipeline, one against Litton Industries Inc. and another that is under court seal, that could bring the government "staggering" amounts.

UNDERMINING VOLUNTARY EFFORTS?

Not surprisingly, many of the defense industry are aghast at the new False Claims Act—and, specifically, its *qui tam* provisions. The law has created "enormous concern in the defense industry," says Alan R. Yuspeh, a government-contracts attorney and partner in Howrey & Simon in Washington, D.C. Some fear that cases may proliferate and people with essentially technical disagreements may bring suits in the hope of reaping payoffs from an out-of-court settlement.

The *qui tam* provisions encourage "bounty hunting" and undermine voluntary ethics efforts, add critics. Why should an employee report wrongdoing to his company when he can hold out and earn millions from the government? And from the larger ethical perspective: Shouldn't people report fraud because it's the right thing to do, and not because they hope to reap a windfall profit?

"I think personally that the provision of bounties is misguided," said Gary Edwards, president of the Ethics Resource Center, a nonprofit education and consulting organization based in Washington, D.C. "It creates an incentive for individuals in companies that are trying to do a better job—not to report wrongdoing, but to gather data so as to participate in the reward."

"Encouraging tittle-tattles is destructive," declares Charles Barber, former chairman and CEO of Asarco, Inc., a *Fortune* 500 company that produces nonferrous metals. "The integrity of the organization has to be built another way," such as with corporate ombudsman offices. "You can't run a defense company if everyone is being watched."

"I deplore the way we have developed into such a litigious society in which everyone is jumping on the bandwagon to sue about anything that comes up," says Sanford N. McDonnell, chairman emeritus of McDonnell Douglas Corp., the nation's largest defense contractor.

"IF WE ALL LIVED IN AN IDEAL WORLD . . ."

Phillips, who is generally credited with drafting the amended False Claims Act, responds: "If we all lived in an ideal world, where all did the right thing on principle, we would have no need for such a law. But we don't live in such a world." People who bring charges against their companies take great risks—to their jobs, their families and their careers, he says.

Most agree that the plight of the corporate whistle-blower has historically been a bleak one. A survey of 85 whistle-blowers by the Association of Mental Health Specialties (now Integrity International) in College Park, Md., in the late-1980s found that 82 percent experienced harassment after blowing the whistle, 60 percent got fired, 17 percent lost their homes, and 10 percent reported having attempted suicide. "You can't expect them to [report fraud] when there is nothing but risk and heartache down the road," says Phillips. Sharing in the recovery of damages is one way to right the balance.

Yuspeh, for one, isn't convinced. It is an "unsound piece of legislation. It almost invites disgruntled former employees who may have had some technical disagreement to go out and file a lawsuit." (It should be added that in recent years, large contractors have increasingly reported instances of wrongdoing or fraud to the government voluntarily, before evidence came to public light.)

Congressman Berman says the law works precisely as intended: By providing marketplace incentives, it encourages people to protect the government and the public from waste, fraud and abuse. "I'm not only happy with the law, I'm proud of it," he tells *Across the Board.*

Morally problematic"? "You mean like: If you have any information about a wanted criminal, we'll pay a reward?" asks Berman, rhetorically.

Those companies that commit fraud don't like the Act, suggests Berman, while those in compliance with the law aren't troubled by it. And he is skeptical of detractors who claim that these are merely technical disputes. "The test here is commission of fraud," he says.

HARKS BACK TO THE CIVIL WAR

The original False Claims Act dates back to the Civil War, where it was used to prosecute manufacturers who substituted sawdust for gunpowder in Union army supplies. Employees who exposed contractors who overcharged the government could, theoretically, earn 10 percent of the amount recovered. But under the old law, federal prosecutors who took over cases had the option of removing private plaintiffs, leaving whistle-blowers high and dry.

—Continued

Continued

PORTRAIT OF A WHISTLE-BLOWER

Corporate whistle-blowers have traditionally been treated as malcontents, troublemakers, and misfits. And many have paid a steep price for their actions.

A 1987 survey of 87 whistle-blowers by Dr. Donald Soeken, president of Integrity International in college Park, Md., noted: "All but one respondent reported experiencing retaliation which they attributed to their whistle-blowing. And that one individual merely indicated that 'nothing could be proved.'"

Soeken, who was a government whistle-blower himself, compares the whistle-blower to a cross between a bloodhound and a bulldog. "He will track it down [i.e., the wrongdoing] and stand his ground. . . . His conscience is very strong, unwavering. He's the first one to feel guilty when something happens.

That certainly applies to Richard Walker, a whistle-blower in the era *before* the amended False Claims Act. A scientist with a Ph.D. in physics, Walker worked for 27 years at American Telephone & Telegraph Co.'s (AT&T) prestigious Bell Laboratories.

In 1971, as head of a team of scientists working on a high-level military project for the U.S. Navy, he discovered serious errors in Bell Labs' computer projections. He informed his superior of the errors, and said they had better report them to the Navy. When his boss refused, Walker took matters into his own hands.

He decided to give a corporate seminar within Bell Labs, which was his prerogative as a manager. Walker spent an hour exposing the errors he had found and explaining how the company had overestimated the effectiveness of the project. "The way to avoid corruption is to get it out in the open," he told *Ethikos* in a 1987 interview, recalling his thinking at the time.

The immediate response within the company to his seminar seemed positive. "I thought, in view of his feedback, that I had gotten through to these people," said Walker.

He was mistaken, Several months later, Walker's boss wrote a letter to a high Bell Labs officer questioning Walker's technical competence. "On the basis of that criticism, I was moved out of that area and put into a totally inappropriate assignment. It was just a way of getting rid of me."

There was a succession of increasingly demeaning and meaningless assignments. He spent three-and-a-half years in a marine-cable engineering department, followed by a supervisory appointment at a "planning" center in which "for three-and-a-half years, they wouldn't tell me what my responsibilities were."

In 1979, Bell Labs fired Walker for allegedly not taking an active interest in his assigned work. In 1982, Walker brought suit against AT&T, charging that he had been fired without good cause. Walker devoted himself full time to his case. He had an entire room in his apartment set aside to store depositions and other evidence relevant to his case. He spent $50,000 of his own money pressing the litigation. During this time, his wife divorced him and he was forced to sell the house he designed in affluent Mendham, N.J., where he raised his four children.

On March 23, 1987, *Walker vs. Bell* came to trial. Eight days later, the New Jersey judge dismissed the case that Walker had brought.

According to AT&T, justice was served. "Dr. Walker had ample opportunity to prove his allegations before the court, and the court rejected those allegations as being totally unfounded," the AT&T attorney who tried the case commented.

Walker took the defeat hard. Despite the advice of people like Soeken and others, he refused to let the matter rest. For years he tried to interest journalists, government officials and employee-rights organizations in this case. He barraged AT&T officers and directors with letters seeking redress for the wrong he felt he had suffered. All to no avail.

Eventually, Walker moved back to his home state of Michigan, where he remarried and is now working to establish a retreat for whistle-blowers.

Walker may have been ahead of his time. New Jersey has since passed legislation to protect whistle-blowers. AT&T now has an excessive network of corporate ombudsman to handle cases like his. And the amended False Claims Act has since been enacted.

John Phillips, an attorney who has represented other whistle-blowers and a principal author of the amended False Claims Act says that one key effect of the amended Act is that it no longer requires a "heroic" figure to blow the whistle. The Act could also bring forth a higher order of whistle-blower, he suggests. In the past, whistle-blowers "were not always the most stable people," noted Phillips in a 1989 interview with *Ethikos*. Many, he said, had a "need to confess" or to "point the finger at someone."

The people whom Phillips sees coming forward now to report wrongdoing by government contractors are still idealistic in some ways, but in many ways they are "far more credible, substantial, senior people than whistle-blowers, from the pre-[False Claims Act] amendment era."—**A.W.S.**

—Continued

Continued

"Very few people were willing to do it under the old system," either through fear of losing their jobs, being black-balled within their industry, or shunned by their friends, says Phillips, a partner in the Los Angeles law firm of Hall & Phillips. It took a kind of heroic figure to blow the whistle, he says.

The amended False Claims Act aimed to fix some of those problems, "We tried to rebuild the law, to give it some teeth," explains Berman. "Where the government is not privy to information about fraud, the taxpayers are represented by private parties."

Even more important than the sheer amounts of money recovered, says Phillips, is the preventive effect of the statute on corporations. "The law has shaken up their internal practices. People who were previously inclined to go along with questionable practices are now doing the right thing," he says.

But companies say the statute undermines their voluntary ethics efforts. "I know their argument," replies Phillips. "But there's no basis to it. They're saying, 'We have a whole system set up. You should come to us first.' With fraud, he says, the government has an interest in being the first to know. The government is saying, 'We want information to come directly to us in cases of fraud.' "

"It will enhance corporate efforts, because companies can get socked with treble damages for fraud," says Berman. "Companies will become more vigilant."

Does he know of any contractors who support the amendments? "The goal of the act is not to please government contractors," snaps Berman. "The goal is to protect the government and the public."

THE GE CASE

The case involving General Electric's aircraft-engine division is one of the more interesting False Claims Act actions to arise. Employees in the division conspired with an Israeli general, Rami Dotan, to submit fraudulent claims for work done for the Israeli Air Force. General Electric eventually pleaded guilty to four federal criminal-fraud charges. It agreed to pay the Justice Department $9.5 million in fines for the criminal charges and $59.5 million for the civil case brought under the False Claims Act.

The Justice Department said the company's employees helped divert as much as $40 million to Dotan and others, money that ultimately came from the U.S. government. The scheme became known through a lawsuit filed by Chester Walsh, who served as general manager of the aircraft-engine division's Israeli unit from 1984 to 1988.

What irks General Electric is that Walsh reported the matter first to the government instead of the company, despite the fact that Walsh, like others at GE, signed an ethics statement each year affirming that he would report wrongdoing to the company if and when it was discovered.

"The man involved decided not to report wrongdoing," says Bruce Bunch, a GE spokesman. "He took no steps to stop it. "He participated in it, and all the time he signed our written statement each year that he would report any improprieties to management." It is General Electric's position that Walsh gathered information from 1986 to 1990 and then filed his lawsuit, from which he hoped to gain personally. Walsh could receive 25 percent of the nearly $60 million recovered by the government as a result of the civil suit. (A hearing that will determine the exact amount is set to begin in November in Cincinnati.)

If he had reported the corruption immediately, the case would have come to light, continues Bunch. "We had an ombudsman telephone number at the corporate office, outside of the business loop. Additionally, he could have called the Department of Defense ombudsman."

A case of bounty hunting? "That clearly appears to be what happened here," says Bunch.

Phillips, who represents Walsh, claims that General Electric has smeared his client. "They claim Walsh is a money grubber. That's their party line." (GE Chairman John F. Welch, Jr. had been quoted in the *Corporate Crime Reporter*, a weekly legal publication, labeling Walsh as "a money-grubbing guy who sat back and waited in the weeds so the damages would mount." Bunch declines to comment on the accuracy of that quote.) Phillips tells a different story: "It was his dream job. It was very painful for him to do this."

Walsh feared for his job and even his life, Phillips says. He worried that anything he told GE would get back to Dotan, whom Phillips characterizes as a ruthless, violence-prone individual. His superiors at the aircraft-engine division were all aware of the arrangement with Dotan, Walsh believed, "He says that Dotan had people removed from their jobs at GE. The idea that he would go back and write a letter to Cincinnati [where the aircraft-engine division is based] about what he had seen was simply not credible," says Phillips.

As proof that Walsh's suspicions were well-founded. Phillips points to the fact that Dotan is now serving 13 years in prison in Israel. The general was charged by the Israeli government with kickbacks, theft, fraud, obstruction of justice and conspiring to kidnap and harm a fellow Israeli Ministry of Defense official.

Couldn't Walsh have gone to General Electric's corporate ombudsman, who is based in Fairfield, Conn., and is presumably outside the aircraft-engine division loop? "He doesn't know who's on the other end," answers Phillips. For all Walsh knew, Phillips says, the ombudsman might just get on the phone with Cincinnati to find out what was going on.

—Continued

Continued

But couldn't he have called anonymously? "It's an 800 number. They can find out where it came from. There was no way he could protect his anonymity." Or so Walsh believed, Phillips says.

"The idea that people will call up blindly some number is ludicrous," Phillips says. "I don't think people have confidence in the GE program." (Subsequent to this interview, *The Wall Street Journal* ran a front-page story on the company headlined: "GE's Drive to Purge Fraud Is Hampered by

---

FALSE CLAIMS SUITS GROWING

How does the government view the False Claims Act? "It is hardly a secret that the Act is critical to the government's anti-fraud effort," Stuart Gerson, assistant attorney general, acknowledged last year, Gerson added, however, that the statute's *qui tam* provisions, which allow private citizens to bring actions on behalf of the government, have been controversial, affecting as they do "the climate of government contracting and the dynamics of a corporation's relationship with its employees."

As of April 1, six years since the amendments passed, 407 *qui tam* suits had been filed. The government took over 66 of these cases; it is currently litigating 29 cases and has settled or obtained judgements in 37 others. The total recoveries of $147 million from *qui tam* suits under the Act comprise about 13.5 percent of the governments's total fraud recoveries for the six-year period. Individuals who brought suits had won $14.5 million as of April, but 75 cases were still under investigation. (The dollar amount doesn't include the large recoveries in July from the General Electric Co. case reported in the main story.)

The number of *qui tam* suits has grown steadily since 1986, notes Gerson, and it is expected to rise further. Thirty-three were filed in all of fiscal-year 1987, for example, while 78 were filed in the first eight months of fiscal-year 1991 alone. Cases involving the Department of Defense are by far the most numerous, but now actions being taken in other areas, including health care, agriculture, and the Department of Housing and Urban Development.

"In short, as attention is focused on the whistle-blower suits, and significant recoveries have been reported, this form of action is proliferating," said Gerson.

However, some government officials recently have expressed second thoughts about the potentially large awards to individual whistle-blowers. In the GE fraud case, Gerson said he had reservations about just how much credit and money the whistle-blower and his lawyers should receive. It remains to be seen whether attempts will be made to curb such awards.—**A.W.S.**

Workers' Mistrust," which appeared to support many of Phillips' assertions.)

"A DETRIMENTAL EFFECT"

Whatever the whys and wherefores of the GE case, it seems clear that the *qui tam* provisions are causing havoc among those in charge of compliance at some defense companies. "Pandemonium" was how the ombudsman at one large defense company characterized the provisions and the large suits now being filed.

"I've heard from some company representatives who believe the availability of the *qui tam* rewards have had a detrimental effect, that they have caused people not to use their internal systems," says the Ethics Resource Center's Edwards.

"No company can be happy with *qui tam* procedures," says John Impert, director of corporate ethics policy and assistant general counsel at The Boeing Co., even though his company has been virtually untouched by the False Claims Act. "It provides incentives to employees to take an adverse position. This is illustrated graphically in the GE case."

It's important that people report matters of ethical concern, says McDonnell of McDonnell Douglas, "But I don't think they should receive remuneration for that," he says.

Won't this help eliminate the steep price whistle-blowers have paid for coming forward?" "I'm sure it will stimulate more action, more people coming forward, but I'd rather see it come from individuals who take it to the company ombudsman, and report it without attribution," says McDonnell.

DEPUTIZING CITIZENS

Attorney Yuspeh and others are fundamentally at odds with the notion that individuals should bring lawsuits on the part of the U.S. government. "The role of initiating [lawsuits] on the part of the government is a role for the officer of the U.S. government. I have a big problem with individuals who have a personal profit motive, who have inside information, and who may be disgruntled because of downsizing, having the power of the government to advance a personal agenda."

Yuspeh notes that plaintiffs' lawyers tend to profit from the amended False Claims Act and its controversial *qui tam* provisions: "There's a lot of money for them to make." He would prefer an arrangement where informants would get some money from the government, but would not bring suit themselves. "At least the government is then deciding whether to bring a suit." This would also cut out the plaintiffs' legal fees.

"The problem with *qui tam* suits is that someone who would otherwise do this as part of their normal duties might now wait until they are no longer employed, or until they have an opportunity to enrich themselves," says LeRoy J. Haugh, who is vice president for procurement and finance of the

—Continued

Continued

Aerospace Industries Association, an organization based in Washington, D.C.

"Our biggest concern with *qui tam* proceedings is that someone who wants to bring a suit is at no risk at all," Haugh says. "If they can get a lawyer to handle it on a contingency basis and they win, they stand to win a great deal of money. And if they lose, they haven't lost anything, except the lawyer's time."

Answers Congressman Berman: "The situation here is that no one gets anything unless fraud is committed. Lawyer's won't take cases if they're not legitimate."

Still, Haugh says, the negative publicity generated from such suits—even if the company accused of wrongdoing is eventually found to be not guilty—"often overshadows efforts over the last seven or eight years on the part of many companies to comply with Defense Industry Initiative guidelines [a set of voluntary guidelines developed by the nation's largest defense contractors to promote ethical business conduct] and to put into place adequate checks and balances."

IMPORTANCE OF BUILDING TRUST

"I'm not saying that every suit that is brought is a frivolous suit," says Yuspeh, who served as coordinator of the Defense Industry Initiative (DII) steering committee. (He makes clear that he is speaking only for himself in making these comments, not the DII companies.) "Clearly some cases are meritorious. But it makes more sense to have officials of the U.S. government handle them."

Ethics Resource Center's Edwards doesn't quarrel with the notion that whistle-blowers have historically been treated very badly. But he points out that today they have protection under the law against retaliation, and that many excellent voluntary corporate programs have been initiated since the amendments were passed. Many companies today have ethics hotlines, ombudsman offices, extensive ethics-training programs and ethics committees. "Maybe several years ago it was necessary to entice them to blow the whistle," he says. But that isn't the case in many major American corporations today. "A well-developed ethics program should obviate the need for that," he adds.

Even Phillips concedes that voluntary corporate ethics efforts could be effective. "But you've got to convince people that the corporation wants you to do this, and that the corporation will reward you," he says.

Phillips may have hit on something there. Or to put the problem in quasi-dialectical terms: If the *thesis* back in the 1980s was egregious defense-industry waste and abuse, and the *antithesis* was the punitive (at least, from the industry perspective) bounty-hunting provisions of the False Claims Act, the *synthesis* could well be voluntary corporate ethics efforts that enjoy the full confidence of employees—and that really work.

"It takes time, no doubt about it," says McDonnell, referring to building trust within a company. "You can't just mandate it. It has to be built up by actual cases, and it's difficult to advertise it, because that [confidentiality] is the sort of thing you're trying to protect. But when it's done right, it gets the desired result."

SOURCE: *Across the Board*, November 1992, pp. 16–22. Reprinted with permission.

Law Case Summary: Caremark National Inc.

L.J. Brooks

Late in 1996, the Chancery Court of the State of Delaware—a very influential court in corporate matters—handed down a decision that changed the expectations of directors for monitoring the affairs of the organizations they direct. The change held in the Caremark National Inc. case was to require directors to monitor organizational activities even when there is no cause for suspicion of wrongdoing.

Until the Caremark decision, the guiding case was the Delaware Supreme Court's 1963 decision in *Graham v. Allis-Chalmers Manufacturing Co.* In *Allis-Chalmers*, a case involving director's liability for violations of U.S. antitrust laws, the court had found that, "absent cause for suspicion," a board of directors had no legal duty to create a system for monitoring of or compliance with organizational activities. This allowed directors to argue an "ostrich" defense in the event of wrongdoing to the effect that they had "seen no evil nor heard no evil" and had made their decisions in good faith and to the best of their ability. As a result, the fiduciary duties of directors and the duty of care were somewhat circumscribed from the level of responsibility that some stakeholders felt reasonable.

The Chancery Court took the view, in the *Caremark Case*, a derivative lawsuit to one involving kickbacks to health care providers in violation of the Federal Anti-Referral Payments Law, that the directors could be liable for recovery of some of the company's $250 million in fines from its directors for breach of their duty of care by failing to take good faith measures to prevent or remedy the violations. The court noted, since employee actions could prevent a corporation from achieving its strategic goals, "that a director's obligation includes a duty to assure in good faith that [an] information reporting system, which the Board concludes is adequate, exists and that failure to do so under some circumstances may, in theory at least, render a director liable for losses caused by non-compliance with applicable legal standards." Moreover, due to the issuance of the U.S. Sentencing Guidelines on November 1, 1991, and their subsequent integration into expectations, directors must now consider the "due diligence defense" criteria that those guidelines have spawned when advancing their "good faith" defense. This means that the Chancery Court no longer considers a corporate compliance and monitoring program to be optional.

For further information, the reader is referred to an article by Frank M. Placenti in *The National Law Journal* on Monday June 23, 1997 (pages B5, B6). Further insights are possible if higher courts modify the Chancery Court's Caremark decision, but, until then, directors are well-advised to be ethically proactive in the development of strategic plans and operating policies and in the monitoring of performance.

Chapter Two

Governance, Accounting, and Auditing, Post-Enron

Purpose of the Chapter

Enron and the subsequent Arthur Andersen and WorldCom fiascoes have triggered a "sea change" of new expectations for governance in the accounting profession in the United States and Canada, and are in the process of informing expectations around the world. These fiascoes created such a serious crisis of credibility in the corporate accounting, reporting, and governance processes that U.S. politicians created new frameworks of accountability and governance within the Sarbanes-Oxley Act to restore sufficient confidence to allow capital markets to return to normal functioning. In essence, the fiascoes accelerated and then the Sarbanes-Oxley Act crystallized heightened expectations for ethical behavior by businesspeople and members of the accounting profession.

Understanding the issues, principles, and practices involved in these new expectations is essential to the anticipation and consideration of what will be appropriate future governance and behavior for corporations and professional accountants. Faced with applying a stream of new guidelines and regulations, including many spawned by the Sarbanes-Oxley Act, businesspersons and professional accountants will find their task facilitated by understanding the essence—the ethical underpinnings—of the new initiatives.

Governance and Accountability Reform

OVERVIEW AND TIMELINE OF EVENTS AND DEVELOPMENTS

Multiple huge shocks generated a crisis of investor confidence in the corporate and professional ethics that underpin North American capital market values and the trust that allows modern commerce. President Bush and leaders around the world were calling for solutions to ensure compliance with fair values that the public could support and the public interest demanded. Ultimately, corporate governance and the accounting profession were shown to need reform, which—based on ethical guidelines—is on the way.

In mid-October 2001, vaunted giant Enron restated manipulated earnings, and on December 2 filed for bankruptcy, destroying billions in value—especially of retirement investment—in the process. Amid stories of huge sham and fraudulent off-statement transactions, it became clear that senior executives enriched themselves beyond belief while the board of directors and Arthur Andersen, the auditor, apparently were unaware or worse. Frequently, Enron executives claimed bad memories, ignorance, or the Fifth Amendment in front of Senate and Congressional committees. Government and the SEC seemed at a loss to deal with the situation.

Stories also began to surface about a blatant, self-interested, and apparently in-your-face shredding of Enron audit documents by Arthur Andersen, which ultimately produced charges on March 7, 2002, and, after protracted jury deliberations, an obstruction of justice conviction on June 15, 2002. Throughout the period from October 2001 to June 2002, Arthur Andersen's client base and practice disintegrated. A firm of 85,000 worldwide was essentially gone. 24,000 employees in the United States lost their jobs because of the decisions of less than 100 colleagues.

On June 25, 2002, when Senate and Congress hearings were well along and some governance changes were starting to be considered, came the incredible specter of giant WorldCom also applying for bankruptcy protection. When it became known that executives had again manipulated profits through accounting shenanigans and the CEO had essentially loaned himself over $400 million without the apparent oversight of the board, the Congress and Senate were galvanized to produce the Sarbanes-Oxley Act (SOX) on July 30, 2002.

SOX provides frameworks for reform of the corporate governance system based on integrity and accountability, and for the accounting profession based on independence and fiduciary duty to the public interest. The provisions of SOX will be observed by U.S. SEC registrants, by the world's largest corporations that want access to U.S. capital markets, and by their auditors.

The worlds of corporate governance, governance of the accounting profession, and of business ethics have entered a time warp on fast forward. Understanding what happened and why, and what the impact will be on corporations, the accounting profession, and upon business ethics will assist in interpreting future developments.

The Enron Debacle: A Discussion Covering the Powers Report Summary, Senate Subcommittee Summary, and Key Subcommittee Submissions

BACKGROUND

With hindsight, most observers agree that Enron's problems were caused by a failure of the board of directors to exercise adequate oversight. This allowed the misuse of special purpose entities, a form of partnership, to manipulate financial reports, mislead investors, and self-remunerate the perpetrators. Arthur Andersen, Enron's audit firm, has essentially disintegrated, and the accounting profession, as well as corporate governance, will be forever altered. All of this was not apparent until almost the end of the story.

Throughout the late 1990s, as shown in Figure 2.1, Enron's stock rose slowly on the New York Stock Exchange, within a trading range from $20 to $40. Within a few months of the start of the new millenium, Enron's stock price leapt to $70, based upon the overall buoyancy of the stock markets in general, the favorable assessment accorded the company by analysts, and Enron's own reports of earnings and prospects.

During 2000, Enron's stock traded in a range of $60 to $90, peaked in August at $90.56, and closed the year near $80. In 2001, however, the stock price fell precipitously downward until an Enron share was virtually worthless. Rumors of Enron's demise had been circulating for months when the company, on December 2, 2001, filed for protection from creditors under Chapter 11 of the U.S. Securities Act. On April 2, 2002, a share of Enron stock was worth only 24 cents on the over-the-counter market.

How and why did this occur? Who was to blame? What were the repercussions? Investors were scandalized, pensioners lost their life savings, the public was outraged, and the credibility of the financial markets and of the corporate world was shaken. How could the alleged financial manipulations have occurred under the watchful eyes of Enron's auditor, Arthur Andersen, and a blue-ribbon board of directors? Amid allegations that Enron alumni had infiltrated the U.S. government and its agencies, the ability and resolve of the Securities and Exchange Commission (SEC) and of the U.S. Justice Department were questioned.

Officials and politicians hurriedly looked for answers that would restore that credibility and the trust that had been lost. So great was the concern that President Bush himself pledged that the guilty would be punished aggressively by government agencies. The president also called for governance reforms and offered a 10-point plan for legislative action.[1]

FIGURE 2.1

ENRON STOCK CHART,
WEEKLY PRICES, 1997–2002

Reprinted courtesy of NAQ, Inc.

---

[1]Speech of March 7, 2002. The speech can be viewed on the Texas Society of Certified Public Accountants Website (see *http://brooks.swlearning.com*).

After considerable delay and outcry, Enron's audit firm, Arthur Andersen LLP (AA), the fifth largest audit firm in the United States and one of the largest in the world, was charged on March 7, 2002, with obstruction of justice for shredding documents allegedly important to the government's investigation. As a condition of the charge the SEC placed restrictions on AA to serve its SEC-registered clients, thus AA's ability to continue as a firm was jeopardized and ultimately it disintegrated and was taken over piecemeal by competitors. A separate section is included in this chapter that contains a full discussion of the troubles of Arthur Andersen, and how less than 100 employees were responsible for the disaster that ruined a once-revered firm that employed 85,000 worldwide. In addition, the self-regulatory framework that the profession had enjoyed in the United States was further eroded.

Not surprisingly, the desire to know why the Enron disaster occurred spawned many investigations, including the following that may be reviewed and downloaded from the text's Website:

http://brooks. swlearning.com

- *The Powers Report* by a specially formed subcommittee of Enron's board—February 1, 2002 (Powers)
- *The Role of the Board of Directors in Enron's Collapse* by the U.S. Senate's Permanent Subcommittee on Investigations—July 8, 2002 (Senate)
- *The Accounting Treatment of Prepays* by Robert Roach, Counsel and Chief Investigator, U.S. Senate's Permanent Subcommittee on Investigations—July 27, 2002 (Roach)

In addition, new governance initiatives continued to be issued and become relevant throughout the Enron fiasco period, including:

- The Joint Toronto Stock Exchange/Canadian Institute of Chartered Accountants Report on Governance
- The New York Stock Exchange Blue Ribbon Task Force Report and Regulations
- NASDAQ Governance Regulations
- Toronto Stock Exchange Regulations
- U.S. Securities and Exchange Commission Guidance
- Ontario Securities Commission Guidance

WHAT HAPPENED? WHO WAS TO BLAME?

The Powers Report

The Powers Report was prepared by a three-person subcommittee of the Enron board chaired by William Powers, Jr., who joined the board in September 2001 and resigned in February 2002. The Powers subcommittee was appointed on October 26, 2002, with the mandate to investigate related-party transactions that had surprised the board and resulted in several restatements of issued financial statements and reports. In the Powers Report's own words:

> On October 16, 2001, Enron announced that it was taking a $544 million after-tax charge against earnings related to transactions with LJM2 Co-Investment, L.P. ("LJM2"), a partnership created and managed by Fastow. It also announced a reduction of shareholders' equity of $1.2 billion related to transactions with that same entity.

Less than one month later, Enron announced that it was restating its financial statements for the period from 1997 through 2001 because of accounting errors relating to transactions with a different Fastow partnership, LJM Cayman, L.P. ("LJM1"), and an additional related-party entity, Chewco Investments, L.P. ("Chewco"). Chewco was managed by an Enron Global Finance employee, Kopper, who reported to Fastow.

The LJM1- and Chewco-related restatement, like the earlier charge against earnings and reduction of shareholders' equity, was very large. It reduced Enron's reported net income by $28 million in 1997 (of $105 million total), by $133 million in 1998 (of $703 million total), by $248 million in 1999 (of $893 million total), and by $99 million in 2000 (of $979 million total). The restatement reduced reported shareholders' equity by $258 million in 1997, by $391 million in 1998, by $710 million in 1999, and by $754 million in 2000. It increased reported debt by $711 million in 1997, by $561 million in 1998, by $685 million in 1999, and by $628 million in 2000. Enron also revealed, for the first time, that it had learned that Fastow received more than $30 million from LJM1 and LJM2. These announcements destroyed market confidence and investors' trust in Enron. Less than one month later, Enron filed for bankruptcy.[2]

After investigation, the Powers Report presented the following in its Summary of Findings:

- Employees enriched themselves by millions without proper approvals— Fastow by $30 million, Kopper by at least $10 million, and two others by at least hundreds of thousands of dollars.

- Partnerships—Chewco, LJM1, and LJM2—were established and used to enter into transactions that (1) could not be arranged with independent entities, (2) were designed "to accomplish favorable financial statement results, not to achieve *bona fide* economic objectives or to transfer risk,"[3] and (3) did not conform to U.S. accounting rules that could have enabled the hiding of assets and liabilities (debt).

- Other transactions were improperly entered into to hedge or offset almost $1 billion in losses on Enron's merchant investments and thus improperly keep reported profit approximately $1 billion higher between the third quarters of 2000 and 2001. Only Enron had assets at risk in these transactions.[4]

- The original accounting treatments for the Chewco and LJM1 transactions were wrong, as were many others, in spite of extensive involvement and advice from Arthur Andersen. AA was paid $5.7 above their audit fees for the Chewco and LJM1 advice.[5]

- Much of the need for restatement arose because of the failure to satisfy two conditions required for special purpose entities (SPEs) to be independent from Enron. They are: "(1) an owner independent of the company must make a substantive equity investment of at least 3% of the

---

[2]Powers Report, 2, 3.

[3]Ibid., 4.

[4]Ibid., 4.

[5]Ibid., 5.

SPE's assets, and that 3% must remain at risk throughout the transaction; and (2) the independent owner must exercise control of the SPE."[6] If these conditions had been satisfied, according to U.S. accounting rules, Enron could have recorded gains and losses on transactions with the SPE, and the assets and liabilities of the SPE would not have been included in Enron's balance sheet, even though Enron and the SPE were closely related.

The Senate Subcommittee Report

The Senate Permanent Subcommittee on Investigations released its *Report on The Role of The Board of Directors in the Collapse of Enron* on July 8, 2002.

Based upon the evidence before it, including over one million pages of subpoenaed documents, interviews of thirteen Enron Board members, and the Subcommittee hearing on May 7, 2002, the U.S. Senate Permanent Subcommittee on Investigations makes the following findings with respect to the role of the Enron Board of Directors in Enron's collapse and bankruptcy.

1. **Fiduciary Failure.** The Enron Board of Directors failed to safeguard Enron shareholders and contributed to the collapse of the seventh largest public company in the United States, by allowing Enron to engage in high risk accounting, inappropriate conflict of interest transactions, extensive undisclosed off-the-books activities, and excessive executive compensation. The Board witnessed numerous indications of questionable practices by Enron management over several years, but chose to ignore them to the detriment of Enron shareholders, employees and business associates.

2. **High Risk Accounting.** The Enron Board of Directors knowingly allowed Enron to engage in high risk accounting practices.

3. **Inappropriate Conflicts of Interest.** Despite clear conflicts of interest, the Enron Board of Directors approved an unprecedented arrangement allowing Enron's Chief Financial Officer to establish and operate the LJM private equity funds which transacted business with Enron and profited at Enron's expense. The Board exercised inadequate oversight of LJM transaction and compensation controls and failed to protect Enron shareholders from unfair dealing.

4. **Extensive Undisclosed Off-The-Books Activity.** The Enron Board of Directors knowingly allowed Enron to conduct billions of dollars in off-the-books activity to make its financial condition appear better than it was and failed to ensure adequate public disclosure of material off-the-books liabilities that contributed to Enron's collapse.

5. **Excessive Compensation.** The Enron Board of Directors approved excessive compensation for company executives, failed to monitor the cumulative cash drain caused by Enron's 2000 annual bonus and performance unit plans, and failed to monitor or halt abuse by Board Chairman and Chief Executive Officer Kenneth Lay of a company-financed, multi-million dollar, personal credit line.

6. **Lack of Independence.** The independence of the Enron Board of Directors was compromised by financial ties between the company and certain Board members. The Board also failed to ensure the independence of the company's auditor, allowing Andersen to provide internal audit and consulting services while serving as Enron's outside auditor.[7]

---

[6]Ibid., 5.
[7]Senate Subcommittee Report, 3.

These findings led the Senate Subcommittee to make recommendations for (1) strengthening the oversight of directors and (2) strengthening the independence of directors, the audit committee, and auditors of publicly traded companies.[8]

FAILURE OF THE DIRECTORS TO OVERSEE OR GOVERN ENRON ADEQUATELY

What Are Directors Expected to Do?

According to the Senate Subcommittee, the governance model should function as follows:

> **Fiduciary Obligations of Boards of Directors.** In the United States, the Board of Directors sits at the apex of a company's governing structure. A typical Board's duties include reviewing the company's overall business strategy; selecting and compensating the company's senior executives; evaluating the company's outside auditor; overseeing the company's financial statements; and monitoring overall company performance. According to the Business Roundtable, the Board's "paramount duty" is to safeguard the interests of the company's shareholders.[9]

Directors operate under state laws that impose fiduciary duties on them to act in good faith, with reasonable care, and in the best interest of the corporation and its shareholders. Courts generally discuss three types of fiduciary obligations. As one court put it:

> Three broad duties stem from the fiduciary status of corporate directors: namely, the duties of obedience, loyalty, and due care. The duty of obedience requires a director to avoid committing ... acts beyond the scope of the powers of a corporation as defined by its charter or the laws of the state of incorporation. ... The duty of loyalty dictates that a director must act in good faith and must not allow his personal interest to prevail over the interests of the corporation. ... [T]he duty of care requires a director to be diligent and prudent in managing the corporation's affairs.[10]

> In most states, directors also operate under a legal doctrine called the "business judgment rule," which generally provides directors with broad discretion, absent evidence of fraud, gross negligence or other misconduct, to make good faith business decisions. Most states permit corporations to indemnify their directors from liabilities associated with civil, criminal or administrative proceedings against the company. In addition, most U.S. publicly traded corporations, including Enron, purchase directors' liability insurance that pays for a director's legal expenses and other costs in the event of such proceedings.

> Among the most important of Board duties is the responsibility the Board shares with the company's management and auditors to ensure that the financial statements provided by the company to its shareholders and the investing public fairly present the financial condition of the company. This responsibility requires more than ensuring the company's technical compliance with generally accepted accounting principles. According to the Second

---

[8]Ibid., 4.

[9]*Statement of Corporate Governance*, The Business Roundtable, (September 1997), at 3.

[10]*Gearheart Industries v. Smith International*, 741 F.2d 707, 719 (5th Cir. 1984).

Circuit Court of Appeals, this technical compliance may be evidence that a company is acting in good faith, but it is not necessarily conclusive. The "critical test," the Court said, is "whether the financial statements as a whole fairly present the financial position" of the company." [11]

Within this governance framework, Enron's directors were responsible for overseeing Enron's lines of business and strategies for financing them. One of the lines of business—the online energy trading business—required access to large lines of credit to ensure settlement of trading positions at the end of each day. At the same time, the nature of this business caused large earnings fluctuations from quarter to quarter, which made it a challenge to maintain a low credit rating, and therefore to access low-cost financing. Other lines of business such as optical fiber networks (that were mostly not in use) represented cash drains as well. Therefore, according to the Senate Subcommittee:

> In order to ensure an investment-grade credit rating, Enron began to emphasize increasing its cash flow, lowering its debt, and smoothing its earnings on its financial statements to meet the criteria set by credit rating agencies like Moody's and Standard & Poor's.

> Enron developed a number of new strategies to accomplish its financial statement objectives. They included developing energy contracts Enron called "prepays" in which Enron was paid a large sum in advance to deliver natural gas or other energy products over a period of years; designing hedges to reduce the risk of long-term energy delivery contracts; and pooling energy contracts and securitizing them through bonds or other financial instruments sold to investors. Another high profile strategy, referred to as making the company "asset light," was aimed at shedding, or increasing immediate returns on, the company's capital-intensive energy projects like power plants that had traditionally been associated with low returns and persistent debt on the company's books. The goal was either to sell these assets outright or to sell interests in them to investors, and record the income as earnings which top Enron officials called "monetizing" or "syndicating" the assets. A presentation made to the Finance Committee in October 2000 summarized this strategy as follows. [12] It stated that Enron's "[e]nergy and communications investments typically do not generate significant cashflow and earnings for 1–3 years." It stated that Enron had "[l]imited cash flow to service additional debt" and "[l]imited earnings to cover dilution of additional equity." It concluded that "Enron must syndicate" or share its investment costs "in order to grow."

> One of the problems with Enron's new strategies, however, was finding counterparties willing to invest in Enron assets or share the significant risks associated with long-term energy production facilities and delivery contracts. [13] The October 2000 presentation to the Finance Committee showed that one

---

[11] *U.S. v. Simon*, 425 F.2d 796, 805-6 (2nd Cir. 1969), quoting, in part, the trial judge. See also 15 USC 77s and 78m. ("Every user ... shall ... keep books, records, and accounts, which, in reasonable detail, accurately and fairly reflect the transactions and disposition of the assets of the issuer.")

[12] Hearing Exhibit 39, "Private Equity Strategy," Finance Committee presentation, October 2000.

[13] As part of its asset light strategy, during the summer of 2000, Enron worked on a transaction called "Project Summer" to sell $6 billion of its international assets to a single purchaser in the Middle East. Enron's directors indicated during their interviews that this deal fell through when the purchaser's key decision maker became ill. Enron then pursued the asset sales on a piecemeal basis, using Whitewing, LJM, and others.

solution Enron had devised was to sell or syndicate its assets, not to independent third parties, but to "unconsolidated affiliates"—businesses like Whitewing, LJM, JEDI, the Hawaii125-0 Trust and others that were not included in Enron's financial statements but were so closely associated with the company that Enron considered their assets to be part of Enron's own holdings. The October 2000 presentation, for example, informed the Finance Committee that Enron had a total of $60 billion in assets, of which about $27 billion, or nearly 50 percent, were lodged with Enron's "unconsolidated affiliates."

All of the Board members interviewed by the Subcommittee were well aware of and supported Enron's intense focus on its credit rating, cash flow, and debt burden. All were familiar with the company's "asset light" strategy and actions taken by Enron to move billions of dollars in assets off its balance sheet to separate but affiliated companies. All knew that, to accomplish its objectives, Enron had been relying increasingly on complicated transactions with convoluted financing and accounting structures, including transactions with multiple special purpose entities, hedges, derivatives, swaps, forward contracts, prepaid contracts, and other forms of structured finance. While there is no empirical data on the extent to which U.S. public companies use these devices, it appears that few companies outside of investment banks use them as extensively as Enron. At Enron, they became dominant; at its peak, the company apparently had between $15 and $20 billion involved in hundreds of structured finance transactions.[14]

How Was Enron's Board Organized, and How Did It Function?

In 2001, Enron's Board of Directors had 15 members, several of whom had 20 years or more experience on the Board of Enron or its predecessor companies. Many of Enron's Directors served on the boards of other companies as well. At the hearing, John Duncan, former Chairman of the Executive Committee, described his fellow Board members as well educated, "experienced, successful businessmen and women," and "experts in areas of finance and accounting." [15] The Subcommittee interviews found the Directors to have a wealth of sophisticated business and investment experience and considerable expertise in accounting, derivatives, and structured finance.

Enron Board members uniformly described internal Board relations as harmonious. They said that Board votes were generally unanimous and could recall only two instances over the course of many years involving dissenting votes. The Directors also described a good working relationship with Enron management. Several had close personal relationships with Board Chairman and Chief Executive Officer (CEO) Kenneth L. Lay. All indicated they had possessed great respect for senior Enron officers, trusting the integrity and competence of Mr. Lay; President and Chief Operating Officer (and later CEO) Jeffrey K. Skilling; Chief Financial Officer Andrew S. Fastow; Chief Accounting Officer Richard A. Causey; Chief Risk Officer Richard Buy; and the Treasurer Jeffrey McMahon and later Ben Glisan. Mr. Lay served as Chairman of the Board from 1986 until he resigned in 2002. Mr. Skilling was a Board member from 1997 until August 2001, when he resigned from Enron.

The Enron Board was organized into five committees.

1. The **Executive Committee** met on an as needed basis to handle urgent business matters between scheduled Board meetings. Its members in

---

[14]Senate Subcommittee Report, 7, 8.
[15]Hearing Record at 34.

2001 were Mr. Duncan, the Chairman; Mr. Lay, Mr. Skilling, Mr. Belfer, Dr. LeMaistre and Mr. Winokur.

2. The **Finance Committee** was responsible for approving major transactions which, in 2001, met or exceeded $75 million in value. It also reviewed transactions valued between $25 million and $75 million; oversaw Enron's risk management efforts; and provided guidance on the company's financial decisions and policies. Its members in 2001 were Mr. Winokur, the Chairman; Mr. Belfer, Mr. Blake, Mr. Chan, Mr. Pereira and Mr. Savage.

3. The **Audit and Compliance Committee** reviewed Enron's accounting and compliance programs, approved Enron's financial statements and reports, and was the primary liaison with Andersen. Its members in 2001 were Dr. Jaedicke, the Chairman; Mr. Chan, Dr. Gramm, Dr. Mendelsohn, Mr. Pereira, and Lord Wakeham. Dr. Jaedicke and Lord Wakeham had formal accounting training and professional experience. Dr. Mendelsohn was the only Committee member who appeared to have limited familiarity with complex accounting principles.

4. The **Compensation Committee** established and monitored Enron's compensation policies and plans for directors, officers and employees. Its members in 2001 were Dr. LeMaistre, the Chairman; Mr. Blake, Mr. Duncan, Dr. Jaedicke, and Mr. Savage.

5. The **Nominating Committee** nominated individuals to serve as Directors. Its members in 2001 were Lord Wakeham, the Chairman; Dr. Gramm, Dr. Mendelsohn and Mr. Meyer.

The Board normally held five regular meetings during the year, with additional special meetings as needed. Board meetings usually lasted two days, with the first day devoted to Committee meetings and a Board dinner and the second day devoted to a meeting of the full Board. Committee meetings generally lasted between one and two hours and were arranged to allow Board members, who typically sat on three Committees, to attend all assigned Committee meetings. Full Board meetings also generally lasted between one and two hours. Special Board meetings, as well as meetings of the Executive Committee, were typically conducted by telephone conference.

Committee chairmen typically spoke with Enron management by telephone prior to Committee meetings to develop the proposed Committee meeting agenda. Board members said that Enron management provided them with these agendas as well as extensive background and briefing materials prior to Board meetings including, in the case of Finance Committee members, numerous deal approval sheets ("DASHs") for approval of major transactions. Board members varied in how much time they spent reading the materials and preparing for Board meetings, with the reported preparation time for each meeting varying between two hours and two days. On some occasions, Enron provided a private plane to transport Board members from various locations to a Board meeting, and Board members discussed company issues during the flight. Enron also organized occasional trips abroad which some Board members attended to view company assets and operations.

During the Committee meetings, Enron management generally provided presentations on company performance, internal controls, new business ventures, specific transactions, or other topics of interest. The Finance Committee generally heard from Mr. Fastow, Mr. Causey, Mr. Buy, Mr. McMahon and, occasionally, Mr. Glisan. The Audit Committee generally heard from Mr. Causey, Mr. Buy, and Andersen personnel. The Compensation Committee generally heard from the company's top compensation official, Mary Joyce, and from the company's compensation consultant, Towers Perrin. On occasion, the Committees heard from other senior Enron officers as well. At the full Board meetings, Board members typically received presentations from each Committee Chairman summarizing the Committee's work and recommendations, as well as from Enron management and, occasionally, Andersen or the company's chief outside legal counsel, Vinson & Elkins. Mr. Lay and Mr. Skilling usually attended Executive, Finance, and Audit Committee meetings, as well as the full Board meetings. Mr. Lay attended many Compensation Committee meetings as well. The Subcommittee interviews indicated that, altogether, Board members appeared to have routine contact with less than a dozen senior officers at Enron. The Board did not have a practice of meeting without Enron management present.

Regular presentations on Enron's financial statements, accounting practices, and audit results were provided by Andersen to the Audit Committee. The Audit Committee Chairman would then report on the presentation to the full Board. On most occasions, three Andersen senior partners from Andersen's Houston office attended Audit Committee meetings. They were D. Stephen Goddard, head of the Houston office; David Duncan, head of the Andersen "engagement team" that provided auditing, consulting and other services to Enron; and Thomas H. Bauer, another senior member of the Enron engagement team. Before becoming head of the Houston office, Mr. Goddard had led the Enron engagement team for Andersen. Mr. Duncan became the "worldwide engagement partner" for Enron in 1997, and from that point on typically made the Andersen presentations to the Audit Committee. The Audit Committee offered Andersen personnel an opportunity to present information to them without management present.

Minutes summarizing Committee and Board meetings were kept by the Corporate Secretary, who often took handwritten notes on Committee and Board presentations during the Board's deliberations and afterward developed and circulated draft minutes to Enron management, Board members, and legal counsel. The draft minutes were formally presented to and approved by Committee and Board members at subsequent meetings. Outside of the formal Committee and Board meetings, the Enron Directors described very little interaction or communication either among Board members or between Board members and Enron or Andersen personnel, until the company began experiencing severe problems in October 2001. From October until the company's bankruptcy on December 2, 2001, the Board held numerous special meetings, at times on almost a daily basis.

Enron Board members were compensated with cash, restricted stock, phantom stock units, and stock options.[16] The total cash and equity compensation of Enron Board members in 2000 was valued by Enron at about $350,000 or more than twice the national average for Board compensation at a U.S. publicly traded corporation.[17, 18]

---

[16]See Hearing Exhibits 35a and 35b on Enron Board Member compensation, prepared by the Subcommittee based upon information in Enron filings with the Securities and Exchange Commission. Phantom stock units at Enron were deferred cash payments whose amounts were linked to the value of Enron stock.

[17]See "Director Compensation; Purposes, Principles, and Best Practices," Report of the Blue Ribbon Commission of the National Association of Corporate Directors (2001), page V (average total board compensation at top 200 U.S. public corporations in 2000 was $138,747).

[18]Senate Subcommittee Report, 8–11.

ENRON'S QUESTIONABLE TRANSACTIONS

An understanding of the nature of Enron's questionable transactions is fundamental to understanding why Enron failed. What follows is an abbreviated summary of the essence of the major important transactions with the SPEs, including Chewco, LJM1, LJM2, and the Raptors.

Chewco Transactions

Chewco Investments LP[19] was created in November 1997 to buy the 50 percent interest owned by CalPERS, the California Public Employees' Retirement System, in a joint venture investment partnership called Joint Energy Development Investment Limited Partnership (JEDI). JEDI had operated since 1993 as a non-consolidated SPE. Enron wanted to create a larger unit with capital of $1 billion, and CalPERS asked to be bought out. Chewco was created as a vehicle to attract a replacement for CalPERS and to buy out CalPERS' interest in JEDI.

Originally Andrew Fastow proposed that he be appointed to manage Chewco temporarily until an outside investor, or counterparty, could be found. According to the Powers Report, Enron lawyers advised against this since his senior officer status would have required proxy disclosure. Instead, Michael Kopper, who worked at Enron for Fastow, a fact known only to Skilling on the board of directors,[20] was appointed.

Enron planned to guarantee loans for bridge financing to buy out CalPERS' interest in JEDI, which had been valued at $383 million. The intention was to replace the bridge financing with the investment of an outside investor, but none was found. Enron's financial year end passed on December 31, 1997; and without an independent, controlling outside investor with at least 3 percent of the capital at risk, $11.5 million in this case (3 percent of $383 million), the activities of both JEDI and Chewco had to be consolidated into Enron's financial statements and on a retroactive basis. Whether through negligence or inability to find a proper counterparty, the accounts of Enron had to be restated to include the dealings of JEDI.

"In November and December of 1997, Enron and Kopper created a new capital structure for Chewco, which had three elements:

- $240 million unsecured subordinated loan to Chewco from Barclays Bank PLC, which Enron would guarantee;
- $132 million advance from JEDI to Chewco under a revolving credit agreement; and
- $11.5 million in equity (representing approximately 3% of total capital) from Chewco's general and limited partners.

Kopper invested approximately $115,000 in Chewco's general partner and approximately $10,000 in its limited partner before transferring his limited partnership interest to William Dodson [Kopper's domestic partner]."[21] The rest of the $11.5 million—$11.4, to be exact—was loaned by Barclays bank to Kopper/Dodson, although the original wording was unusual in that it implied that the monies were for "certificates" that would generate a "yield."[22]

---

[19]Chewco was named for "Chewbacca," the Star Wars character.

[20]Powers Report, 41.

[21]Powers Report, 49.

[22]Ibid., 50.

Ultimately, Kopper and Dodson created a series of limited partnerships (LLPs) and limited companies (LLCs) through which to operate their interests, but Kopper was *de facto* the managing general partner of Chewco. This meant there was no outside investor with three percent of equity at risk. Moreover, Barclays asked that $6.6 million be reserved against the $11.4, and the $6.6 million was pledged/deposited with them, so that the resulting net of $4.8 million did not satisfy the three percent rule for nonconsolidation. According to the Powers Report, the existence of $6.6 reserve was well-known at Enron.[23] However, in Congressional Committee testimony, the CEO of Arthur Andersen stated that they had reviewed and approved the financial arrangement as qualifying under the three percent rule, and received $80,000 for this advice.[24] The $6.6 million reserve was created as part of a transfer of $16.6 million from JEDI through Chewco to two of the limited partnerships controlled by Kopper and Dodson, namely Big River Funding LLC and Little River Funding LLC.

The entire complicated structure created for the Chewco financing transaction can be viewed on page 51 of the Powers Report.

The Powers Report goes on to detail several subsequent transactions that took place before Enron unraveled in late 2001 that appear not to be in the best interests of Enron, including:

- Management and other fees paid to Kopper amounted to $2 million for essentially little work, some of which was done by Fastow's wife. Most of the rest of the work was on time that Kopper was being paid as an Enron employee.

- The fee for Enron guaranteeing the Barclays loan was under that called for by the market risk assumed.

- When it was decided to liquidate JEDI, the buyout of Chewco's interest was valued at a premium of $1 million by Jeffrey McMahon (then senior vice president of finance and treasurer of Enron). He told Fastow, who undertook to negotiate with Kopper and came back indicating that Skilling had approved a $10 million payment.[25] Fastow denied this to the Powers committee but declined to comment on a handwritten note from Kopper that confirmed Fastow's participation. Ultimately, a premium of $10.5 was paid. This represented a return of 360 percent.

- Kopper demanded and received $2.6 million in September 2001 as an indemnification against the tax consequences of the $10.5 million premium. Enron's in-house counsel had originally declined this request, but was overruled by Fastow, who told them that Skilling had approved.

- Upon closing the repurchase of JEDI, Chewco was not required to repay the $15 million it had loaned on an unsecured and nonrecourse basis to Kopper and Dodson for them to invest in Osprey trust certificates. Osprey was a limited partner in Whitewing Associates, an other-related company that will be discussed later.

- The Powers Report also noticed that from December 1997, Enron began to incorrectly pre-book revenue for services not yet provided in regard

---

[23]Ibid., 52.
[24]Ibid., 53.
[25]Ibid., 61.

to the Barclays guarantee fee and the JEDI management fee arrangement that Chewco assumed, in the amounts of $10 million and 25.7 million, respectively.

When Enron's affairs began to unravel in public, the board started an investigation that led to the bankruptcy filing on December 2, 2001. The Powers Report states:

> In late October 2001, the Enron Board (responding to media reports) requested a briefing by Management on Chewco. Glisan [Ben F. Glisan, Jr., the Enron "transaction support" employee with principal responsibility for accounting matters in the Chewco transaction, signed many of the documents on Enron's behalf] was responsible for presenting the briefing at a Board meeting on short notice. Following the briefing, Enron accounting and legal personnel (as well as Vinson & Elkins) undertook to review documents relating to Chewco. This review identified the documents relating to the finding of the Big River and Little River reserve accounts in December 1997 through the $16.6 million distribution from JEDI.

> Enron brought those documents to the attention of Andersen, and consulted with Andersen concerning the accounting implications of the funded reserve accounts. After being shown the documents by Enron and discussing the accounting issues with Enron personnel, Andersen provided the notice of "possible illegal acts" that Andersen's CEO highlighted in his Congressional testimony on December 12, 2001.

> Enron's accounting personnel and Andersen both concluded that, in light of the funded reserve accounts, Chewco lacked sufficient outside equity at risk and should have been consolidated in November 1997. In addition, because JEDI's non-consolidation depended on Chewco's status, Enron and Andersen concluded that JEDI also should have been consolidated in November 1997. In a Current Report on Form 8-K filed on November 8, 2001, Enron announced that it would restate its prior period financials to reflect the consolidation of those entities as of November 1997.[26]

LJM Partnerships and the Raptors: LJM1

On June 28, 1999, the Enron board approved Fastow's proposal that he invest $1 million and become the sole managing/general partner of LJM1 (LJM Cayman LP), which would raise funds from outside investors that could be used to hedge the possible loss of market value of Enron's investment in Rhythms NetConnections, Inc. (Rhythms for short). Fastow said that he would receive fees, that the Enron Code of Conduct would require special action (suspension of the code) by the chairman, and that his participation "would not adversely affect the interests of Enron."[27] The Powers Report continues: "LJM1 was formed in June 1999. Fastow became the sole and managing member of LJM Partners, LLC, which was the general partner of LJM Partners, LP. This, in turn, was the general partner of LJM1. Fastow raised $15 million from two limited partners, ERNB Ltd. ... and Campsie Ltd. ... " A diagram of the financing of LJM1 can be found on page 70 of the Powers Report.

LJM1 ultimately "entered into three transactions with Enron: (1) the effort to hedge Enron's position in Rhythms NetConnections stock, (2) the

---

[26]Powers Report, 66, 67.
[27]Ibid., 69.

purchase of a portion of Enron's interest in a Brazilian power project (Cuiaba), and (3) a purchase of certificates of an SPE called 'Osprey Trust.'"[28]

The Rhythms hedge transaction is significant because it introduces the basic form for future hedge transactions. Per the Powers Report on page 77:

> In March 1998, Enron invested $10 million in the stock of Rhythms NetConnections, Inc. ("Rhythms"), a privately-held internet service provider for businesses using digital subscriber line technology, by purchasing 5.4 million shares of stock at $1.85 per share. On April 7, 1999, Rhythms went public at $21 per share. By the close of the trading day, the stock price reached $69. By May 1999, Enron's investment in Rhythms was worth approximately $300 million, but Enron was prohibited (by a lock-up agreement) from selling its shares before the end of 1999. Because Enron accounted for the investment as part of its merchant portfolio, it marked the Rhythms position to market, meaning that increases and decreases in the value of Rhythms stock were reflected on Enron's income statement.

Skilling was concerned about mitigating the volatility caused by these mark-to-market increases and decreases, and Fastow and Glisan devised a hedging transaction to do so. The arrangement also resulted in Enron recognizing the appreciation in value of Enron's own stock—a recognition that GAAP does not normally permit except under strict conditions where cash is received for the stock confirming the market value. Their proposal was to capitalize an SPE with Enron stock, and have the SPE hedge the value of the Rhythms investment so that the SPE would pay Enron if the Rhythms investment decreased. This payment would be shown as revenue by Enron and offset the loss in the Rhythms investment on Enron's books.

Ultimately, $95 million in lost Rhythms value was offset, and, as a result, Enron's income was higher. In addition, Enron recorded profit on the Enron shares transferred. Unfortunately, LJM1 did not qualify as having three percent invested by an independent, controlling general partner (since Fastow was not independent), and the Enron stock was paid for by a promissory note, not cash. Moreover, it became clear that the creditworthiness of the SPE depended upon the Enron shares transferred, and since the value of Enron shares declined in 2000 and 2001, that creditworthiness was eroded below the level required to pay Enron its offsets. Enron, it became obvious, was attempting to hedge itself—largely a game of smoke and mirrors in the absence of outside investment to absorb the economic risk. In spite of these problems, Arthur Andersen and Enron's law firm, Vinson & Elkins, indicated that the hedge was reasonable, and that it could go ahead as Fastow and Glisan intended. Ultimately, however, upon reexamination by Arthur Andersen, it was determined (in October 2001) that the financial statements for 1999–2001 had to be restated. In November, Enron announced that "it would restate prior period financial statements to reflect the consolidation retroactive to 1999, which would have the effect of decreasing Enron's net income by $95 million in 1999 and $8 million in 2000."[29]

The Powers Report describes the Rhythms transaction beginning on page 79, with a diagram on page 81 and a discussion of the hedge beginning on page 82. It is noted on page 83 that the equity of the SPE used for the transaction (Swap

---

[28]Ibid., 70.
[29]Powers Report, 84.

Sub, of which LJM1 owned part) was negative and thus the transaction could not have qualified for the three percent nonconsolidation rule. This sprung from the fact that: "At its formation on June 30, 1999, Swap Sub had negative equity because its liability (the Rhythms put, valued at $104 million) greatly exceeded its assets ($3.75 million in cash plus $80 million in restricted Enron stock).[30] This was what Arthur Andersen found upon reexamination in October 2001. AA's CEO said:

> In evaluating the 3 percent residual equity level required to qualify for non-consolidation, there were some complex issues concerning the valuation of various assets and liabilities. When we reviewed this transaction again in October 2001, we determined that our team's initial judgment that the 3 percent test was met was in error. We promptly told Enron to correct it.[31]

Within two weeks after the transaction closed on June 30, 1999, it was realized that the volatility of earnings had not improved to the degree desired[32] and four more derivative actions were entered into to make the hedge act more like a swap. These did not cure the problem sufficiently, and due to the continuing concern for the erosion of creditworthiness, the decision was made to liquidate the hedge. In February or March 2000, Enron's risk manager Vincent Kaminski estimated that there was a 68 percent probability that the structure would default, and he claims he relayed this to the accounting group.[33]

In early March 2000, negotiations to unwind Swap Sub were begun between Causey and Fastow, with Fastow giving the impression that he had no personal interest in the outcome—which he was just negotiating for the limited partners of LJM1. On March 8, 2000, Enron gave Swap Sub a put on 3.1 million shares of Enron at $71.31 per share, which was $4.12 over the closing price, thus conveying approximately $12.8 million in value to Swap Sub. Perhaps this was by mistake. Subsequently, Fastow proposed that Swap Sub receive $30 million from Enron for the unwind, and this was agreed to. The unwind was completed per an agreement dated March 22, 2000, which was not subjected to an independent fairness examination, nor was the board advised, nor DASH sheets executed. Arthur Andersen reviewed the deal, but said nothing. Not until later was it realized that the value ascribed to the shares reacquired by Enron was as unrestricted shares, and no discounting was employed to reflect that they were restricted. *As a result, an estimated $70 million more than what was required was transferred to Swap Sub, and ultimately to Fastow and his associates.*[34] *In addition, LJM1 was allowed to retain 3.6 million post-split Enron shares related to the original transaction, which, on April 28, 2000, had an undiscounted value of $251 million at closing price.*[35]

Many of Enron's employees were involved in these transactions, but none were approved to benefit as required by the Enron Code of Conduct, and the board apparently did not know of their involvement. However, the employees benefited mightily, as is detailed later.

---

[30] Ibid., 83.

[31] Ibid., 84.

[32] Ibid., 85. See Footnote 30 of the Powers Report. Because the put provided one-sided protection, Enron was exposed to income statement volatility when Rhythms' price increased and subsequently decreased. In addition, Enron was subject to income statement volatility from the time value component of the put option.

[33] Ibid., 87.

[34] Ibid., 91.

[35] Ibid., 91.

In May, as noted earlier, McMahon expressed his reservations about Enron accounting and deals to Fastow and was reassigned. Glisan became the new treasurer of Enron.

LJM Partnerships and the Raptors: LJM2

In October 1999, Fastow proposed a second LJM partnership, LJM2 Co-Investment LP (LJM2), where he would serve as a general partner through intermediaries to encourage up to $200 million of outside investment that could be used to purchase assets that Enron wanted to syndicate. This, Fastow said, would provide Enron the funds needed to grow quickly and at less cost than by other means. This was not done blindly, as the following shows:

> The minutes and our interviews reflect that the Finance Committee discussed this proposal, including the conflict of interest presented by Fastow's dual roles as CFO of Enron and general partner of LJM2. Fastow proposed as a control that all transactions between Enron and LJM2 be subject to the approval of both Causey, Enron's Chief Accounting Officer, and Buy, Enron's Chief Risk Officer. In addition, the Audit and Compliance Committee would annually review all transactions completed in the prior year. Based on this discussion, the Committee voted to recommend to the Board that the Board find that Fastow's participation in LJM2 would not adversely affect the best interests of Enron.[36]

Later the board reviewed the discussion and gave their approval. LJM2 was formed in October 1999, and its general partner was LJM2 Capital Management, LP. Limited solicitation developed approximately 50 limited partners, raising $394 million including the contributions of the general partner. Again, Fastow arranged a series of intermediaries as follows: "The general partner, LJM2 Capital Management, LP, itself had a general partner and two limited partners. The general partner was LJM2 Capital Management, LLC, of which Fastow was the managing member. The limited partners were Fastow and, at some point after the creation of LJM2, an entity named Big Doe LLC. Kopper was the managing member of Big Doe.[37] (In July 2001, Kopper resigned from Enron and purchased Fastow's interest in LJM2.)"

A diagram of this structure is given on page 74 of the Powers Report. Subsequently, a management agreement was executed between Enron and LJM2 that specified which full-time Enron employees were to work on LJM2 matters.

Once again, the issue arises of whether LJM2 qualified for nonconsolidation. A series of transactions were entered into that created profit on Enron's earnings statement based upon the assumption that LJM2 was not to be consolidated under the three percent rule. Fastow was not a completely independent third party who possessed the risks and rewards of ownership. However, he was able to be removed by a 75 percent (and later 66 percent) vote of the limited partners. Were these restrictions enough? Initially Arthur Andersen and Enron's lawyers, Vinson & Elkins, thought so, but the Powers Committee was not so certain.[38]

---

[36]Powers Report, 71.

[37]Ibid., 73.

[38]Ibid., 76.

LJM2 and the Raptors

In aggregate, the Raptors, which were Rhythms-like hedging arrangements for various of Enron's other merchant investments, had a huge impact on Enron's financial results. Unfortunately, three of the four were modeled after the ill-fated Rhythms and they had the same shortcomings, so that their impact had to be reversed when their lack of creditworthiness was exposed. They acted as dampeners of the accounting volatility related to earnings, but they were not useful hedges of economic risk. The termination of the Raptor arrangements in the third quarter of 2001 was one of the mighty blows that undermined investor confidence in Enron.

Table 2.1 shows the impact of the Raptors and appears on page 133 of the Powers Report.

The Report also discloses that shareholders' equity was overstated by $1.2 billion due to improper accounting for Enron stock transferred as stock sold, as seen in the following excerpt.

> The transactions between Enron and LJM2 that had the greatest impact on Enron's financial statements involved four SPEs known as the "Raptors." Expanding on the concepts underlying the Rhythms transaction (described above), Enron sought to use the "embedded" value of its own equity to counteract declines in the value of certain of its merchant investments. Enron used the extremely complex Raptor structured finance vehicles to avoid reflecting losses in the value of some merchant investments in its income statement. Enron did this by entering into derivative transactions with the Raptors that functioned as "accounting" hedges. If the value of the merchant investment declined, the value of the corresponding hedge would increase by an equal amount. Consequently, the decline—which was recorded each quarter on Enron's income statement—would be offset by an increase of income from the hedge.
>
> As with the Rhythms hedge, these transactions were not true economic hedges. Had Enron hedged its merchant investments with a creditworthy, independent outside party, it may have been able successfully to transfer the economic risk of a decline in the investments. But it did not do this. Instead, Enron and LJM2 created counter-parties for these accounting hedges—the

TABLE 2.1

IMPACT OF THE RAPTORS ON
EARNINGS, IN MILLIONS

QUARTER	REPORTED EARNINGS	EARNINGS WITHOUT RAPTORS	RAPTORS' CONTRIBUTION TO EARNINGS
3Q 2000	$ 364	$ 295	$ 69
4Q 2000	286	(176)	462
1Q 2001	536	281	255
2Q 2001	530	490	40
3Q 2001	(210)	(461)	251
TOTAL	$1,506	$ 429	$ 1,077

*Third quarter 2001 figures exclude the $710 million pre-tax charge to earnings related to the termination of the Raptors.

Raptors—but Enron still bore virtually all of the economic risk. In effect, Enron was hedging risk with itself.

In three of the four Raptors, the vehicle's financial ability to hedge was created by Enron's transferring its own stock (or contracts to receive Enron stock) to the entity, at a discount to the market price. This "accounting" hedge would work, and the Raptors would be able to "pay" Enron on the hedge, as long as Enron's stock price remained strong and especially if it increased. …When the value of many of Enron's merchant investments fell in late 2000 and early 2001, the Raptors' hedging obligations to Enron grew. At the same time, however, the value of Enron's stock declined, decreasing the ability of the Raptors to meet those obligations. These two factors combined to create the very real possibility that Enron would have to record at the end of first quarter 2001 a $500 million impairment of the Raptors' obligations to it. Without bringing this issue to the attention of the Board, and with the design and effect of avoiding a massive credit reserve, Enron Management restructured the vehicles in the first quarter of 2001. In the third quarter of 2001, however, as the merchant investments and Enron's stock price continued to decline, Enron finally terminated the vehicles. In doing so, it incurred the after-tax charge of $544 million ($710 million pre-tax) that Enron disclosed on October 16, 2001 in its initial third quarter earnings release.

Enron also reported that same day that it would reduce shareholder equity by $1.2 billion. One billion of that $1.2 billion involved the correction of accounting errors relating to Enron's prior issuance of Enron common stock (and stock contracts) to the Raptors in the second quarter of 2000 and the first quarter of 2001; the other $200 million related to termination of the Raptors.[39]

Details of these activities are available in the Powers Report on pages 98–133. Table 2.2 is provided for reference purposes.

Raptors I and II were capitalized in almost identical manners. For Raptor I (Talon), in April 2000, LJM2 contributed $30 million cash. Enron contributed (through a wholly-owned subsidiary) $1,000 cash; a $50 million promissory note; and Enron shares, or rights to shares, worth $537 million that could not be sold, pledged, or hedged for three years. The value of the shares was therefore discounted by 35 percent, which agreed with a fairness evaluation by PricewaterhouseCoopers (PwC). Enron received a promissory note from Talon in the amount of $400 million.

An interesting arrangement apparently was not reflected in the setup documents seen by the board, but was understood by those working on the deal,

TABLE 2.2

ENRON'S RAPTORS—SELECTED DETAILS

	NAME	APPROVED IN 2001	DIAGRAM ON	CAPITAL (MIL.) FROM LJM2	REQUIRED (MIL.) LJM2 RETURN	EXPECTED (MIL.) HEDGE CAP. USED
Raptor I	Talon	May	101	$30	$41	$500
Raptor II	Timberwolf	June 2		30	41	513
Raptor III	Porcupine	Not/	116	30	39.5	Only TNPC
Raptor IV	Bobcat	Aug. 7		30	41	Nil

[39]Powers Report, 97, 98.

namely that Talon could not write any derivatives until LJM2 received at least its capital back plus $11 million ($41 million) or 11 percent annualized return. If this return was not received in six months, Enron could be forced to buy back its shares at their unrestricted value. Enron was to get any return after the $41 million was paid.

These arrangements were very generous to LJM2. In addition, however, $41 million in profit was created for Talon by Enron purchasing from Talon a put option that would require Talon to purchase Enron shares in six months at a $41 million premium. This was strange and generous because Enron was betting its own stock would go down, and the terms of the put did not reflect the lack of creditworthiness of Talon.[40]

The option was settled early, on August 3, 2000, by Causey on behalf of Enron and Fastow. Since Enron stock had gone up, only $4 million of the $41 million was returned to Enron. Talon paid $41 million to LJM2, which earned 193 percent, plus Enron paid its accounting fees and a management fee of $250,000 per year. Talon was free to start hedging, which it did.

Unfortunately, the capacity of Talon to hedge Enron's merchant investments was limited by Talon's ability to pay Enron as the value of the merchant investment(s) declined. This ability, or creditworthiness, depended in turn upon Talon's assets, which included some cash but mostly shares of Enron. As the market price of those Enron shares declined in the fall of 2000, the possibility that Talon could not pay—thus forcing Enron to record losses—grew so large that Enron sought to shore up Talon's creditworthiness by using a "costless collar" arrangement. The Powers Report describes the arrangement as follows:

> To protect Talon against a possible decline in Enron stock price—which would decrease the value of Talon's principal asset, and thereby decrease its credit capacity on October 30, 2000, Enron entered into a "costless collar" on the approximately 7.6 million Enron shares and stock contracts in Talon. The "collar" provided that, if Enron stock fell below $81, Enron would pay Talon the amount of any loss. If Enron stock increased above $116 per share, Talon would pay Enron the amount of any gain. If the stock price was between the floor and ceiling, neither party was obligated to the other. This protected Talon's credit capacity against possible future declines in Enron stock.[41]

Unfortunately, the protection was only designed to protect within a narrow range and Enron's stock was destined to fall below the $81 level. Based on Talon's revised contract, its creditworthiness would only protect Enron for about another $10 per share fall below the $81 level. If Enron's share price was to fall below $71, Talon could not pay off and Enron would have to record net losses on its merchant investments.

In addition, the "costless collar" dealt with Talon's Enron shares as if they were not restricted, thus not honoring the 35 percent discount for the three-year restriction period that underlay the original fairness valuation and setup calculations. To make the "costless collar" arrangements legal, Causey signed a waiver of the three-year restrictions (worth $187 million), thus conveying more even more value to Talon than was originally expected.[42]

---

[40]Powers Report, 103, 104.
[41]Ibid., 110.
[42]Ibid., 111.

Before there were any hedge transactions between Talon (Raptor I) and Enron, Fastow told Enron's executive committee that "there had been tremendous utilization by the business units of Raptor I,"[43] and asked for the establishment of Raptor II on June 22, 2000. The presentation requesting the establishment of Raptor IV was made on August 7, 2000, by Ben Glison, who "noted that Raptor I was almost completely utilized and that Raptor II would not be available for utilization until later in the year."[44] This deferred availability of Raptor II reflects the need to repay LJM2 its $41 million similar to the Raptor I arrangements before hedging could start.

The arrangements to capitalize Raptors II and IV were indeed similar to that used for Raptor I, as the Powers Report states:

> Just as it had done with Talon in Raptor I, Enron paid Raptor II's SPE, "Timberwolf," and Raptor IV's SPE, "Bobcat," $41 million each for share-settled put options. As in Raptor I, the put options were settled early, and each of the entities then distributed approximately $41 million to LJM2. Although these distributions meant that both Timberwolf and Bobcat were available to engage in derivative transactions with Enron, Enron engaged in derivative transactions only with Timberwolf. These transactions, entered into as of September 22, 2000 and December 28, 2000, had a total notional value of $513 million.[45]

Raptor II did enter into merchant investment hedge transactions with Enron. Raptor IV never did because, due to the continued erosion of both merchant investment values and Enron share prices, on March 26, 2001, Raptor IV's creditworthiness had to be combined with that of the other Raptors to shore up the entire Raptor program. However, prior to the creation of a combined Raptor credit pool, for the same reasons as noted for Raptor I, Enron arranged "costless collars" for Raptors II and IV on November 27, 2000, and January 24, 2001, respectively. Again, the impact of the collars was limited and the restricted share values factored into the setup transfer valuations was waived.

Raptor III was different from the other Raptors because it was intended to hedge only the merchant investment in The New Power Company (TNPC), and it did not hold Enron shares or rights to Enron shares as assets. Instead Enron provided it warrants or rights to purchase TNPC shares at a very low value, which essentially amounted to the same thing as holding shares. This avoided seeking board approval to use Enron shares, and avoided the dilutive effect on Enron's EPS (earnings per share) that using such shares would have produced.

On September 27, 2000, Enron (through a subsidiary named "Pronghorn") and LJM2 created the Raptor III SPE "Porcupine" as shown in the diagram on page 116 of the Powers Report. Once again, Enron's contribution followed the earlier Raptor framework except for the substitution of TNPC shares/rights, and LJM2 contributed $30 million. This left the Raptor III hedge in the position of having to pay Enron for declines in the value of TNPC from assets largely consisting of TNPC shares or rights. If the shares of TNPC declined, the need to pay would rise and the means to pay decreased. This "doubling" of the importance of TNPC meant that the risk of default was

---

[43]Ibid., 112.
[44]Ibid.
[45]Ibid., 113, 114.

higher than for other Raptors, and certainly more sensitive to declines in the share values of Enron's TNPC merchant investment. Arthur Andersen and Enron's lawyers Vinson & Elkins both received fees for pre-clearing the Raptor III arrangements. Enron's board did not appear to have approved the creation of Raptor III, and no DASH sheets were prepared. LJM2's return was set at $39.5 million or 30 percent per year, and LJM2 received the $39.5 million in one week—yielding a return of 2,500 percent.

By mid-December 2000, the assets of Raptors I and III had declined; their liabilities had increased so much that both had negative equity and therefore did not have the ability to pay off Enron in regard to the hedges undertaken. Unless something was done quickly, Enron would have had to reflect significant losses on the year-end statement for 2000 due to this lack of creditworthiness. Therefore, according to the Powers Report,

> ... Enron's accountants, working with Andersen, decided to use the "excess" credit capacity in Raptors II and IV to shore up the credit capacity in Raptors I and III. A 45-day cross-guarantee agreement, dated December 22, 2000, essentially merged the credit capacity of all four Raptors. The effect was that Enron would not, for year end, record a credit reserve loss unless there was negative credit capacity on a combined basis. Enron paid LJM2 $50,000 to enter into this agreement, even though the cross-guarantee had no effect on LJM2's economic interests. We have seen no evidence that Enron's Board was informed of either the credit capacity problem or the solution selected to resolve that problem. Enron did not record a reserve for the year ending December 31, 2000.[46]

It is noteworthy that the Powers Report goes on to say in a footnote that:

> At the time, Andersen agreed with Enron's view that the 45-day cross-guarantee among the Raptors to avoid a credit reserve loss was permissible from an accounting perspective. The workpapers that Andersen made available included a memorandum dated December 28, 2000, by Andersen's local audit team, which states that it consulted two partners in Andersen's Chicago office on the 45-day cross-guarantee. The workpapers also include an amended version of the December 28, 2000 memorandum, dated October 12, 2001, stating that the partners in the Chicago office advised that the 45-day cross-guarantee was not a permissible means to avoid a credit reserve loss.[47]

In early 2001, Enron's stock price continued to decline as did its merchant investments. As a result, the cross-quarantee proved to be insufficient and a more permanent solution was sought. On March 26, 2001, the Raptor arrangements were restructured by a cross-collateralization of the Raptors, and by the infusion of more Enron shares. Essentially, Enron assigned its interest in hedge payments from any Raptor to any other Raptor that could not pay for its hedge commitments. Consequently, Enron was protected by the creditworthiness of all the Raptors taken together. However, the credit problems of Raptors I and III were too great for Raptors II and IV to carry, and (1) in return for notes receivable totaling $260 million, Enron had to agree to advance Raptors II and IV up to 18 million Enron shares that could not be sold, hedged, or hedged for four years (necessitating a 23 percent discount); (2) to increase credit capacity, Enron sold 12 million shares of Enron's stock to raptors II and IV in

---

[46]Powers Report, 120.
[47]Ibid.

exchange for notes receivable totaling $568 million; and (3) Enron hedged any restricted shares held by the Raptors. This last hedging, however, overtook the 23 percent discount calculations for the notes receivable, a fact that was brought forward to the auditors and Enron's accountants by Kaminski. "Restructuring the Raptors allowed Enron to avoid reflecting the $504 million credit reserve loss in its first quarter financial statements. Instead, it recorded only a $36.6 million credit reserve loss."[48]

Ultimately, in the late summer of 2001, the continuing decline of Enron and TNPC share values caused a further large deficiency of Raptor creditworthiness. In addition:

> The collaring arrangements Enron had with the Raptors aggravated the situation, because Enron now faced the prospect of having to deliver so many shares of its stock to the Raptors that its reported earnings per share would be diluted significantly.

> At the same time, an unrelated, but extraordinarily serious, Raptor accounting problem emerged. In August 2001, Andersen and Enron accountants realized that the accounting treatment for the Enron stock and stock contracts contributed to Raptors I, II and IV was wrong. Enron had accounted for the Enron shares sold in April 2000 to Talon (Raptor I), in exchange for a $172 million promissory note, as an increase to "notes receivable" and to "shareholders' equity." This increased shareholders' equity by $172 million in Enron's second, third and fourth quarter 2000 financial reports. Enron made similar entries when it sold Enron stock contracts in March 2001 to Timberwolf and Bobcat (Raptors II and IV) for notes totaling $828 million. This accounting treatment increased shareholders' equity by a total of $1 billion in Enron's first and second quarter 2001 financial reports. Enron accountants told us that Andersen was aware of, and approved, the accounting treatment for the Enron stock contracts sold to the Raptors in the first quarter of 2001. Andersen did not permit us to interview any of the Andersen personnel involved.

> In September 2001, Andersen and Enron concluded that the prior accounting entries were wrong, and the proper accounting for these transactions would have been to show the notes receivable as a reduction to shareholders' equity. This would have had no net effect on Enron's equity balance. Enron decided to correct these mistaken entries in its third quarter 2001 financial statements. At the time, Enron accounting personnel and Andersen concluded (using a qualitative analysis) that the error was not material and a restatement was not necessary. But when Enron announced on November 8, 2001 that it would restate its prior financials (for other reasons), it included the reduction of shareholders' equity. The correction of the error in Enron's third quarter financial statements resulted in a reduction of $1 billion ($172 million plus $828 million) to its previously overstated equity balance.

> In mid-September, with the quarter-end approaching, Causey met with Lay (who had just recently reassumed the position of CEO because of Skilling's resignation) and Greg Whalley (Enron's COO) to discuss problems with the Raptors. Causey presented a series of options, including leaving the vehicles in place as they were, transactions to ameliorate the situation, and terminating the Raptors. Lay and Whalley directed Causey to terminate the Raptors. Enron did so on September 28, 2001, paying LJM2 approximately $35 million. This

---

[48]Powers Report, 125.

purchase price apparently was the result of a private negotiation between Fastow (who had sold his interest in LJM2 to Kopper in July), on behalf of Enron, and Kopper, on behalf of LJM2. This figure apparently reflected a calculation that LJM2's residual interest in the Raptors was $61 million. Enron accounted for the buy-out of the Raptors under typical business combination accounting, in which the assets and liabilities of the acquired entity are recorded at their fair value, and any excess cost typically is recorded as goodwill.

However, Andersen told Enron to record the excess as a charge to income. As of September 28, 2001, Enron calculated that the Raptors' combined assets were approximately $2.5 billion, and their combined liabilities were approximately $3.2 billion. The difference between the Raptors' assets and liabilities, plus the $35 million payment to LJM2, resulted in a charge of approximately $710 million ($544 million after taxes) reflected in Enron's third quarter 2001 financial statements.

It is unclear whether the accounting treatment of the termination was correct. Enron's transactions with the Raptors had resulted in the recognition of earnings of $532 million during 2000, and $545 million during the first nine months of 2001, for a total of almost $1.1 billion. After taking the unwind charge of $710 million, Enron had still recognized pre-tax earnings from its transactions with the Raptors of $367 million. Thus, it may have been more appropriate for Enron to have reversed the full $1.1 billion of previously recorded pre-tax earnings when it bought back the Raptors.[49]

Unbelievably, Fastow reported to the LJM2 investors in October 2000 that the Raptors had brought returns of 193, 278, 2,500, and 125 percent, which were far in excess of the 30 percent annualized returns described to the finance committee in May 2000. Moreover, since Enron retained the economic risks involved, these returns are evidently for something else. The Powers Report concludes by identifying seven accounting issues raised by the Raptors that are alleged to be questionable.[50]

ENRON CULTURE, CONFLICTS OF INTEREST, AND WHISTLE-BLOWERS

How could the employees of Enron, Arthur Andersen, and Vinson & Elkins stand by when the returns to the Enron SPEs were so incredibly high? The returns to individuals involved were also spectacular even though they already being paid by Enron, as Table 2.3 shows.

TABLE 2.3

PAYMENTS TO FASTOW & HELPERS

	INVESTMENT	RETURN, IN MILLIONS	OTHER, IN MILLIONS
A. Fastow	$25,000	$4.5 in 2 months	$30 + stock options
M. Kopper	125,000	10.0 incl. Dodson	$2 in fees
B. Glisan	5,800	1.0	
K. Mordaunt	5,800	1.0	

---

[49]Powers Report, 125–128.
[50]Ibid., 129–132.

Many Enron employees knew about the lack of integrity of the SPE dealings, but few came forward, and the ears of the board did not hear their stories. Perhaps more would have come forward, or made a more determined effort to contact the board, if conditions within Enron were different.

Enron's culture was lacking in integrity to a surprising degree. For example, it is reported that a sham energy trading floor was created to mislead a group of stock analysts. The floor was complete with computers, desks, chairs, and traders. What employee would have thought that such an elaborate hoax could be created without the knowledge of the senior executives? And who would come forward with other tales of wrongdoing knowing that the senior officials encouraged or acquiesced to such outrageous behavior? A further example of major malfeasance is the reciprocal wash trading engaged in with other energy companies during the California energy crisis of the summer of 2000, which was designed to inflate demand and Enron revenues without generating any profits since there was no substantive transaction. An Enron employee would have to be an ethical hero to come forward to report ethical problems when Enron's culture and senior officers were apparently willing to go along with, or even lead in, the wrongdoing.

Some employees did come forward, however. Not surprisingly, they made little impact on the minds and actions of senior Enron management, and none on Enron's directors. As Table 2.4 shows, some came to Andrew Fastow and others to Kenneth Lay. Fastow was clearly making himself wealthy and not about to turn himself in, or change his ways. Ken Lay consulted Enron's lawyers about Sherron Watkins' initially anonymous letter, but they had been paid as consultants to set up the SPE strategy and were not likely to report that they had made a mistake. Whether Lay did this purposely or not will probably never be known. In any event, the board of directors failed to pick up on many red flags, and apparently remained blissfully in the dark until too late. The board trusted Lay and Fastow to serve their interests and those of the shareholders, and the shareholders, pensioners, and employees paid the price.

The Sherron Watkins letter, sent on August 15, 2001, and which is available, along with her Senate Subcommittee testimony of February 14, 2002, from the

TABLE 2.4

ENRON WHISTLE-BLOWERS

	BLEW TO	ACTION	SUBSEQUENTLY
Cliff Baxter, Vice Chair	Lay	None	Exercised $32 million in stock options, had just agreed to testify to Congress when found shot dead in his car—an apparent suicide—on Jan. 25, 2002
McMahon, Treasurer	Fastow	None	Reassigned, later returned as CEO
Kaminski, Risk Mgr.	Fastow and others	None	Continued
Sherron Watkins	Lay	None	Discussed with Skilling and asked Vinson & Elkins to review

http://brooks.swlearning.com

text's Website, is discussed at some length in the Powers Report beginning on page 172. Sherron was a competent professional accountant who had worked for Arthur Andersen for many years before joining Enron. She complained that the aggressive accounting being practiced by Enron would implode, and it did. When Ken Lay apparently did not change things because of her letter and their meetings, she was prepared to testify before investigating committees. If a few knowledgeable board members had heard her concerns perhaps action could have been taken earlier. Sherron is a highly principled woman, who knew what could happen and feared the worst. She realized the stakes were so high that she ultimately put her concerns for her own self-interest aside and came forward. Initially, however, she sent her letter anonymously—an indication of her concern about the reception and treatment she expected.

One of the unexplained Enron conundrums is why the following men who occupied senior positions at Enron, and all of whom had continuous interaction with board members, apparently did not come forward with concerns:

Richard Causey, chief accounting officer
Richard Buy, chief risk officer
Ben Glisan, treasurer and senior accountant

Why weren't they loyal agents of Enron? Perhaps they were just too anxious to keep Andrew Fastow happy. Perhaps their lack of loyalty had something to do with the desire to please Fastow and Ken Lay, who had a significant influence over Enron's stock option incentive plan. The plan was particularly lucrative as Table 2.5 shows.

TABLE 2.5

ENRON STOCK PROCEEDS, OCTOBER 1998 TO NOVEMBER 2001, OVER $30 MILLION

Lou Pal	Chairman, Enron Accelerator	$353.7 million
Ken Lay	Chairman	101.3
Rebecca Mark-Jusbasche	Director	79.5
Ken Harrison	Director, Portland General Electrics	75.2
Kenneth Rice	Chairman, Enron Broadband	72.8
Jeffrey Skilling	Director (former CEO)	66.9
Mark Frevert	Vice Chairman	50.3
Stanley Horton	Global Chairman	45.5
Joseph Sutton	Vice Chairman	40.1
J. Clifford Baxter	Vice Chairman	35.2
Joseph Hirco	CEO, Enron Broadband	35.2
Andrew Fastow	Chief Financial Officer	30.5

SOURCE: © 2002, *The Washington Post.* Reprinted with permission.

Startlingly, many boards of directors took the view that stock options were of no cost to the issuing companies because they were not recorded on the financial statements when earmarked for the recipient. Prevailing practice in the United States was to record stock options only when and if exercised, and then only at the exercise price, not at market. The chairman of Enron's compensation committee implied this during his Senate Subcommittee testimony on the subject of Ken Lay's overall compensation of $141 million for 2001, the stock option portion of which was approximately $130 million.[51]

[51]Testimony of Charles LeMaistre on May 7, 2002, (see *http://brooks.swlearning.com*).

ARTHUR ANDERSEN'S ROLE

Arthur Andersen (AA) was, as Enron's auditor, supposed to be a professional fiduciary looking out for the interests of Enron's shareholders and their representatives, Enron's board of directors. As outlined more fully in the accompanying case, *Arthur Andersen's Troubles*, the once-proud firm that defined the standard for integrity occupied the following roles with regard to Enron:

- Auditor
- Consultant on accounting and other matters, including SPE transactions
- Internal auditor, since this function was contracted out by Enron to AA
- Advisor on tax matters
- Advisor, reviewer of financial disclosure

For the year 2000, AA is said to have received fees of approximately $52 million: $25 million for audit work and $27 million for other services. There is little doubt that Enron was one of AA's largest clients, and was growing. AA's internal culture was reportedly driven by the desire for revenue, so Enron was one of AA's prize possessions.

Given these facts, AA and its personnel were confronted by several conflicts of interest, which may have impinged upon and weakened their resolve to act in their fiduciary relationship as auditors, including:

- Auditing their own work as SPE consultants, leading to a lack of objectivity.
- Self-interest versus the public's interest, leading to wishing not to upset Enron management and thus:
  - Losing a very large, prestigious audit and a huge audit fee:
    - Partners not liked by Enron were removed from the audit.
    - Noncompliance with company policies and codes was not brought to the attention of the board.
    - AA's internal debates over Enron's questionable accounting treatments and business risks were not aired with the audit committee to ensure that the members were knowledgeable.
    - Public disclosures were not satisfactory to inform investors.
  - Audit staff wishing to leave AA and join Enron lose their chances to make the change.

Of course, AA's shortcomings may be due, in part, to:

- A lack of competence, such as displayed in the Rhythms decisions.
- A failure of AA's internal policies whereby the concerns of a quality control or practice standards partner can be and were overruled by the audit partner in charge of the Enron account. AA was the only one of the Big 5 accounting firms to have this flaw and it left the entire firm vulnerable to the decision of the person with the most to lose by saying no to a client.
- Lack of information caused by Enron staff not providing critical information, or failure on the part of AA personnel to ferret it out.
- A misunderstanding of the fiduciary role required by auditors.

Regardless of the causes, AA did not live up to the expectations of the public, the board, current shareholders, the accounting profession, and regulators.

Ultimately, AA was indicted and convicted for the obstruction of justice because personnel in several cities shredded Enron audit papers. AA claimed these were not important, but this lacked credibility and could not be substantiated since the shredding had taken place. The impact of this conviction was that AA's ability to audit companies who were SEC registrants (required for share listing and trading on the New York Stock Exchange or NASDAQ, was initially in doubt, and finally withdrawn. The reputation and ability of the firm to function was eroded. AA personnel joined other accounting firms in the United States and around the world. AA was finished as a firm, and the Big 5 firms became the Big 4.

In addition, the accounting profession was altered forever in the United States, and received a "wake up" call in other parts of the world. Independence, objectivity, fiduciary duty, and the primacy of the public interest came into sharper focus.

ENRON'S GOVERNANCE AND CONTROL SYSTEM WAS SHORT-CIRCUITED

In view of the conflicts of interest of Fastow and his helpers, of the rest of the senior management team, of Enron's lawyers, and particularly those of Arthur Andersen, it is clear that Enron's directors were unable to rely on the information they were receiving, or upon Enron's company policies being followed. Enron's management was out of control. This was the directors' own fault. They failed to understand their role included a challenge and compliance cycle, and trusted too much when there were many red flags warning that questions should have been pressed. Figure 2.2 shows the elements of Enron's system that were short-circuited, and therefore not reliable for the governance of Enron in the shareholders' best interests.

FIGURE 2.2

ENRON'S GOVERNANCE AND CONTROL STRUCTURE WAS SHORT-CIRCUITED

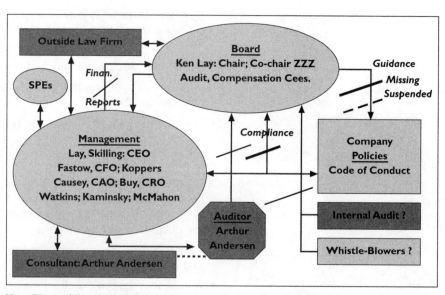

Note: Diagonal lines indicate missing, suspended, or conflicted relationships.

BANKS WHO WERE WILLING ACCOMPLICES IN ENRON "PREPAYS"

Many of the schemes used by Fastow to mislead investors and strip money out of Enron relied upon the participation of large financial institutions like Barclays Bank in the Rhythms hedge transaction. The Senate Investigations Committee has undertaken a review of some of these arrangements, known as "prepays," to see if there is evidence that the banks knew that the transactions involved had no economic substance.[52] If so, the banks were knowledgeable accomplices in the schemes to defraud Enron's investors, and will probably face sanctions and lawsuits from aggrieved investors, pensioners, and others. The report of investigator Roach identified two banks, JPMorgan Chase (12 deals worth $3.7 billion) and Citigroup (14 deals worth $4.8 billion), as the primary sources of Enron "prepay" funding, and concludes that "the parties involved in the Enron prepays were aware of the entire structure and its accounting purpose."[53]

Enron's "prepays" were mechanisms for Enron to record prepayments for future energy delivery as current operating earnings and cash flow rather than as cash flow from financing operations. The Roach Report states:

> Under the Enron prepay structure, a participating bank would send cash (the money destined for Enron) to the third party, in exchange for the future delivery of a fixed amount of a commodity. The third party, in turn, would enter into an identical arrangement with Enron, and effectively serve as a pass through for the bank funding to get to Enron. Enron would repay the funding in a fixed amount of the commodities, which would pass through the third party en route to the bank. Up to this point this appears to be a "real" trade because all three parties bear the risk that the price of the underlying commodity will change. This is called price risk and it is an essential element in a true trading transaction.

> But, Enron prepays also entailed a transaction known as a "swap" in order to mitigate price risk. Under a swap agreement, Enron exchanged (with the bank) the floating price of the commodity for the fixed price of the commodity. The net effect is to cancel out any price risk to all parties in the trade. … the third party was not independent and the terms of the prepay were predetermined based on Enron's decision as to how much operating cash flow it needed to report …[54]

The linked structure used by Enron did not comply with AA's internal criteria that were established "to distinguish true trading activity from loans."[55] An AA June 1999 audit memo found by Roach clearly shows that AA recognized the problem and how it needed to be rectified. The Roach Report does not state whether the AA memo was followed by Enron.

An additional complication has arisen. One bank that has reinsured their loans to Enron is finding that the reinsurors are refusing to pay up, arguing that the banks knew that the underlying transactions were a sham. Therefore, they argue that the reinsurance arrangements were not made in good faith, that risks were beyond the norm, and therefore the reinsurance for subsequent loss is void.[56]

---

[52]See the testimony of Senior Investigator Roach on July 23, 2002.

[53]Roach Report, Appendix A, A-8.

[54]Ibid.

[55]Ibid., A-7.

[56]The Royal Bank of Canada is involved in lawsuits with Rabobank, a reinsuror, seeking to recover a $500 million loan.

The prospect of either direct lawsuits for complicity, or the possibility that reinsurance will be declared void, will have a sobering effect on the participation of banks in the future. The banks will be screening partners and deals much more carefully and will be less ready to participate in arrangements that may look legal, but are probably unethical. This may be one of the most significant outcomes of the Enron debacle.

ENRON'S TAX AVOIDANCE

Enron's banks were not the only willing accomplices in the company's questionable transactions. Several accounting firms, investment bankers, and law firms allegedly provided highly questionable advice on twelve large structured transactions that sheltered over $2 billion in tax from 1995 until its bankruptcy on December 2, 2001. While these transactions may barely adhere to the letter of the law, they have been branded as unethical by members of the Senate Committee on Finance.

According to the Senate Committee's *Report*,[57] Enron's management discovered that tax transactions could not only save tax, but could be used to generate financial statement earnings. Thereafter, Enron's tax department was looked upon as a "profit center."[58]

Generally, four strategies were used in the structured transactions:

- Duplication of a single economic loss (i.e., deduction of the same loss twice),
- Shifting of tax basis from a nondepreciable asset to a depreciable asset with little or no outlay,
- Generation of tax deductions for the repayment of principal, and
- Generation of fees for serving as an accommodation party for another taxpayer.[59]

Enron recorded the credits arising from the first two strategies as financial income.

Unfortunately, the Senate's analysis of Enron's structured transactions (summarized on Table 3 of the Senate *Report*) revealed "*a pattern of behavior showing that Enron deliberately engaged in transactions that had little or no business purpose in order to obtain favorable tax and accounting treatment.*"[60] Although a proper business purpose is a fundamental prerequisite for such tax benefits, according to the Senate *Report*, "Enron represented the business purpose of the transaction, and Enron's counsel did not bother to look beyond the representation."[61] Most proposed transactions received a "Should comply with technical tax law requirements" assurance opinion from advisers or counsel.[62]

---

[57] *Report of the Investigation of Enron Corporation and Related Entities Regarding Federal Tax and Compensation Issues, and Policy Recommendations, Volume 1: Report*, U.S. Senate Committee on Finance, February 2003, released 2/22/03, (see *http://brooks.swlearning.com*).

[58] Ibid., p. 8.

[59] Ibid., p. 8.

[60] Ibid., p. 16.

[61] Ibid., p. 16.

[62] Ibid., p. 16.

Moreover, the Senate *Report* indicates that the transactions were exceedingly complicated, thus precluding a meaningful review by tax auditors. This complexity was engineered with the advice of a small pool of sophisticated outside advisers. Sometimes these advisers counseled Enron directly, and sometimes each other. The following names appeared as promoter and/or primary tax opinion provider on the twelve structured transactions:

- Arthur Andersen   4 times
- Bankers Trust   5 "
- Vinson & Elkins   3 "
- Deloitte & Touche   2 "
- Akin, Gump, Strauss, …   2 "
- 6 others   1 "   including Chase Manhattan, Deutsche Bank, Ernst & Young

The Senate *Report* comments[63] that:

> A critical component of many of Enron's transactions was the involvement of an accommodation party such as an Enron employee or the party promoting the transaction. Enron's activities show that, in general, when transactions can be structured by parties that have the shared goal of obtaining favorable tax treatment, the tax rules do not function as intended and may produce undesirable results.

> Enron's aggressive interpretation of business purpose, the cooperation of accommodation parties, the protections provided by tax opinions, the complex design of transactions, advantages over IRS—all were factors that contributed to Enron's ability to engage in tax-motivated transactions. Until the costs of participating in tax-motivated transactions are substantially increased, corporations such as Enron will continue to engage in transactions that violate the letter or the spirit of the law.

Time will tell whether the exposure generated by the Senate *Report*, or the proposed tightening of loopholes and increases in sanctions and penalties, will change the practice of these and other tax advisers in the future. Their actions may be legal, but in the case of Enron, not considered ethical because they offended the public interest.

THE AFTERMATH

The aftermath for Arthur Andersen and the accounting profession are dealt with above and in the accompanying case, *Arthur Andersen's Troubles.*

The Senate Investigations Committee deliberations were noted above with regard to the role of Enron's management and directors. Their report appeared on July 8, 2002. Prior to this, the Enron bankruptcy and the Senate Hearings had raised the awareness of the public, politicians, and regulators to

---

[63]Ibid., p.16.

governance failures and their impact. As noted in the previous discussion of the governance timeline, many groups had brought forward changes in governance structures. On June 26, 2002, WorldCom announced that it had discovered a $4.3 billion manipulation of earnings. The resulting outrage galvanized the construction and passage of the Sarbanes-Oxley Act on July 30, 2002, which provides the blueprint for a new framework for governance to be developed in the United States and which will inform developments around the world. Not surprisingly, the key concepts will include accountability, transparency, independence, objectivity, fiduciary duty, and the primacy of the public interest.

As Enron executives and accomplices are indicted, and as the SEC and other regulators respond to the Sarbanes-Oxley Act, the long-run changes in corporate governance and practice and the accounting profession will emerge.

DOWNLOADABLE ENRON CASE SOURCE DOCUMENT FILES

To assist readers of this case, the following downloadable files are available from the text's Website.

http://brooks.
swlearning.com

- The Powers Report
- The Senate's Permanent Subcommittee on Investigations Report on The Role of the Board of Directors in the Collapse of Enron
- Senate Subcommittee Testimony of Robert Roach, Appendices
- Sarbanes-Oxley Act of 2002

Arthur Andersen's Troubles: A Review and Analysis

Once the largest professional services firm in the world, and arguably the most respected, Arthur Andersen LLP (AA) has disappeared. The Big 5 accounting firms are now the Big 4. Why did this happen? How did it happen? What are the lessons to be learned?

Arthur Andersen, a 28-year-old Northwestern University accounting professor, co-founded the firm in 1913. Tales of his integrity are legendary, and the culture of the firm was very much in his image. For example, "Just months after [Andersen] set up shop in Chicago, the president of a local railroad insisted that he approve a transaction that would have inflated earnings. Andersen told the executive there was "not enough money in the City of Chicago" to make him do it."[64] In 1954, consulting services began with the installation of the first mainframe computer at General Electric to automate its payroll systems. By 1978, AA became the largest professional services firm in the world with revenues of $546 million, and by 1984 consulting brought in more profit than auditing. In 1989, the consulting operation, wanting more control and a larger share of profit, became a separate part of a Swiss partnership from the audit operation. In 2000, following an arbitrator's ruling that a break fee of $1 billion be paid, Andersen Consulting split completely and changed its name to Accenture. AA, the audit practice, continued to offer a limited set of related services such as tax advice.[65]

---

[64]"Fall from Grace," *Business Week*, August 12, 2002, 54.
[65]Ibid., see table on page 53.

TABLE 2.6

SELECTED ENRON FINANCIAL
STATEMENT DETAILS

	2000	1999	1998
Summary Income Statement *(in millions)*			
Revenues	$100,789	$40,112	$31,260
Operating income	1,953	802	1,378
IBIT	2,482	1,995	1,582
Net income before cumulative accounting changes	979	1,024	703
Net income	979	893	703
EPS (in dollars) - basic	1.22	1.17	1.07
- diluted	1.12	1.10	1.01
Detail of IBIT *(in millions)*			
Transport & distribution			
Trans. Services	$ 391	$ 380	$ 351
Portland General	341	305	286
Wholesale services	2,260	1,317	968
Retail energy services	165	(68)	(119)
Broadband services	(60)		
Exploration & prod.	-	65	128
Corporate and other	(615)	(4)	(32)
IBIT	**2,482**	**1,995**	**1,582**
Summary Balance Sheet *(in millions)*			
Current assets (in billions)	$ 30.4	$ 7.3	
Investments, other	23.4	15.4	
Property, plant, equip, net	11.7	10.7	
Total Assets	**65.5**	**33.4**	
Current liabilities	28.4	6.8	
Long-term debt	8.6	7.2	
Deferred credits and other	13.8	6.5	
Other, including minority interests	3.2	3.3	
Shareholders' equity	11.5	9.6	
Total Liab. & Shareholders' Equity ...	**65.5**	**33.4**	

CHANGING PERSONALITIES AND CULTURE

Throughout most of its history, AA stood for integrity and technical competence. The firm invested heavily in training programs and a training facility in St. Charles, a small town south of Chicago, and developed it until it had over 3,000 residence beds and outstanding computer and classroom facilities. AA personnel from all over the world were brought to St. Charles for training sessions on an ongoing basis. Even after the consulting and audit operations split, both continued to use the facility.

Ironically, AA was the first firm to recognize the need for professional accountants to study business and professional ethics formally. In the late

1980s, AA undertook a number of programs to stimulate that formal education, including the development of ethics cases, the creation of an approach to the resolution of professional ethical problems, and the hosting of groups of 100 accounting academics to get them started in the area. Most had no formal ethics training and were uncertain how to begin teaching ethics, or even if they should. It is likely that AA's far-sighted policies are responsible for the genesis of much of the professional ethics education and research in accounting that is going on today.

What happened to the AA culture that focused on integrity and technical competence? What changed that would account for AA's involvement in the major financial scandals noted in Table 2.7 as the audit firm that failed to discover the underlying problems?

Some observers have argued that a change in AA's culture was responsible. Over the period when the consulting practice was surpassing the audit practice as the most profitable aspect of the firm, a natural competitiveness grew up between the two rivals. The generation of revenue became more and more desirable, and the key to merit and promotion decisions. The retention of audit clients took on an increasingly greater significance as part of this program, and since clients were so large, auditors tended to become identified with them; many audit personnel even looked forward to joining their clients. In any event, the loss of a major client would sideline the career of the auditors involved at least temporarily, if not permanently. For many reasons, taking

TABLE 2.7

ARTHUR ANDERSEN'S
PROBLEM AUDITS

CLIENT	PROBLEM MISSED, DATE	LOSSES TO SHAREHOLDERS	JOB LOSSES	AA FINE
WorldCom	$4.3 billion overstatement of earnings announced on June 25, 2002	$179.3 billion	17,000	N.A.
Enron	Inflation of income, assets, etc., bankrupt Dec. 2, 2001	$66.4 billion	6,100	$.5 million (for shredding)
Global Crossing	Candidate for bankruptcy	$26.6 billion	8,700	
Waste Management*	Overstatement of income by $1.1 billion, 1992–1996	$20.5 billion	11,000	$7 mil.
Sunbeam*	Overstatement of 1997 income by $71.1 million, then bankruptcy	$4.4 billion	1,700	
Baptist Foundation of Arizona	Books cooked, largest nonprofit bankruptcy ever	$570 million	165	

* Cases are at the end of the chapter.

SOURCE: "Fall from Grace," *Business Week*, August 12, 2002, 54.

a stand against the management of a major client required a keen understanding of the auditor's role, the backing of senior partners in your firm, and courage.

The pressure for profit was felt throughout the rest of the audit profession, not just at Arthur Andersen. Audit techniques were modified to require higher levels of analysis, and lower investment of time. Judgment sampling gave way to statistical sampling, and then to strategic risk auditing. While each was considered better than its predecessor, the trend was toward tighter time budgets and the focus of the audit broadened to include the development of value-added non-audit outcomes, suggestions, or services for clients. Such non-audit services could include advice on the structuring of transactions for desired disclosure outcomes and other work upon which the auditor would later have to give an audit opinion.

According to discussions in the business and professional press, many audit professionals did not see the conflicts of interest involved as a problem. The conflict between maximizing audit profit for the firm and providing adequate audit quality so that the investing public would be protected was considered to be manageable so that no one would be harmed. The conflict between auditing in the public interest with integrity and objectivity that could lead to the need to roundly criticize mistakes that your firm or you had made in earlier advice was considered not to present a worry. In addition, the conflict between the growing complexity of transactions, particularly those involving derivative financial instruments, hedges, swaps, and so on, and the desire to restrain audit time in the interest of profit was thought to be within the capacity of auditors and firms to resolve. The growing conflict for auditors between serving the interests of the management team, which was often instrumental in making the appointment of auditors, and the interests of shareholders was recognized but did not draw reinforcing statements from firms or professional accounting bodies. Some professional accountants did not understand whether they should be serving the interests of current shareholders or future shareholders, or what serving the public interest had to do with serving their client. They did not understand the difference between a profession and a business.

Ethical behavior in an organization is guided by the ethical culture of that organization, by any relevant professional norms and codes, and particularly by the "tone at the top"[66] and the example set by the top executives. Also, presumably the selection of the CEO is based partly on the choice of the values that an organization should be led toward. Joe Barardino was elected AA's CEO on January 10, 2001, but he had been partner-in-charge of AA's U.S. audit practice for almost three years before. He was the leader whose values were driving the firm from 1998 onward, and probably continued those of his predecessor. What were his values? Barbara Ley Toffler, a former Andersen partner during this period and before has provided the following insight:

> When Berardino would get up at a partners meeting, all that was ever reported in terms of success was dollars. Quality wasn't discussed. Content wasn't discussed. Everything was measured in terms of the buck. … Joe was blind to the conflict. He was the most aggressive pursuer of revenue that I ever met.[67]

---

[66]This is a concept emerging in new governance standards that boards of directors are to monitor.
[67]"Fall from Grace," 55, 56.

ARTHUR ANDERSEN'S INTERNAL CONTROL FLAW

Given this "tone at the top," it is reasonable to assume that AA partners were going to be motivated by revenue generation. But if too many risks are taken in the pursuit of revenue, the probability of a series of audit problems leading to increasingly unfavorable consequences becomes greater. That is exactly what happened. Unfortunately, the leaders of AA failed to recognize the cumulative degree to which the public, the politicians, and the SEC were angered by the progression of AA audit failures.

If they had recognized the precarious position they were in, the AA leadership might have corrected the flaw in the AA internal control that allowed the Enron audit failures to happen. AA was the only one of the Big 5 to allow the partner in charge of the audit to override a ruling of the quality control partner. This meant that at AA the most sensitive decisions were taken by the person who was most concerned with the potential loss of revenue from the client in question, and who was most likely to be subject to the influence of the client. In all of the other Big 5 firms, the most sensitive decisions are taken by the person whose primary interest is the compliance with GAAP, the protection of the public interest, and the reputation of the firm.

On April 2, 2002, the U.S. House Energy and Commerce Committee released a memo dated December 18, 1999, from Carl Bass, a partner in AA's Professional Services Group in Chicago, to David Duncan, the AA partner in charge of the Enron account.[68] That memo asked for an accounting change (believed to be in regard to SPE transactions) that would have resulted in a $30–$50 million charge to Enron's earnings. In February 2000, Bass emailed Duncan to object to the setting up of an LJM partnership because he indicated that "this whole deal looks like there is no substance."[69] On March 4, 2001, Bass wrote that "then-chief financial officer Andrew Fastow's role as manager of special partnerships compromised deals Enron made with the entities."[70] Duncan overruled Bass on the first issue, and Bass was removed from Enron audit oversight on March 17, 2001, less than two weeks after he questioned Fastow's role in Enron's SPEs. In any other Big 5 firm, Duncan would not have been able to overrule a quality control partner on his own. History might have been different if a quality-focused internal control procedure had been in place at AA, rather than one that was revenue focused.

ARTHUR ANDERSEN'S APPARENT ENRON MISTAKES

The "Enron Debacle" section presented previously covers in detail many of the questionable accounting transactions, legal structures, and related disclosures that AA reviewed as auditors of and consultants to Enron. Without repeating these in detail, it is possible to provide the following summary of significant issues that AA could be questioned about in court proceedings:

- AA apparently approved as auditors and consultants (and collected fees for the consulting advice) the structure of many special purpose entities

---

[68]"Andersen Under Fire over Memos: Carl Bass Documents," *Financial Post*, April 4, 2002, FP1, FP10.

[69]"Andersen Partner Warned on Enron in '99: Questioned Partnerships," *Financial Post*, April 3, 2002, FP9.

[70]"Anderson Under Fire," FP1.

(SPEs) that were used to generate false profits, hide losses, and keep financing off Enron's consolidated financial statements, failed to meet the required outsider 3 percent equity at risk, and decision control criteria for nonconsolidation.

- AA failed to recognize the generally accepted accounting principle (GAAP) that prohibits the recording of shares issued as an increase in shareholders' equity unless they are issued for cash (not for notes receivable).
- AA did not advise Enron's audit committee that Andrew Fastow, Enron's CFO, and his helpers were involved in significant conflict of interest situations without adequate alternative means of managing these conflicts.
- AA did not advise the Enron audit committee that Enron's policies and internal control were not adequate to protect the shareholders' interests even though AA had assumed Enron's internal audit function.
- Many transactions between Enron and the SPEs were not in the interest of Enron shareholders since:
  - Enron profits and cash flow were manipulated and grossly inflated, misleading investors and falsely boosting management bonus arrangements.
  - Extraordinarily overgenerous deals, fees, and liquidation arrangements were made by Fastow, or under his influence, with SPEs owned by Fastow, his family, and Kopper, who was also an employee of Enron.
- AA apparently did not adequately consider the advice of its quality control partner, Carl Bass.
- AA apparently did not find significant audit evidence, or did not act upon evidence found, related to the:
  - Erroneous valuation of shares or share rights transferred to SPEs.
  - Side deals between Enron and banks removing the banks' risk from transactions such as the:
    - Chewco SPE Rhythms hedge.
    - numerous prepay deals for energy futures, even though AA made a presentation to Enron on the GAAP and AA requirements that preclude such arrangements.[71]

WHY DID ARTHUR ANDERSEN MAKE THESE APPARENT MISTAKES?

The term "apparent" is used because AA's side of the story has not been heard. The so-called mistakes may have logical, reasonable explanations, and may be supportable by other accounting and auditing experts. That stated, these apparent mistakes may have been made for several reasons, including:

- Incompetence, as displayed and admitted in the Rhythms case.
- Judgment errors as to the significance of each of the audit findings, or of the aggregate impact in any fiscal year.
- Lack of information caused by Enron staff not providing critical information, or failure on the part of AA personnel to ferret it out.

---

[71]Testimony of Robert Roach to the Senate Permanent Subcommittee on Investigations, July 23, 2002, Appendix A, A-6.

- Time pressures related to revenue generation and budget pressures that prevented adequate audit work and the full consideration of complex SPE and prepay financial arrangements.
- Desire not to confront Enron management or advise the Enron board in order not to upset management, and particularly Fastow, Skilling, and Lay.
- A failure of AA's internal policies whereby the concerns of a quality control or practice standards partner can and was overruled by the audit partner in charge of the Enron account. AA was the only one of the Big 5 accounting firms to have this flaw and it left the entire firm vulnerable to the decision of the person with the most to lose by saying no to a client.
- A misunderstanding of the fiduciary role required by auditors.

Since AA has now disintegrated, it is unlikely that the cause of specific audit deficiencies will ever be known. However, it is reasonable to assume that all of the causes listed played some part in the apparent mistakes that were made.

A review of additional cases of failure where Arthur Andersen was the auditor, such as the Waste Management and Sunbeam failures that appear at the end of the chapter, reveal that AA's behavior was striking similar to that in the Enron debacle. In each case, AA appears to have been so interested in revenue generation that they were willing not to take a hard line with their clients. AA personnel apparently believed that there was no serious risk of default and that, over time, accounting problems could be worked out. At the very least, AA's risk assessment process was seriously flawed. Also, when AA's client had a combined chairman of the board and CEO who intimidated or was willingly helped by his CFO, neither other professional accountants working for the corporations nor other non-accounting personnel who knew of the accounting manipulations raised their concerns sufficiently with AA or the audit committee of their board of directors to stimulate corrective action. This lack of courage or understanding of the need and means to stimulate action left AA, the board, and the public vulnerable.

SHREDDING ENRON AUDIT DOCUMENTS: OBSTRUCTION OF JUSTICE

The final disintegration of AA was not caused directly by the Enron audit deficiencies, but by a related decision to shred Enron audit documents and the conviction on the charge of obstruction of justice that resulted. This charge, filed on March 7, 2002, raised the prospect that, if AA were convicted, the Securities and Exchange Commission would withdraw AA's certification to audit SEC registrant companies.[72] That would preclude those large public companies that needed to be registered with the SEC to have their shares traded on U.S. stock exchanges (the NYSE and NASDAQ) or raise significant amounts of capital in the United States.

Since these clients represented the bulk of AA's U.S. and foreign accounting practices, if convicted, AA would be effectively reduced to insignificance unless a waiver could be arranged from the SEC. The SEC, however, was very angry about the Enron audit deficiencies, particularly in view of the earlier similar cases involving the AA audits of Waste Management and Sunbeam. In

---

[72]AA could also face probation for up to five years and a $500,000 fine as well as fines for up to twice any gains or damages the court determines were caused by the firm's action.

regard to the Waste Management debacle, "The commission argued that not only did Andersen knowingly and recklessly issue materially false and misleading statements, it failed to enforce its own guidelines to bring the company in line with minimally accepted accounting standards."[73] As a condition of the $7 million fine paid in June 2001 settling AA's Waste Management audit deficiencies, AA had agreed to rectify its audit inadequacies, and the SEC believed that AA had not honored this undertaking. Because AA's behavior in the Enron debacle was so similar, the SEC provided only a temporary and conditional waiver pending the outcome of the trial.[74]

The conviction was announced on June 15, 2002, but many large clients had already transferred their work to other audit firms. Some boards of directors and CEOs thought that AA's reputation was so damaged by the Enron fiasco that they no longer wanted to be associated with AA, or that such an association might weaken their company's ability to attract financing at the lowest rates. The outrage of the public was so intense that other boards could not face the lack of credibility that continuing with AA would have produced with their shareholders. Still other boards realized that if AA were convicted, there would be a stampede to other firms, and their company might not be able to make a smooth transition to another SEC-certified audit firm if they waited to switch. By the time the conviction was announced, only a small percentage of AA's largest clients remained. Even though AA's chances of acquittal upon appeal were considered by some observers to be good, AA was a shell of its former self and was essentially finished as a firm in the United States, and ultimately around the world.

The chain of events that led to the shredding of some of AA's Enron audit documents begins before Enron decided to announce a $618 million restatement of earnings and a $1.2 billion reduction of equity on October 16, 2001. An SEC investigation was launched into Enron's accounting on October 17 and AA was advised on October 19. However, AA had advised Enron that such an announcement was necessary to correct its accounting for SPEs and on October 9, as the 8-page indictment states, "retained an experienced New York law firm to handle further Enron-related litigation."[75] Eleven days later, the subject of shredding was discussed as part of an emergency conference call to AA partners, and shredding began three days after that.[76]

Shredding was undertaken in AA's Houston office, as well as in London, Chicago, and Portland. "...according to the U.S. government, ... the destruction was 'wholesale,' with workers putting in overtime in order to get the job done." "Tonnes of paper relating to the Enron audit were promptly shredded as part of the orchestrated document destruction. The shredder at the Andersen office at the Enron building was used virtually constantly and to handle the overload, dozens of large trunks filled with Enron documents were sent to Andersen's Houston office to be shredded."[77]

---

[73]"'Back Time' May Catch Andersen," *Toronto Star*, March 21, 2002, D11.

[74]"SEC Announces Actions for Issuers in Light of Indictment of Arthur Andersen LLP," SEC Release 2002-37.

[75]Grand jury indictment on the charge of obstruction of justice, United States of America against Arthur Andersen, LLP, filed in the United Sates District Court Southern District of Texas on March 7, 2002, 5

[76]"'Back Time' May Catch Andersen."

[77]Ibid.

At the trial, AA argued differently. AA's lawyer attempted to clarify the purpose of Chicago-based AA lawyer Nancy Temple's e-mail of October 10 to Michael Odom of AA's Houston office. In that e-mail she wrote that "it might be useful to consider reminding the (Enron audit) team that it would be helpful to make sure that we have complied with the policy."[78] "which calls for destruction of extraneous and redundant material."[79] This lack of relevance, of course, was difficult to prove after the documents in question had been destroyed. Essentially, AA contended that "the order to follow the document retention policy was an innocent effort to organize papers, e-mails and computer files and eliminate extraneous material."[80]

David Duncan, however, testified against AA. He had been fired from AA (where he had been the partner in charge of the Enron audit) on January 15, one day after he met with the Justice Department. He said: "I obstructed justice ... I instructed people on the (Enron audit) team to follow the document retention policy, which I knew would result in the destruction of documents."[81]

The jury deliberated for many days, emerged, and was sent back for additional deliberations. Ultimately, AA was declared guilty. Although AA planned to appeal, it agreed to cease all audits of public companies by the end of August. Ironically, AA's conviction turned upon the jury's view that the shredding was part of a broad conspiracy, and that rested upon testimony that was reread to the jury indicating that an AA memo (or memos) was altered. The acts of shredding alone were not enough for conviction. The jury was reported as concluding that:

> Duncan eventually pleaded guilty to one count of obstruction and testified on the government's behalf, but jurors said afterwards that they didn't believe his testimony.
>
> Instead, the jury agreed that Andersen in-house attorney Nancy Temple had acted corruptly in order to impede the SEC's pending investigation. Speaking to reporters, juror Jack Gallo said that one of Temple's memos was critical in helping the jury reach its verdict. The memo, from last October, was a response to an email from Duncan about Enron's third quarter earnings statement. Enron wanted to describe a massive earnings loss as "non-recurring," but Duncan advised Enron against using that phrase.
>
> Temple's memo advised Duncan to delete any language that might suggest that Andersen disagreed with Enron, and further advised Duncan to remove her own name from his correspondence, since she did not want to be called as a witness in any future litigation stemming from Enron's earnings announcements.[82]

On October 16, 2002, AA was fined the maximum of $500,000 and placed on five years probation. AA's lawyer stated the AA would appeal out of principle, even though only 1,000 employees remained.

LINGERING QUESTIONS

Within a few months, arrangements had been made for the AA units around the world to join other firms, but not before many staff had left, and not all

---

[78]"Auditor Evidence Attacked," *Toronto Star*, May 22, 2002, E12.
[79]Ibid.
[80]Ibid.
[81]"Andersen Partner Admits Wrongdoing," *Toronto Star*, May 14, 2002, D3.
[82]Greg Farrell, "Arthur Andersen Convicted of Obstruction of Justice," *USA TODAY*, June 15, 2002.

those remaining were hired by the new employers. A firm of 85,000 people worldwide, including 24,000 in the United States, was virtually gone.

Was this an appropriate outcome? Perhaps only 100 AA people were responsible for the Enron tragedy, but 85,000 paid a price. Will the reduced selection of large accounting firms, the Big 4, be able to serve the public interest better than the Big 5? What if another Big 4 firm has difficulty—will we see the Big 3, or are we now facing the Final Four? Will other individual AA partners and personnel be brought to justice in the courts beyond David Duncan, or by the AICPA through the exercise of its code of conduct? Will a similar tragedy occur again?

EMERGING RESEARCH

These questions, and others, have stimulated the accounting research community to investigate them. Conferences are being held, and research articles are appearing.

An early study by Chaney and Philipich, entitled "Shredded Reputation: The Cost of Audit Failure,"[83] provided insights into the impact of AA's problems on its other corporate clients and their investors. On January 10, 2002, AA admitted shredding Enron's documents, and in the ensuing three days the stock prices of most of AA's 284 other large clients that were part of the Standard & Poor's 1,500 Index fell. Over that time, these stocks dropped an average of 2.05 percent and lost more than $37 million in market value. This was the largest movement observed for the four critical information events tested. The other events were November 8, 2001, when Enron announced its restatements; December 12, 2001, when AA's CEO admitted AA made an error; and February 3, 2002, the day following the release of the Powers Report when AA hired former Federal Reserve Chairman Paul Volcker to chair an Independent Oversight Board to shore up AA's credibility. Volcker later resigned when it became evident that AA was unwilling to embrace significant changes.

Additional research studies have examined many aspects of the conduct of the directors, executives, lawyers and accountants involved in the Enron, Arthur Andersen and WorldCom tragedies. In addition, the role of regulators, of directors, and of professional independence has and will come under scrutiny. These studies are to be found in many academic and professional journals as well the popular business press. In particular, useful articles can be found or will be forthcoming in the *Journal of Business Ethics, Business Ethics Quarterly, The Journal of Accounting Research, Canadian Accounting Perspectives*, the *Journal of Research in Accounting Ethics*, and *Business Week*.

Governance and Accounting Changes up to WorldCom

Even before the Enron scandal appeared and resulted in a filing for bankruptcy protection on December 2, 2001, there had been some recognition that governance and accounting changes were desirable. After Enron, there was a turmoil and growing outrage over the cavalier way that Enron executives claimed ignorance, bad memories, or pleaded the Fifth Amendment. Arthur Andersen representatives did not help in their testimony, and there was a growing concern that no one was being

---

[83]Paul R. Chaney and Kirk L. Philipich, "Shredded Reputation: The Cost of Audit Failure," *Journal of Accounting Research*, Vol. 40, No. 4, September 2002, 1235, 1240.

brought to justice. There seemed to be no accountability, or little will on the part of justice officials to get tough with the culprits that had caused so much anxiety and loss, and had enriched themselves so handsomely in the process.

The following Table 2.8 is a partial list of key guideline and regulatory changes that had been brought into being before and after the Enron fiasco, and before WorldCom's cataclysmic restatement on June 25, 2002.

TABLE 2.8

SOME KEY GUIDELINES AND
REGULATORY CHANGES

ANNOUNCED	SOURCE OF CHANGE
1994	*The Dey Report,* "Where Were the Directors?" Toronto Stock Exchange To review corporate governance and make recommendations for best practice.
1999	*Five Years to the Dey,* Report on Corporate Governance, Toronto Stock Exchange and The Institute of Corporate Directors To survey and analyze governance procedures at TSE companies.

May 2000	*The Combined Code: Principles of Good Governance and Principles of Best Practice*
	    Based on the Hempel (1998), the Cadbury (1992) and Greenbury Reports (1995), used by
	    companies listed on the London Stock Exchange.

2000	*Guidance for Directors on the Combined Code* The Turnbull Report See Combined Code purpose.

Nov. 21, 2001	*The Saucier Report,* "Beyond Compliance: Building a Governance Culture"
	Joint Committee on Corporate Governance, CICA/TSE
	    To review the current state of corporate governance in Canada, compare Canadian and
	    international best practices, and make recommendations for changes that will ensure Canadian
	    corporate governance is among the best in the world.

Apr. 26, 2002	*Toronto Stock Exchange (TSX) Guidelines,* Amended Revisions effective Dec. 31, 2002, to adopt some Saucier Report recommendations.
Apr. 4, 2002	SEC Blue Ribbon Committee Discussions
2002 Various	Business Roundtable—various statements

June 6, 2002	*NYSE Corporate Governance Listing Requirements*
	Effective Aug. 2002, after SEC approval
	    A review at the request of Harvey Pitt, SEC Chairman, to enhance the accountability,
	    integrity, and transparency of companies listed on the NYSE.

June 28, 2002	SEC Order effective Aug. 14, 2002 CEO and CFO to certify 8-K, quarterly, and annual financial reports
July 9, 2002	President George Bush's Proposals Speech

Visit the text's Website for links to the organizations' Websites.

http://brooks.
swlearning.com

http://brooks.
swlearning.com

A synthesis of the 2002 proposals as of July 17, 2002, is available at Torys, LLP, "The Corporate Governance Crisis – Regulatory Initiatives by the SEC, NYSE and NASDAQ," No 2002-16T.

WorldCom: The Catalyst

WORLDCOM LIGHTS THE FIRE

WorldCom, Inc., the second largest U.S. telecommunications giant and almost 70 percent larger than Enron in assets, announced on June 25, 2002, that it had overstated its cash flow by $3.8 billion.[84] This came as a staggering blow to the credibility of capital markets. It occurred in the middle of the furor caused by:

- The Enron bankruptcy on December 2, 2001, and the related Congress and Senate hearings and Fifth Amendment testimony by Enron executives.
- The depression of the stock markets.
- The pleas by business leaders and President Bush for restoration of credibility and trust to corporate governance, reporting, and the financial markets.
- Responsive introduction of governance guidelines by stock exchanges and the Securities and Exchange Commission.
- Debate by the U.S. Congress and Senate of separate bills to improve governance and accountability.
- Arthur Andersen's conviction for obstruction of justice on June 15, 2002.

WORLDCOM'S ACCOUNTING MANIPULATIONS

WorldCom's accounting manipulations involved very basic, easy-to spot types of fraud.[85] Overstatements of cash flow and income were created because one of WorldCom's major expenses, line costs—"fees paid to third party telecommunication network providers for the right to access the third parties networks"[86]—were accounted for improperly. Essentially, line costs that should have been expensed, thus lowering reporting income, were offset by capital transfers or charged against capital accounts, thus placing their impact on the balance sheet rather than the income statement.

---

[84]Simon Romero and Alex Berenson, "WorldCom Says It Hid Expenses, Inflating Cash Flow $3.8 Billion," *The New York Times*, June 26, 2002.

[85]Bruce Myerson, "A WorldCom Primer," Associated Press, June 26, 2001.

[86]Complaint: SEC v. WorldCom, Inc., U.S. Securities and Exchange Commission, June 26, 2002, para 5, (see *http://brooks.swlearning.com*).

The aggregate overstatement of income quickly rose to more than $9 billion[87] by September 19, 2002, for the following reasons:

- $3.85 billion for improperly capitalized expenses, announced June 25, 2002.[88]
- $3.83 billion for more improperly capitalized expenses in 1999, 2000, 2001, and the first quarter of 2002, announced on August 8, 2002.[89]
- $2.0 billion for manipulations of profit through previously established reserves, dating back to 1999.

Key senior personnel involved in the manipulations at WorldCom included:

- Bernard J. Ebbers, CEO
- Scott D. Sullivan, CFO
- Buford Yates, Jr., Director of General Accounting
- David F. Myers, Controller
- Betty L. Vinson, Director of Management Reporting, from January 2002
- Troy M. Normand, Director of Legal Entity Accounting, from January 2002

According to the SEC's complaint against Vinson and Normand:

4. WorldCom fraudulently manipulated its financial results in a number of respects, including by improperly reducing its operating expenses in at least two ways. First, WorldCom improperly released certain reserves held against operating expenses. Second, WorldCom improperly recharacterized certain operating costs as capital assets. Neither practice was in conformity with generally accepted accounting principles ("GAAP"). Neither practice was disclosed to WorldCom's investors, despite the fact that both practices constituted changes from WorldCom's previous accounting practices. Both practices artificially and materially inflated the income WorldCom reported to the public in its financial statements from 1999 through the first quarter of 2002.

5. Many of the improper accounting entries related to WorldCom's expenses for accessing the networks of other telecommunications companies ("line costs"), which were among WorldCom's major operating expenses. From at least the third quarter of 2000 through the first quarter of 2002, in a scheme directed and approved by senior management, and participated in by VINSON, NORMAND and others, including Yates and Myers, WorldCom concealed the true magnitude of its line costs. By improperly reducing reserves held against line costs, and then—after effectively exhausting its reserves—by recharacterizing certain line costs as capital assets, WorldCom falsely portrayed itself as a profitable business when it was not, and concealed the large losses it suffered. WorldCom's fraudulent accounting practices with respect to line costs were designed to and did falsely and fraudulently inflate its income to correspond with estimates by Wall Street analysts and to support the price of WorldCom's common stock and other securities.

---

[87]David E. Royella, "WorldCom to Reveal More Bogus Accounting," Associated Press, September 19, 2002, and "WorldCom Faces Two New Charges, Misstatement Grows," *Financial Post*, November 6, 2002, FP4.
[88]WorldCom Inc., Form 8-K, Current Report Pursuant To Section 13 Or 15(D) Of The Securities Exchange Act Of 1934, August 14, 2002, para. 2, (see *http://brooks.swlearning.com*).
[89]Ibid., para. 3.

6. More specifically, in the third and fourth quarters of 2000, at the direction and with the knowledge of WorldCom's senior management, VINSON, NORMAND and others, by making and causing to be made entries in WorldCom's books which improperly decreased certain reserves to reduce WorldCom's line costs, caused WorldCom to overstate pretax earnings by $828 million and at least $407 million respectively. Then, after WorldCom had drawn down WorldCom's reserves so far that the reserves could not be drawn down further without taking what senior management believed was an unacceptable risk of discovery, VINSON, NORMAND and others, again at the direction and with the knowledge of senior management, made and caused to be made entries in WorldCom's books which improperly capitalized certain line costs for the next five quarters, from the first quarter 2001 through the first quarter 2002. This accounting gimmick resulted in an overstatement of WorldCom's pretax earnings by approximately $3.8 billion for those five quarters.[90]

The motivation and mechanism for these manipulations is evident from the SEC's description of what happened at the end of each quarter, after the draft quarterly statements were reviewed.

27. In or around October 2000, at the direction and with the knowledge of WorldCom senior management, VINSON, NORMAND and others, including Yates and Myers, caused the making of certain improper entries in the company's general ledger for the third quarter of 2000. Specifically, after reviewing the consolidated financial statements for the third quarter of 2000, World-Com senior management determined that WorldCom had failed to meet analysts' expectations. WorldCom's senior management then instructed Myers, and his subordinates, including Yates, VINSON and NORMAND, to make improper and false entries in WorldCom's general ledger reducing its line cost expense accounts, and reducing—in amounts corresponding to the improper and false line cost expense amounts—various reserve accounts. After receiving instructions through Yates, VINSON and NORMAND ensured that these entries were made. There was no documentation supporting these entries, and no proper business rationale for them, and they were not in conformity with GAAP. These entries had the effect of reducing third quarter 2000 line costs by approximately $828 million, thereby increasing World-Com's publicly reported pretax income by that amount for the third quarter of 2000.[91]

Manipulations followed the same pattern for the fourth quarter of 2000, but a change was required for the first quarter of 2001, for fear of discovery.

29. In or around April 2001, after reviewing the preliminary consolidated financial statements for the first quarter of 2001, WorldCom's senior management determined that WorldCom had again failed to meet analysts' expectations. Because WorldCom's senior management determined that the company could not continue to draw down its reserve accounts to offset line costs without taking what they believed to be unacceptable risks of discovery by the company's auditors, WorldCom changed its method of fraudulently inflating its income. WorldCom's senior management then instructed Myers, and his subordinates, including Yates, VINSON and NORMAND, to make entries in WorldCom's general ledger for the first quarter of 2001 which fraudulently reclassified line cost expenses to a variety of capital asset accounts without any

---

[90]Complaint: SEC v. Betty L. Vinson, and Troy M. Normand, U.S. Securities and Exchange Commission, modified October 31, 2002, para 4, 5, 6 (see *http://brooks.swlearning.com*).
[91]Ibid.

supporting documentation or proper business rationale and in a manner that did not conform with GAAP.

30. Specifically, in or around April 2001, at the direction and with the knowledge of WorldCom's senior management, defendants VINSON, NORMAND and others, including Yates and Myers, fraudulently reduced first quarter 2001 line cost expenses by approximately $771 million and correspondingly increased capital asset accounts, thereby fraudulently increasing publicly reported pretax income for the first quarter of 2001 by the same amount. In particular, in or about April 2001, NORMAND telephoned WorldCom's Director of Property Accounting (the "DPA") and instructed him to adjust the schedules he maintained for certain Property, Plant & Equipment capital expenditure accounts (the "PP&E Roll-Forward") by increasing certain capital accounts for "prepaid capacity." NORMAND advised the DPA that these entries had been ordered by WorldCom's senior management. Correspondingly, a subordinate of NORMAND made journal entries in WorldCom's general ledger, transferring approximately $771 million from certain line cost expense accounts to certain PP&E capital expenditure accounts.[92]

In future periods, the increase of certain accounts for "prepaid capacity" remained the manipulation of choice.

WORLDCOM'S OTHER REVELATIONS

WorldCom, which applied for bankruptcy protection on July 21, 2002, had also announced that it might write off $50.6 billion in goodwill or other intangible assets when restating for the accounting errors previously noted. Apparently other WorldCom decisions had been faulty.

The revelations were not yet complete. Investigation revealed that Bernard Ebbers, the CEO, had been loaned $408.2 million. He was supposed to use the loans to buy WorldCom stock or for margin calls as the stock price fell. Instead he used it partly for the purchase of the largest cattle ranch in Canada, construction of a new home, personal expenses of a family member, and loans to family and friends.[93]

WHY DID THEY DO IT?

Ebbers was not an accountant. However, he was ably assisted in these manipulations by Scott Sullivan, his chief financial officer, and David Myers, his controller. Both Sullivan and Myers had worked for Arthur Andersen before joining WorldCom. According to U.S. Attorney General John Ashcroft:

> the alleged Sullivan-Myers scheme was designed to conceal five straight quarterly net losses and create the illusion that the company was profitable.[94]

In view of Ebbers' $408.2 million in loans, which were largely to buy or pay margin calls on WorldCom stock and which were secured by WorldCom stock, he would be loathe to see further deterioration of the WorldCom stock price. In short, he could not afford the price decline that would follow from lower WorldCom earnings.

---

[92]Ibid.

[93]David E. Royella, "WorldCom Faces Two New Charges, Misstatement Grows," *Financial Post*, November 6, 2002, FP4.

[94]"WorldCom Accounting Fraud Rises to $7 billion," *The Baltimore Sun*, August 9, 2002.

In addition, according to the WorldCom's 2002 Annual Meeting Proxy Statement, at December 31, 2001, Ebbers had been allocated exercisable stock options on 8,616.365 shares and Sullivan on 2,811,927.[95] In order to capitalize on the options, Ebbers and Sullivan (and other senior employees) needed the stock price to rise. A rising or at least stable stock price was also essential if WorldCom stock was to be used to acquire more companies.

Finally, if the reported results became losses rather than profits, the tenure of senior management would have been shortened significantly. In that event, the personal loans outstanding would be called and the stock option gravy train would stop. In 2000, Ebbers and Sullivan had each received retention bonuses of $10 million so they would stay for two years after September 2000. In 1999, Ebbers received a performance bonus allocation of $11,539,387, but he accepted only $7,500,000 of the award.[96]

AN EXPERT'S INSIGHTS

Former Attorney-General Richard Thornburgh was appointed by the U.S. Justice Department to investigate the collapse and bankruptcy of WorldCom. In his Report to the U.S. Bankruptcy Court in Manhattan on November 5, 2002, he said:

> One person, Bernard Ebbers, appears to have dominated the company's growth, as well as the agenda, discussions and decisions of the board of directors…

> A picture is clearly emerging of a company that had a number of troubling and serious issues…[relating to] culture, internal controls, management, integrity, disclosure and financial statements.

> While Mr. Ebbers received more than US $77 million in cash and benefits from the company, shareholders lost in excess of US $140 billion in value.[97]

THE CONTINUING SAGA

The WorldCom saga continues as the top executives are charged with fraud and the company tries to stabilize its finances. So far, the SEC has filed complaints (which can be found on its website) against the company, and also separately against Myers, Yates, Vinson, and Normand. All have consented to the filing of judgment against them. Further discussions are apparently underway with other executives.

In response to each of the complaints filed, the Court has granted the injunctive relief the SEC sought. The individuals were enjoined from further such fraudulent actions, and subsequently banned by the SEC from practicing before it. Myers and Yates were banned by the Court from acting as officers or directors in the future. Monetary relief will be decided in the future by the Court upon a motion by the SEC, or at the instance of the Court.

---

[95]WorldCom's 2002 Annual Meeting Proxy Statement, SEC Edgar File, April 22, 2002 (see *http://brooks.swlearning.com*).

[96]Ibid.

[97]Don Stancavish, "WorldCom Dominated by Ebbers," Bloomberg News, in *Financial Post*, November 5, 2002, FP13.

WorldCom, as a company, consented to a judgment:

> imposing the full injunctive relief sought by the Commission; ordering an extensive review of the company's corporate governance systems, policies, plans, and practices; ordering a review of WorldCom's internal accounting control structure and policies; ordering that WorldCom provide reasonable training and education to certain officers and employees to minimize the possibility of future violations of the federal securities laws; and providing that civil money penalties, if any, will be decided by the Court at a later date.[98]

The Catalyzed Outcome—The Sarbanes-Oxley Act of 2002

The announcement by WorldCom of their massive accounting earnings manipulation fraud struck the capital markets, media, and politicians like a lightening bolt. Senator Paul Sarbanes, a Democrat, was trying to push forward a bill of governance and accounting reforms through the Senate. Congressman Michael Oxley, a Republican, was trying to do the same through the House of Representatives. Opposition was stiff to both bills, but immediately after the WorldCom announcement, the two men joined forces and the Sarbanes-Oxley Act of 2002 was passed by both the House and the Senate and became law on July 30, 2002. It was an amazing galvanization and an unexpected but hoped for outcome.

SARBANES-OXLEY ACT (SOX): FUTURE GOVERNANCE FOR CORPORATIONS AND THE ACCOUNTING PROFESSION

SOX has the potential to be the most far-reaching U.S. security law enacted since the Securities Act of 1933 and the Securities Exchange Act of 1934, which spawned the Securities and Exchange Commission in 1934 to administer the Acts. Many of the Act's provisions require SEC action for implementation, and future studies to assess the best path for future guidance.

SOX will create an international regulatory framework for corporations seeking access to the U.S. capital markets and their auditors. SOX sets new standards for governance that will ultimately impact on all SEC registrant companies, including those large foreign companies that are listed on the U.S. exchanges. One hundred and seventy-seven of Canada's largest companies, and many other large international enterprises, will have to comply with any new rules when ultimately put in place by the SEC, NYSE, and NASDAQ. Also, SOX establishes a new framework for the U.S. accounting profession that replaces self-regulation by the profession with a Public Company Accounting Oversight Board (PCAOB). The PCAOB will oversee all accounting firms— U.S. and foreign—that audit SEC registrants.

Prior financial disasters, including the Enron, Arthur Andersen, and WorldCom governance debacles, raised the awareness in the United States, Canada, Australia, and the United Kingdom that the governance frameworks had to be improved. Specifically, in order to deal with the governance credibility crisis and

---

[98]SEC Litigation Release No. 17883/December 6, 2002 (see *http://brooks.swlearning.com*).

restore confidence in the current corporate capital markets system, action was needed to meet public expectations in regard to the following matters:

- Clarification of the roles, responsibilities, and accountabilities of the board of directors, its subcommittees, of the directors themselves, and of the auditors.

- Reduction of the conflicts of interest influencing the directors, executives, and auditors so that they would exercise loyalty, independent judgment, and objectivity in the best interest of the shareholders or the company; or in the case of the auditor, in the public interest.

- Ensure that the directors were sufficiently informed on corporate plans and activities, the adequacy of company policies and internal controls to ensure compliance, and actual compliance including whistle-blowers' concerns.

- Ensure that directors possess adequate financial competence and other expertise where required.

- Ensure that financial reports were accurate, complete, understandable and transparent.

- Ensure that accounting standards are adequate to protect investor's interests.

- Ensure that the regulation and oversight of auditors of public companies, as well as their appointment and operating parameters, are adequate and appropriate to serve the public interest.

The developments proposed in SOX to remedy these problem areas are discussed next within the context of the new governance frameworks for corporations and for the auditing profession, as well as other matters. A .pdf version of SOX is available on the text's Website together with a summary of certain SOX provisions relevant to oversight of the accounting profession.

http://brooks. swlearning.com

NEW SOX CORPORATE GOVERNANCE FRAMEWORK

The new SOX framework takes the perspective that honest and full accountability to shareholders, and therefore to the public, is of paramount importance. Such accountability is identified as a prime responsibility of corporate directors to ensure and senior corporate officers to deliver, and that they are free from bias in doing so. In addition, since the accuracy and integrity of such an accountability regime depends upon the independent scrutiny of auditors, directors are charged with ensuring that, through the audit subcommittee of the board, the auditors are free from conflicts of interest, have access to and report to the board, and so on. These matters are provided for in SOX through the introduction of specific provisions related to:

- Clarification of the responsibility of directors and officers for public accountability and its integrity.

- Enhanced conflict of interest provisions designed to ensure sufficient directors are independent from management, and

- Clarification of the role, responsibility and membership of audit sub-committees of the board, so that:
  - The audit subcommittee:
    - Is "directly responsible for the appointment, compensation, and oversight of any public accounting firm employed by that issuer."[99] including the resolution of any disputes with management.
    - Must establish procedures to receive and address complaints regarding accounting, auditing and internal controls, including establishing procedures to allow employees to submit anonymous complaints.[100]
    - Must approve any non-audit services to be provided by the auditors.
  - Only independent[101] directors serve on the audit subcommittee.
  - All members must be financially competent.
  - One must be, and be identified to be, a financial expert.[102]
  - Auditors are report to the audit subcommittee, and are to be met without management present, and vice versa.
  - The subcommittee must be given adequate budget and time to complete its work, including the right to hire and consult outside experts.
- Additional disclosures:
  - To allow scrutiny of transactions between principal stockholders and management.
  - To report upon the corporation's internal controls including management's responsibility for establishing, maintaining, and assessing their effectiveness.
- Accelerated reporting of corporate disclosures and stock trades.
- Management assessment and signed certification to the Board and SEC of the integrity of:
  - Quarterly and annual financial reports, and SEC forms.
  - The systems of internal control underlying and ensuring that integrity.
- Requirement for a code of ethics and compliance thereto for senior financial officers.
- The illegality of exercising any undue influence on the conduct of audits.
- Proper action by insiders for stock trading and dealing with stock analysts.
- Sanctions for wrongdoing including forfeiture of bonuses and profits, officer and director bans from service, and penalties.

---

[99]SOX, Section 301 (2), p. 33.

[100]SOX, Section 301 (4), p. 34.

[101]SOX, Section 310 (3), p. 33 states that independence requires that "a member of an audit committee may not, other than in his capacity as a member of the audit committee, the board of directors, or any other board committee—(i) accept any consulting, advisory, or other compensatory fee from the issuer; or (ii) be an affiliated person of the issuer or any subsidiary thereof."

[102]A "financial expert" is defined in SOX, SEC 407 (b), p. 47, as a person who has "(1) an understanding of GAAP and financial statements, (2) experience in (A) the preparation or auditing of financial statements of generally comparable issuers, and (B) the application of such principles in connection with the accounting for estimates, accruals and reserves; and (3) experience with internal accounting controls; and (4) an understanding of audit committee functions."

NEW SOX FRAMEWORK FOR THE U.S. ACCOUNTING PROFESSION

Auditors, as previously noted, will be more responsive to the audit subcommittee of the board who will arrange their appointment and reappointment, and less to senior management who have traditionally played a, if not the, significant role. In this regard they will be working with financially competent, independent directors whose interests should be more directed than they may have been toward clear, comprehensive public reports.

Auditors must report directly to audit committees on the following matters:

- All critical accounting policies and practices to be used.

- All alternative treatments of financial information under GAAP that have been discussed with management.

- The ramifications of the use of the alternative treatments and disclosures and the treatment preferred by the auditor.

- All other material written communications between the auditor and management, including any management letter and schedule of unadjusted differences.

- Their review of and attestation on management's assessment of the company's internal controls, including:

  - "whether the internal control structure and procedures include maintenance of records that accurately and fairly reflect the company's transactions and disposition of assets;

  - whether there is reasonable assurance that the transactions are recorded as necessary to permit the preparation of financial statements in accordance with GAAP and made in accordance with proper authorization by management and directors; and

  - a description of material weaknesses in internal controls found on the basis of testing done and material non-compliance."[103]

http://brooks.
swlearning.com

In addition, SOX establishes a Public Company Accounting Oversight Board (PCAOB) that will:

- Consist of five members (only two of which can be CPAs) with five-year staggered terms.

- Inspect, discipline, and write rules governing accounting firms that audit public companies.

- Establish auditing and attestation standards, including quality control and independence standards for the audit of public companies.

- Maintain a register of foreign firms that audit SEC registrants, and who will be subject to PCAOB regulations and discipline.

In order to stop auditors from auditing results of their own non-audit services, auditors will be prohibited from offering the non-audit services listed below, and may offer other non-audit services such as tax services to SEC registrants only if permitted by the client's audit subcommittee:

- "bookkeeping and other services related to the accounting records or financial statements of the client;

- financial information system design and implementation;

---

[103]"The Sarbanes-Oxley Act," *Financial Reporting Release*, PricewaterhouseCoopers, August 2002, 3.

- appraisal or valuation services;
- fairness opinions, or contribution-in-kind reports;
- actuarial services;
- internal audit outsourcing services;
- management functions or human resources;
- broker or dealer, investment adviser, or investment banking services;
- legal services and expert services unrelated to the audit; and any other service the PCAOB determines by regulation is not permissible."[104]

Finally, an audit partner may not serve as the engagement partner or the concurring partner for over five concurrent years.

NEW SOX FRAMEWORKS FOR OTHER MATTERS

SOX has provisions covering/requiring the need for a code of conduct for attorneys serving registrants, the treatment of analyst conflicts of interest, and penalties for fraud and white collar crime. In addition, SOX requires the following studies to chart the best course ahead:

- U.S. General Accounting Office (GAO)—problems associated with the consolidation of major accounting firms.
- Comptroller General—mandatory rotation of audit firms.
- SEC—adoption of "principles-based" accounting system, role and function of credit rating agencies, actions of violators and violations, enforcement actions, possible complicit earnings manipulation activities of investment banks and financial advisers.

Finally, SOX states that it is a crime to knowingly destroy, alter, or falsify records needed in federal investigations and bankruptcy proceedings, with such crime to be punishable by a fine and/or imprisonment of up to 20 years.[105]

IMPLEMENTATION BY THE SEC

The SEC has been charged with introducing new regulations or changes in its regulations to implement the proposed SOX frameworks within defined time frames. In some cases, studies must be done and analyzed to find the best course of action.

It should be noted, however, that while the proposed SOX frameworks push governance and accountability reform a long way, the SEC may push the reforms even further. One such case is the proposed SEC rule for lawyers that discover a violation. As the proposal stands, lawyers would have to report any material violation of securities laws, fiduciary duty, or similar material violation to their client's chief legal counsel or to the CEO. If there is no appropriate response the attorney must report to the audit committee, the board, or a committee of outside directors. If this "up-the-ladder" reporting does not generate an appropriate response, and the violation would likely result in substantial injury to the financial interest or property of the issuer or of investors, the outside attorney

---

[104]Ibid., 4.
[105]SOX, Section 802 (a), p. 57.

would have to make a "noisy exit." A noisy exit involves withdrawal from representation of the issuer, notification to the SEC of the withdrawal, and repudiation of any submission to the SEC that the lawyer believes is tainted.

Law firms are arguing that the proposed rule goes further than SOX intended and proposes to turn them into whistle-blowers. They are arguing that the noisy withdrawal provision is inconsistent with fundamental rights such as attorney-client privilege and confidentiality. Time will tell whether outside lawyers have responsibilities worthy of action to those outside the SEC client.[106]

Impact on Governance, Accountability and Reporting, and Management Practice

The new SOX governance framework will focus the attention of directors and management on issues that are of critical importance to the proper governance and reporting process. In particular, the following developments will bring positive and long-overdue changes:

- New and specific focus on improved accountability and reporting to public shareholders, and related internal control and whistle-blower systems, and certification by CEO and CFO.
- Strengthening of the role of the audit committee, the full independence of serving directors, information flow and the ability of auditors to report on and engage the committee in meaningful discussion.
- Clarification of roles, responsibilities, and competencies of directors and board subcommittees.
- Definition and emphasis on avoiding conflict of interest situations, as well as codes of conduct for the CFO and others.
- Increased penalties for wrongdoing.

However, the provision of financial experts to serve as directors, and as identified directors on audit committees, will be a challenge. Time requirements will escalate forcing the reduction of the number of boards on which one can sit, and time requirements as well as increased legal risk will necessitate much higher board fees and special fees for sitting on audit committees. Training in director competencies will become the norm.

It is unlikely that smaller companies and foreign companies will want to voluntarily fully adopt the new governance regime due to its time-consuming nature and cost. This may create a two-tier governance system that may not favor some investors. Some corporations will resign their SEC registration and remove themselves from the U.S. capital markets, as Porsche already has done.

In the end, if the purposed SOX governance system had been in place, would the Enron, WorldCom, and other financial disasters have been avoided? Certainly the probability of avoidance would have been much higher.

Impact on the Accounting Profession and Auditing Practice

The U.S. accounting profession has lost its relatively unfettered ability to offer non-audit service to clients based solely on the judgment and self-regulation

---

[106]"SEC Aims to Make Lawyers Whistle-blowers," Torys LLP, December 19, 2002 (see *http://brooks.swlearning.com*).

of accountants. Services offered will be circumcised and less efficient or more costly to provide to non-audit clients. Audit service margins will probably increase from their current low state, but the overall profitability of professional firms will not return to that of prior unfettered times.

In U.S. and foreign jurisdictions, it is probable that some firms will forego auditing SEC or stock market registrants because they will want to avoid dealing with the PCAOB, and wish to maintain the nature and margins of their current integrated practices. This may mean that a two-tier system of auditors develops throughout the world—one for the large corporations and another for the small. A two-tier system for GAAP for big or small corporations may also become more attractive.

While the strengthening of independence standards, and of the relationship of the auditor to the audit subcommittee, will help the auditor serve the public interest, a full appreciation of what SOX will bring must wait until the SEC acts, and various studies are completed. A suggestion such as the rotation of audit firms is rather unlikely given the reduction to the Big 4, of which the auditor is one, and the requirement that non-conflicted, non-audit consulting be probably done by another one.

Impact on Business Ethics Trends

There is no doubt that the Enron, Arthur Andersen, and WorldCom cases have produced much greater awareness of ethical issues and trends that were underway, including conflicts of interest and the control of self-interest, fiduciary duty of directors to shareholders/company and of auditors to the public interest, and the general good business sense of developing an ethical culture. That ethical culture should be based upon honesty, fairness, compassion, integrity, predictability, and responsibility, and focused on the development of trust and the respect for stakeholder interests. In fact, U.S. and foreign corporations that have good governance and accountability do embrace these, and have indicated that they have already been doing, in substance, what SOX recommends.

The infamous debacles cited have also produced a new awareness that ethics and reputation are linked much more sensitively than were earlier thought to be the case. Moreover, as in most product liability cases, the fine for Arthur Andersen of $500,000 (or the largest earlier fine of $7 million) proved insignificant compared to the loss of future revenue. Most importantly, the concept of franchise risk has taken on an entirely new reality since Arthur Andersen, a firm of vaunted reputation and 85,000 employees, has essentially disappeared in less than one year, and two of the world's most highly regarded corporations are in bankruptcy proceedings. Comprehensive risk management must include ethics risks and higher estimates for franchise risk.

The modern strategic, risk-oriented audit approaches now practiced by three of the four big international firms will have to incorporate ethics risks and higher estimates for franchise risk as well. Corporate internal control systems should include ethics risk monitoring and new systems should be spawned to do so.

Professional accountants had tended to subjugate fiduciary values to revenue generation considerations until AA's debacle. Will professional accounting bodies and firms consolidate the learning from AA, or will they continue to put their own business concerns before quality? Will the switch from self-regulation in the United States be beneficial if applied around the world, or will a two-or multi-tier regime emerge that will leave the public interest at risk?

Finally, the need for business and professional ethics education, which illustrates through cases like Enron, Arthur Andersen, and WorldCom how important ethics are to corporate and professional accounting firm culture, and performance, has never been more evident.

QUESTIONS FOR DISCUSSION

1. What were the common aspects that were necessary for the Enron and WorldCom debacles to occur?

2. What actions by directors, executives, and professional accountants could have prevented the Enron and WorldCom debacles?

3. Was the enactment of the Sarbanes-Oxley Act (SOX) necessary? Why or why not?

4. What are the three most important improvements in the governance structure that could result from SOX?

5. What were the common elements in Arthur Andersen's approach that appeared to allow the disasters at Enron and WorldCom.

6. What is wrong with Enron's banks financing transactions they knew were without economic substance?

7. How should boards of directors change incentive remuneration schemes for executives to lessen the risk of motivating executives to risk manipulations to enrich themselves?

8. What lessons should be learned from reviewing the events described in this chapter?

CASES

The cases included in the text of the chapter, Enron, Arthur Andersen, and WorldCom, and those that follow, Waste Management and Sunbeam, have become icons in the history of governance and accountability. Taken together, they reflect the greed of fraud-intent management, the failure of conflicted governance systems and the integrity of the corporate reporting systems, and the misunderstanding of the fiduciary duties of directors and professional accountants. The seeds of Arthur Andersen's downfall are evident throughout.

Questions are presented for the first three cases, and the full case and questions for the last two.

- *The Enron Debacle*—the massive fraud that revealed the flaws in corporate and professional accounting governance.

- *Arthur Andersen's Troubles*—the story of the once revered, but systemically flawed auditor of all these companies that forgot to whom fiduciary duty was owed.

- *WorldCom: The Catalyst*—the timely and massive fraud that triggered meaningful reform of corporate and professional accounting governance.

- *Waste Management, Inc.*—one of Arthur Andersen's early audit failures where the accounting manipulations of management and a dominated corporate governance system led to bankruptcy.

- *Sunbeam Corporation and Chainsaw Al*—Arthur Andersen failed to stop Chainsaw Al Dunlap, who hoodwinked his board and intimidated his accounting staff into manipulating financial reports.

PRINCIPAL REFERENCES, all to be found on *http://brooks.swlearning.com.*

Sarbanes-Oxley Act of 2002.

SEC Reports, Press Releases, and Complaints, regarding Enron, Arthur Andersen, and WorldCom.

Testimony of Robert Roach, Appendices, U.S. Senate Permanent Subcommittee on Investigations.

The Powers Report, 2001.

The Role of the Board of Directors in the Collapse of Enron, The U.S. Senate's Permanent Subcommittee on Investigations Report, 2002.

Ethics case

The Enron Debacle

The following questions are presented for discussion of the significant issues raised in the case, which appears on pages 56–86 of the chapter.

1. Which segment of its operations got Enron into difficulties?

2. How were profits made in that segment of operations (i.e., what was the business model)?

3. Did Enron's directors understand how profits were being made in this segment? Why or why not?

4. Enron's directors realized that Enron's conflict of interests policy would be violated by Fastow's proposed SPE management and operating arrangements because they proposed alternative oversight measures. What was wrong with their alternatives?

5. Ken Lay was the chair of the board and the CEO for much of the time. How did this probably contribute to the lack of proper governance?

6. What aspects of the Enron governance system failed to work properly, and why?

7. Why didn't more whistle-blowers come forward, and why didn't some make a significant difference? How could whistle-blowers have been encouraged?

8. What should the internal auditors have done that might have assisted the directors?

9. Identify conflicts of interest in the following activities:
   - SPE activities
   - Arthur Andersen's activities
   - executive activities

10. How much time should a director of Enron have been spending on Enron matters each month? How many large company boards should a director serve on?

11. How would you characterize Enron's corporate culture? How did it contribute to the disaster?

Arthur Andersen's Troubles

The following questions are presented for discussion of the significant issues raised in the case, which appears on pages 86–95 of the chapter.

1. What did Arthur Andersen contribute to the Enron disaster?

2. What Arthur Andersen decisions were faulty?

3. What was the prime motivation behind the decisions of Arthur Andersen's audit partners on the Enron, WorldCom, Waste Management, and Sunbeam audits—the public interest or …? Cite examples that reveal this motivation.

4. Why should an auditor make decisions in the public interest rather than in the interest of management or current shareholders?

5. Why didn't the Arthur Andersen partners responsible for quality control stop the flawed decisions of the audit partners?

6. Should all of Arthur Andersen have suffered for the actions or inactions of less than 100 people? Which of Arthur Andersen's personnel should have been prosecuted?

7. Under what circumstances should audit firms shred or destroy audit working papers?

8. Answer the "Lingering Questions" on page 94.

WorldCom: The Catalyst

The following questions are presented for discussion of the significant issues raised in the case, which appears on pages 97–102 of the chapter.

1. Describe the mechanisms that WorldCom's management used to transfer profit from other time periods to inflate the current period.

2. Why did Arthur Andersen go along with each of these mechanisms?

3. How should WorldCom's board of directors have prevented the manipulations that management used?

4. Bernard Ebbers was not an accountant, so he needed the cooperation of accountants to make his manipulations work. Why did WorldCom's accountants go along?

5. Why would a board of directors approve giving its chair and CEO loans of over $408 million?

6. How can a board ensure that whistle-blowers will come forward to tell them about questionable activities?

Sunbeam Corporation and Chainsaw Al

In July 1996, Albert J. Dunlap was hired as CEO and Chairman by Sunbeam's board of directors to revive the company from a period of lagging sales and profits, and make it an attractive acquisition target. "Chainsaw Al," as he was known for his staff- and cost-cutting style as a turn-around expert, had a reputation for results that immediately propelled the price of Sunbeam stock upward by 60 percent to $18.63.[1] By 1997, he planned to eliminate half of Sunbeam's 6,000 employees and 87 percent of its products.[2] "According to Sunbeam managers, it … resulted in near-total chaos."[3] However, 1997 reported sales rose by $184 million or 18.7 percent.[4]

In March 1998, Sunbeam paid $2.5 billion to buy the companies manufacturing Coleman stoves, Mr. Coffee coffee makers, and First Alert smoke detectors. Dunlap was rewarded with a $2 million annual salary and stock options

worth millions.[5] Sunbeam's stock peaked at $52.

Unfortunately, Chainsaw had used manipulative accounting techniques to inflate Sunbeam's financial results. When properly restated, for example, Sunbeam's reported net income for 1997 was reduced from $109.4 million to $38.3 million.[6]

In early 1998, the lack of real success in the selling of Sunbeam's products could no longer be easily masked and the manipulations had to offset the lowered sales and be larger than earlier manipulations in order to create an attractive percentage gain in sales and profits. Moreover, since some of the manipulations used in 1996 and 1997 had recorded future sales too early, there were even fewer sales to count in 1998, and using the same manipulative techniques at ever larger levels raised issues of credibility.

Interestingly, at least two people were not fooled: Deidra DenDanto, a 26-year-old, recently hired member of Sunbeam's internal audit staff, and Andrew Shore, a stock analyst at Paine Weber, Inc.[7] Deidra challenged the manipulative practices from the start, but got little support from her superiors. She finally resigned on April 3 after sending a letter to the board of directors.[8] Shore became wary of the high inventory and accounts receivable levels Dunlap was creating as early as the second quarter of 1997.

On April 3, 1998, Sunbeam had to announce that revenue and orders would be 5 percent lower than expected. Chainsaw Al did not put forward a credible front during the conference call. In addition, Andrew Shore had just found that two senior officers had

1. "Chainsaw Al: He Anointed Himself America's Best CEO. But Al Dunlap Drove Sunbeam into the Ground," *BusinessWeek*, October 18, 1999.

2. Ibid.

3. Ibid.

4. Sunbeam Corporation's 1997 Annual Report SEC 10-K Filing, March 2, 1998 (see *http://brooks.swlearning.com*).

5. Sunbeam 1999 Annual Meeting Proxy Statement, SEC Edgar Filing, May 14, 1999 (see *http://brooks.swlearning.com*).

6. "Andersen's Other Headache: Sunbeam," *BusinessWeek*, January 29, 2002.

7. "Chainsaw Al."

8. Ibid.

FIGURE I

STOCK PRICE MOVEMENT DURING THE STEWARDSHIP OF MR. DUNLAP

Reprinted with permission of Shyam V. Sunder, from Working Paper Series ACC-99-07 Sunbeam, Inc, Stearns School of Business, NYU.

—Continued

Continued

left—Rich Goudis, chief of investor relations, resigned on April 3,[9] and Donald Uzzi, executive vice president for worldwide consumer products, had been fired earlier[10]—and Shore had downgraded his rating of the company's shares. The company's share price fell by almost 25 percent to $34.375.[11]

The accounting manipulations used were unraveling, and stories began to appear in the press. The most damaging appeared in *Barron's*, and an impromptu board meeting was held on June 9 during which Dunlap, Russell A. Kersh, the CFO; and Robert J. Gluck, the controller, refuted the charges.[12] Kersh did, however, reveal that it would be tough to make 1998 projections. At the end of the meeting, Dunlap demanded the board's support or he (and Kersh) would leave the company. The directors were stunned and incredulous. They did some checking with other executives including David C. Fannin, Sunbeam's executive vice president and chief counsel. They met again with Fannin on June 13 and

Chainsaw Al was fired by phone later that day along with the CFO.[13] He asked for, but was given no explanation. Sunbeam then announced that its prior financial statements could not be relied upon. In the same month, the Securities and Exchange Commission began their investigation into Sunbeam's accounting practices.

A new management team was hired, but the fundamental weaknesses of Sunbeam products in their markets were tough to remedy. In November 1998, Sunbeam issued restated financial statements for the fourth quarter of 1996, all quarters of 1997, and the first quarter of 1998. As a result, Sunbeam's stock price declined to approximately $7 from $52 in March, eight months earlier.

On February 5, 2001, Sunbeam filed for protection while reorganizing under Chapter 11 of the U.S. Bankruptcy Code.[14]

On May 15, 2001, the SEC charged Dunlap, former CFO Russell A. Kersh, controller Robert J. Gluck, and vice presidents Donald R. Uzzi and

Lee B. Griffin, as well as Arthur Andersen LLP partner Phillip Harlow, with fraud. The SEC also announced the settlement of similar charges against Sunbeam's former counsel, David Fannin.[15]

SEC Findings

The SEC based its fraud charges on the following summary of its findings:

From the last quarter of 1996 until June 1998, Sunbeam Corporation's senior management created the illusion of a successful restructuring of Sunbeam in order to inflate its stock price and thus improve its value as an acquisition target. To this end, management employed numerous improper earnings management techniques to falsify the Company's results and conceal its deteriorating financial condition. Specifically, senior management created $35 million in improper restructuring reserves and other "cookie jar" reserves as part of a year-end 1996 restructuring, which were reversed into income the following year. Also in 1997, Sunbeam's

—Continued

---

9. Ibid.
10. "How Al Dunlap Self-Destructed," *BusinessWeek*, July 6, 1998.
11. Ibid.
12. Ibid.
13. Ibid.

14. "Order Instituting Public Administrative Proceedings, Pursuant to Section 8A of the Securities Act of 1933 and Section 21A of the Securities Exchange Act of 1934, Making Findings, and Imposing a Cease-And-Desist Order", Securities Act of 1933 Release No. 7976/May 15, 2001, Securities Exchange Act of 1934 Release No. 44305/May 15, 2001, Accounting and Auditing Enforcement Release

No. 1393/May 15, 2001, Administrative Proceeding File No. 3-10481, Securities and Exchange Commission, May 15, 2001, (SEC Litigation Release) (see *http://brooks.swlearning.com*).

15. "SEC Sues Former CEO, CFO, Other Top Officers of Sunbeam Corporation in Massive Fraud," SEC News Headline Report 2001-49, May 15, 2001 (see *http://brooks.swlearning.com*).

Continued

management engaged in guaranteed sales, improper "bill and hold" sales, and other fraudulent practices. At year-end 1997, at least $62 million of Sunbeam's reported income of $189 million came from accounting fraud. The undisclosed or inadequately disclosed acceleration of sales through "channel-stuffing" also materially distorted the Company's reported results of operations and contributed to the inaccurate picture of a successful turnaround.

When these measures did not lead to a sale of the Company by year-end 1997, senior management took increasingly desperate measures to conceal Sunbeam's mounting financial problems, meanwhile attempting to finance the acquisition of three other companies in part through the public sale of debt securities. Management engaged in additional accelerated sales and sales for which revenue was improperly recognized, deleted certain corporate records to conceal pending returns of merchandise, and misrepresented the Company's performance and future prospects in press releases and in meetings with analysts and lenders.

In June 1998, negative statements in the press about the Company's sales practices prompted Sunbeam's Board of Directors to begin an internal investigation. This resulted in the termination of certain members of senior management, including

Sunbeam's chief executive officer and chief financial officer, and, eventually, in an extensive restatement of the Company's financial statements from the fourth quarter of 1996 through the first quarter of 1998. As a result, Sunbeam's restated 1997 income was approximately one-half of the amount previously reported.[16]

The details[17] of the manipulative techniques that were uncovered by the SEC are of particular interest, as follows:

- Overstatement of 1996 restructuring charges, thus creating inflated or "cookie jar" reserves to be reversed later to bolster future profits. This overstatement of restructuring charges by a newly installed management team is known as the "big bath" approach because of the attribution of large losses to ousted management, leaving it clean for the new group. At least $35 million of the total restructuring charge of $337.6 million was improperly created, including:

  - $18.7 million of overstated restructuring costs not in conformity with generally accepted accounting principles (GAAP).
  - $6 million overstatement of a $12 million reserve against a future environmental litigation/remediation (this litigation was settled late in 1997 for $3 million).

---

16. SEC Litigation Release, op. cit.
17. Ibid.

- $2.1 million overstatement of inventory loss by erroneously considering some good inventory as bad, and then selling it at inflated margins in 1997.

- $2.3 million overstatement of 1996 advertising expenses for service to be rendered in 1997.

- Overstatement of part of the $21.8 million reserve for cooperative advertising for local retailers.

These "cookie jar" reserves were drawn down throughout 1997, having an effect on reported figures. See table on the next page.

- Nondisclosure of unusual or "infrequent" sales:

  - $19.6 million of deeply discounted products (a one-time sale) were sold in the first quarter of 1997 without disclosure, thus conveying to investors a false picture of sustainable sales.

- Recording of accelerated and false sales, through:

  - Contingent sales

    - In March 1997, Sunbeam booked as a sale $1.5 million revenue from an arrangement where a wholesaler held barbeque grills over the quarter end but could return all unsold grills for credit after the quarter end with Sunbeam paying all costs of shipment and storage. No risks of ownership were assumed by the wholesaler.

—Continued

Continued

- "Early-buy incentives," including offering excessive discounts and other incentives to induce customers to place orders before they would otherwise have done so. This practice was not disclosed so investors were unaware of lowered margins and future sales would be jeopardized.

- "Bill and hold" sales began to be used in the second quarter of 1997. If customers would order goods before they needed them, Sunbeam offered to hold the goods in Sunbeam's warehouse until they requested later delivery. Sunbeam would pay all storage, shipment, and insurance expense. Unsold goods could be returned for full credit. The SEC considered these transactions "little more than projected orders disguised as sales."

- The preceding three techniques would be considered "channel-stuffing"—the overloading of distribution channels by inducing or forcing the channel members (i.e., wholesalers, distributors, retailers, etc.) to acquire goods before they would otherwise order them. This practice causes the goods ordered prematurely to clog up the channel and delay further orders until the backlog is sold. For example, according to an internal Sunbeam

memo, by May 1998, "Wal-Mart Stores, ... which prefers four weeks inventory, was loaded with 23.6 weeks of Sunbeam appliances."[18] Obviously there will be a delay before a company can attain normal sales levels—unless the channel is stuffed to a greater degree.

- Recording of rebates from suppliers for purchases in later periods as income in the period the rebate was received or negotiated. $2.75 million was falsely recorded in the second quarter of 1997 as early sales instead of reductions in the cost of goods sold in later periods. An additional $1.9 million was recorded in the third quarter.

- Purported sale of spare parts inventory to a company that had serviced Sunbeam

products for a fixed fee per unit. $11 million in revenue and $5 million in income was recorded. However, Arthur Andersen, Sunbeam's auditor, found that Sunbeam had guaranteed a five percent profit margin to the "customer" on resale of the inventory, and a fee for service of an indeterminate value, and indicated that Sunbeam's revenue recognition was improper. Sunbeam reserved $3 million against the value of the transaction, but refused to reverse it. Arthur Andersen regarded the restated net transaction as not material and therefore did not qualify their opinion for it.

- Improper deletion from Sunbeam's computer system of all product return authorizations in the first quarter of 1998. Although Sunbeam

18. "Chainsaw Al."

—Continued

QUARTER OF 1997	COOKIE JAR RESERVE	IMPROVEMENT OF INCOME
Q1	$4.3 million – non-GAAP	13%
	$2.1 million – inventory	6%
	$330,000 – advertising expense	
Q2	$8.2 million – non-GAAP	
	$5.6 million – coop advertising	
Q3	$2.9 million – non-GAAP	
	$663,000 – advertising expense	
Q4	$1.5 million – non-GAAP	
	$9.0 million – litigation	

Continued

had to honor their agreements, many returns were delayed past the quarter end so that the company's reserve for returns appeared to be adequate when, in fact, it was understated and income correspondingly overstated. At the end of 1997, Sunbeam reduced its reserve from $6.5 million to $2.5 million without reasonable justification. At the end of January 1998, Sunbeam further reduced it by another $1 million when, in fact, there was approximately $18 million in impending returns and the company's established approach should have called for a reserve of $4.5 million.

- Extending the first quarter of 1998 from March 29 to March 31 to capture more sales in the quarter.

The SEC further claims that no acquisitor had surfaced for Sunbeam, and the financial picture was so grave in early 1998 that Chainsaw Al negotiated the purchase of three companies—Coleman, First Alert, and Signature Brands—with the view of creating another restructuring or "cookie jar" reserve. The 1998 manipulations described above, and others, were intended to maintain the illusion of favorable momentum to facilitate the placement of $700 million of zero coupon bonds and raise a sufficient revolving line of credit ($1.7 billion) to complete the purchases. Sunbeam completed the acquisition on March 30, 1998, but never disclosed that the increase in gross sales for the two extended days, March 30 and 31, amounted to $38 million.

While Sunbeam executives were manipulating the company's financial reports, they were also making a continuous stream of misleading statements to financial analysts, the SEC, and to the investing public. These are detailed in the SEC's Litigation Release.

The SEC's claim, in summary, was that these manipulations accounted for an overstatement of Sunbeam's income by 50 percent during 1997, and that this fraudulent misrepresentation was significant to the decisions of the investing public.

How Did They Do It?

According to published reports, soon after Chainsaw Al was hired, he recruited Russell Kersh, with whom he had worked before, to be his CFO. Then he gave huge stock options to 250 of the 300 top officers at Sunbeam—so significant that many would have had to forego gains of $1 million or more if they resigned before the three-year vesting period. This potential gain was obviously why these senior executives endured Dunlap's intimidating performance review sessions, which were referred to as "Hair Spray Days" due to the stream of air from Dunlap's mouth that blew back the executive's hair. "It was like a dog barking for hours, ... He just yelled, ranted and raved. He was condescending, belligerent, and disrespectful."[19]

Dunlap's cost-cutting measures resulted in the firing of so many people that normal functions could not be carried out. At one stage, the Sunbeam computer system broke down during an upgrade and couldn't be fixed for months due to lack of technicians that had been fired. During this period Sunbeam reportedly lost track of shipments, could not bill customers properly, and could not collect accounts receivable.[20]

Making the projected quarterly numbers was always a difficult exercise. "But in the fourth quarter [of 1997], however, no amount of game playing or beating up on people could produce the numbers Dunlap had promised investors. So he turned to his longtime ally and CFO, Russell Kersh, who had been with him through his stints at Lily Cup and Scott Paper. In the often esoteric interpretations that are made in accounting, Kersh

—Continued

---

19. "Chainsaw Al."
20. Ibid.

Continued

was rarely conservative or bashful about his creative competence during his tenure as Sunbeam's CFO. In a self-congratulatory tone, he would point to his chest and boast to fellow executives that he was 'the biggest profit center' the company had. Dunlap knew it as well. At meetings, executives recalled, Dunlap would say: 'If it weren't for Russ and the accounting team, we'd be nowhere.' Several executives heard Dunlap shout at subordinates: 'Make the goddamn number. And Russ, you cover it with your ditty bag.'"[21]

"To investors who made millions by following him, Dunlap was, if not a god, certainly a savior. He parachuted into poorly performing companies and made tough decisions that quickly brought shareholders sizable profits. 'We're all seduced by the possibility of big wins,' says Paine Webber Inc. analyst Andrew Shore."[22]

Arthur Andersen's Role

With all this going on, it is reasonable to ask how Arthur Andersen staff members could not have known about the poor internal controls on sales, accounts receivable, and inventory associated with the computer system breakdown. Did they not review internal

audit reports? If their audit procedures were more strategic or analytical than procedural, why did they not identify the abnormal growth of inventory and accounts receivable that Andrew Shore did? Perhaps the auditors did not exercise sufficient professional skepticism[23] in recognizing the abnormality or, if they recognized it, in exploring the explanations received from Sunbeam's management.

Deidra DenDanto, one of Sunbeam's internal auditors and formerly of Arthur Andersen, knew of the accounting manipulations. Why didn't Arthur Andersen? Perhaps Arthur Andersen recognized many of the problems discussed above (as the SEC claims), but regarded them as not material. In one instance the SEC notes that the auditor may have regarded a partially adjusted matter (the recording as revenue of the purported sale of Sunbeam's spare parts inventory) as not material in relation to Sunbeam's reported figures, but implies that this was too simplistic an analysis. The comparisons necessary for a proper assessment of materiality should be based on the client's adjusted figures,

and on many more factors than most would expect.[24]

Whether Arthur Andersen knew about Sunbeam's problems, and how much they knew, will probably never be known with certainty. In their defense against the SEC claims, Andersen claimed that "revisions found in the restatement were purely the result of changes in approach mandated by Sunbeam's new management."[25] Lawyers and Sunbeam executives regarded this position as "Andersen doing anything to evade blame."[26]

Board of Director's Role

Given this defense, however, it is possible that Andersen did not review all accounting, internal control, and other concerns with the audit committee of the board or the board of directors itself or, if it did, Andersen may not have branded them as material.[27] One reason for this could be that Chainsaw Al was both the CEO and chair of the board, so open discussion and questioning of management may not have been encouraged.

—Continued

---

21. Ibid.
22. "How Al Dunlap Self-Destructed."

23. See "Auditor Scepticism and Revenue Transactions," Jimmy W. Martin, *The CPA Journal*, New York, August 2002.

24. See FASB, Concepts Statement No. 2, p. 125, and SEC Staff Accounting Bulletin: No. 99—Materiality, August 12, 1999, p. 4.
25. "Andersen's Other Headache: Sunbeam."
26. Ibid.
27. Ibid.; SEC Litigation Release.

Continued

Another reason could be that Andersen wanted to protect its audit and non-audit fees.

Nonetheless, the board of directors is not supposed to accept what the external auditors say without any probing or discussion. If issues were raised, questions about the nature of the transactions and the auditors' judgments about materiality should have been posed by board members. These might have surfaced information on the company's practices or the auditor's judgments that required further investigation.

In addition, the board is expected to ensure that the company has proper policies and internal controls so that the policies are followed. This area is the specific mandate of the controller and internal audit group. Although Deidra DenDanto had made numerous reports about her concerns, these do not appear to have reached the board, except perhaps too late in March or early April 1998. Perhaps a whistle-blowing program reporting to the audit committee might have assisted the Sunbeam board. The board seems to have been out of touch with the reality of Sunbeam's operations.

One matter the board did not handle properly was the investigation of Chainsaw Al's resume and background before it hired him. Apparently, there were several years missing from his resume, thus hiding a period "a quarter century ago [when] he was also fired from Nitec Paper Corp. amid similar allegations; in both cases, amazingly high profits were reported and used to justify huge payouts to Dunlap, only to have auditors later conclude that profits were fictitious."[28] Dunlap denied any wrongdoing.

Results of the SEC Charges

In April 2001, Arthur Andersen agreed to pay Sunbeam shareholders $110 million to settle a class action lawsuit.[29]

On September 4, 2002, the SEC announced[30] that, without admitting or denying the SEC's allegations, Dunlap and Kersh consented to the entry of judgments before the court:

(1) permanently enjoining each of them from violating the antifraud, reporting, books and records, and internal controls provisions of the federal securities laws; (2) permanently barring each of them from serving as officers or directors of any public company, and (3) requiring Dunlap to pay a civil

---

28. "The Incomplete Resume: A Special Report; An Executive's Missing Years: Papering Over Past Problems," Floyd Norris, *The New York Times*, July 16, 2001.
29. "Andersen's Other Headache: Sunbeam."
30. "Former Top Officers of Sunbeam Corp. Settle SEC Charges …", SEC Litigation Release No. 17710/September 4, 2002, Accounting and Auditing Enforcement Release No. 1623/September 4, 2002.

penalty of $500,000 and Kersh to pay a civil penalty of $200,000.

The Release further notes that:

Dunlap paid $15,000,000 and Kersh $250,000 out of their own funds to settle a related class action. Neither Dunlap nor Kersh sold Sunbeam stock or received performance-based bonuses during the relevant period.

The Commission's action against three other former officers of Sunbeam, Robert J. Gluck, Donald R. Uzzi and Lee B. Griffith, and against Phillip Harlow, the audit partner on the Arthur Andersen engagements to audit Sunbeam's 1996, 1997 and 1998 year-end financial statements, remains pending. Trial is scheduled for January 2003.

Questions

1. Explain how Chainsaw Al used "cookie jar" reserves to inflate Sunbeam's profit.

2. Can "bill and hold" practices ever be considered sales that should be recorded in the period in which the goods are initially "held"?

3. Why didn't Sunbeam's board of directors catch on to the manipulations?

4. How should a board make sure that it gets the information it needs to monitor management actions and accounting policies?

—Continued

Continued

5. If you are a professional accountant who reports an ethical problem to your superior who does nothing, what more should you do?

6. What problems can you identify with Arthur Andersen's work as auditor of Sunbeam?

7. How should a board assess the performance of their company's auditors?

8. While it is attractive to have a CEO that is a strong person with a high profile, how should a board manage or keep track of such a person without demotivating them?

9. Can a board effectively monitor a CEO who is also the chair of the board?

Ethics case

Waste Management, Inc.

Waste Management, Inc. (WMI), founded by cousins Dean Buntrock and Wayne Huizenga, first came to public attention in 1971 when the founders began to buy up many small family-owned waste haulers in a successful effort to consolidate the waste disposal industry in the United States. By 1990, as a result of strong growth through acquisitions and operations, WMI had become the largest waste management company in the United States. Wayne Huizenga left WMI in 1984 to found his Blockbuster empire.[1]

Unfortunately, real growth was bolstered by "aggressive accounting policies" and, when profitability and real growth slowed in the early 1990s,[2] Dean Buntrock and his associates began to manipulate the company's financial reports to keep to its appearance of success.[3] Without this successful appearance, the company's stock price would have fallen, making WMI stock far less

—Continued

Waste Management Stock Chart, Weekly Prices, 1998–2003

Reprinted courtesy of NAQ, Inc.

---

1. "Can Waste Management Climb Out of the Muck?" *Business Week*, March 23, 1998.

2. Ibid. The decline was due to a surplus of dump space and declining prices, and a slowing of stock-based acquisitions due to low attractiveness of company stock.

3. Actually, the use of aggressive or liberal accounting policies and questionable disclosure probably began prior to 1992. "Burying Trash in Big Holes—On the Balance Sheet," *Business Week*, May 11, 1992.

Continued

useful in acquiring additional haulers, as well as making executive stock options worth far less.

Ultimately, the lack of real growth came to light, management was changed, and investigations began. In February 1998, WMI announced the restatement of its 1992–1996 reported earnings, acknowledging that profits had been overstated by $3.54 billion pre-tax. The impact on WMI's share price was not favorable, and although steep declines did not emerge until the second half of 1998, the stock's growth trend was broken.

The U.S. Securities and Exchange Commission investigated and laid charges citing massive fraud against former WMI officials; Arthur Andersen, WMI's auditor; and several of Arthur Andersen's partners. Significant fines and sanctions were applied. Arthur Andersen paid a fine of $7 million, and key partners were fined and banned from practicing before the SEC. In order to settle two class action lawsuits with irate shareholders, WMI paid $677 million, with Arthur Andersen contributing $95 million. WMI refused to pay pensions and severance to the senior officers implicated in the scandal.

Arthur Andersen was the company's auditor throughout this period, and the firm was well aware of WMI's

accounting practices. Why didn't they stand up to their client? What could they have done? What should they have done? Did this experience change their approach to risk management?

Discovery

Dean Buntrock retired as CEO in June 1996, but continued as the chairman of WMI's board of directors. He appointed his longtime second-in-command Phillip B. Rooney, the company's president and chief operating officer, as CEO, but Rooney resigned in February 1997 due to pressure from unhappy WMI shareholders, and Buntrock was pressed back into service. In July 1997, Buntrock turned over his chairman's title to Ronald T. Lemay, who was formerly an executive at Sprint Corp. However, on October 29, after only three months, Lemay resigned and went back to Sprint. A former Chrysler vice chairman, newly named director and turn-around expert, Robert S. Miller, was appointed interim chairman and CEO. According to Miller, LeMay got "a whiff of the accounting problems" and "He left because it was deep enough and he hadn't hit bottom yet."[4]

4. "Where it Hurts: An Accounting Scandal Endangers Big Payout For A Retired CEO—Waste Management's Board Withholds $40 Million From Buntrock, Others—Alma Mater Loses $3 Million," Jeff Bailey, *The Wall Street Journal*, May 19, 1999.

Nonetheless, LeMay had initiated an investigation into the accounting manipulations that subsequently became the starting point for recognizing the 1992–1996 financial reports needed restatement to correct numerous overstatements, and the point of departure for the ensuing SEC investigation. According to the SEC's information release of March 26, 2002, the defendants, WMI's senior officers (Buntrock; Rooney; James E. Koenig, executive vice president and CFO; Thomas C. Hau, vice president, corporate controller, and chief accounting officer; Herbert Getz, senior vice president general counsel, and secretary; and Bruce D. Tobecksen, vice president of finance), aided by Arthur Andersen and its partners, "perpetrated a massive financial fraud lasting more than five years."[5] The information release goes on to state that in its related complaint the SEC alleges the following:

> Defendants fraudulently manipulated the Company's financial results to meet predetermined earnings targets.

—Continued

5. "Waste Management, Inc. Founder and Five Other Former Top Officers Sued for Massive Earnings Management Fraud," Litigation Release No. 17435/ March 26, 2002, Accounting and Auditing Enforcement Release No. 1532, U.S. Securities and Exchange Commission (see *http://brooks.swlearning.com*).

Continued

The Company's revenues and profits were not growing fast enough to meet these targets, so defendants instead resorted to improperly eliminating and deferring current period expenses to inflate earnings. They employed a multitude of improper accounting practices to achieve this objective. Among other things, defendants

- avoided depreciation expenses on their garbage trucks by both assigning unsupported and inflated salvage values and extending their useful lives,

- assigned arbitrary salvage values to other assets that previously had no salvage value,

- failed to record expenses for decreases in the value of landfills as they were filled with waste,

- refused to record expenses necessary to write off the costs of unsuccessful and abandoned landfill development projects,

- established inflated environmental reserves (liabilities) in connection with acquisitions so that the excess reserves could be used to avoid recording unrelated operating expenses,

- improperly capitalized a variety of expenses, and

- failed to establish sufficient reserves (liabilities) to pay for income taxes and other expenses.[6]

6. Ibid.

The Impact

These manipulations gave rise to the following aggregated amounts over the period from 1992–1996, as indicated by the cumulative restatement announced in early 1998, as reported in the SEC complaint:

The Restatement—Then the Largest in Corporate History

293. The accounting review started in mid-July by Buntrock's successor continued through the end of the year, with the same long-time Company controllers conducting the review. AA continued as the Company's auditor, but a new engagement team was assembled to audit the Company's restated financial statements. The audit committee oversaw the work on the Restatement and engaged another big 5 accounting firm to shadow the audit work of AA and advise the committee

regarding the various accounting issues.

294. The details of the massive Restatement finally came in early 1998. In February 1998, Waste Management announced that it was restating its financial statements for the period 1992 through 1996 and the first three quarters of 1997. At the time, the Restatement was the largest in history. In the Restatement, the Company admitted that, through the first three quarters of 1997, it had materially overstated its reported pre-tax earnings by approximately $1.7 billion and understated certain elements of its tax expense by $190 million. See table below.

295. Additionally, contemporaneous to the Restatement, the Company also recorded approximately $1.7 billion in impairment losses and other charges. The total amount of the Restatement and fourth

—Continued

Cumulative Restatements of Pre-Tax Income (through 12/31/96)	(in millions)
Vehicle, equipment and container depreciation expense	$ 509
Capitalized interest	192
Environmental and closure/post-closure liabilities	173
Purchase accounting related to remediation reserves	128
Asset impairment losses	214
Software impairment reversal	(85)
Other	301
Pre-tax subtotal	**$ 1,432**
Restatements of Pre-Tax Income (1/1/97 through 9/30/97)	$ 250
Income Tax Expense Restatement (through 9/30/97)	$ 190
Total Restated items	**$ 1,872**

Continued

quarter charges was approximately $3.6 billion.[7]

The WMI restatement acknowledged that its reported net after-tax income had been misstated by the following amounts in each of the years from 1992 to 1996 inclusive, as reported in the SEC complaint:

14. In the Restatement, the Company acknowledged that its original financial statements had misstated its net after-tax income as in the table below.

The Company acknowledged that, in total, it had overstated its net after-tax income by over $1 billion.[8]

Who Did It, and Why?

The complaint goes on to explain each defendant's participation in the fraud, essentially indicating that Buntrock masterminded the fraud, and that the other defendants actively participated in and/or knew or recklessly disregarded facts indicating that WMI's financial statements or disclosures contained material misstatements and omissions. In the process, the:

defendants received the following estimated ill-gotten gains, from their bonuses,

retirement benefits, trading and charitable giving alone:

	Ill-gotten Gains
Buntrock	$16,917,761
Rooney	$9,286,124
Koenig	$951,005
Hau	$640,100
Getz	$472,500
Tobecksen	$403,779[9]

For these wrongdoings, the SEC made the following claims against all or some of the defendants: securities fraud, filing false periodic reports, falsification of books and records, and lying to auditors.[10] In summary, the SEC sought:

a final judgment as to each defendant that permanently enjoins him, orders the disgorgement of ill-gotten gains plus prejudgment interest, imposes civil penalties as a lesson to him and to others, and prohibits him from serving as an officer or director of a public company.[11]

---

9. Ibid., 5.
10. Ibid., 79–81.
11. Ibid., 6.

Arthur Andersen's Role

The SEC's Litigation Release does not mince words about the role of Arthur Andersen's partners. It states:

Defendants were aided in their fraud by the Company's long-time auditor Arthur Andersen LLP ("Andersen"), which repeatedly issued unqualified audit reports on the Company's materially false and misleading annual financial statements. At the outset of the fraud, management capped Andersen's audit fees and advised the Andersen engagement partner that the firm could earn additional fees through "special work." Andersen nevertheless identified the Company's improper accounting practices and quantified much of the impact of those practices on the Company's financial statements. Andersen annually presented Company management with what it called Proposed Adjusting Journal Entries ("PAJEs") to correct errors that understated expenses and overstated earnings in the Company's financial statements.

—Continued

---

7. *Complaint:* SEC v. Dean Buntrock, Phillip B. Rooney, James E. Koenig, Thomas C. Hau, Herbert A. Getz, and Bruce D. Tobecksen, No. 02C 2180, U.S. Securities and Exchange Commission, March 26, 2002, 64–65 (see *http://brooks.swlearning.com*).
8. Ibid., 4–5.

YEAR	ORIGINALLY REPORTED (THOUSANDS)	AS RESTATED (THOUSANDS)	PERCENT OVERSTATED
1992	$850,036	$739,686	15
1993	$452,776	$288,707	57
1994	$784,381	$627,508	25
1995	$603,899	$340,097	78
1996	$192,085	$(39,307)	100+
Q1–Q3 1997	$417,600	$236,700	76

Continued

Management consistently refused to make the adjustments called for by the PAJEs. Instead, defendants secretly entered into an agreement with Andersen fraudulently to write off the accumulated errors over periods of up to ten years and to change the underlying accounting practices, but to do so only in future periods. That signed, four-page agreement, known as the Summary of Action Steps (attached to the Commission's complaint), identified improper accounting practices that went to the core of the company's operations and prescribed thirty-two "must do" steps for the company to follow to change those practices. The Action Steps thus constituted an agreement between the company and its outside auditor to cover up past frauds by committing additional frauds in the future.

Defendants could not even comply with the Action Steps agreement. Writing off the errors and changing the underlying accounting practices as prescribed in the agreement would have prevented the company from meeting earnings targets and defendants from enriching themselves.[12]

In a separate announcement[13] of settlements reached on June 19, 2001, the SEC

detailed its findings against Arthur Andersen and the following of its partners:

- Robert E. Allgyer, partner responsible for the audit, who was "known as the 'rainmaker' inside Andersen for his skill at winning business by pitching consulting, tax and other non-audit services."[14]

- Edward G. Maier, the risk management partner for Andersen's Chicago office.

- Walter Cercavschi, the concurring partner on the WMI audit.

- Robert Kutsenda, then Central Region audit practice director for Andersen.

The SEC findings as detailed beginning on page 3 of the June 19 Litigation Release, or in the longer Administrative Proceedings of the same date,[15] provide an interesting year-by-year expansion of the summary noted above. In addition, the Litigation Release makes the following salient points:

- As reported to the audit committee, between 1991 and

1997, Andersen billed Waste Management corporate headquarters approximately $7.5 million in audit fees. Over this seven-year period, while Andersen's corporate audit fees remained capped, Andersen also billed Waste Management corporate headquarters $11.8 million in other fees, much of which related to tax, attest work unrelated to financial statement audits or reviews, regulatory issues, and consulting services.

- A related entity, Andersen Consulting, also billed Waste Management corporate headquarters approximately $6 million in additional non-audit fees. Of the $6 million in Andersen Consulting fees, $3.7 million related to a Strategic Review that analyzed the overall business structure of the Company and ultimately made recommendations on implementing a new operating model designed to "increase shareholder value." Allgyer was a member of the Steering Committee that oversaw the Strategic Review, and Andersen Consulting billed his time for these services to the Company. In setting Allgyer's compensation, Andersen took into account, among other things, the Firm's billings to the Company for audit and non-audit services.

—Continued

---

12. SEC Litigation Release No. 17435, 3.

13. "Arthur Andersen … and Partners Settle …," Litigation Release No. 17039/ June 19, 2001, Accounting and Auditing Enforcement Release No. 1410/ June 19, 2001, U.S. Securities and Exchange Commission (see *http://brooks.swlearning.com*).

14. David Ward and Loren Steffy, "How Andersen Went Wrong," *Bloomberg Markets*, May 2002.

15. "Order Instituting Public Administrative Proceedings, Making Findings and Imposing Remedial Sanctions Pursuant to the Commission's Rules of Practice," Securities Exchange Act of 1934, Release No. 44444/June 19, 2001, Accounting and Auditing Enforcement Release No. 1405/June 19, 2001, Administrative Proceeding File No. 3-10513, Securities and Exchange Commission (see *http://brooks.swlearning.com*).

Continued

- As the Commission stated in its Order as to Andersen,
  - [u]nless the auditor stands up to management as soon as it knows that management is unwilling to correct material misstatements, the auditor ultimately will find itself in an untenable position: it either must continue issuing unqualified audit reports on materially misstated financial statements and hope that its conduct will not be discovered or it must force a restatement or qualify its report and thereby subject itself to the liability that likely will result from the exposure of its role in the prior issuance of the materially misstated financial statements.
- The Commission in this case found that
  - Andersen failed to stand up to management to prevent the issuance of materially misstated financial statements. Instead, Andersen allowed the Company to establish—and then continue for many years—a series of improper accounting practices. As a result, Andersen found itself in 1998 in the position of auditing the Restatement and issuing an unqualified audit report in which it acknowledged that the prior financial statements on which it had issued unqualified audit reports were materially misstated.
- The Commission ultimately found in its Order as to Andersen that
  - the circumstances of this case, including the positions within the Firm of the partners who were consulted by the engagement team, the gravity and duration of the misconduct, and the nature and magnitude of the misstatements mandate that the Firm be held responsible for the acts of its partners in causing the Firm to issue false and misleading audit reports in the Firm's name.
- The Commission's Complaint alleges and the Commission's Order found that Andersen knew or was reckless in not knowing that the unqualified audit reports that it issued for the years 1993 through 1996 were materially false and misleading because the audits were not conducted in accordance with GAAS and the financial statements did not conform to GAAP. The Complaint further alleges that Andersen violated section 10(b) of the Exchange Act and rule 10b-5 thereunder. The Commission's Order as to Andersen finds that Andersen engaged in improper professional conduct within the meaning of rule 102(e)(1)(ii) of the Commission's Rules of Practice.[16]

As a result of the Commission's complaint, and without admitting or denying the allegations or findings in the Commission's complaint and orders, Arthur Andersen and the partners consented to the actions in the accompanying table.

Surprisingly, Arthur Andersen was not fired as WMI's auditor until 2001. According to audit committee members, Arthur Andersen was kept on to help with the accounting probe. "If you want to find where the bones are buried, … 'you've got to use the dog.'"[17]

Other Impacts

Arthur Andersen and Waste Management, Inc., have been sued in numerous class actions by irate shareholders. To date they have paid out the following amounts:

- Regarding the restatement of earnings: $220 million (Andersen $75 mil.)[18]
- Securities violations: $457 million (Andersen $20 mil.)[19]

---

16. "Arthur Andersen … and Partners Settle."
17. "Where It Hurts."
18. Ibid.
19. Calmetta Coleman, "Waste Management to Pay $457 Million To Settle Shareholder Class-Action Lawsuit," *The Wall Street Journal*, November 8, 2001.

Continued

Not surprisingly, the confidence that shareholders were willing to place in WMI management and future earnings announcements was severely eroded.

On a personal level, Mr. Buntrock and other senior executives discovered in May 1999 that the approximately $40 million due them for pension and deferred compensation was withheld by the WMI board until the accounting investigation was completed. This followed the precedent set in the case of the former Sunbeam CEO, Albert J. Dunlap, who expected $5.5 million. Cendant Corp., however, which found its pretax profits were overstated by $500 million, paid retiring CEO, Walter A. Forbes, the full $35 million in severance due in July 1998.[20] Now that the precedent appears to have shifted, the question arises as to whether executives found to have knowingly or unknowingly, but negligently, contributed to a financial scandal should be forced to pay towards class action settlements reached.

20. "Where It Hurts."

Questions

1. Why didn't Arthur Andersen stand up to WMI management?

2. What aspects of their risk management model did the Arthur Andersen partners incorrectly consider?

3. To whom should Arthur Andersen have complained if WMI management was acting improperly?

4. Did the WMI board and audit committee do their jobs?

5. Were the fines levied high enough?

6. Should you use the same "dog" to discover the "bones" in an accounting scandal?

SEC SANCTIONS RELATED TO IMPROPER AUDIT PRACTICES WITH REGARD TO THE AUDITS FOR 1992–1997 OF WASTE MANAGEMENT, INC.			
	Permanent Injunction Enjoining From Future Violations of Sections or Rules of the Securities Exchange Act	**Civil Penalty (Fine)**	**Censure under Rule 102(e) for improper professional conduct Denial of right to appear or practice before the SEC as an accountant, with the right to request reinstatement after…**
Arthur Andersen	Section 10(b) [1934] Rule 10b-5 [1934]	$7 million	Censure
Robert Allgyer	Section 10(b) [1934] Rule 10b-5 [1934] Section 17(a) [1933]	$50,000	Censure Denial, 5 years
Edward Maier	Section 10(b) [1934] Rule 10b-5 [1934] Section 17(a) [1933]	$40,000	Censure Denial, 3 years
Walter Cercavschi	Section 10(b) [1934] Rule 10b-5 [1934] Section 17(a) [1933]	$30,000	Censure Denial, 3 years
Robert Kutsenda	-	-	Censure Denial, 1 year

Part Two

Ethical Governance and Accountability

Chapter 3	Corporate Ethical Governance and Accountability
Chapter 4	Professional Accounting in the Public Interest, Post-Enron

Introduction

Part 1 provided an understanding of the ethical concerns and expectations that directors, executives, and professionals are facing that are shaping the future. Both traditional stakeholder concerns and the Sarbanes-Oxley Act acceleration provided by the Enron, Arthur Andersen, and WorldCom debacles are responsible for redefining the accountability and governance frameworks for organizations and particularly the accounting profession. The downside for organizations that fail to understand and provide for the shift is significant. Their directors and executives, and any professionals involved will face serious consequences because they will be seen as not fulfilling their newly defined, due diligence expectations as fiduciaries. To avoid this result, organizations and professions are providing more guidance about expected behavior.

Chapter 3 examines how ethics can be incorporated into modern accountability and governance mechanisms that respond to stakeholder expectations. An effective guidance system requires an ethical culture, code of conduct, trust, ethics risk management, whistle-blower mechanism, reinforcement, and compliance. Threats to good governance such as conflicts of interest and poor risk management are also discussed.

Chapter 4 goes on to discuss the role and responsibilities of professional accountants in the new accountability and governance framework. Their role, both as external auditors and as employees of the corporations, is a key component in the credibility of corporations and their reports. The future prestige of the accounting profession depends upon embracing the role of fiduciary that public expectations demand.

Chapter Three

Corporate Ethical Governance and Accountability

Purpose of the Chapter

Businesses, directors, executives, and professional accountants are facing increasingly demanding expectations from shareholders and other stakeholders for what organizations are doing and how they are doing it. At the same time, the environments that organizations operate in are increasingly complex, as are their ethical challenges. Organizational governance and accountability mechanisms are therefore under considerable strain, and improvement is highly desirable.

Trial-and-error decision making involves too high a risk of unfortunate consequences for the reputation and achievement of strategic objectives of the organization, its directors, executives, employees, and professional accountants. Consequently, corporate leaders, and those of the accounting profession and accounting firms are expected to put in place governance programs that provide ethical guidance and accountability programs that satisfy expectations. Ethical governance and accountability programs are voluntary, and while some organizations will choose not to introduce them, those directors, executives, and professional accountants who wish to reduce the risks involved in ethical malfeasance and enjoy the benefits of continuing stakeholder support will.

Directors, executives, and professional accountants all have essential roles to play in the emerging framework for ethical governance and accountability. They are all serving mostly the same set of expectations, but have different levels of duty and responsibility. This chapter deals with both the common and distinct aspects related to each role. The emerging framework is developed, then common threats to good governance are discussed, followed by matters relating to the corporation and those relating to professional accountants.

NEW EXPECTATIONS—NEW FRAMEWORK

Chapter 1 explained the concerns that organizations, and particularly corporations, are facing with regard to what they are doing and how they are doing it. Even before the Enron, Arthur Andersen, and WorldCom debacles, the public was pressing corporations over misleading financial reports and scandals; protection of the environment, worker, customer, and human rights; instances of bribery, undue influence, and incredible greed; and failure to govern within the bounds expected by stakeholders and to be accountable to them.

Stakeholders found that they could have significant impacts on a corporation's consumer markets, capital markets, and on the support offered the corporation by other stakeholder groups such as employees and lenders. A corporation's reputation could be significantly affected by irate stakeholders. Directors and executives watching boycotts, reduced revenue and profit streams, or turn-downs by outstanding recruits or employees found that the support of stakeholders was essential to the optimal achievement of medium- and long-term corporate objectives. Some directors and executives wanted that support and, with the help of academics and others, a new governance and accountability framework was developed, complete with new tools and techniques.

Then along came the Enron, Arthur Andersen, and WorldCom debacles. They showed the world the faults and vulnerabilities inherent in the old style shareholder-only governance and accountability model. The credibility of North American corporations, professional accountants, and capital markets was so severely eroded in the minds of the public that President Bush and business leaders had to call repeatedly for reforms. Finally, as Chapter 2 described, the U.S. Congress and Senate were galvanized to rise above partisan politics to amalgamate two proposals and pass the Sarbanes-Oxley Act (SOX) within one month and a few days of WorldCom's declaration of bankruptcy.

SOX has reformed the governance and accountability framework for corporations wishing to raise funds and have their shares traded on U.S. stock markets. The framework laid out in SOX will be put in place by the Securities and Exchange Commission (SEC) over time. It will apply to both U.S. and foreign SEC registrant corporations and to the professional accountants and outside lawyers who serve them. This means, for example, that 177 of Canada's largest companies, whose securities are traded on U.S. markets, will have to comply, as will their professional accountants and outside lawyers. Over time it will be the standard on which governance and accountability frameworks around the world are based.

Expectations from decades of stakeholder concerns and about the immediate need to restore credibility have given rise to the new framework of governance and accountability. SOX represented a response to an acceleration of stakeholder concerns brought on by the scandals that affected the lives of investors, and particularly pensioners, employees and their dependants, and many others. In the end, the shortfall in expected behavior was so egregious that only quick reform—a new framework—could restore the necessary trust in corporate governance and accountability.

ACCOUNTABILITY TO SHAREHOLDERS OR STAKEHOLDERS?

The growing capacity of nonshareholder stakeholders to influence the achievement of corporate objectives and their increasing sensitivity made it attractive for corporations to encourage stakeholder support. The Enron, Arthur Andersen, and WorldCom scandals showed that corporate activities designed to favor current executives, directors, and some shareholders were not necessarily in the interest of future or current shareholders who wished for long-term success such as pensioners-investors, employees, and lenders. Executives, directors, and investors who were focused on the short term jeopardized the credibility of the entire corporate governance and accountability process.

The SOX reforms were designed to refocus the governance model on the responsibility of directors on their fiduciary duty, beyond their own self-interest to that of shareholders as a whole and to the public interest. To quote the Senate Subcommittee[1] that investigated the Enron fiasco:

> **Fiduciary Obligations of Boards of Directors.** In the United States, the Board of Directors sits at the apex of a company's governing structure. A typical Board's duties include reviewing the company's overall business strategy; selecting and compensating the company's senior executives; evaluating the company's outside auditor; overseeing the company's financial statements; and monitoring overall company performance. According to the Business Roundtable, the Board's "paramount duty" is to safeguard the interests of the company's shareholders.[2]

Directors operate under state laws that impose fiduciary duties on them to act in good faith, with reasonable care, and in the best interest of the corporation and its shareholders. Courts generally discuss three types of fiduciary obligations. As one court put it:

> Three broad duties stem from the fiduciary status of corporate directors: namely, the duties of obedience, loyalty, and due care. The duty of obedience requires a director to avoid committing ... acts beyond the scope of the powers of a corporation as defined by its charter or the laws of the state of incorporation. ... The duty of loyalty dictates that a director must act in good faith and must not allow his personal interest to prevail over the interests of the corporation. ... [T]he duty of care requires a director to be diligent and prudent in managing the corporation's affairs.[3]

Given the recent corporate scandals and the documented capacity of stakeholders to influence the achievement of corporate objectives, it would be well within the directors' duty to safeguard the interests of shareholders, and prudent to take into account the interests of stakeholders when creating their governance structure.

Because stakeholder interests can potentially conflict with some shareholder interests, many states have formally modified the statutes by which corporations are created to allow directors to take stakeholder interests into account when appropriate. Directors may have to examine the trade-offs between shareholders and stakeholders and chose one or the other, or a blended solution. Fortunately, a longer-term shareholder perspective frequently coincides with stakeholder interests.

---

[1] *Report on The Role of The Board of Directors in the Collapse of Enron,* U.S. Senate Permanent Subcommittee on Investigations, July 8, 2002.

[2] *Statement of Corporate Governance,* The Business Roundtable (9/97) at 3.

[3] *Gearheart Industries v. Smith International,* 741 F.2d 707, 719 (5th Cir.1984).

Based on the reality of stakeholder pressures and the desire to encourage stakeholder support, corporations realize that they are accountable to stakeholders and are governing themselves to minimize the risks and maximize the opportunities inherent in the stakeholder accountability framework. *De facto,* corporations are increasingly realizing that they are accountable to all or a subset of the stakeholders shown in Figure 3.1.

FIGURE 3.1

MAP OF CORPORATE
STAKEHOLDER
ACCOUNTABILITY

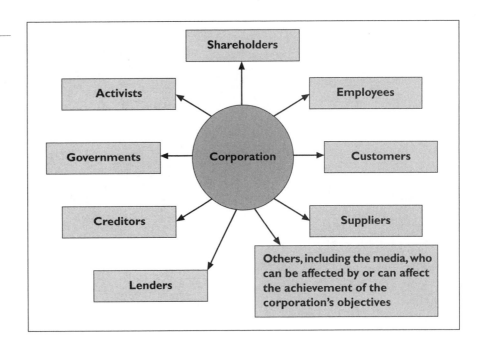

GOVERNANCE FOR BROAD STAKEHOLDER ACCOUNTABILITY

Governance Process Based on Stakeholder Interests

Once a corporation's directors and/or executives realize that the corporation is accountable legally to shareholders, but strategically to additional stakeholders who can significantly affect the achievement of its objectives, they understand the logic and desirability of governing the corporation with the interests of all important stakeholders in mind. Shareholders are, in fact, a stakeholder group—and probably the most important on a continuing basis—but they are no longer the only stakeholder group whose interests should influence corporate actions, nor are those interests homogenous.

In order to minimize harmful stakeholder reactions and optimize opportunities in the future, corporations should assess how their actions impact upon the interests of their important stakeholder groups. This has been the underlying focus for environmental scanning and issues management for decades. What has changed is that *stakeholder impact analysis* has become significantly more developed as have the tools employed in examining, ranking, and assessing stakeholder interests—to the point that incorporating them into the governance process is now both feasible and desirable.

In a stakeholder accountability oriented governance process (SAOG), the board of directors must, as shown in Figure 3.2, take all stakeholder interests into account and make sure that they are built into the company's vision, mission, strategy, policies, codes, practices, compliance mechanisms, and feedback

FIGURE 3.2

STAKEHOLDER
ACCOUNTABILITY ORIENTED
GOVERNANCE PROCESS

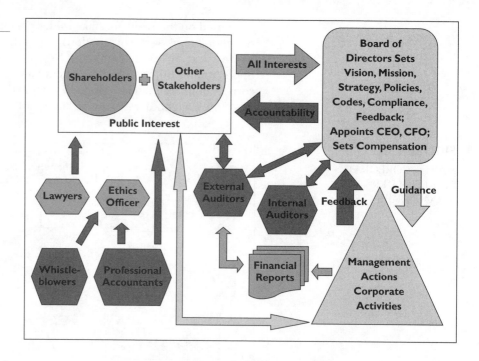

arrangements. If this is not done, the company's actions may fail to take important interests into account, and the company may lose the support of one or more stakeholder groups. For example, not enough emphasis on customer value or safety, or too much on short-term profit, may cost the support of customers. The Ford/Firestone case at the end of this chapter illustrates such a problem.

Appropriate guidance reinforced by feedback mechanisms and an ethical culture must be given to management, or else management can honestly say that no one told them what boundaries they should be operating within. This guidance will influence the preparation of financial reports and other sources of feedback, as well as the behavior exhibited in dealings with customers, employees, and other stakeholders.

The board of directors may be advised by several agents if management behavior is questionable. Shareholders usually elect the external auditors to provide an expert opinion on whether the financial statements prepared by management present fairly the results of operations and financial position of the company and are in accordance with generally accepted accounting principles (GAAP). As Chapter 2 pointed out, Enron and other scandals have rededicated the audit profession to protecting the public interest when applying GAAP, not the interests of the senior management or current directors. External auditors are required to meet with the audit committee of the board and discuss the financial statements, as well as their work and opinions, and the state of the company's internal control measures.

In addition, a company's internal auditor's role is to assess whether its policies are comprehensive and are being observed. They should regularly report directly and in person to the audit committee, without management being present, even though they may report on a day-to-day basis to the CEO.

Due to the SOX proposals, the company's lawyers will be expected to make the board of directors aware of problems if management does not respond appropriately when told of improprieties.

An important element of modern SAOG systems should be an ethics officer (EO) or ombudsperson who watches over the ethical culture and serves as the person to whom whistle-blowers report anonymously. The EO should report to the audit committee of the board and be the conduit through which a generic report of whistle-blower's concerns reaches the board. Similar to the internal auditors, the EO may report on a day-to-day basis to the CEO, and should be ready to whistle-blow inside their corporation and, per the SOX reforms, probably specifically to the audit committee on questionable financial matters.

Professional accountants in the company's employ are called upon by their professional codes of conduct to serve the pubic interest. Consequently, they should report financial wrongdoing to the CFO and, if appropriate action is not taken, to the EO and auditors. They are not allowed to be involved with misrepresentation and should be ready to whistle-blow inside their corporation and, per the SOX reforms, specifically to the audit committee of the board.

Identifying Organizational Values—The Foundation of Behavior

The new framework for accountability is based on responding to shareholder and other stakeholder interests, and the modern governance framework should direct corporate employees to integrate those interests into their strategies, planning, and decision making. Chapters 1 and 2 showed that the public has expectations not only about what is done, but how it is accomplished. Consequently, discovering what those interests are, which are the most important, and where the risks are that should be managed is a necessary sequence that should precede the establishment of an organization's vision, mission, strategies, policies, and procedures.

This process is represented in Figure 3.3. The specific measures use to identify, assess, and rank the stakeholder interests faced by a specific organization are discussed in Chapter 4.

FIGURE 3.3

STAKEHOLDER INTERESTS, RANKING, RISK ASSESSMENT, AND USAGE

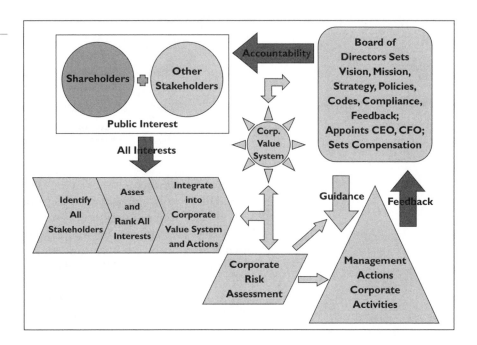

In essence, what is required is an exploration of the stakeholder interests and expectations for the organization, so that respect for these can be built into the values that drive behavior. This will lessen the chance that employees will be motivated to make decisions and take actions that are not in the interests of stakeholders.

This linkage between motivation and action is reflected in Figure 3.4. Individuals hold beliefs about what is right or improper. Those beliefs stem from many sources, but principally from the values that individuals hold. Some values were taught directly or through example by their parents, respected individuals, bosses, friends, and so on, but other values spring from the rules and motivational systems in place (or absent) at the organization. Beliefs motivate people to act.

The actions of individual employees are understood collectively to be the "corporation's behavior." The corporation per se is inanimate. *People make things happen, so it is essential that their motivations are aligned with stakeholder expectations. This can only be reliably accomplished by ensuring that the values underlying corporate motivational elements (i.e. culture, codes, policies, etc.) are similarly aligned.* Ensuring this alignment is a vital responsibility for directors whether they are considering stock option bonus systems, penalties for malfeasance, or paper medals (awards) for outstanding exemplars.

FIGURE 3.4

ALIGNING VALUES FOR ETHICAL MOTIVATION, ACTION

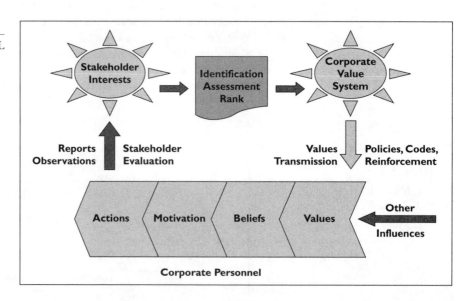

The identification, assessment, and ranking of stakeholder interests should develop a comprehensive set of values for an organization. However, it should be recognized that values and their priority vary in different cultures. This will present increasing complexities as the number of cultures that an organization deals with increases. Some cultures place a high importance on the rights of individuals. Others place primacy on duty to family, the company, religious beliefs, and so on.

In the face of competing value systems for the motivation of employees, corporations should consider which set of values most aligns with those of their shareholders, and of their most important stakeholders—perhaps those that can influence their largest consumer and capital markets. Modern media coverage is shrinking the world, so activities that take place on the other side of the globe will be known—and quickly—by interested stakeholders everywhere. Greenpeace and CNN will see that pollution incidents, for example, are quickly brought to everyone's attention.

Researchers are studying this multicultural diversity of values problem, in order to identify a set of universal values or *hypernorms* that could be embedded in corporate values systems. Although their strict interpretation differs somewhat depending on the culture, six relatively universally respected values have been identified. These universal values are honesty, fairness, compassion, integrity, predictability, and responsibility (Table 3.1).

TABLE 3.1

CULTURAL VALUES AND
HYPERNORMS

Sphere/Culture	Basis of Value System
North America	Rights-based: rights, justice, utility
Sino-Confucian	Duty-based: obligation to family
Japan	Duty-based: obligation to company
Middle East	Duty-based: obligation to savior
Europe	Personal rights
South America	Duty-based: obligation to family, religious values

Impact Exident On:

Dealing with people...hiring, gender
Bribery
Motivation for doing business
Short- and long-term time horizons
Importance of quality-of-life issues

Hypernorm Values:

Honesty, Fairness, Compassion, Integrity, Predictability, Responsibility

Directors should consider embedding these hypernorms in their corporate values systems in order to ensure that all important values are included, and that maximum acceptance and respect is assured in dealings with many cultures.

GUIDANCE MECHANISMS—CODE OF CONDUCT AND ETHICAL CULTURE

The values that a corporation's directors wish to guide and motivate the beliefs and actions of its employees need to be conveyed successfully. Usually, such guidance takes the form of a code of conduct that states the values selected, the principles that flow from those values, and any rules that are to be followed to ensure that appropriate values are respected. As noted later, research has been done into the improvement of the effectiveness of a code. For example, principles are more useful than just rules because principles facilitate interpretation when the precise circumstances encountered do not fit the rule prescribed exactly. A blend of principles and rules is often optimal.

Unfortunately, a code on its own may be nothing more than "ethical art" that is rarely studied or followed. *Experience has revealed that, to be effective, a code must be reinforced by a comprehensive ethical culture.* Developing an ethical culture involves continuing significant effort, applied over several dimensions. A code should be the subject of a training session for new recruits upon joining an organization, with yearly update sessions. Moreover, the ethical behavior expected must be referred to in speeches and newsletters by top management as often as they refer to, for example, their health and safety program, or else it will be seen as less important by employees. If employees never or rarely hear about ethical expectations, they will know that they will not be taken as a serious priority. Similarly, there should be an ethical behavior reporting mechanism linked to feedback, recognition, and promotion systems. Whistle-blowers are also part of a needed monitoring, risk management, and remediation system. More often than not, a corporation that has a code of conduct without supporting in it an ethical culture is simply engaging in window dressing, not in providing effective ethical guidance.

The development of effective codes of conduct, and of the necessary supportive ethical culture, are discussed later in this chapter.

Threats to Good Governance and Accountability

The assumption that employees will automatically be motivated to behave as the owners want is no longer valid. People are more motivated by self-interest than in the past, and are likely to come from different cultures that emphasize different priorities of duty. As a result, there is a greater need for clear guidance and for identifying and effectively managing threats to good governance and accountability. Three significant threats are discussed next.

MISUNDERSTANDING OBJECTIVES AND FIDUCIARY DUTY

Even when different cultures are not an issue, employees can misunderstand the organization's objectives and their own role and fiduciary duty. For example, many directors and employees of Enron evidently believed that the company's objectives were best served by actions that brought profit:

- Through ethical dishonesty—manipulation of energy markets in California, or sham displays of trading floors
- That was illusory—SPE transactions
- That benefited themselves at the expense of other stakeholders—payment of extraordinary fees and commissions to SPEs

Frequently employees are tempted to cut ethical corners, and they have done so because: they believed that their top management wanted them to, they were ordered to do so, or they were encouraged to do so by misguided or manipulatable incentive programs. These actions occurred when the board of directors would have preferred (sometimes with hindsight) that they had not. Employees simply misunderstood what was expected by the board because guidance was unclear, or they were led astray and did not understand that they were to report the problem for appropriate corrective action, or to whom or how.

Lack of proper guidance or reporting mechanisms may have been the result of directors and others not understanding their duty as a fiduciary. As noted previously, directors owe shareholders and regulators several duties, including obedience, loyalty, and due care; safeguarding of assets; accurate, comprehensive and transparent reports; and so on. Many directors have been looking out for their own interests, and they have spent little time protecting shareholders, other stakeholders, and the public interest from top management. Even where good guidance was in place, compliance mechanisms were nonexistent, rusty, or neglected because most directors concentrated on moving the company forward, not protecting it from ethical downsides.

Fortunately, the Sarbanes-Oxley Act (SOX) has clarified much of this lack of understanding of fiduciary relationships for directors, executives, and also for professional accountants. Professional accountants at Arthur Andersen forgot they should have been serving the public interest when giving their opinion that Enron's financial statements were in accordance with generally accepted accounting principles, (GAAP). Instead, by failing to contradict the initiatives of management, Arthur Andersen allowed unreported variations that prejudiced the interest of shareholders wanting to retain their stock, and those wishing to buy in the future, as well as the interests of employees, long-term lenders, and others.

Fortunately, the ensuing investigation and SOX has clarified the primacy of the public interest as the foremost concern of professional accountants. This clarification is not only for external auditors, but also for professional accountants employed by organizations. As employees, they owe a loyalty to their employer, but this does not supersede their duty to the public interest, their profession, or themselves. When acting as executives or managers, professional accountants must observe their professional code of conduct and, for example, cannot be associated with misrepresentations. These priorities of duty will be discussed more fully later.

Similarly, as discussed in Chapter 2, external lawyers who discover serious illegalities that are not rectified by management may be expected to reveal these matters to the board through a "noisy departure" process being contemplated by the SEC. Amazingly, many law firms are arguing against the imposition of this process, asserting that such disclosure may not be in the company's interest. A silent departure would certainly favor the interests of management, who already probably know what is going on, rather than the directors, investors, and other stakeholders who do not.

FAILURE TO IDENTIFY AND MANAGE ETHICS RISKS

Recognition of the increasing complexity, volatility, and risk inherent in modern corporate interests and operations, particularly as their scope expands to different countries and cultures, has led to the requirement for risk identification, assessment, and management systems. In the late 1990s, it became a requirement that board of directors ensure that their company's risk management process was effective,[4] and a number of studies were published illustrating how such a system might be developed and what types of risk might be targeted.[5]

However, *the systematic search for ethics risks—those where the expectations of stakeholders may not be met—has not been targeted* and should be now that the need for

---

[4]The Toronto Stock Exchange, for example, identified risk management as a matter requiring oversight by directors in 1995.

[5]See for example, AICPA/CICA and Institute for Internal Auditors publications on risk management identified in Chapter 1.

stakeholder-oriented accountability and governance is emerging. Table 3.2 illustrates the aspects of risk that are usually investigated by corporate examiners.

TABLE 3.2

AREAS OF CORPORATE RISK
ASSESSMENT

Governance and objectives
Areas of impact
     Reputation
     Assets, revenues, costs
     Performance
     Stakeholders
Sources of risk
     Environmental
     Strategic
     Operational
     Informational
Specific hazards
Degree of control over risk—little, some, great deal
Documentation

Usually there is an examination designed to safeguard assets by internal auditors who will also ensure compliance with policies. External auditors examine statements to see that internal controls are in place that will ensure accurate financial statements and reports. Given the Enron, WorldCom, and other recent fiascos, both types of auditor are now expected to spend more time searching for fraudulent activities where there is intent to deceive. External auditors have resisted being charged with full responsibility for this in the past, because fraud is very difficult to discover and the costs of doing so are much greater than boards of directors have been willing to authorize and management has been willing to incur.

In only a very few companies has there been a systematic annual process designed to focus the attention of directors, executives, and advisors on those areas where the company's actions may not meet the expectations of stakeholders. Dow Corning has had an "ethics audit process" but, based on the silicone breast implants case (see page 192), its orientation has apparently been toward avoiding scientifically justified, legal liability rather than making sure the interests of customers and other stakeholders are met. The Tylenol recall is an example of where planning ahead for customer interests made Johnson & Johnson famous. Dow Corning, on the other hand, resorted to bankruptcy protection, and their parent companies went public with a plea that the legal liability not reach upward to them. As usual in product liability cases, the fine paid was small relative to the damage to its reputation, ongoing business relationships, and the support of stakeholders.

All of Dow Corning's stakeholders would have benefited by a broader definition of ethics risk—one that identified where the expectations of stakeholders may not have been met. The Dow Corning audit process, which was also somewhat flawed, can be readily repaired to serve as one approach to the discovery of ethical risks. Other approaches could involve making an annual reflection routine part of annual ethics sign-off and/or training processes. Charging internal auditors with responsibility for identification and assessment, and the ethics officer with ongoing responsibility for discovery, assessment, and reporting to the CEO and audit committee of the board, are logical steps to take as well. Reward recognition should be accorded to employees who bring issues forward. Prevention is the most important aspect of crisis management and ethics risks have a nasty way of becoming crises if not diagnosed early enough.

The principles of ethics risk management are summarized in Table 3.3. As the importance of maintaining the support of stakeholders becomes more apparent and widely accepted, ethics risk management will become a normal element of the due diligence requirements for a board of directors and a significant part of management's responsibility.

TABLE 3.3

ETHICS RISK MANAGEMENT
PRINCIPLES

Normal definitions of risk are too narrow for   Stakeholder-oriented accountability and governance   An *ethics risk* exists where   the expectations of a stakeholder may not be met.   *Discovery and remediation* are essential in order to   avoid a crisis or the loss of the support of stakeholders.   *Assign responsibility, develop annual processes, board review*

CONFLICT OF INTERESTS

Conflict of interests has been a subject of extreme importance in recent scandals where agents and professionals failed to exercise proper judgment on behalf of their principals. In the Enron fiasco, senior officers, lawyers, and professional accountants acted in their own self-interest rather than for the benefit of the shareholders of Enron. The conflict between the self-interest of the decision makers and the interest of the shareholders interfered with the judgment being applied, causing the interests of the shareholders to be subjugated to the self-interest of the decision makers. As a result, Enron declared bankruptcy, investors lost their savings, and capital markets lost credibility and fell into a turmoil. As a result, the governance frameworks for corporations and professional accounting will be changed forever.

Stated simply, a conflict of interest occurs when the independent judgment of a person is swayed, or might be swayed, from making decisions in the best interest of others who are relying on that judgment. An executive or employee is expected to make judgments in the best interest of the company. A director is legally expected to make judgments in the best interest of the company and its shareholders, and to do so strategically so that no harm and perhaps some benefit will come to other stakeholders and the public interest. A professional accountant is expected to make judgments that are in the public interest.

Decision makers usually have a priority of duties that they are expected to fulfill. A conflict of interest confuses and distracts the decision maker from that priority of duty, resulting in harm when legitimate expectations are not fulfilled. This situation is illustrated in Figure 3.5 where a decision maker (D) "has a conflict of interest if, and only if, (1) D is in a relationship with another (P) requiring D to exercise judgment in P's behalf and (2) D has a special interest tending to interfere with the proper exercise of judgment in that relationship."[6]

---

[6] *Conflict of Interest in the Professions*, edited by Michael Davis and Andrew Stark, Oxford University Press, 2001, Note that D and P can be a person or a corporate body. Davis uses only P.

FIGURE 3.5

CONFLICT OF INTEREST FOR A
DECISION MAKER

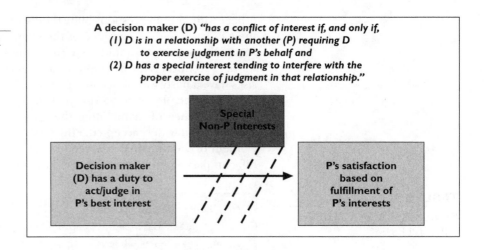

FIGURE 3.6

TYPES OF CONFLICT OF
INTEREST

A conflict of interest is *potential* if, and only if, D is not yet in a situation where he or she must (or, at least, should) make that judgment. A conflict of interest is *actual* if, and only if, D is in a situation where he or she must (or, at least should) make that judgment.[7] Sometimes the term *apparent* conflict of interest is used, but it is a misnomer because it refers to a situation where no conflict of interest exists, even though due to lack of information someone other than D would be justified in concluding (however tentatively) that D does have one.[8] Figure 3.6 illustrates these concepts.

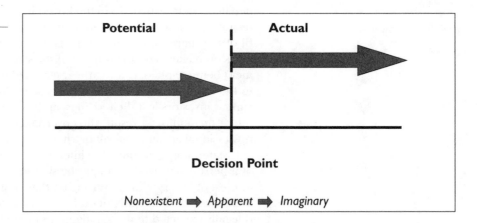

A special or conflicting interest could include "any interest, loyalty, concern, emotion or other feature of a situation tending to make D's judgment (in that situation) less reliable than it would normally be, without rendering D incompetent. Financial interests and family connections are the most common sources of conflict of interest, but love, prior statements, gratitude, and other subjective tugs on judgment can also be"[9] relevant. Table 3.4 provides a list of causes of conflicting interests.

---

[7]Ibid. 15.
[8]Ibid. 18.
[9]Ibid. 9.

TABLE 3.4

CAUSES OF CONFLICTING
INTERESTS

How might judgment be swayed ...
- Any interest, influence, loyalty, concern, emotion, or other feature tending to make judgment less reliable than normal

Self-interest ...
- Bribes, kickbacks — payments or property to decider, family, designees
- Gifts, free travel, favors
- Special advantages — nonmarket discounts on goods
- Special treatment — flattery, social involvement
- Dealings with family, relatives, or relations

Fraud ...
- Misappropriation of funds or property
- Cheating on expense accounts
- Falsifying documents
- Stealing cash, assets, or resources
- Falsifying results to obtain bonuses, merit pay, or promotion

Misunderstanding ...
- Confused signals or incentives
- Boss/everybody's doing it
- Cultural differences

Slippery Slope ...
- Where a small favor leads to ever larger demands

Concern over a conflict of interest stems from:

- The fact that people who are relying upon D's decision may be harmed if D does not respond or compensate.
- If D knows or should have known, but does not tell P, then D is perpetrating a deception.
- If D's judgment will be less reliable than it ordinarily is.

A conflict of interest is more than just bias, which can be measured for and adjusted. However, due to the unknown nature and therefore extent of the influences, *concern should be for any tendency toward bias.*[10]

Management to Avoid and Minimize Consequences

To remedy the concerns over a conflict of interest, three general approaches should be considered: (1) avoidance, (2) disclosure to those stakeholders relying upon the decision, and (3) management of the conflict of interest so that the benefits of the judgment made outweigh the costs.

Avoidance is the preferred approach if the appearance of having a conflict of interest can be avoided as well the reality. The appearance of having a conflict can often be as harmful to the decision maker's reputation as having a real conflict because it is almost impossible to recover lost credibility and reputation without extreme effort and cost, and then only with luck. Consequently, for example, it is advisable to provide rules against giving or receiving kickbacks since it is difficult to argue later that they really didn't matter.

---

[10]Ibid. 11, 12.

Management of potential conflicts is a potentially useful approach if avoidance is not possible and the cost-benefit trade-off of management measures is favorable. The probability that reputation will be lost and the related cost must be taken into account in the trade-off analysis. The important aspects related to the management of conflicts of interest are identified in Table 3.5.

TABLE 3.5

MANAGEMENT OF
CONFLICTING INTERESTS

> ### Steps To Be Taken
> Ensure awareness through:
> - Codes of conduct and
> - Related initial and ongoing training
>
> Create a program to provide an understanding of:
> - Employer's concerns regarding conflict of interests
> - Major issues:
>   - Avoidance is preferable
>   - Slippery slope
>   - Management techniques:
>   - Annual code sign-off, confirming review and compliance
>   - Guidelines for gifts, behavior
>   - Counseling, reporting, reinforcement
>   - Chinese walls/firewalls, scrutiny

The first step in the process of managing to defend against these influences is to ensure that all employees are *aware* of their existence and consequences. This can be done through codes of conduct and related training. One of the items that should be covered in the training is the slippery slope problem where an individual can be enticed into a relationship by a seemingly innocuous request for a small favor, then a larger one, and then find that they are told that unless they go along with a serious infraction, their past secrets will be revealed. The start of the slope is too gentle for some to notice, but the slope becomes steeper and more slippery very quickly.

The second step is to *create an understanding* of the reasons: why the employer cannot afford unmanaged conflict of interest situations; and why guidelines have been developed to prevent their occurrence, their exploration through counseling if recognized, their reporting if they have occurred, as well as penalties for their occurrence and nonreporting. Annual written confirmations of ethical behavior and adherence to the employer's code of conduct should include reference to conflicts of interest encountered by the signatory, and those identified involving others.

One set of guidelines that can prove helpful are those that specify when it may be acceptable to give or accept a gift or preferential treatment. Useful questions to ask in this regard are shown in Table 3.6. They are intended to assess whether the offering is likely to sway the independent judgment of the professional. Obviously something worth a very modest amount, perhaps under $100, that is offered to a group of people as a publicity venture is much less of a problem than a high-value item offered to one person who has considerable influence over the fortunes of the giver.

Additional reinforcement of problems and good examples through publicity will also serve to keep the awareness and understanding fresh. Compliance

TABLE 3.6

GUIDELINES FOR ACCEPTANCE
OF GIFTS OR PREFERENTIAL
TREATMENT

1. Is it nominal or substantial?
2. What is the intended purpose?
3. What are the circumstances?
4. What is the position of sensitivity of the recipient?
5. What is the accepted practice?
6. What is the firm/company policy?
7. Is it legal?

systems must be in place to provide another type of reinforcement, with appropriate penalties for significant wrongdoings.

Agency Theory, Ethics and Sears

Directors, executives, and professional accountants should appreciate that incentive systems that they use to motivate employees can provide appropriate or inappropriate reinforcement, depending on the way in which they are designed. In many ways, the stock option plans available to executives in the Enron, WorldCom, Waste Management, and Sunbeam cases were responsible for motivating them to the detriment of all stakeholders involved.

According to agency theorists, shareholders expect and hope managers, and in turn nonmanagerial employees, will behave in line with the goals set for the corporation. In their terms, the principals or shareholders hope that their agents will be motivated to act as the principals wish. Incentive systems and punishment systems are created to try to influence the agents to stay on the right path. Clearly, as the public's expectations for corporate performance now include ethical standards, the reward and punishment systems set up should also reflect ethical dimensions or shareholders will be disappointed. In fact, the corporation's strategic plans should include ethical dimensions to ensure that their agents, both inside and outside the corporation, are properly influenced and conflicts of interest are avoided. One recent case in point involves the incentive system put in place by Sears for the managers of their auto service stores. The managers' remuneration depended upon the volume of sales made by the store, but this led to the selling of services that customers didn't need to boost the managers' earnings. A national scandal erupted, and Sears apologized for creating a misleading incentive system.

Chinese Walls/Firewalls

An important system for preventing ethical malfeasance, the "Chinese wall" or "firewall" concept, deserves further comment. This practice uses the analogy of an impervious wall to describe those measures and methods that would prevent the transmission of client information from one part of an organization to another. Such firewalls or Chinese walls are not tangible in a three-dimensional sense, but refer to a multidimensional set of measures such as:

- Instructions to keep information confidential
- Instructions not to read, listen to, or act on specific types of information
- Educational programs and reinforcements by top management
- Monitoring and compliance sign-off procedures

- Scrutiny of insider or key-person trading of securities
- Physical barriers to information transmission, such as:
  - Separate computer- or physical-storage systems
  - Segregation of duties to different employees
  - Segregation of information in a different location or building, etc.
  - Different lock systems
- Appointment of a compliance officer who will monitor the effectiveness of the wall
- Disciplinary sanctions for breach of the wall

Chinese walls or firewalls have been a normal part of business and professional operations for many years. For example, when a client is involved in the preparation of a public offering of securities, those members of the offering team (lawyers, professional accountants, and underwriters) are expected not to divulge advance details of the underwriting to the other members of their respective firms, or to anyone else. The public issuance of securities, as presently known, would be impossible without the Chinese wall construct. Fortunately, even though in the final analysis a Chinese wall relies upon the integrity of the employees involved for its effectiveness, such arrangements are considered effective to protect the public interest and to safeguard the interest of current clients as well as former clients.

Forensic Experts and Evidence: The 20/60/20 Rule

The time may come when a director, executive, or professional accountant must consider whether a conflict of interest has led to serious breach of duty, a fraudulent act, or a matter that must be recovered pursuant to an insurance policy. In such instances, an investigative and forensic expert may be called upon if existing company employees would benefit from assistance. The expert will employ appropriate techniques based upon their understanding of the situation.

Many managers may believe that their associates and employees would rarely engage in unethical behavior. However, forensic experts indicate that their experience suggests that the general population can be divided into three groups:

- 20 percent would never commit a fraud.
- 60 percent would seek to commit a fraud depending on the circumstances.
- 20 percent would seek to commit a fraud.

The important questions, then, are who would commit a fraud and what are the circumstances that could come into play in the decision.

The GONE Theory:
Identifying Potentially Harmful Situations and Likely Perpetrators

Forensic experts point out that in most instances of fraud or opportunistic behavior, they can begin to identify prospective perpetrators through the use of the GONE Theory. The acronym, GONE, stands for circumstances that account for motivation of illicit behavior, where:

- G – Greed
- O – Opportunity to take advantage
- N – Need for whatever is taken
- E – Expectation of being caught is low

The experts point out that identifying employees who have or exhibit these characteristics can head off problems if adequate precautions are taken. These would include additional review and diligence on the part of supervisors, transfer to less vulnerable areas, signaling that extra review or audit procedures were in place, etc. For example, if an employee exhibited signs of a lifestyle well beyond his or her means, then extra scrutiny might be warranted.

Duty Depends Upon a Person's Role

While this analysis of conflict of interests has focused on the individual, it should be noted that the elements are similar for groups of individuals within a corporation, organization, or profession. But either as individuals or groups of individuals, it is often the roles taken on, and therefore the duties assumed based upon the expectations of those relying on the actions to be taken, that define the nature of conflicts of interest. For example, it is unlikely that a professional accountant auditing or judging financial statements can audit objectively her or his own work without bias, or maintain objectivity if asked to assume an advocacy role by a client. In order to ensure sufficient objectivity to maintain their duty to serve the public interest, professional accountants have developed standards designed to ensure independence.[11] These will be discussed later in the next chapter.

Corporate Governance and Accountability

DEVELOPING, IMPLEMENTING, AND MANAGING AN ETHICS CULTURE

Directors, owners, and senior management are realizing that they and their employees need to understand that (1) their organizations would be wise to consider the interests of stakeholders, not just shareholders; and that (2) appropriate ethical values are to be considered when decisions are being made. *Because organizational, professional, and personal values provide the framework to decision making, it is vital that organizations create an environment or culture where appropriate values are created, understood, fostered, committed to and used by all concerned.* This cannot be reliably achieved by simply leaving ethics solely to the judgment of individuals in a workforce of divergent experiences and backgrounds to work out by trial and error. Nor can it be achieved simply by sending a letter urging employees to be on their best behavior, or by just publishing a code of conduct. In order to ensure commitment to the ethical principles or values considered appropriate for the organization, it must be evident to the members of the organization that top management is fully supportive

---

[11]See for example the International Federation of Accountants (IFAC) Code of Ethics for Professional Accountants, November 2001, (see *http://brooks.swlearning.com*).

and that such support is evident throughout the organization's governance systems.

A most important aspect of an ethics program designed to ensure an effective understanding and commitment to the organization's ethical principles is the choice of program orientation. According to researchers, there are five orientations for the design and operation of ethics programs. These are described in Table 3.7.

TABLE 3.7

ETHICS PROGRAM
ORIENTATION TYPES

ORIENTATION	PRIMARY FOCUS
Compliance-based	Preventing, detecting, and punishing violations of the law
Integrity or values-based	Defines organizational values and encourages employee commitment
Satisfaction of external stakeholders	Improvement of image and relationships with external stakeholders (customers, the community, suppliers)
Protect top management from blame	"CYA" or cover your ___
Combinations of the above	Values- and compliance-based, for example

SOURCES: Treviño, Weaver, Gibson, and Toffler, 1999, 135–139; Paine, 1994, 111; Badaracco & Webb, 1995, 15.

The researchers went on to evaluate the effectiveness of the impact of these orientations by administering over 10,000 surveys to randomly selected employees in six large American companies from a variety of industries. The dimensions upon which the impact was evaluated were:

1. Unethical/illegal behavior
2. Employee awareness of ethical issues that arise at work
3. Looking for ethics/compliance advice within the company
4. Delivering bad news to management
5. Ethics/compliance violations are reported in the organization
6. Better decision making in the company because of the ethics/compliance program
7. Employee commitment to the organization

According to their research, which confirms the author's experience gained when consulting organizations on the design of their ethics programs, *the most important factor in encouraging employee observance is that the employees perceive that the ethics program is values-based.* This produced significantly more positive outcomes on all seven dimensions. Compliance and external orientations also produced favorable outcomes on the seven dimensions, but not as positive as for the values-based approach. The external orientation outcomes were less than the compliance-based approach. CYA was considered a "harmful" approach, as it resulted in negative outcomes across all dimensions. It was suggested that combined approaches could be effective, such as if a values orientation were "backed up with accountability systems and discipline for violators" where "values can include concern for customers, suppliers, and the community as well as shareholders and internal stakeholders such as employees" (Treviño et al., 1999, 139).

The study also provides some useful insights into the important aspects of an ethical culture. These are included in Table 3.8.

TABLE 3.8

ETHICAL CULTURE:
IMPORTANT ASPECTS

An ethical culture combines formal and informal elements to guide employee thought and action, including:

- Ethical leadership by executives and supervisors*
- Reward systems to incorporate ethical considerations*
- Perceived fairness, fair treatment of employees*
- Open discussion of ethics in the organization*
- Authority structure that emphasizes an employee's accountability and responsibility to question his or her own actions, and an obligation to question authority when something seems wrong*
- Organizational focus that communicates care for employees and the community, rather than self-interest
- Official policies and procedures (code of ethics, practice, conduct)
- Supporting offices (e.g., ethics officer, ombudsperson)
- Supporting structures (e.g., telephone hotline, whistle-blower protection, code sign-off, training, etc.)

* Most influential factors as found by Treviño et al.

http://brooks.swlearning.com

The findings presented in Table 3.8 can be particularly useful for a company that is assessing what it might do to institute a new ethics program or improve its current ethical culture. It would appear that there is quite a lot that could still be accomplished in the development of ethical cultures based upon the status of indicators shown in Table 3.9 recommended for a healthy corporate culture. Table 3.9 has been prepared from U.S. *Fortune 1000* data published in a study by Weaver, Treviño, and Cochran (1999a) and from Canadian large-firm data published as part of the *1999 KPMG Business Ethics Survey: Managing for Ethical Practice,* which is available in full on the KPMG website.

The figures in Table 3.9 show that while most companies have embraced the concept of written ethical guidance, they have fallen far short of embracing many of the supportive mechanisms that are important to the development and maintenance of a healthy ethical culture. Among the omissions of most concern are lack of CEO involvement, lack of training, failure to renew employee commitment to the code annually, and the lack of communications and meetings dealing with ethics. From other sources, we find concerns raised about lack of formal program follow-through; inappropriate placement of the ethics function within the legal department, which focuses on compliance rather than on employee and other stakeholder welfare; employing "quick fix" approaches rather than building a long-term solution; training by people who don't have a commitment to live with the result—top management should be more prominent; and telephone answering by distant outsiders who callers have difficulty believing that the company cares and is taking their calls seriously (Treviño et al., 1999).

TABLE 3.9

ETHICS PROGRAM ELEMENTS
EMPLOYED IN NORTH AMERICA

RESPONSE RATE	U.S. USAGE % IN 1995 25.7% OF 990	CANADIAN USAGE % IN 1998 16.6% OF 1225
Formal Documents	98	85
Codes/mission statements	78	68
Values and principles		83
Guidelines		48
Policy manuals	67	45
Other (speeches, letters, memos, etc.)	22	30
Ethics Policy: Dissemination to 80 percent of		
High-level executives	100	
Middle managers and professionals	98	
Lower-level management/superv. staff	87	
Nonsupervisory staff	75	
Internally/externally		93/36
Acknowledgement of Receipt/Obedience		
At least once in an employee's career	90/85	60
Annually	45/51	
Ethics Personnel and Officers		
Report to: CEO/exec. vice president	18/54	
Single officer assigned responsibility	54	40
Within: Legal dept.	33	
Ethics/compliance	32	
Audit	10	
Human resources	9	
General admin.	10	
Specific ethics office or dept.	30	
Ethics office staff: at most 1 staff	55	
Support system, incl. hotline		47
Whistle-blower Protection (up from 22 percent in 1997)		38
External Assessment of Ethical Performance	50 approx.	
Assessment of Program: yes/one year/external		32/41/32
Standard Procedures for Dealing with Problems	70	
Telephone Reporting	51	
Internal department answers	34	
Called...hotline/...helpline (value-oriented)	57/19	
CEO Involvement		
Communications per year 0/1–2/2+	20/46/34	
Meetings per year 0/1/2+	32/30/38	
Communications—once per Year or Less	75 approx.	
Training (approx.)		27
Never/at hiring/every few years/annually	28/12/38/19	

In addition, when the current evidence about the scope and orientation of ethics programs is compared to what they could be as control systems, they were found to be suboptimal. According to a study by Weaver, Treviño, and Cochran (1999b), formal ethics programs usually include the dimensions listed in Table 3.10.

TABLE 3.10

ETHICS PROGRAMS' USUAL DIMENSIONS

1. Formal ethics codes
2. Ethics committees developing policies, evaluating actions, investigating and adjudicating policy violations
3. Ethics communications systems
4. Ethics officers or ombudspersons coordinating policies, providing education, or investigating allegations
5. Ethics training programs to raise awareness and help employees respond to ethical problems
6. Disciplinary processes for unethical behavior

Weaver et al. reuse the surveys received in their previously reported study to examine the motivation of top management for their commitment to ethics and how this affects the scope and orientation of ethics programs of the *Fortune 500* companies. They argue that the degree to which a values or a compliance orientation characterizes an ethics program's mode of control can be seen in the program's emphases on encouraging shared values, supporting employee aspirations, communicating values, and building trust and confidence. They conclude that the dominant influence of the U.S. Sentencing Guidelines has been to orient top management commitment and corporate ethics programs toward compliance rather than integrity or values. This orientation—according to the earlier Treviño et al. study—will not provide the best adherence to desired ethics values. Hopefully, over time, top management will learn that a values orientation that involves encouraging shared values, supporting employee aspirations, communicating values, and building trust and confidence will produce significant benefits, and ethics programs will move in that direction.

It is worth noting that current research suggests that the values-oriented ethics program can have benefits other than those previously described. In particular, building trust within an organization can have favorable impacts on employees' willingness to share information and ideas, thereby enhancing the innovation quotient of the enterprise and its ability to adapt and take advantage of its opportunities. This process is called *ethical renewal*. Properly cultivated trust can also create commitment to organizational goals and enhance productivity, all of which will raise the ability of the enterprise to profit and compete. This can all be fostered with appropriate attention in the design of the code of conduct (Brooks, 2000). Others are also working on trust as is evidenced by entire special volumes of journals such as *Business Ethics Quarterly*, Vol. 8, No. 2, April 1998; and *Academy of Management Review*, Vol. 23, Issue 3, July 1998.

The discussion to this point has provided an understanding of why organizations—be they corporations, not-for-profit organizations, or professional firms—should develop an ethical culture, what shape that culture should take, and why. Table 3.11 puts these ideas together in an orderly sequence, with additional ideas found in later chapters that a manager, ethics officer, or professional accountant can use to develop and maintain an ethical corporate culture. Information obtained from the Ethics Officer Association and the Center for Business Ethics at Bentley College would be helpful in keeping abreast of current developments.

http://brooks. swlearning.com

The design and introduction of the type of system proposed is well within the capacity of professional accountants because of their exposure to the nature, purpose, and workings of internal control systems. It is not surprising that several large professional accounting firms have developed services such as the KMPG Ethics & Integrity Practice, which "focuses on managing for ethical practice—establishing effective compliance and control, developing ethical awareness within the workforce, and addressing ethical risk through a managed ethics process" (KPMG, Ethics & Integrity website, 1999). Four specific services are mentioned:

- Business Ethics Process Review (an ethics audit)
- Implementation and Integration of Ethics Process Initiatives
- Ethics and Integrity for Boards of Directors
- Ethics and Integrity Awareness and Training

http://brooks. swlearning.com

Similar practices are offered by most of the large professional accounting firms. (See the text's website.)

CORPORATE CODES OF CONDUCT

Purpose, Focus, and Orientation

According to The Conference Board,

> The foundation of most corporate ethics programs is the company code or business conduct statement. Company business ethics principles statements stress two objectives: (1) improving employee capability for making decisions that are in accord with policy and legal requirements; and (2) giving concrete expression to the company's sense of mission and its view of the duties and responsibilities that corporate citizenship entails[12]

An effective code is the embodiment of an organization's values. It represents the major organizational structure in which to implement ethical policy (see Murphy, 1988, attached as a reading) and to signal and communicate behavioral expectations and culture, as well as to provide strategic and legal positioning for the organization. It is an essential part of a modern system of internal control. Unless employees are told, in writing, how they are expected to behave, managers, executives, and directors are vulnerable to charges that they failed to provide adequate guidance to their workers. If so, the company and its officers and directors can be fined heavily, and in some jurisdictions the officers and directors can go to jail. More importantly, it has been suggested that the fines and court costs involved in ethical dilemmas are usually smaller than the lost future profit margin due to the disenchantment of customers. Whistle-blowing outside the corporation may also be prevented by effective

---

[12] *Global Corporate Ethics Practices: A Developing Consensus,* The Conference Board, New York, 1999, 16.

TABLE 3.11

DEVELOPMENT AND
MAINTENANCE OF AN ETHICAL
CORPORATE CULTURE

STEP	PURPOSE
Assign responsibility: 　Chairman or CEO 　Ethics officer 　Ethics committee	Successful initiatives usually involve: ■ top level accountability and adequate budget ■ champions, arbiters ■ monitoring, feedback, advice, and cheerleading
Ethics Audit	To understand the organization's ethical practices and its network of stakeholders and interests
Ethics risk assessment	To identify important ethics problems that could arise (see Chapter 6)
Top management support	Absolutely vital to successful adherence
Develop consensus on key ethical values	Necessary to frame policies and procedures
Develop code of conduct, ethical decision-making criteria and protocols, incl. sniff tests	Provide guidance for employees and all other stakeholders
Develop ethics program: 　Leaders involvement 　Launch 　Training 　Reinforcement policies: 　　Compliance sign-off 　　Measurements of performance 　　Include in strategic objectives and managers' objectives 　　Include in monitoring and reward structures 　　Communications programs 　　Exemplar award system 　Ethics inquiry service 　Crisis management	To successfully present and provide supporting mechanisms for the guidance process Information, investigation and whistle-blower protection To ensure that ethics are part of survival reactions
Establish a review mechanism	

ethical codes because they can help to create an ethical culture in which employees believe doing what is right is expected and bringing forward concerns over unethical behavior will not result in ethical martyrdom.

Codes can be drafted to fulfill different rationales and to provide different depths of coverage. Table 3.12 describes four common levels of coverage.

TABLE 3.12

DEPTHS OF CODE COVERAGE

Credo	Inspirational short statement on key values
Code of Ethics	Deals with ethics principles (short)
Code of Conduct	Deals with principles plus additional examples, etc.
Code of Practice	Detailed rules of practice

The rationales[13] for developing codes that were identified by The Conference Board in its 1999 survey of global ethics practices included:

1. *Instrumental* — to make employees aware that "employee adherence to the company's ethical principles is critical to bottom-line success"

2. *Compliance* — to provide a "statement of do's and don'ts to govern employee conduct"

3. *Stakeholder Commitment* — to offer a discussion of what is expected behavior in stakeholder relationships

4. *Values/Mission* — to establish "certain ethics principles, modes of behavior, and habits of mind as essential to what is means to be an employee or representative of the company" (see Johnson & Johnson credo in the reading by Murphy)

5. *None or a composite* of the above

The Conference Board found that the use of these rationales varied depending on the country or region involved. In the United States, the dominant "instrumental" choice reflects the pressures from stakeholders and the legalistic environment faced in which potentially heavy sanctions have been created for misdeeds due to the advent of the U.S. Foreign Corrupt Practices Act and the U.S. Sentencing Guidelines. Elsewhere, except in Latin America, the values/mission approach was most popular. The choices of rationale, by region, are noted in Table 3.13.

The research findings of Weaver et al. (1999b), Treviño et al. (1999), and others noted earlier in the chapter indicate that a corporate code with an integrity or values orientation will be more effective in engendering adherence to desired ethical standards than other alternatives. Most successful will be a code that is a combination in which the focus is on the important values that the corporation wants to apply in its stakeholder relationships, reinforced by sanctions inherent in the compliance approach. Such a composite orientation code would encourage shared values, support employee aspirations, communicate values, and build trust and confidence, while indicating that processes were in place to monitor and judge ethical performance. The composite orientation

---

[13]Ibid., 24–27.

TABLE 3.13

DOMINANT RATIONALES FOR
CODES BY REGION[14]

	UNITED STATES	CANADA	EUROPE	LATIN AMERICA	JAPAN
Instrumental	64%	30%	-	50%	17%
Stakeholder	5	10	30	-	17
Legal Compliance	14	-	-	25	33
Values/Mission	14	40	60	25	33
None	2	20	10	-	-
N = 72					

code would also provide motivation to employees in all six stages of Kohlberg's model of moral reasoning (see Table 4.3).

The form and nature in which guidance is given and action expected can also limit or foster optimal motivation for moral reasoning. Four alternatives are possible for the nature of the guidance provided. The alternative chosen will provide a signal to employees about the way the organization thinks about its control structure, ranging from an autocratic, imposed control structure on one end of the spectrum to self-imposed control on the other. Table 3.14 identifies the four alternatives and the nature of control they signal.

TABLE 3.14

CODE GUIDANCE
ALTERNATIVES AND THE
CONTROL/MOTIVATION
SIGNALED

GUIDANCE PROVIDED	CONTROL/MOTIVATION SIGNALED
Obey these rules	Imposed Control
Seek advice before acting	
Act on your best judgment, but disclose what you have done	
Guiding principles that indicate "this is what we are and what we stand for"	Self-control

SOURCES: Clarkson & Deck, 1992, Clarkson, Deck & Leblanc, 1997.

In view of the findings of Maslow (1954) and McGregor (1960), and subsequently others who argued that an autocratic management style was less effective than a democratic or participative approach, it is likely that using only imposed control techniques could be similarly suboptimal. Maslow argued that autocratic

---

[14]Ibid., 28.

management techniques involved influence attempts directed at the lower level of his hierarchy of human needs (physiological, safety), whereas a democratic or participative approach was directed at higher-level needs (affiliation, esteem, and self-actualization) and therefore was more likely to provide a sustainable and more engaging level of motivation. In a world that has since moved toward employee empowerment rather than imposed control (Simons, 1995), a code that employs only imposed control is likely to be less effective than one that encourages self-control. A code that successfully encourages self-control would appeal to individuals in all of Kohlberg's six stages of moral reasoning, whereas the imposed control code would motivate only for the lower four stages. In keeping with the reasoning in favor of a composite-oriented, values-based, and compliance-based code, consulting experience has shown that the most successful codes encourage self-control or empowerment, with absolute rules being introduced where necessary. These codes usually provide a set of principles with explanations or rationales being given for each. These principles and their rationales are to be used by employees to reason how to deal with the decisions they face, or to determine whom to contact if they need counsel.

Code Content and Scope

http://brooks.
swlearning.com

Numerous readings are available that outline the topics that are covered in different codes, such as these by Clarkson & Deck (1992), White & Montgomery (1980), Mathews (1987), Berenbeim (1987), and Brooks (1989). Examples of different codes are available on the websites of major corporations.

The choice of orientation of the code and its topics depends somewhat on the scope of the code. Is the code intended to provide guidance to the company's own employees, its suppliers and vendors, and/or its joint venture partners? Geographic locale, union contracts, legal restrictions, competitive practices, and the degree of ownership and/or partner support inherent in the scope decision are critical to the orientation and choice of topics to be included. If a company cannot be comfortable about the guidance to be given, then it should consider whether the arrangement is too high a risk to be undertaken. For example, to do business with a partner or in a repressive regime that does not respect human rights, should give rise to consideration of non-involvement.

In the late 1990s, Nike's suppliers used sweatshop and child labor to produce low-cost products, but this triggered boycotts and necessitated the development of monitoring and reporting mechanisms. Recently, stakeholder activists have become much more aggressive in making companies accountable for the actions of suppliers and joint ventures. Three organizations are

http://brooks.
swlearning.com

leading the development of supplier/workplace standards and codes of conduct: Social Accountability International (SAI) and Fair Labor Association (FLA), Maquila Solidarity, and the International Labor Office (ILO). SAI has developed the SA 8000, which is a standard designed to improve working conditions globally, and it is engaged in the training of auditors for the certification of companies adhering to SA 8000. It is modeled after the ISO standards.

Table 3.15 presents a representative list of topics a company might consider including in its codes for its employees, suppliers, and joint ventures.

TABLE 3.15

SUBJECTS FOUND IN CODES

Ethical principles—honesty, fairness, compassion, integrity, predictability, responsibility

Respect for stakeholder rights, and duties owed to each stakeholder

Vision, mission, and key policies tied into the above

Ethical decision-making frameworks, sniff tests, rules of thumb, and guidance on making trade-offs between competing objectives

When to seek counsel, and whom to seek it from

Specific topics found in over 5 percent of employee, supplier, and joint venture codes:

- Bribery/improper payments or influences
- Conflict of interest
- Security of proprietary information
- Receiving gifts
- Discrimination/equal opportunity
- Giving gifts
- Environmental protection
- Sexual harassment
- Antitrust
- Workplace safety
- Political activities
- Community relations
- Confidentiality of personal information
- Human rights
- Employee privacy
- Whistle-blowing and protection programs
- Substance abuse
- Nepotism
- Child labor

SOURCE: The Conference Board Research Report, *Global Corporate Ethics Practices*, 1999, 29.

Each company should undertake a review of its code when issues and risks emerge that require adjustment of the coverage. For example, codes have been modified in reaction to the external shocks identified in Table 3.16.

TABLE 3.16

EXTERNAL SHOCKS AND INFLUENCES TRIGGERING CODE MODIFICATION

Antibribery legislation—U.S. Foreign Corrupt Practices Act of 1977
  This act provided an early motivation for codes
U.S. Sentencing Guidelines of 1991
  Brought provision for "due diligence" defense
Environmental responsibility:
  Acid rain, air pollution, ozone depletion
    (U.N. Brundtland Commission Report of 1987)
  New environmental protection statutes
  Exxon Valdez oil tanker spill triggers Valdez (now CERES) Principles
Fair treatment for:
  Employees:
    Feminism: sexual harassment, equal opportunity for pay and promotion
    Minorities: discrimination*
    Health, safety, and well-being
      Supplier employees—no sweat shop or child labor
    Drug problems—privacy vs. safety
    Whistle-blowers**
  Customers—buyer beware slowly becomes seller beware:
    Health & safety concerns—auto recalls (see Ford/Firestone case)
    Ethical consumerism, quality
  Shareholders:
    Misuse of inside information
    Conflict of interests
    Mandate and operations are ethical—Enron's banks engage in
      transactions without economic substance, designed to mislead

* See Texaco's Jelly Bean case in Chapter 6.
** See GE case described in reading by Andrew Singer in Chapter 1.

Looking ahead, it is likely that codes will be modified to encompass the following:

http://brooks.swlearning.com

- New antibribery statutes enacted in early 1999 by about thirty countries in the OECD who have responded to the call of Transparency International for standards that will outlaw bribery of foreign officials and allow cross-border investigation and litigation by competitors (see the text's website).
- Adherence to company principles by suppliers, particularly in foreign operations with respect to child labor, fair wages, no forced labor, etc.
- Integrity or values orientation
- Self-control instead of only imposed control

http://brooks.
swlearning.com

According to page 6 of the 1999 KPMG Business Ethics Survey (see the text's website), over 50 percent of Canadian respondents indicated the following to be issues of greater concern over the next three to five years, so their treatment in codes is likely to be modified during that period:

- Security of information
- Environmental management and performance
- Governance principles—clarification of accountability to the board of directors and stakeholders, transparency, risk management for regular and ethics risks
- Ethicality of objectives and competitive practices
- Sexual harassment

These modifications will also be guided by the application of measures of the effectiveness of codes. Codes can be scored or reviewed for comprehensiveness of coverage and for the nature of control signaled. Other measures have been identified, such as surveys of employee awareness and understanding of key aspects covered in the code and in training programs, as well as their ability to apply these to ethical dilemmas proposed.

Benchmarking of codes is done by many consultants. Company employees can also do so by comparing their code against the subjects that information services report upon or that are included in the Global Reporting Initiative (GRI).

Helpful advice on the preparation of codes can be obtained from several organizations including the following:

http://brooks.
swlearning.com

- Institute of Business Ethics (IBE)
- Centre for Applied Ethics, University of British Columbia

Effective Implementation

Because a code of conduct is critical to organizational success, it is important to ensure that a code is both effectively drafted *and implemented*. A properly functioning code is essential to:

- The development and maintenance of an ethical corporate culture
- An effective internal control system
- A "due diligence defense" for directors and officers
- Effectively empower employees to make ethical decisions
- Send proper signals to external stakeholders

In order to avoid implementation problems, the following issues should be kept in mind. First, *top management must endorse and support the code* and be seen to act in accord with it, or it will only be given lip service by management and workers. It is critical that management "walk the talk" or the entire program will be a waste of time and money.

The orientation, tone, and content of the code must be such that *general principles are favored instead of only specific rules*, or else employees will find the code oppressive and hard to interpret, and *background reasons must be given* to permit understanding sufficient for useful interpretation when specifics are not available. Experience has shown that codes designed as extensive rulebooks are rarely useful because they are too difficult to consult. If the underlying reason for a specific pattern of behavior is given, employees find it easier to understand and they buy-in, rather than fight the code or dismiss it. Getting the buy-in is essential.

Guidance should be provided for trade-offs between short-term profit and social objectives. If employees believe profit is to be earned at all costs, then unethical behavior based on short-term thinking can get the company into trouble.

A complete "due diligence" defense should be in place for environmental matters, including the items noted in Table 3.17.

TABLE 3.17

ESSENTIAL FEATURES TO DEMONSTRATE A DUE DILIGENCE DEFENSE IN RESPECT TO ENVIRONMENTAL MATTERS

1. A written environmental policy, made known to appropriate employees
2. Operating practices that guard against environmental malfeasance, including contingency plans to cover mishaps to ensure full-scale, timely cleanup
3. Employees briefed on their duties and responsibilities under the policy, as well as their potential personal liability and the liability of others
4. Employees informed of legal requirements, including notice to government, complete with a contact list
5. A person who is primarily responsible for environmental matters and monitoring compliance
6. Consideration of an environmental audit or consultation with an expert to start the protection process and monitor progress
7. Monitoring of pollution control systems and reporting of mishaps on a timely basis
8. Regular review of reports on compliance, potential problems, environmental charges, conviction, and employee training
9. Management that keeps abreast of new legislation, makes an internal review of compliance and advises directors of the results, and allocates a real and satisfactory budget to achieve these features

Employees should be empowered to make ethical decisions. This should involve setting up *decision protocols* that will require employees to use and be able to defend their decisions against a set of criteria or questions that are outlined further in Chapter 4. Part of the decision process should involve the use of *sniff tests*—quick, simple questions that will alert the decision maker when to undertake an in-depth ethical analysis or to seek counsel. When in doubt over the proper conduct, *employees should be encouraged to seek counsel.* Rather than have them act inappropriately, or waste time needlessly, a company should encourage employees to consult their superior, use a hotline, or consult an ethics officer.

A *fair and confidential hearing process should be assured* or whistle-blowers will not come forward. They don't want to risk paying the price for snitching, even though it is in the best interests of the company. Nor do they want a person accused to be dealt with in a cavalier way—they want a speedy, fair hearing process with protection for both parties. *Whistle-blowing should be legitimized,* and whistle-blowers that come forward should be protected.

Someone should be charged with the *ongoing responsibility for updating the code* so that issues can be referred as they come up. Otherwise, many issues will be lost in the pressures of day-to-day activity or because people won't know where to send their suggestions.

The Code should be distributed to all employees so that none will be able to claim they were not told how to behave. It is surprising that many companies believe their line workers don't have responsibility for environmental acts, for actions toward fellow workers, etc. Not only do excellent suggestions come from the plant, but bad actions are noticed, and support for the company's general activities is enhanced by including these employees.

Training in support of the code is essential. Training should focus on awareness of issues, interpretation of the code in accord with top management wishes, approaches to ethical analysis to enable decisions beyond the code, realistic cases for discussion, and legitimizing the discussion of ethical issues and of whistle-blowing. Codes are written by committees who spend long hours over each paragraph, so how is each employee supposed to know all the thought that went into its construction just by quickly reading the passage? Training is essential to help understand what is meant, and how the code applies to new problems.

Reinforcement of and compliance with the code should be furthered by mechanisms of encouragement, monitoring, and facilitation of the reporting of wrongdoing. These issues should not be left to chance, otherwise the organization might miss an opportunity to head off a disaster or to accomplish an ethical performance objective. These methods are summarized in Table 3.18.

TABLE 3.18

MECHANISMS FOR COMPLIANCE
ENCOURAGEMENT
MONITORING, AND REPORTING
WRONGDOING

Compliance encouragement
>   Awards, bonuses
>   Inclusion in performance reviews, remuneration decisions, and promotion
>   Reprimands, suspension, demotion, fines, dismissal

Monitoring
>   Ethics audit or internal audit procedures
>   Reviews by legal department
>   Annual sign-off by all or some employees
>   Employee surveys

Facilitation of reporting of wrongdoing
>   Assurance of a fair hearing process
>   Protection: absolute confidentiality, whistle-blower protection plan
>   Counseling/information: ombudsperson program, hotline, human resources
>   Committee oversight assured: ethics committee of board, audit committee

Reinforcement of the code should be undertaken through measurement of the code's effectiveness; reporting of ethical performance for management purposes; featuring ethical performance in company publications; and ensuring that other company policies are supportive, including a linkage with the remuneration systems. If you can't measure performance (techniques are discussed in Chapters 4 and 5), it is very hard to manage it. Reporting performance has the impact of producing a scorecard that people are induced to improve for the next report. Publicizing good results can have a salutary effect on subsequent performance as well, and including that performance in the corporation's reward systems will go a long way to underscore how important ethical issues are to top management.

To have an effective corporate culture, not only do codes need constant upgrading under the watchful eye of an ethics officer, but constant attention must also be given to improving training programs, measures and reports of performance, and compliance and whistle-blowing mechanisms. In addition, it is essential to have a formal external or internal review of the corporation's culture, code, and other mechanisms on a periodic basis. This is often referred to as an ethics audit. Although it may be undertaken by the internal audit staff or a team of budding managers, such as in the Dow Corning case at the end of the chapter, an outside consulting service can provide useful feedback.

Finally, it should be understood that it is unlikely that employees will see the merit of ethical behavior in regard to one area of the company's operations if they believe management wants or is prepared to tolerate questionable behavior in other areas. Whistle-blowers will not come forward, for example, unless there is a feeling of trust that they and the parties they accuse will be dealt with fairly and confidentially. Consequently, the development of a broadly based ethical culture within the company is an essential precursor for an effective code of conduct, and vice versa.

PUBLIC ACCOUNTABILITY BENCHMARKS

One of the recent developments that a board of directors needs to consider when developing the values, policies, and principles that undergird their corporation's culture and the actions of their employees is the recent surge in scrutiny and public accountability. Never before has there been such interest in what a corporation is doing, and how it is doing it.

http://brooks.
swlearning.com

In the United States, Canada, and the United Kingdom rating services exist that examine and score corporate governance systems and performance against competitors and external benchmarks. New visibility is being given U.S., U.K., and Canadian companies through social rating services linked to the London Stock Exchange FTSE4Good service. New standards for social performance and disclosure are emerging that will provide comparisons that corporations will watch and build into their mechanisms, performance assessments, and public disclosures. It is doubtful that corporations will be regarded as responsible corporate citizens if their operations are seen not to compare well based on these new comparators. Therefore, at the very least, corporations should maintain a watching brief over developments identified in Table 3.19.

Conclusion

In an era of increasing scrutiny, where stakeholders without legal claim can influence the achievement of corporate objectives profoundly, it is very much in the interest of shareholders, directors, and executives that their company's

TABLE 3.19

EMERGING PUBLIC
ACCOUNTABILITY STANDARDS
AND INITIATIVES

http://brooks.
swlearning.com

GRI	Global Reporting Initiative
	A framework for economic, social, and environmental reporting.
AA1000	AccountAbility
	An assurance standard designed to provide assurance on the quality of an organization's public reporting and the quality of its underlying systems and processes.
FTSE4Good	
	FTSE4Good is an index made up of companies judged acceptable using an objective global standard for socially responsible investment. The FTSE4Good Selection Criteria cover 3 areas:
	- Working towards environmental sustainability
	- Developing positive relationships with stakeholders
	- Upholding and supporting universal human rights
Domini 400 Social index	
	400 predominantly U.S. corporations are ethically screened on 11 criteria and included in the index for use by ethical investors.
The Jantzi Social Index	
	Similar to the Domini and FTS4Good indices, 400 Canadian companies that are socially and environmentally screened.
SA 8000	Social Accountability International (SAI)
	SAI is developing the SA 8000 standard to provide guidance with regard to workplace conduct and specifically with regard to sweatshops. Auditors are also trained.

See the text's website for links to these resources.

governance system provides appropriate guidance and accountability. Only in this way can directors show due diligence in the management of the company's business and ethics risks.

Directors must ensure that an effective ethical culture prevails in their company. This requires the development of a code of conduct and the essential means of creating an awareness of appropriate behavior, reinforcing that behavior, and making sure that the underlying values are embedded in corporate strategy and operations. The company's positions on conflicts of interest, sexual harassment, and similar topics need to be worked out in advance, with watchful updating to keep the company's culture abreast of current expectations.

If directors are able to recognize and prepare their company for the new era of stakeholder accountability through an effective, ethical governance system, not only will they reduce risks, but they will also produce a competitive advantage with customers, employees, partners, environmentalists, and other stakeholders—which will surely be attractive to shareholders.

QUESTIONS FOR DISCUSSION

1. What is the most important contribution of a corporate code of conduct?

2. Are one or more of the fundamental principles found in codes of conduct more important than the rest? Why?

3. Why should codes focus on principles rather than on specific detailed rules?

4. How can a corporation integrate ethical behavior into their reward and remuneration schemes?

5. What is the role of an ethical culture and who is responsible for it?

6. How could you monitor compliance with a code of conduct in a corporation?

7. Descriptive commentary about corporate social performance is sometimes included in annual reports. Is this indicative of good performance, or is it just window dressing? How can the credibility of such commentary be enhanced?

8. Should professional accountants push for the development of a comprehensive framework for the reporting of corporate social performance? Why?

9. Do professional accountants have the expertise to audit corporate social performance reports?

CASES

■ *Ford/Firestone Tire Recall* presents how two companies, with a history of earlier recalls, failed to learn from them, or use what they learned. Information was available, but not used. Risks were not assessed properly, nor were crises effectively dealt with. The tension between doing what is right to maintain the confidence of consumers and following advice to minimize legal liability is explored.

■ *Conflicts of Interest on Wall Street* captures New York's Attorney General Elliot Spitzer's challenge of the traditional conflicted ways that brokers have been doing business on Wall Street. While purporting to act for their investing clients, they have been profiting by misleading investors with over-hyped investment analyses.

■ *RT Capital* had a manager of several mutual funds who engaged in "high closing" to manipulate the end-of-period closing prices for stocks held in his funds in order to overstate his performance and attract more investors to his funds. Because it was only temporary, some observers couldn't see the harm involved.

■ *Bankers Trust: Learning from Derivatives* is the story of how the competitive culture of an enterprise got out of control and affected the company's clients, personnel, and fortunes.

■ *Barings Bank: Rogue Trader* reveals why Barings is no longer the oldest family-owned bank in Britain. Was it the fault of a rogue trader in derivatives, or was it that the corporate culture sabotaged a greedy management?

■ *Philip Services Corp....Into the Dumper* is about what was the largest waste management/metals recycler in the world in late 1997. Shares that traded as high as $17.90 were worth about $0.20 each on November 24, 1998. How did this happen? Who is to blame? Could things have been different?

■ *Dow Corning Silicone Breast Implants* illustrates the pitfalls of a company with an excellent code and a world-class, follow-up monitoring procedure—yet they still had problems with effectiveness.

■ *Playing God* reveals the dilemma of Trish Ohling, who needs to choose a technique for a capital budgeting analysis. What basic ethical values should guide her?

REFERENCES

1999 KPMG Business Ethics Survey: Managing Ethical Practice, KPMG Ethics & Integrity Services, (see *http://brooks.swlearning.com*), March 1999.

Badaracco, J. L., and Webb, A. P., "Business Ethics: A View from the Trenches," *California Management Review*, Vol. 37, Issue 2, Winter 1995, 8–28.

Berenbeim, R. E., *Corporate Ethics*, a Report of The Conference Board, Inc., New York, 1987.

Brooks, L. J., "Ethical Codes of Conduct: Deficient in Guidance for the Canadian Accounting Profession," *Journal of Business Ethics*, Vol. 8, No. 5, May 1989, 325–336.

_____, "A Survey on the Effectiveness/Compliance of Corporate Codes of Conduct in Canada," Unpublished manuscript, 1990.

_____, "No more trial and error: It's time we moved ethics out of the clouds and into the classroom," *CAmagazine*, March 1993, 43–45.

_____, "Codes of Conduct: Trust, Innovation, Commitment and Productivity: A Strategic-Cultural Perspective," *Global Outlook: An International Journal of Business, Economics, and Social Policy*, Vol. 12, No. 2, 2000, 1–11.

Brooks, L. J., and Fortunato, V., "Discipline at the Institute of Chartered Accountants of Ontario", *CAmagazine*, May 1991, 40–43.

Centre for Applied Ethics, University of British Columbia, (see *http://brooks.swlearning.com*).

Clarkson, Max B. E., and Deck, M., "Applying the Stakeholder Management Model to the Analysis and Evaluation of Corporate Codes," Clarkson Centre for Business Ethics, University of Toronto, 1992.

_____, "Towards CSR₄: Defining Economic and Moral Responsibilities," Unpublished manuscript, November 1989.

Clarkson, Max, Deck, M., and Leblanc, R., *Codes of Ethics, Practice and Conduct*, The Society of Management Accountants of Canada, 1997. An excellent practical guide that incorporates part of the material in Clarkson & Deck, 1992.

Conflict of Interest in the Professions, edited by Michael Davis and Andrew Stark, Oxford University Press, 2001.

Corporate Ethics Monitor, a bi-monthly publication published by EthicScan Canada, Toronto, Canada.

Council on Economic Priorities, *SA8000: Guideline for Social Accountability*, New York, updated continuously, (see *http://brooks.swlearning.com*).

Enterprise Risk Management: Trends and Emerging Practices, The Institute of Internal Auditors Research Foundation, 2001.

Global Corporate Ethics Practices: A Developing Consensus, The Conference Board, New York, 1999.

Guidance for Directors—Governance Processes for Control, Canadian Institute of Chartered Accountants, Toronto, Canada, December 1995.

IFAC Code of Ethics for Professional Accountants, International Federation of Accountants, November 2001, (see *http://brooks.swlearning.com*).

Institute of Business Ethics (IBE), (see *http://brooks.swlearning.com*).

Managing Risk in the New Economy, AICPA & CICA, 2001.

Maslow, A., *Motivation and Personality*, Harper and Brothers, New York, 1954.

Mathews, M. C., "Codes of Ethics: Organizational Behaviour and Misbehaviour," *Research in Corporate Social Behaviour*, JAI Press Inc., 1987, 107–130.

McGregor, D. D., *The Human Side of Enterprise*, McGraw-Hill, New York, 1960.

Paine, L. S., "Managing for Integrity," *Harvard Business Review*, March–April 1994, 106–117. Reproduced as a reading in Chapter 1.

Report of the Toronto Stock Exchange Committee on Corporate Governance in Canada, Toronto Stock Exchange, Toronto, December 1994, paragraphs 4.3 and 4.4, p. 17.

Report on The Role of The Board of Directors in the Collapse of Enron, U.S. Senate Permanent Subcommittee on Investigations, July 8, 2002, (see *http://brooks.swlearning.com*).

Simons, R. "Control in an Age of Empowerment," *Harvard Business Review*, 41, Issue 2 (1995), 131–151.

Statement of Corporate Governance, The Business Roundtable, (September 1997).

Treviño, L. K., Weaver, G., Gibson D. G., and Toffler, B. L., "Managing ethics and legal compliance: What works and what hurts," *California Management Review*, Vol. 41, Issue 2, Winter 1999, 131–151.

U.N. Brundtland Commission Report, *Our Common Future*, World Commission on Environment and Development, Oxford University Press, Oxford, 1987.

U.S. Sentencing Guidelines, United States Sentencing Commission, Washington, D.C., November 1, 1991.

Valdez (CERES) Principles, Environmental management principles created by a coalition of environmental interest groups (hence CERES), including the Sierra Club, shortly after the Exxon Valdez went aground.

Weaver, G. R., Trevino, L. K., and Cochran, P. L., "Corporate Ethics Practices in the mid-1990's: An Empirical Study of the Fortune 1000," *Journal of Business Ethics*, Vol.18, 1999, 283–294.

Weaver, G. R., Trevino, L. K., & Cochran, P. L., "Corporate Ethics Programs as Control Systems: Influences of Executive Commitment and Environmental Factors," *Academy of Management Journal*, Vol. 42, Issue 1, February 1999, 41–57.

White, B. J., and Montgomery, R., "Corporate Codes of Conduct," *California Management Review*, Winter 1980, 80–87.

Ford/Firestone Tire Recall

On August 9, 2000, 6.5 million Firestone tires were recalled in the United States.[1] 15" ATX, ATXII, and Wilderness AT tires installed on Ford Explorers were to be replaced at company cost due to evident defects, public outcry, government investigation, and earlier recalls in Venezuela, Malaysia, Thailand, Colombia, Ecuador, and Saudi Arabia. Early estimates of costs of the recall were in the range of $300 to $600 million,[2] but these did not include loss of future revenues due to loss of consumer confidence, nor costs of future litigation. Further recalls followed.[3] As of September 2001, an estimated 192 deaths and over 500 injuries had been attributed to these tires.[4]

As the prospect of having to recall faulty tires increased, Firestone and Ford had a falling out. Firestone, or Bridgestone/Firestone as it became known, alleged that the Ford Explorer suspension accounted for at least part of the problem. Ford charged that Firestone had failed to advise them of potential problems and provide their data for analysis. Ultimately, both companies were "invited" to face questioning and testify before U.S. Congress and Senate Subcommittees.

Déjà vu, All Over Again

Firestone and Ford had been in recall debacles before.

Firestone had to recall tires in 1977, 1978, and 1980. The 1978 recall was so large (14.5 million units) that it threatened the financial viability of the company. In fact, Bridgestone, a Japanese company and the No. 3 tire maker in the world, had to rescue Firestone, then the No. 2 tire maker, from financial collapse in May 1988. Consequently, although most design and operating decisions preceded the takeover, much of the decision making with regard to the recall in 2000 was under the Bridgestone/ Firestone regime. Many Firestone people, however, continued to be involved.

Ford had suffered significantly during the Pinto fires fiasco.[5] Introduced in 1970, the small Pinto would burst into flames when struck from the rear at a speed of 21 miles per hour. This was due to a design flaw that permitted the rupturing of the Pinto's gas tank. Many lawsuits persisted until the late 1970s.

Multiple failures of Ford and Firestone people—and of government regulators at the National Highway Traffic Safety Administration (NHTSA) to recognize such problems early, and to deal with them effectively—raise interesting questions, including: Why did the companies get involved in yet another recall debacle? Did the companies and the NHTSA know about the need to investigate and recall the Wilderness tires much earlier than their official investigations began? If not, why not? Did the companies deal with the recall ethically? What lessons can be learned about crisis management?

The key events of the recall are summarized in Table 1.

---

1. 14.4 million tires were produced, but at the recall date only 6.5 million were estimated to still be on the road.
2. "Ford/Firestone Tire Recall Time Line," Virginia Trial Lawyers Association.
3. Statement of Michael P. Jackson…before the Subcommittees on…U.S. House of Representatives, June 19, 2001, (see *http://brooks.swlearning.com*). Mr. Jackson advises of the recall details as follows:

- On August 9, 2000, Firestone recalled all of its ATX and ATX II tires of the P235/75R15 size manufactured since 1991. It also recalled Wilderness AT tires of that size made at its Decatur plant, for a total of 14.4 million tires.
- On May 22, 2001, Ford announced a tire replacement program that includes all other Firestone Wilderness tires on certain Ford, Mercury, and Mazda SUVs and light trucks. This replacement action totals approximately 13 million tires.

4. "Engineering Analysis Report and Initial Decision Regarding EA00-023: Firestone Wilderness AT Tires," National Highway Traffic Safety Administration (NHTSA) (see *http://brooks.swlearning.com*).

5. See the Ford Pinto case in this book for additional information.

—Continued

Continued

TABLE I

FORD/FIRESTONE TIRE RECALL
TIME LINE

November 1978: Firestone recalled 14.5 million of the Firestone 500 series tires after reports of accidents and deaths due to tread separation on steel-belted radial tires.

May 1988: Bridgestone, the world's No. 3 tire maker, acquired Firestone, the No. 2 tire maker. The takeover rescued Firestone from potential financial collapse due to the 1978 recall.

February 1989: Arvin/Calspan Tire Research Facility of Alexandria, Virginia, an independent research lab hired by Ford, measured the performance of 17 Firestone tires. The lab reported 3 belt-edge separation failures of the 17 tires tested.

March 1990: The Explorer was introduced as a 1991 model. The Explorer was redesigned to its current chassis design in 1995.

1991: Bridgestone/Firestone ATX, ATX II, and Wilderness AT tires became original equipment for the Ford Explorer (1991–2000), Ford Ranger (1991–2000), F-150 truck (1991–1994), Mercury Mountaineer (1996–2000), Mazda Navajo (1991–1994) and B-Series pickup truck (1994–2000). Eventually, over 14.4 million tires would be manufactured.

1992: Bridgestone/Firestone began investigating allegations of safety problems with its tires. Ford began receiving complaints regarding Firestone tires on its light truck models.

1994–1996: The workers at the Firestone Decatur Illinois, plant went out on strike. Firestone used replacement workers during this period to continue production.

July 1998: State Farm Insurance research analyst Sam Boyden sent an e-mail to the National Highway Transportation Safety Administration (NHTSA) reporting 21 tread separation cases involving the Firestone ATX tire. Boyden continued to send e-mails to NHTSA about subsequent Firestone tread separation accidents.

October 1998: Ford noted tread separation problems on Ford Explorers in Venezuela, and sent samples to Bridgestone/Firestone for analysis. A Ford-affiliated dealer in Saudi Arabia wrote to Ford Motor Co. complaining of problems with Firestone tires.

March 12, 1999: Ford memorandum noted that Ford and Bridgestone/Firestone executives discussed notifying U.S. safety authorities about a planned tire recall in Saudi Arabia. Ford decided to replace the tires overseas without telling federal regulators.

April 1999: NHTSA's Uniform Tire Grading Report gave Firestone ATX II and Wilderness AT tires the lowest grade on stress test temperature. The overwhelming majority of comparable tires received higher grades. It is believed that overheated tires lead to tread separation.

August 1999: Ford began replacing Firestone tires on Explorers sold in Saudi Arabia after reports of tread separation problems. Ford did not report the safety concerns, but called the replacement program a "customer notification enhancement action."

January 19, 2000: Internal documents showed Firestone executives knew about rising warranty costs due to accidents caused by the ATX, ATX II, and the Wilderness AT tires.

February 2000: Houston, Texas, TV station KHOU does a story on tread separation of Firestone tires used on Ford Explorers. The TV station gives the NHTSA 800 telephone number for consumers to report complaints. Consumers start calling in with reports of tread separations of Firestone tires.

—Continued

Continued

TABLE I CONTINUED

FORD/FIRESTONE TIRE RECALL
TIME LINE

March 6, 2000: Based on the information NHTSA received, primarily from complaints stemming from the Houston, Texas, TV story, the agency begins its Initial Evaluation (IE) of Firestone Tires.

May 2000: Ford changed Explorer's standard equipment to Goodyear tires in Venezuela while waiting for Firestone to come to a resolution regarding the tire separation problems. Ford recalled Firestone tires in Malaysia, Thailand, Colombia, and Ecuador. The entire overseas recall reached 46,912 SUVs.

May 2/8, 2000: NHTSA launched a formal investigation (PE-0020) into the tread separation cases involving the Firestone ATX and Wilderness tires.

May 10, 2000: NHTSA sends letters to Ford and Firestone requesting information in connection with PE-0020.

June 8, 2000: Ford requests that Firestone provide all information that they gave to NHTSA relating to PE-0020. This information includes the claims data that will demonstrate the high accident rate of the tires.

July 28, 2000: Ford receives Firestone's information, and begins an analysis.

August 4, 2000: Ford found a pattern in the data pointing to the 15" ATX, ATX II, and Wilderness AT tires made at the Decatur, Illinois, plant and called in the Firestone experts. They found that older tires produced late in each production year from 1994–1996 had a higher failure rate.

August 9, 2000: Bridgestone/Firestone announced a region-by-region recall of more than 6.5 million AT, ATX II, and Wilderness AT tires. Approximately 2 million Ford Explorers were named as subjects to the recall. The cost estimate for the recall ranged from $300 to $600 million. The hot weather regions were scheduled for tire replacement first, with other regions to follow. NHTSA reports that Firestone tire separations were responsible for 46 deaths.

August 10, 2000: Plaintiff attorneys involved with Firestone litigation over the past decade note they know of 107 related tire cases, with 90 of those having a direct link to the recalled tires.

August 10, 2000: Ford claimed it became aware of the tire separation problem one year ago, from anecdotal reports from Saudi Arabia.

August 16, 2000: NHTSA increased the number of deaths connected to the Firestone tread separations to 62.

September 1, 2000: NHTSA announced another 24 Firestone tire models showed rates of tread separation exceeding those of the recalled tires. NHTSA also increased the estimate of deaths attributed to Firestone tires from 62 to 88. Venezuelan authorities report that at least 47 people died because of the Firestone tires.

Sources: "Ford/Firestone Tire Recall Time Line", Virginia Trial Lawyers Association, (see *http://brooks.swlearning.com*).

"Firestone Tire Recall Timeline", Democratic Staff of the Commerce Committee, (see *http://brooks.swlearning.com*).

The Safety Problems: Firestone Tire Tread Separation and Ford Explorer Design

The tread separation problem and the related NHTSA findings were summarized in the Executive Summary of NHTSA's Engineering Analysis Report and Initial Decision,[6] as follows:

> Belt-leaving-belt tread separations, whether or not

accompanied by a loss of air from the tire, reduce the ability of a driver to control the vehicle, particularly when the failure occurs on a rear tire and at high speeds. Such a loss of control can lead to a crash. The likelihood of a crash, and of injuries or

—————————————
6. "Engineering Analysis Report"

—Continued

Continued

fatalities from such a crash, is far greater when the tread separation occurs on a SUV than when it occurs on a pickup truck.

Tread separation claims included in the Firestone claims database involving the recalled and focus tires have been associated with numerous crashes that have led to 74 deaths and over 350 injuries (as of March 2001). Tread separation complaints from all sources included in the ODI consumer complaint database (including the Firestone claims data) that can be identified as involving these tires have reportedly led to 192 deaths and over 500 injuries (as of September 2001).

The belt-leaving-belt tread separations in the recalled and focus tires generally occur only after several years of operation. Thus, since the focus tires have not been on the road as long as the recalled ATX tires, the absolute number of failures of those tires, and the unadjusted failure rate of those tires, are less than those of comparable ATX tires. Claims in the Firestone claims database involving the focus tires have been associated with 17 deaths and 41 injuries, with additional crashes and casualties reported in the ODI complaint database, including reports of six additional fatalities. However, on a plant-by-plant basis, the focus tires manufactured at the Wilson and Joliette plants have exhibited tread separation failure trends that are similar to those

experienced by the recalled ATX tires at similar service intervals.

These failure trends indicate that it is likely that, if they are not removed from service, the focus tires—at least those manufactured before May 1998—will experience a similar increase in tread separation failures over the next few years, leading to a substantial number of future crashes, injuries, and deaths. The tread separation failure experience of the focus tires is far worse than that of their peers, especially that of the Goodyear Wrangler RT/S tires used as original equipment on many Ford Explorers.

The belt-leaving-belt tread separations that have occurred and are continuing to occur in the recalled and focus tires begin as belt-edge separation at the edge of the second, or top, belt. This is the area of highest strain in a steel belted radial tire and is a region with relatively poor cord-to-rubber adhesion because bare steel is exposed at the cut ends of the cords. Once belt-edge separations have initiated, they can grow circumferentially and laterally along the edge of the second belt and develop into cracks between the belts. If they grow large enough, they can result in catastrophic tread detachment, particularly at high speeds, when the centrifugal forces acting on the tire are greatest.

ODI conducted a non-destructive analysis of numerous randomly collected focus tires and peer tires from southern

states, where most of the failures have occurred, using shearography, which can detect separations inside a tire. This shearography analysis demonstrated that the patterns and levels of cracks and separations between the belts were far more severe in the focus tires than in peer tires. Many of the focus tires that were examined were in the later stages of failure progression prior to complete separation of the upper belt. The shearography results for tires manufactured at Wilson were similar to those manufactured at Joliette.

A critical design feature used by tire manufacturers to suppress the initiation and growth of belt-edge cracks is the "belt wedge," a strip of rubber located between the two belts near the belt edges on each side of the tire. The belt wedge thickness, or gauge, in the ATX tires and the Wilderness AT tires produced prior to May 1998 is generally narrower than the wedge gauge in peer tires, and the wedge gauge in cured tires was often less than Firestone's target for this dimension. The tires with this wedge did not adequately resist the initiation and propagation of belt-edge cracks between the steel belts. During March and April 1998, Firestone changed the material composition and increased the gauge of the wedge in its Wilderness AT tires (and some other tire models).

Another important feature of radial tires related to the prevention of belt-leaving-belt

—Continued

Continued

separations is the gauge of the rubber between the two steel belts, or "inter-belt gauge." The inter-belt gauge initially specified by Firestone for the focus tires is generally narrower than the inter-belt gauges in peer tires and is narrower than Firestone's original specification for the ATX tires in the early 1990s. Moreover, the actual measured gauge under the tread grooves in several of the focus tires measured by ODI was far less than Firestone's minimum design specification. Since an inadequate inter-belt gauge reduces the tire's resistance to crack growth and its belt adhesion capabilities, this narrow inter-belt gauge may be partially responsible for the relatively low peel adhesion properties of the focus tires compared to peer tires. In August 1999, after becoming concerned about the adequacy of the inter-belt gauge in the cured Wilderness AT tires, especially in the regions directly under the tread grooves, Firestone changed the inter-belt gauge specification back to the original dimension.

Another relevant feature is the design of the shoulder pocket of the focus tires, which can cause higher stresses at the belt edge and lead to a narrowing, or "pinching," of the wedge gauge at the pocket. The focus tires exhibit a series of weak spots around the tire's circumference, leading to the initiation and growth of cracks earlier than in competitor tires and in other Firestone tires

produced for light trucks and SUVs. In addition, many of the focus tires exhibited shoulder pocket cracking similar to that which Firestone identified as a significant contributor to the risk of tread detachment in the recalled ATX tires.

Because the tread separations at issue in this investigation occur only after several years of exposure, almost all of the failures on which ODI's analysis of field experience was based involved tires manufactured before May 1998, when Firestone increased the dimensions and improved the material of the belt wedge. In theory, these modifications to the wedge would tend to inhibit the initiation and propagation of the belt-edge cracks that lead to tread separations. If these modifications actually improved the resistance of the focus tires to belt-edge separations, the historical failure trends described above may not predict the future performance of the newer tires. However, because tread separation failures rarely occur in the focus tires until at least three years of use, it is not now possible to ascertain from field experience whether their actual performance has improved significantly.

The rate of tread separation failures on Ranger pickups is lower that the rate of such failures on Explorers for a variety of reasons, including the fact that the Explorer generally carries higher loads and is a more demanding application,

and the tires on the Explorer had a significantly lower recommended inflation pressure (especially on the rear wheels). The risk of such a separation on Rangers remains a cause for possible concern. Nevertheless, because the likelihood of a crash due to a tread separation, and of deaths and injuries resulting from such a crash, is substantially lower when the separation occurs on a pickup than on a SUV, NHTSA's initial defect decision does not apply to focus tires installed on pickup trucks.

Under the National Traffic and Motor Vehicle Safety Act, in order to compel a manufacturer to conduct a recall, NHTSA has the burden of proving that a safety-related defect exists in the manufacturer's products. The record of this investigation supports a determination that a safety-related defect exists in the focus tires manufactured by Firestone prior to its 1998 modifications to the belt wedge that are installed on SUVs. Although the agency has concerns about the possibility of future tread separations in focus tires manufactured after the wedge change, the available evidence at this time does not clearly demonstrate that a safety-related defect exists in those focus tires. NHTSA will, however, continue to closely monitor the performance of these tires.

Therefore, on the basis of the information developed during the ODI investigation, NHTSA has made an initial decision that

—Continued

Continued

a safety-related defect exists in Firestone Wilderness AT P235/75R15 and P255/70R16 tires manufactured to the Ford specifications prior to May 1998 that are installed on SUVs. These tires were manufactured primarily at Wilson and Joliette and, to a lesser extent, at Oklahoma City. The initial decision does not apply to the P255/70R16 tires produced at Decatur or any of the Wilderness AT tires produced at Aiken, since these tires were all manufactured after May 1998.

At the request of Bridgestone/Firestone's chairman, the NHTSA also investigated the claims that the Ford Explorer had a design defect, probably in its suspension, that contributed to the tread separation in Wilderness tires. In his Statement to the U.S. Congressional Committees, NHTSA Deputy Secretary, Michael P. Jackson, comments that: "…NHTSA has had no credible evidence that the Ford Explorer's design is in any way responsible for *causing* tread separation or other such catastrophic tire failure."[7]

When Did the Companies Know of Problems and What Did They Do About Them?

According to the time line information, both Ford and Firestone received information about tire tread separations as early as 1992. These investigations may have been limited in some way, perhaps focused on or influenced by legal liability considerations. In any event, they do not appear to have raised "red flags" for Ford or Firestone such that either company was actively following up looking for further evidence.

Actually, Ford had received an earlier warning in February 1989, when an independent testing lab it hired found 3 of 17 tires tested had tread separations. Again, this information does not appear to have been carried forward as part of an ongoing formal risk assessment program.

Interestingly, in 1992, Ford chose the P235 tires that were later recalled over the smaller P225 tires that had tested better in turning (a prelude to rollover) tests. A memo shows Ford management was aware of the potential risk. Moreover, in order to improve the stability of the Explorer, Ford lowered the recommended tire pressure to 26 p.s.i. from the normal 30–35 p.s.i. that Firestone usually recommended. Firestone later insisted that this low pressure recommendation increased tire heat and caused the tire separations. At the time, however, Firestone went along; when Ford found that the mushier tires worsened fuel economy and asked for a fix,

Firestone reduced the tire weight by about 3 percent.[8]

Unlike General Motors, which has their own in-house tire safety and research unit,[9] neither Ford nor Firestone had an ongoing tire safety, testing, and database analysis program. Perhaps, if they had, they would have been aware of and following the work of Sam Boyden, the State Farm insurance analyst who began to e-mail NHTSA and have person-to-person conversations with NHTSA about Firestone tire problems in July 1998. Unfortunately, these e-mails and conversations do not appear to have been followed up until May 2, 2000, when the official investigation started. Even the NHTSA has admitted that they did not have an ongoing database project. Ford had to wait for Firestone to send them data, and Firestone initially had only cursory warranty data and needed to build a more comprehensive and useful dataset. NHTSA had to assemble data from various sources, including the companies, as well. Neither of the companies nor NHTSA was putting together a complete picture on an ongoing basis— they were all reacting, focused on short-term concerns, and using makeshift resources.

---

8. John Greenwald, "Inside the Ford/Firestone Fight," *TIME Online Edition*, May 29, 2001 (see *http://brooks.swlearning.com*).

9. Information from a student.

—Continued

---

7. Statement of Michael P. Jackson.

Continued

Ford and Firestone became aware of tire failures in warm climates in October 1998. The companies discussed the problems and Ford proposed a recall in Saudi Arabia. According to an internal Ford memo dated March 12, 1999, Firestone had asked Ford to handle it on a case-by-case basis so that the U.S. Department of Transport would not have to be notified, and so that the Saudi government would not overreact.[10] Ford had apparently told Firestone that the recall should be reported since the tires were also sold in the United States, but ultimately did not do so. Later, Ford maintained that it was not obligated to report the foreign recalls to U.S. regulators.[11]

Ford asked Firestone to do some tests in November 1999. These tests, which became known as the "Southwest Study," were completed in April 2000, but no evidence of a problem was discovered.[12]

Ultimately, when facing inflamed public reactions in specific locales to mounting accidents and deaths, Ford recalled Firestone tires in Saudi Arabia, Venezuela, and four other countries between June 1999 and May 2000. Firestone continued to advise Ford that there were no problems with the tires, and recalls were unwarranted. Note that these recalls were undertaken before recalling the same tires in North America—a fact not lost on consumers and commentators when the salient facts began to surface.

A TV station in Houston, Texas, KHOU, aired a 10-minute story on the tread separations on tires on Ford Explorers in February 2000. They gave the 800 telephone number for the NHTSA and complaints started to roll in. The news secrecy bubble had finally burst in the United States, and on March 6 the NHTSA began its Initial Evaluation (IE) of Firestone tires.[13] Subsequent analysis of Firestone warranty claims and other data showed a high accident rate for the tires, and led to the recall on August 9. Again, actions were in response to public pressure.

Findings were ultimately identified, in part, from Firestone warranty data that could have been assessed much earlier. Whose responsibility should that have been? Who would have benefited? On Friday, July 28, 2000, Ford engineers picked up the Firestone warranty data and then set up a "war room" at Ford headquarters in Dearborn, Michigan.[14] Working with Firestone personnel, after ten long days the investigators decided that "the problem tires appear[ed] to have come from the plant in Decatur, Ill., during specific periods of production. The bulk of the tire-separation incidents had occurred in hot states: Arizona, California, Florida and Texas. This correlated with information from overseas."[15]

"The rate of warranty claims on tires for Explorers surged in the mid-1990s, and the bulk of them involved tires made at Decatur. For the three years from 1994 through 1996, tread-separation claims attributed to ATX tires produced at the Decatur plant came in at rates ranging from roughly 350 to more than 600 tires per million. During the same years, tires of the same model produced at all

10. Stephen Power, "Tire Check: The Recall Rolls On: Bridgestone Fretted About Replacements," *The Wall Street Journal,* September 6, 2000.

11. Ibid.

12. "Firestone Tire Recall Timeline," Democratic Staff of the Commerce Committee, (see *http://brooks.swlearning.com*).

13. Ibid.

14. Robert L. Simison et al., "Blowout: How the Tire Problem Turned into a Crisis for Firestone and Ford—Lack of a Database Masked the Pattern That Led To Yesterday's Big Recall—The Heat and the Pressure," *The Wall Street Journal,* August 10, 2000.

15. Ibid.

—*Continued*

Continued

other Firestone plants had claim rates of 100 per million tires."[16]

At least two factors may have contributed to these higher tread separation rates at Decatur. In preparation for a product liability suit in Florida, a retired worker has sworn that he saw inspectors pass tires without inspecting them on a daily basis in 1993 and 1994.[17] Secondly, Firestone used 2,300 scab or replacement workers when United Rubber Workers local 713 went on strike from 1994 to 1996. After the very acrimonious strike was settled Firestone made the scab workers permanent hires.[18] An interesting question remains: Did Firestone fully appreciate and manage these risks effectively?

Misunderstanding the Risks

Perhaps the tread separation problems were found earlier, and actions were suppressed in the United States due to concerns over potential legal ramifications and ensuing costs. Unfortunately, this is probably a correct line of reasoning, and it reflects an erroneous understanding of the significant risks of delay in dealing with a product safety matter.

Specifically, delay in dealing with a product safety matter can lead to a serious erosion of reputation and confidence among customers, and result in a loss of future revenues and profits. Frequently, the cost of opportunities lost is the largest item to be taken into account in a cost-benefit analysis of the decision to recall a product. Moreover, failing to remedy a problem at the earliest point of recognition can lead to an inflation of the number of claims and the cost of satisfying them. If the executives had seen the cost-benefit analysis in Table 2, they would have seen the logic in speeding up their analysis and recognition of the tread separation problem.

Using an Ethical Decision-Making Framework

Had Ford and Firestone executives used an ethical decision-making framework such as those discussed in Chapter 5, they would have recognized the risks allowing legal defense strategy to dominate their thinking. Moreover, they might have considered the application of alternative remedies such as the use of a nylon cap or safety layer between the steel belts and tread to keep the ends of the belts from chafing the tread rubber and contributing to tread separation. The nylon cap was apparently used in late-production Firestone tires in Venezuela at a cost of $1 per tire. According to engineers, the extra cost was the only reason not to use them widely.[19] Bridgestone does use them on some tire lines, as does Pirelli on nearly all of its U.S.-market tires.[20]

The Aftermath

Not surprisingly, the sales of Ford Explorers dropped, as did Firestone's sales. In Venezuela, for example, Ford Explorer sales dropped 37 percent in 2000. In December 2000, Saudi Arabia banned new and used vehicles with Firestone tires. Firestone announced that it believed the ban was unjustified.

Both the U.S. Congress and Senate held hearings, and a new act was passed on October 11, 2000, called the Transportation Recall Enhancement, Accountability, and Documentation Act (TREAD). The TREAD Act:

- Strengthens the reporting requirements for manufacturers of motor vehicles and motor vehicle equipment (including the reporting of defects first discovered in a foreign country);

16. Timothy Aeppel et al., "Road Signs: How Ford, Firestone Let The Warnings Slide By As Debacle Developed—Their Separate goals, Gaps in Communication Gave Rise to Risky Situation—Bucking the Bronco Legacy," *The Wall Street Journal*, September 6, 2000.

17. Ibid.

18. James R. Healey & Sara Nathan, "Could $1 Worth of Nylon Have Saved People's Lives? Experts: Caps on Steel Belts May Have Stopped Shredded Tires," *USA Today*, August 9, 2000.

19. Ibid.
20. Ibid.

—Continued

Continued

- Increases the civil penalties for violations of safety regulations (e.g., fines for certain violations of Title 49 were raised from $1,000 to $5,000 for each violation, and the maximum penalty for a related series of violations was raised from $800,000 to $15,000,000);

- Provides additional criminal penalties (e.g., for any knowing and willful false statement that was intended to mislead NHTSA with respect to a defect that causes death or grievous bodily harm, the possible prison term was raised from 5 years to 15);

- Requires NHTSA to revise and update its safety standards for tires;

- Increases the number of years that a defect must be remedied without charge to the owner (from three years to five for tires);

- Increases the authorization for funding NHTSA;

- Requires the Secretary of Transportation to report to Congress within a year on the criteria, procedures, and methods that NHTSA uses in determining whether to open an investigation of a possible defect; and

- Contains other safety-related provisions.[21]

Questions

1. Why didn't Ford and Firestone learn from their past recall debacles?

2. Why didn't Ford, Firestone, and the NHTSA discover the nature and seriousness of the tread-separation, product-liability problem earlier?

3. Why didn't Ford or Firestone report the problem to U.S. authorities earlier?

BRIDGESTONE'S STOCK CHART

Ford's Stock Chart

Reprinted Courtesy of NAQ, Inc.

---

21 "Lawyer's Silence and Highway Deaths," United States Republican Policy Committee, July 9, 2001 (see *http://brooks.swlearning.com*).

—Continued

Continued

TABLE 2

COST-BENEFIT ANALYSIS OF
DECISION TO USE AS A NYLON
CAP SAFETY LAYER

BENEFITS		
SAVINGS	**UNIT COST**	**TOTAL**
203 Deaths[1]	$977,000	$198,331,000
700 Injuries[2]	$327,925	$229,547,500
Avoid Legal Fees & Settlements		
Avoid Recalling Tires		
Avoid Damage to Reputation[3]		$1,272,121,500
Total Benefits		$1,700,000,000
COSTS		
COST	**UNIT COST**	**TOTAL**
Nylon Safety Cap for 10,000,000 recalled tires[4]	$1	$10,000,000
Total Costs		$10,000,000

[1]The unit cost of death was obtained from an NHTSA study in 2000 on "The Economic Impact of Motor Vehicle Crashes" (see *http://brooks.swlearning.com*).

[2]The unit cost of injury was determined by applying the percentage cost of injury/death in 1971 from the Ford Pinto case ($67,000/$200,000 = 33.5%) to the unit cost of death estimated by the NHTSA survey from 2000: $977,000 × 33.5% = $327,295.

[3]The investment banking firm of UBS Warburg estimated that the tire problems could cost Firestone and Ford between $719 million and $2.7 billion. We assumed the total cost to be $1.7 billion (a number in the middle). Therefore, since we know the total cost to Ford & Firestone is $1.7 billion, we can calculate the residual amount to be allocated to the avoidance of legal fees, settlement fees, cost of recalling tires, and the cost of the loss of reputation: $1,700,000,000 − $427,878,500 = $1,272,121,500 (see *http://brooks.swlearning.com*).

[4]An article written in *USA Today* on August 9, 2000, by James R. Healey & Sara Nathan, proposed that a nylon safety cap could have prevented the tread separation problem. The article states that a nylon safety layer between the steel belts and the tread would keep the ends of the belts from chafing the tread rubber and contributing to tread separation. The article also cited that affidavits from tire engineers said that cost is the only reason not to use them. The estimated cost was $1 per tire to cover the radial piles with a nylon cap. We determined the number of tires affected as follows:

August 9, 2000	6.5 million tires were recalled
September 4, 2000	3.5 million additional tires were recalled
Total recalled	10.0 million

SOURCE: Master of Management & Professional Accounting (MMPA) degree students at the Rotman School of Management, University of Toronto: Meghan Davis, Theresa Yim, Paul Spitzen, Michael Krofchick, and Katy Yeung. Group project, Fall 2002.

—Continued

Continued

4. Ultimately, which was the largest cost to Ford and Firestone: fines, lawsuit settlements, or the loss of reputation leading to loss of future revenue and profits?

5. What errors should be corrected in the cost-benefit analysis presented?

6. What were the ethical risks, if any, involved in this tire recall situation?

7. If you were advising Ford and Bridgestone, what should each include in their risk management program?

Ethics case

Conflicts of Interest on Wall Street

On December 20, 2002, New York's Attorney General, Eliot Spitzer, announced a $1.4 billion settlement ending a multi-regulator probe of ten brokerages that alleged that "investors were duped into buying over-hyped stocks during the '90s bull market."[1] But the settlement may represent only the tip of the iceberg as aggrieved investors review the findings when they are released in 2003, and sue the brokerages for redress of their personal losses estimated to be $7 trillion since 2000.[2] Nonetheless, it promises an overdue start on the reform of Wall Street's[3] flawed conflict of interest practices. As such, the revisions ultimately adopted will provide a template for investment advisors around the world.

The story behind the probe is also an interesting one. It shows the capacity of a state's Attorney-General to force the U.S. Securities and Exchange Commission (SEC), which has regulatory authority over U.S. capital markets, to act when they appeared reluctant to take on Wall Street in a direct, public, and serious manner. In fact, Spitzer was able to bring together his office, the SEC, the National Association of Securities Dealers, the New York Stock Exchange, and a group of state regulators, as well as the major brokerages involved, to arrange a settlement.

The accepted settlement, while indicating the complicity of the ten firms involved, will probably do more to restore lost confidence in the capital markets than to weaken it. Regulators have been seen to act, brokerages are on notice that the old practices will no longer be tolerated, and the right of investors to have unbiased advice is reinforced. The resulting sharpening of ethics awareness on the part of advisors, their firms, and the regulators, together with the emergence of more ethical practices, should assist in the restoration of investor trust in the capital markets.

The Settlement

Ten firms have agreed "to pay $1.435 billion, including $900 million in penalties, $450 million for research over the next five years and $85 million for investor education."[4] The list of payment, in millions, is shown in Table 1. Two other firms that had been part of the settlement talks did not participate in the announced settlement.

Some observers hailed the settlement and resulting

1. "Wall Street firms to pays fines of $1.4 billion U.S.," *Toronto Star*, December 21, 2002, D3.

2. Alex Berenson and Andrew Ross Sorkin, "How Wall Street Was Tamed," *The New York Times*, December 22, 2003.

3. Wall Street is used in this case to signify the U.S. investment advisory/brokerage community, which is centered on Wall Street in New York City.

4. Randall Smith, "Ten Firms Must Pay $1.4 Billion Over Misleading Stock Research," *The Wall Street Journal*, December 23, 2002.

—Continued

Continued

changes to be "the dawn of a new day for Wall Street."[5] Others felt that the fines were a drop in the bucket. "Citicorp, for example, averaged about $65 million in profit each business day in the third quarter, meaning one good week would cover its payment."[6] If the payments turn out to be tax deductible, the impact would certainly be minor in size, but would possess a significant signaling value.

What Caused Concern?

Conflicts of interest have been common practice in the brokerage business since its inception. For example, most brokerages, and brokers, have investments upon which they take speculative positions, and upon which they make investment recommendations to investors. In the case of the brokerages, they are usually required to disclose to prospective investors when they are selling shares as a principal, but the presumption of unsuspecting investors has been that brokerage employees—analysts and investment advisers—were acting in the best interest of the investors they were advising. How wrong they were!

According to *Forbes.com*, Spitzer's office found e-mails showing Merrill Lynch (and other firms') analysts... privately trashing the stocks they publicly recommended."[9] In addition, "there is the widespread phenomenon of research departments commencing coverage of companies their (investment) banks recently took public. This coverage is always positive."[10] Moreover, "...analysts almost never say 'sell.' According to Thompson Financial/First Call, fewer than 2% of all financial analysts are 'sell' or 'strong sell.' ... Third, there are cases like Enron that

TABLE I

WALL STREET BROKERS SETTLEMENT PAYMENTS[7]

FIRM	INDEPENDENT INVESTOR			
	FINES	RESEARCH	EDUCATION	TOTAL
Saloman Smith Barney parent, Citigroup Inc.	$300	$75	$25	$400
Credit Suisse First Boston	150	50	0	200
Merrill Lynch	100*	75	25	200
Morgan Stanley	50	75	0	125
Goldman Sachs	50	50	10	110
Bear Stearns	50	25	5	80
Deutsche Bank	50	25	5	80
J. P. Morgan Chase	50	25	5	80
Lehman Brothers	50	25	5	80
UBS Warburg	50	25	5	80
Total	$900	$450	$85	$1,435

*Merrill Lynch agreed to pay an additional $100 million seven months earlier in response to Spitzer's original charges.[8]

5. Ibid.
6. "Wall Street firms."
7. Smith.
8. "Wall Street firms."
9. Dan Ackerman, "Everyone Wants A Shot At The Analysts," *Forbes.com*, May 1, 2002.
10. Ibid.

—Continued

Continued

are not recent initial public offerings but companies that do massive and repeat business with Wall Street. The analysts can say they are not swayed by their firm's interests, and they can claim they were defrauded, but how do they explain the uniformity of their recommendations."[11]

Brokerages have long relied upon the notion of the Chinese wall or a firewall that they claim can stop information known to investment bank personnel who develop and price independent public offerings from reaching stock analysts or brokers serving retail clients. However, there are those who doubt that Chinese walls are fully effective. According to Richard Epstein, a law professor at the University of Chicago: "The only thing [the analyst] needs to know [about the investment banking client] if he is inclined to swing his recommendation is that it is a client."[12] Since analysts have been remunerated partly on the basis of underwriting revenues, and/or on the basis of retail commissions, or total broker-age revenues, there is built-in remuneration motivation for promoting the stock of known or potential underwriting clients.

On other occasions, the attempts to influence analysts have been quite direct. "Perhaps the most startling example came in mid-November, when Citigroup chief executive Sanford

Weill said he told Jack Grubman to re-examine his rating of AT&T and admitted that he helped get Grubman's children gain admission to a prestigious Manhattan nursery school."[13]

In addition to providing investment advice that lacked integrity, Wall Street firms have been playing favorites. They have been offering shares of hot public offerings to the executives of companies regarded as good prospects for investment banking deals. This is known as "spinning," and due to the pent-up demand for the new offerings, a profit is virtually assured.

Proposed Structural Reforms

In order to help ensure that "stock recommendations are not tainted by efforts to obtain investment banking fees"[14] and other benefits, the settlement proposes several changes in the way investment business is done, including:

- "Each firm's research unit will reside in a unit separate from the investment banking unit, with its own legal and compliance staff, and which doesn't report to investment banking,...
- ...decisions to terminate [ana-lyst] coverage must be made by research and not invest-ment bankers, and can't sub-stitute for a rating downgrade.
- ...analysts can't be compen-sated based on investment

banking work or input from bankers, and should be paid based partly on the accuracy of their stock picks...."

Some problems still exist, and further framework changes will emerge, but a start has been made on cleaning up some of the conflicts of interest facing investors and the brokerage community.

On April, 2003, a Joint Release was issued and lodged on the SEC Press website by the five regulatory agencies involved, which had the following headlines:

Ten of Nation's Top Investment Firms Settle Enforcement Actions Involving Conflicts of Interest Between Research and Investment Banking

Historic Settlement Requires Payments of Penalties of $487.5 Million, Disgorgement of $387.5 Million to Fund Investor Education and Mandates Sweeping Stuctural Reforms

Questions:

1. Identify and explain the conflicts of interest referred to in this case.

2. What additional rules should the SEC make?

3. What should be included in the investor education that the settlement funds are earmarked for?

4. Was it appropiate for the New York Attorney General's Office to have become invloved in securities regulation, or should this have been left to securities regulators?

---

11. Ibid.
12. Ibid.
13. "Wall Street firms."
14. Smith.

In the late summer of 1998, the surveillance department of the Toronto Stock Exchange (TSE) became concerned about the possible "upticking" or "high closing" of some stock prices at the end of the trading day. This process involves buying stock at the end of the day at a price above the market level so that the valuation of the share is shown at a "boosted" or "juiced" price. Managers of portfolios holding the stock benefit because the performance of their portfolio is improved. Inflated results that are reported in the press and other prospectus documents encourage investors to invest in the mutual and other funds, and are used to determine the bonuses of the portfolio managers. Investors joining the funds pay inflated prices to do so. The market returns to normal prices within a few moments of opening on its next trading day.

On a wintry day in December 1998, the TSE's surveillance team noted some suspicious trading patterns at RT Capital Management Inc., the third largest institutional money manager in Canada with $28.9 billion in assets under management, and the pension fund management arm of its parent the Royal Bank of Canada.[1] They were looking for end-of-day trades that sent stock prices up sharply without any apparent reason, and they found several instances that raised concerns over the next few months. By May 1999, the TSE team headed by Neil Winchester had isolated at least three instances where RT Capital personnel were suspected of boosting stock prices.[2]

Having delegated the power to regulate directly the stockbrokerages that are members of the TSE to the Investment Dealers Association (IDA), the TSE was not in a position to act alone to pursue a full investigation into its concerns and discipline those responsible for misdeeds. Perhaps believing the IDA would not able to mete out the sanctions required, the TSE passed its findings to the Enforcement Branch of the Ontario Securities Commission (OSC), the regulator that oversees matters relating to investors in Ontario.

A joint OSC/TSE investigation ensued involving requests of records, tape recordings of phone calls,[3] and interviews of about 25 people in regard to selected trades. No one was advised of the target of the investigation until October, when formal written notification was sent to the top five managers of RT Capital, including Reay Mackay, the vice chairman of the Royal Bank in charge of the wealth management division. After this date, the bank required the OSC to subpoena any Royal Bank employees required to give interviews.

Investigations continued until 8 P.M. on June 26, when a telephone call was made to RT Capital advising them what "the OSC had in its draft statement of allegations, and what a settlement would take: $2.6 million plus $100,000 for each of the 26 illegal trades. The OSC was also asking for permanent trading bans against the employees involved and sanctions against RT Capital's most senior executives."[4]

Also on June 26, four employees of RT Capital were suspended: Peter Larkin, chief strategist for Canadian equity team; Gary Baker, vice president for oil and gas investments; and Pat Shea and Marion Gillespie, senior equity traders. These employees were to be paid until settlement was reached or the case adjudicated.

Early on, the Royal Bank wished to negotiate a settlement with OSC to prevent a public hearing and embarrassment of employees. However, the initial proposed settlement was not

1. "What Set Off the Alarms?" *Financial Post,* June 28, 2000, C1.

2. "When Ambition, Arrogance Collide: RT Capital Scandal," *Financial Post,* July 1, 2000, D1, D4, D5.

3. Phone calls for orders to brokers to buy and sell shares are taped in the brokerage industry to resolve later disputes and to provide a trail for investigations.

4. "When Ambition, Arrogance Collide," D4.

—*Continued*

Continued

accepted, partly because the problem was not sufficiently significant in Royal Bank's perspective. "By the time the numbers were crunched and the auditors had performed their last bit of wizardry, the Royal Bank figured it had a $10,000 problem on its hands. That's the amount the bank's internal audit yielded when it scoured the complex myriad of trades and their revenues to Messrs. Larkin and Baker (who were the key strategist at RT Capital and vice president, respectively). In other words, activities that allegedly inflated Mr. Larkin's portfolios by $30.2 million and Mr. Baker's funds by $8.4 million actually netted them less than $10,000 in performance bonuses and commissions. In fact, Royal's audit estimates RT Capital's Canadian equity funds only moved 0.04%—or four basis points—higher as a result of stock manipulation. 'It's a pittance,' said a lawyer close to the investigation. 'It wasn't about a financial motive and it isn't as sinister as it looks either.' In fact, members of the country's largest financial community shake their heads in disbelief that Mr. Larkin and Mr. Baker would have risked their reputations—and their million-dollar salaries—for a few thousand extra dollars."[5]

So why did Peter Larkin do what he did? A competing money manager said, "Peter didn't do this for the money. It's about proving that he's smarter."[6] A former classmate said, "He risked millions of dollars not to make money but to prove something. He wanted not only to be the best manager in Canada, but the best plus a little bit more."[7]

This attitude reminds some observers of a "gunslinger" or "cowboy" mentality that they believe exists in the brokerage community. They argue that the intensely competitive, highly subjective, fast-paced, fast buck, buyer beware, highly conflicted, performance-driven culture that most people ascribe to the brokerage industry permits— and some would even say even fosters—a gunslinger attitude. According to Fred Ketchen, managing director of equity trading at ScotiaMcLeod Inc. in Toronto, "We have talked [about it] in our business before when firms have gotten into difficulty about a gunslinger attitude."[8]

Ketchen doesn't approve of the attitude, but some of his compatriots do. In fact, the opinion on "the street" was reported as highly divided over whether the violation was

serious, or just a technical breach grossly exaggerated by overzealous regulators. For example, Claude Lamoreux, head of a $70 billion teachers pension plan fund, commented that, "When I look at high closing, yes, it's an offence. But in the order of sin, this is a minor sin—although when you have traders bragging on tape that they would never get caught... if you are the OSC, you can't let people get away with that."[9] Other senior executives worried about a rush to justice where the OSC, in its haste to make a strong example, was overdoing the sanctions, particularly in view of the fact that the Royal Bank admitted its wrongdoing. In addition, they noted that high closing was something that many people did.

In spite of the fact that the Royal Bank admitted its wrongdoing, the settlement negotiations did not proceed quickly or smoothly. In fact, on July 14, John Cleghorn, the chairman of the Royal Bank, apologized to the investing public using full-page advertisements in the major Canadian newspapers. His ad stated that: "I apologize to our

---

5. "When Ambition, Arrogance Collide," D4.

6. "When Ambition, Arrogance Collide," D4.

7. "When Ambition, Arrogance Collide," D4.

8. "When Ambition, Arrogance Collide," D4.

9. "Royal probed RT staff last June," *Toronto Star*, June 29, 2000, C01. A portion of the tapes allegedly include an RT Capital employee telling a trader who balks at a request to high-close or 'juice' a stock that the TSE's market surveillance boss, Neil Winchester, would never catch on.

—Continued

Continued

clients and to the community at large for this situation… We have taken and will continue to take steps to ensure that there will not be a recurrence of these activities."[10] However, one of the 13 brokers charged with manipulating the market refused to settle and, with the Royal Bank, forced the scheduling of a hearing before the commissioners of the OSC to adjudicate the charges. As far as the broker was concerned, he had done nothing wrong, and was merely exercising his right to set a proper, higher valuation for a security where the market had failed to do so.

Finally, however, a settlement was reached, and on July 20 a hearing was held in front of the commissioners of the OSC to approve the penalties involved. The penalties were announced and details are on the OSC website at *http://brooks.swlearning.com* They included fines for RT Capital and offending personnel, a lifetime ban for one trader and shorter-term bans from trading for others, bans from serving as directors, payment of costs for the proceedings, and so on. At the end of the OSC website are specific comments relating to the alleged misdeeds and their impacts. In particular, the summary of impacts on the capitalization is noteworthy as it

shows the range of manipulation involved.

The reaction to the scandal has been interesting. Editorials have differed with one declaring it to be like a tempest[11] in a teapot, with another calling for the TSE to apologize for allowing such a scandal to occur,[12] and yet another prior to the Royal Bank apology declaring that: "As simple as it is, the Royal still doesn't seem to get it: Anyone who seeks to manage other people's money must be—and be seen to be—above reproach."[13]

Clients of the Royal Bank have also reacted, and the Royal has gone to some lengths to comfort them. On July 21 it was announced that Michael Wilson, a former senior broker and former Government of Canada senior Cabinet minister of ethical repute, had been appointed chairman and chief executive of RT Capital. Deloitte & Touche was hired to assess the brokerage practices and recommend changes to ensure that the problem could not reoccur. Nonetheless, institutional clients were actively considering whether they could place further or new monies

with RT Capital for management. Some clients were concerned that high-performing Peter Larkin's absence would lessen the return their funds would generate,[14] while others felt that the explanation of why their mutual fund clients would use a scandalized RT Capital would be difficult for their investors to accept.[15] Although he wanted to know what the company's asset base would be in six months time, Michael Wilson revealed on August 17 that RT Capital's assets under management had fallen by $1 billion to $37.1 billion in July 2000. He went on to say that, "The impact of this was broader than RT Capital because it reflected on the integrity of the whole group."[16]

Questions

1. How much was lost due to the "juicing" or "high closing"?

2. Was this episode of high closing a serious problem? Why or why not?

---

10. "Royal Chief Apologizes for Improper Trading," *Toronto Star*, July 15, 2000.

11. Terence Corcoran, "The Court of Public Manipulation," *Financial Post*, July 1, 2000.
12. Dalton Camp, "Time for TSE to Come Clean in This Royal 'Juicing' Scandal," *Toronto Star*, July 19, 2000.
13. "Royal mess," *Toronto Star*, July 12, 2000.

14. "Larkin's Absence Has RT Clients Contemplating Jumping Ship," *Financial Post*, July 1, 2000.
15. "OSC Said Seeking $2.6 Million Fine," *Toronto Star*, E1, E7.
16. "RT Capital's Business Hurt by Scandal, Wilson Says," *Toronto Star*, August 17, 2000.

—Continued

Continued

3. Were the sanctions appropriate in the circumstances?

4. What caused the problem that precipitated the scandal?

5. What could Royal Bank have done to avoid this problem entirely?

6. Did Royal Bank manage its crisis well? What would an improved approach have involved?

7. Should the directors of RT Capital and/or the Royal Bank be sanctioned? How?

Prepared in October 2000 by Prof. L. J. Brooks, with assistance from Cara Greenberg and Jeffrey Tannenbaum while both were students in the Rotman School's Master of Management & Professional Accounting Program.

RT Capital Scandal— Timeline

- December 1998 – The surveillance system at TSE picks up suspicious trading patterns at RT Capital.

- Next few months – TSE's surveillance team finds several instances of end-of-day trades that sent stocks up sharply without any apparent reason.

- July 1999 – The problem is brought to the attention of the OSC director of enforcement.

- May 1999 – At least three cases of stock price manipulation at RT Capital are isolated by the TSE.

- September 1999 – OSC investigation is in full swing; RT Capital changes taping procedures of phone calls.

- October 1999 – RB executives receive official notice of investigation by OSC.

- June 23, 2000 – OSC investigation into RT becomes public. People are questioned, and tapes are requested.

- June 24, 2000 – The investigation widens to include other provinces (BC, Quebec).

- June 26, 2000 – Four employees of RT are suspended (Peter Larkin, chief strategist for Canadian equity team; Gary Baker, vice president for oil and gas investments; Pat Shea and Marion Gillespie, senior equity traders). These employees will continue to be paid until a settlement is reached or the case is settled. OSC seeks $2.6 million (substantial amount for OSC; $100,000 for each stock admitted to be manipulated between October 30, 1998, and March 31, 1999), suspension of several staff from stock trading, and other settlement conditions. RB wants to negotiate settlement with OSC to prevent public hearing and embarrassment of employees. OSC offer is rejected by RBC (RBC thinks OSC is demanding too much).

- June 29, 2000 – Formal proceedings against RT Capital commence. Nine RT Capital employees and directors are charged by the OSC, 13 stock traders from 11 investment dealers, including Merrill Lynch and CIBC World Markets, are charged by the OSC for making trades on behalf of RT Capital, lying to authorities, hampering investigation, and boosting stock prices and company values. Larkin and Baker are charged with heading up the scandal (Larkin and Baker give orders to Shea and Gillespie, who relay buy and sell orders to traders at 11 investment dealers). The CEO and others now face allegations (Timothy Griffin, president; Donald Webster, senior vice president; Michael Edwards, chief executive and former chairman of TSE); OSC wants to make an example of RT by demanding large punitive damages.

- As of June 30, all but 1 of 13 stock traders agree to settle with TSE and OSC.

- June 30, 2000 – City of Toronto discloses it has halted transfer of any more pension money to RT Capital. RT Capital doesn't want to lose Larkin, therefore it does not settle with OSC.

- July 14, 2000 – RBC chairman publishes apology advertisement in major newspapers. Five senior employees (Thomas Griffin, president; Gary Baker, vice president; Peter Larkin, senior vice president and chief strategist; Patrick Shea and Marion Gillespie, equity traders) accused of stock manipulation are expected to be fired as part of the OSC package settlement agreement; five people have agreed to permanent termination.

- July 18, 2000 – OSC hearing; deal failed to be negotiated.

- July 19, 2000 – OSC hearing to strike deal over allegations.

- July 20, 2000 – TSE panel set to approve penalties negotiated with 13 traders charged with

—Continued

Continued

filling RT Capital's improper trades. Nine RT employees asked to appear at OSC hearings to approve penalties, which leads to heated debate over individual penalties. RT agrees to package deal set out by OSC, including admission to stock manipulation and inadequate policing of employees. Securing a settlement avoids the embarrassment of a public hearing. RT is fined $3 million and one-tenth of the workforce is suspended or banned. Fines up to $8,000 are levied for nine staff members;

chairman Michael Edwards is demoted but remains as director. He is replaced by Michael Wilson as chairman and chief executive running day-to-day operations. President Wilson Timothy Griffin resigned, as well as the four main players in the scandal. Peter Larkin receives a lifetime ban from the securities industry. Other staff penalties include trading bans and suspension of roles as officers and directors of RT and any other company for specific time periods. RT is also

fined $150,000 for investigation costs, and is ordered to be audited and to reinstate its telephone-taping system. Eleven stock traders are fined a total of $400,000 and suspended for up to 10 weeks by TSE.

- Aftermath: RBC pension arm has lost $1 billion in assets under management over a month after the admission to the fraud. There was a short-term loss of clients and money due to Larkin's leave, and long-term damage to reputation.

Bankers Trust: Learning from Derivatives*

Bankers Trust (BT) was one of the most powerful and profitable banks in the world in the early 1990s. Under the stewardship of Chairman Charles Sanford, Jr., it had transformed itself from a staid commercial bank into "a highly-tuned manufacturer of high-margin, creative financial products—the envy of wholesale bankers."[1] BT prided itself on its innovative trading strategies, which used derivatives to manage risks; its performance-driven culture; and its profits: the bank made a profit of over $1 billion US in 1993.[2]

Key to BT success was the dominance of its business in derivatives—contracts in which companies make payments to each other based on some underlying asset such as a

commodity, a financial instrument, or an index.[3] The value of the payments—and thus the contract—is derived from those assets. Companies can use derivatives to lower financing costs, manage risk, or speculate on interest and currency rates. It is estimated that almost $400 million of BT's 1993 profits came from its leveraged derivatives business.

Derivatives, with their high margins, held a preeminent position with BT management, with their fervent focus on the bottom line. At BT, each product and each trader was given a value that was based on what income the product or trader could bring the firm.[1] The bank's intense focus on the bottom line decreased attention on products and services which

had low margins but which fostered and nurtured client relationships. BT was known for courting customers only insofar as they would buy high-margin products.[1] In 1990 Charles Hill, former co-head of merchant banking, left with thirty members of his department because he saw no room at BT for offering clients impartial financial advice and deal structuring. One source within the company explained: "we got rid of the nurturers and builders—the defensive guys—and kept the offensive guys."[1] Those who remained describe a firm driven by intense internal rivalry, endless politicking, and discussions about profit and losses. They describe a

—Continued

Continued

"coliseum" mentality at the top level: "we look on while the guys are out there fighting the lions."[1] What remained was a bank where the customer's interests appeared to come second to the bank's.

It was within this context that BT, once one of the most powerful banks in the world, was disgraced by a series of highly publicized lawsuits brought forth by several of its clients in 1994 and 1995 over losses they incurred as a result of derivative products sold to them by BT. The clients contended that BT sold them the derivatives without giving them adequate warning and information regarding their potential risks. BT countered that these derivative deals were agreements between the bank and sophisticated clients who were now trying to escape from their loss-making contracts by crying foul.[2] At issue was whether the clients were naïve and should have known what they were getting into or whether BT deliberately deceived them (p. 110).[4]

There were more than half a dozen companies that suffered losses as a result of derivatives due to BT's allegedly fraudulent sales practices (Appendix 1), but the Procter & Gamble (P&G) case is representative of the other cases.

The relationship between P&G and BT's derivatives unit was established in January 1993 when the company set up a broad agreement with the bank for derivatives contracts. In November 1993, P&G agreed to buy a leveraged derivative product; P&G would make large profits if interest rates decreased and would lose money if interest rates increased. Leveraged derivatives products are a complex type of derivative, and their value can fluctuate to a greater degree than ordinary derivatives. The derivative worked fine at first, and P&G was sufficiently satisfied to agree to a second leveraged derivative contract in February 1994. However, interest rates began to rise that same month, significantly increasing P&G's payments to BT.

It is unclear whether P&G knew the cost of getting out of the contract, and P&G has since acknowledged that its internal procedures were not followed when it agreed to this derivative. P&G claimed that Bankers fraudulently induced it to buy complex derivatives, misrepresented their value, and then induced P&G to buy more for alleged gains or to staunch losses. However, P&G appeared to be an active market player. It had $5 billion in long-term debt, and its treasury managed a large, sophisticated portfolio of derivatives. P&G has acknowledged that its internal procedures were not followed when it entered into the derivatives contracts in November 1993. Ed Artzt, P&G's CEO, said the executives who bought the derivatives ignored policies against such speculation and were "like farm boys at a country carnival." His treasurer, Ray Mains, didn't read the contract he signed, didn't ask the right questions, and didn't assess risk by seeking outside help. Artzt also said Mains "failed to tell his boss when he knew he had a problem, . . . delayed while losses piled up, . . . and misled his boss into believing the loss was much smaller than it was."[5] P&G's CFO, Erik Nelson, relied on Mains instead of getting outside advice and did not inform Artzt or the board of the problems with the deal.

P&G's court filings include taped conversations that took place at Bankers Trust. In November 1993, Kevin Hudson, a managing director and salesman on the P&G deal, told his fiancee that the transaction would bring BT a profit of $7.6 million. She asked, "Do they understand that? What they did?" He replied, "No. They understand what they did but they don't understand the leverage." She warned Hudson that the deal would blow up on him. He replied, "I'll be looking for a new opportunity at the bank by then anyways." When the Fed raised interest rates in February 1994, P&G lost $157 million and when asked if "they were dying" Hudson replied, "They don't know." He

—Continued

Continued

was even then trying to sell P&G a second leveraged derivative and said, "Let me just get the deutsche mark trade done first; then they can ask." By April 12 that year, P&G announced a $157 million derivatives bath. Hudson's bonus for 1993 was $1.3 million. (He and his fiancee were married on November 5, 1994, live in London, and are still working for BT.[5])

P&G contended that, when it asked for an explanation of the costs, it learned that the bank was using a proprietary model to calculate the costs which it would not share with P&G.[4] P&G alleged that in April BT gave the company charts which showed that it would have had to pay a penalty to get out of its November contract almost from the day it was initiated.

Further evidence points to taped conversations between BT employees in which a BT salesman, discussing P&G's decision to enter into the November contract, says "we set 'em up."[4*] P&G finally locked in interest rates on both the derivatives; however, it claimed that by the time it finished doing so, its financing costs were $195.5 million higher than they should have been (p. 110).[4]

P&G asserted that BT employees were trying to deceive it from the day the derivatives contract was initiated. As evidence, P&G points to a taped conversation between Bankers employees about the November contract

where one asks: "Do they [P&G] understand that? What they did?"[4] The other employee replies: "No. They understand what they did but they don't understand the leverage, no."[4] The first employee then says: "But I mean . . . how much do you tell them. What is your obligation to them?"[4] The second employee responds: "To tell them if it goes wrong, what does it mean in a payout formula . . ."[4] P&G sued BT in October 1994, alleging that the bank "deliberately misled and deceived it, keeping the company in the dark about key aspects of the derivatives the bank was selling (p. 106)."[4]

BT countered that P&G was an active and sophisticated player in the financial markets and knew how its derivatives would perform. In court filings, BT described P&G as "sophisticated, experienced, and knowledgeable about the use of interest-rate derivative contracts and the risks presented by those contracts (p. 109)."[4] It added: "Although P&G would like this court to believe that it is a naive and unsophisticated user of derivatives transactions, the fact is that as part of its regular course of business and with authorization from top management, P&G's Treasury Department managed a large and sophisticated portfolio of derivative transactions (p. 109)."[4] BT asserted that P&G knew how the derivatives would perform and had

included a taped conversation in its court filings in which a BT employee shows a P&G treasury employee how to calculate its rate on the November derivative.[4] BT also produced evidence in court filings that P&G top executives blamed their own personnel for the investments. "Rather than putting its own house in order, and accepting its losses, P&G chose instead to bring this lawsuit (p. 111)."[4]

On September 1, 1995, P&G filed a motion in the U.S. District Court, which was approved, to add RICO (racketeer-influenced and corrupt organization) charges to the allegations against BT. A company found guilty of RICO charges is liable for three times the damages and plaintiff's legal costs. Banker's counter-filing called this "blackmail", saying P&G was hoping to vilify BT by the sheer number of its charges.

The lawsuit was settled out of court in May 1996.

Questions

1. What do you think the basis of settlement should have been?

2. Did BT have a duty to disclose all the information it had regarding the transactions to P&G, including pricing, mark to market value, and risk, or should P&G, a multibillion-dollar company, have ensured that it knew and understood

—Continued

Continued

these figures and risks prior to engaging in the transactions?

3. Did BT have an ethical duty to ascertain the suitability of these products for P&G, or did its responsibilities end with providing its client with the product it demanded?

4. Was the maxim of "buyer beware" more appropriate than "seller beware"?

5. What other ethical issues are raised by the case?

References

1. Shirreff, Y. D. "Can Anybody Fix Bankers Trust?" *Euromoney* (April 1995): 34–40.
2. "Bankers Trust Blurred Vision." *Economist* (April 8, 1995): 67–68.
3. Edwards, G. A., & Eller, G. E. "Overview of Derivatives Disclosures by Major US Banks." *Federal Reserve Bulletin* (September 1995): 817–31.
4. Holland, Kelly and Linda Himelstein and Zachary Schiller. "The Bankers Trust Tapes." *Business Week* (October 16, 1995): 106–111.
5. Loomis, C. J. "Bankers Trust Times— More Dirt About Derivatives." *Fortune Magazine,* November 27, 1995, 34.

*Prepared by L. J. Brooks, with assistance from student papers of Linda Rutledge, Deryk Angstenderger, Kelly Kang, Nilou Makarechian, Roman Masley, Khalid Rashid, and Chao Xu.

APPENDIX I

COMPANIES THAT PROCTER & GAMBLE SAYS LOST MONEY ON DERIVATIVES DUE TO BANKERS TRUST'S ALLEGEDLY FRAUDULENT SALES PRACTICES

COMPANY	LOSS (MILLIONS $US)
Procter & Gamble	195.5
Air Products	105.8
Sandoz	78.5
P.T. Adimitra Rayapratama	50.0
Federal Paper Board	47.0
Gibson Greetings	23.0
Equity Group Holdings	11.2
Sequa	7.5
Jefferson Smurfit	over 2.4

SOURCE: Business Week, October 16, 1995.

Barings Bank: Rogue Trader

It was early on a Friday morning in London—7:15 A.M. on February 24, 1995, to be exact—that the phone call came for Peter Baring from Peter Norris. Barings's family had been in banking since 1763. They enjoyed the patronage of the Queen of England and had financed the Napoleonic Wars and the transcontinental railway in Canada. Barings, London's oldest merchant bank, would soon be owned by foreign interests because of Norris's news.

Early on the previous day, Norris, the head of investment banking, had been summoned to Singapore by James Bax, the regional managing director of Baring Securities. Its star trader, Nick Leeson, hadn't been seen since Wednesday afternoon Singapore time and it appeared that he had left major unhedged securities positions that Barings might not be able to cover. If not, Barings would be bankrupt, or owned by others who could pay off what

was owed when the uncovered commitments came due.

At the beginning, Barings officials weren't sure what had happened, or the extent of the potential losses and commitments. When they did discover the nature of their obligations, they realized that the securities contracts were still open, so that the upper limit of their losses would not be known until the closing date of the contracts. If the markets involved sank further by that

—Continued

Continued

time, Barings's losses would grow. This was a complete shock because Leeson was supposed to deal in fully hedged positions only, making his money on short-term price changes with virtually no chance of losing a significant amount of money. What had happened?

Norris found confirmation of what Bax had told him. Essentially, Leeson had built up two huge securities positions. He had arranged futures contracts committing Barings to buy US $7 billion worth of Japanese equities and US $20 billion or more of interest rate futures at future dates. Unfortunately, due to the Kobe earthquake in Japan, the Japanese stock market was falling, so the equity contracts were worth less than he had paid, and the projected losses were growing but not yet at their maximum. In fact, it was estimated that every 1 percent decline in the stock market raised the losses by US $70 million.

When Peter Baring, the chairman of the bank, advised the Bank of England on Friday at noon that his bank had a potential problem, he estimated the combined losses at £433 million (US$650 million), a figure that was close to the shareholders' equity of £541 million. The governor of the Bank of England, Eddie George, was recalled from his skiing holiday in France, and his deputy, Rupert Pennant-Rea, called other British bankers to meet at the Bank of England to

pledge funds to help meet Barings's problem. Prospective purchasers were canvassed throughout Saturday, but the loss estimate rose to £650 million with no cap in sight. On Sunday, several options were pursued, including contacting the world's richest man, the Sultan of Brunei. The British bankers met again at the bank at 10 A.M. and by 2 P.M. they had agreed to provide £600 million. The question of what their return would be for advancing the money was being debated, but the issue of someone providing an upper cap to the losses remained. An offer arrived from the sultan to do so, which included the taking over of Barings. Unfortunately, this offer was withdrawn before a deal was consummated, and Eddie George had to sign an Administration Order that essentially put Barings under the administration of the Bank of England. At 10:10 P.M., the Bank of England announced that Barings had failed. Two hundred thirty-three years of stewardship by the Barings family was over.

One of the prospective buyers, ING, the second largest insurance firm in The Netherlands, was still interested and had sent a squad of at least thirty people to complete due diligence examinations. ING was particularly interested in assessing the degree of risk of other losses and of the complicity of personnel in the London and Singapore offices

in the Leeson problems. And Jacobs, the chairman of ING, agreed to buy Barings for £1 two hours before the Japanese market opened on Tuesday, February 28. As part of the deal, he agreed to keep the Barings name on the bank. In addition, he subsequently agreed to pay out most of the £105 million in bonuses that the Barings management had agreed to give its staff two days prior to the famous phone call.

How did this debacle happen? Bits and pieces of the puzzle came out slowly until the Report of the Bank of England's Board of Banking Supervision emerged. On Tuesday the 28th, Nick Leeson still had not been found, and he would not be detained until he and his wife arrived in Frankfurt on Thursday, March 2, having spent time in Kuala Lumpur and Kota Kinabalu, Malaysia. He would ultimately make a deal to assist investigators but would still be sent back to Singapore to stand trial.

Nick Leeson had gone to Singapore as the head of a unit that traded in futures, and he had prospered. He made money by buying and selling futures contracts for baskets of Japanese stocks known as Nikkei 225 futures. These Nikkei 225 futures contracts were traded on both the Osaka stock exchange and the SIMEX, the Singapore financial futures exchange. Since the prices on each exchange were slightly different,

—Continued

Continued

a sharp-eyed trader could buy on one and sell on the other exchange, making money on the spread. This was relatively safe, since for every purchase there was an immediate sale—if not, Barings would be exposed to very large risks, since the transactions were highly leveraged. In 1992 his unit made £1.18 million, in 1993 £8.83 million, and in the first seven months of 1994 it made a total of £19.6 million, or more than one-third of the total profit for the whole group. Nick was a star.

Barings did send out its internal auditors to see that all was well. Although the twenty-four-page report condemned the lack of controls and particularly having one man in charge of both the front (investing) and back (recordkeeping) offices, it was not acted on for fear that Leeson would be aggravated and leave for a job at another broker. Leeson's profits, after all, provided bonuses for everyone. Even though Leeson's behavior was getting somewhat bizarre, no action was taken. For example, five months before, he was fined $200 (Singapore) for dropping his pants in a pub and daring a group of women to use his cell phone to call the police.

It appears that his ego and the pressure to make more and more profits pushed him in the direction of more risky investments, and he began to make unhedged transactions in which there was no immediate sale or purchase to offset the initial transaction. As a result, since the market was declining, his transactions required funds to meet margin calls. Since he did not report to Mr. Bax but directly to the head office in London, he contacted the head office, and £454 million was sent in late January and early February.

Somehow he had convinced them that his operations were safe—but how? It seems that his ability to control the back office provided him the opportunity to do so. Earlier, when he began to trade heavily, the back office was swamped with transactions that included lots of errors made in the trading pits at the stock exchanges. He had been allegedly advised by Gordon Bowser, former derivatives trading chief, to set up a fictitious account, Error Account No. 88888, to put trading problems through and not to send reports to London so that the auditors would not be aroused. Instead, Leeson used the account as the hiding place for his losses, which totaled £2 million in 1992, £23 million in 1993, £208 million by the end of 1994, and £827 million by February 27, after Barings went into receivership. When the computer reports came off the printer for the fake account, Leeson destroyed them.

By happenstance, Anthony Hawes, the treasurer of Barings, visited Singapore. Over a sumptuous lunch on Wednesday the 22nd, he told Leeson that he was to get a bonus of at least $2 million (Singapore) on Friday the 24th. In addition, he told Leeson that the bank had a new policy of control, that he wanted to review the back room operation and check the accounting operation. Pleading that his wife was having a miscarriage and needed him, Leeson rushed from a meeting with Hawes on Thursday and left for Kuala Lumpur. He had evidently realized that the jig was about to be up and he would be caught.

Later, after he was caught, Leeson's wife revealed that the pressure for profits had become too much and that he had begun to take more risks. At the end, he was just trying to make back the losses. Before he was caught, Leeson reportedly phoned a friend from his Malaysian hotel and said, "People senior to me knew exactly the risks I was taking. Lots of people knew. . . . But it went wrong and now they're trying to lump all the blame on me."[1] Will we ever really know for sure?

Questions

1. How would you deal with a star trader who would be extremely sensitive to additional controls that implied he or she wasn't trusted or would generate more time on paperwork and explanations?

1. *The Observer,* "Busting the Bank," March 5, 1995, p. 25.

—Continued

2. What ethical and accounting controls would you advise ING to institute at Barings?

3. Who was more at fault—top management or Nick Leeson?

SOURCES: *Financial Post.* "Leeson Expected to Receive a Light Sentence," December 2, 1995, p. 12.

Financial Post. "Police Hunt Rogue Trader Who Torpedoed Barings," February 28, 1995, p. 3.

Financial Post. "Buyers Circle Barings' Corpse," March 1, 1995, p. 5.

Financial Post. "Death Came Sudden and Swift for Barings," March 4, 1995, pp. 6, 7.

Financial Post. "Leeson Says Barings Told Him to Set Up a Secret Account," February 14, 1996, p. 10.

Financial Post. "Ex-Barings Directors Sued by Auditors," November 30, 1996, p. 15.

Manchester Guardian Weekly. "Barings Bank Goes Bust in 17 Bn Scam," week ending March 5, 1995, p. 1.

The Observer. "Busting the Bank," March 5, 1995, pp. 23–25.

The Observer. "Barings' Dutch Master," March 12, 1995, p. 8/Business.

Toronto Star. "Leeson's Resignation," March 7, 1995, p. D1.

Toronto Star. "Barings Loss Expands 50% as Takeover Approved," March 7, 1995, p. D6.

Manchester Guardian Weekly. "Barings Saved, but City Faces Inquiry," March 12, 1995, p. 1.

The Observer. "Norris Was a Director in Singapore," March 12, 1995, p. 1.

Philip Services Corp. . . . into the Dumper

At its zenith in late 1997, Philip Services Corporation was the largest waste management/metals recycler conglomerate in the world, and its co-founders, Philip and Allen Fracassi, were on top of the heap. Its combined annual sales were supposedly in the order of US$1.8 billion and its net profit a sizable positive figure. Goodwill, largely from acquisitions of smaller competitors at prices above their book values, was said to be in the neighborhood of $1,150 million.[1] On November 17, 1997, a major 20 million-share issue financing was completed at US$16.50 per share to trade on the New York Stock Exchange.[2] All was apparently well in the Philip world.

1. *Financial Post.* "Philip Weighs Up Problems," February 3, 1998, pp. 1, 2.
2. *Financial Post.* "Philip Plans Further Probe of Copper Trading Losses," August 1, 1998, p. 2.

Then, in 1998, came the bumps in the road. First, an anonymous letter arrived, citing large unreported losses. Then, the head of the company's metal division, Robert Waxman, resigned. A mountain of copper was missing. Many of the acquisitions made by the company, which fueled its rising sales and profit figures, were found to be money losers. Much of the US$1.15 billion in goodwill largely created from purchasing companies at valuations above book value had to be written off. Philips revised its 1995, 1996, and 1997 reported financial results five times, including several after the company's auditors had certified them. Cash was short, lenders got antsy, and regulators and top management was shuffled, with some departing to make room for more credible outsiders. Charges and counter-charges flew back and forth as

current and ousted managers and directors laid blame at the door of the others. In the end, Carl Icahn, a vulture fund-type investor took a run at the company, and, as 1998 closed, it made a proposal to creditors for voluntary insolvency and reorganization protection. *Lenders were to receive value worth 18 cents on the dollar, and the company's shares that had traded as high as US$17.90 on October 31, 1997, finished up at US$3/16 on November 24, 1998.* More than twenty class action lawsuits were filed, charging that Philip's directors and management had misrepresented the company's financial status when the share issue of November 1997 was made, and when shares at high valuations were used for acquisitions. Class action participants were afraid the reorganization would nullify their claims.

—Continued

Continued

Questions abound. Were the directors and top management guilty of misrepresentation, as alleged? If so, why did they do it? How was it done? Why didn't the company's auditors discover the problems? Were they negligent? What could the company's directors, officers, accountants, and auditors have done differently? What could the accounting profession do to improve the situation? Selected details of how Philip fortunes changed during 1998 follow.

A SELECTED CHRONOLOGY OF PHILIP SERVICES CORPORATION'S 1998 SLIDE INTO THE DUMPER
[CLOSING STOCK PRICES ARE SHOWN IN SQUARE BRACKETS.]

Jan. 5: Robert Waxman, head of the metals division, resigns. Earlier, on December 4, an anonymous letter claimed that Waxman diverted and sold copper and would be fired. The company branded it "hate mail" and denied Waxman was to be sacked.[3]

Feb. 3: A "US$200 million after tax writedown to cover a mountain of its copper inexplicably missing from its inventory"[4] [US$8 1/8]

Feb. 3: A writedown on goodwill of between US$60 and 85 million to provide for acquisitions between 1993 and 1996[5]

Feb. 20: Seventh lawsuit is filed alleging misrepresentation of "true financial condition" before issuing US$379.5 million of shares in November 1997.[6]

Mar. 5: A company press release details "special and non-recurring charges totaling US$310.5 million, including a US$92.2 million pretax loss in copper trading built up in 1995 ($27.2 million) and 1996 ($65 million) caused by rogue trading (outside the company's normal business practices) by people who "were no longer with the company."[7] Questions are raised about how such losses could be hidden from top management, accountants, and auditors because they amounted to more than the company's net earnings in those years. The company's press releases are not clear, but prepaid or inventory accounts were hinted at as hiding places. Even so, the drain on cash reserves should have been noticed.

Mar. 31: The company files a 10K submission with the Securities and Exchange Commission, including a report signed off on by the company's auditors, Deloitte & Touche, on March 4 that details "special and non-recurring charges" at US$346.2 million, or *$35.7 million more* than reported on March 5. Questions are asked and the company responds, saying that an additional US$13.6 million of nonrecurring charges were discovered *after* March 5 and the 10K filing identifies US$22.1 million as a restatement of revenue for the recording of revenue in the wrong period, thus overstating both revenues and accounts receivable.[8]

Apr. 23: Another press release announces that "Philip and its auditor, Deloitte & Touche, had determined its financial statements for 1997 ... understated the company's liabilities by ... US$30 million. The company also determined that adjustments to balance sheet accounts of approximately US$5 million are also required"[9]

Apr. 24: SEC and Ontario Securities Commission regulators are said to be probing why the company had reported five versions of 1995, 1996, and 1997 financial results, some of which were at variance with audited reports.[10]

---

3. *Financial Post.* "Philip Charges Waxman," July 31, 1998, p. 1.
4. *Financial Post.* "Philip weighs up problems," February 3, 1998, p. 2.
5. Ibid., p. 2.
6. *Financial Post.* "Philip Now Facing Seven Lawsuits," February 20, 1998, p. 5.
7. *Financial Post.* "Questions Remain on Philip," March 12, 1998, pp. 1, 2.
8. *Financial Post.* "Philip Reports Don't Add Up," April 4, 1998, p. 5.
9. *Financial Post.* "Philip Takes Another Hit," April 24, 1998, p. 1.
10. *Financial Post.* "Canadian and US Regulators Probe Philip After Latest 'Losses,' " April 25–27, 1998, pp. 1, 2.

—Continued

Continued

A SELECTED CHRONOLOGY OF PHILIP SERVICES CORPORATION'S 1998 SLIDE INTO THE DUMPER, CONTINUED
[CLOSING STOCK PRICES ARE SHOWN IN SQUARE BRACKETS.]

Apr. 24: Some investors are said to be losing their patience with Philip; some are not. "Asked what the feeling was among investors who had been supporting Philip, the analyst said: 'Absolute disbelief would be an understatement. Astonishment gets you closer.'" Another broker said that the stock was "very cheap" and "we are not getting off this position," but his firm was reported as a net seller of stock in April.[11]

May 7: Philip announces changes to senior management and its board of directors. Felix Pardo, Robert Knauss, and Allen Fracassi are appointed president and CEO, chairman, and executive vice chairman. Howard Beck resigns as chairman and director; Marvin Broughton resigns as CFO; Philip Fracassi, co-founder of the company, resigns as president of the Metals Services Group and Chief Operating Officer; and Robert Chiste resigns as executive vice president. Harland Riker of Cambridge, MA agrees to stand for election to the board and an additional independent director is being searched for.[12] [lost $1 1/2 to close at US$6]

May 7: First quarter 1998 results are released, showing a net loss of US$565,000 caused by losses totaling about $5.1 million due to withdrawing from its copper business after a gain of $14.7 million from a break-up fee related to its participation in an unsuccessful bid for Safety-Kleen. The company also announces that its auditors had "not concluded their examination of the Company's financial statements for 1997" ... but "the company believes that liabilities for the year ended December 31, 1997 were understated by US$26.0 million, resulting in an overstatement of the Company's after tax earnings for the year of US$19.0 million. In addition, the Company believes that accounts receivable and prepaid expenses were overstated by US$4.8 million."[13]

May 7: Philip is alleged to have stretched accounting rules since it went public in 1990, according to sources close to Philip's accounting department. "The company (allegedly) capitalized minor expenses to boost assets and earnings, under reported liabilities, and kept shareholders in the dark in other ways." The same sources allege that "these practices were pressed on reluctant staff by intimidation exercised by its principal executives, Allen and Philip Facassi." "'If the results were not good Philip [Fracassi] came screaming to the [accountants].'" "...This was described as 'management by intimidation.' Internally, the accounting standard, Generally Accepted Accounting Principles was jokingly referred to as Generally Accepted Accounting at Philip. The company also took sophisticated measures to keep the auditors, Deloitte & Touche, from taking a negative view of its books.... People who really understand Philip have many reasons for not speaking to the media. One is a valid fear of being caught up in a lawsuit.... The company sued former accountant Michael Hilson for $30 million after he criticized Philip."[14]

May 16: Auditor Deloitte & Touche signs off a second time on 1997 financial statements that show a net loss of US$126 million, which is some $22 million more than first detailed in April. Felix Pardo cautions the investment community that a further loss of $23 million could result from the sale of $58 million of copper inventory.[15] [US$5 7/16]

---

11. *Financial Post.* "Investors Losing Their Patience with Philip," April 25, 1998, p. 4.
12. Philip Services Press Release, May 7, 1998.
13. Second Philip Services Press Release, May 7, 1998.
14. *Financial Post.* "Philip Stretched Rules," May 7, 1998, pp. 1, 2.
15. *Financial Post.* "Deloitte Signs Off Again on Philip's Results," May 16, 1998, p. 5.

—Continued

Continued

A SELECTED CHRONOLOGY OF PHILIP SERVICES CORPORATION'S 1998 SLIDE INTO THE DUMPER, CONTINUED
[CLOSING STOCK PRICES ARE SHOWN IN SQUARE BRACKETS.]

May 20: CEO Felix Pardo states that whoever is responsible for trading losses and accounting errors will be held accountable. "Pardo blamed some of Philip's problems on the 18 accounting systems in use in its industrial services division following the acquisition of dozens of companies in 1997.... The result was that the reports upper management received were not timely and lacked segmented data."[16]

May 27: Graham Hoey, senior vice president of finance, discloses that the $26 million loss not discovered until the end of the first quarter of 1998 was disguised and masked by the issuance of a repayable note created by someone with substantial clout to do outside financings.[17] No names are revealed.

June 3: Plans are made to sell the metals division, which accounted for approximately 60 percent of 1997's $1.8 million in sales.[18] [US$3 15/16]

June 4: Lenders want to see sale of assets bring in at least $550 million to pay off at least half of $1.1 billion owed in debt[19] as the company's debt covenant has become a problem. [US$4 1/2]

July 30: Robert Waxman, former head of Philip's metals division is sued for $150 million, along with others for $90 million plus costs for all twenty-seven shareholder class action suits for allegedly defrauding the company in a copper trading scheme, hiding the nature of the transactions, removing significant sums of cash for his own use, trading with and through a company he owned an interest in, inflating metals group profits to inflate his bonus, and improperly obtaining payments for personal expenses. In response, Waxman says: "Any allegations raised by Philip are totally frivolous. The company was aware at all times and approved any and all of my activities during my employment there."[20]

July 30: On the same day he is sued, Robert Waxman breaks his seven-month silence and tells reporters of a number of incidents of accounting trickery at Philip, including

- In 1997 a commodity financing group gave Philip a short-term loan of $30 million against Philip's inventory. This was recorded as a sale, not a loan, thus inflating sales and understating liabilities.

- When the $30 million was repaid, part of the payback was recorded as a consultant's fee for an unrelated acquisition rather than as a payback to the lender.

- Funds received from accounts receivable factors were recorded without reflecting the need to pay to the factoring company any receivables collected.[21]

July 31: Robert Waxman denies company allegations and issues a statement with company memos attached. He says, "A review of these documents suggests that the management, the board and, perhaps, the external auditors were aware or should have been aware on a progressive basis of the accumulating losses of the company well before the end of 1997. The figure of US$192,670,000 of losses was known by the summer of 1997 and a 'restructuring charge' to account for these losses was discussed in September, 1997."[22] [US$2 9/16]

---

16. *Financial Post.* "Philip to Say Who Is Responsible for Losses," May 21, 1998, p. 7.
17. *Financial Post.* "Philip Executive Breaks Silence on Tangled Finances," May 28, 1998, pp. 1, 2.
18. *Financial Post.* "Philips Hopes to Keep Afloat by Tossing Metals Unit over the Side," June 3, 1998, pp. 1, 2.
19. *Financial Post.* "Philip Faces Another Writedown," June 4, 1998, p. 3.
20. *Toronto Star.* "Philip Sues Ex-staff for Fraud," July 31, 1998, pp. E1, 3.
21. *Financial Post.* "Waxman Accuses Philip of 'Accounting Trickery,'" July 31, 1998, p. 7.
22. *Toronto Star.* "Intrigue Mounts in Philip Case," August 1, 1998, p. E1.

—Continued

Continued

A SELECTED CHRONOLOGY OF PHILIP SERVICES CORPORATION'S 1998 SLIDE INTO THE DUMPER, CONTINUED
[CLOSING STOCK PRICES ARE SHOWN IN SQUARE BRACKETS.]

Aug. 6: "Voodoo accounting, allegedly used by Philip Services Corp. to bamboozle investors dates back as far as 1992 according to a file unsealed by a Hamilton court. . . . The allegations were made three years ago by Michael Hilson, a chartered accountant and former employee." "Doug Hodgson, a Philip lawyer, said in court that Hilson's allegations are lies. The file containing them was sealed by court order in 1996 because, Hodgson said, Hilson had revealed confidential Philip information and, in doing so, had breached his fiduciary duty as a member of the Canadian Institute of Chartered Accountants. . . . Philip has also made other accusations against Hilson. . . . 'He drank heavily, sometimes to the point of stupidity [and he was depressed . . .]' . . . . When he heard these allegations in court, Hilson laughed."[23]

Aug. 6: "US financier Carl Icahn said he had upped his holding of Philip's stock to 11.5% from 9% 'for investment reasons.'"[24]

Aug. 14: Five executives (Allen Fracassi, Howard Beck, Colin Soule [senior VP], Marvin Broughton, and Peter Chodos [executive VP]) are sued for misrepresentation in regard to the purchase of the Steiner-Liff metals group in November 1997. Of the US$157 million purchase price, US$56 million was in the form of Philip shares, which were worth US$17 3/8 on October 31, 1997, and US$2 1/8 today.[25]

Aug. 21: Bank lenders install overseers for Philip management to receive cash flow reports and monthly financial statements, and give approval for acquisitions and for paying the fees of bank legal and forensic advisors.[26] [US$1 1/2]

Sept. 1: Sale of a small glass recycling business and an electrical instrument company collapses.[27] [US$1 1/4]

Oct. 6: After investigation by a legal firm, McCarthy Tetrault, aided by Pricewaterhouse-Coopers, Philip denies Waxman's charges of senior personnel involvement or personal benefit in the fraudulent trading and improper accounting in the metals division.[28] [US$13/16]

Oct. 14: Province of Ontario officials asked Philip to halt shipments of cyanide-laced sludge from the United States to Canada. Apparently the U.S. shipping manifest describes a waste too hazardous to be dumped, but the Canadian manifest describes it differently. For two years, Philip has been treating this waste in Hamilton, Ontario, and dumping it nearby.[29] Moreover, the dumpsite that has been opened for only two years may not be able to handle hazardous waste in the future.

Oct. 15: Alan Facassi is fired as CEO and a turnaround specialist, John McGregor, is hired primarily to "work with our banks."[30] [US$9/16]

Nov. 12: In a lengthy interview responding to Philip's charges in its US$150 million lawsuit against him, Robert Waxman details several of the accounting issues that gave rise to unreported losses. For example, a pile of copper wire was valued as having a copper content of 8 percent for a total value of $8 million, but the recycler could find only

23. *Financial Post.* "Philip Court Battle Heats Up," August 7, 1998, p. 5.
24. Ibid., p. 5.
25. *Financial Post.* "Philip Managers Hit with Lawsuit," August 15, 1998, pp. 1, 2.
26. *Financial Post.* "Bank 'Minders' Installed at Philip," August 21, 1998, p. 5.
27. *Financial Post.* "New Setback for Philip as Seco Sale Collapses," September 1, 1998, p. 7.
28. *Financial Post.* "Philip Turns Up Heat on Former Metals Division Boss," October 6, 1998, p. 3.
29. *Financial Post.* "Philip Waste Situation in a Muddle," October 14, 1998, p. 6.
30. *Financial Post.* "Beleaguered Philip Fires CEO," October 15, 1998, p. 3.

—Continued

Continued

A SELECTED CHRONOLOGY OF PHILIP SERVICES CORPORATION'S 1998 SLIDE INTO THE DUMPER, CONTINUED
[CLOSING STOCK PRICES ARE SHOWN IN SQUARE BRACKETS.]

2 percent. The erroneous valuation was not written off in the second quarter of 1997, as the accountant was instructed not to do so. In another scheme alleged by Waxman, Philip purchased copper on thirty-day payment terms but sold it the next day to create a cash bulge. When payment for the first batch was required, another batch was purchased and sold on the second day to get the cash, and so the process started over again. "Under the system, Philip, forced to dump copper on the market and pay interest on copper for which it owed money, racked up losses, according to a memo from then-Philip Treasurer Fred Cranston. . . . Mr. Cranston wrote that in one particular case the copper trading losses were the equivalent of a loan at 47% interest. There was a master plan, Mr. Waxman says. 'Allen Fracassi was trying to get the company so big that he could just write off the $150 million [US] as accounting problems and nobody would notice.'"[31]

Nov. 21: Alan Fracassi becomes the CEO again, after two days of talks in New York with corporate raider Carl Icahn collapses and Philip offers to turn the company over to its lenders. According to the agreement filed with the SEC, forty banks and vulture funds that hold US$1.1 billion in debt will receive 90 percent of the shares of a new Philip and will continue to hold US$200 million of secured debt. Current shareholders will receive 10 percent of the new shares. Other lenders must agree to accept US$300 million in new notes. Mr. McGregor is to be freed up to work on the tight deadlines involved to file involuntary insolvency proceedings by February 28, 1999, and to complete them by July 30.[32]

Nov. 24: Amid fears that the agreement announced on Friday, November 21, would allow escape from class action suits, investors trade the company's shares wildly on Monday.[33] [US$3/16]

31. *Financial Post.* "Scrapping over Philip's Troubles," November 12, 1998, p C9.
32. *Financial Post.* "Allen Fracassi Takes Back Helm at Philip Services," November 21, 1998, pp. D1, 3.
33. *Financial Post.* "Banks in Line to Get 18c to the Dollar on Philip's Debt," November 24, 1998, p. C3.

Ethics case

Dow Corning Silicon Breast Implants

On January 6, 1992, the "growing controversy over the safety factor led the U.S. Food and Drug Administration to call for a moratorium on breast implants."[1] As January wore on, the crisis deepened until, on January 30, the Toronto *Globe & Mail* carried a New York Times Service report entitled "Dow Corning Fumbles in Damage Control." Among other critical points, that article stated:

Regardless of whether Dow Corning Inc. ever convinces regulators its silicone-gel breast implants are safe, the company seems likely to be branded as bungling in its handling of the problem, say public relations and crisis management experts.

"It's a textbook case of crisis management," . . . "it looks like the lawyers are in charge, trying to limit their liability." "But the damage is much worse to the corporation if they lose in the court of public opinion than if they lose in the court of law."

—*Continued*

1. Feder, Barnaby. "Dow Corning Fumbles in Damage Control." *Toronto Globe & Mail* (January 30, 1992): 3.

Continued

Consultants concede that, because Dow Corning argues there is little evidence supporting many of the injury claims, it is difficult for the company to act sympathetically without appearing to undermine its legal strategy. (p. B1)

The controversy escalated until, on March 20, one month after the U.S. authorities called for sharply restricted use and their Canadian counterparts opted for a moratorium, Dow Corning canceled its breast implant line. The company also offered up to $1,200 each to women in the U.S. not covered by private insurance who needed to have their implants removed. In addition, $10 million was to be spent by the company on research into breast implants.[2]

Among the issues raised by this unfortunate controversy is how

2. McKenzie, Rob. "Dow Cancels Implant Line." *The Financial Post* (March 20, 1992): 3.

Dow Cancels Implant Line

Rob McKenzie

Financial Post, March 20, 1992 Beseiged Dow Corning Corp quit the breast implant business yesterday, offering money to some women in the U.S. who need their implants removed, but leaving Canadian taxpayers to fund any medical costs here.

Bert Miller, president of subsidiary Dow Corning Canada Inc., said the number of medically necessary removals will not be as high as critics expect.

"I honestly don't think it's a huge amount," he said.

Dow Corning insisted its gel-filled sacs are no health hazard.

"Our reasons for not resuming production and sales, therefore, are not related to issues of science or safety, but to the existing condition of the marketplace," Dow Corning chairman and chief executive Keith McKennon said in a statement.

Miller told reporters in Toronto he was "personally quite convinced that there's been no unnecessary risk that wasn't worth the benefit."

He added: "We at Dow Corning stand by our product."

Many women say the company's silicone-gel implants maimed them or caused other health problems, either by leaking or bursting.

On Feb. 20, a panel of the U.S. Food and Drug Administration recommended use of the implants be sharply restricted. In Canada the Department of Health and Welfare has imposed a moratorium on their use.

Dow Corning, a Michigan-based joint venture of Dow Chemical Co. and Corning Inc., sold more than 600,000 breast implants, including an estimated 27,000 in Canada.

Besides ceasing production and sales, the company said it will spend US$10 million on research into breast implants. In the U.S., it will offer up to US$1,200 each to women who for medical reasons need their implants excised, but are not covered by private health insurance.

Miller said such surgery in Canada is covered by health-care programs.

Women who fear their implants will harm them, but as yet show no ill effects, are not eligible for aid.

"If she has no physical manifestation and the implant is not giving any problems, she should be calmed," Miller said.

Bryan Groulx, a manager of business development for the Canadian unit, added: "We're not here to provide unnecessary surgery."

One of Dow Corning's strongest critics, Ottawa consultant and breast-implant expert Dr. Pierre Blais, said yesterday's announcement was "a courageous and an appropriate decision."

Breast implants account for about 1% of Dow Corning's sales.

—Continued

Continued

faulty breast implants could come to be sold by Dow Corning, a company that had been lionized for almost a decade in three Harvard cases for its outstanding ethics program. The basic details of this program* are as follows:

Six managers serve three-year stints on a Business Conduct Committee; each member devotes up to six weeks a year on committee work.

Two members audit every business operation every three years; the panel reviews up to 35 locations annually.

*Further details of the program are described in "Dow Corning Corporation: Business Conduct and Global Values (A)," Harvard Business School case #9-385-018. See also pages 200 and 201 of the article by P. E. Murphy, which is a reading in this chapter.

Three-hour reviews are held with up to 35 employees. Committee members use a code of ethics as a framework and encourage employees to raise ethical issues.

Results of audits are reported to a three-member Audit & Social Responsibility Committee of the Board of Directors.[3]

Interestingly, although the silicone breast implant operation had been audited four times since 1983, and the ethics audit approach had failed to uncover any signs of problems, Jere Marciniak, an area vice president who is chairman of the Conduct

3. Byrne, John A. "The Best Laid Ethics Programs." *Business Week* (March 9, 1992): 67–69.

Committee, has stated that "he has no plans to touch . . . the ethics program. . . . 'It will still aid and guide us through this difficult time.'"

Questions

1. Why didn't the Dow Corning ethics audit program reveal any concerns about the silicone-gel breast implant line?

2. What are the critical factors necessary to make such an ethics audit program work effectively?

3. Was the announcement on March 20 well advised and ethical?

4. Are there any other ethical dilemmas raised by the case?

SOURCE: "Dow cancels implant line." *Financial Post* (March 20, 1992).

Playing God

Trish Ohling was the controller of South East Converters, Inc., a subsidiary of a small conglomerate in the paper industry, which was owned by Evan Trist, a man in his seventies. She was involved in the preparation of submissions for new capital funding which would go to the owner for his decision along with all of the rest of the submissions from the other subsidiaries. Trist had never created a tightly controlled management structure or specified the form of presentation or analytical techniques to be used in these submissions, because, as he said, "I prefer to hire only fully qualified people and then rely upon them to look after my interests."

"I'm in trouble," Trish began, thinking aloud. "If I use the optimistic estimates my management teammates have developed, we will surely get the capital we want, but we may not be able to achieve the results I forecast. If I use the 'best guess' figures we have developed it will be touch and go as to whether we are successful in getting the money or not. We need this project to maintain our competitive position; otherwise, I and many others are ultimately out of a job."

—Continued

Continued

"There is another way, of course. Our project will pay off very quickly, but there will be a big cleanup and storage problem when our sludge by-product gets too large for our current in-ground storage facility, which will happen in about seven years. I could just submit our projections for the first five years, and our project will look terrific. If I just use the payback period method of presentation, the seventh-year problem will never show up. Besides, Evan will be in his late seventies by then and probably won't remember anything about this. I may not even be working here by then."

Questions

1. Who are the stakeholders in this instance?

2. In this situation, why would Evan Trist's interest be better protected by a fully qualified professional rather than just a knowledgeable bookkeeper employee?

Readings

Creating Ethical Corporate Structures

Patrick E. Murphy

Sloan Management Review, Winter 1989, pp. 81–87

ETHICAL BUSINESS PRACTICES stem from ethical corporate cultures, the author writes. How does an organization go about developing that kind of culture? The most systematic approach is to build and nurture structures that emphasize the importance of ethical considerations. This paper outlines several companies' experiences with three types of ethics-enhancing structures: corporate credos, programs such as training workshops and ethics "audits," and codes tailored to the specific needs of a functional area. Ed.

WHAT IS AN ETHICAL COMPANY? This question is not easy to answer. For the most part, ethical problems occur because corporate managers and their subordinates are *too* devoted to the organization. In their loyalty to the company or zest to gain recognition, people sometimes ignore or overstep ethical boundaries. For example, some sales managers believe that the only way to meet ambitious sales goals is to have the sales reps "buy" business with lavish entertaining and gift giving. This overzealousness is the key source of ethical problems in most business firms.

Employees are looking for guidance in dealing with ethical problems. The guidance may come from the CEO, upper management, or immediate supervisors.[1] We know that ethical business practices stem from an ethical corporate culture.

Key questions are, How can this culture be created and sustained? What structural approaches encourage ethical decision making? If the goal is to make the company ethical, managers must introduce structural components that will enhance ethical sensitivity.

In this paper, I examine three promising and workable approaches to infusing ethical principles into business:

- corporate credos that define and give direction to corporate values;

- ethics programs where companywide efforts focus on ethical issues; and

- ethical codes that provide specific guidance to employees in functional business areas.

Below I review the virtues and limitations of each and provide examples of companies that successfully employ these approaches.

CORPORATE CREDOS

A corporate credo delineates a company's ethical responsibility to its stakeholders; it is probably the most general approach to managing corporate ethics. The credo is a succinct statement of the values permeating the firm. The experiences of Security Pacific Corporation (a Los Angeles–based national bank that devised a credo in 1987) and of Johnson & Johnson illustrate the credo approach.

—Continued

---

1. P. E. Murphy and M. G. Dunn, "Corporate Culture and Marketing Management Ethics" (Notre Dame, IN: University of Notre Dame, working paper, 1988).

Continued

Security Pacific's central document is not an ethical code per se; rather, it is six missionlike commitments to customers, employees, communities, and stockholders. The credo's objective is "to seek a set of principles and beliefs which might provide guidance and direction to our work" (see Table 1).

More than 70 high-level managers participated in formulating a first draft of the commitments. During this process, senior managers shared the analyzed examples of ethical dilemmas they had faced in balancing corporate and constituent obligations. An outside consultant, hired to manage the process, helped to draft the language. Ultimately more than 250 employees, from all levels of the bank, participated in the credo formulation process via a series of discussion groups.

Once the commitments were in final form, management reached a consensus on how to communicate these guiding principles to the Security Pacific organization. Credo coordinators developed and disseminated a leader's guide to be used at staff meetings introducing the credo; it contained instructions on the meeting's format and on showing a videotape that explained the credo and the process by which it was developed. At the meetings, managers invited reactions by posing these questions: What are your initial feelings about what you have just read? Are there any specific commitments you would like to discuss? How will the credo affect your daily work? Employees were thus encouraged to react to the credo and to consider its long-run implications.

Security Pacific's credo was recently cited as a model effort, and it serves internally both as a standard for judging existing programs and as a justification for new activities.[2] For example, the "commitment to communities" formed the basis for a program specifically designed to serve low-income constituents in the area. However, this credo should not be considered the definitive approach to ethics management. First, the credo could be interpreted simply as an organizational mission statement, not as a document about ethics. Indeed, the examples supporting the credo and the videotape itself do stress what might just be called good business practice, without particular reference to ethical policies. And second, the credo has not been in place long enough for its impact to be fully assessed.

Any discussion of corporate credos would be incomplete without reference to Johnson & Johnson, whose credo is shown in Table 2. This document focuses on responsibilities to consumers, employees, communities, and stockholders. (The current J&J president, David Clare, explains that responsibility to the stockholder is listed last because "if we do the other jobs properly, the stockholder will always be

served.") The first version of this credo, instituted in 1945, was revised in 1947. Between 1975 and 1978, chairman James Burke held a series of meetings with J&J's 1,200 top managers; they were encouraged to "challenge" the credo. What emerged from the meetings was that the document in fact functioned as it was intended to function; a slightly reworded but substantially unchanged credo was introduced in 1979.

Over the last two years, the company has begun to survey all employees about how well the company meets its responsibilities to the four principal constituencies. The survey asks employees from all fifty-three countries where J&J operates questions about every line in the credo. An office devoted to the credo survey tabulates the results, which are confidential. (Department and division managers receive only information pertaining to their units and composite numbers for the entire firm.) The interaction at meetings devoted to discussing these findings is reportedly very good.

Does J&J's credo work? Top management feels strongly that it does. The credo is often mentioned as an important contributing factor in the company's exemplary handling of the Tylenol crises several years ago. It would appear that the firm's commitment to the credo makes ethical business practice its highest priority. One might question whether the credo is adequate to deal with the multitude of ethical problems facing a multinational firm; possibly additional ethical guidelines could serve as reinforcement, especially in dealing with international business issues.

When should a company use a corporate credo to guide its ethical policies? They work best in firms with a cohesive corporate culture, where a spirit of frequent and unguarded communication exists. Generally, small, tightly knit companies find that a credo is sufficient. Among large firms, Johnson & Johnson is an exception. J&J managers consciously use the credo as an ethical guidepost; they find that the corporate culture reinforces the credo.

When is a credo insufficient? This approach does not offer enough guidance for most multinational companies facing complex ethical questions in different societies, for firms that have merged recently and are having trouble grafting disparate cultures, and for companies operating in industries with chronic ethical problems. A credo is like the Ten Commandments. Both set forth good general principles, but many people need the Bible, religious teachings, and guidelines provided by organized religion, as well. Similarly, many companies find that they need to offer more concrete guidance on ethical issues.

ETHICS PROGRAM

Ethics programs provide more specific direction for dealing with potential ethical problems than general credos do. Two

---

2. R. E. Berenbeim, *Corporate Ethics* (New York: The Conference Board, research report no. 900, 1987), p. 15, pp. 20–22.

—Continued

Continued

TABLE I

THE CREDO OF SECURITY
PACIFIC CORPORATION

Commitment to Customer

The first commitment is to provide our customers with quality products and services which are innovative and technologically responsive to their current requirements, at appropriate prices. To perform these tasks with integrity requires that we maintain confidentiality and protect customer privacy, promote customer satisfaction, and serve customer needs. We strive to serve qualified customers and industries which are socially responsible according to broadly accepted community and company standards.

Commitment to Employee

The second commitment is to establish an environment for our employees which promotes professional growth, encourages each person to achieve his or her highest potential, and promotes individual creativity and responsibility. Security Pacific acknowledges our responsibility to employees, including providing for open and honest communication, stated expectations, fair and timely assessment of performance and equitable compensation which rewards employee contributions to company objectives within a framework of equal opportunity and affirmative action.

Commitment of Employee to Security Pacific

The third commitment is that of the employee to Security Pacific. As employees, we strive to understand and adhere to the Corporation's policies and objectives, act in a professional manner, and give our best effort to improve Security Pacific. We recognize the trust and confidence placed in us by our customers and community and act with integrity and honestly in all situations to preserve that trust and confidence. We act responsively to avoid conflicts of interest and other situations which are potentially harmful to the Corporation.

Commitment of Employee to Employee

The fourth commitment is that of employees to their fellow employees. We must be committed to promote a climate of mutual respect, integrity, and professional relationships, characterized by open and honest communication within and across all levels of the organization. Such a climate will promote attainment of the Corporation's goals and objectives, while leaving room for individual initiative within a competitive environment.

Commitment to Communities

The fifth commitment is that of Security Pacific to the communities which we serve. We must constantly strive to improve the quality of life through our support of community organizations and projects, through encouraging service to the community by employees, and by promoting participation in community services. By the appropriate use of our resources, we work to support or further advance the interests of the community, particularly in times of crisis or social need. The Corporation and its employees are committed to complying fully with each community's laws and regulations.

Commitment to Stockholder

The sixth commitment of Security Pacific is to its stockholders. We will strive to provide consistent growth and a superior rate of return on their investment, to maintain a position and reputation as a leading financial institution, to protect stockholder investments, and to provide full and timely information. Achievement of these goals for Security Pacific is dependent upon the successful development of the five previous sets of relationships.

—Continued

Continued

TABLE 2

JOHNSON & JOHNSON CREDO

We believe our first responsibility is to the doctors, nurses, and patients, to mothers and all others who use our products and services. In meeting their needs everything we do must be of high quality. We must constantly strive to reduce our costs in order to maintain reasonable prices. Customers' orders must be serviced promptly and accurately. Our suppliers and distributors must have an opportunity to make a fair profit.

We are responsible to our employees, the men and women who work with us throughout the world. Everyone must be considered as an individual. We must respect their dignity and recognize their merit. They must have a sense of security in their jobs. Compensation must be fair and adequate and working conditions clean, orderly, and safe. Employees must feel free to make suggestions and complaints. There must be equal opportunity for employment, development, and advancement for those qualified. We must provide competent management, and their actions must be just and ethical.

We are responsible to the communities in which we live and work and to the world community as well. We must be good citizens—support good works and charities and bear our fair share of taxes. We must encourage civic improvements and better health and education. We must maintain in good order the property we are privileged to use, protecting the environment and natural resources.

Our final responsibility is to our stockholders. Business must make a sound profit. We must experiment with new ideas. Research must be carried on, innovative programs developed and mistakes paid for. New equipment must be purchased, new facilities provided, and new products launched. Reserves must be created to provide for adverse times. When we operate according to these principles, the stockholders should realize a fair return.

companies—Chemical Bank and Dow Corning—serve as examples. Although the thrust of the two programs is different, they both illustrate the usefulness of this approach.

Chemical Bank, the nation's fourth largest bank, has an extensive ethics education program. All new employees attend an orientation session at which they read and sign off on Chemical's code of ethics. (This has been in existence for thirty years and was last revised in May 1987.) The training program features a videotaped message from the chairman emphasizing the bank's values and ethical standards. A second and more unusual aspect of the program provides in-depth training in ethical decision making for vice presidents.[3]

The "Decision Making and Corporate Values" course is a two-day seminar that occurs away from the bank. Its purpose, according to a bank official, is "to encourage Chemical's employees to weigh the ethical or value dimensions of the decisions they make and to provide them with the analytic tools to do that." This program began in 1983; more than

250 vice presidents have completed the course thus far. Each meeting is limited to twenty to twenty-five senior vice presidents from a cross-section of departments, this size makes for a seminarlike atmosphere. The bank instituted the program in response to the pressures associated with deregulation, technology, and increasing competition.

The chairman always introduces the seminar by highlighting his personal commitment to the program. Most of the two days is spent discussing case studies. The fictitious cases were developed following interviews with various Chemical managers who described ethically charged situations. The cases are really short stories about loan approval, branch closings, foreign loans, insider trading, and other issues.[4] They do not have "solutions" as such; instead, they pose questions for discussion, such as, Do you believe the individual violated the bank's code? Or, What should X do?

Program evaluations have yielded positive results. Participants said they later encountered dilemmas similar to the

---

3. A more detailed discussion of Chemical's comprehensive program, and of Johnson & Johnson's, appears in *Corporate Ethics: A Prime Business Asset* (New York: Business Roundtable, February 1988).

4. One of the case studies appears in "Would You Blow Whistle on Wayward Colleague?" *American Banker* 17 June 1988, p. 16.

—Continued

Continued

cases, and that they had developed a thinking process in the seminar that helped them work through other problems. This program, while it is exemplary, only reaches a small percentage of Chemical's 30,000 employees. Ideally, such a program would be disseminated more widely and would become more than a one-time event.

Dow Corning has a longstanding—and very different—ethics program. Its general code has been revised four times since its inception in 1976 and includes a seven-point values statement. The company started using face-to-face "ethical audits" at its plants worldwide more than a decade ago. The number of participants in these four-to-six-hour audits ranges from five to forty. Auditors meet with the manager in charge the evening before to ascertain the most pressing issues. The actual questions come from relevant sections in the corporate code and are adjusted for the audit location. At sales offices, for example, the auditors concentrate on issues such as kickbacks, unusual requests from customers, and special pricing terms; at manufacturing plants, conservation and environmental issues receive more attention. An ethical audit might include the following questions.

- Are there any examples of business that Dow Corning has lost because of our refusal to provide "gifts" or other incentives to government officials at our customers' facilities?

- Do any of our employees have ownership or financial interest in any of our distributors?

- Have our sales representatives been able to undertake business conduct discussions with distributors in a way that actually strengthens our ties with them?

- Has Dow Corning been forced to terminate any distributors because of their business conduct practices?

- Do you believe that our distributors are in regular contact with their competitors? If so, why?

- Which specific Dow Corning policies conflict with local practices?

John Swanson, manager of Corporate Internal and Management Communications, heads this effort; he believes the audit approach makes it "virtually impossible for employees to consciously make an unethical decision." According to Swanson, twenty to twenty-three meetings occur every year. The Business Conduct Committee members, who act as session leaders, then prepare a report for the Audit Committee of the board. He stresses the fact that there are no shortcuts to implementing this program—it requires time and extensive interaction with the people involved. Recently the audit was expanded; it now examines internal as well as external activities. (One audit found that some salespeople believed manufacturing personnel needed to be more honest when developing production

schedules.) One might ask whether the commitment to ethics is constant over time or peaks during the audit sessions; Dow Corning may want to conduct surprise audits, or develop other monitoring mechanisms or a more detailed code.

When should a company consider developing an ethics program? Such programs are often appropriate when firms have far-flung operations that need periodic guidance, as is the case at Dow Corning. This type of program can deal specifically with international ethical issues and with peculiarities at various plant locations. Second, an ethics program is useful when managers confront similar ethical problems on a regular basis, as Chemical Bank executives do. Third, these programs are useful in organizations that use outside consultants or advertising agencies. If an independent contractor does not subscribe to a corporate credo, the firm may want to use an ethical audit or checklist to heighten the outside agency's sensitivity to ethical issues.

When do ethics programs come up lacking? If they are too issue centered, ethics programs may miss other, equally important problems. (Dow's program, for example, depends on the questions raised by the audit.) In addition, the scope of the program may limit its impact to only certain parts of the organization (e.g., Chemical Bank). Managers who want to permanently inculcate ethical considerations may be concerned that such programs are not perceived by some employees as being long term or ongoing. If the credo can be compared with the Ten Commandments, then ethics programs can be likened to weekly church services. Both can be uplifting, but once the session (service) is over, individuals may believe they can go back to business as usual.

TAILORED CORPORATE CODES

Codes of conduct, or ethical codes, are another structural mechanism companies use to signal their commitment to ethical principles. Ninety percent of Fortune 500 firms, and almost half of all other firms, have ethical codes. According to a recent survey, this mechanism is perceived as the most effective way to encourage ethical business behavior.[5] Codes commonly address issues such as conflict of interest, competitors, privacy, gift giving and receiving, and political contributions. However, many observers continue to believe that codes are really public relations documents, or motherhood and apple pie statements; these critics claim that codes belittle employees and fail to address practical managerial issues.[6]

5. Touche Ross, *Ethics in American Business* (New York: Touche Ross & Co., January 1988).
6. Berenbeim (1987), p. 17.

—Continued

Continued

Simply developing a code is not enough. It must be tailored to the firm's functional areas (e.g., marketing, finance, personnel) or to the major line of business in which the firm operates. The rationale for tailored codes is simple. Functional areas or diversions have differing cultures and needs. A consumer products division, for example, has a relatively distant relationship with customers, because it relies heavily on advertising to sell its products. A division producing industrial products, on the other hand, has fewer customers and uses a personal, sales-oriented approach. A code needs to reflect these differences. Unfortunately, very few ethics codes do so.

Several companies have exemplary codes tailored to functional or major business areas. I describe two of these below—the St. Paul Companies (specializing in commercial and personal insurance and related products) and International Business Machines (IBM).

The St. Paul Companies revised their extensive corporate code, entitled "In Good Conscience," in 1986. All new employees get introduced to the code when they join the company, and management devotes biannual meetings to discussing the code's impact on day-to-day activities. In each of the five sections, the code offers specific guidance and examples for employees to follow. The statements below illustrate the kinds of issues, and the level of specificity, contained in the code.

- Insider Information. For example, if you know that the company is about to announce a rise in quarterly profits, or anything else that would affect the price of the company's stock, you cannot buy or sell the stock until the announcement has been made and published.

- Gifts and Entertainment. An inexpensive ballpoint pen, or an appointment diary, is a common gift and generally acceptable. But liquor, lavish entertainment, clothing, or travel should not be accepted.

- Contact with Legislators. If you are contacted by legislators on matters relating to the St. Paul, you should refer them to your governmental affairs or law department.

The "Employee Related Issues" section of the code is the most detailed; it directly addresses the company's relationship to the individual, and vice versa. This section spells out what employees can expect in terms of compensation (it should be based on job performance and administered fairly), advancement (promotion is from within, where possible), assistance (this consists of training, job experience, or counseling) and communications (there should be regular feedback; concerns can be expressed without fear of recrimination). It also articulates the St. Paul Companies' expectation of employers regarding speaking up (when you know something that could be a problem), avoiding certain actions (where the public's confidence could be weakened), and charting your career course.

The company also delineates employee privacy issues. The code outlines how work-related information needed for hiring and promotion is collected. (Only information needed to make the particular decision is gathered; it is collected from the applicant/employee where possible. Polygraphs are not used.) The St. Paul informs employees about what types of information are maintained. Finally, information in an individual's file is open to the employee's review.

The code covers other important personnel issues in depth, as well. It touches on equal opportunity by mentioning discrimination laws, but the emphasis is on the company recognition of past discrimination and its commitments to "make an affirmative effort to address this situation in all of its programs and practices." Data acquired from the St. Paul supports this point. Between 1981 and 1986, hiring and promotion increased 60 percent for minorities in supervisory positions and 49 percent for women in management—even though overall employment rose only about 3 percent during this time. In addition, the code informs employees that the company will reimburse all documented business expenses. And it covers nepotism by stating that officers' and directors' relatives will not be hired; other employees' relatives can be employed, so long as they are placed in different departments.

Being an ethical company requires providing clear guidelines for employees. The St. Paul Companies' extensive discussion of personnel policies does just that. Employees may strongly disapprove of certain policies, but they are fully informed. The termination policy, for example, states that employment is voluntary and that individuals are free to resign at any time; the company, too, can terminate employees "at any time, with or without cause." Some people may consider that policy unfair or punitive, but at least the rules of the

—Continued

Continued

game are clear. One limitation of the code is that all sections are not uniformly strong. For example, the marketing section is only one paragraph long and contains few specifics.

The second illustration is of a code tailored to the company's major line of business. IBM's "Business Conduct Guidelines" were instituted in the 1960s and revised more recently in 1983. New employees receive a copy and certify annually that they abide by the code. It has four parts; the most extensive section is entitled "Conducting IBM's Business." Since IBM is, at its core, a marketing and sales organization, this section pertains primarily to these issues.

Six subsections detail the type of activities IBM expects of its sales representatives. First, "Some General Standards" include the following directives, with commentaries: do not make misrepresentations to anyone, do not take advantage of IBM's size, treat everyone fairly (do not extend preferential treatment), and do not practice reciprocal dealing. Second, "Fairness in the Field" pertains to disparagement (sell IBM products on their merits, not by disparaging competitors' products or services). In addition, it prohibits premature disclosure of product information and of selling if a competitor already has a signed order. Third, "Relations with Other Organizations" cautions employees about firms that have multiple relationships with IBM (deal with only one relationship at a time, and do not collaborate with these firms).

The fourth and fifth sections address "Acquiring and Using Information for or about Others." The code spells out the limits to acquiring information (industrial espionage is wrong) and to using information (adverse information should not be retained). Employers must determine the confidentiality of information gathered from others. The final section outlines IBM's policy on "Bribes, Gifts, and Entertainment." The company allows customary business amenities but prohibits giving presents that are intended to "unduly influence" or "obligate" the recipient, as well as receiving gifts worth more than a nominal amount.

One might contend that it is easy for a large, profitable company like IBM to have an exemplary code. On the other hand, one could also argue that a real reason for the company's continued success is that its sales representatives do subscribe to these principles. Is this a perfect code? No. The

gifts area could use more specificity and, even though the company spends millions of dollars a year on advertising, that subject is not addressed in any section of the code. Further, IBM's legal department administers the code, which may mean that problems are resolved more by legal than ethical interpretation.

When should a company use a tailored code of ethics? If a company has one dominant functional unit (like IBM), or if there is diversity among functional areas, divisions, or subsidiaries, then a tailored code might be advisable. It allows the firm to promulgate specific and appropriate standards. Tailored codes are especially useful to complex organizations because they represent permanent guidelines for managers and employees to consult.

When should they be avoided? If a firm's leaders believe specific guidelines may be too restrictive for their employees, then a tailored code is an unsatisfactory choice. Codes are not necessary in most small firms or in ones where a culture includes firmly entrenched ethical policies. If a credo is similar to the Ten Commandments, and programs are similar to religious services, then tailored credos can be considered similar to the Bible or to other formal religious teachings. They provide the most guidance, but many people do not take the time to read or reflect on them.

CONCLUSION

My research on ethics in management suggests several conclusions that the corporate manager may wish to keep in mind.

- **There Is No Single Ideal Approach to Corporate Ethics.** I would recommend that a small firm start with a credo, but that a larger firm consider a program or a tailored code. It is also possible to integrate these programs and produce a hybrid: in dealing with insider trading, for example, a firm could develop a training program, then follow it up with a strongly enforced tailored code.[7]

- **Top Management Must Be Committed.** Senior managers must champion the highest ethical postures for their

---

7. G. L. Tidwell, "Here's a Tip—Know the Rules of Insider Trading." *Sloan Management Review,* Summer 1987, pp. 93–99.

—Continued

Continued

companies, as James Burke of J&J does. This commitment was evident in all the companies described here; it came through loud and clear in the CEO's letters, reports, and public statements.

- **Developing a Structure Is Not Sufficient by Itself.** The structure will not be useful unless it is supported by institutionalized managerial processes. The credo meetings at Security Pacific and the seminars at Chemical Bank are examples of processes that support structures.

- **Raising the Ethical Consciousness of an Organization Is Not Easy.** All the companies mentioned here have spent countless hours—and substantial amounts of money—developing, discussing, revising, and communicating the ethical principles of the firm. And in fact there are no guarantees that it will work. McDonnell Douglas has an extensive ethics program, but some of its executives were implicated in a recent defense contractor scandal.

In conclusion, let me add that managers in firms with active ethics structures—credos, programs, and tailored codes—are genuinely enthusiastic about them. They believe that ethics pay off. Their conviction should provide others with an encouraging example.

The author would like to thank Bernard Avisbai, Gene Laczniak, Michael Mokwa, Lee Tavis, and Oliver Williams, C.S.C., for their helpful comments on an earlier version of this article.

SOURCE: Reprinted from "Creating Ethical Corporate Structures", Patrick E. Murphy. *Sloan Management Review,* Winter 1989, pp. 81–87, by permission of the publisher. Copyright © 1989 by Sloan Management Review Association. All rights reserved.

Patrick E. Murphy is Associate Professor of Marketing at the College of Business Administration, University of Notre Dame. Dr. Murphy holds the M.B.A. degree from the University of Notre Dame, the M.B.A. degree from Bradley University, and the Ph.D. degree from the University of Houston. He is currently editor of the Journal of Public Policy and Marketing.

Chapter Four

Professional Accounting In the Public Interest, Post-Enron

Purpose of the Chapter

When the Enron, Arthur Andersen, and WorldCom debacles triggered the Sarbanes-Oxley Act of 2002 (SOX), a new era of stakeholder expectations was crystalized for the business world and particularly for the professional accountants that serve in it. The drift away from the professional accountant's role as a fiduciary to that of a businessperson was called into question and reversed. The principles that the new expectations spawned and renewed resulted in changes in how professional accountants are to behave, what services are to be offered, and what performance standards are to be met. These standards are to be embedded in a new governance structure and in guidance mechanisms, which will have domestic and international components. The influence of the International Accounting Standards Board (IASB) and the International Federation of Accountants (IFAC) will be as important as that of SOX in the long run.

This chapter examines each of these developments, and provides insights into important areas of current and future practice. Building upon the understanding of the new stakeholder accountability framework facing clients and employers developed in earlier chapters, the chapter explores public expectations for the role of the professional accountant and the principles that should be observed in discharging that role. This leads to consideration of the implications for services to be offered, and of the key "value added" or competitive edge that accountants should focus their attention on to maintain their reputation and vitality. Sources of ethical governance and guidance are also introduced. Prior reading of Chapter 2 is essential to understanding Chapter 4.

Both the increase in importance of traditional stakeholder concerns discussed in Chapter 1, and the impact of the Enron, Arthur Andersen, and WorldCom debacles discussed in Chapter 2, gave rise to a crisis of credibility for the business community, its reports and capital markets, and for professional accountants who were seen to be part of the problem. The public was looking for a return to credibility founded upon values such as trust, integrity, transparency of reports, and so on. The answer came in the form of SOX, which required the Securities and Exchange Commission (SEC) to create regulations bringing governance reforms for both corporations and the accounting profession.

The reforms called for businesses to be more openly accountable to the investing public, and for professional accountants to remember that they were professionals who were expected to protect the interests of investors and other stakeholders. Professional accountants were not expected to be involved in misrepresentations in order to assist management, or to avoid the risk of losing audit revenues—or their jobs if they were employees.

At the same time, the concerns of non-investor stakeholders such as customers, employees, or environmentalists were becoming serious barriers to the achievement of corporate objectives. Damage to reputation caused by ethical problems was recognized to be so significant as to be potentially fatal as in the case of Arthur Andersen.

Consequently, both business and professional accountants recognized that their future success depended upon meeting new regulations, and upon meeting the ethical expectations of stakeholders. Governance mechanisms for both business and the accounting profession now, more than ever, need to provide assurance that these expectations will be met.

Rededication of the Role of a Professional Accountant

Fortunately, the Enron, Arthur Andersen, and WorldCom debacles have made clear that professional accountants owe their primary loyalty to the public interest. This rededication to the public interest is critically important. Unless professional accountants clearly and properly understand their role, they cannot consistently answer important questions in an ethically responsible way, and as a result will probably offer questionable advice and make decisions that leave them and their profession exposed to criticism or worse. For instance, a clear understanding of role is essential to respond appropriately to questions about ethical trade-offs encountered and proper services to offer, such as:

- Who really is our client—the company, the management, current shareholders, future shareholders, the public?
- In the event I have to make a decision with ethical ramifications, do I owe primary loyalty to my employer, my client, my boss, my profession, the public, or myself?
- Am I a professional accountant bound by professional standards, or just an employee?
- Is professional accounting a profession or a business? Can it be both?
- When should I not offer a service?

- Can I serve two clients with competing interests at the same time?
- Is there any occasion when breaking the profession's guideline against revealing confidences is warranted?

PUBLIC EXPECTATIONS OF ALL PROFESSIONALS

There is little doubt that the public has different expectations of behavior for a member of a profession, such as a doctor or lawyer, than they do of a non-professional, such as a sales or personnel manager. Why is this? The answer seems to have to do with the fact that a professional often works with something of value where trust in how competently they will function or how responsibly they will conduct themselves is particularly important. Ultimately, the public's regard for a particular profession will govern the rights it enjoys: to practice, frequently with a monopoly on the services offered; to control entry to the profession; to earn a relatively high income; and to self-regulation or to be judged by one's peers rather than government officials. If a profession loses credibility in the eyes of the public, the consequences can be quite severe, and not only for the offending professional.

What makes a profession? In the final analysis, it is a combination of features, duties, and rights all framed within a set of common professional values—values that determine how decisions are made and actions are taken.

The thoughts of Bayles (1981) and Behrman (1988), which are summarized in Table 4.1, are useful in focusing on the important features. Professions are established primarily to serve society. The services provided to society are so important that high levels of expertise are required, which, in turn, call for extensive educational programs focused primarily on intellectual rather than mechanical or other training and skills. The most highly regarded professions normally are licensed to practice on the public with a high degree of autonomy from the "red tape" of government or other regulation as evidenced by the degree of control exercised by the profession over education, standard-setting, disciplinary, and licensing programs.

It is worth noting the importance of autonomy to a profession. Autonomy, or freedom from government regulations and regulators, allows members of a profession to be judged by their informed, objective peers, rather than by

TABLE 4.1

WHAT MAKES A PROFESSION

Essential Features   (Bayles)
- Extensive training
- Provision of important services to society
- Training and skills largely intellectual in character

Typical Features
- Generally licensed or certified
- Represented by organizations, associations, or institutes
- Autonomy

Foundation of Ethical Values   (Behrman)
- Significantly delineated by and founded on ethical considerations rather than techniques or tools

politically appointed regulators, and sanctions to be meted out without raising the attention of the public. This allows a profession to manage its affairs efficiently and discreetly, so that the public has the impression that the profession is responsible and able to discharge its duties to members of the public properly. If, however, the public becomes concerned that these processes are not fair or objective, or that its interest is not being protected, the government will step in to ensure that protection. Here, as it is in dealings with clients, the maintenance of the credibility of the profession is extremely important.

This lack of credibility due to recent financial scandals was responsible for the introduction in 2002 by the SEC and the Canadian Institute of Chartered Accountants (CICA) of Public Accounting Oversight Boards (PAOBs). The U.S. PAOB oversees professional accountants who are able to practice before the SEC on large companies whose stock is traded on U.S. stock exchanges—which means that its oversight will affect the practice of large professional accounting firms worldwide.

The services provided by a profession are so important to society that society is prepared to grant the profession the rights previously outlined, but it also watches closely to see that the corresponding duties expected of the profession are discharged properly. In general terms, the duties expected of a profession are the maintenance of:

- *Competence* in the field of expertise
- *Objectivity* in the offering of service
- *Integrity* in client dealings
- *Confidentiality* with regard to client matters
- *Discipline* over members who do not discharge these duties according to the standards expected

These duties are vital to the quality of service provided, a condition made more significant because of the *fiduciary relationship* a professional has with his or her clients. A fiduciary relationship exists when service provided is extremely important to the client, and where there is a significant difference in the level of expertise between the professional and the client such that the client has to trust or rely upon the judgment and expertise of the professional. *The maintenance of the trust inherent in the fiduciary relationship is fundamental to the role of a professional*—so fundamental that professionals have traditionally been expected to make personal sacrifices if the welfare of their client or the public is at stake.

In the past, some have argued that to be a true professional the individual had to offer services to the public—that a person serving as an employee in an organization did not qualify and, could be excused from following the ethical code of the profession involved. It was presumed that the need to serve the employer should be dominant. Unfortunately, the failings of this limited perspective were exposed in cases where buildings and other structures collapsed due to cheap construction, and, as with Enron, the disclosure of financial results was favorable to current management instead of current and future shareholders. In both instances, the professions involved—engineering and accounting—lost credibility in the eyes of the public. As a result, prior to Enron, some engineering and accounting professions decided to make their responsibility to the public explicit in their code of conduct.

The U.S. Senate, SOX, and the SEC have made it clear that service to the public interest is paramount. The concept of *loyal agency* just to an employer has been refuted by philosophers, and is clearly out of step with the expectations of today's public. The conditions of a fiduciary relationship—the necessity to trust or rely on the judgment and expertise of a professional—are as applicable to professionals who serve within organizations as employees as to those who offer services directly to the public. The public views the provision of services within organizations as indirectly for the public's benefit in any event.

In order to support this combination of features, duties, and rights, it is essential that the profession in question develop a set of values or fundamental principles to guide its members, and that each professional possess personal values that dovetail with these. Normally, desired personal values would include honesty, integrity, objectivity, discretion, courage to pursue one's convictions, and strength of character to resist tempting opportunities to serve themselves or others rather than the client. Without these values, the necessary trust required to support the fiduciary relationship cannot be maintained, so efforts are usually made by the profession to assess whether these values are possessed by candidates for the profession and by its members. Such screening is usually undertaken during the prequalification or articleship period, as well as by a discipline committee of the profession. Usually, criminal activity is considered cause for expulsion, and failure to follow the standards of the profession, which are expressed in its code of conduct, can bring remedial measures, fines, suspension of rights, or expulsion.

PUBLIC EXPECTATIONS OF A PROFESSIONAL ACCOUNTANT

A professional accountant, whether engaged in auditing or management, or as an employee or a consultant, is expected to be both an accountant and a professional. That means a professional accountant is expected to have special technical expertise associated with accounting and a higher than layman's understanding of related fields such as management control, taxation, or information systems. In addition, he or she is expected to adhere to the general professional duties and values previously described and to adhere to those specific standards laid out by the professional body to which he or she belongs. Sometimes a deviation from these expected norms can produce a lack of credibility for or confidence in the whole profession. For example, when an individual or a profession puts its own interests before those of the client or the public, a lack of confidence can develop that can trigger public enquiries into the affairs of the profession in general. Such was the case with the Treadway Commission (1987) in the United States and the Macdonald Commission (1988) in Canada. Recommendations from such enquiries for the revision of professional accounting are difficult to ignore.

Not surprisingly, professional accounting conforms quite well to the combination of features, duties, and rights in a framework of values as previously described for professions in general. These have been summarized specifically for professional accounting in Table 4.2.

DOMINANCE OF ETHICAL VALUES RATHER THAN ACCOUNTING OR AUDIT TECHNIQUES

Many accountants, and most nonaccountants, hold the view that mastery of accounting and/or audit technique is the *sine qua non* of the accounting profession. But relatively few financial scandals are actually caused by methodological errors in the application of technique—most are caused by *errors in*

Features

- Provision of important fiduciary services to society
- Extensive knowledge and skill are required
- Training and skills required are largely intellectual in character
- Overseen by self-regulating membership organizations
- Accountable to governmental authority

Duties Essential to a Fiduciary Relationship

- Continuing attention to the needs of clients and other stakeholders
- Development and maintenance of required knowledge and skills
- Maintenance of the trust inherent in a fiduciary relationship by behavior exhibiting responsible values
- Maintenance of an acceptable personal reputation
- Maintenance of a credible reputation as a profession

Rights Permitted in Most Jurisdictions

- Ability to hold oneself out as a designated professional to render important fiduciary services
- Ability to set entrance standards and examine candidates
- Self-regulation and discipline based on codes of conduct
- Participation in the development of accounting and audit practice
- Access to some or all fields of accounting and audit endeavor

Values Necessary to Discharge Duties and Maintain Rights

- Honesty
- Integrity
- Objectivity, based on independent judgment
- Desire to exercise due care
- Competence
- Confidentiality
- Commitment to place the needs of the public, the client, the profession, and the employer or firm before the professional's own self-interest

judgment about the appropriate use of a technique or the disclosure related to it. Some of these errors in judgment stem from misinterpretation of the problem due to its complexity, while others are due to lack of attention to the ethical values of honesty, integrity, objectivity, due care, confidentiality, and the commitment to the interests of others before those of oneself.

Examples of placing too much faith in technical feasibility rather than proper exercise of ethical values or judgment are readily available. For example, a conceptually brilliant accounting treatment will lack utility if it is biased or sloppily prepared. Suppression of proper disclosure of uncollectible accounts or loans receivable prior to bankruptcy is often not a question of competence but one of misplaced loyalty to management, a client, or oneself rather than to the public who might invest in the bank or savings and loan company.

It should be noted, however, that sometimes a disclosure problem is so complex or the trade-offs so difficult that suppression of disclosure seems a reasonable interpretation at the time the decision is made. For example, accountants are often confronted with the decision of when and how much to disclose about a company's poor financial condition. It is possible that the corporation may work out of its problem if sufficient time is allowed, but to disclose the weakness may trigger bankruptcy proceedings.

Particularly in these situations of uncertainty, accountants must take care that their decisions are not tainted by failing to observe proper ethical values. At the very least, ethical values must be considered on a par with technical competence—both qualify as *sine qua non*. However, the edge in dominance may be awarded to ethical values on the grounds that, when a professional finds a problem that exceeds his or her current competence, it is ethical values that will compel the professional to recognize and disclose that fact. *Without ethical values, the trust necessary for a fiduciary relationship cannot be sustained, and the rights allowed the accounting profession will be limited,* reducing the effectiveness that an independent profession can bring to society.

From time to time, other members of other professions have made the mistake of doing something because it is technically possible without regard to the ethical consequences. Genetic cloning may be an example of this practice, which is referred to as the *technological imperative*—meaning that if something can be done, it should be done. When this arises in accounting, it is usually because existing accounting standards do not prohibit the practice, and it is therefore presumed to be permitted. However, there are many examples of practices that were employed, such as pooling of interests or renegotiation of overdue mortgage loans which were then disclosed as current, only to be reversed, constrained, or changed when they were found not to satisfy the public interest fairly and objectively—in other words, in accord with fundamental ethical principles. Consequently, even though technical feasibility may govern the short-term decisions of some accountants, in the longer term, ethical considerations are dominant. Whether the interest of the profession is well served by adopting technical methods without thoroughly exploring their potential consequences is a question worth examining. Conceivably, the problems associated with pooling-of-interest merger consolidations or Enron's special purpose entities could have been foreseen and constraints devised if an "ethical screen" had been more explicitly in place.

PRIORITY OF DUTY, LOYALTY, AND TRUST IN A FIDUCIARY

Who should be the real client of a professional accountant? Since the primary role of the professional accountant is to offer important fiduciary services to society, the performance of those services often involves choices that favor the interests of one of the following at the expense of the others: the person paying your fee/salary; the current shareholder/owner of the organization; potential future shareholder/owners; and other stakeholders, including employees, governments, and lenders. A decision will have differing impacts in the short and long term, depending on the interest and situation of each stakeholder, and each should be examined carefully where a significant impact is anticipated. The intricacies of stakeholder impact analysis are discussed in depth in Chapter 5, but several general observations are worthy of mention for auditors and accountants.

A professional accountant is given the right to provide important fiduciary services to society because he or she undertakes to maintain the trust inherent in the fiduciary relationship. Not only must the professional accountant have expertise, but he or she must apply that expertise with courage, honesty, integrity, objectivity, due care, competence, confidentiality, and avoidance of misrepresentation in order to ensure that those relying on the expertise can trust that proper care is taken of their interests.

History has shown, however, that these values, characteristics, and principles are not enough, on their own, to ensure predictability and best practice in the choice of accounting treatments or audit approach. Consequently, in order to narrow the range of acceptable choices of accounting treatment or auditing practice, professional accountants are expected to adhere to generally accepted accounting principles (GAAP) and generally accepted auditing standards (GAAS). These generally accepted principles and standards have been created so that the choices made according to them will be fair to the multiplicity of users of the resulting financial reports and audits (i.e., *fair to the public interest*). This means, for example, that audited financial statements are intended to be fairly presented from the perspectives of all of the current shareholders, future shareholders, lenders, management, government, and so on. If audited financial statements are biased in favor of one user group over another, the trust fundamental to that fiduciary relationship will have been broken. The professional accountant involved will not be worthy of the trust placed in him or her, and will bring his or her fellow professionals into disrepute, thus affecting the reputation and credibility of the profession.

The need to adhere to the ethical values previously articulated and to GAAP is as important for professional accountants working in management, as employees, or as consultants as it is for those who are auditing financial reports. The difference between a skilled manipulator of numbers and a professional accountant is that a user can rely upon or have trust in the integrity of the professional's work. Any involvement with misrepresentations or biased reports or unethical activities will break the trust required in a professional's fiduciary relationships, and will bring other members of the profession into disrepute.

If a person wants to be a professional accountant, he or she must be prepared to act with integrity always, not just sometimes. He or she should not, for example, be involved with misrepresentations or illegalities due to a misguided sense of loyalty to an immediate client or employer. Loyalty is owed first to the public interest and then to the accounting profession through the observance of the principles articulated in its code of conduct and its standards.

Auditors are specifically appointed by shareholders or owners as their agents to examine the activities of an organization and to report upon the soundness of the financial systems and the reasonableness of the annual statements. This is done to protect the interests of the shareholders/owners from a number of problems, including the unscrupulous conduct of management. Audited financial reports are used and relied upon by both existing and prospective shareholders and creditors, as well as by governments and others. This reliance is critical to the effective running of commerce in general. The choice of accounting or disclosure treatment that maximizes current income at the expense of future income could breach the trust required for the fiduciary arrangement with the public—an outcome that could lead to charges of misrepresentation and loss of reputation for the auditor and the profession as a whole. The Enron choices triggered such a reaction. Accordingly, *an auditor's loyalty to the public should not be less than the loyalty to existing shareholders/owners, and should not be primarily to the management of the organization.*

In the case of accountants employed by organizations or by audit firms, there is no statutory or contractual duty to shareholders or the public. However, in the performance of their duties to their employer, professional accountants are expected to exercise the values of honesty, integrity, objectivity, and due care. These values prohibit professional accountants from being associated with a misrepresentation, so improper acts by an employer should cause professional accountants to consider their responsibility to other stakeholders, including those who would be disadvantaged by the act, and their professional colleagues whose reputation would be tarnished by association. From this perspective, the paramount duty of professional accountant employees is to ensure the accuracy and reliability of their work for the benefit of the end user—the public. It is not surprising that professional codes of conduct require disassociation from misleading information and misrepresentations. Unfortunately, some current codes do this with the requirement of silence or confidentiality, thus leaving unsuspecting stakeholders to their fate. Logic would dictate that maintenance of the trust required in specific fiduciary relationships is based on the broader trust between the public and the profession as a whole, so in the long term codes should change to protect the public-at-large rather than a specific stakeholder.

In summary, if the interest of the public is not the prime motivator of actions by both professional accountants in public practice and those who are employees, and the codes of conduct of the profession were seen to permit this, confidence in and support for that profession would be eroded. Government pressure would be brought to bear to reform the profession or to create a new group free of bias and loyal to the public's interest. The Treadway and Macdonald Commissions are examples of such pressure, and each has offered suggestions for change. As discussed in Chapter 2, the lack of credibility precipitated by the Enron, Arthur Andersen, and WorldCom disasters gave rise to the SOX reforms that brought new regulation and a rededication to the accounting profession.

Sometimes clients or employers are confused in their thinking that a professional accountant has a real or implied contract with them and must act only in the best interest of the client or employer. It is imperative to note, however, that the contract is one where the professional is understood to be answerable to the ethical codes of his or her profession—so it is unreasonable to expect absolute loyalty to the client or employer rather than the profession and ultimately to the public. On the other hand, it is reasonable for the client/employer to expect that a professional accountant will place the client/employer interest before that of the professional's self-interest. To do otherwise would undermine the trust required for a fiduciary arrangement to work. Legitimate confidences about business problems would not be shared for fear the interest of the client/employer would be subverted or obviated by premature release, or misused for personal gain, so the professional accountant would not be able to work effectively or on sensitive matters. As a result, the scope of an audit could be constrained to the detriment of the auditor, the profession, and the public. To prevent the release of client/employer confidences, most codes of conduct require confidences not to be divulged except in a court of law or when required by the discipline process of the profession.

In the final analysis, a professional accountant facing a difficult choice should make that choice so as to preserve the trust inherent in the fiduciary relationships: first with the public, then with the profession, then with the client/employer, and finally with the individual professional. The usual practice of placing the client/employer's interests first is valid only if those interests will be overridden by the interests of the public and the profession in circumstances where a proposed treatment would not be in the public interest or profession's interest, either legally or ethically. Any doubt about the primacy of the public interest should be erased by remembering that the once-revered, mighty, 85,000-strong Arthur Andersen disappeared within a year of being discovered abusing the public's trust at Enron.

CONFIDENTIALITY: STRICT OR ASSISTED

The previous analysis places the professional accountant in the unenviable position of having to keep confidential those aspects of the client/employer that he or she might not agree with, but which may not impact on the financial activities of the company sufficiently to be of concern to the public. If, for example, the professional is dismissed for refusing to misrepresent the receivables as current, he or she would have to seek other employment but could not discuss the reason for leaving the former employer. He or she could not discuss client/employer problems with anyone not bound by a code of confidentiality (i.e., someone in the accounting firm or a lawyer hired specifically for the purpose). Unless their professional society has an ethics adviser (some now have) who could be called upon, this leaves the professional accountant in a disadvantaged position from many perspectives. It also gives unscrupulous client/employers an opportunity to get away with wrongdoing.

Professional societies have begun to recognize that this strict level of confidentiality is not in the interest of several stakeholders, including the public, and have introduced a limited, confidential consultation service to ensure the professional has cost-free help to make the right decision, to call for a response from the client/employer and perhaps resolve the problem, and to reassure prospective employers. It is also noteworthy that, generally speaking, professional accountants are not yet expected to report problematic accounting treatments to securities regulators, taxation authorities, or their professional societies. It will be interesting to see if such a reporting responsibility emerges further. It has already done so in Canada, where all chartered accountants must report apparent breaches of the rules of conduct and for auditors of financial institutions who must report viability problems to the superintendent of financial institutions. Also, in England and Wales, chartered accountants are required to report money laundering for drugs and terrorists. Professional accountants in doubt about such responsibilities should check with their society.

Implications for Services Offered

ASSURANCE AND OTHER SERVICES

Professional accountants have developed fiduciary services in the following traditional areas:

- Accounting and reporting principles, practices, and systems
- Auditing of accounting records, systems, and financial statements
- Financial projections: preparation, analysis, and audit
- Taxation: preparation of tax returns and advice

- Bankruptcy: trustee's duties and advice
- Financial planning: advice
- Decision-making: facilitation through analysis and approach
- Management control: advice and design of systems
- Corporate and commercial affairs: general advice

These services are all bounded by the professional accountant's primary area of competence, accounting. However, as management needs changed, it was recognized that accounting expertise in the measurement, disclosure, and interpretation of data could be applied to provide services outside of the traditional area of accounting. For example, nonfinancial indicators of quality have become an important part of control systems, and they are far more timely than traditional financial reports.

More importantly, when examining the future vision of CPAs in the United States and CAs in Canada, it was realized that there were many so-called *assurance services* that could be offered *where the professional accountant could add value by adding credibility or assurance to a report or process.* In particular, the proper discharge of these services relies on the understanding possessed by professional accountants of fiduciary responsibilities, evidence-gathering and evaluation skills, scepticism, objectivity, independence and integrity, and reporting skills. In 1997, the AICPA Special Committee on Assurance Services estimated that while traditional audit services would generate approximately $7 billion per annum, new assurance services would generate $21 billion. The Special Committee developed a list of over 200 possible new assurance services and then winnowed it down to assurance services concerning:

- Risk assessment
- Business performance measurement
- Information systems reliability
- Electronic commerce (Website seal of approval)
- Health care performance measurement
- Eldercare

Additional details can be obtained from the AICPA Website. See the text's Website.

http://brooks.
swlearning.com

NEW SEC INDEPENDENCE RULES

What the Special Committee did not anticipate was the inability of its members to manage the inherent conflict of interest situations that arise when audit and other services are offered to the same client. This failure was responsible for the Enron, Arthur Andersen, and WorldCom disasters, and the reaction of SOX, discussed in Chapter 2, in setting limits on the services that could be offered by SEC auditors to their SEC registrant clients. Conflict of interest management was discussed in Chapter 3 and continues in this section.

The limitations introduced by SOX and ordered by the SEC restrict the auditor of an SEC registrant corporation—one that trades its stock on U.S. stock exchanges or raises funds from the U.S. public—from auditing his or her own work, or assuming an advocacy position for the client. This is to avoid those situations where the independent judgment that must be employed by an auditor to fairly judge the positions taken by an audit client is likely to be impaired or swayed from protecting the public interest. When auditing an information system installed by the audit firm, an auditor's self-interest (pride or wishing to retain the audit client revenue) may prevent him or her from pointing out an error or the result of an error. Advocating a client position may sway an auditor's position with regard to disclosure in accordance with GAAP to further the interests of current shareholders or management. Although most auditors have been managing most of these conflict situations successfully for decades, the Enron, WorldCom, and other disasters illustrate the serious consequences that can come from not properly managing the risks involved.

To avoid these conflict of interest risks in large company audits, and thereby protect the public interest, SOX required the SEC to ban the following non-audit services that would impair an accounting firm's independence from being offered by auditors to their SEC registrants:

- Bookkeeping or other services related to the accounting records or financial statements of the audit client;
- Financial information systems design and implementation;
- Appraisal or valuation services, fairness opinions, or contribution-in-kind reports;
- Actuarial services;
- Internal audit outsourcing services;
- Management functions or human resources;
- Broker or dealer, investment adviser, or investment banking services; and
- Legal services and expert services unrelated to the audit. …

The Commission's principles of independence with respect to services provided by auditors are largely predicated on three basic principles, violations of which would impair the auditor's independence: (1) an auditor cannot function in the role of management, (2) an auditor cannot audit his or her own work, and (3) an auditor cannot serve in an advocacy role for his or her client.[1]

The SEC also adopted other measures beyond limiting the specific services offered, that will:

- require that certain partners on the audit engagement team rotate after no more than five or seven consecutive years, depending on the partner's involvement in the audit, except that certain small accounting firms may be exempt from this requirement;
- establish rules that an accounting firm would not be independent if certain members of management of that issuer had been members of the accounting firm's audit engagement team within the one-year period preceding the commencement of audit procedures;
- establish rules that an accountant would not be independent from an audit client if any "audit partner" received compensation based on the partner procuring engagements with that client for services other than audit, review and attest services;
- require the auditor to report certain matters to the issuer's audit committee, including "critical" accounting policies used by the issuer;

---

[1]*Final Rule: Strengthening the Commission's Requirements Regarding Auditor Independence*, U.S. Securities and Exchange Commission, (see *http://brooks.swlearning.com*), modified 2/6/2003.

- require the issuer's audit committee to pre-approve all audit and non-audit services provided to the issuer by the auditor; and

- require disclosures to investors of information related to audit and non-audit services provided by, and fees paid to, the auditor.[2]

These SOX/SEC limitations will have an interesting impact on professional accounting because they apply only to the services offered to SEC registrants around the world. They could continue to be offered to non-SEC registrant audit clients and to audit clients of other firms. Moreover, the vast number of professional accounting firms around the world do not service large SEC registrant companies, or those trading securities on exchanges that will emulate the SOX/SEC position, so they will likely continue to offer these services to their audit clients. Consequently, within large worldwide firms and in smaller firms, professional accountants will still have to use their best judgment about which assurance service to offer, how to conduct them, and how to manage the conflict of interest risks involved.

CRITICAL VALUE ADDED BY A PROFESSIONAL ACCOUNTANT

A professional accountant's judgment about what services to offer and how to do so should be based, in part, upon an understanding of the critical value added by a professional accountant. *Credibility* is the critical value added by professional accountants in the newer assurance services as well as the traditional ones. This has become much more apparent during the recent visioning exercises.

Competence is, of course, a fundamental factor, and high levels of competence can and do provide a competitive advantage. But it is apparent that high competence can be acquired by nonprofessionals and is therefore not, by itself, the critical value added by a professional accountant. *Credibility to the immediate client/employer and to the public at large depends upon the reputation of the entire profession, and reputation stems from the professional values adhered to and the expectations those create in the persons being served.* In particular, the critical value added by a professional accountant lies in the expectation that whatever services are offered will be based on integrity and objectivity, and these values, in addition to an assured minimum standard of competence, lend credibility or assurance to the report or activity. These individual ethical values, reinforced by the standards of the profession, provide a competitive advantage to professional accountants and ensure that their services are in demand. In the words of Stanton Cook, President of the (Chicago) Tribune Company, accountants, entrepreneurs, manufacturers, salespeople, and even lawyers all say, "The product we are ultimately selling is credibility" (Priest, 1991).

STANDARDS EXPECTED FOR BEHAVIOR

The public, and particularly a client, expects that a professional accountant will perform fiduciary services with competence, integrity, and objectivity. While not obvious, *integrity* is important because it assures that whatever the service, it will be performed fairly and thoroughly. No detail will be omitted,

---

[2] *Commission Adopts Rules Strengthening Auditor Independence*, U.S. Securities and Exchange Commission (see *http://brooks.swlearning.com*).

understated, or misstated that would cloud the truth, nor would an analysis be put forward that misleads users. *Honesty*, or accuracy or truthfulness, is implied in all aspects of data gathering, measurement, reporting, and interpretation. Similarly, *objectivity* implies freedom from bias in the selection of measurement bases and disclosure, so as not to mislead those served. Objectivity cannot be maintained unless the professional accountant is *independent*-minded, or free from undue influence from any stakeholder. Independence is an issue developed at greater length in the later conflict of interest discussion.

Integrity, honesty, and objectivity are essential to the proper discharge of fiduciary duties. They are, with competence, so important to the critical value added from belonging to a profession that they must be protected by the profession in order to assure its future. Consequently, professional accounting organizations take pains to investigate and discipline members whose conduct is questionable with regard to these ethical values.

Judgment and Values

IMPORTANCE TO VALUE ADDED

The proper discharge of the ethical values of competence, integrity, honesty, and objectivity relies substantially, if not primarily, upon the personal ethical values of the professional accountant involved. If the profession itself has high standards, the individual professional can choose to ignore them. Often, however, a professional is simply not sufficiently aware of potential ethical dilemmas or the appropriate values to properly discharge his or her duties. Additionally, a professional may err in her or his judgment about the potential outcome of an ethical dilemma or about the seriousness of the outcome for those who must bear the impact. The credibility of the profession, therefore, rests on the values it espouses, the personal and professional ethical values of each individual member, and the quality of judgment exercised.

DEVELOPMENT OF JUDGMENT AND VALUES

How do professional accountants develop the judgment they must apply to ethical dilemmas? In the past, trial and error has been the established mode—largely experienced when growing up, or on the job by learning from others who have problems or pass on their own experience. But the limitations of trial and error are obvious, as significant costs may be borne by the learner, the client, society, and the profession. In addition, an orderly framework for thinking about future problems may never be developed, nor may the level attained by a professional be adequate to safeguard the profession's stakeholders, including the professionals themselves.

Trial and error can never be entirely supplanted by organized training or educational experiences, but many of the deficiencies previously noted can be remedied by a well-ordered, stimulating program that deals with the major issues to be faced and suggests practical, ethical approaches to their resolution. In this regard, it is helpful to consider how far a student's ethical reasoning capacity has progressed and how to advance that capacity. A model developed by Lawrence Kohlberg is helpful in this regard (Kohlberg, 1981, 1984; Colby & Kohlberg, 1987).

Kohlberg argues that individuals pass through six progressive stages of moral development, which are described in articles on accountants by Ponemon (1992); Ponemon & Gabhart (1993); Etherington & Schulting (1995); Cohen, Pant, and Sharp (1995); and Thorne and Magnan (1998). These six stages and the motivation that leads individuals to make decisions at each stage can be helpful, as is pointed out by W. Shenkir (1990), in designing an educational program to expose students to the six levels. Such exposure can enable students to develop their awareness, knowledge, and skills for dealing with ethical problems and may, through understanding the motivations involved, shift their moral reasoning to higher stages. The motivations, which influence people at each of Kohlberg's stages of moral reasoning, are identified in Table 4.3.

TABLE 4.3

MOTIVES INFLUENCING PEOPLE AT KOHLBERG'S SIX STAGES OF MORAL REASONING

STAGE DESCRIPTION	MOTIVE FOR DOING RIGHT
Preconventional	**Self-interest**
1. Obedience	Fear of punishment and authorities
2. Egotism—instrumental and social exchange	Self-gratification, concern only for oneself "Let's make a deal"
Conventional	**Conformity**
3. Interpersonal concordance	Role expectation or approval from others
4. Law and duty (social order)	Adherence to moral codes or to codes of law and order
Post-conventional, Autonomous, or Principled	**Interests of Others**
5. General individual rights and standards agreed upon by society	Concern for others and broader social welfare
6. Self-chosen principles	Concern for moral or ethical principle

Researchers have found that students in business facing ethical decisions are largely in cognitive stages 2 or 3, so there is quite a bit of growth that is possible and desirable (Weber & Green, 1991). Other researchers have found that business students believe that their success is more dependent on questionable ethical practices than do nonbusiness students, so orderly ethics education would appear desirable lest these attitudes pervade the students who enter the ranks of professional accounting (Lane & Schaup, 1989). Leaving the cognitive development of students for the accounting profession and graduate accountants to trial and error rather than significant thought and formal training could, in itself, be unethical. Exposure to educational material, linked to traditional course work and particularly to realistic cases, should provide students and graduate practitioners with a better understanding of the ethical issues, dilemmas, approaches to their resolution, and the values necessary to make good ethical judgments than would the vicissitudes of trial and error.

There are several sources of guidance available to professional accountants. The codes of conduct or ethics of their professional body and of their firm or employer rank as important reference points. However, many other inputs should also be taken into account when appropriate, because professional accountants must respond to a body of expectations and standards created by various professional accounting organizations in their own country and internationally together with standard setters, regulators, the courts, politicians, financial markets, and the public.

Expectations for behavior of professional accountants are and will be embodied in:

- Standard setters (FASB, IASB, CICA, ICAEW, and so on)
  - Generally accepted accounting principles (GAAP)
  - Generally accepted auditing standards (GAAS)
- Commonly understood standards of practice
- Research studies and articles
- Regulator's guidelines (SEC, OSC, NYSE, TSX, etc.)
- Court decisions
- Codes of conduct from:
  - Employer (i.e., corporation or accounting firm)
  - Local professional accounting bodies
  - International Federation of Accountants (IFAC)

No one organization has a monopoly on the creation of the environment of expectations or standards that a professional accountant in the United States, Canada, or elsewhere should meet. However, with the support of securities commissions around the world for harmonized global standards of accounting measurement, disclosure, and behavior, the FASB, IASB, and IFAC pronouncements are becoming more important sources of guidance. This convergence is reinforced by the desire of IFAC members—the professional accounting bodies including the AICPA, ICAEW, CICA, and most others around the world—to harmonize their accounting standards and ethical codes to those of the IASB and IFAC, and will mean that FASB, IASB, and IFAC standards should emerge as a dominant set and framework by 2005.

Currently, however, there are five national and international professional accounting organizations operating in North America, plus their subsets in each U.S. state or Canadian province (i.e., The Institute of Chartered Accountants of Ontario or a state society of certified public accountants). They and their functional and geographic mandates are listed in Table 4.4.

The regulatory frameworks of each country occupy an important place in the creation of the professional accounting environment because written standards usually flow from them. Table 4.5 provides an overview of the contributions of organizations important to the North American environment.

It is important to note that although a national body can develop a code of conduct, in all cases the local state or provincial subset organization controls its own members by enacting its own code of conduct (using the national code as a guide but not always adopting all its provisions), and policing and disciplining its members. Consequently, the standard of ethical expectation varies somewhat

TABLE 4.4

NATIONAL AND INTERNATIONAL ACCOUNTING ORGANIZATIONS OPERATING IN NORTH AMERICA

NAME	DESIGNATION	PRIME MANDATE(S)	LOCATION
American Institute of Certified Public Accountants (AICPA)	CPA	Auditing, management accounting	United States, some Canadian provinces
Institute of Management Accountants (IMA)	CMA	Management accounting	United States
Canadian Institute of Chartered Accountants (CICA)	CA	Auditing, management accounting	Canada
Society of Management Accountants of Canada (SMAC)	CMA	Management accounting	Canada
Certified General Accountants Association of Canada (CGAAC)	CGA	Management accounting, auditing	Canada, some provinces

from jurisdiction to jurisdiction, and from organization to organization. Fortunately, basic principles of ethical conduct apply to all organizations, and the convergence toward global ethics principles, accounting, and auditing standards holds considerable promise.

Professional Codes of Conduct

PURPOSE AND FRAMEWORK

Professional codes of conduct are designed to provide guidance about the conduct expected of members in order that the services offered will be of acceptable quality and the reputation of the profession will not be sullied. If that reputation is sullied, some aspect of a fiduciary relationship has been breached, and a service has not been performed in a professional manner. Alternatively, it may mean that a member has offended the rules of society in some way so as to bring the profession's name into disrepute and thereby damage the public trust required for its members to serve other clients effectively.

To be effective, codes of conduct need to blend fundamental principles with a limited number of specific rules. If a code were drafted to cover all possible problems, it would be extremely voluminous—probably so voluminous that few members would spend the time required to become familiar with it and to stay abreast of the constant flow of additions. With practicality in mind, most professional codes have evolved to the framework outlined in Table 4.6.

FUNDAMENTAL PRINCIPLES AND STANDARDS

The fundamental principles and standards described in Table 4.7 are found in most codes.

The maintenance of the *good reputation* of the profession is fundamental to the ability of the profession to continue to enjoy its current rights and privileges, including autonomy in the discipline of its members, the setting of accounting standards, and the recognition by the public and government that new competing professional organizations need not be created to serve the *public interest*

TABLE 4.5

CONTRIBUTIONS TO THE NORTH AMERICAN REGULATORY FRAMEWORK FOR PROFESSIONAL ACCOUNTANTS

ORGANIZATION	CONTRIBUTION GOVERNING ORGANIZATION'S MEMBERS/USERS
AICPA	Statements of Auditing Standards (SAS), research studies, journal articles, code of conduct
IMA	Statements of accounting practice, research studies, journal articles, code of conduct
Financial Accounting Standards Board (FASB)	Financial Accounting Standards (FAS)
CICA	Accounting and auditing standards in Canada, research studies, journal articles, code of conduct
SMAC	Statements of accounting practice, research studies, journal articles, code of conduct
CGAAC	Statements of accounting practice, research studies, journal articles, code of conduct
U.S. Securities and Exchange Commission (SEC)	Regulations related to U.S. public securities markets including corporate disclosure and governance, GAAP, GAAS, and behavior of auditors and other professionals practicing before the SEC. Regulation in respect to disclosure for companies raising funds in the USA. Standards of independence for CPAs auditing SEC companies
Ontario Securities Commission (OSC)	Regulations related to financial disclosure in Canada's principal securities market (Ontario), whose regulations are accepted by the SEC
U.S. and Canadian courts	Common law decisions affecting legal liability
International Federation of Accountants (IFAC) and the International Accounting Standards Board (IASB)	International Code of Ethics, and accounting and auditing standards that may facilitate international harmonization
Public Accounting Oversight Boards	Oversight in the U.S. and Canada

TABLE 4.6

TYPICAL FRAMEWORK FOR A CODE OF CONDUCT FOR PROFESSIONAL ACCOUNTANTS

Introduction and purpose
Fundamental principles and standards
General rules
Specific rules
Discipline
Interpretations of rules

more effectively. The phrase *at all times* is significant because the public will view any serious transgression of a professional accountant, including those outside business or professional activity, as a black mark against the profession as a whole. Consequently, if a professional accountant is convicted of a criminal offense or fraud, his or her certification is usually revoked.

Maintenance of standards of care is also imperative for the proper service to clients and the public interest. *Integrity, objectivity* and *honesty,* in the preparation

TABLE 4.7

FUNDAMENTAL PRINCIPLES
IN CODES OF CONDUCT FOR
PROFESSIONAL ACCOUNTANTS

Members should:

- at all times maintain the good reputation of the profession and its ability to serve the public interest,
- perform with:
  - integrity,
  - due care,
  - professional competence,
  - independence,
  - objectivity,
  - confidentiality, and
- not be associated with any misleading information or misrepresentation.

of reports, choice of accounting options, and interpretation of accounting data will ensure that neither the client nor the public will be misled. Sometimes reports or opinions can lack integrity if the professional involved has failed to maintain *independence* from one of the persons likely to benefit or be harmed by the report, and this causes the professional to bias the report, decisions, or interpretations toward the favored party.

Charges of bias are very hard to refute, so professionals are often admonished to avoid any situation or relationship that might lead to the *perception of bias*. This is why, even though in the past many professionals have served successfully as bookkeeper, auditor, shareholder, and director of an organization, modern codes of conduct recommend against situations involving such apparent conflicts of interest. The prospect of an auditor misstating a report for his or her own gain, or that of fellow shareholders, was judged to be too tempting a prospect to allow. Similar reasoning has led to the introduction of the separation of duties within an organization and, wherever possible, between the bookkeeping and audit functions. In simplistic terms, from the profession's viewpoint, why leave freshly baked cookies on the open windowsill to cool if the temptation presented may someday lead someone to sneak one? It is interesting to speculate as to who is more at fault, the person leaving the cookies in a vulnerable position or the person succumbing to temptation.

It would be impossible for a professional accountant to offer services at the level a client or employer has the right to expect if the professional has failed to maintain his or her *competence* with regard to current standards of disclosure, accounting treatment, and business practice. However, beyond understanding and developing facility with current standards, a professional accountant must act with due care.

The exercise of *due care* involves an understanding of the appropriate levels and limits of care expected of a professional accountant in different circumstances. For example, a professional accountant is not expected to be all-knowing and all-seeing with regard to incidents of fraud that occur at a client or employer. However, if the professional becomes aware of these (and there are new expectations for U.S. auditors to search out fraud), there are expectations for follow-up and reporting that need to be observed. Similarly, audit procedures need not specifically cover 100 percent of an organization's transactions; judgment sampling and statistical sampling may be applied to reduce specific coverage to a level deemed appropriate according to professional judgment.

That level will be set with reference to what other professionals regard as providing sufficient evidence for the forming of an opinion based on due care. In a court of law, expert witnesses will be called to testify as to what levels of judgment represent the exercise of due care.

Confidentiality is fundamental to fiduciary relationships from several perspectives. First, these relationships are very important to the well-being of the client or employer. They usually involve personal information, or information that is critical to the activities of the organization and which would result in some loss of privacy or of competitive advantage if it were disclosed to specific individuals or to the public. Advice, for example, about a business transaction, could be used in bargaining if known by the other party to the transaction. Second, it is not beyond the realm of possibility that such information could be used for the professional's own purposes for profit or to gain some other advantage. Finally, if it were suspected that a professional accountant was not going to maintain a client's or employer's information in confidence, it is unlikely that full information would be shared. This would put an audit and other services on a faulty foundation, which could lead to substandard and potentially misleading opinions and reports.

Keeping information confidential should not, however, lead to illegal behavior. For example, codes of conduct usually specify that a professional accountant *should not be associated with any misrepresentations.* If the professional cannot induce revision by persuasion, then the professional is usually required by his or her code to disassociate from the misrepresentation by resignation. Professional accountants are also usually prohibited from disclosing the misrepresentation, except subject to a disciplinary hearing or in a court of law. That this resignation and nondisclosure of a misrepresentation *does not benefit* the public, the profession, or the professional is a matter that should be redressed in revisions to professional codes by measures suggested in Brooks (1989).

RULES: GENERAL AND SPECIFIC

Professional accountants are expected to apply the fundamental principles previously outlined in order to protect the public interest as well as the interest of the profession and of the member themselves. There are, however, matters that lend themselves to coverage in general or specific rules such as proper relations between members or the organization and conduct of a professional practice. The appropriate form of advertising would be one of the administrative matters covered in rules.

DISCIPLINE

Customarily, codes of conduct provide information about the operation of the discipline process of the professional association. Members should know how and to whom to report a concern over conduct, what the process is for investigation of the concern, what the hearing process entails, how decisions will be made, what fines and other penalties are possible, how results will be reported, and how appeals will be considered. Unless these facts are known, together with some examples of sanctions levied, a professional is likely to misjudge how important the ethical conduct of its members is to the profession and to society.

Sanctions for unethical behavior can include any of the items listed in Table 4.8. It should be noted, however, that the sanctions identified are not all levied by every professional accounting body or regulatory agency.

TABLE 4.8

POSSIBLE SANCTIONS FOR
UNETHICAL BEHAVIOR UNDER
PROFESSIONAL ACCOUNTING
CODES OF CONDUCT AND
REGULATORY AUTHORITIES

	LEVIABLE ON THE	
	PROFESSIONAL	ACCOUNTING FIRM
Caution	Yes	Yes
Reprimand	Yes	Yes
Review by peer	Yes	Yes
Requirement to complete courses	Yes	No
Suspension:		
■ for a specified period	Yes	No
■ for an indefinite period	Yes	No
■ until specific requirements are completed	Yes	No
■ from appearing before regulatory agencies (SEC, OSC)	Yes	Yes
■ from auditing SEC or OSC registrant companies	Yes	Yes
Expulsion from membership	Yes	No
Compensation for damage	Yes	Yes
Fine	Yes	Yes
Costs of hearing	Yes	Yes
Ancillary orders		
■ for community work	Yes	No
■ financial support, etc.	Yes	Yes

SOURCE: Distillation of discipline cases from the professional accounting and regulatory bodies in the United States and Canada.

Usually the discipline process begins with a complaint being lodged at the professional organization about the ethical conduct of a member or firm. Alternately, the conviction on a legal charge of consequence (fraud, etc.) may also trigger the discipline process. The complaint or legal charge is investigated by staff, and a decision is made to lay a charge or not. Laying a charge necessitates a hearing to determine guilt or innocence, and the hearing process can be quite cumbersome. It can be held on camera or in public. It can involve lawyers for the plaintiff (the staff of the professional body) and defendant, and a tribunal or panel to hear the case, which often includes an outside layperson to ensure that proper procedures are followed and the public interest is served.

The cost of the hearing can be substantial in terms of out-of-pocket costs and also lost work time, which could be billed to clients. In the end, the largest cost involved is the lost reputation of the guilty accountant—in the audit world, credibility is what professionals strive to protect the most, since it is evidence of the value of their audit opinion. Without it, their audit services would be without demand.

When a professional accountant or firm is found guilty, the details of the case are made public, usually in the newsletter of the professional organization. It is essential that full details be published to warn other members of ethical problems and the sanctions they might encounter, and to preserve the profession's upstanding image as a profession worthy of policing itself (i.e., worthy of the trust of the public).

A guilty professional can look forward to more than one sanction. For example, he or she might receive a reprimand, a fine, and the bill for the costs of the lawyers and hearing. Alternatively, the penalty might be a suspension from membership until a set of required courses are completed, plus compensation for damages and costs. If the professional appears to need supervision for a while, the penalty might include the review of all work by a peer.

Fines can range in size from less than $1,000 to more than the damage done to the injured party. The amounts are growing over time, and in the United States, fines in the millions have been levied particularly against Arthur Andersen and some of its partners as was outlined in Chapter 2 (see Table 2.7). If the penalty involves the prohibition from practice, or appearance before the securities commissions, the lost revenue can be very large indeed. The inability to appear before the SEC or audit SEC registrant companies appears to be a very powerful sanction to use against accounting firms. It should be noted, however, that although Arthur Andersen was destroyed by the actions of the SEC, it is not likely that this will happen again due to the public's perception that it would be fair for only the guilty few individuals to be punished, not the whole firm.

INTERPRETATIONS OF RULES

Sometimes when the profession finds that a concern arises in the profession due to a debate over the proper application of a rule, a clarification is issued in the form of an interpretation. These interpretations are often an addendum or appendix to the code, which can be added to as circumstances require.

MOTIVATION FOR CHANGES IN PROFESSIONAL CODES

The motivation for changes in professional codes has been surprisingly similar and cyclical over the years. Usually, roughly every decade, pressure has come upon the accounting profession due to a financial or accounting scandal that has eroded the credibility of the profession.[3] Generally, the pressure has been greatest when the North American economy has been weak, and this weakness caused companies and individuals to engage in fraud, misstatement of financial results, or the use of loopholes to take unfair advantage. In reaction, professional codes have been revised to provide more and stronger guidance to avoid such problems in the future.

Two factors are different with the motivations at the start of the new millennium. First, the Enron, Arthur Andersen, and WorldCom debacles occurred in good economic times—even though they gave rise to an erosion of credibility that drove down confidence and, in turn, the economy. This change suggests that ethics problems can and will play a more serious and significant role than earlier imagined. Second, the desire for global convergence or harmonization of standards to facilitate global business and capital flows is providing a driver of change that is somewhat beyond the previously normal domestically dominated, political and corporate lobbying influences. As such,

---

[3]Presentation of Mary Beth Armstrong, February 2, 2003, at the American Accounting Association Accounting Programs Leadership Group Conference in New Orleans.

convergence may yield stronger standards and more rapid continuous changes than heretofore possible. Time will tell, however, if the needed companion regulatory or compliance framework, best exemplified by the SEC and the OSC, will be replicated in Europe and around the world to realize the possible improvement fully.

To appreciate the potential of the future, an understanding of the issues facing the accounting profession in the late 1980s is useful. At that time, the Metcalf investigation, the Treadway Commission (1987), and the Macdonald Commission (1988) were public or quasi-public processes of *investigation of how the members of the AICPA and the CICA were serving the public interest*. These investigations would not have been necessary unless some doubt existed about the

---

The Treadway Commission: Fraudulent Financial Reporting

In June 1985 the Independent National Commission on Fraudulent Financial Reporting, sponsored by the American Institute of CPAs, the American Accounting Association, the National Association of Accountants, the Institute of Internal Auditors and the Financial Executives Institute, was formed at the AICPA's initiative.

The commission's aims have been to determine what factors contribute to fraudulent financial reporting and to develop practical, constructive recommendations for reducing the incidence of this problem.

MULTIDIMENSIONAL PROBLEM

A commission early finding was that fraudulent financial reporting is a multidimensional problem with multiple causal influences.

According to Chairman James C. Treadway, Jr., solutions can be determined only by studying the entire financial reporting process, and everyone involved in it, including management, the audit committee and the independent public accountant as well as internal controls, corporate culture and law enforcement.

In Treadway's view, many approaches have potential for reducing fraud and no simple answers exist. The commission is emphasizing the "big picture" to identify and air the issues, create heightened awareness and offer concrete guidance on how to minimize the incidence of fraud. It has stressed that no single conclusion can be separated from the totality of its recommendations.

MANAGEMENT'S RESPONSIBILITY

The commission's initial conclusions in the exposure draft, issued this month, highlight management's ultimate responsibility for financial statement accuracy and its duty to set a tone of personal and professional ethics within the company.

In addition, numerous recommendations focus on enhancing internal controls with a greater role for the audit committee, the obligation of the public accountant to detect fraud, mandatory auditor involvement is quarterly financial reports, mandatory membership for auditors of public companies in a professional quality assurance program, more public representation of the AICPA auditing standards board, and enhanced law enforcement and stiffer penalties as a deterrent to management fraud.

RETAINING PUBLIC CONFIDENCE

Following a 60-day comment period ending July 1, the commission plans to publish its final report early this fall.

The report will have an impact on issuers, regulators, auditors, educators, directors, law enforcers and professional organizations. The ultimate aim of reducing fraudulent financial reporting is to protect the integrity of the financial reporting system and to retain public confidence in the accounting profession and its ability to regulate itself, thereby reversing the escalation in litigation and liability and avoiding government intervention.

National Commission on Fraudulent Financial Reporting

Chairman
James C. Treadway, Jr.

Commissioners
William M. Batten
William S. Kanaga
Hugh L. Marsh, Jr.
Thomas I. Storrs
Donald H. Trautlein

Executive Director
G. Dewey Arnold

Research Director
Jack L. Korgstad

General Counsel
Catherine Collins McCoy

service being provided. Although there were some specific problems that triggered these studies, concern over the credibility of financial reporting was essentially responsible. From the perspective of the accounting profession this manifested itself as an *expectations gap* "between what the public expects or needs and the auditors can reasonably expect to accomplish" (Macdonald, 1988, p. iii).

Excerpts from the Treadway and Macdonald Commissions are provided for reference. In response to the Treadway Commission, a committee of the AICPA was struck under the chairmanship of W. Anderson, which redesigned the AICPA Professional Standards: Ethics and Bylaws (Anderson, 1985, 1987). Paramount in the revisions proposed to the U.S. and Canadian codes by both the Anderson Committee and the Macdonald Commission was the desire for restoration of the public's faith that the profession was serving the public interest. The categorization of the principal recommendations of the Macdonald Commission, shown in Table 4.9, makes this general objective abundantly evident.

CURRENT CODES OF PROFESSIONAL CONDUCT

Current codes of the major industrial nations of the world—which have resulted from the concerns, investigations, commissions, and committees of the late 1980s—are expected to converge over the next decade on the principles embedded in the *IFAC Code of Ethics*. However, since the process of change has just begun, it is worthwhile to study the existing representative codes from the AICPA and the ICAO, which are included in this chapter. Discussions of the provisions of each code may also be covered elsewhere in this book. For instance, discussion of the need to keep client information confidential is included in this chapter and Chapter 3.

TABLE 4.9

THE MACDONALD COMMISSION: OVERVIEW OF PRINCIPAL RECOMMENDATIONS

Recommendations to strengthen auditor independence/integrity:
- Improvement of auditor relationships (#11)
- Strengthen professional standards (7)
- Strengthen professional code of conduct (3)

Recommendations to strengthen auditor professionalism:
- Increase responsiveness to public concerns (6)
- Emphasize vital role of professional judgment (4)
- Improve self-regulation (2)

Recommendations to improve financial disclosure:
- Expand accounting standards and improve financial disclosures (13)
- Greater auditor responsibility for those disclosures (2)

Recommendations to lessen public misunderstanding of the auditor's role:
- Publish a statement of management responsibility (24)
- Expand audit report to clarify auditor's role and the level of assurance the audit provides (25)
- Audit committee to report annually to shareholders (3)

SOURCE: The Macdonald Commission: *The Report of the Commission to Study the Public's Expectation of Audits*, CICA, Toronto, June 1988.

SUMMARY OF THE AMERICAN INSTITUTE OF CERTIFIED PUBLIC ACCOUNTANTS (AICPA)
CODE OF PROFESSIONAL CONDUCT*

Principles:

Responsibilities: In carrying out their responsibilities as professionals, members should exercise sensitive professional and moral judgments in all their activities. (Article I)

The Public Interest: Members should accept their obligation to act in a way that will serve the public interest, honor the public trust, and demonstrate commitment to professionalism. (Article II)

Integrity: To maintain and broaden public confidence, members should perform all professional responsibilities with the highest sense of integrity. (Article III)

Objectivity and Independence: A member should maintain objectivity and be free of conflicts interest in discharging professional responsibilities. A member in public practice should be independent in fact and appearance when providing auditing and other attestation services. (Article IV)

Due Care: A member should observe the profession's technical and ethical standards, strive continually to improve competence and the quality of services, and discharge professional responsibility to the best of the member's ability. (Article V)

Scope and Nature of Services: A member in public practice should observe the Principles of the *Code of Professional Conduct* in determining the scope and nature of services to be provided. (Article VI)

Rules:		**Important Interpretations/Issues Covered:**
101	Independence	▪ will be impaired by various transactions, relationships and interests, including: direct or material financial interests, performance of certain nonattest services, common investments, loans; family relationships, or official office such as: director, officer, employee, promoter, underwriter, trustee, or borrower (except under normal terms from a financial institution for auto, home, credit cards); and the threat of litigation.
102	Integrity and objectivity	▪ no conflicts of interest ▪ no misrepresentations – reporting requirement to avoid subordination of judgment
201	General standards	▪ professional competence ▪ due professional care ▪ planning and supervision ▪ sufficient relevant data
202	Compliance with standards	▪ necessary if service involves auditing, review, compilation, management consulting, tax, or other professional services
203	Accounting principles	▪ no departures from generally accepted accounting principles, *unless a misleading statement would result*; then must state why a departure is warranted and approximate effects – authorization of FASB, GASB, FASAB pronouncements
301	Confidential client information	▪ no disclosure without consent, except for proper court or CPA proceedings ▪ no use for personal gain
302	Contingent fees	▪ not allowed for audit, review, compilation, examination of prospective financial information, or tax return or claim for tax refund – some exceptions listed
501	Discreditable acts	▪ not permitted: discrimination, harassment, deviation from gov. standards, negligence
502	Advertising and solicitation	▪ cannot be false, misleading, or deceptive, or involve coercion, over-reaching, or harassment
503	Commissions and referral fees	▪ not allowed for audit, review, compilation, examination of prospective financial information, otherwise requires disclosure ▪ cannot be paid or accepted without disclosure to the client
505	Form of organization and name	▪ permits non-CPA minority ownership, provided CPA's remain ultimately responsible, financially and otherwise, for the attest work performed to protect the public interest, but cannot hold themselves out as CPA's, and must follow AICPA Code.

*Code of Professional Conduct, AICPA, Updated to Jan. 10, 2003, see http://brooks.swlearning.com

CONTINUED

SUMMARY OF *RULES OF PROFESSIONAL CONDUCT AND COUNCIL INTERPRETATIONS**
OF THE INSTITUTE OF CHARTERED ACCOUNTANTS OF ONTARIO (ICAO)

Foreword ...covering the philosophy underlying the *Rules* governing a Chartered Accountant's responsibilities for:	
Characteristics of a profession	▪ 8 elements including the subordination of personal interest to the public good/interest
Principles governing the conduct of members and students	▪ derived from the public's reliance on sound and fair financial reporting, and competent advice on business affairs
	▪ maintenance of the profession's good reputation and its ability to serve the public interest
	▪ perform with integrity and due care, sustain professional competence, comply with *Rules*
	▪ no influences, interests or relationships which would impair professional judgment or objectivity, or appear to do so to a reasonable observer
	▪ duty of confidence, and no exploitative use, in respect information about a client's affairs
	▪ practice development based upon professional excellence, not on self-promotion
	▪ exhibit courtesy and consideration in dealings with professional colleagues
	▪ observance of fiduciary duties, and professional duties, where applicable
Principles governing the responsibilities of firms	▪ establish, maintain, and uphold policies and procedures in accord with the *Rules*
	▪ failure to comply may trigger sanctions for the whole firm or just the knowledgeable and responsible partners
Personal character and ethical conduct	▪ as per principles and *Rules*, honorable conduct beyond the letter of the prohibition
Application of the *Rules*	▪ to all members engaged in public accounting <u>*and/or*</u> where the public and/or associates rely upon the individual based upon that person's membership in the ICAO
	▪ to non-members supervised by or in partnership with a member
	▪ in jurisdictions outside Ontario, a member must observe the local rules, but not bring disrepute upon the ICAO
Interpretation of the Rules	▪ Rules must be interpreted in light of the matters discussed in the Foreword.
Rules:	**Important Interpretations/Issues Covered:**
General	
101 Compliance with bylaws, regulations and rules	▪ is mandatory ▪ employing students
102 Conviction of criminal or similar offenses	▪ may result in a charge of professional misconduct
102.2 Reporting suspensions for disciplinary reasons	▪ promptly notify the Institute of any suspensions
103 No association with misrepresentation	▪ on a letter, report, statement or representation, or related to candidacy as a student or member
104 Must reply in writing to Institute correspondence	
Standards Affecting the Public Interest	
201 Maintenance of the good reputation of the profession and its ability to serve the public interest	▪ at all times, both members and students ▪ conviction in other Canadian jurisdictions results in charges by the ICAO ▪ advocacy services requirements
202 Integrity and due care	
203 Maintenance of professional competence	*CONTINUED*

203.2	Cooperation with inspections and investigations	▪ Must cooperate with the Institute's appointed personnel conducting practice investigations or investigating professional conduct
204	Independence and objectivity	▪ those who give opinions on financial statements or are undertaking an insolvency engagement must be free of any influence, interest or relationship which would impair professional judgement or objectivity, or has the appearance of doing so
		▪ there must be written disclosure of anything that a reasonable observer might consider impairs the member's independence and objectivity
205	False or misleading statements	▪ no association even where a disclaimer is given
		▪ covers letters reports, representations, financial statements, written or oral
		▪ covers omissions, material misstatements, non-compliance
206	Compliance with professional standards	▪ with generally accepted accounting principles and generally accepted auditing standards as set out in the *CICA Handbook*
207	No unauthorized benefits	▪ from client or employer
208	Maintenance of confidential information about a client's affairs	▪ no disclosure unless client has knowledge and consent, or pursuant to the proceedings of lawful authority, Council, or the Professional Conduct Committee or subcommittees
		▪ no improper use for personal advantage, advantage of a third party, or to disadvantage the client
		▪ responsibility for subcontracted agents
210	Conflict of interest	▪ responsibility to detect before accepting engagement
		▪ no acceptance of a conflicted (self vs. client, or client vs. client) engagement by a member, student, or firm unless all affected parties are advised and consent
211	Duty to report apparent breaches of member, student, or applicant or firm	▪ of rules of conduct
		▪ of any information raising doubt as to competencies, reputation or integrity
		▪ unless specific exemption, or would breach statutory duty or solicitor-client privilege, etc.
212	Handling of trust funds and other property	▪ in accord with trust and trust law
		▪ segregation, records
213	No unlawful activity	▪ association of person, name, or services
214	Fee quotations	▪ Only when requested by a client, and after obtaining adequate information about the assignment
215	Contingent fees	▪ none allowed, except for an insolvency engagement, or under very specific conditions where there will be no real or apparent conflict of interest and where the client consents
216	No referral fees or compensation	▪ none allowed, except in sale or purchase of an accounting practice
217	Advertising restrictions	▪ advertising cannot be false or misleading, in bad taste, contrary to professional courtesy; reflect unfavorably on competence or integrity, or includes unsubstantiated statements
		▪ no solicitation is permitted
		▪ endorsements are possible under strict conditions, and after suitable investigations
218	Retention of documentation and working papers	▪ for a reasonable time period

Relations with Fellow Members or Firms, and Non-members Engaged in Public Accounting

302	Acceptance of appointment where there is an incumbent auditor	▪ Not allowed without asking outgoing auditor if there are circumstances which should be taken into account
		▪ Response is required from incumbent, fraud must be reported if suspected
303	Co-operation with successor	▪ Required if written request received

CONTINUED

304	Joint appointments	<ul><li>carry joint and several liability</li><li>must advise other accountant of activities</li></ul>
305	Communication of special assignments to incumbent	<ul><li>must communicate with incumbent unless client makes such a request in writing before the engagement is begun</li></ul>
306	Responsibilities on special assignments	<ul><li>no action to impair the position of the other accountant</li><li>no services beyond original referral terms, except with consent of referring member</li></ul>

Organization and Conduct of a Professional Practice

401	Practice Names	<ul><li>in good taste, approved by institute, not misleading or self-laudatory</li></ul>
404	Responsibilities conveyed with use of style	<ul><li>public accountants must use "chartered accountant(s)" or "public accountant(s)"</li></ul>
	Operation of offices	<ul><li>offices must be under the charge of a licensed public accountant normally in attendance</li><li>no part-time offices except per regulations</li><li>cannot use "chartered accountants" if a non-CA shares a proprietary interest.</li></ul>
405	Association with firms	<ul><li>only if at least one partner of the other firm is chartered accountant</li></ul>
406	Responsibility for non-members	<ul><li>public accountants are responsible for the failure of non-members associated with the practice to abide by the *Rules of Conduct*</li></ul>
407	Related business or practice	<ul><li>*Rules of Conduct* apply</li></ul>
408	Association with non-member in public practice	<ul><li>only if maintains good reputation of profession, and adheres to *Rules of Conduct*</li></ul>
409	Office by representation	<ul><li>not to be done if a member is only represented by a non-member/firm and *vice versa*</li></ul>
410	Practice of public accounting in a corporate form	<ul><li>prohibited except under specific circumstances – refer to current code</li></ul>

Rules Applicable Only to Firms

501	Establish, maintain & uphold	<ul><li>must have those necessary for compliance with *Rules of Conduct*</li></ul>
502	policies and procedures	<ul><li>and those necessary for compliance with Competence and Conduct of firm members</li></ul>
503	Association with Firms	<ul><li>only if at least one partner of the other firm is chartered accountant</li></ul>

* ICAO, Toronto, Canada, updated to Dec. 12, 2002, see *http://www.brooks.swlearning.com*

INTERNATIONAL COMPARISON OF PROFESSIONAL CODES

It is interesting for several reasons to compare the professional codes or rules of conduct from a variety of professional bodies drawn from around the world, and that is the purpose of Appendix A to this chapter. For instance, each code is revised from time to time, so that generally those with the latest revision dates may contain evidence of ideas to come when older codes are revised. Second, although most codes deal with the same issues, different wording can be used, and a review of that wording can provide an enriched understanding of the topic. Third, there are issues that may be slow in coming into force in a particular code due to political considerations, but which a professional accountant should be aware of. Finally, as professional accountants become involved with foreign activities directly or indirectly through multinational reporting or capital markets, they would do well to be sensitive to professional accounting codes in foreign locales.

Appendix A is organized to review code provisions in comparison to those of the AICPA Code. Where additional issues are raised, those provisions are listed at the end of the appendix.

In particular, the following observations are noteworthy:

- All of the codes identify serving the public interest as a primary obligation or responsibility, but the two management accounting associations (IMA and SMAC) identify "stakeholders" as well. This is helpful in reminding professional accountants to consider their duty to stakeholder groups, thus adding specificity to the concept of the "public interest."

- All of the codes apply to members of the associations, rather than to the firms themselves. Does this reduce the perceived or real responsibility of the governors of the firms from the level of "due diligence" required of corporation executives in building an ethical culture? Can a firm and/or its governors be sanctioned for the misdeeds of its members?

- Procedures for resolution of ethical conflicts vary. Most codes imply what the SMAC code states, which is that the Society's Code is to take precedence over management's code. Some suggest confidential counselling or legal advice, but only the ICAEW proposes consultation with the Institute. None of the codes appear to have considered the interest of the public to be worthy of breaching a client or employer confidence to bring it to the attention of the public, although several require the reporting of breaches (presumably by members) of the code to the professional body (ICAO, ICAEW, IMA, SMAC).

- The IFAC code contains several provisions not covered by the other country-specific codes, including:

  - An explicit standard approving the advancing of a client's best tax position, provided that it does not conflict with any laws. Note that the ICAEW spells out that tax avoidance is legal, but tax evasion is illegal.

  - A requirement for observing the most strict ethical code if required to work in multiple countries.

- The IFAC code goes beyond other codes to specify that information should be presented fully and honestly *to be understood in its context.* This extends the simpler prohibition against involvement with misrepresentations that is in many other codes. Sometimes the disclosure of an otherwise correct fact, out of context, results in a misinterpretation.

With the passage of time, it is possible that the professional codes of specific professional bodies will lag behind those of other countries, or of the expectations of the public. In those cases, other regulatory agencies may put forward requirements to protect the public interest. In view of the current thrust toward the provision of multiple assurance services, or of the development of multidisciplinary firms housing lawyers, engineers, and other professionals with different ethical standards but who are serving the same client, it may be necessary for some outside body to resolve conflicting ethical standards. The SEC, for example, has seen fit to require the licensing of auditors of SEC registrants and to enlarge upon standards expected for independence and other matters.

SHORTFALLS WITH AND IN PROFESSIONAL CODES

In the past, most professional accountants have tended to view their codes as being less relevant than the technical material they were required to deal with. In some cases, lack of awareness of the significance of the code was at the root of the problem, while in other instances inability to interpret the general principles and rules was responsible. As our ethics environment has changed and ethical shortfalls have become recognized as serious threats to professional practice, there have been numerous calls for renewed interest, understanding, and commitment on the part of professionals themselves (see, for example, Gunning, 1989; Brooks, 1993; and a dedicated issue of *Accounting Education*, March 1994). Ethics education is now an official requirement for the formal education of professional accountants according to the AACSB and many professional bodies.

Although it would be theoretically attractive for professional codes of conduct to solve all the problems professional accountants face, in reality their application requires the use of judgment based upon a full set of principles and rules. In this regard, many codes have the following deficiencies:

- Consultation on ethical matters is not uniformly encouraged, and may require the hiring of outside counsel rather than counseling through the professional association. This leaves both the professional and the profession involved at some risk that competent counseling will take place and/or appropriate action will be taken.

- A fair reporting/hearing process is not indicated, so members are uncertain whether to come forward.

- Protection is not offered to a whistle-blower.

- Sanctions are often unclear and their applicability is not defined.

Aside from these flaws, there is a tendency for codes of conduct and the training related to them to focus on what may not be done rather than on how to do something positively. This negativism has been recognized, and recent revisions of codes, both professional and corporate, are beginning to stress the fundamental principles that are essential to the maintenance of strong ethical and fiduciary capabilities. The code of conduct, particularly of leading-edge corporations, is being seen as part of a message to employees as to how to proceed, rather than a proscription on how not to act. It is being seen as a motivating document for action and consultation, rather than a list of rules. Time will tell how far this trend will go.

One of the unresolved issues in many professional codes (with the notable exception of the SMAC code) is the overlap between professional codes and those of the firm or corporation for which the professional works as an employee. The professional accountant is governed by both, and the internal control system and integrity of the organization depends upon its code, so an understanding of corporate codes in general and of the employer's code is essential to the day-to-day activities of employed professionals.

ISSUES NOT USUALLY RESOLVED IN CORPORATE CODES OF CONDUCT

Having examined the nature, content, and shortcomings of both corporate and professional accounting codes of conduct, it is appropriate to turn to the overlap between them. Several issues are often not resolved in codes of conduct that could be faced by employees, including professional accountants. Accordingly, some thought should be given to the following matters when a corporate code is being set up or revised:

1. *Conflicts between codes.* Professionals and other employees will be subject to the company/employer's code and also another code such as a

professional code for engineers or accountants. To avoid placing the person in an ethical dilemma of debating which code to follow, at the very least consultation with an ethics officer/ombudsperson should be advised.

2. *Conflicts between competing interests or corporate stakeholders.* Sometimes the priority of competing interests can be made clear in training sessions. If not, then protected routes for consultation should be available. This subject is discussed here and in Chapter 3.

3. *When should a professional blow the whistle, and to whom?* A protected, internal route for discussion and reporting should be available for professional accountants. An employer should realize that every professional accountant has a professional duty to uphold, which could supersede loyalty to the employer. It would be helpful if the professional's accounting society were to provide consultation to the professional on a confidential basis to assist in these decisions, as is the case in the United Kingdom and some other jurisdictions.

4. *Adequate protection of whistle-blowers.* The most successful arrangements for whistle-blowing involve reporting, in confidence, to an autonomous individual of high rank or to one who reports to a person of very high rank in the organization, for example, an ombudsperson who will follow up on concerns without revealing the informant's name or exposing the informant, and who reports, without informant names, directly to the chairperson of the organization. With this level of apparent support, investigations can be undertaken without interference. The ombudsperson should report back to the informant.

5. *Service decisions involving judgment.* Codes of conduct should be fashioned so as not to rule out the exercise of a professional's values when those are required for the judgments they must make. In the final analysis, it is the exercise of these values and the judgments based on these that can save the individual, the firm or employer, the profession, and the public from ethical problems. The challenge is to develop codes and cultures that do not force the abandonment of personal values but foster the development and exercise of values and judgment processes that will embrace all stakeholders' interests.

Conflicts of Interest and Global Independence Standards

One of the most bedeviling aspects of a professional accountant's life is the recognition, avoidance, and/or management of conflict of interest situations. This is because *conflict of interest situations threaten to undermine the reason for having an accounting profession—to provide assurance that the work of a professional accountant will be governed by independent judgment focused to protect the public interest.* For this reason, the independence standards that the accounting profession must live by are fundamental to the continued success of the profession, its members, and their firms.

A professional accountant is called upon in his or her professional code to *"hold himself or herself free from any influence, interest or relationship in respect of his or her client's affairs, which impairs his or her professional judgment or objectivity or which, in the view of a reasonable observer would impair the member's professional judgment or objectivity.*"[4] Consequently, there are two distinct aspects to be kept in mind: the reality of having a conflict of interest, and the appearance that one might be present. Therefore, the traditional definition—*a conflict of interest is any influence, interest, or relationship that could cause a professional accountant's judgment to deviate from applying the profession's standards to client matters*—covers only part of the conflict of interest risk faced by a professional accountant.

With one notable exception, a professional accountant's view of conflict of interest situations is very similar to that of a director, executive, or other employee as discussed in Chapter 3. Consequently, the discussion in Chapter 3 covering basic concepts, terms—*potential, actual, and apparent conflicts of interest*—causes, and Figures 3.5 and 3.6 and Table 3.4 should be reviewed since it is applicable to professional accountants and the environment they face.

The notable exception is that a professional accountant is a fiduciary that must protect his or her client or employer, but not at any cost, and not if the public interest will suffer. *A professional accountant must adhere to a set of rules aimed at neutrality and at protecting the public interest—he or she should not go to absolutely any lengths to serve a specific client's interests unless the public interest is also served.* The services rendered by a fiduciary must be able to be trusted, and the professional accountant's independence of judgment is essential to that trust.

A GLOBAL PERSPECTIVE FROM THE IFAC CODE

The IFAC Code of Ethics for Professional Accountants[5] provides the most up-to-date treatment of independence requirements and conflicts of interest. For that reason, and because most IFAC member country codes are pledged to be harmonized to it in the future, the IFAC Code provides a useful approach to examine.

The IFAC Code is structured as indicated in Figure 4.1.

FIGURE 4.1

IFAC CODE OF ETHICS VALUES FRAMEWORK

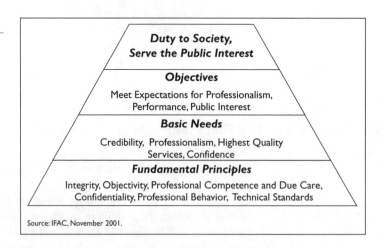

Duty to Society, Serve the Public Interest

Objectives
Meet Expectations for Professionalism, Performance, Public Interest

Basic Needs
Credibility, Professionalism, Highest Quality Services, Confidence

Fundamental Principles
Integrity, Objectivity, Professional Competence and Due Care, Confidentiality, Professional Behavior, Technical Standards

Source: IFAC, November 2001.

---

[4]*Rules of Professional Conduct and Council Interpretations,* Institute of Chartered Accountants of Ontario (ICAO), Toronto, 1997, Foreword, p. 5 05, updated continuously.

[5](See *http://brooks.swlearning.com*)

The sections of the IFAC Code relevant to this framework and to independence and conflict of interests are as follows:

9. A distinguishing mark of a profession is acceptance of its responsibility to the public. The accountancy profession's public consists of clients, credit grantors, governments, employers, employees, investors, the business and financial community, and others who rely on the objectivity and integrity of professional accountants to maintain the orderly functioning of commerce. This reliance imposes a public interest responsibility on the accountancy profession. The public interest is defined as the collective well-being of the community of people and institutions the professional accountant serves.

10. A professional accountant's responsibility is not exclusively to satisfy the needs of an individual client or employer.

14. The Code recognizes that the objectives of the accountancy profession are to the highest standards of professionalism, to attain the highest levels of performance and generally to meet the public interest requirements set out above. These objectives require four basic needs to be met:

- Credibility
- Professionalism
- Quality of Services
- Confidence

15. In order to achieve the objectives of the accountancy profession, professional accountants have to observe a number of prerequisites or fundamental principles.

16. The fundamental principles are:

- Integrity: A professional accountant should be straightforward and honest in performing professional services.
- Objectivity: A professional accountant should be fair and should not allow prejudice or bias, conflict of interest or influence of others to override objectivity.
- Professional Competence and Due Care
- Confidentiality
- Professional Behavior
- Technical Standards

The IFAC Code then points out the central role of judgment, and the importance of maintaining the objectivity of that judgment, when it states:

Part A, Sect. 1.2: Regardless of service or capacity, professional accountants should protect the integrity of their professional services, and maintain objectivity in their judgment.

It goes on to indicate in the following definitions that *objectivity is a function of a professional's independence of mind and of appearance.*

Independence of mind—the state of mind that permits the provision of an opinion without being affected by influences that compromise professional judgment, allowing an individual to act with integrity, and exercise objectivity and professional skepticism.

Independence of appearance—the avoidance of facts and circumstances that are so significant a reasonable and informed third party, having regard knowledge of all relevant information, including any safeguards applied, would reasonably conclude a firm's, or a member of the assurance team's integrity, objectivity or professional skepticism had been compromised.[6]

Diagrammatically, these components and relevance of proper judgment are represented in Figure 4.2.

The IFAC Code goes on to indicate that threats to independence of mind and appearance should be identified, and then avoided or nullified through the application of safeguards. Figure 4.3 identifies the terms and concepts involved.

FIGURE 4.2

IFAC CODE'S FRAMEWORK FOR PROPER JUDGMENT

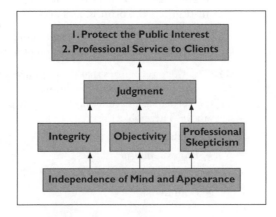

FIGURE 4.3

ASSURING INDEPENDENCE OF MIND AND APPEARANCE

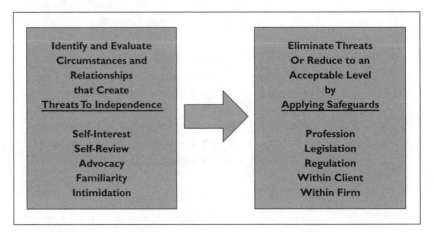

Professional accountants should be alert to conflict of interest problems and the potential difficulties that they could create. The IFAC Code lists five basic conflicts that could sway the professional accountant from acting in the public interest: self-interest; review of one's own work; advocating a client's position; familiarity with the management, directors, or owners of the client corporation; and intimidation by management, directors, or owners. Self-interest, or the desire to protect or enhance one's position, certainly has been known to influence a professional accountant's judgment. Arthur Andersen provides a glaring example of this, as they wanted to retain the audit revenue from several clients, including Enron, WorldCom, Waste Management, and Sunbeam. Auditing

---

[6]*IFAC Code*, 2001, p. 4.

one's own work is a variant of the self-interest problem wherein auditors are reluctant to criticize themselves and lose face with client management. Advocacy of client's positions to a third party occasionally puts a professional accountant in a poor position to argue a different and better position with regard to GAAP or disclosure with the client. Familiarity with client personnel may create interpersonal bonds that leave a professional accountant not wanting to disappoint or offend the friends or close associates that familiarity has created. Finally, there are many cases whereby the senior management of a corporation have intimidated professional accountants working for the corporation, thereby forcing them into misrepresentations, illegalities, and/or poor accounting choices. The Sunbeam and WorldCom cases in Chapter 2 illustrate this problem vividly.

Identification of any of these potential conflict of interest situations should be followed by their avoidance, elimination, or reduction of their risk through the application of safeguards. The IFAC Code suggests that safeguards can be found in techniques and approaches found in professional guidelines, legislation, regulation, or within client or professional accounting firm systems and practices. The examples provided in the IFAC Code are listed in Table 4.10.

TABLE 4.10

SAFEGUARDS REDUCING
THE RISK OF CONFLICT OF
INTEREST SITUATIONS

Safeguards Created by the Profession, Legislation, or Regulation
- Education, training, experience requirement for entry
- Continuing education
- Professional standards, monitoring, and disciplinary processes
- External review of firm's quality control system
- Legislation governing independence requirements of the firm

IFAC Code, 8.37

Safeguards Within a Client
- Appointment of auditors ratified/approved by other than management
- Client has competent staff to make managerial decisions
- Policies and procedures emphasizing client's commitment to fair financial reporting
- Internal procedures to ensure objective choices in commissioning non-assurance engagements
- A corporate governance structure, such as the audit committee, that provides appropriate oversight and communications regarding a firm's services

IFAC Code, 8.38

Safeguards Within a Professional Accounting Firm's Own Systems and Procedures
- Leadership stressing importance of independence, and expectation of service/action in the public interest
- Policies and procedures to implement and monitor control of assurance engagements
- Documented independence policies regarding the identification and evaluation of threats to independence; applications of safeguards to eliminate or reduce those threats to an acceptable level
- Policies and procedures to monitor and manage the reliance on revenue from a single assurance client
- Using partners with separate reporting lines for the provision of non-assurance services to an assurance client
- Six other firm-wide and nine other specific items

IFAC Code, 8.41,2

Most professional accountants take the proper handling of conflict of interest situations very seriously because it is fundamental to the maintenance of fiduciary relationships. Many professional accounting firms, including the largest, have additional codes of conduct or practice that offer the firm's guidance. Members of a multi-office firm often sign a document in which they promise not to discuss the affairs of, or trade in securities of, clients of any office in their firm, and a restricted list of clients' names is maintained for reference. Members of the firm are told that, even if they do not personally possess information on a client's activities, they may be presumed to do so by members of the public. Care must be taken to avoid the appearance of conflict as much as the reality. Reputation is too hard, and too costly, to restore. Consequently, most firms employ several techniques in the management of conflicts of interest to minimize potential harm, including:

- Firm codes to augment those of professional bodies
- Training sessions and reinforcing memos
- Client lists from all locales for reference and sign-off procedures signifying noninvestment
- Scrutiny of securities trading, particularly related to new issues
- Firewalls or Chinese walls to prevent information flows within firms
- Reporting to and consultation with senior officers
- Avoidance
- Rules for serving clients with potentially conflicting interests
- Rules for taking on new clients or providing new services, and for termination of client relations

TYPES OF CONFLICTS OF INTEREST

With the foregoing background, it is useful to consider what the most common conflicts of interest are for accountants. Conflicts of interest can be grouped into four categories as to stakeholder impact:

1. Self-interest of the professional conflicts with the interests of the other stakeholders
2. Self-interest of the professional and some stakeholders conflicts with that of some other stakeholders
3. Interests of one client are favored over the interests of another client
4. Interests of one or more stakeholders are favored over the interests of one or more other stakeholders

SPHERES OF ACTIVITY AFFECTED

The first category pits the professional accountant against the other stakeholders in several spheres of activity. The undermined independent judgment of the professional can be evident in the services offered, the improper use of influence, and the misuse of information. The second category, where the professional sides with some stakeholders to the disadvantage of others, also offers opportunities for poor judgment in terms of the services offered, as does the third category, which refers specifically to clients. The fourth category, which involves stakeholder groups but where self-interest may not come into play except sometimes on the disadvantaged side, focuses primarily on the proper use of information and particularly on issues of confidentiality. These relationships are summarized in Table 4.11, and it is to a discussion of how judgment can be undermined in each of these spheres of activity that we now turn.

TABLE 4.11

CONFLICTS OF INTEREST FOR PROFESSIONAL ACCOUNTANTS: CATEGORIES, SPHERES OF ACTIVITY AFFECTED, AND EXAMPLES

STAKEHOLDER CATEGORY	SPHERE OF ACTIVITY AFFECTED	EXAMPLES
Self vs. others	Services offered	Conflicting services, shaving quality
	Improper use of influence	Improper purchases of client goods
	Misuse of information	Improper investments by relatives
Self & others vs. others	Services offered	Overinvolvement with management or directors erodes objectivity
Client vs. client Employer vs. employer	Services offered	Serving competing clients at the same time
Stakeholder vs. stakeholder	Misuse of information (confidentiality)	Whistle-blowing, reporting to government or regulators

CONFLICTS OF INTEREST AFFECTING SERVICES OFFERED

Self-interest is a powerful motivator that can disadvantage clients, the public, and other stakeholders through a degradation of the services offered by a professional accountant, whether the professional is in the role of auditor or management accountant. Many of the temptations auditors succumb to arise because the auditor's "business" side dominates his or her "professional" side, and the drive for profit or personal gain dominates the values that are needed to maintain the trust expected in a fiduciary relationship. When the needed trust breaks down, it does so because one or more of the essential aspects of professional service expected are not delivered in a manner that protects or furthers the interests that the professional should be serving before the professional's own interest.

For instance, the desire for profit can lead to services being performed at *substandard levels of quality*. Due to the pressures of rising costs, or in an effort to increase profit, services may be performed at substandard levels of quality. This may happen through the use of junior or unskilled staff, or if staff are not adequately supervised by senior, and more costly, personnel. It may lead to pressures on staff to increase their working hours beyond reasonable levels, or to encourage staff to work long hours but not to charge the clients for the total time spent. In either of these cases, the fatigue factor that results is not only unfair to staff but also can result in diminished capacity to detect errors on the audit. While diminished services clearly affect clients and the public, these working conditions also present the staff involved with the very real ethical problem of how to react: should they complain and, if so, how much and to whom. These issues will be addressed later in this chapter.

The quality of services provided can suffer for other reasons as well. A professional may be tempted to *lowball fee quotations* to clients in an effort to gain new business or retain old clients. Later, the reality of the low fee may present the dilemma of having to meet audit budgets that are too tight, which can again lead to substandard service quality and/or pressures on staff to bury or forget about time spent beyond budget allowances. Lowballing is occasionally justified on the basis of anticipated future price increases for audit services or the garnering of additional high margin work in tax or consulting services. This hope is not always incorporated into audit planning, so budgets are occasionally set too tight. Moreover, the anticipated high-margin revenue sources may not materialize. These exigencies have been understood for a long time, and were the major reason why many professional societies prohibited the quotation of *fixed fees*. When something unexpected occurs, in a fixed or lowballed fee situation the additional time spent comes right out of the auditor's pocket—an obvious conflict of interest. Fees set on the basis of hourly rates per level of staff employed allow the need for quality service to be incorporated in the total fee even where unexpected problems arise during an audit.

Self-interest can also lead to the offer of services in situations leading to conflicts of interest with other stakeholders. For example, an auditor is in an excellent position to offer *management advisory services* or *assurance services* because the audit has developed a thorough knowledge of the client's affairs and personnel. On the other hand, if an auditor accepts an engagement to install an internal control system, there may be a reluctance to acknowledge its flaws when these become clear during a subsequent audit. Such reluctance can arise even where non-audit personnel from the same firm are used. Unfortunately, living with a faulty system of internal control is like living with a time bomb, with the enhanced risk being borne by the client and the public. Another example, which presents itself frequently, involves a partner who is negotiating with a client's chief financial officer (CFO) on the adequacy of a provision for bad debts, knowing that next week the CFO will be making a decision on whether to award his or her firm, or a competitor, a very large consulting assignment. The threat to objectivity is obvious and overwhelming, yet the partner is expected to be objective nonetheless.

What are the remedies for such situations involving so-called *conflicting services* that involve self-criticism? Refusal to provide such services is one option, but could lead to the client incurring unnecessary costs and the professional losing revenue. At present, although now changed for SEC registrant companies, the established position of the accounting profession is to rely on the personal integrity of the professionals involved to be able to criticize themselves in the event they or their associates perform conflicting services. Whether this reliance is misplaced remains to be seen, but it is interesting to note that the future of such activities depends upon the values, strength of character, and ethical awareness of the professionals involved.

The self-interest of professional accountants can cause the professional to want to side with certain stakeholder groups, to the detriment of others. Professional accountants can easily and inadvertently become over-involved with clients or suppliers or other stakeholders. Sometimes this *overinvolvement* can make the professional's judgment susceptible to bias in favor of his or her new-found friends or compatriots. Gifts can create pressures for continuance. Involvement in management friendships and decisions can create the desire not to be critical, as can the continued, close involvement of an auditor with the board of directors. To borrow from the hierarchy of human needs developed by Maslow (1954), professionals can be subject to influence attempts directed at their ego, social needs, or even their basic financial needs because of overinvolvement with other stakeholders, which threatens the professional's independence. Frequently, overinvolvement begins very innocuously and builds imperceptibly to a condition that the professional does not expect (the slippery slope problem noted earlier). Constant vigilance is required to stay out of the difficulty of putting the interests of management and directors ahead of shareholders and the public.

Sometimes a professional accountant develops a mutuality of interest with a client or becomes overinvolved with senior management at a client, to the extent that the professional's skepticism and critical perspective is suspended. Friendship, partnerships, the desire to protect existing revenue streams or garner more, and the prospect of social interaction or admiration may all impact on the professional's independence of judgment to the detriment of the public interest. Care must be taken to ensure that a professional accountant or his or her firm does not become so dependent on the revenue from one client that decisions contrary to the public interest become difficult to make. This appears to have happened, as noted in Chapter 2, in the case of Arthur Andersen and several of its audit clients, including Enron, WorldCom, and Waste Management.

Concern over the impact of consulting and other services on the independence of professional accountants alarmed the accounting profession and its regulators, particularly in the United States prior to the demise of Arthur Andersen. In 1998, PricewaterhouseCoopers (PwC) discovered[7] in a post-merger review that its predecessor firms (Price Waterhouse and Coopers & Lybrand) had failed to properly supervise their consulting and audit partners and personnel and almost 50 percent of PwC's U.S. partners held improperly sanitized[8] investments in the firm's audit clients—thereby violating PwC and SEC conflict of interest guidelines. This led, in part, to the issuance of a proposed revision of the SEC's Auditor Independence Requirements[9] for auditors of companies that file SEC documentation in the United States. Among other guidance provided, the revised rule sought to clarify those services that an auditor of SEC registrant companies can and cannot engage in to preserve independence of judgment in fact, as well as the perception of independence. It should be noted that the matters dealt with in the proposed revision were overtaken by the SOX reforms and the resulting new SEC pronouncements[10] discussed on page 214 of this chapter.

While embarrassed by the initial publicity of the PwC violations, PwC, the accounting profession, and regulators such as the SEC have not required complete separation between audit or assurance services and consulting services.

---

[7]SEC's Independent Consultant's *Report of the Internal Investigation of Independence Issues at PricewaterhouseCoopers LLP*, January 6, 2000, SEC website link at *http://brooks.swlearning.com*

[8]Investment where PwC had pre-cleared that no conflict of interests had or would occur.

[9]See *http://brooks.swlearning.com* for the *Proposed Rule: Revision of the Commission's Auditor Independence Requirements*, July 17, 2000, p. 109. A *Final Rule* was released in January 2003.

[10]See *http://brooks.swlearning.com* for the SEC's Final Rule: Strengthening the Commission's Requirements Regarding Auditor Independence, U.S. Securities and Exchange Commission, modified February 6, 2003 and Commission Adopts Rules Strengthening Auditor Independence, U.S. Securities and Exchange Commission, January 22, 2003.

As previously noted, SOX has required the SEC to specify those services that can be offered to audit clients. However, even though some large firms have sold off service lines, such as advice on information systems, they will continue to operate multidisciplinary consulting practices.

This continuation in non-attest activity will require a strong set of guidelines and organizational culture to prevent the erosion of independent judgment and professional skepticism. Professional accountants will have to continue to resist the temptation of focusing on the development of high-profit services to the detriment of low-margin audit services. An instance of this might be a new perversion of risk management in tax matters, where the client is advised to take a questionable action based on the probability that government tax auditors are unlikely to appear because of other time demands, not because the tax treatment is in doubt. An additional aspect of a multidisciplinary firm that could cause difficulties is the potential conflict between the professional codes and practices of accountants, lawyers, and engineers. For example, accountants are not generally expected to blow the whistle on clients, but engineers are required to report any endangerment to life from a dangerous process or poorly maintained building[11]—which profession's rules should prevail? Similarly, lawyers have a different standard of confidentiality that prevents them from advising competing clients, whereas professional accountants do it frequently. We are already seeing some assurance services downgraded to the status of a non-audit review or consulting services to lessen the legal liability involved in an effort to bolster profits. Increased attention to ethical principles for managing such conflicts of interest will be essential to the maintenance of the accounting profession's reputation in the future, as well as the reputations of the other professions involved.

The examples of overindulged self-interest cited in Table 4.11 put the professional's reputation at risk because the interest of the client, employer, or public may not be considered before the professional's self-interest as is expected in a fiduciary relationship. The lure of personal profit from investment positions in clients may lead to the manipulation of accounting disclosure or the choice of accounting principles, which do not communicate the real state of affairs to shareholders because the stock price gains for the investor-professional accountant are too alluring to pass up. Fortunately, such investment has been barred for years in most professional codes. Similarly, skimping on quality of service, particularly of audit service, has proven difficult to resist in the past. As competition on the basis of price of services becomes more intense, professionals would be well advised to consider the longer-term possibilities of loss of reputation, fines, and higher insurance premiums.

It is possible but very risky for a professional accountant and his or her clients to *represent more than one client in a transaction*. Even if a professional is very knowledgeable about the matter, such as would be the case if an audit client were being sold, and the buyer and seller are good friends, it is very difficult to do your best for one except at the expense of the other. Later, if the buyer or seller becomes disenchanted, he or she may suspect that his or her interest has been short-changed and launch a lawsuit. Therefore, even if more

---

[11]Presumably, this difference in treatment is due to the higher priority attached by society (and therefore by engineers) to physical well-being as opposed to financial well-being. Society is willing to endorse the reporting of one, but not yet the other.

than one client who is party to a transaction wants a professional accountant to act on their behalf, the clients should at least be warned that each should have independent representation. Sometimes, it will be advisable to select and serve only one of the clients, even if they are insistent. Whenever more than one client is served in a transaction, the professional accountant must be able to show that all reasonable precautions were taken to avoid failing to act in the best interests of all parties.

For the accountant in management, it is similarly risky to consider *serving two or more employers*. Serving two or more masters has, over the years, proved very difficult because of the real, latent, and imaginary conflicts of interest that inevitably arise even where the employers are not competitors. Where the employers are competitors, it is sheer folly. A variant of this ethical problem surfaces when an accountant in management *invests in a competitor*. Care must be taken to ensure that conflicting interests do not adversely influence judgment or work performance for the employer.

Blind self-interest can prove to be the undoing of professional accountants, just as blind ambition has proven to be the bane of many managers. Frequently, however, professional accountants do not suffer from blind or rabid self-interest, but they do lose sight of *whether they are in a profession or in business*. They would do well to remember that few businesses are accorded the privilege of engaging in fiduciary relationships. A balance is called for which involves placing the interest of the public, the client, the profession, and the firm or employer before the professional's own self-interest.

CONFLICTS OF INTEREST INVOLVING IMPROPER USE OF INFLUENCE

The desire to improve the professional's own lot can lead to the improper use of influence such that the independent judgment of the professional can be undermined. For example, a professional accountant employed by a corporation might be successful in arranging for a friend to be hired by the company. In so doing, however, the professional may put himself or herself in a position to be approached by management who want a *favor in return*, which may take the form of nondisclosure of a financial matter, the delay of such disclosure, or the minimization of the disclosure. The public, shareholders, other management, and the auditors can be misled in the process.

An auditor may also be unsuspectingly trapped by use of his or her influence. From time to time, auditors will want, and be encouraged by clients, to *purchase goods or services from the client* at substantial discounts beyond those available to the public. The risk is that the desire to do this or the satisfaction experienced will create a desire to subjugate public interests in favor of the interests of the management who control this privilege. Similarly, a professional employed by a corporation may wish to *buy goods or services from a supplier* at a discount. Is this a reasonable thing to do? The answer depends on the circumstances.

Alternatively, a professional in audit practice or employed by a corporation can be offered a *gift, a meal, entertainment, a trip, or preferential treatment* by a client or a supplier. Is it ethical to accept such a gift? Again, the answer depends on the circumstances. Fortunately, the guidelines outlined in Table 3.6 can be used to avoid the real or potential conflicts of interest that could develop when the giver expects a favor in return.

CONFLICTS OF INTEREST INVOLVING USE OR MISUSE OF INFORMATION (CONFIDENTIALITY)

The misuse of information by a professional accountant can be detrimental to other stakeholders of the client or company involved. For example, the use of information by the professional before others have the right to use such information is unfair and considered unethical. This is the basic problem for anyone who is privy to *inside information* about a company by virtue of being the auditor or an employee—i.e., an "insider"—to use that information personally or indirectly for *insider trading*. In order to ensure the basic fairness of stock markets so that the public and other noninsiders will wish to enter the market, regulatory bodies such as the Securities and Exchange Commission or the Ontario Securities Commission require management insiders to wait until the information is released to the public before allowing insiders to trade, and then they must disclose these trades so the public will know what has happened. The prospect of a "rigged game" would not be in the public interest or in the interest of the corporations using the market for fund-raising in the long run. Insider trading rules also apply to the families of the insider, extending to those who are not part of the immediate family but for whom the insider has an obvious ability to influence. Some individuals with high-profile jobs in the public service go even further to avoid such conflicts of interest. In order to be seen to be entirely ethical, some politicians have gone so far as to place their holdings, and those of their dependants, in so-called "blind trusts," which are managed by someone else with instructions not to discuss trades or holdings with the politician.

The situation for auditors is somewhat different in that the ownership of shares or financial instruments of a client is forbidden based on of the real or potential conflict of interest that would be created, as discussed in earlier segments of this book. Most auditing firms extend this ban in two ways. First, the ban is applied to the auditor's family and persons who would be considered significant dependants or subject to influence. Second, the ban often applies to any client of the firm, even if that client is serviced through a wholly separate office (for international firms, even in another country) with which the individual does not have contact on a normally occurring basis. The extent of attention to the prevention of insider trading and the perception of it is indicative of the alarm with which most firms view its prospect.

Confidentiality is the term used to describe keeping confidential information that is proprietary to a client or employer. The release of such information to the public, or to competitors, would have a detrimental effect on the interests of the client, and it would be contrary to the expectations of trust of a fiduciary relationship. In the case of an auditor, this expectation of trust and privacy is vital to the client's willingness to discuss difficult issues, which are quite germane to the audit, to get the opinion of the auditor on how they might be dealt with in the financial statements and notes. How frank would the discussion of a contentious contingent liability be if there were a possibility the auditor would reveal the confidence? How could a contentious tax treatment be discussed thoroughly if there was the possibility of voluntary disclosure to the tax collection authorities? It is therefore argued that the maintenance of client confidences is essential to the proper exercise of the audit function, and to the provision of the best advice based on full discussion of the possibilities.

There are, however, limits to privacy that some professions have enshrined in their codes of conduct, or where these limits are spelled out in regulating frameworks. Engineers, for example, must disclose to appropriate public officials when they believe a structure or mechanism is likely to be harmful to the users, as in the potential collapse of a building due to violations of the building code. In Canada, the recent bankruptcy of two chartered banks has resulted in the requirement to report lack of client viability directly to the Federal Office of the Superintendent of Financial Institutions. In the United Kingdom, money laundering for drugs and terrorism must be reported. There appears to be an increasing focus on the public responsibility of auditors and an increasing expectation of action rather than silence.

This trade-off between the interests of client, management, public, regulators, the profession, and management promises to be a growing conundrum for accountants in the future. One issue that is not well understood is the consequences of a professional accountant observing strict confidentiality about the malfeasance of his or her employer, and being directed by the professional code to resign if the employer cannot be convinced to change its behavior. This would follow from the codes of conduct that require no disclosure of client/employer confidences except in a court of law or subject to a disciplinary hearing, and at the same time requiring resignation in order to avoid association with a misrepresentation. In the event of a resignation in silence, the ethical misdeed goes unrecognized by all stakeholders except the perpetrators and the silent professional. How does this protect the interests of the public, the shareholders, or the profession? A discussion of this issue earlier in the book gave rise to an argument for the modification of the strict confidentiality of codes and the introduction of assisted confidentiality involving consultations with officials of the relevant professional institute. Perhaps through such consultations, a means can be found to better judge what needs to be kept confidential, when and how disclosure ought to be made, and how the professional's and public's interests can be protected. For an auditor, the situation is different. When an auditor is discharged or replaced, the incoming auditor has the right to ask the outgoing auditor (and the client) what the circumstances were that led to the dismissal or resignation. In some jurisdictions, the removed auditor even has the right to address the shareholders at their annual meeting, or by mail, at the expense of the corporation involved.

One of the first items that ought to be examined is what action should be taken when a professional accountant realizes that a client or employer is engaging in *tax evasion*. Tax evasion involves the misrepresentation of facts to the taxation authorities, resulting in the commission of a fraud and the cheating of the public treasury. At present, the established practice is not to be involved in the misrepresentation, to counsel against it, but not to report the problem to the authorities. As a result, the perpetrators need not fear their misdeed will be reported by a *whistle-blower* to the tax authorities or the public. Consequently, the interests of the public and, when the deed is found out, the shareholders and the profession will suffer. Hopefully, the corporation will recognize the large cost of not encouraging whistle-blowers to come forward through protected internal channels so that unknown problems can be corrected and public disgrace, and fines, can be avoided.

Looking the other way when confronted with tax evasion doesn't appear to make ethical sense. In some cases the professional involved may believe that the interpretation involved is debatable so that the problem is one of *avoision*, and its borderline nature is worthy of support until the authorities find and rule on the problem. Avoidance of taxes is, of course quite legal; avoision reflects borderline practices, and evasion is both illegal and unethical (Lynch, 1987). The boundaries are blurred, so access to confidential consultation on these matters is essential to proper ethical action.

Enron's use of tax avoidance strategies that is reported in Chapter 2 offers an interesting case of avoidance and probably qualifies as avoision, according to a U.S. Senate Committee on Finance report[12]. The reaction to Enron's tax avoidance transactions may lead to the closing of loopholes such as using accommodation parties, to the increased scrutiny of the business purpose of transactions, and to increased sanctions for extra aggressive interpretations. The resulting publicity, potential loss of reputation, and potential for lawsuits may also cause responsible advisers to consider ethical guidelines for limiting involvement with and the ethics risks inherent in such activities. This would represent a significant change in thinking for many professionals engaged in tax practice.

Another tax practice, that of *risk management*, is worthy of comment here. If the risk management relates to a tax matter that is in doubt, that is an issue of avoision and worthy of estimation of the risks and support. However, if the risk management involves estimating if a known illegality will be found because tax auditors are few and far between, then the practice would appear to represent support for an evasion of tax.

Laws and Jurisprudence

Professional accountants can also refer to legal cases and lawyers for interpretations of their legal liability and potential defenses. To assist the reader, an analysis of trends and a synopsis of important legal decisions is included in Appendix B, "Trends in the Legal Liability of Accountants and Auditors and Legal Defenses Available." It documents an early trend to a broadening of liability from strict "privity of contract" with existing shareholders to "foreseeable parties" who might use the financial statements. Partly to counteract the trend to very excessive liability, recent cases such as *Hercules Managements Ltd. et al. v. Ernst & Young* (1997) have been decided in favor of very limited liability for auditors. Since this case was defended on the rather bizarre basis that financial statements should not be used for investment purposes, and therefore an auditor has no legal liability to shareholders and investors, most observers believe that it is a temporary diversion in a progression toward greater auditor liability. In fact, the U.S. Senate Permanent Subcommittee on Investigations stated in its *Report on the Collapse of Enron* that financial statements and the auditor's independent opinions thereon were essential to the public investment process and its credibility.

To counter the trend to greater auditor liability, safe-harbour or limited liability arrangements are emerging for auditors. As noted in the later discussion of limited liability partnerships (LLPs), these will limit the dollar value of legal damages each partner has to bear from each lawsuit. LLPs, however, will not stop lawsuits.

---

[12]*Report of the Investigation of Enron Corporation and Related Entities Regarding Federal Tax and Compensation Issues, and Policy Recommendations, Volume 1: Report*, U.S. Senate Committee on Finance, February 2003, released 2/22/03 (see *http://brooks.swlearning.com*).

Caution should be exercised in the application of legal standards to ethical problems, however, for three reasons. First, the law appears to offer timeless wisdom when in reality it is continuously changing as it tries to catch up to the positions society believes are reasonable. In other words, the law generally lags what society views as ethically desirable. Second, and more importantly, *what is legal is not always ethical.*

According to former U.S. Supreme Court Justice Potter Stewart, ethics is "knowing the difference between what you have the right to do and what is right to do." There are plenty of examples of this difference between legal, moral, and ethical standards. For example, a company may be able to pollute in a way that is harmful to the health of its workers in a third world country because the local standards are less stringent than at home in North America. Sometimes the legal standard is clear, such as in tax matters or bribery, but large portions of society do not adhere to it, so the mores or norms expected are different. What behavior is right? Legal, moral, and ethical standards are different and should be recognized as such.

The third reason for caution in placing too much reliance on legal interpretations and remedies is that they appear not to be highly relevant to the launching of or final disposition of lawsuits, particularly in the United States. Of 800 allegations of audit failure during the period 1960–1990 against the 15 largest audit firms in the United States, only 64 were tried to a verdict (Palmrose, 1991, p. 154). Although some cases were still underway, less than 10 percent were submitted to judge or jury: a rate, which drops to 2.1 percent for the 1985–1989 period.

By far the highest percentage of cases cited in the Palmrose study were settled for practical reasons rather than legal precedent. Usually, audit firms found it cheaper to settle rather than fight in court. The cost to their pocketbooks in legal fees and lost billable time, and particularly to their reputation, rarely made recourse to the courts a sensible option, even where lawsuits were without legal foundation.

The reasons for this bizarre situation are outlined in a position statement authored by the Big 6 audit firms in August 1992, entitled "The Liability Crisis in the United States: Impact on the Accounting Profession." This statement, which is included as a reading in this chapter, indicates that several quirks which have developed in the legal framework and process are responsible for an intolerable level of liability for audit professionals—a level that has resulted in individuals who have been offered partnerships hesitating or declining the offer, and in the bankruptcy in 1990 of one of the largest audit firms, Laventhol & Horwath. As the heads of the Big 6 said, "To restore equity and sanity to the liability system and to provide reasonable assurance that the public accounting profession will be able to continue to meet its public obligations requires substantial reform of both federal and state liability laws" (p. 6). Several reforms were suggested in the statement, but they have been slow to appear because of the multiple jurisdictions involved and the entrenchment of the practice of contingent legal fees and of the principle of joint and several liability.

Two developments are worthy of comment. In December 1995, the U.S. Congress enacted the Private Securities Reform Act, which changes auditor liability from having to share equally with his or her partners to having to bear a portion allocated by the jury involved (Andrews & Simonette, 1996, p. 54). Secondly, the organizational form of the accounting firm was allowed to be altered to a limited liability partnership (LLP) in some jurisdictions to provide limited liability for nonculpable partners of the firm. Historically, accounting firms were required to be partnerships where, if the firm was sued, each partner was required to pay the full loss from their investment in the firm, plus any additional losses if required from their personal assets. Afterward they could sue others who were also liable for recovery of their fortunes if these other people had resources left. This meant that partners could lose their investment in their firm and their personal assets as well, even though someone else was at fault. This was draconian, but it was considered an appropriate way to ensure that professional accountants were focused on providing competent service. The LLP provided that the negligent partner would be required to settle up with both his or her investment in the firm plus his or her personal assets, whereas the "innocent" partners could lose only the assets they had invested in the firm. Their personal assets were protected. Ernst & Young became the first LLP in New York on August 1, 1994. Other jurisdictions are enacting similar legislation.

Given this scenario, in which the legal "cure" for a problem is still unpalatable—where a lawsuit can bankrupt a firm, although most of the partner's personal assets are untouched—"preventative medicine," or not getting into the dilemma in the first place, is preferred if at all possible. Instilling high standards of professional ethics into the values and culture of accounting professionals and their organizations can prove to be a significant safeguard against getting into practice dilemmas. Even in legal jurisdictions such as Canada or the United Kingdom, where the liability crisis is not quite as alarming, high ethical standards and skill in their application can eliminate or reduce professional exposure.

When Codes and Laws Don't Help

Frequently, professional accountants find themselves facing situations that are not covered explicitly in codes of conduct, nor sufficiently close to jurisprudence to benefit from those sources of guidance. Sometimes a professional accounting body will provide its members with consultation services through a so-called director of ethics. Most often, however, the professional accountant will be left to his or her own devices. He or she may hire an advisor from the ranks of legal or ethical experts, but ultimately the accountant will have to rely upon his or her own knowledge, values, and judgment to decide what is right.

Broadening Role for Professional Accountants

The need for integrity, independent judgment, expertise, and savvy in the preparation and presentation of financial analyses and reports is not abating, rather it is increasing.

In addition to this traditional fiduciary role, professional accountants are best suited to play the dominant or supporting roles in *design, preparation, and management* of the following areas that are vital to good governance in the emerging era of stakeholder accountability:

- Stakeholder interests assessment
- Stakeholder-focused performance indicators and incentive systems
- Stakeholder-oriented reports for management, board, and public

- Ethical corporate culture
- Corporate codes of conduct
- Ethics compliance mechanisms and reporting to the board
- Ethical decision-making guidance frameworks
- Ethics risk management systems

Professional accountants understand the problems that caused the Enron, WorldCom, Arthur Andersen, and other recent fiascos, and understand the potential contribution of an organization's internal control system as well as the pitfalls of an unethical culture. While the professional accountant's focus has been on financial reporting, there is a need to refocus on future performance and how to guide and manage it to help ensure that ethics are built into strategic plans, board compliance reviews, and corporate incentive systems.

Boards of directors have not been equipped to consider and deal with these new necessities. That inability and lack or awareness resulted in the Enron problem and many others. Professional accountants can assist boards greatly in the new, ethics-sensitive era if they are ready to broaden their horizons.

Conclusion

Recent events like the Enron, Arthur Andersen, and WorldCom disasters have rededicated the focus of professional accountants on their expected role as fiduciaries for the public interest. The reputation and future standing of the profession has suffered, and its redistinction and success depends upon this rededication.

The professional accountant must develop judgment and values that embrace the public's expectations which are inherent in the emerging stakeholder-oriented accountability and governance framework. New codes of conduct sections and standards are emerging to guide professional accountants and assure that unrestrained self-interest, bias, and/or misunderstanding do not cloud the professional's independent state of mind or give rise to an appearance that independence may be lacking.

Globalization has begun to influence the development of codes and harmonization of standards for professional accountants, and will surely continue. Just as the governance mechanism for corporations has outgrown domestic jurisdiction and boundaries, stakeholders around the world will be more important in determining the performance standards for professional accountants. Their work will serve global capital markets and global corporations, and their success will require the respect of employees and partners drawn from a much wider set than in the past.

Given their knowledge and skills, it will be interesting to see if professional accountants can seize the opportunities that present themselves for broadening their role. They are particularly well placed to assist in the further development of those mechanisms that will provide and ensure ethical guidance for their organization. They know that codes don't cover every possible challenge. Developing the ethical decision-making frameworks covered in Chapter 5 and understanding the special issues covered in Chapter 6 will assist those who choose to make the most of future opportunities.

QUESTIONS FOR DISCUSSION

1. Answer the seven questions in the opening section of this chapter.

2. What is meant by the term "fiduciary relationship"?

3. Why are most ethical decisions accountants face complex rather than straightforward?

4. When should an accountant place his or her duty to the public ahead of his or her duty to a client or employer?

5. Which would you choose as the key idea for ethical behavior in the accounting profession: "Protect the public interest" or "Protect the credibility of the profession." Why?

6. Why is maintaining the confidentiality of client or employer matters essential to the effectiveness of the audit or accountant relationship?

7. Why did the SEC ban certain non-audit services from being offered to SEC-registrant audit clients even though it has been possible to effectively manage such conflict of interest situations?

8. Where on the Kohlberg framework would you place your own usual motivation for making decisions?

9. Why don't more professional accountants report ethical wrongdoing? Consider their awareness and understanding of ethical issues, as well as their motivation and courage for doing so.

10. Which type of conflict of interest should be of greater concern to a professional accountant: actual or apparent?

11. An auditor naturally wishes his or her activity to be as profitable as possible, but when, if ever, should the drive for profit be tempered?

12. If the provision of management advisory services can create conflicts of interest, why are audit firms still offering them?

13. If you were an auditor, would you buy a new car at a dealership you audited for 17 percent off the list price?

14. If you were a management accountant, would you buy a product from a supplier for personal use at 25 percent off the list price?

15. If you were a professional accountant who discovered your superior was inflating his or her expense reports, what would you do?

16. Can a professional accountant serve two clients whose interests conflict? Explain.

17. If an auditor's fee is paid from the client company, isn't there a conflict of interest that may lead to a lack of objectivity? Why doesn't it?

18. Why does the IFAC Code consider the appearance of a conflict of interest to be as important as a real, but nonapparent, influence that might sway the independence of mind of a professional accountant?

19. What is the most important contribution of a professional or corporate code of conduct?

20. Are one or more of the fundamental principles found in codes of conduct more important than the rest? Why?

21. Was the expectations gap that triggered the Treadway and Macdonald Commissions the fault of the users of financial statements, the management who prepared them, the auditors, or the standard setters who decided what the disclosure standards should be?

22. Why should codes focus on principles rather than specific detailed rules?

23. Is having an ethical culture important to having an effective system of internal control? Why or why not?

24. What should an auditor do if he or she believes that the ethical culture of a client is unsatisfactory?

25. Are the governing partners of accounting firms subject to a "due diligence" requirement similar to that for corporation executives in building an ethical culture? Can a firm and/or its governors be sanctioned for the misdeeds of its members?

26. An engineer employed by a large multidisciplinary accounting firm has spotted a condition in a client's plant that is seriously jeopardizing the safety of the client's workers. The engineer believes that his or her professional engineering code requires him to report this condition to the authorities, but professional accounting codes do not. How should the head of the firm resolve this issue?

27. Why don't codes of conduct or existing jurisprudence provide sufficient guidance for accountants in ethical matters?

CASES

The following cases have been selected to expose situations that shed light upon the role of auditors and management accountants as they discharge their fiduciary duties. Specifically, the issues covered are as follows:

- *Arthur Anderson, Enron, WorldCom, Sunbeam,* and *Waste Management* cases are located in Chapter 2.

- *Allan Eagleson: The Eagle Has Landed* is a fascinating story of a brilliant, powerful man who lost sight of what it meant to be a fiduciary and played an unethical game against some of the greatest hockey players. He landed in jail.

- *The Lang Michener Affair* shows how legal professionals can take to the slippery slopes of shady deals, conflicts of interest, self-interest, passing the buck, and failing to step forward when they should to protect themselves, their firm, and their profession. It also illustrates the frustrations of a whistle-blower and the workings of a self-regulating profession.

- *Dilemma of an Accountant* portrays an auditor who is caught between his principles and the desire of his superior to have a clean file and a clean opinion. What is he to do?

- *Societal Concerns* asks the reader to consider how realistic and short-sighted our traditional financial statements and reports are. Can accountants go beyond this traditional framework to take on environmental and other issues? Should they?

- *Management Choice* focuses on Sue, a management accountant who has a choice of accounting policy and practice to make. She can probably get away with it. Should she?

- *Maple Leaf Gardens Shenanigans* reveals how a former owner of the Maple Leaf Hockey Team and the Toronto Raptors came to power. The story involves conflicts of interest, faithless fiduciaries, and insider information.

- *To Qualify or Not?* introduces the real-life dilemma of wanting to qualify an audit opinion, but realizing that doing so might cause the company to become insolvent.

- In *Economic Realities or GAAP*, Stan Jones is asking penetrating questions about the fundamental utility of traditional financial reports and the role of the auditor.

- *Multidisciplinary Practices—Ethical Challenges* asks questions about managing the new assurance service, expanded practices. If we don't get the answers right, could the accounting profession be in for a black eye?

- *Team Player Problems* deals with the situation faced by a professional accountant who is to be part of a team, but not the leader of it, when he or she disagrees with the use and presentation of data in the report. What would you advise?

- *Locker Room Talk* presents a fascinating case on confidentiality and its strange treatment in professional accounting codes.

- *Minimal Disclosure* investigates how an audit partner would deal with a client who wanted to avoid disclosing the amount of income made from derivative securities, details of a lawsuit, and the financial situation in a consolidated subsidiary.

- *Opinion Shopping* looks at some reasons for seeking a new auditor, and at the responsibility of an auditor likely to lose an audit to a firm willing to be more lenient in deciding on the acceptability of some accounting practices.

- *Lowballing a Fee Quotation* is a common temptation. Are there reasons why it is appropriate?

- *Tax Return Complications* introduces the prospect of "bending the rules" to keep the client happy, as well as having to decide to admit an error or attempt to hide it. This case provides a very good illustration of the "slippery slope" problem.

- *Risk Management of Taxes Payable—Is it Ethical?* spotlights a new practice that can get the accountant into trouble if he or she is not careful.

READINGS

The article by J. Michael Cook provides an excellent historical recount of the issues that lay behind the evolution of the professional code of the American Institute of Certified Public Accountants in its quest to serve the public and to deserve its trust. Appendix A provides an interesting and informative look at the difference between the professional codes of major professional accounting associations. G.D. Anderson's article provides background on the reasons for the current structure of the AICPA code, deficiencies that remain in codes, and how to think about, approach and use codes. The position statement of the six largest accounting firms in the United States on the legal liability crisis highlights the reality faced by the accounting profession and underscores the value of ethical behavior as an approach to the minimization of vulnerability to the legal process. Tom Lynch's article offers insights into the interesting and challenging world of tax advice. Appendix B provides insights into trends in legal liability and defenses available to professional auditors in public practice.

REFERENCES

Anderson, G. D., "A Fresh Look at Standards of Professional Conduct," *Journal of Accountancy*, September 1985, 93–106.

_____, "The Anderson Committee: Restructuring Professional Standards," *Journal of Accountancy*, May 1987, 77.

Andrews, A. R. and Simonette, G., Jr., "Tort Reform Revolution," *Journal of Accountancy*, September 1996, 54.

Bayles, M. D., *Professional Ethics*, Wadsworth Publishing Company, Belmont, California, 1981, 7, 8.

Behrman, J. N., *Essays on Ethics in Business and the Professions*, Prentice-Hall, New Jersey, 1988, 96.

Brooks, L. J., "Ethical Codes of Conduct: Deficient in Guidance for the Canadian Accounting Profession," *Journal of Business Ethics*, Vol. 8, No. 5, May 1989, 325–336.

_____, "No more trial and error: It's time we moved ethics out of the clouds and into the classroom," *CAmagazine*, March 1993, 43–45.

_____, "Codes of Conduct: Trust, Innovation, Commitment and Productivity: A Strategic-Cultural Perspective," *Business & The Contemporary World*, Global Outlook: An International Journal of Business, Economics, and Social Policy, Vol. 12, No. 2, January 11, 2000.

Brooks, L. J., and Fortunato, V., "Discipline at the Institute of Chartered Accountants of Ontario," *CAmagazine*, May 1991, 40–43.

Cohen, J., Pant, L., and Sharp, D., "An Exploratory Examination of International Differences in Auditor's Ethical Perceptions," *Behavioral Research in Accounting*, Vol. 7, 1995, 37–64.

Colby, A., and Kohlberg, L., *The Measurement of Moral Judgment: Theoretical Foundations and Research Validations, and Standard Scoring Manual*, Volumes 1 and 2, Cambridge University Press, 1987.

Cook, J. M., "The AICPA at 100: Public Trust and Professional Pride," *Journal of Accountancy*, May 1987, 307–379.

Etherington, L. D., and Schulting, L., "Ethical Development of Accountants: The Case of Canadian Certified Management Accountants," *Research in Accounting Ethics*, JAI Press, Vol. 1, 1995, 235–251.

Final Rule: Strengthening the Commission's Requirements Regarding Auditor Independence, U.S. Securities and Exchange Commission (see *http://brooks.swlearning.com*), modified 2/6/2003, and *Commission Adopts Rules Strengthening Auditor Independence*, U.S. Securities and Exchange Commission (see *http://brooks.swlearning.com*), January 22, 2003.

Gunning, K. S., "Completely at Sea," *CA Magazine*, April 1989, 24–37.

IFAC Code of Ethics for Professional Accountants, International Federation for Accountants, London, England, November 2001 (see *http://brooks.swlearning.com*).

Kohlberg, L., *Essays in Moral Development, Volume I: The Philosophy of Moral Development*, Harper & Row, 1981.

_____, *Essays in Moral Development, Volume II: The Psychology of Moral Development*, Harper & Row, 1984.

Lane, M. S., and Schaup, D., "Ethics in Education: A Comparative Study," *Journal of Business Ethics*, Vol. 8, No. 12, December 1989, 58–69.

Lynch, T., "Ethics in Taxation Practice," *The Accountant's Magazine*, November 1987, 27, 28.

Macdonald Commission, see *The Report of the Commission to Study the Public's Expectations of Audits*, Canadian Institute of Chartered Accountants, June 1988.

Maslow, A., *Motivation and Personality*, New York: Harper and Brothers, 1954.

Metcalf, Lee, spearheaded a senatorial investigation of the large U.S. accounting firms and the AICPA in the 1970s: in response the AICPA established the Cohen Commission.

O'Malley, S. F., "Legal Liability is Having a Chilling Effect on the Auditor's Role," *Accounting Horizons*, Vol. 7, No. 2, June 1993, 82–87.

Palmrose, Z-V, "Trials of Legal Disputes Involving Independent Auditors: Some Empirical Evidence," *Journal of Accounting Research*, Vol. 29, Supplement 1991, 149–185.

Ponemon, L. A., "Ethical Reasoning and Selection-Socialization in Accounting," Accounting, *Organizations & Society*, Vol. 17, No. 3/4, 1992, 239–258.

Ponemon, L. A., and Gabhart, *Ethical Reasoning in Accounting and Auditing*, CGA-Canada Research Foundation, Vancouver, Canada, 1993.

Priest, S., "Perspective: The Credibility Crisis," *Ethics in the Marketplace*, The Center for Ethics and Corporate Policy, Chicago, June 1991, 2.

SEC's Independent Consultant's Report of the Internal Investigation of Independence Issues at PricewaterhouseCoopers LLP, SEC website, January 6, 2000, Press Release at *http://brooks.swlearning.com*, link to Report at Press Release 2000-4 on *http://brooks.swlearning.com*.

Shenkir, W. G., "A Perspective from Education: Business Ethics," *Management Accounting*, June 1990, 30–33.

The Liability Crisis in the United States: Impact on the Accounting Profession, Arthur Andersen & Co., Coopers & Lybrand, Deloitte & Touche, Ernst & Young, KPMG Peat Marwick, Price Waterhouse, August 6, 1992.

Thorne, L., and Magnan, M., "The Generic Moral Reasoning Development and Domain Specific Moral Reasoning of Canadian Public Accountants," *Journal of Accounting Ethics*, forthcoming.

Treadway Commission, see the *Report of the National Commission on Fraudulent Public Reporting*, AICPA, 1987.

U.S. Sentencing Guidelines, United States Sentencing Commission, Washington, D.C., November 1, 1991.

Weber, J., and Green, S., "Principled Moral Reasoning: Is It A Viable Approach to Promote Ethical Integrity," *Journal of Business Ethics*, Vol. 10, No. 5, May 1991, 325–333.

Allan Eagleson: The Eagle Has Landed

Allan Eagleson is a brilliant, likeable, engaging, opportunistic man—a terrific success. Why, then, did some people grow to loathe him so much that he ended up in jail?

Eagleson began his career as a lawyer interested in sports. He soon found that he could make a handsome living as an agent for players in the National Hockey League (NHL). He would negotiate their salaries and their contracts for endorsement of products, as well as invest their money and even become a partner with some in their ventures. On his staff was an accountant and a lawyer, as well as other personnel. He attracted all types of players, but he particularly enjoyed working with the stars, such as Bobby Orr, Wayne Gretsky, Phil Esposito, Paul Henderson, and their like. He knew everyone, including many of the top politicians in the United States and Canada. In fact, he was very active in political circles.

As time went on, Eagleson realized that there was room for him on a broader stage—that of head of the NHL Players Association (NHLPA)—so he fostered it and became its first executive director. In this position, he was able to negotiate with the owners of the NHL teams for minimum salary levels, standards of work, pension benefits, and terms by which players could move from team to team. Such movement was called "free agency" and was much sought after because otherwise team owners could prevent movement and thereby hold down salaries. Eagleson created a governance structure at the NHLPA wherein he reported to an executive committee made up mainly of the stars in the league (most of whom happened to be his clients). There were also player representatives on each team who met irregularly, as well as an annual meeting of all players. In time, Eagleson became the executive director of the NHLPA, its chief negotiator, and its investment decision maker—all within the governance structure, of course.

One of the major rivalries in the hockey world was over who were the best hockey players—NHLers or Russians. There was an amateur competition every four years at the Olympics, but everyone knew that the Russians paid their best players to play for the Red Army team, whereas in North America our best hockey players turned pro in the NHL and were therefore not eligible to compete in the Olympics. Our best amateurs were competing against Russian pros, and the Russians began to win. Eagleson saw the opportunity to create a series in which NHLers could compete directly against the Russian pros, and thanks to incredible negotiating skills and persistence he organized the Canada Cup Series. Eagleson oversaw the whole process and deserves the credit, along with the players, for this marvelous experience. Eagleson emerged as "the Eagle," a sort of a "folk hero" to sports buffs.

There were rumblings heard from time to time, but these were attributed to malcontents and given low credibility. After all, weren't the likes of Carl Brewer and Terry O'Reilly known to be fiery complainers, known to pick fights and do their own thing? It was known that Bobby Orr and the Eagle had a falling out, but why was not known. The rosy glow, however, began to fade when Eagleson was charged with professional misconduct in 1990 by a fellow agent, Rick Winter. Carl Brewer hired a lawyer and pension expert, Mark Zigler, who reported in September 1990 that there was a players pension surplus of $24 million and the owners had used some $13 million to reduce their own contributions, while the benefits to retired players such as Gordie Howe, Bobby Hull, and Andy Bathgate were kept absurdly low. Russ Conway, a reporter for the *Eagle-Tribune* of Lawrence, Massachusetts, began an investigative series in 1991 called

—*Continued*

Continued

"Cracking the Ice," which dug up many allegations of wrongdoing, as did a book by David Cruise and Allison Griffiths called *Net Worth.* Conway later wrote a book called *Gross Misconduct,* which incorporated the worst allegations against the Eagle.

Legal action was slow to start, perhaps because Eagleson was so well respected. Ultimately, however, the Eagle faced legal proceedings in both the United States and Canada. Among the allegations were that he

- was friendly to the owners
- acted for the owners in holding down salaries
- held back the onset of free agency
- didn't tell Bobby Orr of the Boston Bruins offer of 10 percent of the Boston Bruins if he would sign with them, instead counseling Bobby to sign with his friend, Mr. Wirtz, the owner of the Chicago Black Hawks
- made loans to friends and family members or enterprises that he controlled
- charged excessive expenses
- pocketed the rental revenue from advertising on rink boards during the Canada Cup Series
- charged Mike Gillis $41,250 for settling a disability claim that he knew was already settled

Ultimately, in early January 1998, after refusing to cross the border to face U.S. charges in the United States, the Eagle pleaded guilty to a reduced list of charges and apologized to the players he had harmed. He paid a fine of $1 million Canadian and received a Canadian jail sentence of eighteen months. Many would have preferred a harsher sentence, including U.S. Attorney Donald Stern, but the negotiated settlement involving the U.S. and Canadian legal systems, he suggested, was serious enough to send a message appropriate to the seriousness of the charges involved.

The Eagle had landed . . . in jail. But his trials and tribulations were not over. As soon as his trials were over, an outcry started to have him removed from the Hockey Hall of Fame. Many star players who were also members of the Hall of Fame refused to allow their names to stay in the Hall unless Eagleson was ousted, and he was.

Why did Eagleson do what he did? According to U.S. Attorney Stern, "He did this all in the name of greed. . . . The guy who had a lot wanted still more. . . . He basically dipped into the till and took money from players' pockets."[1]

---

1. *Toronto Star,* "Fraudster Eagleson 'Did It All in the Name of Greed' Attorney Says," January 7, 1998, A1, 4.

It is rumored that, when he wasn't working in the prison laundry or library, the Eagle took time to read books on business ethics.

Questions

1. What conflicts of interest can you identify?
2. How would you avoid or manage each one?
3. What better principles of governance might have avoided this entire debacle?

SOURCES: *Financial Post,* "US Court Fines Eagleson $1M," January 7, 1998, 43.

Financial Post, "Eagleson Sentenced to 18 Months," January 8, 1998, 51.

Financial Post, "A strong lesson for business," January 12, 1998, 10.

Game Misconduct: Allan Eagleson and the Corruption of Hockey, Conway, R., Macfarlane Wolter & Ross, 1995.

Toronto Star, "Fraudster Eagleson 'Did It All in the Name of Greed' Attorney Says," January 7, 1998, A1, 4; "Eagle Downed by US Reporter," A4; "Hockey Veterans Savour Admission of Guilt," A5; "Prison Inmates Required to Work, A5; "The Eagle's Long Fall From Grace," A16.

Toronto Star, "Humbled Eagleson Jailed," January 8, 1998, A1, 8; several other articles on A6–8.

Toronto Star, "Teflon Con Man," January 10, 1998, B1, 5; several other articles on B3, B6.

The Lang Michener Affair

Martin Pilzmaker was a young, aggressive lawyer from Montreal who was invited in 1985 to join the law firm Lang Michener in Toronto. It was expected that his immigration law practice "could enrich the (firm's) coffers by $1 million a year catering to the needs of Hong Kong Chinese already starting to panic over the crown colony's 1997 return to China's control."

Although rumors of Pilzmaker's questionable practices began to surface and were reported to the firm's executive committee in December, it wasn't until early February 1986 that a senior colleague, Tom Douglas, "drew aside Ament and Wiseman (Pilzmaker's junior colleagues) and grilled them on their boss's activities. They told him that Pilzmaker not only smuggled regularly but that he was running a double-passport operation. . . . The scam involved the false reporting of lost Hong Kong passports by his clients, which, in fact, would be kept by Pilzmaker in Canada. On their replacement passports, the clients could travel in and out of the country at will. When the time came to apply for citizenship—which requires three years' residence—they could supply the original 'lost' passports to show few if any absences from Canada."

Douglas told the executive committee of this activity, by memo, on February 10. The executive committee

"speculated that Pilzmaker's admissions may have consti-tuted only knowledge of wrongdoing on the part of certain clients and not active complicity. The committee decided to send (two members) Don Wright and Donald Plumley back to Pilzmaker to ask him, in the words of Farquharson's instructing memo, 'if he would be willing to agree' not to participate in any client violation of the Immigration Act."

Early in June 1986, angered that Pilzmaker had not been expelled, Tom Douglas sought advice from Burke Doran, "a colleague he regarded as a personal friend but moreover, one who was a bencher, or governor, of the Law Society. Doran went on to advise him to keep his head down and his mouth shut—a caution Doran later said he had no recollection of giving."

While mulling over this advice and some from another lawyer, Brendon O'Brien, a foremost authority on professional conduct, Douglas discovered a further problem. "This was a pro-posal by Pilzmaker to Brian McIntomny, a young associate lawyer, who was in the market to buy a house. The idea was that McIntomny would put up $50,000 for a $200,000 house, the balance supplied by a Pilzmaker client in Hong Kong. The client would officially own the house, have the phone and utilities registered in his name,

while McIntomny lived in it and held a secret deed. After three years, he would pay the client the interest-free $150,000, register the deed to place title in his own name and benefit from the accrued increase in value. The client, meanwhile, would have 'proof' of having resided in Canada for the three years required for citizenship." Douglas arranged for Bruce McDonald, a member of the firm's new executive committee, now consisting of McDonald, Don Wright, Albert Gnat, Donald Plumley, and Bruce McKenna, to be informed.

An investigation was begun and "at a July 28th Executive Committee meeting, a vote was taken on whether or not to expel Pilzmaker." The vote was three to two in favor of his staying. Douglas was allowed to address the meeting only after the vote was finalized, and he was enraged.

"On August 6, the night before McKenna's report was submitted but in partial knowledge of what it would likely contain, Douglas had dinner with Burke Doran again, this time in the company of a mutual colleague, Bruce Drake. Drake and Douglas subsequently claimed that when he was asked whether the firm had an obligation to report at least Pilzmaker's double-passport scam to the Law Society, Doran said no, 'because no white men have been hurt.'

—*Continued*

Continued

(Neither man took this as a racist remark but as meaning it was a victimless crime, with the clients knowingly involved.) The following morning at the office, Drake said he asked Doran if his remarks of the night before could be taken as official advice from the chairman of the Law Society. Doran said yes."

Doran has always denied that, confining his explanation to the dinner and not the morning after: "It's far-fetched to say I was sitting at a social dinner in my capacity as chairman of discipline." Don Wright would later testify, however, that it was Doran's view throughout the period "that we did not have any obligation to report to the Society."

On August 7, McKenna filed a scathing fifteen-page report to the executive committee, listing fifteen breaches of unethical behavior both inside and outside the firm by Pilzmaker, noting that "I am not aware of any material statement of fact made by him to me that I have checked out and has proven to be true." Furthermore, "I am concerned that I now have a personal responsibility, as a member of the Law Society and an officer of the court, to report the situation. If each of you review the facts closely, you will have similar concerns about your own obligations." 'On August 20, the executive committee did finally decide

Pilzmaker had to go, subject to confirmation by the entire partnership.'

After this, events proceeded at a faster pace:

September 4: Brendon O'Brien, hired to counsel the firm, advised that "they couldn't afford not to report to the Society."

September 5: A general meeting of the firm's partners is called to review the matter.

September 18: The requisite two-thirds of the 200 votes was obtained to force expulsion.

September 26: Pilzmaker's files were secured at the firm.

October 1: The Executive Committee debated the impact on the reputation of the firm and of high-profile partners "such as Jean Chretien (who is now the Prime Minister of Canada) and Burke Doran."

November 6: Douglas wrote Don Wright, urging the firm to report to the society.

November 18: Pilzmaker's lawyer filed suit to have Pilzmaker's files transferred to him.

November 21: The Law Society received a report from O'Brien "that (a) Pilzmaker had been expelled, (b) that he had been wrongly billing into the general, not trust, account and (c) that there was more than $300,000 in unpaid fees where Pilzmaker had either not done the work or had not even been retained in the first place." The society's investigator, Stephen Sherriff, began his investigation and subsequently called for a fuller report from the firm.

December 5: Pilzmaker's request for his files was granted by Justice Archibald Campbell, who "was given no hint that the files contained evidence that at some point might need to be looked at by the Law Society."

December 8: A fuller report is presented to the Law Society.

Twenty-five months later, "in January, 1989, Sherriff filed a lacerating 138-page confidential report that recommended a professional misconduct charge be laid against Burke Doran for placing himself in a conflict-of-interest situation in which he chose the interests of the firm over his responsibility as the Society's then chairman of discipline. Separate charges of professional misconduct were recommended against eight others in the firm. Sherriff contended that (a) they had failed to inform clients that Pilzmaker had likely given them unethical advice and to seek independent counsel and (b) they had failed to report in a timely manner what they knew about his behavior, indeed they reported only when Pilzmaker's lawsuit gave them no alternative."

An Ottawa lawyer, David Scott, was retained to help the society by analyzing what to do about Sherriff's recommendations. His report of March 2, 1989, was presented to Paul Lamek, the new chair of discipline for the society. "The ball was now

—Continued

Continued

in Lamek's court. He says he saw his job as twofold: To define who Scott meant by 'Managing partners and/or group' and to decide whether a charge could be made against Doran on a basis different from Sherriff's— namely, that as a bencher and chair of discipline, Doran had a 'higher duty' to report than did his colleagues. Although it wouldn't be officially disclosed until this spring, Lamek initially did opt to charge all eight, subject to clarifying just who exactly was on the executive committee from the crucial time on— a period Lamek pinned at June, 1986. That clarification consequently dropped several senior people out of the picture. As for Doran, 'after agonizing analysis' Lamek concluded that no complaint of any kind should be issued."

What was the outcome of these charges/events?

In the Spring of 1989, when it became obvious that Douglas would have to testify against his colleagues that fall, he finally did resign—three years after he'd first threatened to.

On October 31, without waiting for the panel's ruling, a disillusioned Sherriff resigned from his job: "What could have been a testament to the integrity of the Society had ended up sullying it. I had no choice but to quit." His departure, coupled with growing media speculation that there might be a

"whitewash of a cover-up" in process, had many other members of the Society adding to the chorus of concern.

At a convocation meeting of the benchers last September [1989], lawyer Clayton Ruby, who'd been given a copy of the investigation report by Sherriff, presented a motion that Lamek's decision be set aside and the original recommendations adopted. Ferrier ruled the motion out of order. "Douglas and Sherriff are right-wingish, not my kind of guys," [said] the notoriously left-leaning Ruby. "But I really felt that Lamek's decision to charge only five made it look as if we (the Society) were covering something up."

At a general members meeting the following month, former bencher Paul Copeland tried to table a motion demanding simply an explanation for why only five had been charged. He says he too was "cut off" by Ferrier.

On January 5 of this year [1990], the five who'd been charged were found guilty of professional misconduct for not reporting their concerns about Pilzmaker three months earlier than they did, specifically at the time McKenna made his damning report. The panel, however, found that the same concerns had not "imposed a duty on them" to inform clients that Pilzmaker had been expelled or that he might have given them unethical advice or that they should get independent legal advice.

Due to the ensuing controversy, on February 7, "the Society hired retired Manitoba former Chief Justice Archibald Dewar to review its handling of the entire affair." But his findings didn't please everyone. "Dewar did not find any evidence of impropriety or favouritism in Lamek's charges. The Doran decision was a judgment call, he wrote, and while debatable, to proceed with a charge now would only satisfy critics but "Not be seen as adding lustre to the discipline process."

What he did find, however, was a catalog of complaints against Sherriff. Sherriff was incensed. "The big deal, first," says Sherriff, "is that the real bad guy (Pilzmaker) almost went free. The big deal, second, is that the self-governing ability of this profession was compromised. 'Lawyers have special privileges, therefore, special responsibilities. Protecting the public is chief among them. That's the big deal. If you're a man of principle, you won't walk away from it.' "*

---

*Martin Pilzmaker was disbarred by the Law Society of Upper Canada in January 1990. Five other partners of his firm—Lang, Michener, Lash, and Johnston—were also found guilty and reprimanded. But the scandal refused to die, culminating in a major article in the "Insight" section of the *Toronto Star* on Sunday, July 22, 1990. The quotations in the case are from that article.

Postscript: Martin Pilzmaker committed suicide.

—Continued

Continued

Questions

1. Are professionals bound to meet a higher standard of ethical behavior than nonprofessionals? If so, why?

2. In what respects were the actions of the lawyers involved in the Lang Michener Affair not up to the ethical standard you would expect? Consider:

   a. Pilzmaker's conduct,

   b. the conduct of members of the executive committee

   at Lang Michener—in particular, Burke Doran, and

   c. the investigation and proceedings by the Law Society.

   What obligations did each owe to clients, the legal profession, the Law Society, the public?

3. Do the same considerations apply to other professionals as to lawyers?

4. Is the self-regulation of a profession on ethical

   matters effective from the perspective of

   a. the members of the profession?

   b. the public?

   c. clients?

5. Would you agree with the argument, which was used to exonerate members of the management team, that "when a professional makes a serious mistake, the error is of no consequence, if it is honestly made" (Bud Jorgensen, *Globe & Mail*, February 5, 1990, B9)?

Dilemma of an Accountant*

In 1976 Senator Lee Metcalf (D-Mont.) released a report on the public accounting industry which rocked the profession. Despite a decade of revisions in rules and regulations (variously established by the Securities and Exchange Commission, Accounting Principles Board, and Financial Accounting Standards Board), public

---

Copyright © 1980 by the President and Fellows of Harvard College. Harvard Business School case 380-185. This case was prepared by Laura Nash under the direction of John B. Matthews as the basis for class discussion rather than to illustrate either effective or ineffective handling of an administrative situation. Reprinted by permission of the Harvard Business School.

accounting firms were still perceived by many on Capitol Hill as biased in favor of their clients, incapable of or unwilling to police themselves, and at times participants in cover-ups of client affairs. Senator Metcalf even went so far as to suggest nationalizing the industry in light of these activities.

Just prior to the Metcalf report, Daniel Potter began working as a staff accountant for Baker Greenleaf, one of the Big Eight accounting firms. In preparation for his CPA examination, Dan had rigorously studied the code of ethics of the American Institute of Certified Public Accountants (AICPA)

and had thoroughly familiarized himself with his profession's guidelines for morality. He was aware of ethical situations which might pose practical problems, such as maintaining independence from the client or bearing the responsibility for reporting a client's unlawful or unreasonably misleading activities, and he knew the channels through which a CPA was expected to resolve unethical business policies. Dan had taken the guidelines very seriously; they were not only an integral part of the auditing exam, they also expressed to him the fundamental dignity

—Continued

Continued

every independent auditor was obligated to maintain and calling of the profession—namely, to help sustain the system of checks and balances on which capitalism has been based. Daniel Potter firmly believed that every independent auditor was obligated to maintain professional integrity, if what he believed to be the best economic system in the world was to survive.

Thus, when Senator Metcalf's report was released, Dan was very interested in discussing it with numerous partners in the firm. They responded thoughtfully to the study and were concerned with the possible ramifications of Senator Metcalf's assessment. Dan's discussions at this time and his subsequent experiences during his first year and a half at Baker Greenleaf confirmed his initial impressions that the firm deserved its reputation for excellence in the field.

Dan's own career had been positive. After graduating in economics from an Ivy League school, he had been accepted into Acorn Business School's accountant training program, and was sponsored by Baker Greenleaf. His enthusiasm and abilities had been clear from the start, and he was rapidly promoted through the ranks and enlisted to help recruit undergraduates to work for the firm. In describing his own professional ethos, Dan endorsed the Protestant work ethic on which he had been raised, and combined this belief with a strong faith in his own worth and responsibility. A strong adherent to the assumptions behind the profession's standards and prepared to defend them as a part of his own self-interest, he backed up his reasoning with an unquestioning belief in loyalty to one's employer and to the clients who helped support his employer. He liked the clear-cut hierarchy of authority and promotion schedule on which Baker Greenleaf was organized, and once had likened his loyalty to his superior to the absolute loyalty which St. Paul advised the slave to have towards his earthly master "out of fear of God" (Colossians 3:22). Thus, when he encountered the first situation where both his boss and his client seemed to be departing from the rules of the profession, Dan's moral dilemma was deep-seated and difficult to solve.

The new assignment began as a welcome challenge. A long-standing and important account which Baker had always shared with another Big Eight accounting firm needed a special audit, and Baker had reason to expect that a satisfactory performance might secure it the account exclusively. Baker put its best people on the job, and Dan was elated to be included on the special assignment team; success could lead to an important one-year promotion.

Oliver Freeman, the project senior, assigned Dan to audit a wholly-owned real estate subsidiary (Sub) which had given Baker a lot of headaches in the past. "I want you to solve the problems we're having with this Sub, and come out with a clean opinion (i.e., confirmation that the client's statements are presented fairly) in one month. I leave it to you to do what you think is necessary."

For the first time Dan was allotted a subordinate, Gene Doherty, to help him. Gene had worked with the project senior several times before on the same client's account, and he was not wholly enthusiastic about Oliver's supervision. "Oliver is completely inflexible about running things his own way—most of the staff accountants hate him. He contributes a 7:00 A.M. to 9:00 P.M. day every day, and expects everyone else to do the same. You've *really* got to put out, on his terms, to get an excellent evaluation from him." Oliver was indeed a strict authoritarian. Several times over the next month Dan and Oliver had petty disagreements over interpretive issues, but when Dan began to realize just how stubborn Oliver was, he regularly deferred to his superior's opinion.

Three days before the audit was due, Dan completed his files and submitted them to Oliver for review. He had

—Continued

Continued

uncovered quite a few problems but managed to solve all except one: one of the Sub's largest real estate properties was valued on the balance sheet at $2 million, and Dan's own estimate of its value was no more than $100,000. The property was a run-down structure in an undesirable neighborhood, and had been unoccupied for several years. Dan discussed his proposal to write down the property by $1,900,000 with the Sub's managers, but since they felt there was a good prospect of renting the property shortly, they refused to write down its value. Discussion with the client had broken off at this point, and Dan had to resolve the disagreement on his own. His courses of action were ambiguous, and depended on how he defined the income statement: according to AICPA regulations on materiality, any difference in opinion between the client and the public accountant which affected the income statement by more than 3 percent was considered material and had to be disclosed in the CPA's opinion. The $1,900,000 write-down would have a 7 percent impact on the Sub's net income, but less than 1 percent on the client's consolidated net income. Dan eventually decided that since the report on the Sub would be issued separately (although for the client's internal use only), the write-down did indeed represent a material difference in opinion.

The report which he submitted to Oliver Freeman contained a recommendation that it be filed with a subject-to-opinion proviso, which indicated that all the financial statements were reasonable subject to the $1.9 million adjustment disclosed in the accompanying opinion. After Freeman reviewed Dan's files, he fired back a list of "To Do's," which was the normal procedure at Baker Greenleaf. Included in the list was the following note:

1. Take out the pages in the files where you estimate the value of the real estate property at $100,000.

2. Express an opinion that the real estate properties are correctly evaluated by the Sub.

3. Remove your "subject-to-opinion" designation and substitute a "clean opinion."

Dan immediately wrote back on the list of "To Do's" that he would not alter his assessment since it clearly violated his own reading of accounting regulations. That afternoon Oliver and Dan met behind closed doors.

Oliver first pointed out his own views to Dan:

1. He (Oliver) wanted no problems on this audit. With six years of experience he knew better than Dan how to handle the situation.

2. Dan was responsible for a "clean opinion." Any neglect of his duties would be viewed as an act of irresponsibility.

3. Any neglect of his duties would be viewed as an act of irresponsibility.

4. The problem was not material to the Client (consolidated) and the Sub's opinion would only be used "in house."

5. No one read or cared about these financial statements anyway.

The exchange became more heated as Dan reasserted his own interpretation of the write-down, which was that it was a material difference to the Sub and a matter of importance from the standpoint of both professional integrity and legality. He posited a situation where Baker issued a clean opinion which the client subsequently used to show prospective buyers of the property in question. Shortly thereafter the buyer might discover the real value of the property and sue for damages. Baker, Oliver, and Dan would be liable. Both men agreed that such a scenario was highly improbable, but Dan continued to question the ethics of issuing a clean opinion. He fully understood the importance of this particular audit and expressed his loyalty to Baker Greenleaf

—Continued

Continued

and to Oliver, but nevertheless believed that, in asking him to issue knowingly a false evaluation, Freeman was transgressing the bounds of conventional loyalty. Ultimately a false audit might not benefit Baker Greenleaf or Dan.

Freeman told Dan he was making a mountain out of a molehill and was jeopardizing the client's account and hence Baker Greenleaf's welfare. Freeman also reminded Dan that his own welfare patently depended on the personal evaluation which he would receive on this project. Dan hotly replied that he would not be threatened, and as he

left the room, he asked, "What would Senator Metcalf think?"

A few days later Dan learned that Freeman had pulled Dan's analysis from the files and substituted a clean opinion. He also issued a negative evaluation of Daniel Potter's performance on this audit. Dan knew that he had the right to report the incident to his partner counselor or to the personnel department, but was not terribly satisfied with either approach. He would have preferred to take the issue to an independent review board within the company, but Baker Greenleaf had no such board. However, the negative evaluation would

stand, Oliver's arrogance with his junior staff would remain unquestioned, and the files would remain with Dan's name on them unless he raised the incident with someone.

He was not at all sure what he should do. He knew that Oliver's six years with Baker Greenleaf counted for a lot, and he felt a tremendous obligation to trust his superior's judgment and perspective. He also was aware that Oliver was inclined to stick to his own opinions. As Dan weighed the alternative, the vision of Senator Metcalf calling for nationalization continued to haunt him.

Societal Concerns

Two accounting students, Joan and Miguel, were studying for their final university accounting exam.

"Miguel, what if they ask us whether the accounting profession should speak out about the shortcomings in financial statements?"

"Like what, Joan? We know they don't show the value of employees or the impact of inflation, or the economic reality or market value of many transactions—is that what you mean?"

"No, I mean the advocacy of disclosures which will lead to a better world for all of us. For example, if we could only get companies to start disclosing their impacts on society, and particularly our environment, they would be induced to set targets and perform better the next year. We know that lots of externalities, like pollution costs, are not included in the financial statements, but we could speak out for supplementary disclosures."

"Joan, you go right ahead if you like. But I'm going to

stick to the traditional role of accountants—to the preparation and audit of financial statements. It got us this far, didn't it?"

"Yes, but do medical doctors refrain from commenting on health concerns, or do lawyers refrain from creating laws that govern our future? Why should we shy away from speaking out on issues that we know something about that mean a lot to our future?"

Questions

1. Is Joan or Miguel right? Why?

Management Choice

Anne Distagne was the CEO of Linkage Construction Inc., which served as the general contractor for the construction of the air ducts for large shopping malls and other buildings. She prided herself on being able to manage her company effectively and in an orderly manner. For years there had been a steady 22–25 percent growth in sales, profits, and earnings per share, which she wanted to continue because it facilitated dealing with banks to raise expansion capital. Unfortunately for Sue Fault, the chief financial officer, the situation has changed.

"Sue, we've got a problem. You know my policy of steady growth—well, we've done too well this year. Our profit is too high: it's up to a 35 percent gain over last year. What we've got to do is bring it down this year and save a little for next year. Otherwise, it will look like we're off our well-managed path. I will look like I didn't have a handle on our activity. Who knows, we may attract a takeover artist. Or we may come up short on profit next year."

"What can we do to get back on track? I've heard we could declare that some of our construction jobs are not as far along as we originally thought, so we would only have to include a lower percentage of expected profits on each job in our profit this year. Also, let's take the $124,000 in R&D costs we incurred to fabricate a more flexible ducting system for jobs A305 and B244 out of the job costs in inventory and expense them right away."

"Now listen, Sue, don't give me any static about being a qualified accountant and subject to the rules of your profession. You are employed by Linkage Construction and I am your boss, so get on with it. Let me know what the revised figures are as soon as possible."

Questions

1. Who are the stakeholders involved in this decision?
2. What are the ethical issues involved?
3. What should Sue do?

Maple Leaf Gardens Shenanigans

Harold Ballard was a larger than life personality, and he packed almost enough living into his lifetime to satisfy two ordinary people. He had run the Toronto Maple Leafs, a National Hockey League (NHL) team, as his own private toy and had strong supporters and powerful detractors.

As he approached the end of his life, he decided that he would have his estate make some modest payments with the residual being left to seven named charities. He appointed three executors whose acumen he respected to oversee his estate: Steve Stavro, a self-made millionaire grocer; Don Giffen, the head of a group of metal companies; and Don Crump, the long-time treasurer of Maple Leaf Gardens. These executors were authorized to sell or buy property at "fair market value, supported by two independent appraisals, without court authorization."[1]

---

1. *Financial Post*, "Former MLG Shareholders to Get Top-Up Cash," April 12, 1996, 5.

Don Giffen subsequently died and was replaced by a lawyer, Terry Kelly.

On April 11, 1990, Harold Ballard died in a Miami hospital. He left three children, to whom he had transferred the shares of Maple Leaf Gardens (MLG) Ltd. (MLG owned the Toronto Maple Leafs) many years before as part of an estate freeze arrangement. Each child had 25 percent of the MLG, but two of the three had subsequently sold their shares back to Harold.

—Continued

Continued

In order to complete these repurchases, Harold had borrowed $20 million from the Molson Company Limited, the owner of the Montreal Canadians NHL hockey team, even though the NHL forbade dealings between teams and their owners. One of his children, Bill, did not sell his shares back to Harold.

When the $20 million loan to the Molson Company came due on December 31, 1990, attempts to repay the loan were unsuccessful, and 19.99 percent of the MLG shares pledged as collateral were lost to the Molson Company. In January 1991, Stavro offered to loan the estate the money in return for the exclusive right to buy the estate's MLG shares that represented 60 percent of the company. Bill Ballard challenged Stavro's right to do so but, in April 1990, the Ontario Court of Justice decided to allow the arrangement to proceed. In September, the Molson Company agreed to sell its 19.99 percent of MLG stock to Stavro, and on September 20 Stavro also bought Bill Ballard's 25 percent of MLG for $21 million.

In 1990, a special report was commissioned by MLG management in which Ralph Mellanby, a TV expert, was asked to render a report on future prospects for TV revenue. In it, he speculated that broadcasting rights would triple in value, making them worth 17 percent of revenue. Unfortunately, this report was not given to two independent brokerage firms, which were asked to value the MLG shares in October 1993. Their valuations ranged from $25.83 to $29.92 per share by Burns Fry to $27 to $34 per share by Dominion Securities.

Negotiations commenced with the trustees for Stavro to buy the estate's shares. Stavro found willing partners and created MLG Ventures LTD. in March 1994 to buy the Molson shares and those of the estate. On April 2, MLG Ventures bought these shares for $34 each, which gave it 80 percent of MLG. Ontario Teacher's Pension Plan Board ended up owning 49 percent of MLG Ventures, with Stavro (41 percent) and Toronto Dominion Bank (10 percent) owning the rest. It does appear, according to a handwritten note later found in the papers of the Toronto Dominion Bank, that Stavro shared information on future TV revenues, which was shared with the bank. On April 8, MLG Venture offered $34 per share for the rest of the shares owned by the public, and 11.2 percent were tendered. MLG Ventures then owned 91.2 percent of MLG.

There was a strong public reaction to keeping the bidding process private, rather than opening it up to other bidders. A former Premier of the Province of Ontario filed an affidavit with Ontario's Public Trustee, stating that his syndicate would have offered more than $34 per share. Based on these concerns and those for the interests of the seven charities that he was sworn to protect, the Public Trustee stepped in and asked for information on April 28, 1994. He subsequently sued Stavro and others for conflict of interest (August 4, 1995), asking for information (through the Ontario Court of Appeal on November 23, 1995) including the records of the Toronto Dominion Bank and commissioning a third appraisal of the MLG shares. This appraisal, which included information on new TV revenues, valued MLG shares from $50 to $53 each. After negotiation, a settlement was reached and on April 4, 1996, approved by the court, whereby the charities and others received the equivalent of $49.50 per share.

On February 22, 1996, Bill Ballard filed a $50 million lawsuit, claiming he had been conned into accepting too low a price for his shares. This lawsuit is still outstanding.

In addition, the Ontario Securities Commission (OSC) took notice that prominent sports figures Harry Ornest and Jim Devellano (general

—Continued

Continued

manager of the Detroit Red Wings), who in aggregate owned about 5 percent of MLG, joined the public trustee's lawsuit on November 2, 1995. In the fall of 1996, the OSC began to review the transactions between Stavro and his partners to determine if insider trading rules had been violated because insufficient information had been given to outsiders. The role of the Toronto Dominion Bank as both lender and owner was also under review.

Questions

1. What conflicts of interest can you identify and explain?
2. How could these have been avoided?
3. Why didn't Harold Ballard's executors properly discharge their fiduciary duties?
4. What steps could have been taken to ensure that the executors did their job properly?
5. Did Steve Stavro violate insider trading rules, even if involuntarily?

SOURCES: *Financial Post,* "Former MLG shareholders to get top-up cash," April 13, 1996, 5.

Toronto Star, "Stavro breaks silence amid Gardens probe," September 21, 1996, A1, 26.

Toronto Star, "Maple Leaf Gardens: The Inside Story," September 21, 1996, C1, 4–9.

Toronto Star, "Gardens deal costs owners $1.6 m," March 30, 1998, A1, 20.

Student assignments by Marni Halpern, Rachel Pollock, Jessica Kim, Yao Li, Domenic Belmonte, Robert Berger, Lorraine Floody, Alistair Maclaine, Pierre Michaud.

To Qualify or Not?*

Jane Ashley was a staff accountant at Viccio & Martin, an accounting firm located in Windsor, Ontario. Jane had been a co-op student while in college and, during her first work term with the firm, she had the privilege of being on several audits of various medium-sized companies in the Windsor area, where she picked up some valuable audit experience. Fresh out of her final academic term, she felt ready to put her scholastic knowledge to work and show the seniors and partners of Viccio & Martin her stuff.

*This case was adapted from an assignment submitted by Phil Reynolds, an MBA (accounting) student at the University of Toronto in the summer of 1994.

In her first assignment, Jane was placed on an audit team consisting of herself and a senior. This senior, Frankie Small, had been a qualified accountant for five years and had been on staff for over ten. He was well respected within the company and was known for his ability to continually bring engagements in under budget.

The client, Models Inc., which was Viccio & Martin's largest, was a private corporation which made its business in the distribution of self-assembly, replica models, toys, and other gaming products. It operated from a central warehouse in Windsor but also distributed from a small warehouse in

Toronto and had a drop-off point in Michigan as it purchased merchandise from companies in the United States. Its year-end was April 30. Since Jane had joined the firm on May 15, she had not been present for the year-end inventory count, which was taken on the year-end date. Frankie S. was present, along with another co-op student, who, incidently, had returned for her final academic term on May 11. Jane asked Frankie how just two people could simultaneously be present for an inventory count at three locations. Frankie responded by telling her that, since the inventory balances

—Continued

Continued

at the Toronto warehouse and Michigan drop-off sites were of immaterial amounts (based on representations by management, company records, and audits in prior years) audit staff had only been present at the Windsor warehouse count. Models Inc. was on a periodic inventory system.

Since she had not been on this engagement before, the evening before her first day of fieldwork, Jane stayed at work late to review the previous year's audit files, this year's audit programs, and the notes on this year's inventory count so she could gain a knowledge of the client's business. After an hour or so of reviewing the information, Jane gained a knowledge of the client, but she couldn't quite understand what was happening with the inventory section because the working papers were messy and disorganized. On reviewing the inventory sheets from this year's count, she found that many of the items were unfamiliar and were referenced only by general product names; there were no serial numbers, no order numbers.

The first day of fieldwork arrived, and Jane was given the responsibility of Accounts Payable Cut-off. On tracing invoices to the master accounts payable ledger, Jane found that she was having a hard time locating many of them. She brought this matter to the attention of the accounts payable clerk, who provided the explanation that invoices received after the year-end date were not yet entered in the current year but should have been. Jane was provided with this list and traced it to the journal entry made to pick up the extra payables. Jane then performed audit procedures on this extra list. She again found that it was incomplete. The total cut-off problem was, in her estimation (of sample to population figures), in excess of $400,000. She also noted that many of the invoices received had invoice dates after April 30, but title to these goods had changed hands (F.O.B. shipping point) prior to April 30.

The financial statements originally provided by management showed healthy profits of $150,000. The current accounts payable (trade) balance was $1.4 million, which was up over a half a million from last year. The current receivables balance was $800,000 which was up about $100,000 from the previous year. Sales had jumped from $8 million in 1988 to $10 million this year. The company had an operating (demand) line of credit with a lending institution of $1 million. The company owned its two warehouses, which had a net equity of approximately $1,600,000 at fair market.

Jane brought the cut-off problem to the attention of Frankie, who was perplexed and surprised by the whole issue. The two returned to the office that evening, and Jane was asked to prepare a memorandum explaining her findings. It was reviewed by the partner in charge, Mr. Viccio, who contacted the appropriate level of management of Models Inc. to explain the discrepancy.

The accounts payable clerk recorded the transactions Jane had found left out, and the audit testing was again performed on the accounts payable cut-off and the rest of the accounts payable section to the satisfaction of the auditors with respect to all financial statement assertions. The total corrections made to accounts payable were in the order of $350,000. The impact of the adjustments was partially to inventory, where traceable, and partly to cost of goods sold. The total effect on the profit figure was $300,000. The financial statements showed a loss of $150,000.

The head manager and 50 percent shareholder of the corporation, Mrs. Hyst,

—*Continued*

Continued

was astonished and panic stricken by the entire situation. She was sure something was wrong and that this problem would be rectified at some point throughout the remainder of the audit.

No problems were encountered throughout the remainder of the audit fieldwork; however, Jane did notice, when she was in the accounts payable clerk's office, that the clerk spent a great deal of time on the phone with suppliers, discussing how Models Inc. could pay down its over-90-day payables such that the company would not be cut off from purchasing further goods.

Toward the finalization of the audit, Mrs. Hyst came to the auditors and told them that there was most likely inventory that had been left out of the count. She provided a listing which amounted to approximately $200,000. In this listing were material amounts of inventory in the Toronto warehouse, the Michigan drop-off point, goods in transit, and goods stored at other locations.

The auditors, who were surprised by the list, decided to perform tests on it and found that it was very difficult and often impossible to track the inventory, given the poor system used by the company. Jane telephoned all of the companies that appeared on the list under "goods stored at other locations" and, in all cases, found that no inventory was being kept on behalf of Models Inc. Suppliers in the United States were telephoned for exact shipment dates, and, based on the evidence of how long it usually takes to bring goods across the border, it was determined that those goods were included in the year-end inventory count. As for the "extra" inventory stored in the Toronto and Michigan sites, there was no reliable evidence that anything not already accounted for was there. However, there was no way to tell for sure. From the items on this extra list, $50,000 was accounted for as either already counted in inventory as of the year-end date or included in cost of goods sold. The whereabouts of the other $150,000 was not determinable.

Mrs. Hyst was asked to discuss this listing. At the meeting, Mr. Viccio, Frankie, and Jane were all present. Mrs. Hyst stated that, if she showed these sorts of losses, the bank would surely call the company's operating loan of $1 million and it would "go under." Mr. Viccio asked the client whether there was any way of determining where the other $150,000 was. She explained that it was hard, given their inadequate inventory system, but she was pretty sure that it was not counted in the year-end inventory count.

After the meeting, Mr. Viccio explained that there was no reason to doubt management's good faith and that the $150,000 most likely should be added to inventory and taken out of cost of goods sold. Frankie went along with this. Jane, however, was astonished. She felt that, since there was no evidence backing up the claims made by the client, the firm should be conservative. She also related her experience to the other two concerning the problems the company was having with keeping up with its trade payables. Mr. Viccio explained to her that the $150,000 should be added to back inventory and that, even if it was the cost of goods sold, the client will most likely recover in the near future, anyway. "In these situations, we must help the client; we cannot be responsible for its downfall. Who are we to say that there isn't an extra $150,000 in inventory—we're just guessing." Frankie added to this by saying that, if the loan were called, there would be plenty of equity in the buildings of the company to pay it off.

Jane went home that day very distraught. She felt that Mr. Viccio's decision was

—Continued

Continued

based on audit fees and that a poor picture on the financial statements would result in the loan being called and Mr. Viccio would not get his fees. Jane was also disappointed with the level of responsibility shown by Frankie, the senior. Jane couldn't believe what was happening, given the fact that the original reason for the

audit was because the bank had requested it several years ago as the operating loan was increasing. Jane was also aware that Model Inc.'s major suppliers were requesting the year-end statements as well and, based on them, would make a decision whether or not to extend the company any more credit.

The next day, Jane expressed her opinion in a morning meeting held in Mr. Viccio's office. Frankie was also present. She was told that the $150,000 would be added back to inventory.

Questions

1. What should Jane do? Why?

Ethics case

Economic Realities or GAAP

Stan Jones was an investor who had recently lost money on his investment in Fine Line Hotels, Inc., and he was anxious to discuss the problem with Janet Todd, a qualified accountant who was his friend and occasional adviser.

"How can they justify this, Janet? This company owns 19.9 percent of a subsidiary, Far East Hotels, which has apparently sustained some large losses.

But these consolidated statements don't show any of these losses, and the investment in Far East hasn't been written down to reflect the loss either. I bought my shares in Fine Line just after its last audited statements were made available but just before the papers reported that the statements didn't reflect any of the losses. What should I do in the future— wait until the papers report the

true economic picture? If I can't rely on audited figures, what's the sense of having an audit? And don't tell me that, if the ownership percentage had been 20 percent, the consolidated statements would have reported the loss. That's just outrageous."

Question

1. How should Janet Todd respond?

Ethics case

Multidisciplinary Practices—Ethical Challenges

Multidisciplinary practices, or MDPs, are probably an inevitable development. Clients want "one-stop shopping," at a professional firm where they

can go for all their needs, and where the partner responsible for their work can keep them briefed on new services that might be worth using. New

services offered currently include

- Legal services
- Actuarial services

—Continued

Continued

- Engineering services
- Investment services
- Risk assessment services
- Ethics and integrity services

These new services, particularly in the area of legal services, have raised a high degree of controversy among existing accounting partners. Trevor, an older partner, and Dhana, a new and younger partner, were deep in discussion about the problems and benefits the new organization would bring.

"Trev, I don't really see what your problem is. We're going to be more helpful to our clients—that's the bottom line, isn't it?"

"I suppose so, D, but all these new services bring their own professionals. Are lawyers or engineers going to set aside their codes of conduct to live by ours? Whom do they report to—I don't have enough legal expertise or engineering expertise to supervise them, so how can I ensure they live up to our accounting standards of service and quality? Aren't I going to be holding myself out as their supervisor on false pretenses? If anything goes wrong, won't we be sued?

"Another thing, D, as the proportion of our operations from these new services grows, won't the entire firm take on a client focus just like any other business? As professional accountants, we are supposed to be serving the public—that's what keeps us from fudging the figures and our audit reports to benefit current management and current shareholders. Do you think that all these new professionals will buy into a 'public' focus rather than a 'client' focus where the bottom line drives decisions? How would we go about keeping them on the straight and narrow, even if we got them on it in the first place?"

"Trev, you sure do have a lot of worries. How close are you to retirement? Well, I just had a call from our CEO, Hajjad. He wants me to think about taking over our Ethics and Integrity practice. Say—you don't have anything I could read up on in that area, do you?"

Question

1. What are your answers to the questions raised in the case?

Ethics case

Team Player Problems

"John, I have questions about that job you want me to do next week—the one where I am supposed to go and be part of that multidisciplinary team to study how the hospitals in Denver ought to be restructured for maximum efficiency, and how they should be reporting that efficiency in the future. As you know, I am a professional accountant, but I'm not going to be the study leader. What happens if I disagree with the study's findings or recommendations? What do I do if I think they haven't used accounting data correctly and have recommended that a hospital be shut down when I don't think it should be? Do I go along? Do I blow the whistle?"

Question

1. Answer the questions put to John.

Locker Room Talk

Albert Gable is a partner in a CPA firm located in a small midwestern city which has a population of approximately 65,000. Mr. Gable's practice is primarily in the area of personal financial planning; however, he also performs an annual audit on the city's largest bank.

Recently, Mr. Gable was engaged by Larry and Susan Wilson to prepare a comprehensive personal financial plan. While preparing the plan, Mr. Gable became personal friends of the Wilsons. They confided to him that they have had a somewhat rocky marriage and, on several occasions, seriously discussed divorce. Preparation of the comprehensive personal financial plan, which is nearing completion, has taken six months. During this period, Mr. Gable also performed the annual audit for the bank.

The audit test sample selected at random from the bank's loan file included the personal loan files of Larry and Susan Wilson. Because certain information in the loan files did not agree with facts personally known to Mr. Gable, he became somewhat concerned. Although he did not disclose his client relationship with the Wilsons, he did discuss their loan in detail with a loan officer. The loan officer is very familiar with the situation because he and Larry Wilson were college classmates, and now they play golf together weekly.

The loan officer mentioned to Mr. Gable that he believed Larry Wilson was "setting his wife up for a divorce." In other words, he was arranging his business affairs over a period of time so that he would be able to "leave his wife penniless." The loan officer indicated that this was just "locker room talk" and that Mr. Gable should keep it confidential.

Mr. Gable's compensation from his firm is based upon annual billings for services. If Mr. Gable resigns as CPA for the Wilsons, it would result in his losing a bonus constituting a substantial amount in annual personal compensation. Mr. Gable is counting on the bonus to contribute to support tuition and expenses for his youngest daughter, who will be starting as a freshman in college next fall.

Questions

1. What are the ethical issues?
2. What should Albert Gable do?

SOURCE: Prepared by Paul Breazeale, Breazeale, Saunders & O'Neil Ltd., Jackson, Mississippi. Drawn from the Ethics Case Collection of The American Accounting Association.

Minimal Disclosure

Ted was the manager and Carl the partner on the audit of Smart Investments Limited, an investment company whose shares were traded on the NASDAQ exchange. They were discussing the issues to be debated at the upcoming Audit Committee meeting to finalize the financial statements and audit for the current year.

"As I see it, Carl, we have three problems that are going to be difficult because it's not in the interests of the CEO, CFO, and some directors to go along with us. Remember that all those stock options that may be exercised next month at $7.50 per share and with the stock trading at $9.50 now—well, they aren't about to upset the price with negative news."

"Anyway, the rules call for segmented disclosure of significant lines of business, and this year the company has made 55 percent of its profit through the trading of derivative securities. It's awfully high risk and I'm not sure they can keep it

—*Continued*

Continued

up, so I think they ought to add a derivative securities disclosure column to their segmented disclosure information. They are going to argue that they are uncertain how much profit relates to derivative securities trading by itself, and how much was realized because the derivative securities were part of hedging transactions to protect foreign currency positions."

"The second issue concerns their reluctance to reveal the potential lawsuit by their client, Bonvest Mutual Funds, for messing up the timing and placement of orders for several mining securities. I believe it should be mentioned in the Contingent Liabilities note, but they may be dragging their feet on calculating the size of the problem. They don't want to disclose an amount, anyway, because they argue that Bonvest will set that figure as the lower bound for its claim."

"Finally, as you know, the statements we are auditing are consolidated and include the accounts of the parent and four subsidiaries. One of these subs, Caribbean Securities Limited, is in tough shape, and I think they may let it go broke. That's the sub which is audited by the Bahamian firm of Dodds & Co., not our own affiliate there. There is no qualification on the Dodds & Co. audit opinion, though, but I know how these guys at Smart think."

"I realize that a lot of this is speculative, but each of these issues is potentially material. How do you want to play each of them?"

Question

1. What should Carl, the partner, plan to do?

Opinion Shopping

"We have had Paige & Gentry as our auditors for many years, haven't we, Jane? They have been here since I became president two years ago."

"Yes, Bob, I have been the Chief Financial Officer for seven years, and they were here before I came. Why do you ask?"

"Well, they were really tough on us during the recent discussions when we were finalizing our year-end audited statements—not at all like I was used to at my last company. When we asked for a little latitude, our auditors were usually pretty obliging. Frankly, I'm a little worried."

"Why, Bob, we had nothing to hide?"

"That's true, Jane, but let's look ahead. We're going to have difficulty making our forecast this year, and our bonuses are on the line. Remember, we renegotiated our salary/bonus package to give us a chance at higher incentives, and we have to be careful."

"Looking ahead, we've got a problem with obsolete inventory that's sure to come to require discussion for a second year in a row. We've got the warranty problem with the electrical harness on mid-range machine which is going to cost us a bundle, but we want to spread the impact over the next three years when the customers discover the problem and we have to fix it up. And don't forget the contaminated waste spill we just had—how much is that going to cost to clean up, if we ever get caught?"

"These are potentially big ticket items. Bill Paige, the guy who is in charge of our audit, is not going to let these go by. He said the inventory problem was almost material this year and we had to argue really hard. You are a qualified accountant; how can we handle this?"

—Continued

Continued

"Well, Bob, we could have some informal discussions with other auditors—maybe even the ones at your old company—to see how they would handle issues like these. The word will get around to Bill and he may be more accommodating in the future, and will probably shave his proposed audit fee for next year when he meets with our Audit Committee next month. If you really wanted to play hardball, we could talk the Audit Committee into calling for tenders from new auditors. After all this time, it's logical to

check out the market, anyway. We would have advance discussions during which we would sound them out on how they would assess materiality in our company's case. Our audit fee in getting pretty large—almost $50,000 this year—so some big firms will be really interested."

"Jane, let's play hardball. Get a list of audit firms together for the tender process, and I will approach the Audit Committee. Be sure to list some small firms, including Webster & Co.,

the firm auditing my old company."

Questions

1. Who are the major stakeholders involved in this situation?

2. What are the ethical issues involved?

3. Is this situation unethical? Why and why not?

4. What should Jane do if Webster & Co. looks like the choice the Audit Committee will make and recommend to the board of directors?

Lowballing a Fee Quotation

"Look, Tim, I've been told that the competition for the audit of Diamond Health Services is really competitive, and you know what it would mean to the both of us to bring this one in. You would be a sure bet for the Executive Committee and I would take over some new audit responsibility as your back-up partner. Let's quote the job really competitively and get it."

"I'm not sure, Anne. After all, we have to make a reasonable profit or we're not pulling our weight. Anyway, you don't know what problems we may meet, so

you should build in a cushion on the front end of the job."

"But, Tim, if we quote this job the usual way—on an hourly rate and estimated total time basis—we are going to miss it! The CFO as much as told me we would have to be lower than the current auditor, and we would have to guaranty the fee for two years. Now, are we in, or not? I plan to put our best staff on the job. Don't worry; they won't blow it. What's the matter? Don't you think I can get the job done?"

"Well, Anne, I suppose there would be some overall saving to

our firm because this audit is the only one of six companies in the Diamond Group that we don't audit. We certainly don't want any other auditors getting a foothold in the Diamond Group, do we? What are you proposing, anyway, a fee that's at a lower margin than normal, or one that's below the projected cost for this job? Either way, It's unethical, isn't it?

Question

1. Answer the question posed to Tim.

As Bill Adams packed his briefcase on Friday, March 15, he could never remember being so glad to see a week end. As a senior tax manager with a major accounting firm, Hay & Hay, on the fast track for partnership, he was worried that the events of the week could prove to be detrimental to his career.

Six months ago, the senior partners had rewarded Bill by asking him to be the tax manager on Zentor Inc., a very important client of the firm in terms of both prestige and fees. Bill had worked hard since then insuring his client received impeccable service and he had managed to build a good working relationship with Dan, the Chief Executive Officer of Zentor Inc. In fact, Dan was so impressed with Bill that he recommended him to his brother, Dr. Rim, a general medical practitioner. As a favor to Dan, Bill agreed that Hay & Hay would prepare Dr. Rim's tax return.

This week a junior tax person had prepared Dr. Rim's tax return. When it came across Bill's desk for review today, he was surprised to find that, although Dr. Rim's gross billings were $480,000, his net income for tax purposes from his medical practice was only $27,000. He discussed this with the tax junior, who said he had noted this also but was not concerned, as every tax return prepared by the firm is stamped with the disclaimer "We have

prepared the return from information provided to us by the client. We have not audited or otherwise attempted to verify its accuracy."

On closer review, Bill discovered that the following items, among others, had been deducted by Dr. Rim in arriving at net income:

a. $15,000 for meals and entertainment. Bill felt that this was excessive and probably had not been incurred to earn income, given the nature of Dr. Rim's practice.

b. Dry-cleaning bills for shirts, suits, dresses, sweaters, etc. Bill believed these to be family dry-cleaning bills that were being paid by the practice.

c. Wages of $100 per week paid to Dr. Rim's twelve-year-old son.

Bill telephoned Dr. Rim and had his suspicions confirmed. When Bill asked Dr. Rim to review the expenses and remove all that were personal, Dr. Rim became very defensive. He told Bill that he had been deducting these items for years and his previous accountant had not objected. In fact, it was his previous accountant who had suggested he pay his son a salary as an income-splitting measure. The telephone conversation ended abruptly when Dr. Rim was paged for an emergency, but not before he threatened to inform his

brother that the accounting firm he thought so highly of was behind the times on the latest tax planning techniques.

Bill was annoyed with himself for having agreed to prepare Dr. Rim's tax return in the first place. He was afraid of pushing Dr. Rim too far and losing Zentor Inc. as a client as a result. He could not anticipate what Dan's reaction to the situation would be. Bill was glad to have the weekend to think this over.

Just as Bill was leaving the office, the tax senior on the Zentor Inc. account informed him that the deadline had been missed for objecting to a reassessment, requiring Zentor Inc. to pay an additional $1,200,000 in taxes. The deadline was Wednesday, March 13. The senior said he was able to contact a friend of his at the Tax Department, and the friend had agreed that if the Notice of Objection was dated March 13, properly signed, and appeared on his desk Monday, March 18, he would process it.

Bill left his office with some major decisions to make over the weekend.

Questions

1. Identify the ethical issues Bill Adams should address.

2. What would you do about these issues if you were Bill?

SOURCE: Prepared by Joan Kitunen, University of Toronto, 1994.

Ethics case on conflicts of interest

Risk Management of Taxes Payable—Is It Ethical?

"At the firm, we've got a new way of looking at tax issues. It's called 'risk management,' and, in your case, John, it means that we can be more aggressive than in the past. In the past, when there was an issue open to interpretation, we advised you to adopt a practice that was relatively safe, so that you would not get into trouble with the tax department. The thinking was that it would be better not to attract attention because that would lead to more audits and more difficult negotiations of questionable issues. We noticed, however, that there are fewer tax auditors now than in the past, particularly in remote areas, so it makes sense to take more chances than in the past—if you are audited, you can always pay up, anyway. It just makes good business sense to take advantage of all the possibilities open to your competitors. More and more of our clients are moving into this area of risk management, and you should think about it too."

Question

1. Is this new practice of risk management ethical?

Readings

The AICPA at 100: Public Trust and Professional Pride

J. Michael Cook
Journal of Accountancy, May 1987

From one perspective, the American Institute of CPA's centennial marks a very short time in the history of accounting. Five thousand years ago, Babylonians and Assyrians kept records of cash receipts and disbursements on clay tablets. Roman bookkeepers reviewed government accounts under contingent fee arrangements 3,000 years later. Double-entry bookkeeping was invented 500 years ago and "audits" started to take place. By those measures, the AICPA and the organized profession are infants; the past 100 years, but a page in a long history.

But from a more useful perspective, the AICPA's centennial marks the end of an important and dramatic era. In a short 100 years we have evolved from bookkeepers and clerks to members of a recognized, respected profession, and the AICPA has become a truly national organization of CPAs.

In these past 100 years we have gained the public's trust in our profession's objectivity and integrity. The words of the president of the Institute, Colonel Robert H. Montgomery, at our 50th anniversary ring as true today as they did in 1937: "We are here today because there was and is a need for us. That demand will continue as long as people feel a need to know the truth, whether or not it hurts. . . . Our profession always has had a vision—this urge to find and to tell the truth—and we should cling to it and continue to strive for its accomplishment."

We have earned the public's trust by keeping ourselves adaptable and sensitive to its changing needs, anticipating those needs when possible and taking a proactive stance on them. We have dealt successfully with a practice environment that has changed markedly, and continues to change, in its social, economic, governmental and legal aspects.

The AICPA now has a century of professional responsiveness and responsibility of which to be proud; these qualities are at work today in the Institute and will continue indefinitely into the future. That's why I've given this article its subtitle—"Public Trust and Professional Pride." These past 100 years demonstrate that we, as a profession, have tackled the tough issues—we've earned the public's trust. Because of this I have, and I believe I share with my fellow members, a strong sense of confidence in our ability to handle present problems and future challenges. We may not be infallible as a profession, but our overall track record is most impressive. And we keep on trying. With the trust of the public and confidence in ourselves, we will have the strength to handle what the future brings.

100 YEARS AT A GLANCE

A short look at the past quickly demonstrates the Institute's responsiveness in meeting the challenges we have faced in the last century.

1887. One hundred years ago corporate leaders did not have a clear idea of the capabilities of accountants. As James T. Anyon wrote in 1925, on the "Early Days of American Accountancy," a great many executives "had very mixed ideas as to just what the business of the expert accountant was and exactly what he professed to do. Some considered that he was an experienced bookkeeper and no more; others looked

—Continued

Continued

upon him as a man whose business it was to detect fraud, embezzlement and stealing, and that his employment was of value only in this direction; while many had a vague idea that he was merely a man of figures, a rapid and unerring calculator who could add up two or three columns of figures at a time, and who could tell you immediately the square or cube root of any given number."

Our predecessors, men such as Edwin Guthrie and James Anyon, British accountants who arrived in New York in the early 1880s, and native Americans such as Charles Waldo Haskins and Charles E. Sprague, changed those perceptions; they also changed the members of the accounting profession in the process. Together, these men set out to see that competence and professionalism were encouraged among practicing accountants and that accountants' capabilities were recognized. They formed in 1887 (by a December 1886 resolution) the American Association of Public Accountants, now the AICPA.

1896. Although the AICPA is not the accounting profession, it is impossible to separate the development of the profession from that of the AICPA. Indeed, the AICPA began with only 31 members, but James Anyon reported that those 31 men constituted almost all the accountants in the United States. And that small group—united in a professional association—began to work toward setting standards and instituting state licensing.

In 1896 New York became the first state to license public accountants. Certification required passage of an examination in accounting theory and practice, auditing, and commercial law. Thus was born the CPA examination. Other states quickly adopted legislation to license CPAs; by World War I, legislation had been enacted in 45 jurisdictions, with the rest adopting legislation in the 1920s or shortly thereafter.

1913. I doubt that the framers of the 1913 federal income tax legislation could have dreamt of its effect on business practices and individuals or of its ultimate effect on the national economy. When it comes to describing this legislation's impact on members of our profession, I can do no better than to quote from the November 1913 issue of this *Journal:*

". . . it is indubitable that the income tax law is to have a more far-reaching effect upon public accountants than upon any other profession or business in the country. Hundreds of [people] who have never seen the necessity for a correct system of accounting now find themselves compelled to prepare statements of income and expenditure; and the work in nine cases out of ten will fall upon the shoulders of the public accountants. . . . The corporation tax law in its administration vastly increased the labors of public accountants, but the work arising from the enactment of that law was far less than that which will result from the new income tax act. . . ."

1916. In 1916, aware that the interstate practice of public accounting was being impeded by the diversity of state licensing requirements, the Institute published its first Model Accountancy Bill. The model bill has proved to be so useful that it has been revised and reissued seven times, with the latest issued in 1984.

1917. Our profession attained two milestones in 1917. First, the Institute issued an official audit procedure in the form of a *Federal Reserve Bulletin* entitled *Approved Methods for the Preparation of Balance-Sheet Statements.* The Institute revised this bulletin in 1929 and 1936. Additional efforts in this standard-setting area will be discussed later.

As the second milestone in 1917, the Institute began to develop the Uniform CPA Examination, which is now required by the boards of accountancy of all 50 states, the District of Columbia, Puerto Rico, Guam and the Virgin Islands. As mentioned earlier, starting with the first CPA exam in New York in 1896, each state offered its own CPA examination as its licensing statute went into effect. The exam's subject matter and level of difficulty varied from state to state, however, which raised doubts that CPAs were meeting comparable licensing requirements.

In response to requests from the states, the Institute made its admission examination available starting in June 1917, when some 250 CPA candidates took the Institute's examination in the states of New Hampshire, Kansas and Oregon. Gradually other states, seeing the merit and practicality of a uniform test, began using the Institute's exam. By 1952 all jurisdictions had adopted the Uniform CPA Examination. Although originally achieved through only an examination, entrance into the profession now requires demonstrated competence, an academic degree and experience in the field.

1932. In the wake of the 1929 stock market crash, the Institute appointed a special committee on the development of accounting principles. In 1932 this committee issued its "basic principles" of accounting, which dealt with unrealized profits, capital surplus, treasury stock, and notes or accounts receivable from officers or employees. The committee also recommended to the New York Stock Exchange that audit certificates for listed companies should state that the financial statements were prepared in accordance with these "accepted principles of accounting."

By 1959 the committee had issued 51 accounting research bulletins. Established as the Accounting Principles Board in 1959, this committee came under heavy attack from federal and business sectors in the mid-1960s. A central theme to the criticism was whether a private professional organization had the right to create accounting standards and to impose them on the public business community.

—Continued

Continued

In 1972 an Institute group appointed to study the establishment of financial accounting standards (the Wheat committee) recommended that an independent foundation and standard-setting board be established outside the Institute to be financed by organizations with a strong interest in accounting. Consequently, the Financial Accounting Foundation, the Financial Accounting Standards Advisory Council and the Financial Accounting Standards Board were founded in 1973.

1934. Aided by information provided in the testimony of Colonel Arthur H. Carter, president of the New York State Society of CPAs and later managing partner of Haskins & Sells, Congress passed the Securities Act of 1933 and the Securities and Exchange Act of 1934, which established the Securities and Exchange Commission and increased the accounting and auditing work required by publicly traded companies. At the time, members of Congress had been contemplating using government auditors for all publicly traded companies, and Carter's testimony was instrumental in persuading them of the benefits of using independent accountants instead.

1936. The American Society of CPAs, which had splintered off from the Institute in the 1920s, merged back into the main group during this year. The differing opinions on policies and programs that had prompted this split were reconciled, and the profession once again presented a united front.

1939. In 1939, in response to concerns arising from the McKesson & Robbins case, the Institute established a committee on auditing procedure. This committee developed recommendations on the examinations of inventories and receivables, the appointment of independent auditors and the form of the accountant's report. The substance of the proposals was published in Statement on Auditing Procedure no. 1, *Extensions of Auditing Procedure.*

At the same time, the SEC was gathering evidence and hearing testimony in the McKesson & Robbins matter. After hearing about the Institute's initiatives, the SEC commended the profession for adopting the new audit requirements that had been set forth in *Extensions of Auditing Procedure* and indicated that it would rely on the profession to adopt further extensions of auditing procedures.

A significant outcome of the McKesson & Robbins matter was the Institute's creation of the committee on auditing procedure. In 1948 the Institute adopted 10 generally accepted auditing standards. Since that time, through this committee, which became the auditing standards executive committee in 1972 and then the auditing standards board in 1977, the Institute has published the most comprehensive body of auditing standards in the world.

1957. The Institute adopted its current name, altering its title from the American Institute of Accountants.

1959. During this year the Institute organized its continuing professional education division, which has grown through the years to become a major Institute function.

In 1971, on the recommendation of the committee on CPE, the AICPA council passed a resolution urging state boards of accountancy to adopt a mandatory CPE requirement for all practicing CPAs. As of 1987, 48 states have mandatory CPE requirements, and the other jurisdictions either mandate CPE as a state CPA society requirement or are in the process of implementing such a requirement.

Late 1960s–early 1970s. The Institute's standard-setting efforts have not always satisfied the profession's critics in Congress, the media and elsewhere. Criticisms come to the boiling point whenever there is a spate of business failures, as there was with some large companies that had attracted considerable investor interest in the late sixties and early seventies. The profession was the subject of hearings in both the House of Representatives and the Senate, hearings that led to the introduction in the House of legislation intended to regulate the accounting profession.

The profession responded to these criticisms and legislative proposals with alacrity. New auditing standards were issued on errors and irregularities and on illegal acts by clients, and an independent Commission on Auditors' Responsibilities (the Cohen commission) was established.

1977. By vote of council at a heated meeting in Cincinnati in 1977, the AICPA established the division for CPA firms.

The division had been gradually evolving at the Institute during the 1970s. In 1971 a voluntary quality review program for local firms had been formed; reviewers were from out of state, and no written reports were issued on the results of the reviews. In 1974 the Institute enlarged this effort to encompass a voluntary multioffice quality control review, which supplemented the program for local firms.

The division for CPA firms is divided into two sections: one for SEC practice and one for private companies practice. Requirements for membership in the division include, among others, CPE and periodic peer reviews.

The formation of the division was a major step in the program of self-regulation. It enabled the Institute for the first time to deal with firms, not just individual members, and recognized quality control compliance reviews—peer reviews—as an essential part of an effective self-regulatory program. It acknowledged that the public had a legitimate need for more information about CPA firms and the quality of their practices and provided for even more oversight by the SEC. And it placed in the hands of the division the power to sanction member firms.

—Continued

Continued

A FINAL HISTORICAL OBSERVATION

The above thumbnail sketches obviously demonstrate a concerned, responsive organization. The AICPA has its flaws and foibles, but overall it is made up of people who are responsible, serious and concerned about their profession and its place in the business world.

The history of our profession has included many challenges, and we have responded to each one. Just think of a few—the crisis in confidence in 1929 and the massive McKesson & Robbins fraud. Each time we responded with measures to ensure that these problems would be avoided in the future. It may be true that those who don't learn from history are doomed to repeat it; if so, we should be all right because we've learned a lot in the past century. We've learned from our challenges, we've responded to them and they've made us grow. We've earned the public's trust in our integrity and professionalism.

Ours is a profession striving to contribute to the public interest; a profession with high standards and even higher ideals. These ideals, which have governed our activities over the past century, are encapsulated and summarized in the Institute's mission statement, adopted by council in 1986. The statement merits reproduction, because it defines our activities today and charts the course of our future.

OUR MISSION IN TODAY'S ENVIRONMENT

We have to interpret and apply our mission statement in a very complex business environment in which there are somewhat conflicting views of our effectiveness as a profession.

On the one hand, according to a recent Louis Harris survey, "certified public accountants emerge strong with the general public, those who are 'knowledgeable' about accounting, stockowners, and the special publics surveyed." Indeed, a majority of the general public agrees that we have and follow high ethical and moral standards, which is gratifying in an era when trust in established institutions is fragile at best. And strong majorities of both general and special publics rank us highly on attributes such as competence, reliability and objectivity. So we have clearly established a positive public perception of CPAs.

On the other hand, we have our share of critics with an interest in auditing and financial reporting who do not fully share that positive perception. The quality of our audits and the effectiveness of our financial reporting system have been challenged in congressional hearings over the past two years. These hearings have been influenced by a number of highly publicized business failures, and our critics continue to pose the question "Where were the auditors?" that was originally asked by Senator Lee Metcalf and

Congressman John Moss in the 1970s. At that time the profession responded in three ways:

- A voluntary program to monitor practice and to improve compliance with performance standards—the division for CPA firms—was set in motion.

- New auditing standards were issued on errors and irregularities, illegal acts, planning and supervision, communicating weaknesses in internal accounting control and more.

- The Cohen commission made an extensive study of the audit process and public expectations and issued a comprehensive report with far-reaching recommendations.

These actions were the first steps of an evolving process that continues today.

In 1986 concerns about business failures and undetected fraud led Congressman Ron Wyden to introduce legislation requiring auditors to search for financial fraud and bring possible irregularities and illegal acts to the attention of corporate management and audit committees, which would be expected to report these acts to regulatory and law enforcement authorities. Congressmen John Dingell, Wyden and others are concerned about the adequacy of regulation of the profession.

We are dealing with these congressional concerns on several levels, all expansions on the three responses initiated in the 1970s:

- The report of the special committee on standards of professional conduct for CPAs (the Anderson committee) proposes numerous changes in the Code of Professional Ethics, recommends a program (required for all AICPA members) to monitor practice and to improve compliance with performance standards, and requires all members who audit SEC registrants to belong to the SEC practice section (SECPS).

- The ASB has addressed a whole range of "expectation gap" issues and has issued 10 exposure drafts proposing significant revisions of existing auditing standards.

- An independent commission, the National Commission on Fraudulent Financial Reporting, is studying ways for all participants in the financial reporting process to improve the prevention and detection of fraud.

AICPA MISSION STATEMENT

The American Institute of Certified Public Accountants is the national professional organization for all certified public accountants. The mission of the AICPA is to act on behalf of its members and provide necessary support to ensure that CPAs serve the public interest in performing quality professional services. In fulfilling its mission, the AICPA gives

—Continued

priority to those areas where public reliance on CPA skills is most significant.

To achieve its mission, the AICPA:

1. Promotes uniform certification and licensing standards for CPAs.

2. Sets requirements for maintaining members' professional competence.

3. Assists members in the continuing development of professional expertise.

4. Provides standards of professional conduct and performance.

5. Monitors professional performance to enforce professional standards.

6. Promotes public confidence in the integrity, objectivity, competence, and professionalism of AICPA members and the services they perform.

7. Encourages highly qualified individuals to become CPAs and promotes the availability of appropriate educational programs.

8. Unites CPAs—whether in public practice, industry, education, or government—in their efforts to serve the public interest.

9. Serves as the national representative of CPAs to government, regulatory bodies, and other organizations.

10. Assists members in understanding and adjusting to changes in the economic, political, and technological environment.

OUR CHALLENGES TODAY

Some would ask why we face the concerns of the late 1970s again, just 10 years later.

In part this situation arises because we will be investigated and criticized whenever there are significant business failures. We know auditors cannot prevent business failures; we also know that business failures are inevitable in a dynamic, volatile and competitive business environment. Consequently, we must be prepared to answer without apology the questions and criticisms that always accompany such business failures. Even though we realize this, we seem to be in a principally defensive position lately. Why is this so, and what should we be doing to strengthen our performance and our ability to answer our critics?

First, as a profession, our communications with our clients and the public have not been as effective as they could be. Our reporting standards and formats need to be clarified. The Cohen commission noted that the standard auditor's report was not read for its information content and that it is an often-unread symbol, a "seal of approval." Can we convincingly deny

a responsibility to insure against business failures when our audit report is regarded as a confirmation of the sound financial health of the entity—as a seal of approval?

Consequently, it is particularly important that the ASB's proposal to revise the audit report receive the support of the profession. We must effectively convey what an audit is and is not, what it can and cannot reasonably be expected to accomplish and the meaning of our opinion on the financial statements.

Second, the profession, with some justification, has been reluctant to accept expansion of the auditor's role and responsibilities in the financial reporting process. Yet we must recognize that professional services that do not evolve to meet the changing needs of the users of those services will decline in value and others will seek to fill the resulting void, often in unsatisfactory ways. Can we deny government's initiatives for us to assume greater responsibilities if we fail to meet the reasonable expectations of the users of our services?

For example, as the ASB has proposed, auditors must become more concerned about the *total* control structure and environment, not just "internal accounting controls." An additional proposal would require auditors to perform certain analytical procedures that would provide a better understanding of the overall business environment. And it is particularly desirable that the profession work to enhance the relevance, reliability and understandability of financial statements. ASB proposals dealing with matters such as continued existence, reporting on management discussion and analysis, and auditing client judgments and estimates are important in that regard.

Third, there is disagreement about the degree of our responsibility for the detection of material errors and irregularities. According to the Louis Harris survey, the general public believes that uncovering material errors and irregularities is the most important function of the independent audit. This is not an easy challenge to accept in today's environment for legal liability, but it can be accepted if we can effectively communicate the distinctions between "responsibility" and "liability" and between an "auditor" and a "guarantor."

The ASB's exposure draft on errors and irregularities makes those distinctions and provides useful guidance on the conduct of an audit. It emphasises that professional skepticism is crucial to an effective audit. The profession needs to embrace that document and its companion document on illegal acts. A failure to do so will be seen as evidence of an unwillingness to serve the public interest.

Finally, I believe it is essential that we act affirmatively on the Anderson committee recommendations. In considering the Anderson report, a key question is whether we are to accept the role and responsibilities of a self-regulatory

—Continued

Continued

organization committed to monitoring the quality of our professional work and responding to the needs of the public on an equal footing with the needs of our members.

The part I favor is for us to stand up for quality—to require CPE and quality reviews and to require all firms that engage in SEC practice to participate in the programs of the SECPS.

Equally important, I believe we must have a strong code of ethics that we are prepared to live by and to enforce vigorously. The decisions the profession makes in this area will have a significant impact on our future.

WHAT LIES AHEAD?

We face many problems and challenges. In addition to those mentioned previously, there are, for example, criticisms of the quality of audits of governmental units and federal financial assistance programs; concerns about the scope of services we provide to audit clients; concerns about the confidentiality that surrounds certain of our self-regulatory activities; and, as we all are so painfully aware, burgeoning legal liability and difficulty in obtaining adequate insurance at a reasonable price. The courts, Congress and the SEC continue to challenge our role and seek to redefine our responsibilities. All of these factors and others discussed in this article will affect our profession in ways we cannot fully comprehend today.

When I consider the upcoming changes and challenges to our profession, I see two different facets of the future—the short term and the long term—that will have to be analyzed and handled in different ways. Dealing with the short-term future requires a practical, pragmatic grasp of the problems and needs in our purview today; analyzing the long-term future lends itself more to the rhetorical, to the visionary questions.

At this noteworthy moment in our professional history, we must grapple with both aspects of our future. The next few years are critical—serious choices must be made that will affect the very essence of our professional lives. Is the AICPA to be regarded as a professional "club," with initial entry requirements and yearly dues, whose principal emphasis is on serving the needs of its members? Or will it be a serious, self-regulatory body, intent on monitoring and demonstrating the quality of our professional services and responding to the needs of the public on an equal footing with the needs of our members? Will we commit ourselves to a communicative, proactive stance on the "expectation gap" issues, or will we continue a defensive posture, seeking to maintain the status quo?

These issues are at the heart of the questions we must come to grips with in the short term, and our decisions in these areas will have an enormous impact on our long-term future. The long term will also be influenced by factors that we cannot identify today.

Who can really predict what our profession will be like in 10 years? I don't think I can. I hope and expect that the AICPA will continue to be a growing, healthy, dynamic organization. Our membership doubled in the decade before 1976 and again in the 10 years between 1976 and 1986, growing from about 60,000 members to over 240,000 members in 20 years.

I see this growth continuing. But as to predicting the nature of an accountant's daily work, and the way in which it will be performed—who really knows? With all of the changes resulting from greater computerization, advances in EDP and the continuous stream of information that these will provide, will we be performing continuous audits? When our markets have a continuous flow of financial information, will they function the same way they do today? What will be the effects of advances in expert systems and artificial intelligence? No one can tell for sure.

Changes are occurring in our profession at a phenomenal rate. For example, who could have predicted 10 years ago, when a small minority of people entering our profession were women, that today that number would approach 50 percent? And the changes we're seeing now are really only the beginning. I believe, as awesome as it might sound, that the next 10 years will bring more changes to our profession than the last 100 have.

But change is not something to fear. The words of the committee on scope and structure are as true today as they were in 1975:

"Every profession is continually changing or being changed. It is changed by the aspirations of its own members—not only by those who cherish its old traditions, but by those who are inspired by a new vision of its function in society. It is changed by the emergence of additional opportunities for service which, if accepted, can stimulate its growth and, if neglected, may reduce its prestige. It is changed by the need to develop new skills—a requirement which may often entail the enlistment of those trained in different disciplines or an apparent incursion into other realms of knowledge. It is changed by the impact of new social and moral values and by the influence of political decisions reflecting those values. It is changed by the spectacular advance of technological innovation. It is changed by the mounting demand for a constantly higher level of competence—not only in terms of a wider span of knowledge, but also a greater depth of knowledge in specialized areas. And a profession successfully adapts to its altered environment or it runs the risk of extinction. For no calling has a valid claim to eternal professional status. It must constantly justify its retention of that privilege by responding, in a creative and responsible manner, to the changing needs of society."

—Continued

Continued

I believe that change and challenge are really just other names for opportunity. And we'll be there, taking advantage of every new opportunity to work with and be responsive to the public, which has vested its trust in us.

The future will bring many challenges, and we must meet them in a positive frame of mind—alert and adaptable, responsive and responsible. I have no doubt that we will do this. All we have to do is look at the caliber of the people around us, at the people who are attracted to accounting as a profession; you never cease to impress me.

Although we may not be able to predict the future, we know that we will always be able to rely on the integrity and professionalism of our fellow members. These really are the greatest qualities we can celebrate during our centennial year, and let's be sure that we do pause to appreciate our two greatest assets— the confidence that we have in ourselves and in the value of our profession, and the honor of the public's trust in our objectivity and integrity. We have much to be grateful for and to be proud

of, and this will give us the ability, enthusiasm and resilience to cope with whatever challenges are ahead of us. I'm certain that our successors will view our second hundred years with the same pride and confidence that we feel today as we look back over the first hundred years of our great organization.

J. Michael Cook, CPA, is chairman of Deloitte Haskins & Sells and 1986–87 chairman of the AICPA board of directors. A former chairman of the AICPA SEC regulations committee, he has also served on council, the auditing standards board, the future issues committee and the executive and peer review committees of the SEC practice section of the division for CPA firms. He serves on the advisory committee of the University of Florida's School of Accountancy and has testified before the House Subcommittee on Oversight and Investigations in defense of self-regulation for the accounting profession.

APPENDIX A

INTERNATIONAL COMPARISON OF MAIN ASPECTS OF PROFESSIONAL CODES OF CONDUCT
(Commentary on Professional Codes of Australia, New Zealand, and Japan is at the end of Table)

	US AICPA	INTERNATIONAL IFAC	CANADA ICAO	UNITED KINGDOM ICAEW	US IMA	CANADA SMAC
DESIGNATION	CPA		CA	CA	CMA	CMA
SOURCES	American Institute of Certified Public Accountants	International Federation of Accountants	Institute of Chartered Accountants of Ontario	Institute of Chartered Accountants in England and Wales	Institute of Management Accountants	Society of Management Accountants of Ontario
Website	www.aicpa.org	www.ifac.org	www.icao.on.ca	www.icaew.co.uk	www.imanet.org/ethics	www.cma-canada.org
Effective date	Dec. 31, 2002	November 2001	Dec. 12, 2002	October 2002	Dec., 31, 2002	Dec./02
Advisory Service	Yes	Not Applicable	Yes	Yes	Yes	Yes
Ethics Decision Questions					Fair? Just? What if friends learn?	
PRINCIPLES	**Responsibilities** In carrying out their professional responsibilities, members to exercise sensitive professional and moral judgment in all their activities.	**Responsibilities** To attain highest levels of professionalism and performance, and to meet the public interest, four basic objectives must be met regarding: credibility, professionalism, quality of services, & confidence. To meet these, the following Principles need to be observed.		*Since the ICAEW Guide to Professional Ethics is declared to be wholly compatible with IFAC Code, the specific details are not listed below.* The Guide is substantially shared with The Institutes of Chartered Accountants of Ireland & Scotland		
	The Public Interest Members have an obligation to act in a way that will serve public interest, honor the public trust and demonstrate commitment to professionalism.	**The Public Interest, 1.9** The Profession has responsibility to the public which relies on it to maintain the orderly functioning of commerce. Standards are heavily determined by the public interest, which is the collective well-being of the community of people	**The Public Interest, 201** Maintenance of good reputation of the profession and its ability to serve the public interest	**The Public Interest** Accountancy has a public interest responsibility as the society depends on it heavily to contribute towards orderly function of commerce	**The Public Interest.** Have an obligation to public – first in list	**The Public Interest** Members have a responsibility for and fidelity to public needs

CONTINUED

APPENDIX A

INTERNATIONAL COMPARISON OF MAIN ASPECTS OF PROFESSIONAL CODES OF CONDUCT
(Commentary on Professional Codes of Australia, New Zealand, and Japan is at the end of Table)—*CONTINUED*

	US AICPA	INTERNATIONAL IFAC	CANADA ICAO	UNITED KINGDOM ICAEW	US IMA	CANADA SMAC
PRINCIPLES		and institutions the professional accountant serves.				
	Integrity To maintain and broaden public confidence, perform all responsibilities with highest sense of integrity.	**Integrity, 1.16** Be straightforward and honest in performing professional services.	**Integrity and due care, 202** Perform his or her professional services with integrity and due care	**Integrity, 1** Not merely honesty but fair dealing and truthfulness	**Integrity** Avoid influences and actual or apparent conflicts of interest Advise of any potential influences Refuse any gift, etc. that would influence or appear to influence Refrain from active or passive subversion	**Integrity and Personal Honour** Must perform duties with honour and professional integrity
	Objectivity Be objective and free of conflicts of interest in discharging responsibilities	**Objectivity, 1.16** Be fair and not allow prejudice or bias, conflict of interest or influence of others to override objectivity	**Objectivity, 204** Opinion on financial statements must be free of any influence and interest or relationship which may impair judgment	**Objectivity, 2** It is the state of mind which has regard for all considerations relevant to task in hand, but no other	**Objectivity** Communicate fairly and objectively Disclose fully all relevant information that could reasonably be expected to influence an intended user's understanding	**Objectivity** Must be objective and impartial
	Independence A member in public practice be independent in fact and appearance when providing	(See below)	**Independence, 204** Interests and relationships may weaken independence or appear to do so	(See below)	See integrity above	**Independence** Must maintain independence of thought and action

PRINCIPLES — auditing and other attestation services

Due care Observe the technical and ethical standards, strive to improve competence and quality of services, and act to the best of ability	**Professional Competence, S9 & Due Care, I.16** Maintain professional knowledge and skill at a level for competent services. Perform professional services with due care, competence and diligence.	**Professional Competence, 203** Duty to maintain professional competence Due care, 202 Compliance with bylaws and regulations is mandatory, 101	**Professional Competence, 3 Due diligence, 4** Only handle tasks for which competent or obtains advice and assistance to competently carry out the task Work with due skill, care, diligence and expedition	**Professional Competence** To constantly develop professional knowledge and skills level	**Competence** Act with competence through devotion to high ideals of personal honour and professional integrity
Scope and nature of services Members in public service should observe the Principles of the *Code of Professional Conduct* in determining the scope and nature of the services to be provided	**Technical standards, I.16** Carry out the professional services in accordance with the relevant technical and professional standards. Duty to carry out with care and skill	**Compliance with Bylaws and Regulations** Observe all bylaws and regulations, 101	**Performance, 4** Employ due skill, care, diligence and expedition, with proper regard for technical and professional standards	**Competence, cont'd** Observe laws, regulations and technical standards Prepare complete and clear reports and recommendations after appropriate analyses of relevant and reliable information	**Scope of Service** Undertake only such work as competence allows, and advise that another person be engaged when appropriate.
(See below)	**Confidentiality, I.16** Maintain the confidentiality of information acquired. No disclosure without proper authority, unless there is legal or professional right or duty to disclose.	**Confidentiality, 208** No improper use of information received in the course of business Maintain confidentiality unless lawful authority requires such information	(See below)	**Confidentiality** No improper disclosure or use of information Inform subordinates and monitor Refrain from misusing info, or appearing to misuse it.	**Confidentiality** No disclosure without proper authority, unless there is legal or professional right or duty to disclose.

CONTINUED

APPENDIX A

INTERNATIONAL COMPARISON OF MAIN ASPECTS OF PROFESSIONAL CODES OF CONDUCT

(Commentary on Professional Codes of Australia, New Zealand, and Japan is at the end of Table)—*CONTINUED*

	US AICPA	INTERNATIONAL IFAC	CANADA ICAO	UNITED KINGDOM ICAEW	US IMA	CANADA SMAC
PRINCIPLES	See above	**Professional Behavior, I.16** Act in a manner consistent with the good reputation of the profession. Refrain from any conduct, which might bring discredit to the profession.	**Maintenance of good reputation, 201** Duty to maintain good reputation of the profession and its ability to serve the public interest	**Courtesy and consideration, 5** Conduct himself with courtesy and consideration towards all in professional work		**Courtesy** Members must show courtesy to all in performing their professional duties
ORGANIZATION	Divided into Principles and Rules for all members	Divided into four parts for members engaged in different job areas: I Introduction A. For all members; B. Public practice; C. Employed.	Foreword gives characteristics and principles that inform the *Rules* for all members.	Fundamental Principles Framework Expansions on: Integrity, objectivity, Independence; Conflicts of Interest, Confidentiality Special areas	*Standards of Ethical Conduct* is a 3 page document covering: Introduction, Competence, Integrity, Objectivity, Resolution of Ethical Conduct	*Code of Ethics* is a 2 page statement of undertakings
APPLICABILITY TO MEMBERS & TO FIRMS				***Wholly compatible with IFAC Code***	**Most principles are covered above**	
RULES	**Independence** Will be impaired by various transactions, relationships and interests, including; direct or material financial interests, performance of certain nonattest functions, common investment, loans, family relationships, or official office such as director, officer,	**Independence, B.8** Should be and appear to be free of any interest when undertaking a reporting assignment. Financial involvement may affect independence. Independence is impaired by financial interest, family relationship and other issues etc. Conceptual approach – see Text Chapter 4 on Conflicts of Interest Section 8 is extensive.	**Independence, 204** Be free of any influences, relationship or interests which may impair professional judgment or have the appearance of doing so. Disclosure requirement.			**Independence** It is the foundation of professional work. Beware of, and inform of all conflicts of interest, and do not give in to outside pressures to act against the ethical code

RULES trustee, employee, underwriter, promoter, and the threat of litigation, etc.

Integrity	Integrity, A.1	Integrity, 202	Integrity	Professional integrity.
No conflicts of interest are allowed. No misrepresentations, must report to avoid subordination of judgment	Integrity implies not merely honesty but fair dealing and truthfulness.	No association with any form of misrepresentation, 103. No association even when a disclaimer is given with a false or misleading statements, 205. Disclosure of material facts and material misstatements covers omissions, non-compliance with GAAP & GAAS, 206	Avoid conflict of interest, gift, pressures, family influences, etc., which can affect decision-making. No form of misrepresentation of facts, etc.	Not to be party to any unlawful act of employer or misrepresentation etc. Disclose all material facts and departures from GAAP.

Objectivity	Objectivity, A.1	Objectivity, 204	Objectivity	Impartiality.
No misrepresentations, must report to avoid subordination of judgment	Objectivity requires accountants to be fair, intellectually honest and free of conflicts of interest	Opinion on financial statements must be free of any influence and interest or relationship which may impair judgment, or appear to do so.	Communicate fairly and objectively	Beware of pressures and conflicts etc.

Compliance with standards	Professional Competence, A.3, 17	Compliance with Bylaws and Regulations	Compliance	Compliance
Necessary if service involves auditing, review, compilation, management consulting, tax or	Consult other professional accountants if special skills required are not available, and take advice.	Observe all bylaws and regulations, 101. Compliance with	To perform in accordance with relevant laws, regulations and standards	Must follow the code of ethics, Personally accountable for their own ethical behavior

CONTINUED

INTERNATIONAL COMPARISON OF MAIN ASPECTS OF PROFESSIONAL CODES OF CONDUCT
(Commentary on Professional Codes of Australia, New Zealand, and Japan is at the end of Table)—*CONTINUED*

	US AICPA	INTERNATIONAL	IFAC CANADA	ICAO	UNITED KINGDOM ICAEW	US	IMA	CANADA	SMAC
RULES	other professional services	Do not portray having expertise or experience that you do not possess.	professional standards, 206						
	General standards, Professional competence Due professional care Planning and supervision Sufficient relevant data	**Maintenance of Professional Competence, A.3** Requires awareness of developments in accountancy profession, other relevant regulations and statutory requirements Should adopt a program designed to ensure quality control in the professional services consistent with appropriate national and international pronouncements.	**Professional Competence** Duty to maintain professional competence, 203 Due care, 202				**Professional Competence** To maintain appropriate level of competence by ongoing development of knowledge and skills	See above	
	Accounting Principles No departure from generally accepted accounting principles, unless a misleading statement would result; then must state why a departure is warranted and its effects.		**Accounting principles, 206** Must comply with professional standards and GAAP			See above			
	Confidentiality Information from client not used for personal gains.	**Confidentiality, A.4** Fully respect confidentiality of information acquired during work, even after the end of the relationship.	**Confidentiality, 209** No improper use of information			**Confidentiality** No disclosure of information except when legally obligated		**Confidentiality** No improper disclosure of information received in course of duties.	**Confidentially**

No disclosure without consent, except for court or CPA proceedings	No disclosure unless specific authority is given or there is professional or legal duty to disclose.	received in course of professional duties To maintain confidentiality of information unless a lawful authority requires such information. Responsible for agents.	
Contingent fees Not allowed for audit, review, compilation, examination of prospective financial information or tax return or refund claim etc.— some exceptions	**Contingent Fees and commission, B.10** Contingent fees not allowed If fixed by court then permitted. Percentage fee is regarded as contingent fee	**Contingent Fees, 215** Not allowed No free services unless for charitable or benevolent organization, No unauthorized benefits allowed from client or employer	
Responsibilities to colleagues Continuing responsibility to cooperate Should not retain client records when a demand for them is received.	**Relations with other accountants in public practice, B.13** In referral, restrict service to that specific area and do not step into existing professional's business. Communication between new and old accountants when they supersede is recommended	**Relations with Members, Firms and Non-Members, 300** Acceptance of appointment where there is an incumbent auditor; 302 Communication of special assignments to incumbent, 305 Responsibilities on special assignments, 306	**Relations with Members** Exhibit fairness and loyalty, courtesy and good faith. No review of other members except with the knowledge of the member, unless terminated.
Discreditable acts Not permitted, any form of discrimination, harassment, deviation from	**Activities incompatible with the practice of public accountancy, B.11** Not to engage in any activity and business which	**Maintenance of the good reputation of the profession, 201** No unlawful activities, association of	**Misconduct** No activity to discredit the profession. Members will not act — **Breach of principles** Discreditable act. No discreditable acts Report breaches of

CONTINUED

APPENDIX A

INTERNATIONAL COMPARISON OF MAIN ASPECTS OF PROFESSIONAL CODES OF CONDUCT

(Commentary on Professional Codes of Australia, New Zealand, and Japan is at the end of Table)—*CONTINUED*

	US AICPA	INTERNATIONAL IFAC	CANADA ICAO	UNITED KINGDOM ICAEW	US IMA	CANADA SMAC
RULES	government standards, negligence	impairs objectivity and independence or affects the good reputation of profession	person, name or services 213		contrary to ethical standards, nor condone such acts	Code to the proper tribunals of the Society
	Advertising and solicitation Cannot be false, misleading or deceptive, or involve coercion, over-reaching or harassment	**Advertising and solicitation, B.14 Publicity, A.7** Aim to inform the public in objective manner No coercion, harassment Be decent, truthful and in good taste Not bring profession into disrepute No exaggerated claims Do not denigrate work of others	**Advertising restrictions, 217** None that are false, misleading or in bad taste. Endorsement only under limited conditions. No solicitation Do not bring disrepute to profession			
	Commission and referral fees Not allowed for audit, review, compilation, examination of prospective financial information, otherwise requires disclosure Cannot be paid or accepted without disclosure to client	**Fees and Commissions, B.10** Fee should fairly reflect value of services provided Based on time and resources spent. If pre-arranged fee is charged, estimates must be reasonable. Commission not allowed.	**Referral Fees or Compensation** Not allowed, except for very few exceptions, 216			**Commission or Non-standard Remuneration** None allowed without disclosure to employer/client and consent therefrom.

CONTINUED

RULES

Names and Forms of organization
Practice public accounting only in a form (see note at end) of organization permitted by state law or regulation whose characteristics conform to resolutions of Council. Permits non-CPA minority ownership, provided CPA is ultimately responsible, financially and otherwise, for attest work performed to protect the public interest; non-CPA must abide by CPA code and requirements, and not hold themselves out as CPA's.

Misleading name or style, 401
Not allowed
Work for public interest must be under the charge of licensed public accountant, 404
Sole and firm's names, 406
Surnames in title limited to active or deceased partners
Practice of public accounting in corporate form limited in many provinces, 408

Resolution of ethical conflicts, A.2
Be conscious and alert to factors which give rise to conflicts of interest.
Should follow established policies to seek their resolution.
Review the conflict problem with the immediate superior or higher levels if problem is not resolved.

Resolution of ethical Matters
Resolve with superiors and follow the ethical guidelines of the Institute
Resign if matter not resolved

Resolution of Conflict
To follow policy of the organization and discuss such issues with superiors, obtain advice from recently (2002) created IMA Ethics Counseling

INTERNATIONAL COMPARISON OF MAIN ASPECTS OF PROFESSIONAL CODES OF CONDUCT
(Commentary on Professional Codes of Australia, New Zealand, and Japan is at the end of Table)—*CONTINUED*

	US AICPA	INTERNATIONAL IFAC	CANADA	ICAO	UNITED KINGDOM	ICAEW	US IMA	CANADA	SMAC
RULES		Seek counseling and advice on a confidential basis If no other recourse on significant matters (e.g., Fraud) resign and to submit an information memorandum to an appropriate representative of that organization.					Service available as a hotline, or if not resolved finally resign and present a memorandum to an appropriate representative of the organization. Depending on the nature of the ethical conflict, consideration should also be given to the notification of other parties.		
		Tax Practice, A.5 Put forward the best position in favor of client, but be consistent with laws. Advise the client if material error noted in previous returns. Do not associate with any return if have reasons to believe it is false.							

Cross Border Activities, A.6
If required to work in another country, follow the stricter of IFAC and local code.
If home country code is mandatory for outside work and stricter than IFAC, follow same

Support for colleagues, C.16
Working as superior, should give due weight to others to develop and hold their own judgment
Deal with differences professionally

Presentation of information, C.18
Present information fully and honestly to be understood in its context.
Give the true nature of business transactions, assets, liabilities, etc.

Presentation of Information, 205
No false reports or misrepresentation.

Presentation of Information
Must disclose fully all relevant information, fairly and objectivity

Responsibility to others
To provide opportunities for professional development and adequate compensation to accountants employed.

Presentation of Information
Members must report all material misstatements or departures from generally accepted accounting principles.

CONTINUED

INTERNATIONAL COMPARISON OF MAIN ASPECTS OF PROFESSIONAL CODES OF CONDUCT

(Commentary on Professional Codes of Australia, New Zealand, and Japan is at the end of Table)—*CONTINUED*

	US AICPA	INTERNATIONAL IFAC	CANADA ICAO	UNITED KINGDOM ICAEW	US IMA	CANADA SMAC
RULES	**Conflict of interest** May occur if a member performs a professional service for a client or employer and the member or his or her firm has financial or family relationship that could, in the member's professional judgment, be viewed by the client, employer, or other appropriate parties as impairing the member's objectivity	**Conflict of loyalties, C.15** Owe duty to employer and profession. Normally must support organization's legitimate objectives and ethics. Resolve any differences with superiors and professionals within the organization. Resign if no recourse left.	**Conflict of interest, 210** Must inform client of conflicting business connections, affiliations or interests, and obtain consent. Responsible for detection before accepting engagement.		**Conflict of Interests** Members must be aware of and avoid conflict of interest, and not be affected	**Conflict of Interests** Inform the client or employers.
		Professional competence, C17 and responsibilities regarding use of non-accountants, B.9 Responsible for others' work Take necessary advice and assistance if not competent	**Responsible for the failure of non-members, 406** Responsible for all associated with the practice to abide by the rules of conduct		**Responsible for others** Responsible for subordinates work to maintain confidentiality of information etc.	See above

RULES	See above			
		Duty to report apparent breaches, 211 Report on conduct, competencies, regulations or integrity	**Duty to report violations** Can not condone violations of ethical code	**Duty to report** Any deviation from code of ethics.
	Client monies, B.12 Should not hold client's monies if reason to believe they were obtained by illegal means. If accepted, safeguard and keep separate accounts fees from such money can be taken if permitted by client.	**Handling of trust funds, 212** To follow trust laws and have separate records		
		Retention of documents and working papers, 218 For a reasonable period of time		

Note: The Ethical Codes of Conduct for Professional Accountants in Australia, New Zealand and Japan were also reviewed. Their findings have been omitted from this table for lack of space. However, the main issues and points were:

- The New Zealand Institute of Chartered Accountants (see *http://brooks.swlearning.com*) has released a revised code designed to reflect the IFAC Code Principles, to be effective in mid-2003. It is available at (see *http://brooks.swlearning.com*). Appendix 3 which appears on page 63 of the .PDF version contains a comparison with the IFAC and Australian Codes.
- The Australian Code (see *http://brooks.swlearning.com*) matches the guidelines of IFAC Code.
- The Japan Institute of Certified Public Accountants Code document dated 1987 contained general principles, and a brief list of responsibilities is available of the Institute's website at *http://brooks.swlearning.com*

The Anderson Committee: Restructuring Professional Standards

Special Committee on Standards of Professional Conduct for Certified Public Accountants
Journal of Accountancy, May 1987

IN OCTOBER 1983 THE SPECIAL committee on standards of professional conduct for certified public accountants was appointed to study the relevance and effectiveness of professional standards in today's environment.

After three years of analysis, consultation and vigorous debate, the committee issued its final report in July 1986— *Restructuring Professional Standards to Achieve Professional Excellence in a Changing Environment.* The report urges the membership to give thoughtful consideration to the committee's recommendations for sweeping revisions in the American Institute of CPAs Code of Professional Ethics and substantial reforms in a way adherence to professional standards is achieved.

The AICPA leadership initiated the study in response to concerns over the profession's ability to serve the public interest and retain public confidence in a rapidly changing environment. The special committee's basic charge was to consider the changing economic, social, legal and regulatory climate, to thoroughly assess the relevance and effectiveness of existing ethical standards, to evaluate the role of the Institute in establishing standards and to recommend a course of action to be taken.

ROOM FOR IMPROVEMENT

Amid criticism in the profession by Congress, the media, regulators and the public, the committee concluded that some legitimate concerns had been raised about CPAs' behavior and commitment to quality. It found a need for greater flexibility and responsiveness in the existing system and substantial room for improvement in the way the profession identifies and deals with substandard work. The final report includes recommendations for changes in four broad areas:

1. Restructure the Institute's Code of Professional Ethics into two sections, including new standards of professional conduct and completely revised rules of performance and behavior.

2. Provide guidance to practitioners in making judgments regarding the scope and nature of services and adherence to professionalism.

3. Establish a new program for the systematic monitoring of practice to improve the quality of service and to assure compliance with performance standards.

4. Establish mandatory continuing professional education for the AICPA membership and postbaccalaureate education requirements for entry into the profession.

REVOLUTIONARY CHANGES

The revolutionary nature of the report's recommendations is expected to have a profound impact on how the profession functions. The Institute and the state CPA societies are working together to encourage their members' careful consideration of the report. The membership has been urged to recognize the report's implications for the profession's continued ability to regulate itself and to counteract the real threat of intrusive outside regulation.

The special committee's report represents a positive response to changing times and revitalizes the concepts that the profession has always valued: the public interest, integrity, independence and objectivity, and due care. It reaffirms the profession's commitment to the highest attainable level of professional service and conduct.

After implementation proposals have been submitted to and cleared by council, they will be presented to the membership for ballot to put the recommendations into effect. The AICPA is requesting whole-hearted support for all of the committee's proposals. Full endorsement and implementation are expected to send a clear message that the profession intends to achieve and maintain the highest standards of excellence as it meets the challenge of the future.

George D. Anderson
Chairman

Robert L. Bunting	Bernard Z. Lee
Joseph P. Cummings	Herman J. Lowe
James Don Edwards	Archie E. MacKay
Robert C. Ellyson	William L. Raby
Francis A. Humphries	Ralph Saul
Richard Kasten	John P. Thomas
James Kurtz	Kathryn D. Wriston

The Liability Crisis in the United States:
Impact on the Accounting Profession
A Statement of Position

Arthur Andersen & Co., Coopers & Lybrand, Deloitte & Touche, Ernst & Young, KPMG Peat Marwick, Price Waterhouse

The tort liability system in the United States is out of control. It is no longer a balanced system that provides reasonable compensation to victims by the responsible parties. Instead, it functions primarily as a risk transfer scheme in which marginally culpable or even innocent defendants too often must agree to coerced settlements in order to avoid the threat of even higher liability, pay judgments totally out of proportion to their degree of fault, and incur substantial legal expenses to defend against unwarranted lawsuits.

The flaws in the liability system are taking a severe toll on the accounting profession. If these flaws are not corrected and the tort system continues on its present inequitable course, the consequences could prove fatal to accounting firms of all sizes. But a liability system seriously lacking in logic, fairness and balance is not just the accounting profession's crisis. It is a business crisis and a national crisis.

This position statement describes these matters in more detail, as well as needed reforms that the American Institute of CPAs (AICPA) and the six largest accounting firms are advocating. In seeking these reforms, the firms are not attempting to avoid liability where they are culpable. Rather, the firms seek equitable treatment that will permit them and the public accounting profession to continue to make an important contribution to the U.S. economy.

AN EPIDEMIC OF LITIGATION

The present liability system has produced an epidemic of litigation that is spreading throughout the accounting profession and the business community. It is threatening the independent audit function and the financial reporting system, the strength of U.S. capital markets, and the competitiveness of the U.S. economy.

The principal causes of the accounting profession's liability problems are unwarranted litigation and coerced settlements. The present system makes it both easy and financially rewarding to file claims regardless of the merits of the case. As former SEC Commissioner Philip Lochner recently pointed out in *The Wall Street Journal*, plaintiffs may simply be seeking to recoup losses from a poor investment decision by going after the most convenient "deep pocket"—the auditor.[1] In too

many cases, moreover, claims are filed with the sole intent of taking advantage of the system to force defendants to settle.

The doctrine of joint and several liability makes each defendant fully liable for all assessed damages in a case, regardless of the degree of fault. In practical terms this means that, even with no evidence of culpability, a company's independent auditors are almost certain to be named in any action filed against that company alleging financial fraud, for no reason other than the auditors' perceived "deep pockets" or because they are the only potential defendant that is still solvent. A particularly egregious example of the abuses encouraged by joint and several liability is the common practice of plaintiffs' attorneys settling with the prime wrongdoers, who don't have a defense or money, at a fraction of what these parties should pay. The attorneys then pursue the case against the "deep pocket" professionals, who as a result of joint and several liability are exposed for 100 percent of the damages even if found to be only one percent at fault.

Other elements in the system also act as incentives for unwarranted litigation leading to forced settlements. For example, American judicial rules make no effective provision for recovery of legal costs by prevailing defendants, even if the plaintiff's case is meritless. In addition, judicial restrictions on the types of cases in which punitive damages may be awarded have been significantly relaxed in recent years, making solvent professional and business defendants a prime target. The prospect of having to pay all damages as a consequence of joint and several liability, the high costs of defense, and possible punitive damages are persuasive factors in coercing settlements.

Abusive and unwarranted litigation is a problem not just for the accounting profession, but for business and the economy generally. A small group of attorneys is reaping millions of dollars by bringing federal securities fraud claims (under SEC Rule 10b-5) against public companies whose only crime has been a fluctuation in their stock price. These attorneys use the threat of enormous legal costs, a lengthy and disruptive discovery process, protracted litigation, and damage to reputation to force large settlements.

The CEO of a high tech company that has been the target of 13 specious Rule 10b-5 suits calls these actions "legalized extortion" and their effects go far beyond the "payoffs" demanded. These meritless suits siphon off funds needed for

---

1. Philip R. Lochner, Jr., "Black Days for Accounting Firms," *The Wall Street Journal*, May 22, 1992, page A10.

—Continued

Continued

research and development, capital investment, growth and expansion. They divert management's time, talent and energy from the principal mission of running the business. They send liability insurance premiums skyrocketing. Ultimately, the direct and indirect costs of these suits are borne by shareholders, along with employees, customers, and all of a company's stakeholders.

Joint and several liability encourages the inclusion of "deep pocket" defendants such as independent accountants, lawyers, directors and underwriters in these suits in order to increase the prospect and size of settlements. Prohibitive legal costs, the unpredictable outcome of a jury trial, and the risk of being liable for the full damages compel even blameless defendants to race each other to the settlement table. And they do this despite the realization that, to the uninformed public, "agreeing" to settle is seen as an admission of wrongdoing.

A survey by the six largest accounting firms of the cases against them involving 10b-5 claims which were concluded in fiscal year 1991 showed that: (i) the average claim subjecting the accounting firm to joint and several liability was for $85 million; (ii) the average settlement by the firm was $2.7 million, suggesting there might have been little or no merit to the original claim against the accountant; yet, (iii) the average legal cost per claim was $3.5 million. It is not surprising that an accounting firm would agree to settle a case for less than what it had already spent in legal fees and, therefore, avoid the risk of liability of over twenty times the settlement by a jury that may be hostile to a business with "deep pockets." However, controlling risk by settling where you did nothing wrong becomes a very expensive strategy for "winning" the liability game.

FINANCIAL CRISIS FOR THE ACCOUNTING PROFESSION

The financial impact of rampant litigation on the six largest accounting firms has been well-publicized. Numerous headlines and articles resulted from the firms' own disclosure that, in 1991, total expenditures for settling and defendant lawsuits were $477 million—nine percent of auditing and accounting revenues in the United States. This figure, a multiple of what other businesses spend on litigation, does not even include indirect costs. It covers only costs of legal services, settlements and judgments, and liability insurance premiums, minus insurance reimbursements. The 1991 figure represents a substantial increase over the 1990 figure of $404 million or 7.7 percent of audit and accounting revenues. And based upon reported settlements through June 30, 1992, there appears to be no end to the continuous upward spiral.

The litigation explosion has affected the entire accounting profession. It has been estimated that there are about $30 billion in damage claims currently facing the profession as a whole. A recent survey by the AICPA indicates that claims against firms other than the six largest rose by two-thirds between 1987 and 1991. Ninety-six percent of those firms having more than 50 CPAs reported an increase in exposure to legal liability. The same group has experienced a 300 percent increase in liability insurance premiums since 1985. Smaller firms must now carry far more coverage, and high deductibles force them to pay even medium-sized claims out-of-pocket. The median amount for deductibles is now $240,000—nearly six times the 1985 median of $42,000. Forty percent of all the firms surveyed are "going bare," largely because liability insurance is simply too expensive.[2]

For the largest firms, the increase in insurance premiums was dramatically higher than that reported by the smaller firms, coupled with drastically reduced policy limits. Deductibles also have risen dramatically and now exceed $25 million for a first loss. The higher rate of increase in liability insurance for the largest firms generally reflects the larger proportion of audit work for publicly-held companies, thereby subjecting them to a greater liability risk.

IMPACT ON CORPORATE ACCOUNTABILITY AND ECONOMIC COMPETITIVENESS

The heavy financial burden placed on accounting firms by runaway litigation affects business and the economy in two major ways: first, through the actual and threatened failure of accounting firms; and, second, through the "survival tactics" firms are forced to employ.

In 1990, Laventhol & Horwatyh, the seventh-largest firm, collapsed—the largest bankruptcy for a professional organization in U.S. history—necessitating that its former partners agree to pay $48 million to avoid personal bankruptcy. While other factors contributed to the firm's demise, the overriding reason was the weight of its liability burden. According to former CEO Robert Levine, L&H, like other accounting firms, was included as a defendant because of the perception of being a "deep pocket" rather than deficiencies in the performance of its professional responsibilities. "It wasn't the litigation we would lose that was the problem," he asserted. "It was the cost of winning that caused the greatest part of our financial distress."

The consequences of L&H's failure reverberated throughout the capital markets. Audits in process were interrupted. New auditors had to be found, with the inevitable time lag that occurs for start-up. Special rules had to be adopted by the SEC to deal with public companies whose prior year financial statements reported on by L&H had to be

---

2. Survey of accounting firms (excluding the six largest), American Institute of Certified Public Accountants, 1992.

—Continued

Continued

reissued in connection with public offerings and periodic public filings. Companies whose financial statements were audited by L&H were placed under a cloud through no fault of their own.

Furthermore, the failure undermined confidence in the ability of the profession to carry out its public obligations by creating concerns about the financial viability of other firms. It also created a deep sense of apprehension throughout the accounting profession that has only grown worse. During 1992, another prominent firm, Pannell Kerr Foster, closed or sold about 90 percent of its offices and opted to reorganize its offices as individual professional corporations. *Accounting Today* quoted a former PKF partner who indicated that liability was one of the reasons for this massive restructuring.

The magnitude of the six largest accounting firms' liability-related costs, as well as the size of some highly-publicized judgments and settlements, has fueled speculation about their survival. This is not surprising. A grim precedent has been set, and without decisive action the liability crisis will grow worse and the six firms' collective liability burden, enormous as it is, will increase.

This potential long-term threat to the survival of the six firms has serious implications for the independent audit function, the financial reporting system and the capital markets. As a group, the six largest accounting firms audit all but a handful of the country's largest and most prominent public companies in every category:

- 494 of the *Fortune* 500 industrials;
- 97 of the *Fortune* 100 fastest growing companies;
- 99 of the *Fortune* 100 largest commercial banks;
- 92 of the top 100 defense contractors; and
- 195 of the 200 largest insurance companies.

In each of these categories, at least one of the six firms audits more than 20 percent of the companies. According to figures from *Who Audits America,* the six firms audit 90 percent (4,748 of 5,266) of the publicly-traded companies in the U.S. with annual sales of one million dollars or more.[3]

The detrimental effects on auditing, financial reporting, and our capital markets are already very much in evidence. They are a natural consequence of the risky and uncertain practice environment which the litigation epidemic has created not only for the six largest firms, but for the entire accounting profession.

The "Tort Tax"

One obvious effect is what the media [have] called "the tort tax"—that is, the increased cost of goods and services caused by runaway litigation. To quote SEC Chairman Richard C. Breeden, "Accounting firms, in particular, pay substantial and increasing costs to litigate and settle securities cases. At some point, these increasing litigation costs will increase the cost of audit services and tend to reduce access to our national securities markets."[4] If companies must pay higher costs for services provided not only by auditors, but by underwriters, attorneys and other frequent "deep pocket" defendants, it will be more expensive for them to raise needed capital. Opportunities for investors will be reduced, and U.S. businesses will be placed at a competitive disadvantage *vis-a-vis* companies in countries with more rational liability systems—virtually every other country in the world.

The Impact of Risk Reduction

The liability burden cannot be measured only in dollars and cents. Other effects are less easy to detect, but are no less costly. For example, groups targeted by frequent litigation now practice risk reduction as a matter of professional survival. Doctors, for instance, are avoiding such fields as gynecology and obstetrics. The result is a scarcity of practitioners in crucial specialties.

Accountants are also practicing risk reduction. The six largest firms are attempting to reduce the threat of litigation by avoiding what are considered high-risk audit clients and even entire industries. High risk categories include financial institutions, insurance companies, and real estate investment firms. Also considered "high risk" are high technology and mid-size companies, and private companies making initial public offerings (IPOs). These companies are a ready target of baseless Rule 10b-5 suits because their stock prices tend to be volatile. Unfortunately, they are also the companies that most need quality professional services, are a key source of innovation and jobs, and play a crucial role in keeping this country competitive.

Risk avoidance is not confined to only the largest accounting firms. Smaller and medium-sized firms are dropping their public clients or abandoning their audit practices altogether. A recent survey of California CPA firms showed that only 53 percent are willing to undertake audit work. This creates serious problems for smaller companies (and their shareholders) that need viable alternatives to the major firms. Additionally, the survey showed that thirty-two percent of the

---

3. *Who Audits America,* 25th Edition, Data Financial Press, Menlo Park, California, June 1991, pp. 393–396.

4. Letter from SEC Chairman Richard C. Breeden to Rep. John D. Dingell (D-MI), Chairman, Committee on Energy and Commerce, U.S. House of Representatives, May 5, 1992.

—Continued

Continued

reporting CPA firms are discontinuing audits in what they consider as high risk sectors. Another survey by Johnson & Higgins found that 56 percent of the mid-sized firms surveyed will not do business with clients involved in industries they consider high risk.

Impact on Professional Recruitment and Morale

Another troubling effect of the litigation explosion on the accounting profession, its clients and the public is one that cuts across all industries and services. The litigious practice environment is making it increasingly difficult to attract and retain the most qualified individuals at every level. The *Atlantic Monthly* has reported that fewer top business students are choosing to go to public accounting firms to do audit work because, among other things, they perceive it as risky.

It is likely that the most serious impact on recruitment and retention of qualified people is yet to be felt, since widespread media and public attention have only recently begun to focus on the accounting profession's liability plight. Recruiters from the six largest firms report that they are encountering more awareness, more questions and more apprehension about the liability risk on college campuses across the country. Transforming public accounting from a secure and respected career to one in which becoming a partner carries with it the threat of personal financial ruin, is no way to ensure the profession's ability to meet its responsibilities to investors and the public.

NEEDED REFORMS

To restore equity and sanity to the liability system and to provide reasonable assurance that the public accounting profession will be able to continue to meet its public obligations requires substantive reform of both federal and state liability laws.

Proportionate Liability

While other serious problems must also be addressed, the principal cause of unwarranted litigation against the profession is joint and several liability, which governs the vast majority of actions brought against accountants at the federal and state levels.

In arguing for an end to joint and several liability, the profession is in no way attempting to evade financial responsibility in cases where accountants are culpable. The profession is merely asking for fairness—the replacement of joint and several liability with a proportionate liability standard that assesses damages against each defendant based on that defendant's degree of fault. SEC Chairman Richard Breeden recently acknowledged that joint and several liability can lead to unfair results by forcing marginal defendants to settle even weak claims. He has also expressed support for reducing the coercive "effect of allegations of joint and several liability in cases of relatively remote connection by the party to the principal wrongdoing."[5]

Proportionate liability will help restore balance and equity to the liability system by discouraging specious suits and giving blameless defendants the incentive to prove their case in court rather than settle. By creating overwhelming pressure on innocent defendants to settle, joint and several liability gives plaintiffs' lawyers a strong incentive to bring as many cases as possible, without regard to the relative merits, include as many defendants as possible without regard to their degree of fault, and to settle these cases at a fraction of the alleged damages. Thus victims of real fraud receive no more (on average 5 to 15 percent of their alleged damages) than so-called "professional" plaintiffs and speculators trying to recoup investment losses. On the other hand, the lawyers bringing these suits typically receive 30 percent of the settlement plus expenses. If plaintiffs' lawyers were not able to use the threat of joint and several liability to compel innocent defendants to settle meritless cases, they would have to focus all of their efforts on meritorious claims. That, in turn, would result in more appropriate awards for true victims.

Current Reform Efforts

The six largest firms have joined with the AICPA and concerned businesses in calling for federal securities reform to curb unwarranted litigation brought under Rule 10b-5. Proposed remedies include replacing joint and several liability with proportionate liability and requiring that plaintiffs pay a prevailing defendant's legal fees if the court determines that the suit was meritless.

Curbing baseless Rule 10b-5 actions will, however, ease but not solve the liability problem. Of the total cases pending against the six largest firms in 1991, only 30 percent contained Rule 10b-5 claims. Of that 30 percent, less than 10 percent were exclusively 10b-5 claims.

The greatest liability exposure resides in the states. Reform of state liability laws affecting accountants is of critical importance to the future viability of the profession. The 10b-5 effort, if successful, will certainly serve as an important precedent for further reform. Beyond proportionate liability, reasonable limitations on punitive damages, as well as disincentives to filing meritless claims ought to be enacted. Reforms could be accomplished either through federal preemption or state-by-state modification of their statutes governing legal liability. The accounting profession will continue to participate in various state liability reform initiatives.

---

5. Letter from SEC Chairman Richard C. Breeden to Sen. Terry Sanford (D-NC), June 12, 1992.

—Continued

Continued

No less important is the need for the accounting profession to remove legislative, regulatory and professional restrictions on the forms of organization that may be used by accounting firms. Accountants must be free to practice in any form of organization permitted by state law, including limited liability organizations. The accounting profession is not seeking special treatment. Importantly, public accountants only seek to practice in forms of organization that are available to the vast majority of American businesses. Such changes will not relieve culpable individuals of legal responsibility for their own actions, but simply end the current inequity of full personal liability on all partners for all judgments against their firms resulting from the actions of others. The six largest firms will continue to aggressively pursue needed state-level liability reform.

The six largest firms are exploring all possible alternatives for reducing the threat that liability poses to their ability to meet their public obligations and to their survival. In this pursuit, the firms cannot support any legislative or regulatory proposal that increases the responsibilities of the profession unless these increased responsibilities are accompanied by meaningful and comprehensive liability reform. The firms will support initiatives at both the federal and state levels that will restore balance to the current system of justice.

August 6, 1992

J. Michael Cook
Chairman and Chief Executive Officer
Deloitte & Touche

Ray J. Groves
Chairman
Ernst & Young

Shaun F. O'Malley
Chairman and Senior Partner
Price Waterhouse

Eugene M. Freedman
Chairman
Coopers & Lybrand

Jon C. Madonna
Chairman and Chief Executive
KPMG Peat Marwick

Lawrence A. Weinbach
Managing Partner-Chief Executive
Arthur Andersen & Co., S.C.

Ethics in Taxation Practice

Tom Lynch
The Accountant's Magazine, November 1987

Tom Lynch draws attention to some problem areas where ethical standards come under pressure in particular tax situations.

Taxation practice is no different from any other professional practice in that it should be conducted in accordance with the highest ethical standards backed by the application of a high degree of skill, know-how and competence, to the affairs of clients whose interests will be foremost in the mind of the practitioner.

Taxation services fall broadly into two categories: compliance and advisory. There are, of course, other services such as advocacy before Tribunals, addressing the members of a trade association client and so on, but these are usually ancillary activities which can be ignored for present purposes.

When the word "ethics" is mentioned in taxation circles the first reaction is that it relates to evasion and avoidance. Evasion is illegal and therefore unethical, while avoidance is entirely in order and therefore ethical. It follows from this that if one does not positively evade taxes all is well, and since no self-respecting accountant would do so or assist others to do so, that is the end of the matter. Beyond this ethics may be ignored. There is, of course, a great difference between evasion and avoidance. One can lead to prison while the other leads only to disappointment.

But life is not quite as simple as that. On the one hand there are degrees of culpability in evasion, while in avoidance there is a distinction to be made between straightforward mitigation

—Continued

Continued

and complex artificial schemes of tax avoidance. Some writers on the subject have even referred to "avoision" as a hybrid word implying that evasion and avoidance may in some circumstances be indistinguishable. The ultimate effect may be the same in that revenue is lost to the Exchequer, but they are different and they are distinguishable. It is in compliance work that tax evasion is normally encountered while generally speaking advisory work is more likely to involve tax avoidance.

EVASION

Evasion can take many forms but the objective is the same: to evade in whole or in part the tax liabilities which arise on the actual expenditure income, gains and wealth of the taxpayer. Given that the accountant in practice would not consciously assist a client to evade taxes it may be argued that evasion does not concern him. But this is not so and, further, it is a dangerous assumption to make. He, or she, can still become involved in evasion—for example, by failing to notice discrepancies in books or accounts or perhaps by finding out after the event that the client has evaded some or all of his tax liabilities.

The practising accountant must strive to ensure—as far as it is humanly possible to do so—that, as agent, no contribution is made to evasion of tax by a client. Compliance work is not a merely passive exercise when it is done by a professional accountant and it is by accepting unsatisfactory information and explanations that the accountant is most at risk. It must be borne in mind too that an accountant's contribution to evasion could be more reprehensible than the evasion itself.

If the accountant comes to the conclusion that his client is evading his tax liabilities, he must point out the risks and penalties; if the client fails to change his ways, the accountant should cease to act for him. Similarly, if an omission in a return or set of accounts comes to light after they have been submitted (and possibly agreed), the client should be advised to report the error—the client is responsible for what is in the return—and if he does not do so the accountant should withdraw his services. It should be made clear to the client, before doing so, that the Inland Revenue's attitude is very different in cases of voluntary disclosure from those where evasion is discovered only after investigation.

COMPLIANCE

Not all taxpayers are both highly literate and highly numerate. Their accounts and financial records can be a mess. But this is no reason to refuse to act for them even if it is necessary to use estimates in order to complete their accounts and returns. The Inland Revenue acknowledges this as a fact of life and is prepared to settle for estimated assessments in many cases. Provided the extent of the estimation is clearly stated, the accountant cannot be faulted even if evasion on the part of the taxpayer is subsequently discovered. But it is necessary to apply professional skills and common sense to the information and explanations on which the estimates are based and to refuse to accept doubtful information.

When the proprietor of a small local business in a rural area in Scotland tells his accountants that his regular trips to Newmarket are solely for business purposes, it would not be prudent to accept this statement without further enquiry. It may well be that what he says is true—perhaps because it is the one place he can be sure to get hold of a certain important supplier or customer; apart from that he may loathe crowds in general and racegoing crowds in particular. But on the face of it further enquiry would be expected.

One of the most common problems is the danger of accepting unsatisfactory explanations (or none) in the preparation of accounts because of the pressure of work and time limits—"the General Commissioners' meeting is tomorrow!" The accountant must ensure that work is properly staffed and where there is client-caused delay the accountant must not be stampeded or tempted to "keep things tidy" by throwing fingers into accounts without weighing up their reasonableness and requiring further explanations where this is necessary. Indeed, the more incomplete the records and the greater the delay in getting information to supplement what is there the more watchful the accountant should be and the more inclined to seek to square the accounts and returns with the client's standard of living and wealth. This will often turn out to be a valuable service to the sort of client who is simply careless and who would otherwise get into deep financial trouble or worse over his tax liabilities.

AVOIDANCE

"Avoidance" is rather an unfortunate word with a rather naughty connotation; in fact it covers everything from a simple and real rearrangement of affairs, which is eminently sensible and pure, to complex schemes where affairs are re-arranged with no real effect—*ie,* with no substance other than to reduce tax liabilities. These artificial schemes are not illegal but are thought by many to be reprehensible and, more importantly, potentially ineffective.

FORM AND SUBSTANCE

The *obiter dicta* in the Duke of Westminster's case about form being preferred to substance and Lord Tomlin's famous words about it being legitimate to arrange one's affairs so as to avoid the Inland Revenue putting its largest shovel into one's store still hold good despite *Furmiss v Dawson* et al. Form is still important. For example, a grandparent may give a grandchild a simple cash gift each year or may choose instead to pay the same cash under a valid deed of covenant. The gift

—Continued

Continued

is the same under either method, but the latter will have a tax saving effect solely because of the form in which the gift is made. The essential point is that the transaction between the grandparent and the grandchild has substance apart from tax saving. It is a real transaction in which real money passes from one person to another. The grandparent's finances would change for the worse after each payment while the grandchild's financial position would correspondingly improve. The form of the transaction is therefore vital.

Where the form of the transaction is not accepted by the courts it is not because the substance is preferred to the form but because there *is* no substance, no real transaction. Whatever form one may choose to give to a nothing, a nonentity, a fiction, it can never be a real transaction and it may therefore be ignored. Such transactions may conveniently be described as artificial avoidance schemes.

ADVISORY SERVICES

Whatever may be said about artificial avoidance schemes, tax mitigation is not reprehensible. Taking advantage of loopholes (with real transactions) may not be quite so commendable, but they are available to all taxpayers and it is up to Parliament to avoid creating them and, where they occur, to close them up as soon as possible.

Clients expect to be given advice on tax planning and mitigation and there is nothing wrong in the accountant giving this sort of advice. A Royal Commission report put it very well:

> "there is no reason to assume that the situation of any one taxpayer at that moment is the fairest possible as between himself and others differently situated: and if there is not, it seems wrong to pronounce any principle that would have the effect of fixing each taxpayer in his situation without allowing him any chance of so altering his arrangements as to reduce his liability to assessment."

A wife who helps her husband in his business may decide not to take a salary. Nevertheless, the true situation is that any profits are jointly earned and if the wife becomes a paid employee or a partner it is possible that the tax liability on the jointly earned income may be less. That the profits are jointly earned is the real substance of a case such as this, but once again it is the form in which the profits are earned that will settle the tax position. The accountant should see that the most tax efficient form is in fact adopted.

The transfer of cash from a building society deposit account (taxed income) to National Savings Certificates (income not taxed) is an example of a transaction which is both tax efficient and entirely acceptable. HM Government itself publicises the tax efficiency of National Savings Certificates using phrases such as "send the taxman away empty handed," phrases which accountants would think twice about using in the exercise of their profession.

On other slightly more complicated matters—such as the timing of an incoming or outgoing partner, or accepting shares rather than cash in a take-over bid—Lord Tomlin's dictum should be followed with enthusiasm, without risk of blame or stigma.

The situation is not so clear when it comes to artificial avoidance schemes. Certainly accountants should advise on them and indeed it is their duty to point out the risks associated with such schemes, the uncertainties and possible changes in the law which might negate them. It would not, however, be part of his duty to devise and promote such schemes if for no other reason than that the scheme so promoted not only has the blessing of the accountant but, because of his expertise, some sort of guarantee of success which if it fails to materialise may sour the relationship with the client. There is no question of morality here, at least so far as the adviser is concerned. Artificial schemes are best left alone simply because they bring trouble and expense in their wake, and often they do not work.

As regards morality, this is a question solely for the taxpayer. It is not the duty of the accountant as tax adviser to advise on what is or is not moral. Not everyone agrees that what is legal must necessarily also be moral or that any act within the law is not only permissible but even praiseworthy. Moral values are often rather higher than minimum legal requirements and it will be a matter for the individual's own conscience to determine which he or she prefers. The accountant/adviser may want, however, to avoid unduly influencing a client's moral judgment by vigorously promoting artificial schemes of tax avoidance.

CONCLUSION

In compliance work it is important not to be "used" either deliberately or willy nilly to assist evasion. It is all too easy to get caught up in this way and accountants must not allow pressures of any kind to distract them from working to a uniformly high standard. It is also necessary to be entirely firm about disclosing omissions in previous accounts and returns.

In advisory work, mitigation advice may and should be given. Advice should also be given on artificial avoidance schemes, but I suggest that accountants should not promote such schemes.

Tom Lynch, CA, FRSA, is visiting Professor of Taxation at the University of Glasgow and a former senior tax partner in Ernst & Whinney.

SOURCE: *The Accountant's Magazine,* November 1987: 27, 28. Reprinted with the permission of the Editor of *CA Magazine,* published by the Institute of Chartered Accounts of Scotland.

Appendix B: Trends in the Legal Liability of Accountants and Auditors and Legal Defenses Available

The traditional sources of legal liability for accountants and auditors have arisen under common law related to breach of contract or to torts for negligence. Recently, however, due to Enron and other financial fiascoes, there is a growing prospect of liability from statutory law particularly in the U.S. and probably in Canada. New constructs such as proportionate liability and the Limited Liability Partnership (LLP) have provided some relief, but the advent of class actions and higher public expectations for auditors such as for the finding of fraud will focus auditors on how to minimize their liability risk.

The burden of liability has shifted over time. As discussed below, early common law restricted liability to situations where there was privity of (a direct) contract between auditor and an investor/plaintiff in order to avoid "liability in an indeterminate amount for an indeterminate time to an indeterminate class" (*Ultramares*, 1931). Subsequently this bound was relaxed to allow liability to plaintiffs that could have reasonably been foreseen by the auditor (*Hedley Bryne & Co.*, 1964 and *Haig v. Bamford*, 1976). However, more recent cases have reduced the exposure to liability by narrowing the "foreseeability" test (*Caparo Industries plc*, 1991 and *Hercules Management Ltd. et al v. Ernst & Young et al*, 1997). The latter case, in a bizarre twist by the Supreme Court of Canada, calls for a duty of care by auditors *only* "when they [audited financial reports] are used 'as a guide for the shareholders, as a group, in supervising or overseeing management.'"[1] On the other hand, a month earlier a lower Canadian Court, the British Columbia Court of Appeal, held in *Stephen Kripps et al v. Touche Ross* (now Deloitte Touche) that the accounting profession could not hide behind "'according to GAAP' if the auditors know … that the financial statements are misleading."[2] The words "present fairly" are particularly important in the auditor's opinion in determining auditor liability.

http://brooks.swlearning.com
Auditors have been liable for malfeasance under statutory law for some time. For example, involvement with misleading statements in a prospectus has, for some time, been actionable under Acts in both the U.S. and Canada. However, since 1997, the will of politicians and the impact of statutory law, regulators and their agents have become greater. While dealing with Enron, the U.S. Senate has articulated that auditors are responsible to investors (see page 263) and has instructed the SEC to create regulations and activate statutes that make this clear. The Public Company Accounting Oversight Board (PCAOB) is one result that will impact on

auditor liability as its mandate unfolds. In Canada, the Ontario Securities Commission has been given similar powers to oversee auditors and a Canadian Public Accountability Board (CPAB) has recently been created.[3] Consequently, there is a strong likelihood that future developments in auditor and accountant liability will arise from statutory and regulatory authority rather than common law.

The burden of legal liability has also been affected by another development that sprang from the cry for reform of tort liability by the Big 6 Firms on August 6, 1992 reproduced as a reading beginning on page 295. That cry documents the debilitating state of affairs that had come to prevail in 1992. It suggests that the joint and several liability of audit firm partners should be replaced by a proportionate responsibility standard. This, it was argued, would remedy the unfairness of plaintiffs going after defendants with deep pockets who had very little if any direct culpability but had to pay and then look for recompense from others who were bankrupt. In fact, proportionate liability did come into being, and the construct of the Limited Liability Partnership (LLP) originated in 1994 in New York. In an LLP framework, 'innocent' partners can lose their business investment, but not their personal assets, in the event of their firm losing a court case.[4]

The development of proportionate liability and the LLP is counterbalanced to some extent by the advent of class action lawsuits that were stimulated in part because by plaintiff's lawyers who are willing to take the case on a contingency fee basis. That is, for the prospect of 30% of the final settlement, they will forgo other guaranteed fees. Some even chase plaintiffs to get their business because the possibility of settlement or winning a large judgement is so high. The reading by the Big 6 accounting firms provides interesting information on the nature and extent of class action liability.

Over the decades, changes in legal liability have had a profound effect on the development of the accounting profession's governance framework and of generally accepted accounting and auditing principles and practices as has been outlined in the reading by J. Michael Cook on page 274. The readings by Cook, the Big 6, and by Anderson provide excellent background for the review presented below.

TRENDS IN THE LEGAL LIABILITY OF ACCOUNTANTS AND AUDITORS

Contract experts contend that stakeholders (including employees, suppliers, customers, creditors) and their interests

---

1. Mathias, Philip, "Auditors Not Legally Liable to Investors, Top Court Rules", *Financial Post*, May 24, 1997, p. 3.
2. Editorial, "Accounting Profession Has A Duty to Shareholders," *Financial Post*, May 20, 1997.

3. Breiger, Peter, "New Auditing Watchdog Recruits Its First Board," *Financial Post*, February 27, 2003, FP11.
4. See earlier discussion at pages 45–46.

—Continued

Continued

are protected adequately through explicit and implicit contracts with a business enterprise. However, there has been a progressive trend over the last 30 years, reflected through changes in the law, that has been predicated on the notion that contracts may be insufficient to protect the interests of certain stakeholders who rely upon the conduct of and statements made by governors of a corporation and the professionals associated with it. Public and stakeholder knowledge, expectations, and sophistication have been heightened, and the law has changed to reflect a third-party duty (foreseeable) owed beyond contract by virtue of the position held within the company and the standard of conduct expected of a professional such as an auditor or an accountant. A precedent-setting Canadian case, *R. v. Bata Industries Ltd.* (1992), 70 C.C.C. (3d) 394 (Ont. Prov. Ct.), established that the courts will in fact pierce the corporate veil to determine the controlling mind and, more particularly, not merely what someone in a position of authority, such as a director, did do or know but what that director could or ought to have done or known under the circumstances.

This broadening trend from that of contractual privity to a duty owed to foreseeable stakeholders is reflected in the common law for auditors and accountants. Both auditors and accountants are now being sued by stakeholders without privity of contract, such as investors, shareholders, suppliers, and creditors. This is sometimes referred to as a "foreseeability" or "fairness" principle and is actually one part of a test of negligence that courts will use in determining whether an accountant or auditor's conduct has been negligent.

In very general legal terms, in order to establish auditor or accountant negligence, a duty of care must be owed by virtue of the relationship that is recognized in law; that standard of care must have been breached; that breadth of duty owed must have caused in a proximate and not remote way the actual damage to a third party (plaintiff) who relied to its detriment on the audit statements; the resultant damage must have been reasonably foreseeable (hence the "foreseeability" test) and, lastly, the conduct of the plaintiff must not be such so as to bar recovery; that is, the plaintiff must not have voluntarily assumed the risk, must not have contributed to the negligence and must be able to show that he or she attempted to mitigate damages.

A significant increase in auditor and accountant litigation has occurred as a result of this trend in the law that broadens standing among third-party stakeholders, who may sue auditors for negligence if the above requirements are met. So now, in addition to the auditor or accountant being bound by contract and fiduciary duty of trust to the client, he or she must, as a result of the above-mentioned foreseeability or fairness principle, assume additional duties to third-party stakeholders.

The trend along the continuum between contractual privity on one end and stakeholder fairness and foreseeability on the other can be demonstrated by a review of how the common law has developed in Canada, England, and the U.S. on this issue. Both the high courts in Canada and England have spoken on the foreseeability test of auditor liability, suggesting that the U.S. Supreme Court may soon speak on this point as well.

The leading Canadian case on auditor liability to foreseeable parties is *Haig v. Bamford et al.* (1976) 72 D.L.R. (3d) 68. The Supreme Court of Canada held in *Haig* that where an accountant has negligently prepared financial statements and a third party relies on them to his or her detriment, a duty of care in an action for negligent misstatement will arise in the following circumstances:

(i) the accountant knows that it will be shown to a member of a limited class of which the plaintiff is a member and which the accountant actually knows will use and rely on the statements;

(ii) the statements have been prepared primarily for guidance of that limited class and in respect of a specific class of transactions for the very purpose for which the plaintiff did in fact rely on them;

(iii) the fact that the accountant did not know the identity of the plaintiff is not material as long as the accountant was aware that the person for whose immediate benefit they were prepared intended to supply the statements to members of the very limited class of which the plaintiff is a member.

In short, *Haig v. Bamford* stands for the proposition that an accountant will be found liable to a third party where the accountant had actual knowledge of the limited class of which the third party is a member and that third party will use and rely on the statement.

In England, in a landmark case establishing the modern role governing liability for professional advisers whose negligence gives rise to economic loss, the House of Lords in *Hedley Byrne & Co. Ltd. v. Heller & Partners Ltd.* [1964] A.C. 562 (H.L.) held that a professional adviser has an implied duty of care in making an oral or written statement to another person whom he or she knows or should know will rely on it in making a decision with economic consequences.

The "foreseeability" test in the above-mentioned Canadian *Haig* case was narrowed recently in *Caparo Industries plc. v. Pickman et al.* [1991] 2 W.L.R. 358 (H.L.). Although *Caparo* is an English case from the House of Lords, it is of precedential value to Canadian jurisprudence and has been followed in both Ontario and British Columbia courts. *Caparo* narrows the scope of the foreseeability doctrine by focusing on whether

—Continued

Continued

the auditor knew the "purpose" for which the third party was to use the financial statements. The *Caparo* foreseeability test is as follows: A duty is said to arise only where the auditor knew the *purpose* for which the financial statements were to be used by the person relying on them and knew that the statements would be communicated to that person either as an individual or as a member of an identifiable class, specifically in connection with a particular transaction or a transaction of a particular kind. The duty extends only to the particular transaction for which the accountants knew their accounts were to be used. Moreover, the advisee must reasonably suppose that he or she was entitled to rely on the advice or information communicated for the very purpose for which it was required. No duty arises in respect of statements put into general circulation and relied on by strangers to the maker of the statement for a purpose that the maker had no reason to anticipate, such as nonshareholders contemplating investment in a company.

Therefore, although both Canada and England have moved from contractual privity to a stakeholder foreseeability test of auditor liability, the British decision *Caparo* restricts *Haig*'s primary emphasis on foreseeability to that of knowledge of purpose. In other words, an auditor may be liable to a foreseeable third party under *Haig* where the accountant had actual knowledge of the third party and that party's intention to rely on the statement. An auditor may be liable to a foreseeable third party under *Caparo* where the accountant knew the purpose for which the third party was to rely upon and use the financial statements. The point is that the trend in auditor and accountant liability toward being liable to foreseeable third parties has been established in both Canada and England and has resulted in increased litigation for auditing firms.

Unlike Canada and England, the United States Supreme Court has never ruled on the duty owed to foreseeable third parties. In fact, state supreme courts are split between considering contractual privity (often termed *intended beneficiary*) versus foreseeable third parties as the required grounds for suit. Two cases are noteworthy here. *Ultramares Corporation v. Touche* 174 N.E. 441 (1931) stands for the proposition that experts who prepare statements or reports for a third party who is not a client will not be held accountable in negligence for any misstatement or misreport to that third party (nonclient). In other words, an immediate legal relationship (contractual privity) must exist between the parties in order for one to be liable in negligence to another.

The trend away from this contractual privity requirement in *Ultramares* to that of foreseeability was apparent in *Credit Alliance Corp. v. Arthur Andersen & Co.* 493 N.Y.S. 2d 435 (1985). In this case, the court reaffirmed yet relaxed the *Ultramares* principle. The court said that a legal relationship approaching that of a contract must exist for an auditor to be held liable in

negligence to a nonclient. The court, however, stated that an auditor will meet the "contractual privity" test where the auditor was aware that his or her statement would be used for a particular purpose and that a known party was intended to rely on it. In addition, some evidence must exist demonstrating a relationship between the auditor and the nonclient third party and demonstrating that the auditor knew that nonclient third party was relying on the auditor's statement.

Despite the fact that the trend from contractual privity to foreseeable third parties is still not being applied uniformly in the U.S., the foreseeability doctrine for auditors and accountants is now good law in both Canada and England as the high courts have spoken. The result of this trend has been "joint and several" liability exposure by auditors and accountants to third-party plaintiffs. Joint and several liability means that all codefendants, including the auditors, must account for all damages. If the client is insolvent, the audit firm's and its partners' assets are exposed regardless of the degree of fault. This is often the case as lawyers are trained to sue "deep pockets"—those entities believed to be most able to bear the burden of the loss, such as an accounting firm.

LEGAL DEFENSES AVAILABLE

This litigation exposure has had a chilling effect on the auditing profession and has resulted in a reluctance to pursue risky engagements such as environmental or social audits; exorbitant legal bills; increases in professional liability insurance premiums; increasing opportunity costs of the litigation; and adverse publicity for the profession as a whole.

Nevertheless, a number of defensive and proactive measures can be offered to auditors and accountants to limit their liability to foreseeable third-party litigants. These defenses include:

1. Due diligence and due care
2. Contributory negligence
3. Engagement letter provisions
4. Documentation and recordkeeping
5. Legal counsel

A cursory overview of each of these will be provided.

1. Due Diligence and Due Care

The defense of due diligence exists both in common law and statute. Due diligence entails a thorough and proper examination (reasonable investigation) of all relevant financial records prior to the rendering of an opinion, advice, or conclusion. Due care includes the application of auditing and financial analysis models and techniques to the existing subject matter. Due diligence is the principal means by

—Continued

Continued

which an accountant or auditor can defend against a negligence claim by a client for an alleged breach of a duty of care and skill.

In common law, there is no definitive law defining the standard of due diligence for an auditor or accountant. Each case is fact-dependent. However, due diligence for an auditor is generally meant to be understood as requiring an auditor to make a complete examination of the matter to be audited before issuing any report or giving any advice.

To illustrate the judicial reasoning in this due diligence defense and the degree to which the courts will intervene in applying the law to the facts, the recent precedent-setting Canadian case *R. v. Bata Industries* (1992), 70 C.C.C. (3d) 394 (Ont. Prov. Ct.) hinged on the due diligence defense. Although the conduct involved applied to a company director, the judicial reasoning and degree of intervention illustrates profoundly the leaning of the courts in evaluating the due diligence defense; this reasoning could and likely would be as applicable in evaluating whether an auditor acted with due diligence. At page 427, Justice Ormstrom addressed effectively the issue of due diligence:

I ask myself the following questions in assessing the defense of due diligence:

(a) Did the board of directors establish a pollution prevention "system" as indicated in *Regina v. Sault Ste. Marie*, i.e., Was there supervision or inspection? Was there improvement in business methods? Did he exhort those he controlled or influenced?

(b) Did each director ensure that the corporate officers have been instructed to set up a system sufficient within the terms and practices of its industry of ensuring compliance with environmental laws, to ensure that the officers report back periodically to the board on the operation of the system, and to ensure that the officers are instructed to report any substantial non-compliance to the board in a timely manner?

I reminded myself that:

(c) The directors are responsible for reviewing the environmental compliance reports provided by the officers of the corporation but are justified in placing reasonable reliance on reports provided to them by corporate officers, consultants, counsel or other informed parties.

(d) The directors should substantiate that the officers are promptly addressing environmental concerns brought to their attention by government agencies or other concerned parties including shareholders.

(e) The directors should be aware of the standards of their industry and other industries which deal with similar environmental pollutants or risks.

(f) The directors should immediately and personally react when they have noticed the system has failed.

Within this general profile and dependent upon the nature and structure of the corporate activity, one would hope to find remedial and contingency plans for spills, a system of ongoing environmental audit, training programs, sufficient authority to act and other indices of a proactive environmental policy.

Applying the preceding judicial reasoning in the due diligence defense, auditors as well may limit their liability by adopting proactive and defensive measures to support a due diligence defense. These measures may include but are not limited to:

- educating and communicating with personnel as to the technical, regulatory, legal, and ethical standards required by the profession and the firm and having reporting procedures implemented to ensure that this occurs;

- ensuring that all personnel are properly trained and supervised and having reporting and information systems to facilitate prompt identification and bottom-up flow of difficulties, problems;

- maintaining confidentiality and independence, and avoiding conflicts of interest and judgment; conforming with one's fiduciary duty of trust to the client;

- understanding industry standards and familiarity with the client's business and reputation for integrity;

- obtaining the necessary engagement letter provisions;

- proper documenting and recordkeeping; and

- supporting senior managing partners and partners and rewarding and compensating the above-desired behaviors.

2. Contributory Negligence

Contributory negligence exists as a defense for the auditor in a negligence claim for a breach of a duty of care and skill. The auditor, in using this defense, submits to the court that the client (often company management) contributed to the breach through an act (or acts) of commission or omission. In other words, the client did or failed to do something, and this contributed to the loss. The contributory negligence defense by auditors exists notwithstanding the policy argument against it; namely, that the auditor should not be permitted to use this defense to reduce liability, for doing so would defeat the purpose of having an auditor act as a check on the conduct of managers of a company through the analysis of financial documents.

3. Engagement Letter Provisions

An engagement letter is an agreement between the auditor and the client identifying whether the audit and/or other

—Continued

Continued

services will be provided, due dates, and fees. To mitigate liability and potential litigation, auditors should attempt to include provisions in the engagement letter that:

- narrow the scope of services to be provided in specific, rather than broad, general, terms. This limits liability to failure to perform the terms of the engagement letter.

- indemnify the auditor for third-party claims arising from services rendered by the auditor to the client in accordance with the engagement letter.

- enable the auditor to modify or withdraw the opinion or conclusion should circumstances warrant, such as, for example, the subsequent discovery of a material misstatement.

- permit liability claims against the auditor to be released completely should litigation claims against the indemnitor be settled.

- enable the auditor to participate fully in the preparation of a public offering document insofar as his or her opinion or conclusion is used or summarized in the final document. This participation would include the right to limit and qualify the scope of the opinion or conclusion prior to it reaching public investors via the public disclosure documents and/or the disclaiming of any fiduciary or agency relationship with shareholders should a public offering not be contemplated but the auditor's opinion or conclusion still used.

4. Documentation and Recordkeeping

Due diligence, due care, and a reasonable investigation can be more effectively demonstrated to a court by an auditor during litigation when he or she has a documentary or computerized record of all working papers, tests, and procedures performed that preceded the opinion or report and all written communications with the client. Also, the auditor should not agree in advance to release original copies of confidential client information to third parties without first seeking legal counsel, for retaining copies of the original document for recordkeeping purposes could aid in litigation defense and regulatory purposes.

5. Legal Counsel

Auditors and accountants should not wait to be sued but should take a proactive approach and seek legal counsel concerning their legal rights, exposure, and obligations. Competent and experienced legal counsel educates, communicates, limits exposure to client and third-party liability and costly litigation, and also aids in establishing due diligence evidence should litigation commence. More particularly, auditors should seek legal counsel in preparing and reviewing engagement and representation letters; developing the due diligence reviews; and reviewing the legal implications impacting and flowing from preliminary and final versions of the auditor's opinions and conclusions.

A REVIEW OF CASES

Ultramares Corporation v. Touche 174 N.E. 441 (1931)

In *Ultramares,* the creditors of the insolvent Ultramares Corporation sued the accountants for negligence in relying on the financial statements to their detriment. Particularly the accounts receivable had been inflated $700,000. The New York Court of Appeals held that the accountants had been negligent but were not liable to the creditors because of privity of contract. Only the contracting parties could sue the accountant(s) for negligent services. At page 444, Justice Cardozo held that "to hold the maker of the statement to be under a duty of care in respect of the accuracy of statement . . . is to find liability in an indeterminate amount for an indeterminate time to an indeterminate class." This case stands for the proposition that contractual privity is required in order to sue an accountant or auditor in negligence for any misstatement or misreport.

Hedley Byrne & Co. Ltd. v. Heller & Partners Ltd. [1964] A.C. 562 (H.L.)

In *Hedley Byrne,* the National Provincial Bank telephoned and wrote to Heller & Partners on behalf of Hedley Byrne to find out whether Easipower Ltd., a customer of Heller & Partners, was of sound financial position and thus a company with which Hedley Byrne would want to do business. Heller & Partners, disclaiming all responsibility to both inquiries by National Provincial Bank, said Easipower Ltd. was of sound financial shape. Hedley Byrne, in reliance on those statements, entered into a contract with Easipower Ltd., who subsequently thereafter sought liquidation.

The House of Lords, in deciding that Heller & Partners Ltd. would have been liable except for the disclaimer established the modern role governing liability for professional advisers whose negligence gives rise to economic loss. A professional adviser has an implied duty of care in making an oral or written statement to another person whom he or she knows or should know will rely on it in making a decision with economic consequences.

—Continued

Continued

Haig v. Bamford et al. (1976) 72 D.L.R. (3d) 68

In *Haig,* the Saskatchewan Development Corporation agreed to advance a $20,000 loan to a financially troubled company in part based on the conditional production of satisfactory audited financial statements. The company engaged Bamford's accountants to prepare the statements. The accountants knew that the statements would be used by Saskatchewan Development Corporation. Relying on the accountants' information, Saskatchewan Development Corporation advanced $20,000 to the company. Later investigation disclosed that a $28,000 prepayment on two uncompleted contracts had been treated as if the contracts had been completed, thereby showing a profit instead of a loss, and the accountants failed to spot the error. The court held that where an accountant has negligently prepared financial statements and a third party relies on them to his or her detriment, a duty of care in an action for negligent misstatement will arise in the following circumstances: The accountant knows that it will be shown to a member of a limited class of which the plaintiff is a member and which the accountant actually knows will use and rely on the statements; the statements have been prepared primarily for guidance of that limited class and in respect of a specific class of transactions for the very purpose for which the plaintiff did in fact rely on them; the fact that the accountant did not know the identity of the plaintiff is not material as long as the accountant was aware that the person for whose immediate benefit they were prepared intended to supply the statements to members of the very limited class of which the plaintiff is a member.

Credit Alliance Corp. v. Arthur Andersen & Co. 493 N.Y.S. 2d 435 (1985)

The contractual privity requirement in *Ultramares* was broadened somewhat by the same New York Court of Appeals, but has not approached in scope the stakeholder foreseeability test of *Haig* in Canada and *Caparo* in England. The court held that in order for a relationship to approach that of privity the auditor must have been aware that the financial statement would be used for a particular purpose by a party known to the auditor and the auditor must have had subjective knowledge that the third party had intended to rely upon the statement. Also, evidence, such as the auditor's conduct, must be presented demonstrating the above requirements and the third-party plaintiff carries this burden.

Caparo Industries plc. v. Pickman et al. [1991] 2 W.L.R. 358 (H.L.)

Caparo, in its takeover of Fidelity plc, had Touche Ross & Co. audit the financial statements of Fidelity. Caparo later alleged that its purchase of shares and subsequent takeover were made in reliance on the accounts which they claimed were misleading and inaccurate in that they showed a pre-tax profit of £1.3 million instead of a loss of £400,000. Caparo sued Touche Ross for negligence, maintaining that Touche Ross owed them a duty of care as shareholders and potential investors with respect to the audit and certification of the accounts.

The House of Lords decided that Touche Ross owed no duty of care to Caparo either as a potential investor before it was registered or as a shareholder thereafter for the following reasons:

> While there is no general principle that will determine the existence and scope of a duty of care in all cases, in order for a duty of care to arise, there must be: the harm said to result from the breach of duty must have been reasonably foreseeable; there must be a relationship of sufficient "proximity" between the party said to owe the duty and the party to whom it is said to be owed; and the situation must be one in which, on policy grounds, the court considers it fair, just and reasonable that the law should impose a duty of a given scope on the part of one party for the benefit of the other.

In the case of negligent misstatements made by such a professional adviser as an accountant, a relationship of proximity sufficient to give rise to a duty of care typically arises where the advice is required for a purpose which is made known to the adviser when the advice was given; the adviser knows that his or her advice will be communicated to the advisee, either specifically or as a member of an ascertainable class in order that it should be used by the advisee for that purpose; it is known that advice so communicated is likely to be acted upon for that purpose without independent inquiry; and it is so acted upon by the advisee to his or her detriment.

The duty extends only to the particular transaction for which the accountants knew their accounts were to be used. Moreover, the advisee must reasonably suppose that he or she was entitled to rely on the advice or information communicated for the very purpose for which it was required. No duty arises with respect to statements put into general circulation and relied on by strangers to the maker of the statement for a purpose which the maker had no reason to anticipate, such as a nonshareholder contemplating investment in a company.

SOURCE: Based in part on an earlier version by L.J. Brooks and R. LeBlanc.

Significant Ethics Issues Facing Business and the Accounting Profession

Chapter 5   Approaches to Ethical Decision Making
Chapter 6   Managing Ethics Risks and Opportunities

Introduction

Part III explores how directors, executives, and accountants should approach specific decisions and the ethical management of key aspects of a corporation's activities within the frameworks for ethical awareness, accountability, and governance developed in Parts I and II.

Chapter 5 provides practical approaches to making ethical decisions. Frequently, an employee or professional cannot discern precisely what action to take from a code or cannot consult a colleague, and must decide for him or herself what to do. The approaches discussed will facilitate the development of both a defensible decision and an improved, proposed action. Both outcomes are likely to be of increasing value in the future.

Chapter 6 develops an understanding of several key ethics opportunities and risks facing corporations and a set of tools to deal effectively with them. Topics covered include:

- Ethics risk management
- Ethics strategies and tactics for effective stakeholder relations
- Workplace ethics
- International operations
- Corporate social responsibility/accountability and audit
- Crisis management

Chapter Five

Approaches to Ethical Decision Making

Purpose of the Chapter

When a businessperson or professional accountant faces an ethical problem, the first recourse for guidance should be to corporate and professional codes of conduct. These often do not apply specifically to the problem faced and require interpretation to fit the circumstances. When this is required, the decision maker should be able to use the principles, approaches, and frameworks discussed in this chapter to make defensible ethical decisions.

Introduction

When the broad principles or specific rules embodied in codes of conduct do not specifically apply to the particular problem a professional accountant is facing, the decision maker can be guided by general ethical principles to arrive at a defensible ethical decision. What are these general ethical principles and how should they be applied? This chapter explores these ethical principles within a framework involving how the proposed action would impact upon the stakeholders to the decision. This framework is generally known as *stakeholder impact analysis*.

Stakeholder Impact Analysis

OVERVIEW

Since John Stuart Mill coined the concept of *utilitarianism* in 1861, an accepted approach to the assessment of a decision and the resulting action has been to evaluate the end results of the action. To most businesspeople, this evaluation has traditionally been based on the decision's impact on the interests of the company's owners or shareholders. Usually these impacts have been measured in terms of the profit or loss involved, because profit has been the measure of well-offness that shareholders have wanted to maximize.

This traditional view of corporate accountability has recently been modified in two ways. First, the assumption that *all* shareholders want to maximize *only* short-term profit appears to represent too narrow a focus. Second, the rights and claims of many nonshareholder groups such as employees, consumers/clients, suppliers, lenders, environmentalists, host communities, and governments who have a stake or interest in the outcome of the decision, or in the company itself, are being accorded status in corporate decision making. Modern corporations are now accountable to shareholders and to nonshareholder groups, both of which form the set of *stakeholders* to which a company responds (see Figure 5.1). It has become evident that a company cannot reach its full potential, and may even perish, if it loses the support of one of a select set of its stakeholders known as *primary stakeholders*. These ideas on stakeholders and their emerging role are fully developed in Chapter 1.

FIGURE 5.1

MAP OF CORPORATE
STAKEHOLDER ACCOUNTABILITY

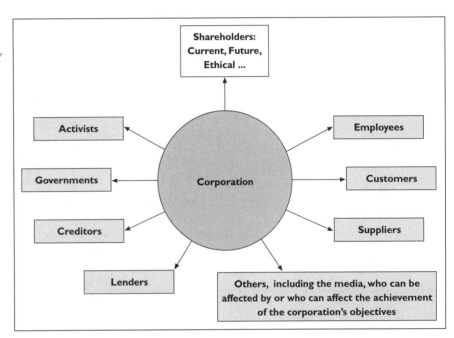

The assumption of a monolithic shareholder group interested only in short-term profit is undergoing modification because modern corporations are finding their shareholders are also made up of persons and institutional investors who are interested in longer-term time horizons and in how ethically business is conducted. The latter, who are referred to as *ethical investors*, apply two screens to investments: do the investee companies make a profit in excess of appropriate hurdle rates, and do they earn that profit in an ethical manner? Because of the size of the shareholdings of the mutual and pension funds, and other institutional investors involved, corporate directors and executives have found that the wishes of this group can be ignored only at their peril. Ethical investors have developed informal and formal networks through which they inform themselves about corporate activity, decide how to vote proxies, and decide how to approach boards of directors to get them to pay attention to their concerns in such areas as environmental protection, excessive executive compensation, and human rights activities in specific countries such as South Africa.

Ethical and many other investors, as well as stakeholder groups, tend to be unwilling to squeeze the last ounce of profit out of the current year if it means damaging the environment or the rights of other stakeholders. They believe in managing the corporation on a broader basis than short-term profit. *Usually, the maximization of profit in a longer than one-year time frame requires harmonious relationships with most stakeholder groups and their interests.* A negative public relations experience can be a significant and embarrassing price to pay for a decision-making process that fails to take the wishes of stakeholder groups into account. Whether or not special interest groups are also shareholders, their capacity to make corporations accountable through the media is evident and growing. The farsighted executive and director will want these concerns taken into account before offended stakeholders have to remind them. *Corporations are finding that in the past they have been legally and practically accountable to shareholders, but they are also becoming increasingly accountable to stakeholders.*

FUNDAMENTAL INTERESTS OF STAKEHOLDERS

The multiplicity of stakeholders and stakeholder groups makes it desirable to identify a set of commonly held interests to be used to focus analyses and decision making on ethical dimensions. Fortunately, decision makers can consolidate the interests of stakeholder groups into the following three commonly held, or fundamental, interests:

1. Their interest(s) should be better off as a result of the decision.
2. The decision should result in a fair distribution of benefits and burdens.
3. The decision should not offend any rights of any stakeholder, including the decision maker.

To some extent, these fundamental interests have to be tempered by the realities facing decision makers. For example, although a proposed decision should maximize the betterment of all stakeholders, trade-offs often have to be made between stakeholders' interests. Consequently, the incurrence of pollution control costs may be counter to the interests of short-term profits that are of interest to some current shareholders and managers. Similarly, there are times when all stakeholders will find a decision acceptable even though one or more of them, or the groups they represent, may be worse off as a result. In recognition of the requirement for trade-offs and for the understanding that a decision can advance the well-offness of all stakeholders in aggregate, even if some individuals are personally worse off, this fundamental interest should be modified to focus on the *well-offness* of stakeholders rather than only on their betterment.

Once the betterment principle is relaxed to become the well-offness principle, the need to analyze the impact of a decision in terms of all three fundamental principles becomes apparent. It is possible, for example, to find that a proposed decision may produce an overall benefit, but the distribution of the burden of producing that decision may be so debilitating to the interests of one or more stakeholder groups that it may be considered grossly unfair. Alternatively, a decision may result in an overall net benefit and be fair, but may offend the rights of a stakeholder and therefore be considered not right. For example, deciding not to recall a marginally flawed product may be cost effective, but it would not be considered "right" if users could be seriously injured. Consequently, *a proposed decision can be declared unethical if it fails to provide a net benefit, is unfair, or offends the rights of a stakeholder* (see Table 5.1). Testing a proposed decision against only one principle is definitely shortsighted, and usually results in a faulty diagnosis.

TABLE 5.1

FUNDAMENTAL INTERESTS OF
STAKEHOLDERS

Well-offness	The proposed decision should result in more benefits than costs.
Fairness	The distribution of benefits and burdens should be fair.
Right	The proposed decision should not offend the rights of the stakeholders and the decision maker.

All three interests must be satisfied for a decision to be considered ethical.

Measurement of Quantifiable Impacts

PROFIT

Profit is fundamental to the interests of shareholders and is essential to the survival and health of our corporations. In inflationary times, profit is essential simply to replace inventory at the higher prices required. Fortunately, the measurement of profit is well developed and needs few comments about its use in ethical decision making. It is true, however, that profit is a short-term measure, and that several important impacts are not captured in the determination of profit. Both of these conditions can be rectified in the following sections.

ITEMS NOT INCLUDED IN PROFIT: MEASURABLE DIRECTLY

There are impacts of corporate decisions and activities that are not included in the determination of the profit of the company that caused the impact. For example, when a company pollutes, the cost of cleanup is usually absorbed by individuals, companies, or municipalities that are downstream or downwind. These costs are referred to as *externalities*, and their impact can often be measured directly by the costs of cleanup incurred by others.

In order to see a complete picture of the impacts of a decision, the profit or loss from a transaction should be modified by the externalities it creates. Frequently, corporations that ignore their externalities over time will find that they have underestimated the true cost of the decision when fines and cleanup costs are incurred, or bad publicity emerges.

ITEMS NOT INCLUDED IN PROFIT: NOT MEASURABLE DIRECTLY

Other externalities exist where the cost is included in the determination of the company's profit, but where the benefit is enjoyed by persons outside of the company. A donation or scholarship are examples of this kind of externality; obviously it would be attractive to include an estimate of the benefits involved in the overall evaluation of the proposed decision. The problem is that neither the benefit nor the cost of some negative impacts, such as the loss of health suffered by persons absorbing pollution, can be measured directly, but they should be included in an overall assessment.

Although it is impossible to measure these externalities directly, it is possible to measure these impacts indirectly through the use of *surrogates* or mirror image alternatives. In the case of the scholarship, a surrogate for the benefit could be the increase in earnings gained by the recipient. The value of the loss of health could be estimated as the income lost plus the cost of medical treatment plus the loss of productivity in the workplace involved as measured by the cost of fill-in workers.

The accuracy of these estimates will depend on the closeness of the mirror-image measure. It is likely, however, that the estimates arrived at will understate the impact involved; in the previous example, no estimate was made for the intellectual gain of the education permitted by the scholarship or the pain and suffering involved as a result of the loss of health. Nevertheless, it is far better to make use of estimates that are generally accurate, rather than make decisions on the basis of direct measures that measure precisely only a fraction of the impact of a proposed decision.

The measurement and use of surrogates to estimate external impacts of corporate decisions is discussed further in the article by Brooks (1979), which appears as a reading a the end of this chapter.

BRINGING THE FUTURE TO THE PRESENT

The technique for bringing future impacts of a decision into an analysis is not difficult. It is handled in a parallel manner to capital budgeting analysis, where future values are discounted at an interest rate that reflects the expected interest rates in future years. This approach is demonstrated as part of *cost-benefit analysis* (CBA) in Brooks (1979). Using the net present value approach of capital budgeting analysis, the benefits and costs of a proposed action can be assessed as follows:

$$\text{Net Present Value of Proposed Action} = \text{Present Value of Benefits} - \text{Present Value of Costs}$$

where benefits include revenues and good externalities, and costs include costs plus bad externalities.

Frequently, executives who have learned the hard way to keep their focus on short-term profit will reject the idea of including externalities in their analyses. However, *what is being advocated here is not that they abandon short-term profit as a yardstick, but that they also consider impacts that are now externalities which have an excellent chance of affecting the company's bottom line in the future.* It is likely, for example, that pollution costs will be turned into fines and/or cleanup will be required. Moreover, the advantages bestowed through donations will strengthen society and allow the corporation to reach its full potential in the future. What cost-benefit analysis allows a decision maker to do is to bring these future benefits and costs into the present for a fuller analysis of a proposed decision. For example, Table 2 of the Cost-Benefit Analysis reading (Brooks, 1979) could be reformatted as Table 5.2 to give the decision maker a clearer view of present and possible future impacts on profit.

DEALING WITH UNCERTAIN OUTCOMES

Just as in capital budgeting analysis, there are estimates that are uncertain. However, a full range of techniques has been developed to factor this uncertainty into the analysis of proposed decisions. For example, the analysis can be based upon best estimates, on three possibilities (most optimistic, pessimistic, and best estimate), on expected values developed from a computer simulation.

TABLE 5.2

COST-BENEFIT ANALYSIS: SHORT- AND LONG-TERM PROFIT IMPACT

	POLLUTION CONTROL EQUIPMENT IMPACT ON PROFIT			UNIVERSITY ADMISSION SCHOLARSHIPS IMPACT ON PROFIT		
	Short-Term	Long-Term	Total	Short-Term	Long-Term	Total
Benefits (Present valued at 10 percent)						
Reduction in worker health costs		$500,000	$500,000			
Increase in worker productivity	$200,000		$200,000			
Improvement in level of earnings of scholarship recipients					$600,000	$600,000
Total benefits	$200,000	$500,000	$700,000		$600,000	$600,000
Costs (Present valued at 10 percent)						
Pollution equipment	$350,000		$350,000			
Scholarships paid				$400,000		$400,000
Total costs	$350,000		$350,000	$400,000		$400,000
Net benefit (costs)	($150,000)	$500,000	$350,000	($400,000)	$600,000	$200,000

All of these are *expected values*, which are combinations of a value and a probability of its occurrence. This is normally expressed as follows:

$$\text{Expected Value of an Outcome} = \text{Value of the Outcome} \times \text{Probability of the Outcome Occurring}$$

The advantage of this expected value formulation is that the cost-benefit analysis framework can be modified to include the risk associated with outcomes to be included. This new approach is referred to as *risk-benefit analysis* (RBA), and can be applied where risky outcomes are prevalent in the following framework:

$$\text{Risk-Adjusted or Expected Value of Net Benefits} = \text{Expected Present Value of Future Benefits} - \text{Expected Present Value of Future Costs}$$

IDENTIFYING STAKEHOLDERS AND RANKING THEIR INTERESTS

The measurement of profit, augmented by externalities discounted to the present and factored by riskiness of outcome, is more useful in assessing proposed decisions than profit alone. However, the usefulness of a stakeholder impact analysis depends upon the full identification of all stakeholders and their interests, and on a full appreciation of the significance of the impacts on the position of each.

There are occasions, for instance, when the simple adding up of benefits and costs does not fully reflect the importance of a stakeholder or of the impact involved, such as when the capacity of a stakeholder to withstand the impact is low. For example, if stakeholders are poor, they will not be able to buy remedial treatment, or alternatively their reserves may be so low that other family members—perhaps children—will suffer. On the other hand, a scholarship to a poor recipient could create a benefit for that person and others of significantly greater impact than to a person who is well-off. In these situations, the values included in the CBA or RBA can be weighted, or the net present values created can be ranked according to the impact created on the stakeholders involved. The ranking of stakeholders and the impacts on them based on their situational capacity to withstand is also used when nonmeasurable impacts are being considered.

Relative financial strength does not provide the only rationale for ranking the interests of stakeholders. In fact, several more compelling reasons exist, including the impact of the proposed action on the life or health of a stakeholder, or on some aspect of our flora, fauna, or environment that is near a threshold of endangerment or extinction. Usually, the public takes a dim view of companies that put profits ahead of life, health, or the preservation of our habitat. In addition, making these issues a high priority will often trigger a rethinking of an offending action so as to improve it by removing its offensiveness.

The illustrative *Castle Manufacturing Inc.* case solution provided at the end of this chapter extends the concept of ranking stakeholders to correlate legal rights, financial and psychological capacity to withstand the impact, and the resulting probable public impact of the action. It is interesting that an item may not be "material" to a lay investor in an accounting sense, but may be quite significant to stakeholders. In the long run, such sensitivity to corporate decisions may redound on the shareholders through the bottom line. In time, the *accounting concept of materiality* as we know it may be inadequate and may need to be expanded.

Two approaches may prove useful in identifying and understanding stakeholder groups and their interactions. In a recent study, Mitchell, Agle, and Wood (1997) suggest that stakeholders and their interests be evaluated on three dimensions: *legitimacy,* or the right (legal or perceived) to influence the organization; *power* to influence the organization through the media, government, or other means; and perceived and real *urgency* of the issues arising. Such an analysis forces the consideration of impacts thought to be very damaging (particularly to external stakeholders) to the fore, so that if an executive decides to go ahead with a suboptimal plan at least the potential downside will be known. The three set of claims are identified in Figure 5.2.

Logic suggests that claims where the three circles overlap in Figure 5.2 (i.e., legitimate and/or viewed as legitimate, urgent, and are held by the powerful)

FIGURE 5.2

STAKEHOLDER IDENTIFICATION AND INTERESTS

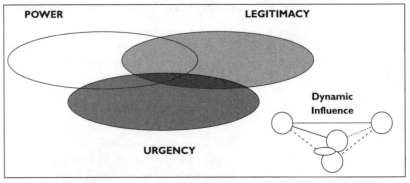

SOURCE: Mitchell, Agle, and Wood, 1997; Rowley, 1997.

will always be the most important. However, this is not necessarily the case. Other urgent stakeholder claims can become the most important if they garner more support of the powerful and those with legitimate claims, and are ultimately seen to have legitimacy.

Many executives forget that an organization's stakeholders change over time, as does the power they wield depending on the urgency they feel about issues brought to their attention. In real life, stakeholders without legitimacy or power will try to influence those with clout, and they succeed. Another researcher, Tim Rowley (1997), has suggested that a set of stakeholders be considered as a *dynamic network*, and that projections be made about who in the network will influence who so as to forecast which issues and interests will become more important. These concepts are developed in the illustrative case *Bribery or Opportunity in China,* located at the end of the chapter.

SUMMARY

The previously discussed approaches to the measurement of impacts of proposed decisions are summarized in Table 5.3.

TABLE 5.3

APPROACHES TO
THE MEASUREMENT OF
QUANTIFIABLE IMPACTS
OF PROPOSED DECISIONS*

A.	Profit or loss only
B.	A. plus externalities (i.e., Cost-Benefit Analysis/CBA)
C.	B. plus probabilities of outcomes (i.e., Risk-Benefit Analysis/RBA)
D.	CBA or RBA plus ranking of stakeholders

*Optimal decisions usually result from the most thorough approach.

Assessment of Nonquantifiable Impacts of Proposed Decisions

FAIRNESS AMONG STAKEHOLDERS

Although the expectation of fair treatment is a right that individuals and groups can properly expect to receive, it is treated here on its own because of its importance to ethical decision making. The concern for fair treatment has been evident in society's recent preoccupation with such issues as discrimination against women and others matters of hiring, promotion, and pay. Consequently, a decision will be considered unethical unless it is seen to be fair to all stakeholders.

Fairness is not an absolute concept. It is evidenced by a relatively even distribution of the benefits and burdens springing from a decision. For example, it is possible that a decision to increase taxes may weigh more heavily on high income earners, but be seen as relatively fair in terms of their capacity to pay those taxes. Reasonability and perspective are required to judge fairness accurately.

RIGHTS OF STAKEHOLDERS

A decision will be considered ethical only if its impacts do not offend the rights of the stakeholders impacted upon, and the rights of the person(s) making the decision. This latter point can be seen in the case of a decision being made by executives who subscribe to values that cause them to be offended by child labor or by low standards of worker safety in third world countries. The executives making the decision are stakeholders to it in their own right.

An individual stakeholder or a stakeholder group in North America may generally expect to enjoy the rights listed in Table 5.4. Some of these rights have been accorded protection under laws and legal regulations, while others are enforced through common law or through public sanction of offenders. For example, employees and consumers are protected under statute for health and safety, whereas dignity and privacy tend to be subject to common law, and the exercise of conscience is subject to public sanction.

TABLE 5.4

STAKEHOLDER RIGHTS

Life
Health and safety
Fair treatment
Exercise of conscience
Dignity and privacy
Freedom of speech

In many cases, even where protection is afforded through statute, considerable judgment is required to know when an individual's rights are being violated. Drug testing in the form of urinalysis, for example, appears to be warranted when the health of the worker and fellow workers is at stake, but the degree of jeopardy has to be severe. Pilots of airliners are considered worthy of urinalysis but, at the moment, drivers of transport trucks are not. There are many reasons for this, including the lack of accuracy and timeliness of the tests, and the stigma that attaches to a false accusation. However, it appears to be reasonable to test a truck driver's reflexes and hand-eye coordination using computer games just prior to his or her shift, so evidently the stigma of failing a computer game related closely to the task to be performed is acceptable in today's society. This complex interplay of statute, regulation, common law, and judgment based on values makes it advisable to give any apparent infringement of a stakeholder's rights careful scrutiny.

Comprehensive Decision-Making Approaches

5-QUESTION APPROACH

The 5-question approach, or 5-box approach as Graham Tucker has called it in a reading at the end of this chapter, involves the examination or challenge of a proposed decision through the five questions in Table 5.5. The proposed decision is to be challenged by asking all of the questions. If a negative response is forthcoming (or more than one) when all five questions are asked, the decision maker can attempt to revise the proposed action to remove the negative and/or offset it. If the revision process is successful, the proposal will be ethical. If not, the proposal should be abandoned as unethical. Even if no negative response is forthcoming when the questions are first asked, an effort should be made to improve the proposed action using the five questions as a guide.

TABLE 5.5

5-QUESTION APPROACH TO
ETHICAL DECISION MAKING

The following five questions are asked about a proposed decision:

IS THE DECISION	STAKEHOLDER INTEREST EXAMINED
1. profitable?	Shareholders'—usually short-term
2. legal?	Society at large—legally enforceable rights
3. fair?	Fairness for all
4. right?	Other rights of all
5. going to further sustainable development?	Specific rights

Question 5 is an optional question designed to focus the decision-making process on a particular issue of relevance to the organization(s) or decision maker involved.

The order of asking the questions is not important, but all of the first four questions must be asked to ensure that the decision maker is not overlooking an important area of impact. Some ethical problems are not as susceptible to examination by the 5-question approach as to the other approaches described in the following sections. For instance, the first question focuses on profit, which is a substantially less comprehensive measurement tool than cost-benefit analysis or risk-benefit analysis, with or without the ranking of stakeholders depending on their ability to withstand the impact of the decision. As it stands, however, the 5-question framework is a useful approach to the orderly consideration of problems without many externalities and where a specific focus is desired by the decision-process designer. For an expanded treatment of this approach, refer to the reading at the end of the chapter by Graham Tucker (1990).

MORAL STANDARDS APPROACH

The moral standards approach to stakeholder impact analysis builds directly on the three fundamental principles of stakeholders that are identified in Table 5.1. It is somewhat more general in focus than the 5-question approach, and leads the decision maker to a more broadly based analysis of net benefit rather than just profitability as a first challenge of proposed decisions. As a result, it offers a framework that is more suited to the consideration of decisions that have significant impacts outside the corporation than the 5-question framework.

The three standards making up the moral standards approach are listed in Table 5.6. Questions that sprang from each standard and that ought to be applied to each decision are also offered.

As shown in Table 5.6 on page 320, the satisfaction of the utilitarian principle is examined through a question that focuses on cost-benefit analysis or risk-benefit analysis rather than just profit. Consequently, the full range of options discussed in Table 5.3 can be employed as befits the need.

In addition, as explained in Velasquez (1992), the examination of how the proposed decision respects individual rights looks at the impact of the decision on each stakeholder's rights as noted in Table 5.4, as well as at the process involved. For example, has deception or manipulation been used, or some type

TABLE 5.6

MORAL STANDARDS APPROACH
TO ETHICAL DECISION MAKING*

MORAL STANDARD	QUESTION OF PROPOSED DECISION
Utilitarian:	
Maximize net benefit to society as a whole	Does the action maximize social benefits and minimize social injuries?
Individual rights:	
Respect and protect	Is the action consistent with each person's rights?
Justice:	
Fair distribution of benefits and burdens	Will the action lead to a just distribution of benefits and burdens?

*All three moral standards must be applied; none is a sufficient test by itself.

of force such as coercion, or has there been some other limit placed on information made available to the individuals impacted upon or upon their freedom to chose a response or limit their redress? If so, their rights have not been respected. One of the interesting questions raised in this connection is whether notification of the intent to undertake an action implies the consent of those individuals impacted upon. Usually, notification does not imply consent unless the notification provides full information, allows time for consideration, and reasonable options are at hand to avoid the impact.

The question focusing on distributive justice, or fairness, is handled in the same way as in the 5-question approach. For a full treatment of the moral standards approach, refer to *Business Ethics: Concepts and Cases* by Manuel G. Velasquez (1992).

PASTIN'S APPROACH

In his book *The Hard Problems of Management: Gaining the Ethical Edge,* Mark Pastin (1986) presents his ideas on the appropriate approach to ethical analysis, which involves examining the four key aspects of ethics noted in Table 5.7.

TABLE 5.7

PASTIN'S APPROACH TO
STAKEHOLDER IMPACT
ANALYSIS

KEY ASPECT	PURPOSE FOR EXAMINATION
Ground rule ethics	To illuminate an organization's and/or an individual's rules and values
End-point ethics	To determine the greatest net good for all concerned
Rule ethics	To determine what boundaries a person or organization should take into account according to ethical principles
Social contract ethics	To determine how to move the boundaries to remove concerns or conflicts

Pastin uses the concept of *ground rule ethics* to capture the idea that individuals and organizations have ground rules or fundamental values that govern their behavior or their desired behavior. If a decision is seen to offend these values, it is likely that disenchantment or retaliation will occur. Unfortunately, this could lead to the dismissal of an employee who acts without a good understanding of the ethical ground rules of the employer organization involved. In order to understand the prevailing ground rules, to correctly gauge the organization's commitment to proposals, and to protect the decision maker, Pastin suggests that an examination of past decisions or actions be made. He calls this approach *reverse engineering* a decision, because an attempt is made to take past decisions apart to see how and why they were made. Pastin suggests that individuals are often guarded (voluntarily or involuntarily) about expressing their values, and that reverse engineering offers a way to see, through past actions, what their values are.

In his concept of *end-point ethics,* Pastin suggests employing the full extent of the treatments summarized in Table 5.3. The application of these techniques to the Ford Pinto case (which appears at the end of this chapter) should illuminate the concept of utilitarianism, and illustrate the pitfalls of focusing an analysis on only short-term profit.

The concept of *rule ethics* is used to indicate the value of rules that spring from the application of valid ethical principles to an ethical dilemma. In this case, the valid ethical principles involve the respect for and protection of the rights of individuals as discussed in Table 5.4, and derivative principles such as the golden rule of "Do unto others as you would have them do to you." The establishment of rules based on respect for individual rights can prove helpful when an interpretation is particularly difficult, or when senior executives want to remove ambiguity about what they believe should be done in certain situations. For example, Pastin suggests that rules, formulated by senior executives to assist their employees, can divide possible actions into those that are obligatory, prohibited, or permissible. Similarly, rules can be crafted so as to make them categorical (i.e., no exceptions allowed) or prima facie (exceptions are allowed in certain circumstances), or to trigger consultation with senior executives. As such, rule ethics represent Pastin's examination of the impact of proposed decisions on the rights of the individuals involved.

The concept of fairness is incorporated by Pastin into his idea of *social contract ethics.* Here he suggests that formulating the proposed decision into an imaginary contract would be helpful because it would allow the decision maker to change places with the stakeholder to be impacted upon. As a result, the decision maker could see if the impact was fair enough to freely enter into the contract. If the decision maker found that he or she were not prepared to enter into the contract with the roles reversed, then the terms (or boundaries) of the contract should be changed in the interests of fairness. This technique of role reversal can prove to be quite helpful, particularly in the case of strong-willed executives who are often surrounded by "yes" men or women. In the case of a real contract, this approach can be useful in projecting how proposed actions will affect the contract, or whether a contract change (such as in a union contract) will be resisted.

EXTENDING AND BLENDING THE APPROACHES

From time to time, an ethical problem will arise that doesn't fit perfectly into one of the approaches described. For instance, a problem may fit the 5-question approach, except that there are significant long-term impacts or externalities that call for cost-benefit analysis rather than profitability as a first-level question. Fortunately, cost-benefit analysis can be substituted or added to the approach to enrich it. Similarly, the concept of ground rule ethics can be grafted onto a non-Pastin approach, if needed in a decision that deals with an in-company setting. Care should be taken when extending and blending the approaches, however, to ensure that each of the areas of well-offness, fairness, and impact on individual rights are examined in a comprehensive analysis, otherwise the final decision may be faulty.

Commons Problems

The term *commons problem* refers to the inadvertent or knowing overuse of jointly owned assets or resources. The concept first arose when villagers in old England overgrazed their livestock on land that was owned in common, or jointly with everyone else in the village, and the term *commons* was used to identify this type of pasture.

The problem of overgrazing could not be stopped because everyone had a right to use the pasture and thus could not be prevented from doing so. Only when the majority of villagers agreed to regulate the commons did the overgrazing stop. Sometimes, when they could not agree, outside authority was called upon to settle the matter. Outdated though these issues seem, the problem of the commons is still with us in modern times. For example, pollution represents the misuse of the environment, a commons we all share. Similarly, if everyone in a business attempts to draw on capital funds, an expense budget, or a service department, the result will be akin to overgrazing.

The lesson to be learned from this is that frequently the decision maker, who is not sensitized to the problem of the commons, will not attribute a high enough value to the use of an asset or resource and therefore will make the wrong decision. Awareness of the problem should correct this and improve decision making. If executives are confronted by the overuse of an asset or resource, they would do well to employ the solutions applied in olden times.

Developing a More Ethical Action

One of the advantages of using a framework such as the 5-question, moral standards, Pastin's, or commons approaches is that the unethical aspects of a decision can be identified and then be modified in order to make the overall impact of the decision acceptable. For example, if a decision is expected to be unfair to a particular stakeholder group, perhaps the decision can be altered by increasing the compensation to that group, or by eliminating or replacing the offending words, image, or specific action. At the end of every application of stakeholder impact analysis there should be a specific search for a win-win outcome.

Experience has shown that there are several pitfalls that unaware decision makers fall into repeatedly. These include:

- *Focusing on short-term profit and shareholder-only impacts.* Often, the most significant impacts (for nonshareholder stakeholders) of a proposed action are those that surface in the future and those that befall nonshareholder stakeholders first. Only after these groups react do shareholders bear the cost for misdeeds. The remedy for this myopia is to ensure an adequate time horizon for the analysis, and to take into account externalities on a cost-benefit basis even though the impact measured is felt initially by a nonshareholder group.

- *Focusing only on legalities.* Many managers are concerned only with whether an action is legal. They argue, "If it's legal, it's ethical." Unfortunately, many find their corporation unnecessarily subject to consumer boycotts, employee slowdowns, increasing government regulation to cover loopholes, and fines. Some don't care because they are intending to stay at this corporation only for a short while. The fact is that laws and regulations lag behind what society wants, but reaction does come and sometimes well before new laws are promulgated. One reason is that corporations lobby against such rule changes. Just because a proposed action is legal does not make it ethical.

- *Limits to fairness.* Sometimes decision makers want to be fair only to groups they like. Unfortunately for them, they do not have the ability to control public opinion and usually end up paying for their oversight. Many executives have been put off by activist organizations such as Greenpeace, but have learned that environmental issues are ignored at their peril. A full review of fairness to all stakeholders is the only way to ensure an ethical decision.

- *Limits to rights canvassed.* Bias is not restricted to fairness. Decision makers should canvass the impact on all rights for all stakeholder groups. Also, decision makers should be encouraged to take their own values into account when making a decision. Courts in North America no longer react favorably to the defense that, "I was ordered to do it by my boss." Employees are expected to use their own judgment, and many jurisdictions have set up protective whistle-blowing and "right to refuse" statutes to encourage employees to do so. Often, managers that force unfortunate actions on subordinates are not speaking in the best interests of shareholders.

- *Conflicts of interest.* Bias based on prejudice is not the only reason for faulty assessments of proposed actions. Judgment can be clouded by conflicting interests—the decision maker's personal interest versus the corporation's best interest, or the interests of a group the decision maker is partial to versus the corporation's best interest can both account for erroneous assessments and decisions.

- *Interconnectedness of stakeholders.* Often decision makers fail to anticipate that what they do to one group will redound to trigger action by another. For example, despoiling the environment in a far-off country can cause negative reactions by domestic customers and capital markets.

- *Failure to identify all stakeholder groups.* The need to identify all stakeholder groups and interests before assessing the impacts on each is self-evident. However, this is a step that is repeatedly taken for granted, with the result that important issues go unnoticed. A useful approach to assist with this problem is to speculate on the downside that might happen from the proposed action, and try to assess how the media will react. This often leads to the identification of the most vulnerable stakeholder groups.

- *Failure to rank the specific interests of stakeholders.* The common tendency is to treat all stakeholder interests as equal in importance. However, those that are urgent usually become the most important. Ignoring this is truly shortsighted, and may result in a suboptimal and unethical decision.

- *Leaving out well-offness, fairness, or rights.* As previously pointed out, a comprehensive ethical decision cannot be made if one of these three aspects is overlooked. Repeatedly, however, decision makers short-circuit their assessments and suffer the consequences.

Summary of Steps for an Ethical Decision

The approaches and issues previously discussed can be used independently or in combination to assist in producing an ethical decision. Experience has shown that completing the following steps provides a sound basis for challenging a proposed decision.

1. Identify all stakeholder groups and interests.
2. Rank the stakeholders and their interests, identifying the most important and weighting them more than other issues in the analysis.
3. Assess the impact of the proposed action on each stakeholder group's interests with regard to their well-offness, fairness of treatment, and impact on other rights using a comprehensive framework of questions and making sure that the common pitfalls previously discussed do not enter into the analysis.

It may be helpful to organize the ethical decision analysis using the steps outlined by the American Accounting Association (1993) as follows:

1. Determine the facts—what, who, where, when, and how.
2. Define the ethical issue(s).
3. Identify major principles, rules, and values.
4. Specify the alternatives.
5. Compare values and alternatives, and see if a clear decision emerges.
6. Assess the consequences.
7. Make your decision.

Conclusion

Stakeholder impact analysis offers a formal way of bringing into a decision the needs of an organization and its individual constituents (society). Trade-offs are difficult and can benefit from such advances in technique. It is important not to lose sight of the fact that the concepts of stakeholder impact analysis that are reviewed in this chapter need to be applied not as single techniques but together as a set. Only then will a comprehensive analysis be achieved and an ethical decision made. Depending on the nature of the decision to be faced, and the range of stakeholders to be affected, a proper analysis could be based on one of the 5-question, moral standards, or Pastin's approaches, taking into account the possible existence of commons problems that might arise.

A professional accountant can use stakeholder analysis in making decisions about accounting, auditing, and practice matters, and should be ready to prepare or assist in such analyses for employers or clients just as is currently the case in other areas. While many hard-numbers-oriented executives and accountants will be wary of becoming involved with the "soft" subjective analysis that typifies stakeholder analysis, they should bear in mind that the world is changing and placing a much higher value on nonnumerical information. They should be wary of placing too much weight on numerical analysis lest they fall into the trap of the economist, who, as Oscar Wilde put it: "knew the price of everything and the value of nothing."

The assessment of stakeholder impacts when combined with the ranking of each stakeholder's ability to withstand the action represents a helpful expansion of the accounting concept of materiality that has guided financial disclosure. As expanded, the "stakeholder significance/materiality" concept could assist in making decisions by projecting their ultimate impact on the company.

Illustrative Applications of Stakeholder Impact Analysis

In order to illustrate and consolidate the techniques of analysis developed in this chapter, two brief cases are described and an approach to a solution offered for each. *Bribery or Opportunity in China* is a real-life example of how a young executive faced the realities of business abroad, and how he came to an innovation solution. *Proposed Audit Adjustment Case* describes the thinking involved in proposing an adjustment to year-end audited financial statements. Both provide useful illustrations of the types of stakeholder impact analysis covered in this chapter.

A further illustrative application is provided to indicate how the fundamental interests of stakeholders described in Table 5.1 ought to generate issues to be considered in a stakeholder impact analysis on the topic of accounting choices, and specifically *When Does An "Aggressive Accounting" Choice Become Fraudulent?*

QUESTIONS FOR DISCUSSION

1. Is it wise for a decision maker to take into account more than profit when making decisions that have a significant social impact? Why?

2. If a framework for ethical decision making is to be employed, why is it essential to incorporate all three considerations of well-offness, fairness, and individual rights?

3. Is the 5-question approach to ethical decision making superior to the moral standards or Pastin's approach?

4. Under what circumstances would it be best to use each of the following frameworks: 5-question, moral standards, and Pastin's approach?

5. How would you convince a CEO not to treat the environment as a cost-free commons?

6. How can a decision to downsize be made as ethical as possible by treating everyone equally?

CASES

■ *Smokers are Good for the Economy — Really* presents an argument that is counter-intuitive in that cigarette smoking can be good. Does this actuarial/economics-based argument take into account all that a comprehensive ethical analysis should?

■ The *Ford Pinto* case is a classic that shows in stark relief the danger of ignoring the social impacts of a decision in favor of maximizing short-run profit. The original cost-benefit analysis was quite faulty, and our appreciation of safety has changed a lot since the Pinto was created, but the same problems continue to recur.

■ The *Kardell Paper Co.* involves the possible pollution of a river with potentially life-threatening consequences. In addition to dealing with uncertainty, the reader learns to appreciate issues such as whistle-blowing, representative corporate governance at the board level, and due diligence requirements on the part of executives and board members.

READINGS

The two readings by Brooks and Tucker that are provided in this chapter are intended to offer the reader further elaboration on cost-benefit analysis and the 5-question approach to ethical decision making.

REFERENCES

American Accounting Association, *Ethics in the Accounting Curriculum: Cases & Readings*, Sarasota, Florida, 1993, updated, see Introduction by William May.

Brooks, L. J., "Cost-Benefit Analysis," *CAmagazine*, October 1979, 53–57.

Mitchell, R. K., Agle, B. R., and Wood, D. J., "Toward a Theory of Stakeholder Identification and Salience: Defining the Principle of Who and What Really Counts," *Academy of Management Review*, Vol. 22, No. 4, 1997, 853–886.

Pastin, M., *The Hard Problems of Management: Gaining the Ethics Edge*, San Francisco, Jossey-Bass Inc., Publishers, 1986.

Rowley, T., "Moving Beyond Dyadic Ties: A Network Theory of Stakeholder Influences," *Academy of Management Review*, Vol. 22, No. 4, 1997, 887–910.

Tucker, G., "Ethical Analysis for Environmental Problem Solving," *Agenda for Action Conference Proceedings*, The Canadian Centre for Ethics & Corporate Policy 1990, 53–57.

Velasquez, M. G., *Business Ethics: Concepts and Cases*, Englewood Cliffs, NJ, Prentice-Hall, 1992.

Bribery or Opportunity in China Case
Note:Names have been changed

John Low, a North American born of Chinese descent, was given the opportunity of his lifetime. He was asked to go to China and set up a manufacturing subsidiary in a medium-sized city in the middle of the country. He had arrived in the city and had attempted to set up a new building and manufacturing facility which would employ thirty people but had run into many delays in dealings with the local authorities. Ultimately, John met with the three senior officials and asked what the problem was. They indicated that things would go a lot faster if John's company was to make them a payment of $100,000 each. This, they said, was quite reasonable in view of what other companies had been paying.

John was in a quandary. When he had been sent to China, his boss had told him that under no circumstances were any bribes to be paid. It was against company policy and it would not be tolerated. On the other hand, John was expected to get his job done, and his boss had told him that, unless he did so, another manager would be sent to take over John's position. John knew that his budget contained a provision for payments to agents, but the total allowed was only $150,000. He knew that if the facility was delayed, every month of delay would cost his company a contribution of approximately $25,000. John told the senior officials repeatedly that there was no way his company would pay them, but they were insistent.

Question

1. Should John pay the bribes? Is there something else he could do instead?

Illustrative Solution

The first step in a stakeholder impact analysis is to identify all stakeholder groups affected by the proposed action and their interests. At the end of the identification process, the stakeholders and their interests are to be ranked in importance. These two steps can be facilitated by means of a tabular analysis as follows:

—Continued

ANALYSIS OF STAKEHOLDERS AND THEIR INTERESTS

STAKEHOLDER	INTEREST	LEGITIMACY/ LEGAL INFLUENCE	POWER TO AFFECT COMPANY	URGENCY OF CLAIM	PRIMARY OR SECONDARY	RANK IN IMPORTANCE: I IS HIGHEST, 3 IS LOWEST
John	Potential success or dismissal, unless a new idea can be found. Probability of discovery estimated at 60 percent.	Yes	Yes	High	Primary	I
Local employees	Delay in job or no job.	No	Not yet	Low	Secondary for now	3
John's boss	John's success is his own, but he runs the risk of sanction if John is found to have bribed.	Yes	Yes	High, but less than John's	Primary	2

CONTINUED

Continued

ANALYSIS OF STAKEHOLDERS AND THEIR INTERESTS—*CONTINUED*

STAKEHOLDER	INTEREST	LEGITIMACY/ LEGAL INFLUENCE	POWER TO AFFECT COMPANY	URGENCY OF CLAIM	PRIMARY OR SECONDARY	RANK IN IMPORTANCE: 1 IS HIGHEST, 3 IS LOWEST
Other managers elsewhere	Company policy will be eroded, so observance will be difficult, since employees will know of breach.	Yes	Yes	Medium	Primary	2
Shareholders	Financial success earlier, but costs of bribes will raise costs, and will be called for in many situations. Possible fines and bad publicity if caught and Foreign Corrupt Practices Act or similar applies so profits down. Prob. 40 percent.	Yes	Yes	High	Primary	1
Chinese officials	$300,000 richer if not caught, then? Prob. 10 percent.	Yes	Yes	Medium/high	Primary	1
Directors and senior executives	Directors same as shareholders. Exec. no bonuses and could be dismissed.	Yes	Yes	High, but less than John's	Primary	1
Elderly Chinese in town (leaders in society)	No benefit until local employment starts, or other benefit created.	No	Yes, very influential	Low	Appears secondary, but could be primary	1
Chinese government	Bribes raise cost of doing business in China.	Yes	Yes, but distant	Low	Secondary for now	3
John's family	Unknown if he has any.					Not applic.

—*Continued*

Illustrative Applicaton of Stakeholder Impact Analysis

Continued

CHALLENGES TO PROPOSED ACTION: PAYMENT OF BRIBES

QUESTION OR CHALLENGE	RESPONSE
1. Is it profitable?	Maybe for company. $25K per month $\times$ 40 percent prob. of being caught less cost of fines and additional bribes elsewhere. For John, probably not, as prob. of being caught is 60 percent.
2. Is it legal?	Not really, but maybe if creative arrangement with an agent is successful and/or this is considered a facilitating payment, not a bribe.
3. Is it fair?	Not to John, or his boss, or top management, to China, or to elderly Chinese.
4. Is it right? generally? per company ground rules? per John?	Everyone is doing it, so maybe. Not per company ground rules and code. Not known what John's views are.
5. Does it provide the highest net benefit for all?	Maybe, unless a better idea is found—see below for an example of *moral imagination*.

In this situation, with the proposed action being to pay the bribes or not, there aren't many externalities, but there are legalities and company ground rules. Consequently, John could use a hybrid ethical decision framework based upon the 5-question, but with the use of net benefit in addition to profit and ground rule ethics. The questions or challenges for the proposed action are therefore as shown in the table above, with responses noted.

Based on this analysis, John found several responses that were negative or not clearly positive, yet he had to bribe or admit failure unless he could find an ethical alternative.

John began to consider the primary stakeholders to the company's long-run success in the area. He realized that the company's relationship with the Chinese elderly was going to be of high long-run significance because the elderly are very influential in Chinese culture. What could he do to satisfy the elderly and perhaps bring the local officials on-side as well? At the same time he did not want to offend his company's ground rules, which were to observe the code and not to bribe.

He had noticed that there wasn't really a good place of the elderly to gather, like his own parents had back home. In the end, he asked his boss if his company ever supported community centers, and the answer was yes. The company's donations budget would provide the funds and company officials were quite interested in paying for a senior citizens' center and park in the Chinese town as part of the company's good corporate citizen program of supporting the communities that they operated in. John proposed this to the senior Chinese officials who wanted the bribes, indicating that his company would not make such payments directly to anyone. The officials, however, would get credit by association with the park and center and would, of course, serve on the Board of Directors of the Center when it was finished.

John's plant was ready in record time, and he was awarded a citation by his company's CEO who was also the person in charge of the company's ethics program. It seemed apparent that he had found a solution that provided the highest net benefit to all—a true win-win-win arrangement.

Proposed Audit Adjustment Case—Castle Manufacturing Inc.

Larry Plant, the Chief Financial Officer of Castle Manufacturing Inc., was involved in a lengthy discussion with Joyce Tang of the company's auditing firm, Bennett & Sange, at the conclusion of the audit fieldwork.

"Look, Joyce, we just can't afford to show that much profit this year. If we do record the $1.5 million after-tax adjustment you proposed, our profit will be 20 percent higher than we had two years ago and 5 percent higher than we reported last year. On the other hand, without the adjustment, we would be close to last year's level. We are just about to enter negotiations with our labor unions, and we have been complaining about our ability to compete. If we show that much profit improvement, they

will ask for a huge raise in wages. Our company will become noncom-petitive due to higher labor rates than our offshore competition. Do you really want that to happen?"

"But, Larry, you really earned the profit. You can't just ignore it!"

"No, I'm not suggesting that, Joyce. But virtually all the goods making up the profit adjust-ment were in transit at our year end—so let's just record them as next year's sales and profits."

"But, Larry, they were all sold FOB at your plant, so title passed to the buyer when they were shipped."

"I know that, Joyce, but that was an unusual move by our overzealous sales staff, who were trying to look good and get a

high commission on year-end numbers. Anyway, the customer hadn't inspected them yet. Just this once, Joyce, let's put it into next year. It's not really a significant amount for our shareholders, but it will trigger a much bigger problem for them if the unions get hold of the higher profit numbers. As you know, about 40 percent of our shares were willed to the United Charities Appeal here in town, and they could sure benefit by higher profits and dividends in the future. I bet the difference in their dividends could be up to $400,000 per year over the life of the next five-year contract."

Question

1. What should Joyce do?

Illustrative Solution

Three approaches to ethical decision making are presented in Chapter 4: the 5-question approach, the moral standards approach, and Pastin's approach. In this illustrative solution, the 5-question framework will be used to start, with expansions, where necessary, drawn from the other approaches.

The 5-question approach calls for the identification of the stakeholders impacted on by the decision and then poses five questions or challenges to assess whether these impacts are

ethical or not. If some aspect of the decision is considered not to be ethical, the proposed decision/action may be altered to mitigate or remove the unethical element.

In this case, the auditor has recommended that a $1.5 million adjustment be made to increase the profitability of the client, Castle Manufacturing Inc. The CFO is resisting, proposing instead that the impact on profit be put into the next year so as to gain a bargaining advantage over the company's unions, who will use

the profit figures to negotiate a new five-year agreement. Joyce Tang, the auditor, must decide whether the proposal to shift the adjustment to the next year is ethical; if not, she must either convince the CFO to record the adjustment or qualify her audit report. It is not immediately apparent whether the adjust-ment is material or not; if it was, the correct action would be to qualify the audit report if the CFO were to hold fast to his proposal.

—Continued

Continued

IDENTIFICATION OF STAKEHOLDERS AND THEIR INTERESTS
THE CFO'S PROPOSAL WOULD IMPACT ON THE FOLLOWING STAKEHOLDERS:

STAKEHOLDERS	INTEREST
Directly Impacted:	
Current shareholders wishing to sell their shares in the short run.	They would want the adjustment recorded in the current year to boost profit and share values.
Current shareholders wishing to hold on to their shares.	They would want the adjustment deferred to minimize the labor settlement and maximize future profits and dividends.
Future shareholders.	They would want an accurate assessment of profitability to properly assess whether or not to buy into the company. If profits are depressed, they might not buy in, so the increased future profits may not be relevant.
Employees.	They would want profits accurately stated to provide a higher basis for negotiation, assuming this would not jeopardize the long-term viability of the enterprise.
Company management.	Depending on their bonus arrangements and their altruism, they would want short- or longer-term recognition of the adjustment
Directors.	They would want the long-run profit improvement, provided they would not be sued for sanctioning something illegal.
Creditors, suppliers, and lenders.	If the labor negotiations result in higher profitability and liquidity, these stakeholders would want the adjustment deferred.
Governments and regulators.	They would want profits accurately stated because this would result in higher taxes and fewer potential complaints from other stakeholders (e.g., unions).
Joyce Tang and her audit firm.	They would want to minimize the chance of legal and professional challenges arising from the audit that could result in fines and/or loss of reputation but also would wish to continue auditing a healthy client.
Indirectly Impacted:	
Recipients of the funds generated by the United Charities Appeal.	They would want the adjustment deferred.
Altruistic management of the United Charities Appeal.	They would want the adjustment properly dealt with, which would probably mean that they would side with the employees.
Host communities.	They would want the highest labor rate settlement possible without jeopardizing the long-term health of the enterprise.
The auditing profession.	It would want to avoid loss of reputation for the profession.

Ranking of Stakeholders' Interests

The stakeholder's interests in the decision identified can be ranked as to their importance on "possessing legal rights," "ability to withstand both financially and psychologically," (a rank of "1" is worst) and "probable public reaction on behalf of" scales, noted in table on the following page.

It is evident from these rankings that the strength of legal rights do not correspond to the rankings of the stakeholders' ability to withstand the decision or to the probable public reaction on behalf of each stakeholder if the decision to defer the adjustment becomes public. Moreover, the legal rights of stakeholders with differing interests are equal. The "probable public reaction"

—Continued

Continued

STAKEHOLDERS IMPACTED	POSSESS LEGAL RIGHTS	RANK OF ABILITY TO WITHSTAND	PROBABLE PUBLIC REACTION FOR
Current shareholders—wishing to sell	First (yes)	3	Low
Current shareholders—wishing to hold	Tie (yes)	3	Low
Future shareholders	Yes	3	Low
Employees—	None (no)	2	Strong
If contract is GAAP-based	Yes	2	Strong
If financial statement is used in negotiation	Yes (poss.)	2	Strong
Company management—dependent on contract	Yes or no	3	Low
Directors	Yes	2	Low
Creditors, suppliers	No	4	Low
Lenders—dependent on contract	No or yes	4	Low
Governments and regulators	Yes	4	Moderate
Joyce and her audit firm	Yes	2	Strong
Recipients of charity funds	No	1	Strong
Altruistic management of charity	No	3 or 2	Strong
Host communities	No	4	Moderate
Auditing profession	No	3	Strong

scale, which corresponds strongly to the "ability to withstand" scale, offers a good idea of how politicians, governments, and regulators will react. Consequently, decision makers would be unwise to focus only on the legality of stakeholders' positions.

Of course, the likelihood of the deferment becoming public has to be estimated. Unfortunately, most decision makers overlook the possibility of an altruistic or disgruntled whistle-blower making the disclosure public or, alternatively, revealing it to the union bargaining team. As a result, the valid probability of revelation is usually far higher than the decision maker's assessment.

Application of the 5-Question Approach

Question 1: Profitability
There is no doubt that the deferment of an upward adjustment of $1.5 million to profit will decrease profit this year and increase it the next. In addition, there is some possibility, if the decision doesn't become public or known to the union, that the company's profits over the life of the contract will rise substantially if the dividends will rise by $1 million per year ($400,000/40 percent). On the other hand, if the decision becomes known, the union may retaliate and bargain harder; lawsuits may be launched

against the company, the executives, and the auditors; and governments may levy tax penalties and fines. Consequently, the outcome on the profitability question is uncertain for the company and therefore for its shareholders and their dependents (and for the auditor, for that matter).

Question 2: Legality
Given that the decision to defer the adjustment is in the gray area of Generally Accepted Accounting Principles (GAAP) (it is not clearly material, nor is it contravening usual company practice, the customers have not inspected the goods as may be their custom, and it is

—Continued

Continued

a conservative treatment), it would probably be declared reasonable in a court of law. However, the legal process, which usually covers the company, its management and directors, and the auditor as being joint and severally liable, will involve legal fees, expert witness testimony, commitment of time (which soaks up billable time), and the potential of having to pursue other co-defendants for restitution if they are found to be culpable rather than the auditor. Of course, the auditor could mitigate these legal consequences by qualifying her report, but that would obviate the exercise and could create ill will with the CFO and possibly the rest of the management and directors. Because the legal interests do not coincide, and a lawsuit is likely if the deferment becomes known, the decision maker may not be able to take comfort from the fact that the deferment could be within the boundaries of GAAP and therefore legal.

Question 3: Fairness

Although the decision to defer the $1.5 million adjustment may not be considered material to an investor making the decision to invest or divest, it may be very significant to the employees and their union, and to the charity and its dependents. Consequently, not to disclose the $1.5 million this year may be unfair to these interest groups. If the decision becomes public, this unfair treatment may result in lawsuits and may bring the company, its auditors, and the auditing profession into disrepute with the public. The claim would be that these parties were not acting in the public interest, that the auditors failed to lend credibility to the financial statements and thereby failed to protect the public.

Question 4: Impact on rights

To the extent that a proposed decision impacts negatively on the rights of stakeholders, in terms of life, health, privacy, dignity, etc. (i.e., rights other than fairness and legal rights, which are canvassed in questions 2 and 3), the decision would be considered unethical. In this case, there are no lives at stake, but conceivably the health and well-being of the employees and particularly the ultimate recipients of the charity are at stake. The extent of this infringement would be revealed by further investigation. Given the information in the case, the degree of infringement on stakeholder rights is unclear.

Question 5: Does it contribute favorably to sustainable development and/or survivability?

From the environmental perspective, the deferment decision appears to have nothing to do with the company's impact on sustainable development. Also, there is probably no impact on the ability of the company to survive because the $1.5 million adjustment appears to be only 5 percent of the after-tax profit before the adjustment. However, it is unlikely that the deferment could be repeated year after year without offending GAAP.

Summary of Findings of the 5-Question Approach

This analysis has shown that the proposed deferment could be legal but may not be profitable, fair, or respectful of stakeholders' rights. Certainly the examination of just a one-year time frame would have proven to be misleading. Further analysis appears needed to reach a conclusive decision on many issues, and even then reflection will be needed to weigh the trade-offs between interests.

Extensions of the 5-Question Approach

As stated earlier, the stakeholder impact challenges inherent in the 5-question approach, the moral standards approach, and Pastin's approach can be grouped into three areas: well-offness, fairness, and rights.

On the dimension of well-offness, it is evident that looking only at the profitability of the decision focuses discussion on the interests of shareholders rather than stakeholders.

—Continued

Continued

The way to broaden the focus is to prepare an analysis over a longer rather than shorter time frame so some of the externalities are included; to use cost-benefit analysis to account for intangibles such as the loss of quality of life; and to use risk-benefit analysis to include probabilities of occurrences. These enhancements have been included intuitively in the previous analysis but could be sharpened with further investigation and presented formally to the decision maker, perhaps in the format opposite.

This presentation would allow the decision maker to see what the short-term and longer-term impact on profit was, and what the overall net benefits were likely to be for all stakeholders. Frequently, the benefits and costs accruing to stakeholders ultimately accrue to shareholders, so this presentation will allow a decision maker to project what may result from the decision. In this case, we do not have enough information to develop estimates for the costs and benefits associated with the positions of many stakeholders.

With regard to fairness, the concept of ranking stakeholders on several dimensions has already been employed. If the fairness of an

Projected	Short-Term Profit	Five-Year Profit	Cost-Benefit Analysis	Risk-Benefit Analysis
Revenues/ cost savings/benefits				
Costs/opportunity costs				
Net profit/net benefits	_____	_____	_____	_____

impact is ever in doubt, one way to assess it is to put yourself in the position of the stakeholder being assessed. If you would be willing to change places with the other party, then the decision is probably fair. If not, the decision may be made fair by altering or reengineering its impact in some way.

The consideration of impacts on stakeholder rights can be enhanced beyond the level employed in this analysis by a heightened awareness of commons problems. Sometimes rights shared with others are taken for granted but should not be. The environment is one example of this, but there may be others on which specific decisions may have an impact.

In this decision, there doesn't appear to be much room for reengineering to make its impact more ethical, so it must be faced as it is.

Conclusion

Although the proposed decision appears to hold some promise of profitability, and could be within GAAP and legal, it does not appear to be fair or right to several stakeholders. *Although its impact may not be material to investors, it is significant to several stakeholders.* Consequently, it is somewhat unethical and may result in significant negative reaction for the directors, auditor, and auditing profession. Because the interests of the public are not being protected, which may lead to repercussions, at the very least the auditor should ensure that the decision and its consequences are fully explained to the Audit Committee of the Board of Directors, who should assess the trade-offs and make the final decision for or against the decision for the client. If the Audit Committee votes for the decision, the full board should be advised and the auditor should consult within her firm to arrive at a consensus position on whether or not to qualify the audit report. In this way, the decision can be shared among those who would be held responsible.

When Does An "Aggressive Accounting" Choice Become Fraudulent?

Fraudulent choices of accounting treatment are those which contain such an element of deception that a reasonably informed and careful investor or other financial report user would be misled to his or her detriment as a result. For instance, revenue or expenses may be misstated to improperly increase current profit (thus diminishing future profits) to raise share prices or increase management bonuses. This would put future shareholders at a disadvantage as they would be buying shares at inflated prices while the company's assets would be reduced by the bonus money paid out.

There are, however, times when generally accepted accounting principles (GAAP) allow a choice among alternative treatments where some are more aggressive than others which are considered conservative usually because of their tendency not to inflate current profits. For instance, a company's management may choose different approaches to depreciate its fixed assets which would give rise to different depreciation charges against profit. Similarly, a range of choices is available for accounting for goodwill, or the recognition of warrantee

expense, or the recognition of revenue from construction contracts. If these accounting choices are made without consideration of all possible accounting practices, current and future shareholders may not be properly served. However, unless there is an effective ethical framework for deciding which of these choices to make, accounting choices may become too aggressive and fraudulent.

The following ethical framework and issues may be helpful in making choices that are aggressive but not fraudulent.

FUNDAMENTAL STAKEHOLDER INTEREST	ISSUES TO BE CONSIDERED
Well-offness	Are current and future shareholders interests reported clearly and accurately, and as the related economic reality warrants?
Fairness	Are the interests of current shareholders, future shareholders, management or other stakeholders unfairly disadvantaged with the benefit being transferred to another stakeholder?

Right(s)	Are the rights of stakeholders observed, including adherence to:
	
	• Professional fiduciary focus on duty to the public
	• Professional standards—objectivity, accuracy, integrity, competency, fair presentation
	• GAAP
	• Securities Commissions guidelines for:
	  • Full, true and plain disclosure
	  • Specific disclosures
	• Company policies such as for clarity and completeness?

Smokers Are Good for the Economy—Really[1]

Antismoking advocates cheered in the summer of 1997 when the U.S. tobacco industry agreed to pay out more than US$368.5 billion to settle lawsuits brought by forty states seeking compensation for cigarette-related Medicaid costs. Mississippi Attorney General Mike Moore, who helped organize the states' legal campaign, called the pact "the most historic public health achievement in history." But were the states right to do what they did?

The fundamental premise of lawsuits, and other anti-tobacco initiatives, is that smokers—and, hence, tobacco companies—place an added tax on all of us by heaping extra costs onto public health care systems. The argument is that those, and other social costs, outweigh the billions in duty and tax revenue that our governments collect from cigarette distribution.

But a basic actuarial analysis of that premise suggests that quite the opposite is true. As ghoulish as it may sound, smokers save the rest of us money because they die sooner and consume far less in health care and in benefits such as pensions. The extra costs they do generate are far outweighed by the subsidies they pay each time they plunk down their money for a pack of cigarettes.

---

1. This case was taken substantially, with permission, from an article written by John Woolsey, a prominent actuary who has been involved in the study of the costs of health care. The article, "Society's Windfall Profit from Smokers," was published in the *Ottawa Citizen* on August 4, 1998.

First of all, let's look at life expectancy consistently over the past decade. In 1994 testimony before the U.S. Senate Finance Committee, the U.S. Office of Technology Assessment showed that the average smoker dies fifteen years earlier than a nonsmoker, so smokers cost society less in health care bills than nonsmokers because they die about a decade earlier. The longer a person lives, the more it costs to treat him or her, especially since the vast majority of health care costs occur in the last few years of life.

One of the paradoxes of modern medicine is that advances in treatments that extend lives have actually increased lifetime health care costs. People who would have died from an acute illness during their working life in the past are now enjoying lengthy retirements, and suffering various debilitating diseases that require high-cost medical intervention. According to an expert, former Colorado governor Richard Lamm, who is now director of the Center for Public Policy and Contemporary Issues at the University of Denver, the average nonsmoker is treated for seven major illnesses during his or her lifetime. The average smoker survives only two major illnesses.

So how much more do nonsmokers add to the national health care bill than smokers? One of the best studies is by Duke University economist Kip Viscusi,[2]

---

2. Viscusi, W. Kip. "Cigarette Taxation and the Social Consequences of Smoking." *Tax Policy and the Economy,* (1995): 51–101.

who conducted an exhaustive comparative analysis in 1994 for a conference on tax policy hosted by the National Bureau of Economic Research in Washington, DC.

Viscusi concluded that smokers, in essence, subsidize the health care costs of nonsmokers. Using government statistics, Viscusi calculated the medical costs of tobacco by adding up things like the percentage of patient days for lung cancer treatment in hospitals that can be attributed to smoking and burn injuries and deaths from fires started by mislaid cigarettes. Viscusi then took into account other costs—by dying younger, smokers deprive society of income tax. Viscusi even added a charge for costs related to second-hand smoke. Viscusi then calculated how much tobacco saves society. Because they receive considerably fewer payments from government and employer pension plans and other retirement benefits, and consume fewer drug benefits, nursing home and hospital dollars, he estimates that the average American smoker saves society on each pack of cigarettes sold in the United States, leaving a net surplus of 31 cents over the costs attributable to smoking (see 3 percent discount column, following page). Adding the 80 cents per package in taxes that American smokers pay brings the total surplus to $1.11 for every pack of smokes.

Other experts have argued that there is a loss of productivity to society because smokers take

—Continued

Continued

more sick days than nonsmokers. But is this cost borne by the economy as a whole, or by individual smokers whose absences mean that they will not reach their full earnings potential due to missed job promotions and merit pay?

The bottom line in all this is that an actuarial approach shows that the facts do not support current political claims about the cost of smoking. Smokers actually leave the economy better off and should be encouraged, not discouraged through taxes, restrictions, and lawsuits.

Questions

1. What can an ethical analysis add to Viscusi's actuarial analysis?

2. Would an ethical analysis change the conclusion reached? Why?

EXTERNAL INSURANCE COSTS PER PACK OF CIGARETTES

SOURCE: Viscusi, W. Kip. "Cigarette Taxation and the Social Consequences of Smoking," *Tax Policy and the Economy*, National Bureau of Economic Research (1995): 74.

	1993 COST ESTIMATE DISCOUNT RATE			1993 COST ESTIMATE WITH TAR ADJUSTMENT DISCOUNT RATE		
	0%	3%	5%	0%	3%	5%
Costs						
Medical care <65	0.288	0.326	0.357	0.330	0.373	0.410
Medical care ≥65	0.375	0.172	0.093	0.384	0.177	0.096
Total medical care	0.663	0.498	0.451	0.715	0.550	0.505
Sick leave	0.003	0.012	0.019	0.000	0.013	0.020
Group life insurance	0.222	0.126	0.084	0.241	0.136	0.091
Nursing home care	−0.584	−0.221	−0.074	−0.599	−0.226	−0.076
Retirement pension	−2.660	−1.099	−0.337	−2.886	−1.193	−0.365
Fires	0.014	0.016	0.018	0.014	0.016	0.018
Taxes on earnings	0.771	0.351	0.107	0.883	0.402	0.122
Total net costs	−1.571	−0.317	0.268	−1.633	−0.302	0.315

Ford Pinto*

In order to meet strong competition from Volkswagen as well as other foreign domestic subcompacts, Lee Iacocca, then president of Ford Motor Co., decided to introduce a new vehicle by 1970, to be known as the Pinto. The overall objective was to produce a car at or below 2,000 pounds with a price tag of $2,000 or less. Although preproduction design and testing

—Continued

---

*More comprehensive cases on the Pinto problem can be found in Donaldson, T., & Gin, A. R. *Case Studies in Business Ethics*. Englewood Cliffs, NJ: Prentice-Hall, 1990, pp. 174–83 (original case by W. M. Hoffman); and Valasquez, M. G. *Business Ethics: Concepts and Cases*. Englewood Cliffs, NJ: Prentice-Hall, 1988, pp. 119–23.

Continued

normally requires about three-and-a-half years and the arrangement of actual production somewhat longer, design was started in 1968 and production commenced in 1970.

The Pinto project was overseen by Robert Alexander, vice president of Car engineering, and was approved by Ford's Product Planning Committee, consisting of Iacocca, Alexander, and Ford's group vice president of car engineering, Harold MacDonald. The engineers throughout Ford who worked on the project "signed off" to their immediate supervisors, who did likewise in turn to their superiors, and so on to Alexander and MacDonald and, finally, Iacocca.

Many reports were passed up the chain of command during the design and approval process, including several outlining the results of crash tests, and a proposal to remedy

the tendency for the car to burst into flames when rear-ended at 21 miles per hour. This tendency was caused by the placement of the car's gas tank between the rear axle and the rear bumper such that a rear-end collision was likely to drive the gas tank forward to rupture on a flange and bolts on a rear axle housing for the differential. The ruptured tank would then spew gas into the passenger compartment to be ignited immediately by sparks or a hot exhaust.

The remedies available to Ford included mounting the gas tank above the rear axle, which would cut down on trunk space, or installing a rubber bladder in the gas tank. Ford experimented with the installation of rubber bladders but apparently decided they were not cost-effective. Later, as part of a successful lobby effort against government regulations for mandatory crash tests

COMPONENT	1971 COSTS
Future productivity Losses	
Direct	$132,000
Indirect	41,300
Medical costs	
Hospital	700
Other	425
Property damage	1,500
Insurance Administration	4,700
Legal and court	3,000
Employer losses	1,000
Victim's pain and suffering	10,000
Funeral	900
Assets (lost consumption)	5,000
Miscellaneous	200
Total per fatality:	**$200,725**

(crash tests were delayed eight years, until 1977), Ford's cost-benefit analysis came to light in

FORD'S COST-BENEFIT ANALYSIS

Benefits: SAVINGS	UNIT COST	TOTAL
180 burn deaths	$200,000	$36,000,000
180 serious burn injuries	67,000	12,060,000
2,100 burned vehicles	700	1,470,000
Total benefits		**$49,530,000**
Costs: NUMBER OF UNITS		
11 million cars	11	$121,000,000
1.5 million light trucks	11	16,500,000
Total costs		**$137,500,000**

—Continued

Continued

a company study entitled "Fatalities Associated with Crash-Induced Fuel Leakage and Fires." As the details previously outlined show, the costs of installing the rubber bladder vastly exceeded the benefits.

Ford took the $200,000 figure for the cost of a death from a study of the National Highway Traffic Safety Administration, which used the estimates in the table on the previous page.

Questions

1. Was the decision not to install the rubber bladder appropriate? Use the 5-question framework to support your analysis.

2. What faults can you identify in Ford's cost-benefit analysis?

3. Should Ford have given its Pinto customers the option to have the rubber bladder installed during production for, say, $20?

Ethics case

The Kardell Paper Co.

Background

The Kardell paper mill was established at the turn of the century on the Cherokee River in southeastern Ontario by the Kardell family. By 1985, the Kardell Paper Co. had outgrown its original mill and had encompassed several facilities in different locations, generating total revenues of $1.7 billion per year. The original mill continued to function and was the firm's largest profit center. The Kardell family no longer owned shares in the firm, which had become a publicly traded company whose shares were widely held.

Kardell Paper Co. was a firm with a record of reporting good profits and had a policy of paying generous bonuses to the chief executive officer and other senior executives.

Kardell's original mill was located near Riverside, a community of 22,000. Riverside was largely dependent on the mill, which employed 500 people. The plant, while somewhat outdated, was still reasonably efficient and profitable. It was not designed with environmental protection in mind, and the waste water that discharged into the Cherokee River was screened only to remove the level of contaminants required by provincial regulation. There were other industrial plants upstream from the Kardell plant.

The residential community of Riverside, five miles downstream from the plant, was home to many of the Kardell plant's management, including Jack Green, a young engineer with two children, ages one and four.

Jack, who was assistant production manager at the Kardell plant, was sensitive to environmental issues and made a point of keeping up on the latest paper mill technology. Jack monitored activity at the plant's laboratory, which in 1985 employed a summer student to conduct tests on water quality in the Cherokee River immediately downstream from the plant.

These tests were taken across the entire width of the river. The tests conducted nearest the plant's discharge pipe showed high readings of an industrial chemical called sonox. Farther away from the plant, and on the opposite shore of the river, the water showed only small trace amounts of sonox. Sonox was used in the manufacture of a line of bleached kraft paper

—Continued

Continued

that Kardell had begun to make at its plant in recent years.

The Issue

The student researcher discovered that the plant lab was not including the high readings of sonox in its monthly reports to management, so the student showed the complete records to Jack. In the summer of 1985, Jack made a report to the CEO with a recommendation that in-depth studies be conducted into the situation and its implications for public health and long-term effects on the ecology.

In recommending that Kardell carry out an "environmental audit" of its operations, Jack pointed out that local doctors in Riverside had been expressing concern over what appeared to be an unusually high rate of miscarriages and respiratory disorders in the community. Jack told the CEO there were data suggesting a possible link between health problems and sonox, but no definite proof. Medical research into sonox's possible effects on humans was continuing.

In bringing his concerns to the CEO's attention, Jack offered as a possible solution the option of Kardell adopting a new processing technology which used recycling

techniques for waste water. This technology, already employed by a handful of plants in Europe, enabled a plant to operate in a "closed cycle" that not only protected the environment but reclaimed waste material, which was then sold to chemical producers. Thus, in the long term the new process was cost-effective. In the short run, however, refitting the existing Kardell plant to incorporate the new technology would cost about $70 million, and, during the retrofit, the plant would have to operate at reduced capacity levels for about a year and possibly be closed down altogether for an additional year to make the change-over.

The Response

Kardell's traditional response to environmental concerns was reactive. The company took its cues from the regulatory climate. That is, the provincial environment ministry would apply control orders on the plant as new limits on emissions of various compounds came into effect, and Kardell would then comply with these orders.

In raising his concerns in 1985, Jack pointed out that the Ministry of Environment, responding to the serious nature of concerns raised by the sonox issue, was

considering internal proposals from its staff that additional research be done into the sources and implications of sonox. Given the early stage of work in this area, Jack could offer no indication of when, if ever, the Ministry would enact new regulations to do with sonox. He argued, however, that the ground rules might change, as they had with previous compounds, and that Kardell should give some thought to the worst-case scenario of how the sonox issue could turn out down the road.

Kardell's CEO was sympathetic to the concerns raised by Jack, a valued employee of the company who had proved himself in the past by identifying many cost-efficiency measures. The CEO felt obliged, however, to match Jack's concerns about sonox against the substantial cost of refitting the plant. The CEO felt there simply was not enough data upon which to base such an important decision, and he was wary of any external force that attempted to influence the company's affairs. The CEO told Jack, "We simply can't let these 'greens' tell us how to run our business."

While the CEO did not feel it would be appropriate for Kardell to adopt the recommendations in Jack's

—Continued

Continued

report, the CEO did take the step of presenting the report to the board of directors, for discussion in the fall of 1985.

Kardell's board of directors represented a cross-section of interest groups. Everyone on the board felt a responsibility toward the shareholders, but, in addition, some members of the board also paid special attention to community and labor concerns. The board was composed of the CEO and president of the firm, along with several "outside" directors: two local businesspeople from Riverside, a representative of the paperworkers' union at the plant, a mutual fund manager whose firm held a large block of Kardell shares on behalf of the fund's investors, an economist, a Riverside city councillor, and the corporation's legal counsel.

Each member of the board spoke to Jack's report from his or her perspective. The Riverside representatives—the city councillor and the two businesspeople—wanted assurances that the community was not in any danger. But they also said, in the absence of any firm proof of danger, that they were satisfied Kardell probably was not a source of harmful emissions.

The lawyer pointed out that legally Kardell was in the clear: it was properly observing all existing regulations on emission levels; in any case, there was no clear indication that the Kardell mill was the only source of sonox emissions into the Cherokee River. While acknowledging the health concerns that had recently arisen over sonox, the lawyer thought it prudent to wait for the government to establish an acceptable limit for sonox emissions. Besides, the lawyer added, while liability actions had been initiated against two or three other mills producing sonox, these claims had been denied through successful defense actions in court on the grounds of lack of clear evidence of a significant health hazard.

The labor representative expressed concern about any compound that might affect the health of Kardell employees living in the area. But the labor official also had to think about the short-term consideration of job loss at the plant and the fact that, with the plant shut down, there were few other employment opportunities in the area to fill the gap. The board representatives from Riverside pointed out that, obviously, the local economy would be severely affected by the shutdown to refit the plant. And the mutual fund manager agreed with the CEO that, at least in the short term, Kardell's profitability and share price would suffer from a decision to undertake a costly overhaul of the facility.

The Decision

After much debate, the board decided to defer consideration of Jack's proposals pending the results of government research into this issue. It also asked Jack to continue monitoring the regulatory climate so that the plant would always be in basic compliance with provincial emission standards.

During the next two years, Jack presented similar warnings to the board regarding sonox and continued to meet with the same response. As a precautionary measure, he kept copies of his reports in his own files so there could never be any question of the timing or substance of his warnings to the board. During this same period, an above-average incidence of miscarriages, birth defects, and respiratory ailments was reported in the Riverside area.

The Kardell case was prepared by David Olive, Graham H. Tucker, Tim J. Leech, and David Sparling.

SOURCE: Agenda for Action Conference Proceedings, the Canadian Center for Ethics & Corporate Policy, 1990, pp. 20–21.

Reprinted with the permission of the Canadian Center for Ethics & Corporate Policy.

Cost-Benefit Analysis

Leonard J. Brooks, Jr., CA
CAmagazine, October 1979

Corporate management has become increasingly aware that business decisions often have an impact that cannot be easily measured by traditional accounting analysis. Governments and special interest groups have been quick to point out that many costs resulting from business decisions are not reflected in (or are external to) corporate accounts. Pollution damage costs, for instance, must be borne by neighbours, not by the companies causing the problems. Understandably, then, corporate executives are searching for analytical techniques that will take account of such external costs and benefits when they are deliberating company policy, resource allocation (to pollution controls, for example), desirability of potentially harmful projects and other programs that will have an impact on the general public. Inevitably, they are looking to their accountants to develop the required cost-benefit analyses to supplement usual rate of return projections.

There are many reasons why management will continue to voluntarily ask for and use cost-benefit analyses. The best managers usually try to reduce uncertainty in their decision making as much as possible, and knowing in advance the costs and benefits of an action could forestall inciting an unpleasant reaction by an angry populance. Furthermore, data developed using cost-benefit techniques can serve as an excellent predictor of cash costs that will show up later in the traditional accounts. Also, the social choices governing the implementation of government programs and regulations are often based on cost-benefit analyses. It may even be that organizations, both profit and non-profit, will someday be forced to justify their social existence in terms of cost-benefit analyses. Already, about 90% of the *Fortune 500* companies make social responsibility disclosures in their annual reports.[1]

There are already many indications that the use of cost-benefit analysis may become mandatory. For example, governments are about to require summaries of social costs and benefits before allowing new chemical plants to be built. A growing number of public-spirited shareholders are demanding increased disclosure of corporate contributions to society. An increasingly burdened electorate is challenging government largesse and is insisting on documented justification of new or further spending programs. Thus, in view of such pressures, accountants would be well-advised to become more familiar with the techniques and potential problems of cost-benefit analysis.

---

1. *Social Responsibility Disclosure: 1977 Survey of Fortune 500 Annual Reports* (Cleveland: Ernst & Ernst, 1977).

Cost-benefit analysis (CBA) can be used to (a) determine whether projects should be undertaken, and (b) to monitor the performance of a company or project. Table 1 provides a partial list of the areas where CBA is now being used in both the private and public sectors of our economy. The format for presentation of these impacts, their scope and other factors will be discussed later; first, it is useful to see how CBA differs from traditional accounting analyses in terms of scope and focus.

SHORTFALLS OF TRADITIONAL ACCOUNTING DATA

In comparison with cost-benefit analysis, traditional accounting analysis falls short on four counts:

1. It focuses on past actions, which are not as relevant as future actions for decision making.

2. It does not take into account external factors.

3. It considers some resources to be free, or to have no cost.

4. Its focus is far more narrow, relating almost always to shareholders' interests, rather than stakeholders' (or society's) interests.

The first shortfall, decision-time orientation, will not be news to most readers. The classic cartoon portraying the manager as an airline pilot flying a plane while looking backwards epitomizes the situation of decision makers using only historical financial reports in their deliberations. Fortunately, CBA looks ahead at what might happen so that decisions can be tempered by foresight.

Not taking external factors into account, the second shortfall, is more serious. In the case of pollution, the cost of clean-up or health damage is rarely shown in the accounts of the corporation responsible, since it is not borne by the company but by someone else. Yet such costs are undeniably real, and to omit them from the net profit figure significantly weakens it as a measure of the polluter's "contribution to society." To be fair, we should point out that the reverse (i.e., costs borne by a company and benefits reaped by society; company-funded scholarships, for example) also exists and should be taken into a corporation's analysis of costs and benefits.

The third type of shortfall noted in traditional accounting analysis is the consideration of many resources as being free. This usually occurs where no market mechanism exists to exact payment for resource use. Air and water are the most ready examples of "free" resources, but governments are

—Continued

Continued

TABLE I

USES OF COST-BENEFIT
ANALYSIS

PRIVATE SECTOR ORGANIZATIONS
▪ Support for government subsidy; grant or tariff.
▪ Estimate of impact of pollution on society.
▪ Valuation of employee time spent on public activities.
▪ Evaluation and allocation of resources to public projects or causes.
▪ Monitor mechanism for net corporate social contribution to society for the year and to date.
▪ Individuals
▪ Support for damage claims arising from loss of life, eyes, limbs, etc.
▪ Valuation of leisure time.
PUBLIC SECTOR
Evaluation of social program alternatives leading to allocation of resources for:
▪ Health programs.
▪ Education programs.
▪ Recreation facilities.
▪ Conservation projects (flood control dams, reservoirs)
▪ Transportation improvement projects (airports, subways, tunnels, etc.)
▪ Formulation of regulations for pollution control.

already moving to regulate their use to protect the interests of other members of society, both present and future. Consequently, capital investment decisions should from now on reflect the potential costs of air and water regulation.

The fourth shortfall, the narrow focus of accounting analysis, is a result of the traditional desire to reflect the impact of corporate actions on the interest of shareholders. But corporations affect, and are responsible to, many other groups in society as well, and these are becoming more vocal in corporate affairs. These groups (employees, neighbours, customers, suppliers, bankers, etc.) are usually referred to as stakeholders, and stakeholder interest has been the focus of a number of recently developed accounting systems.[2]

Currently, however, there is considerable debate over the scope of these new hybrid accounting systems. In 1972, Linowes proposed that a "net social corporate contribution to society" be calculated; curiously, however, he limited the calculations to voluntary expenditures, and did not include, for example, costs involuntarily incurred to comply with government regulations.[3] Abt in 1977, proposed that the cost-benefit analysis leading to the determination of corporate net social equity include both voluntary and involuntary expenditures and be integrated into traditional financial statements.[4] The AICPA agreed that an integrated system would be ideal but, because of costs and the fact that CBA is still in an early stage of development, it has opted for a less sophisticated approach focusing on the organization's impact on, in turn: the environment, human resources, suppliers, etc.[5]

3. D. Linowes, "An Approach to Socio-Economic Accounting, *The Conference Board Record*, Vol. IX, No. 11 (November 1972).

4. C. C. Abt, *The Social Audit for Management* (New York: AMACOM, 1977).

5. Committee on Social Measurement, *The Measurement of Corporate Social Performance* (New York: The American Institute of Certified Public Accountants, 1977).

—*Continued*

2. R. Estes, *Corporate Social Accounting* (New York, N.Y.: John Wiley & Sons, 1976).

Continued

Indeed, although others have suggested even more complex approaches to organizational worth,[6] the long-term answer probably lies in a modification of the Abt Associates, Inc. traditional accounting model plus cost-benefit analysis.[7] But, as the AICPA found, the cost for a moderately large company to set up a system of accounts to duplicate the Abt model, before costing the data assembly each year, could be as much as $300,000—a price too high for most industries to contemplate at this time.[8] In addition, reports generated by this system will be of questionable value until industry standards of comparison are available and the knowledgeability of traditional financial report readers has been improved. Finally, time is required to thoroughly determine the interrelationships of the various comprehensive models.

Obviously, then, costs and other practical considerations will probably mean that the incorporation into financial reports of the disclosure of significant corporate impacts on society will happen gradually, taking into account one area at a time. Yet there should be no illusion that this type of one-dimensional analysis is all that is needed. As a part measure, however, it will make information available to relevant stakeholder groups and allow governments to provide, for instance, pollution standards by which corporate performance can be measured. And, regardless of whether CBAs are used to facilitate decisions or to monitor corporate performance, the basic techniques should be understood.

TECHNIQUES OF COST-BENEFIT ANALYSIS

Instead of the normal captions "revenue," "expense" and "net profit," CBA terminology would be "benefits," "costs" and "excess of benefits over costs." The CBA concepts of benefits and costs are broader than revenues and expenses, because they take into account future and hitherto external values. Projects should be undertaken if benefits exceed costs or the benefits/cost ratio is greater than one. Usually, the larger the benefit/cost ratio, the more attractive the project; but occasionally, if a company has only limited funds to invest, small projects that are attractive from a benefit point of view must be bypassed in favour of larger projects that produce higher absolute levels of benefit. In other words, if only part of the resources available to be invested will be absorbed by the project(s) with the highest benefit/cost ratio, it is preferable to choose a project with a slightly lower benefit/cost ratio which uses more of the resource base and contributes overall benefits.

To illustrate, an unsophisticated yet typical CBA is set out in Table 2. The values used are hypothetical but readily attainable by means we'll discuss later.

The general framework for CBA is identical to the discounted cash flow approach used in capital budgeting analysis. For example, the present value of net costs or net benefits may be derived from the sum of the future values discounted at an appropriate discount rate, or

present value of net costs or net benefit

$$= \frac{B_1 - C_1}{(1+r)^1} + \frac{B_2 - C_2}{(1+r)^2} + \frac{B_3 - C_3}{(1+r)^3} + \dots \dots \infty$$

$$= \sum_{n=1}^{\infty} \frac{B_n - C_n}{(1+r)^n}$$

where:

B is the benefit for the year, accruing at the end of the year.

C is the cost for the year.

r is the discount rate per annum reflecting the opportunity cost for capital invested in projects of comparable risk.

1, 2, 3, . . . n specifies the period/year with n the final period.

THE DISCOUNT RATE

Monies used to finance projects are necessarily withheld from other uses such as private investment or personal consumption. Therefore, the cost of such financing is properly measured by computing the cost of the opportunity foregone, whether that is the lost after-tax marginal rate of return on other investments or the price consumers would be willing to pay not to forego deferring their consumption. Since such alternative costs are not practically available, the results of CBA studies are usually discounted at a weighted average marginal rate based on the projected sources of financing to be employed. The weighted average marginal cost of capital approach has prevailed in practice even though economists have noted that, in some instances, the use of a single discount rate may not produce valid integrations of present and future consumption foregone.[9]

In the case of a corporation, the discount rate is usually its average weighted after-tax cost of capital, plus a risk factor depending on the nature of the project's cash flows, less whatever the amount with which the company wishes to subsidize

---

6. In L. J. Brooks, *Canadian Corporate Social Performance* (Hamilton, Canada: The Society of Management Accountants of Canada), 1986, Chapter 3.

7. Abt. *Op. cit.*

8. *Ibid.* pp. 112–113.

9. M. S. Feldstein, "The Inadequacy of Weighted Discount Rates," in *Cost-Benefit Analysis,* ed. R. Layard (Harmondsworth, Middlesex, Eng.: Penguin Books, Ltd., 1973), pp. 311–322.

—Continued

Continued

TABLE 2

JM CO. LTD. COST-BENEFIT ANALYSIS
OF SOCIAL IMPACT PROPOSALS:
MARCH 1979

	POLLUTION CONTROL EQUIPMENT PROTECTING WORKERS IN PLANT	UNIVERSITY ADMISSION SCHOLARSHIPS
Benefits (Present Valued at 10%)		
Reduction in worker health costs borne by society	$500,000	
Increase in worker productivity	200,000	
Improvements in level of earnings of scholarship recipients		$600,000
	700,000	600,000
Costs (Present Valued at 10%)		
Pollution equipment	350,000	
Scholarships paid		400,000
	$350,000	$200,000
Benefit/cost ratio	2/	3/2
Decision		
(1) if only one project can be funded	X	
(2) if all projects with a positive benefit/cost/ratio can be funded	X	X
Time horizon: 10 years from March 1979		

While there may be some difference of opinion over the validity of considering increased earnings of scholarship recipients as the "benefit" of these payments, such a measure is, on balance, conservative and facilitates a numeric comparison with the project costs and thus results in a more informed decision.

projects with heavy social orientation. A similar approach should be followed for non-profit organizations. For government agencies, however, it has been argued that their size and taxing mandate produces a relatively risk-free cost of capital which, if they used it, would be lower than the cost to firms in the private sector. Over time, the use of the lower governmental rate would result in an increasingly larger rate of investment by the public sector in comparison with that of the private, and the balance of activity would shift further towards the former. To counteract this tendency, the governments of Canada and Britain use a 10% discount rate on most projects.[10]

MEASUREMENT OF COSTS AND BENEFITS

Although there are problems in choosing the appropriate discount rate, they are minor in comparison with the difficulties of identifying and measuring the annual future costs and benefits themselves.

Whenever possible, direct measurement is preferable. For example, when assessing the costs resulting from air pollution caused by a generating station, we can measure the saving (benefit) from the use of coal or natural gas instead of oil. The costs could also be partially measured by a direct survey estimate of the increase in local health costs attributable to

—Continued

---

10. D. B. Brooks, *Conservation of Minerals and of the Environment* (Ottawa: Canada Department of Energy Mines and Resources, 1974).

Continued

respiratory problems and to the increased house mainte-nance costs due to smoke damage.[11]

Unfortunately, many costs and benefits cannot be deter-mined directly, and surrogate or indirect means must be used to estimate the values involved, although, admittedly, it is vir-tually impossible to capture all of the relevant characteristics in the surrogate value. For instance, and continuing our pol-lution example, it is impossible to measure directly the aes-thetic values that will be lost in the cloud of smoke and smell that will enfold the community if coal is used as a fuel. An indirect or surrogate value could be estimated for this aes-thetic loss, however, by surveying the local residents to see how much they would be willing to pay to have the problem improved or removed. From this survey a type of demand curve for smoke and smell abatement could be fashioned and aesthetic values estimated.[12] The cost of a pollution control project could then be compared with the curve to see if the overall demand is large enough to justify going ahead.

Another approach to determining the cost of pollution is to calculate the full cost of health damage incurred based on the value of the time lost by patients while ill. For patients who would not have been working for wages if well, the appropri-ate approach would be to identify the most lucrative oppor-tunity lost by being ill; and, once this is done, the value loss, or opportunity cost, can be estimated by (for instance) esti-mating the cost of task delay or of paying someone else to complete the task. If a patient loses wages while ill, then this would be one measure of the opportunity cost of time lost.

A further example of surrogate measurement is the evalu-ation of the net benefit derived from a company-sponsored training program (total cost $60,000) for 50 personnel. Unable to measure the benefit directly, we make the assump-tion that the benefit will be reflected by increased earnings (say $5,000 per annum) over the expected 20-year average working life of each employee. Hence the net benefit of the courses would be $2,068,500 (calculated as $50 \times \$5,000$ $a_{\overline{20}|}$ 10% [i.e., a 20-year annuity at 10% rate of discount: less $60,000)] before tax.

Additional CBA approaches are outlined in Table 3.[13]

SHORTCOMINGS OF COST-BENEFIT ANALYSIS

Some accountants will argue that CBA is too subjective and too removed from their traditional pursuits to be worth study-ing. But this argument overlooks:

- The longevity of CBA, which has been used since before 1844.[14]
- The prominence of CBA in governmental decision making.
- The apparent likelihood that CBA techniques will be employed in the private sector to provide a focus for deci-sions on corporate programs that will have an impact on society.

Accountants have traditionally assumed a central role in providing data for decisions in the private sector and, if this position is to be maintained, it is in the accountant's best interest to be familiar with CBA techniques and their short-comings. Furthermore, since accountants are often directly involved with (or indirectly subject to) CBA decisions in the public sector, they will be unable to make decisions properly, to advise less-skilled decision makers, or to challenge specific CBA proposals effectively, unless they are aware of the rele-vant CBA techniques and their shortcomings. The reasoning behind our stressing the importance of informed advice will become more apparent when the variety and seriousness of CBA shortcomings are understood. The shortcomings can be grouped into three categories:

- Choices available to the preparer.
- Constraints to be considered by the preparer and user.
- Issues not resolvable by CBA.

THE CHOICES AVAILABLE

The choices are many and, if too inaccurate, would bias a CBA to the point where unwise decisions would result. There are methods by which bias and unreasonableness can be mit-igated, but first the decision maker must understand the potential problems.

When beginning a CBA, the preparer must make certain assumptions such as the rate of discount (r%) and the time horizon over which costs and benefits will be taken into account. Obviously, the choice of a long time horizon might favour some projects, even though the uncertainties of esti-mation are too great to warrant the inclusion of costs and

11. M. O. Alexander and J. L. Livingstone, "What Are the Real Costs and Benefits of Producing "Clean Electric Power?" *Public Utilities Fort-nightly* (August 30, 1973).

12. Estes, *Op. cit.,* pp. 111–114.

13. J. L. Knetsch and R. K. Davis, "Comparisons of Method for Recre-ation Evaluation," in *Water Research,* ed. A. V. Kneese and S. C. Smith (Baltimore: The John Hopkins Press for Resources for the Future, Inc., 1966).

14. J. Dupuit, "On the Measurement of Utility of Public Works" (trans-lated from the French published in 1844). *International Economic Papers,* Vol. 2 (London: Macmillan & Co. Ltd.), 1952.

—Continued

Continued

benefits to be incurred 20–25 years from now. If too high a discount rate is chosen, distant costs and benefits will have less impact on the CBA than they should and, even if no longer-term costs and benefits exist, decision makers might reject proposals when their existing opportunities for investment are far less than r%.

Since it is essential that an accurate opportunity cost be estimated for the monies to be used to finance each CBA project, is the 10% test rate used by Canadian and British governments appropriate? For instance, if 10% is too low, there will be a tendency for the public sector to accept more projects than the private sector would. On the other hand, since private sector capital budgeting decisions do not incorporate all the costs or external factors that public sector CBAs do (thereby inflating projected rates of return), maybe the 10% test rate is acceptable. Surely accountants should have a thorough understanding of this fundamental issue.

Which costs and benefits to include or exclude is another basic choice to be made, one that reflects the special interests of the group making the CBA decision. If the decision makers are an upstream town council, they may be unwilling to include in their analysis the cost incurred by a downstream town to clean up pollution put into the river by the upstream municipality. If, in the same situation, all filtration costs were borne by the province (a larger political jurisdiction to which both towns belong), then the costs of clean-up would be recognized. In other words, decision makers can be led astray if the boundaries of the CBA analysis are not broad enough.

Bias can enter CBA through unfortunate choices of surrogates and of the methods used to assess people's values. Surrogates are rarely mirror images of what one is attempting to measure. Table 3 indicates a wide range of alternatives available to evaluate a park or other recreation facility. Some alternatives listed are more conservative than others, so decision makers should examine surrogates closely to avoid being misled. It should also be kept in mind that the surrogates chosen will most often focus on output or production values, rather than on consumption values. For instance, when evaluating the time of an unemployed person, the conventional CBA approach focusses on his or her production opportunity loss (nil since he/she is unemployed) and he is not asked how much his inactivity or leisure is worth.

Having listed some of the pitfalls, it is comforting to note that a wary review, looking for each item mentioned, can be aided greatly by sensitivity analysis. The discount rate, the time horizon and the choice of surrogate can be varied to see if the CBA outcome changes and in what way. Since CBA is a technique used most frequently to rank several possible projects, it is not essential that a project be valued exactly, but rather that it may be ranked better or worse than other alternatives.

CONSTRAINTS

With respect to the constraints that must be considered by CBA preparers and users, it is imperative that projects be mutually exclusive; or, if a joint project is under consideration, that the CBA analysis include all aspects of the project. Furthermore, accepted projects must meet legal requirements and be amenable to administration. Occasionally, budgetary constraints are removed and decision makers are told to spend their predetermined budget without regard to the opportunity cost (r%) of the money spent. In this case, however, only analyses using an appropriate discount rate will ultimately be defensible.

UNRESOLVABLE ISSUES

The CBA decision maker must realize that many issues can never be fully resolved by CBA techniques. CBA doesn't take into account issues of equity, such as the advisability of penalizing one group to the advantage of another. Moral issues are likewise excluded or abstractly incorporated. For instance,

—Continued

TABLE 3

DIFFERENT METHODS OF EVALUATING THE BENEFITS OF A RECREATION FACILITY

Calculation of:
1. Gross expenditure by users on travel, equipment, etc.
2. Market value of fish caught (production or output value)
3. Production cost of project (input value)
4. Market value of recreation services produced $\times$ number of users.

Survey of:
1. Users' willingness to pay for use
2. Users' (and other interested parties') willingness to pay to prevent deprival of use or enjoyment.

Continued

the $600,000 spent earlier on scholarships might feed 50,000 children in southeast Asia. Similarly, the loss of an eye, limb or human life is valued by the discounted earnings stream foregone, whereas, fortunately, society is willing to pay large amounts to maintain the lives of leukemia victims and provide dialysis equipment for kidney patients whose future incomes may be nil. Even value judgments on issues of less importance than human life may not be handled to everyone's satisfaction. Beauty is in the eye of each beholder and to impute an aesthetic judgment for a whole group based on the average of several individual opinions may not provide an accurate picture. On the other hand, decision makers' judgments often depend on external factors and are therefore enhanced by quantitative CBA analysis, however rough and imperfect.

CBA IS HERE TO STAY

Society in general, public organizations, private corporations and individuals are increasingly looking beyond traditional accounting analysis for broader impact measurements. Traditional accounting will remain valuable, but, in advanced societies, organizations must be aware and take account of their external impacts as well. Governments are already making social choices for all of us based on cost-benefit analysis. Accountants, therefore, would be well advised to increase their understanding of cost-benefit analysis and its pitfalls, or else lose their place at the right hand of decision makers.

Leonard J. Brooks, Jr., MBA, CA, is an associate professor in the Department of Political Economy at the University of Toronto and the discipline representative for commerce at the university's Erindale College in Mississauga. He is also a former audit manager with Touche Ross & Co. in Toronto.

Reprinted with permission, from the October 1979 issue of *CA magazine,* published by the Canadian Institute of Chartered Accountants, Toronto, Canada.

Ethical Analysis for Environmental Problem Solving

Graham Tucker
Canadian Centre for Ethics & Corporate Policy, 1990

INTRODUCTION

Today, no company can claim to be "ethical" unless it is demonstrating a concern for the environment. The focus of this conference is on the tools of ethical analysis and problem solving that can provide a practical framework for action.

Before finalizing a business decision, an executive should ask a series of questions designed to ensure the best possible choice is made both for the shareholders as well as other stakeholders. These questions ought to be asked in the following order to canvass the values shown:

1. Is it profitable? (market values)

2. Is it legal? (legal values)

3. Is it fair? (social values)

4. Is it right? (personal values)

5. Is it sustainable development? (environmental values)

These questions have been built into the "five-box" framework for ethical analysis which is shown in Figure 1.

FIGURE 1 QUESTIONS

The focus on values is critical to the proper analysis of business decisions because morality, which is becoming more and more critical to the health of corporations and society, cannot be legislated. It depends on the value system of corporate leaders and employees. Moreover, the tough choices required among alternatives often defy quantification and must be based on the values of the decision-maker.

Nowadays, it is not safe to judge a prospective action just on its contribution to profits, because the action may not be legal. Even if it is profitable and legal, society will penalize the company if the action is not also perceived to be fair and right. Recently, as the fragility of our global environment has become clear, society has begun to demand that corporate actions fit into the sustainable development of our economy.

The application of the "five-box" framework for analysis will be developed in the analysis of the Kardell Paper Co. case,

—Continued

Continued

after a discussion of some terms used in ethical analysis and the outlining of a framework for ethical problem solving.

SOME IMPORTANT DISTINCTIONS

It's important that we make important distinctions (a) between management and leadership and (b) between being legal and being ethical. Lack of clear distinction in these areas causes a lot of confused thinking in business ethics.

When managers are successful, usually it is because they are high-energy, hard-driving individuals who know how to play by the rules of the game. They efficiently and single-mindedly strive to achieve the goals of the organization. But they may or may not be leaders.

Robert Greenleaf, author of the book *Servant Leadership*, defines leaders as "those who better see the path ahead and are prepared to take the risks and show the way." The characteristic which sets leaders apart from managers is their intuitive insight and the foresight which enables them to go out ahead and show the way. Why would anyone accept the leadership of another, except that the other sees more clearly where it's best to go? The manager, by contrast, tends to be part of the bureaucracy that wants to preserve the status quo.

FIGURE I

A FRAMEWORK FOR ETHICAL ANALYSIS—CHANGING GROUND RULES AND A SUSTAINABLE FUTURE

The managerial role determines the values. Managers do what's expected of them. That role often overrides the managers' personal values.

Role responsibility can be very powerful. The management of Johns-Manville knew for years that its product asbestos was linked by scientists to lung cancer in its employees. Similar situations existed with the Ford Pinto and the Dalkon Shield.

Managers often feel powerless to act outside of their prescribed role; they feel that they don't have the authority to buck the system. The corporate authority may be sanctioning the unethical behavior. It takes the moral authority of a leader to change the system, and this is often notably lacking in both politics and business.

Robert Greenleaf points out that the failure of business-people to use foresight and take creative action before a crisis arises is tantamount to *ethical failure*, because managers in these cases lack courage to act when there is still some freedom to change course. Many managers opt for short-term profit at the expense of long-term viability. On that basis there are probably a lot of people walking around with an air of innocence which they would not have if society were able to pin the label "unethical" on them for their failure to foresee crises and to act constructively when there was freedom to act.

Similarly, it is important that we distinguish between being legal and being ethical. The law is frequently quite distinct from morality. It is mainly concerned with the minimum regulation required for public order, whereas ethics attempts to achieve what is "best" for both the individual and society. Thus it's possible to be operating within the law and yet be unethical. The legal limits for a certain pollutant may have been established before it was discovered to be unsafe at that level. The company may be operating legally. Yet by knowingly endangering the health of workers or the community, the company is acting in an unethical manner.

Many corporate codes of ethics express a commitment to keeping the letter of the law, but that may not protect them from censure when the new data becomes public knowledge. Obviously we have to have laws and regulations to avoid the chaos of a lawless society. However, the ethical crunch that is being experienced by the business world today is that the communications revolution is putting more information in the hands of the public. It used to be possible to exercise power and control by withholding or concealing information. If you don't know that asbestos dust is giving you lung cancer you can't do anything about it. The public now finds out very quickly what is going on, and it is demanding ethical conduct because this affects its well-being.

—Continued

Continued

We have recently witnessed dramatic changes in Eastern Europe, as shared information has empowered previously powerless people to rise up and take control of their own destiny in seeking a better life. Precisely the same power is at work in our society, changing the rules of the game for business. Five years ago, the concern for the environment ranked sixth in the value system of the Canadian public. Today it ranks number one. This in turn is empowering government to enact much tougher regulations. Those companies that are either too entrenched in the old rules or lack the foresight to see the long-term consequences of what is now perceived by the public to be unethical behavior will fail. Whereas those companies which use a combination of ethical foresight and good business, and have the courage to make the changes required, will survive and prosper.

Legislation may provide a level playing field, but legislation alone cannot solve the problem. Similarly, strong corporate statements about environmental values also are useless if business does not have the ethical will to comply with them. The health of our environment depends more than anything else upon corporate moral leadership, which reflects the personal values of executives and employees. And this is where we move from theory to the realm of applied ethics, which is concerned with the practical outcome of business decisions.

VALUE JUDGMENTS

The name of the game is making value judgments in the light of our personal values. I want to say a few words about values so that we can have a common language in this conference.

Values are the criteria by which we make our judgments or choices, and establish our goals and priorities. For most of us, there is a bit of a gap between our ideal personal values and our actual or operative values, and we need to be honest about what our values really are.

The situation is complicated for us today as social values are changing, and this is redefining ethical standards. The ground rules are changing.

Studies have shown the following characteristics resulting from people having clear or unclear values:

Unclear values	Clear values
Apathetic	Know who they are
Flighty	Know what they want
Inconsistent	Positive
Drifter	Purposeful
Role player	Enthusiastic
Indecisive	Decisive

Both individually and corporately, it is to our advantage to develop a clear set of values, because confused values will result in confused ethical decisions.

Ethical analysis usually uncovers value conflicts which occur below the surface of our thinking. They can't be settled by rational argument. Only as we listen respectfully to each other's value perspective is it possible to find a reasonable accommodation of the difference. This is why stakeholder analysis is so important.

RULE ETHICS

This brings us to the two-basic ethical concepts we will apply in our case study today. The first is rule ethics.

Rule ethics states that you make your decisions about right or wrong on the basis of valid ethical principles, norms or ground rules. In other words, we ask, "Will this proposed action be violating civil law, or company policy in the code of ethics?" This is a good place to start, but as mentioned before, it may not produce ethical decisions. The decisions that result may be legal—but if the ground rules have changed, they may not be ethical.

The next level of Rule Ethics consists of the rules or principles that come out of our moral traditions, which in our society are mainly the Judeo-Christian moral norms such as "Thou shalt not kill, steal, lie, cheat or oppress."

The underlying question in Rule Ethics is, Whose rules are you following? It used to be that the corporation had its own rules, which related only to market forces, and it was not felt to be necessary to consider the values of society. That is, "What's good for General Motors is good for the rest of us." Cynically, the Golden Rule has become, "He who has the gold makes the rules."

UTILITARIANISM, OR END-POINT ETHICS

John Stuart Mill said that, "To determine whether an action is right or wrong, one must concentrate on its likely consequences—the end point or end result. What is the greatest benefit for the greatest number?"

This led to cost-benefit analysis: does the benefit justify the cost? And to risk-benefit analysis: does not benefit justify the business risk?

In other words, you begin with Rule Ethics, in which the stakeholders test a decision by asking:

Is it legal?

Is it fair?

Is it right?

Is it environmentally sound?

—Continued

Continued

A FRAMEWORK FOR ETHICAL PROBLEM SOLVING

Consider the following issues while employing the eight steps listed below:

1. **Establish objectivity.**
   Who is doing the analysis and what interests do they represent? What are the ground rules of the company and of the decision-making group?

2. **Scan the situation; identify the problem.**
   Separate out the "core problem" from the subproblems. Whose problem is it? Why is it a problem?

3. **Analyze the problem.**
   Use the "five-box," or "five-question" framework . . . to analyze the situation. What are the operative ground rules or values from the perspective of corporation's existing rules, as well as the legal, public, personal and environmental implications? Who makes the decision? Who are the stakeholders? What are their ground rules? Is it fair to all concerned?

4. **Determine the cause of the problem.**
   Why and how are the rules being broken? Are the rules being broken Prima facie or Categorical? Is there any justification? Specify the cause.

5. **Establish the objective.**
   Describe the desirable outcome, or end-point. Is it achievable? How would you measure it? What is the time frame?

6. **Explore the options.**
   Brainstorm possible solutions. Create alternative cources of action.

7. **Decide on the best solution.**
   Who will be affected by each option? Evaluate the impacts from each option on each group of stakeholders. Which option maximizes the benefits and minimizes the burden? Will it pass the five-box ethics test?

8. **Plan and implement the solution.**

Then you move to the end-point ethics, which seeks the greatest benefit for the greatest number—and this, finally, forces us to make some trade-offs to achieve the greatest good.

So far, we have been considering the process of ethical analysis. However, there is a tendency to think that having analyzed the problem we have solved it. Unless we take it to the next step of rational problem solving, nothing much is going to happen.

The process I am going to introduce is ethically neutral. The thing that makes it ethical is the particular values and ground rules you apply in the process. If the ethical analysis has been done thoroughly, you will have already sorted out the values that you will apply at the various decision points in the problem-solving process.

Creative problem solving involves lateral thinking, or second-order thinking.

First-order thinking is the obvious course of action that first occurs to the mind of the manager or executive.

Second-order thinking involves "reframing" the problem and considering it from a different perspective.

For example, if you look at a business problem from the perspective of each of the five boxes on the chart, you might generate some creative alternatives which might not come to mind if only the corporate box is considered. It will take courage for every business enterprise to make the ethical shift for a sustainable future, but some can and *are* leading the way.

Graham H. Tucker is founder and former director of the King-Bay Chaplaincy in Toronto, and former executive director of the Canadian Centre for Ethics & Corporate Policy. Rev. Tucker is author of *The Faith-Work Connection.*

SOURCE: Tucker, G. "Ethical Analysis for Environmental Problem Solving" *Agenda for Action Conference Proceedings,* The Canadian Centre for Ethics & Corporate Policy, 1990, 53–57.

Chapter *Six*

Managing Ethics Risks and Opportunities

Purpose of the Chapter

Earlier chapters provided an understanding of the changing ethical expectations for business and professional accountants; the new frameworks of stakeholder accountability and governance stimulated by Enron, Arthur Andersen, WorldCom and the Sarbanes-Oxley Act; and how to provide adequate guidance for ethical behavior in the future. Looking ahead, several areas are worthy of specific discussion because of their current and potential significance to the successful future of corporations, directors, executives, and professional accountants. These areas hold risks and opportunities that modern businesspeople and professionals must consider to secure and maintain the support of their stakeholders.

This chapter develops topics that provide an understanding of several key ethics opportunities and risks facing corporations and a set of tools to deal effectively with them, including:

- Ethics risk management
- Ethics strategies and tactics for effective management of stakeholder relations
- Workplace ethics
- International operations
- Corporate social responsibility/accountability and audit
- Crisis management

Ethics Risk and Opportunity Management

LIMITED PERSPECTIVES

Risk management has been a commonly used concept since the late 1990s when major stock exchanges listed it as one of those matters that directors needed to oversee.[1] Leading-edge corporations had employed some form of risk management for years, but most other corporations had not. Even now, after risk management has been endorsed as an important aspect of good governance, many corporations practice it on a limited basis. Few corporations approach risk management within the full *ethics risk management framework* necessary to support the new era of stakeholder accountability and governance. Unless corporations begin to consider a full ethics risk management framework, they will continue to suffer from risks and lose opportunities.

Depending on the organization, risk management has focused on different issues. For example, financial institutions have tended to focus on financial risks such as the bankruptcy of borrowers, or the risk of loss on loans and derivative investments. Other corporations have focused on broad business risks such as are covered in recent studies by the Institute of Internal Auditors (IIA)[2] or in the jointly published study by the AICPA and CICA.[3] Table 6.1 provides a summary of the business risks identified in the two studies.

TABLE 6.1

IDENTIFICATION OF
BUSINESS RISKS

RISK FOCUS/CATEGORIES		AICPA/CICA	INSTITUTE OF INTERNAL AUDITORS
Company objectives		x	
Areas of impact:	Reputation	x	
	Assets, revenues, costs	x	
	Performance	x	
	Stakeholders	x	
Sources of risk:	Environmental	x	
	Strategic	x	x
	Operational	x	x
	Informational	x	
	Financial		x
Specific hazards or perils:	Lawsuits		x
	Fire	x	
	Theft	x	
	Earthquake/natural disasters	x	x
Degree of control over the risk	Little, some, great	x	
Documentation		x	

---

[1]The Toronto Stock Exchange, for example, identified risk management as a matter requiring oversight by directors in 1995.

[2]*Enterprise Risk Management: Trends and Emerging Practices*, Tillinghast-Towers Perrin and the Institute of Internal Auditors Research Foundation, 2001.

[3]*Managing Risk in the New Economy*, American Institute of Certified Public Accountants and the Canadian Institute of Chartered Accountants, 2001.

To further illuminate the nature of risks examined for, Table 6.2 provides a list of those risk events that gave rise to drops of over 25 percent in the stock values of *Fortune 1000* companies from 1993 to 1998 classified according to the IIA study schema.

TABLE 6.2

RISK EVENTS CAUSING A DROP OF OVER 25 PERCENT IN FORTUNE 1000 STOCKS, 1993–1998

		PERCENT
Strategic Risks	Customer demand shortfall	24
	Competitive pressure	12
	M&A integration problems	7
	Misaligned products	6
	Customer pricing pressures	4
	Loss of key customer	2
	Regulatory problems	1
	R&D delays	1
	Supplier problems	1
		58
Operational Risks	Cost overruns	11
	Accounting irregularities	7
	Management ineffectiveness	7
	Supply chain issues	6
		31
Financial	Foreign macroeconomic issues	3
	High input commodity price	2
	Interest ratio fluctuation	1
		6
Hazard	Lawsuits	0
	Natural disasters	0
		0
Unknown		5

SOURCE: Figure 0.3, Mercer Management Consulting, reproduced in IIA Study, xxix.[4]

It should be noted that most of the risks identified have little to do with ethics. However, the 1993–1998 period ends just before the catastrophic chain of Arthur Andersen client bankruptcies began. If the question, "What caused the largest bankruptcies from 1998 to 2002?" were asked, the focus would have been on Sunbeam, Waste Management, Enron, and WorldCom. Each case would have involved ethics malfeasance or moral hazard, and although each could have been attributed to accounting irregularities, they were ultimately the result of poor or inadequate governance, and inadequate ethical/internal controls. Therefore, *although risk management to date has focused on nonethics matters,*

---

[4]*Enterprise Risk Management.*

evidence suggests that avoidance of catastrophic and embarrassing failures should include a focus on ethics risk identification and management processes in the future.

OVERRELIANCE ON EXTERNAL AUDITORS—NEW FRAUD STANDARDS

Some directors and executives presumed that their external auditors were reviewing for risks, and that any risks found would be brought to the attention of management and/or directors. This reliance, however, was misplaced.

Although, as part of their audit, external auditors were to review a corporation's internal controls and sometimes their business risks, the normal external audit mandate required concern only if risks found would have resulted in a material misstatement of the results of operations or financial position of the company. Moreover, since external auditors were only testing, they were not expected to find every problem. In addition, until fiscal periods beginning on or after December 15, 2002, they were not expected to look seriously for fraud. There never has been a requirement for external auditors to search for and report ethics opportunities.

The Enron and WorldCom disasters, and the Sarbanes-Oxley Act of 2002, have raised the need for greater fraud awareness, examination, and reporting thereon, and for external auditors to look for fraud more diligently. In response, the AICPA has released a new Statement of Auditing Standards (SAS 99)[5] that redefines expectations of external auditors in the United States in regard to:

- Mandatory discussion and brainstorming among the audit team of and about the potential and causes for material misstatement in the financial statements due to fraud before and during the audit[6]
- Guidance to be followed about data gathering and audit procedures to identify the risks of fraud[7]
- Mandatory assessment of the risks of fraud based upon the risk factors found, and under revised assumptions of management innocence to guilt,[8] as follows:
  - Presume ordinarily that there is a risk of manipulation of revenues due to fraud and investigate
  - Always identify and assess the risks that management could override controls as a fraud risk
- Increased standards for examination, documentation, and reporting on audit steps taken to assure that manipulation did not occur
- Other measures including:
  - Support of research on fraud
  - Development of antifraud criteria and controls
  - Allocation of 10 percent of CPE credits to fraud study
  - Development of fraud training programs for the public
  - Encouraging antifraud education at universities, as well as appropriate materials[9]

---

[5]"SAS 99," Official Releases column in the *Journal of Accountancy*, January 2003, 105–120.
[6]"Auditor's Responsibility for Fraud Detection," *Journal of Accountancy*, January 2003, 28–36.
[7]Ibid., 30–32.
[8]Ibid., 32.
[9]"Auditor's Responsibility," 36.

According to the Sarbanes-Oxley Act (SOX), management is now expected to report on the system of internal controls, and external auditors must report on the system as well as on management's report.

Even after the adoption of SOX reforms, external auditors will be looking for fraud and/or flaws in controls that will give rise to material misstatements of the financial statements. They will not normally be expected to pursue immaterial or other nonfinancial risks or opportunities. In other words, *they will not normally be expected to raise all ethical risks or opportunities* with management or the audit committee of the board. Consequently, directors and executives, who are responsible for monitoring all ethics risks, must design in-house audit or review processes, or specifically contract with designated outsiders to perform those reviews.

ETHICS RISKS

In view of the newly emerged accountability of corporations to stakeholders, modern governance systems need to reflect the importance of satisfying the interests of stakeholders. Stakeholder satisfaction, in turn, is based upon the respect a corporation shows for the interests of each stakeholder group from whom the corporation wants and needs support to reach its strategic objectives. Within this context, *ethics risks were defined in Chapter 1 as risks of not meeting stakeholder expectations—where not meeting expectations leads to a potential loss of support for a corporation's objectives, and exceeding expectations leads to an opportunity of greater support through the creation of a competitive advantage.* This provides a much broader framework for risk assessment than most corporations have employed. Indeed, most corporations have not looked for the risks of unethical behavior, let alone the broadened risks of not meeting, or the opportunities of exceeding, important stakeholder expectations.

To be fair, there has been some overlap in the traditional risk assessment approaches with the ethics risk/stakeholder interests assessment (ERSIA) approach as is shown in Table 6.3. However, even in cases of overlap, the focus of the non-ERSIA approaches and the mindset of investigators have not been as broad as is now deemed appropriate. That is because the focus has been on what is important from a shareholder rather than a stakeholder perspective. *Without the stakeholder support perspective, an investigator may not recognize risks that could lead to loss of support or opportunities for the creation of competitive advantage based on support.*

ETHICS RISK AND OPPORTUNITY IDENTIFICATION AND ASSESSMENT

The processes involved in ethics risk and opportunity assessment are presented in Figure 6.1.

Phase 1 of a sound ethics risk identification and assessment process should begin with the identification of the corporation's major stakeholders and their interests using the techniques discussed in Chapter 5. Investigators should then rank stakeholder interests in importance using the urgency, legitimacy, and power framework[10] and dynamic influence analysis[11] also developed in Chapter 5. After

---

[10]Mitchell, R. K., Agle, B. R., and Wood, D. J., "Toward a Theory of Stakeholder Identification and Salience: Defining the Principle of Who and What Really Counts," *Academy of Management Review,* Vol. 22, No. 4, 1997, 853–886.

[11]Rowley, T., "Moving Beyond Dyadic Ties: A Network Theory of Stakeholder Influences," *Academy of Management Review,* Vol. 22, No. 4, 1997, 887–910.

TABLE 6.3

OVERLAP OF TRADITIONAL AND ETHICS RISK/STAKEHOLDER INTERESTS ASSESSMENT APPROACHES

| | USUALLY IMPORTANT STAKEHOLDER GROUPS | | | | | |
RISKS	**SHAREHOLDERS**	**CONSUMERS**	**EMPLOYEES**	**GOVERNMENT**	**ENVIRON**	**MEDIA**
Strategic						
Reputation	x	x	Some		Some	Some
Stakeholder	x	x	x	Some	Some	Some
Other	x					
Operations	x	Partial	Partial		Partial	
Financial	x					
Hazard	x	Partial	Partial		Partial	
Ethics	Full	Full	Full	Full	Full	Full

FIGURE 6.1

ETHICS RISK AND OPPORTUNITY
IDENTIFICATION AND
ASSESSMENT

completion of these steps, investigators should have an understanding of which stakeholder interest issues are sensitive and important, and why.

Next, the investigator should confirm these assessments by interacting with a representative stakeholder panel and with important stakeholder groups. This will show concern for their interests and open a dialog that should build trust that could be helpful if unfortunate problems arise later. At the end of this process of stakeholder consultation, a confirmed grid of important stakeholder expectations for performance should emerge.

In Phase 2, investigators should consider their corporation's activities against the mosaic of stakeholder expectations, and assess the risks of not meeting and the opportunities for exceeding expectations. When considering whether expectations have been met, comparisons should be made of relevant input, output, quality, and other performance variables.

In addition, comparison should be made of company activities and stakeholder expectations using the six hypernorm values identified in Chapter 1 that are universally respected in most cultures. *The six hypernorm values are honesty, fairness, compassion, integrity, predictability, and responsibility.*[12] If corporate activities respect these values, there is a good chance that those activities will also respect the expectations of the corporation's important stakeholders, domestic and foreign, now and in the near future.

Finally, the comparison of corporate activities and expectations should be reassessed from the perspective of potential impacts on the corporation's reputation. Charles Fombrun's model[13] where *reputation depends upon four factors—trustworthiness, credibility, reliability, and responsibility*—can be a helpful framework to organize the comparison.

REPORTING AND ACTION

Phase 3 involves preparation of the reports generated by the process. Specific corporate needs should dictate the nature of the reports presented, but consideration should be given to at least the following reports:

- Ethics risks and opportunities:
  - By stakeholder group
  - By product or service
  - By corporate objective
  - By hypernorm value
  - By reputation driver

This set will provide data that will allow directors and executives to monitor ethics risks and opportunities, to plan to avoid and mitigate risks, and to strategically take advantage of opportunities.

Someone such as the corporate ethics officer or corporate social responsibility officer should be charged with the ongoing responsibility of monitoring the assumptions and inputs to the ERSIA model, and for reporting to the relevant subcommittee of the board on a periodic basis. Letting down the corporate guard on this continuing oversight could have serious consequences, as we have recently seen.

Ethics Strategies and Tactics for Effective Stakeholder Relations

Strategies and tactics can be developed for dealing with each stakeholder or group, based upon an assessment of stakeholder interests and possible changes in them. One approach originated by Savage et al. focuses on the potential for stakeholders to pose a threat to the organization, or to cooperate with it. Stakeholders can be susceptible to invitations to collaborate or become co-supporters or, if they are not amenable to the company's position, consideration may be

---

[12]Berenbeim, Ronald E., The Conference Board, Director, Working Group on Global Business Ethics Principles, 1999.

[13]Fombrun, C. J., *Reputation: Realizing Value from the Corporate Image*, Harvard Business School Press, Boston, 1996.

FIGURE 6.2

DIAGNOSTIC TYPOLOGY OF
ORGANIZATIONAL
STAKEHOLDERS

		Stakeholder's Potential for Threat	
		High	**Low**
Stakeholder's Potential For Cooperation	**High**	Type 4 **Mixed Blessing** Strategy **Collaborate**	Type 1 **Supportive** Strategy **Involve**
	Low	Type 3 **Nonsupportive** Strategy **Defend**	Type 2 **Marginal** Strategy **Monitor**

SOURCE: G. Savage et al., "Strategies for Assessing and Managing Organizational Shareholders, "*The Executive*, Vol. 5, No. 2, May 1991, 65.

The model suggests that the most desirable stakeholder group (Type 1) is likely to pose a low threat to an organization's objectives and a high degree of cooperation with them. If possible, it makes sense to *involve* this group more closely with the organization because they are likely to be *supportive*. A stakeholder group that is ranked high on cooperation and high as a potential threat holds some promise (i.e., is a *mixed blessing*), and it is wise to try to *collaborate* with them to keep them as supporters. Where a stakeholder group is ranked as a high threat and a low cooperator, they are considered *nonsupportive* and should be *defended* against. A group low in potential to threaten and low in potential to cooperate is *marginal* to the development of support for company objectives, but it may be wise to *monitor* their expectations in the event that conditions change.

It should be noted that this is a somewhat static analysis. Consequently, any strategy developed should be confirmed through periodic re-analysis that considers possible alliances of stakeholder groups through the use of the urgency, power, and legitimacy framework, and particularly the position of and trends in media coverage. Surprise embarrassment can erode support very quickly. Where possible, advance communication with supporters is attractive in maintaining their support. Of course, the creation of rapport and trust will assist in providing an opportunity to explain problems or tactics if necessary.

It is also worth considering how stakeholders in one cell of the model can be moved to a more supportive position. With this in mind, even if one group is being defended against, continuing to consider how to convert the group to supporters is worthwhile. Therefore, many stakeholder groups should be the focus of more than one strategy at any time.

Workplace Ethics—A Significant Ethical Problem Area

The increasing levels of social conscience and the pressures of activist groups that have been documented elsewhere have had a significant impact on both the internal and external operations of organizations. Consequently, it is appropriate for businesspeople to have an appreciation of the major ethical themes and issues that have emerged or are emerging with regard to the conduct of employees in North American workplaces. The comments that follow are not intended to provide an exhaustive review, but they will raise awareness of the issues and provide some guidance, including when to seek more informed advice.

EMPLOYEE RIGHTS

Since the early 1970s, there has been an increasing awareness that the rights of individual workers were worthy of more respect relative to the rights of the employer. For example, the employer no longer has the right to order his or her employees to pollute, to risk their health or safety or that of others, or to say nothing when the truth is being distorted. Some of the changed rights have become protected by new legislation, while others have been influenced by common law cases, union contracts, and corporate practices that have been sensitive to stakeholder pressures.

Table 6.4 identifies those employee themes in North America that have led to new expectations by employees.

PRIVACY AND DIGNITY

The right of an employer to search the person of an employee, to access any personal information desired, or to search any property has become significantly

TABLE 6.4

EMPLOYEE RIGHTS THEMES IN NORTH AMERICA

Privacy and dignity of person, personal information, and property:
- Boundaries of personal rights, employers' rights, and right of the public
- Proper procedures: notification and consent
- Testing for substance abuse
- Harassment, sexual and otherwise

Fair treatment:
- Discrimination: age, race, sex, employment, pay
- Fair policies
- Is equal treatment fair?

Healthy and safe work environment:
- Expectations: reasonability, right to know, stress, family life, productivity
- Quality-of-life concerns: smoking, health
- Family-friendly workplaces

Ability to exercise conscience:
- Blind loyalty
- Whistle-blowing

Trust—the key to leadership, innovation, loyalty, and performance—depends on ethics:
- Operations: downsizing, contingent workforce

curtailed. North American society now endorses the position that an *individual's personal rights are more important that those of an employer,* unless it can be shown that, in a particular circumstance, the employer's interest is reasonable, legitimate, and morally acceptable. For example, in most locales it is not acceptable to place a surveillance camera in a washroom unless there is a threat to life and health, such as through violent attacks or drug dealing. Even in these cases, outside legal authorities should be consulted prior to the surveillance, and in some cases notification of the intent to use a camera may be called for.

It should be noted, however, that simply notifying workers should not be taken to imply that they have consented to the procedure. Specific conditions must be met before the courts will agree that proper procedures have been followed. In fact, workers must be allowed what is called *informed consent,* wherein they have time to deliberate, have a free choice among reasonable alternatives, and have adequate information to understand the problem and options. In addition, the choice must be one that the courts consider possible to agree to make. An employee, for instance, cannot bargain away his or her right to life or to agree to assume extremely serious health risks. Legal advice is vital before action is taken.

Testing for substance abuse is a related area where North American society has been reluctant to accept invasion of privacy without compelling reason, usually involving the life and health of coworkers or others. Indeed, random drug testing for airplane pilots was only approved by the U.S. Supreme Court in the late 1990s. Drug testing has been relatively inaccurate when measured against the potential harm done to the falsely accused, so that discreet, repeat testing is desirable if an initial test is positive before any accusations are made. Confidentiality should be maintained throughout this time period if at all possible. There have been some testing programs for office workers, but several have been struck down by the courts as being unreasonable. For example, the Exxon program of random testing (started in response to the Exxon Valdez shipwreck, see case at the end of this chapter) was considered to be too unreasonable because it resulted in a reassignment/suspension from the employee's position for up to seven years. The Toronto-Dominion bank program for new recruits was considered not to be sufficiently justified by the bank's desire to ensure that their employees would protect customers' assets properly to warrant allowing the personal intrusion involved. It appears, however, that the stigma associated with drug and alcohol testing programs can be circumvented. Some trucking companies achieve the same ends (protection of the public and their assets) by requiring their drivers to score well on computer games (which feature hand-eye coordination) before they will be given their truck keys. Society does not regard such testing as sufficient invasion of privacy to object to its use.

Harassment is, of course, not only objectionable on grounds of dignity and privacy, but also on grounds of fairness. Definitions of harassment vary depending on the locale, but the trend is toward more stringent tests than most businesspeople or professionals initially contemplate. *Harassment can be defined as any improper behavior directed at you that you find offensive, and that the other person knew or ought reasonably to have known would be unwelcome.* Note that the test is not what the person doing the harassment thought about the act—the important test is what the offended party thought and whether the local authorities think it is reasonable behavior. Usually they side with the offended person. It is therefore imperative if an employee alleges harassment that the claim be investigated immediately and discreetly. If the claim is justified, then the perpetrator should be warned, or dismissed if already warned, and dismissed subject to the due process rules of the company involved. If prompt action is not taken, the manager receiving the complaint and the company can be subject to legal proceedings for failing to provide a harassment-free workplace. In fact, if a traveling salesperson or visiting auditor is harassed, his or her organization must contact the management of the offending company and see that appropriate action is taken, otherwise the complainant's manager and company can be subject to legal proceedings.

FAIR TREATMENT

Discrimination is considered to be unethical and illegal if it involves age, race, gender, and sexual preference. In addition, it is generally held that there should be equal opportunity for employment, and equal pay for equal work, particularly for women and minorities. Many leading-edge companies strive to hire a representative workforce that reflects the population that they are operating in. "The glass ceiling" is a term that is used to describe the barrier women face to promotion within their organizations, and some firms have found a competitive advantage in removing barriers and creating a level playing field for women and men. The Bank of Montreal, for example, found that many outstanding women managers applied for jobs when it did so, thus leaving other Canadian banks facing a dearth of promotable women.

Workers in North America believe that they are entitled to fair policies. These include fair wages, fair hours, fair consideration for promotion, and, for downsizing (see the Texaco's Jelly Beans case at the end of this chapter), a fair hearing. If dismissal is required, they expect that it will be according to appropriate or due process, including adequate notice or pay in lieu of notice. Unjust dismissals are those that do not follow fair due process, and these can result in reinstatement, remedial payments, and/or fines.

It should be noted that persons with disabilities are frequently accorded more than an equal chance for employment. This treatment is considered fair and ethical in view of their disabilities.

HEALTHY AND SAFE WORK ENVIRONMENT

The balance between the rights of workers and owners has shifted to the point that it is considered ethical for workers to expect that their health and safety will not be unreasonably compromised. They must know what the risks are in advance, and many jurisdictions have created right-to-know laws to ensure that organizations make information on hazardous substances, processes, and related treatments readily accessible.

Concern is presently being expressed over extending these arguments to the less tangible areas of excessive stress in terms of hours of overtime expected, extreme levels of productivity, and degradation of family life. No guidelines have yet emerged, but the pressure for them will grow, so a watch should be kept for future developments.

It is apparent that responsible companies are showing respect for the preferences of their workers before they are forced to do so by changing regulations. Smoke-free workplace areas are a case in point. In addition, companies are recognizing the need for fitness and recreation by establishing centers for these on-site. The desire to improve the family-friendliness of workplaces has led to the provision of on-site daycare for children of employees, the institution of flexible work times, and other similar arrangements.

ABILITY TO EXERCISE ONE'S CONSCIENCE

As noted elsewhere, the argument that a worker just did what he or she was ordered to do will no longer provide the worker with protection in many jurisdictions. The concept of *blind loyalty* is not one that many employees are comfortable with, in any case. They would prefer to bring their concerns forward and speak out against pollution or other misdeeds, but they frequently are prevented from doing so by their caution in exposing themselves to the wrath of their coworkers or managers.

Whistle-blowing, while it could contribute to a more ethical organization, is nonetheless something most North Americans were taught not to do when they were growing up, and a stigma continues to be attached to it. To encourage whistle-blowers to come forward within the organization, rather than have them report their concerns outside the enterprise, many companies are creating a whistle-blower protection program. In these programs, an inquiry or allegation is handled by an individual who has credibility with employees to undertake a speedy, fair investigation without revealing the name of the inquirer. If it becomes necessary for the inquirer to testify against the accused, then the inquirer is asked to do so and may decline. Reports of inquiries received are made on an aggregate basis, without revealing the names of the whistle-blowers. Some companies are calling these services Ethics Inquiry Services, rather than more pejorative terms such as a "hotline" or "whistle-blowing" service. There are also a growing number of statutes that seek to protect whistle-blowers. Therefore, and since secrets almost always become public, it would be wise for organizations to facilitate the exercise of employee conscience within the organization, where appropriate action can be taken without ruining the company's reputation.

TRUST AND ITS IMPORTANCE

Only recently have researchers begun to document what farsighted owners and managers have known for some time. As noted earlier, the ethics of an organization are directly related to how leaders are perceived, to whether there is there is sufficient trust for people to share ideas without fear of losing jobs or the respect of their coworkers and managers, and to whether they believe that the organization is worthy of loyalty and hard work (Brooks, 2000). It is increasingly unlikely that employees and managers will be willing to follow the instructions of an untrustworthy or unethical leader if they have any choice. Workers are not willing to contribute to innovation if they fear retribution or erosion of their position in some form, and they may not take the initiative on behalf of the company. Therefore, the organization will find that it may fall behind competitors whose employees trust the company and its leaders.

If employees have sufficient trust in their situation, they will participate wholeheartedly in restructuring sessions (this has been called a process of *ethical renewal*) that may even involve downsizing, and may accept the necessity of shared work assignments or part-time work contracts with greater understanding (this creates what is called a *contingent workforce*). To maintain the trust necessary for these steps, an organization has to be prepared to make trustworthy commitments to recall employees to full-time status when possible or to provide fair termination or contracting arrangements. Continuation of benefits is one such way of maintaining trust with a contingent workforce.

CONCLUSION

Many experts and successful practitioners subscribe to the view that *the way employees view their own treatment by the company determines what the employees think about their company's ethics program.* Consequently, if an organization wants employees to observe a set of corporate ethical values, the workers must be convinced that the organization really means what it says, and there must be a level of trust that permits this belief to flourish. Treating employees right is not only ethical, it is essential to carrying out the organization's ethics program and to achieving its strategic objectives.

International Operations—A Significant Ethical Problem Area

When any corporation operates outside of its domestic market, the normal guidance offered employees must be reconsidered as to:

- How their usual operating practices will impact on the local economy and culture
- Whether different local foreign practices such as widespread gift-giving or even bribery should be endorsed or banned
- The reaction to these changes by domestic stakeholders and particularly by primary stakeholders, including major customers and capital markets

IMPACTS ON LOCAL ECONOMIES AND THEIR CULTURES

Multinational corporations may have a significant impact on local cultures that they would not have domestically. They must be careful not to have unfavorable impacts on local:

- Labor markets: wage rates, availability of supply
- Raw material and other input markets
- Political and legal processes
- Religious and social customs

If, for example, a multinational corporation decides to ignore local religious and/or social customs, it and its workers may be accused of *cultural imperialism,* and may find it difficult to obtain cooperation for future activities. Similarly, by virtue of its size, a multinational corporation may so dominate the locale that there may be an unintended domination of local governments, courts, or elections that, again, may produce a backlash at some point.

CONFLICTS BETWEEN DOMESTIC AND FOREIGN CULTURES

Perhaps the most difficult problems arise when the values of the primary corporate stakeholders differ from that in the local foreign country. Differences noted in the media in recent years include:

- Approval of bribery (Southeast Asia)
- Use of child labor (Dominican Republic, Southeast Asia)
- Use of slave labor

- Unhealthy labor conditions
- Treatment of women
- Support of repressive regimes through location of operations (apartheid, Chile)
- Lack of freedom of association
- Respect for environment
- Dealings with family members are expected, not avoided

Often corporations locate operations in a country just because they want access to cheap labor, lower environmental protection costs, or less governmental red tape, and they are invited to come by the local politicians who do what they can by way of inducements. Why, then, should businesspeople worry about taking advantage of these opportunities when they find them? The reason lies in the new broader and global accountability that stakeholders expect and demand of corporations. Simply put, influential stakeholder groups have made it very difficult for corporations caught offending the values of the group anywhere in the world. Examples include:

- Boycott of clothing made in offensive labor situations:
  - Kathy Lee Gifford's line
  - Nike, Reebok, Adidas, and other shoe manufacturers
- Frustration of the intended scuttling of Shell's Brent Spar oil storage vessel in the depths of the North Sea (see case at the end of this chapter), and boycott of Shell products in Europe
- Worldwide boycott of Nestle products for distributing powdered baby food to mothers in South Africa, who mixed the powder with contaminated water and harmed their babies
- Activist investors in North America have pursued many mining companies for their poor environmental protection practices elsewhere
- Boycott of beef grown on land cleared of the Amazon rain forest

In addition, environmental and personal disasters such as at Bhopal have resulted in lawsuits launched by the same foreign politicians that invited the companies in and even entreated them to stay in adverse circumstances. Lawsuits have also arisen in the these cases in domestic jurisdictions where the offending company's stock has been traded because of investors' and/or foreigners' claims that management was negligent and should have issued warnings of heightened risk due to reduced safeguards. While it seems that some customers want cheap goods and some investors rejoice in high profits, there are others who care about how these are produced, and/or are willing to sue if an opportunity presents itself.

More important than the costs of a trial in terms of time lost, fines, and legal fees paid is the damage to a company's reputation. The impact of lost reputation may not be seen for awhile, but there is no doubt that it translates into lost future revenues of a very large magnitude.

Finally, the impact on the morale of domestic employees engaging in practices not considered worthy should be considered. Their desire to be productive and to produce at high levels of quality may be undermined, with serious consequences.

BRIBERY, FACILITATING PAYMENTS

In their foreign operations, multinational corporations are likely to be asked for facilitating payments or bribes. A *facilitating payment* is usually nominal in value and is made to speed up a result that would have happened anyway given enough time. A bribe is usually larger than nominal, and without which the desired result would not occur. Both payments are intended to influence outcomes, but some observers believe that a facilitating payment is of lesser ethical consequence than a bribe. Others can't see any difference between them.

http://brooks.
swlearning.com

One or both types of payment may be illegal, depending on the jurisdiction. Due to the recent instigation of a multinational group, Transparency International, the United States and other leading OECD (Organization for Economic Development) countries agreed to an OECD protocol whereby each signatory country would enact legislation, similar to the U.S. Foreign Corrupt Practices Act. When fully developed, these acts will allow a corporation that believes its foreign competitor is bribing officials in a third country to pursue the offending corporation through its domestic legal systems. For example, a U.S. corporation that suspected a German company of bribing officials in a South American country could apply to its U.S. legal system, which would, in turn, contact German authorities, who would search the German company's records for proof of the alleged transactions to be put forward in court. This initiative will make it much more risky to make payments to officials of foreign governments. It is a dramatic change from earlier positions where, for example, Germany considered a bribe outside of the country to be ethical and tax deductible, but a bribe inside Germany was considered unethical and illegal.

It should be clear that facilitating payments or bribes are problematic for reasons other than illegality, including:

- Adding to the cost of the operation, good, or service
- Undermining the practice of purchasing based on merit in a country or firm
- Risking possible negative consequences from stakeholder groups should they find out
- Impossibility of enforcing performance (obtaining a contract) after bribes are paid
- Impossibility of assessing sales force effectiveness
- Indicating to employees elsewhere in the multinational corporation that bribes are OK, in spite of what the code of conduct says
- Indicating to seekers of bribes elsewhere that bribes are possible if they ask

As a result, some multinational corporations have banned the giving of bribes or facilitating payments. All corporations should have a policy on paying bribes and facilitating payments, rather than leaving employees to make up their own minds as to when payment is appropriate.

APPARENT CULTURAL CONFLICTS WITH BANNING GIFTS, BRIBES, OR FACILITATING PAYMENTS

In some cultures, particularly in Southeastern Asia, China, and Japan, there is a long tradition of gift giving to cultivate long-term relationships that facilitate business dealings. In addition, it has been popularly believed that a corporation cannot do business in some countries unless payments are made to officials. Consequently, it has been said that, if a corporation wants to do business in certain markets, bribery or facilitating payments is necessary.

In fact, however, some corporations have found that they have been able to do business without such payments, primarily because their products or services are excellent. Allis Chalmers and Citibank are examples of such corporations.

MORAL IMAGINATION

In other corporations, managers have used their *moral imagination* to devise alternatives that answered needs in the host culture but conformed to North American norms for acceptable behavior. For example (see illustrative case in Chapter 5), a manager in China refused to pay officials of a potential host city, citing company policy. When the officials insisted repeatedly, the manager sought and received approval for a corporate contribution toward the establishment of a community center in a local park that would offer services to senior citizens. This appealed to Chinese cultural values and was in line with the corporation's North American policy of community support. It was differentiated from a bribe in that no payment was made to an individual for his or her personal benefit, and all payments were made in public rather than in secret.

GUIDELINES FOR ETHICAL PRACTICE

Two authors have made an extensive study of the ethics of foreign operations, and have written excellent books on the subject. Tom Donaldson (1989) and Richard DeGeorge (1993) have each put forward guidelines that may be useful for corporations to take note of. Their views are summarized in the reading at the end of the chapter by Nancy Roth et al. (1996). Tom Donaldson's (1996) excellent article on bribery and foreign cultures is also reproduced as a reading.

CONCLUSION

The presumption that an organization is best served by a monolithic and rigid ethical culture may not be correct. Certainly, leaving employees to determine how to deal with the various cultures encountered in international operations is a high-risk strategy. All organizations with international operations should sensitize their employees to cultural differences and equip them with an understanding of how the organization wants them to deal with the major issues likely to come up. At the very least, there should be an avenue of consultation with home office officials and a clear understanding of when to use it. Adherence to the six hypernorm values developed in earlier chapters could provide the core of a useful universal guidance regime.

Social Accountability And Audit

Corporations are recognizing that, although they were accountable only to shareholders or owners in the past, they are increasingly accountable to a broader range of stakeholders. *To this extent, a paradigm shift is underway, from accountability to shareholders to accountability to stakeholders.* As a result, organizations are increasingly interested in measuring the performance that various stakeholders are interested in to know what is going on, how management techniques are working, and what to report to board committees and perhaps to the public. This section on social accountability and audit is intended to review developments that should prove useful in deciding what to measure, how others are reporting, and what audit steps may be taken to give assurance to the accuracy of the information being generated and reported. North Americans will be surprised to find that they are probably lagging behind developments in Europe in this area.

There have been many terms used to describe measurement and audit activities in the area of social accountability and audit, such as social accounting (SA) and audit, social performance reporting and audit (SPR), corporate social responsibility (CSR) accounting (CSA) and audit, and corporate ethical performance (CEP) reporting (CEPR) and audit (CEPA). This review of the area will proceed using CSR nomenclature.

ORGANIZATIONAL OBJECTIVES FOR CSR

To develop a comprehensive plan or framework for CSR, an organization should consider its strategic goals, the cultures its operations will encounter, and the interests of its stakeholders, both in domestic and foreign theatres. These considerations, with the understanding of available measures of CSR discussed next, allow the architect of the corporation's systems to match the organization's aspirations with measures that will allow monitoring and reinforcement. Perhaps of equal or greater importance, they will also enable the organization's strategic planners to formulate objectives that are ethical and respectful of the interests of the stakeholders and cultures to be dealt with.

MEASUREMENT OF CORPORATE ETHICAL PERFORMANCE

Measurements or indicators of CSR can take many forms. For example, there are a number of publications such as *Shopping for a Better World* (1994), *Shopping with a Conscience* (1996), and *Conscious Consumption* (2002) that rate the CSR of many companies and can be used as a guide in establishing an appropriate list of measures of interest to ethical investor and ethical consumers. Unfortunately, these measures, such as whether the company deals in armaments or tobacco, may not be useful for management purposes. More relevant measures may be found from the list of almost 80 indicators used by the *Corporate Ethics Monitor* in its "Comparisons of Ethical Performance," one of which is shown in Appendix A. These *measures of fact* are grouped into categories covering:

- Codes or statements of guidance, their currency, and their reinforcement
- Job creation: overall and with regard to women and minority groups
- Relations with communities and local stakeholders, including charitable donations
- Treatment of employees:
  - Progressive staff policies: family, health, training, communications, retirement, benefits programs
  - Gainsharing programs: stock options, profit sharing
  - Labor relations: unionization, safety
- Environmental management programs
- Environmental performance
- Ethical sourcing and trading practices

There are other measures that may be useful in revealing attitudes of managers and employees toward ethical issues. These may be useful in capturing information about actions that are about to happen, or about changes in attitude due to certain signals sent voluntarily or involuntarily by management or perceived by employees. Examples of such *anticipatory measures* are:

- Employee attitude surveys
- Customer or other stakeholder surveys
- Evaluation by paid "shoppers" or solicited customer complainants
- Media commentary assessment

Other measures can concentrate on the operational merit of the organization's fundamental building or support blocks for ethical behavior. This could include *quality assessments* of:

- Code of conduct
- Training programs
- Reinforcement mechanisms, including:
  - Newsletters, correspondence
  - Pay and reward systems
  - Promotion
- Whistle-blowing atmosphere/protection
  - Follow-up on reported problems
  - Speed of response
  - Fairness of hearing process and of the penalty assigned

As with most measurement schemes, *comparison with like organizations and/or with best-practice alternatives* can be helpful. Areas in which this benchmarking may be useful include:

- Environmental management programs and performance
- International operations
- Treatment of employees, customers, etc.

A further source of a measurement scheme can be found in the New York–based Center on Economic Priorities' SA8000 standard for working conditions. It can be accessed through the text's Website.

REPORTING OF CSR

The corporation that embarks on a CSR measurement program needs to consider how it will report on performance, and whether the report will be internal only or available to the public. Internal reports can take on any form, but should be focused on the program's performance objectives.

Public reports are becoming more common. For several years, specific companies and industries have disclosed their performance on dimensions that they know their stakeholders are interested in. For example, there are many corporate reports on environmental performance, and on health and safety performance. Many corporations are including these reports on their Websites, as well as issuing hard copies. Interesting Websites in this regard are listed on the text's Website.

http://brooks. swlearning.com

The most noteworthy comprehensive CSR reports that have been made public and may be viewed upon request or through the Website opposite are those from:

- Shell International
- The Body Shop
- The Co-operative Bank (UK) (Partnership Report)
- VanCity Credit Union (Social Report)

All four of these public reports are at least partially audited.

AUDIT OR VERIFICATION OF CSR REPORTS

Although there have been isolated examples of earlier attempts to audit or verify CSR claims, one of the recent developments is the increase of audited CSR reports, particularly in Europe. European initiatives in environmental protection, and through the International Standards Association (ISO), have had a driving influence on corporate behavior and have required public disclosure of environmental performance. As a result, many individuals and some large audit firms have become involved in attesting to the reports issued. Most of these individuals are not professionally qualified as expected in North America of professional accountants. Therefore, care should be taken when relying on such audits. Also, where KPMG and PricewaterhouseCoopers have certified the Environmental Report for Shell, the wording of their report is very limited as to scope.

In summary, the area of audit verification of CSR reports is in its infancy as far as standards of professionalism are concerned, particularly with regard to scope, techniques, and standard audit reporting. However, this is sure to change as the professional societies take a greater interest in these areas. Moreover, the next phase of ISO reporting (for ISO 14000) may well push currently registered firms beyond documentation of systems to the reporting and audit levels. Indeed, the newer European EMASS process goes farther that the ISO standards. Information on these standards may be accessed on the Website opposite. It should be noted that ISO auditors and SA8000 auditors are certified by the organizations involved.

The current status of environmental reporting and auditing in Canada has been reviewed by Nitkin and Brooks (1998). Most corporations are using their own personnel to audit CSR reports. Internal audit staff may be used, as may managers for other divisions of a company. Questions that may guide auditors of an ethics program are listed in Appendix B to this chapter.

One such managerial audit approach for a broadly based corporate ethics program was used by Dow Corning and was lionized in Harvard Business School cases prior to the unfortunate breast implant scandal. It should be pointed out that the CSR of Dow Corning remains convinced of the worth of the company's ethics audit program, but acknowledges that improvements were warranted. Part of the story appears in the Dow Corning Case on page 192.

A second initiative, called the Mattel Independent Monitoring Council for Global Manufacturing Principles (MIMCO), is discussed in an article by S. Prakash Sethi (1999). Mattel was intent on creating a useful code of conduct and in ensuring that its global manufacturing principles were complied with through an independent monitoring process with the mandate to make its findings public. In so doing, Mattel wished to identify itself "as a socially responsible company and a good corporate citizen." Prior to conducting field audits, the Council developed "highly objective, quantifiable, precise, and strategically rigorous set of instruments ... that cover, among other things:

- Worker's environment, health and safety, and working conditions.
- Wages and working hours.
- Living conditions.
- Communications with the management concerning their living and working conditions, new employee orientation methods, and regular training programs."

This independent review process followed earlier in-house audits, and engagement of suppliers in remediation processes or in termination of relations. The public reports of MIMCO can be found on the Mattel Website Corporate Responsibility page.

CONCLUSION

As the corporate accountability paradigm continues to shift toward increasing accountability to stakeholders, managers and professional accountants will have to become involved as designers, preparers, and as assurance providers. Developing an effective system of social accountability will greatly facilitate better management of an organization's ethical culture and performance. It would be well worth the time to monitor new initiatives in this area, including the Sustainability Reporting Guidelines that are part of the CERES Global Sustainability Reporting Initiative (GRI), and new Standards in Social and Accountability Reporting from the Institute of Social and Ethical AccountAbility.

http://brooks. swlearning.com

Crisis Management – A Significant Ethical Problem Area

Crises are pervasive in the current business environment. In the *1997 Crisis Management Survey of Fortune 1000 Companies,* 71% of the respondents companies had a crisis management plan and/or program in place, and almost a further 12% indicated that one was in development (Questions 1, 2). This is because of the very significant potential impact of a crisis on the reputation of the company and its officers, on the company's ability to reach its objectives, and its ability to survive (Lerbinger, 1997, p. 4). As a result, executives have learned that crises are to be avoided, and if avoidance is not possible, that the crisis is to be managed so as to minimize the harm done. Directors have learned that crisis assessment, planning and management must be part of a modern enterprise risk management program.

Unfortunately, the urgent nature of a crisis causes a focus on survival, and ethical niceties are largely forgotten. According to Lerbinger, a crisis "is an event that brings, or has the potential for bringing, an organization into disrepute and imperils its future profitability, growth, and, possibly its very survival (p. 4)." Effective management of such events involves minimisation of all harmful impacts. In reality, crisis-driven reactions rarely approach this objective unless advance planning is extensive, and is based upon a good understanding of crisis management techniques including the importance of maintaining reputation based upon ethical behavior.

If ethical behavior is considered to be of great importance by a corporation in its normal activities, ethical considerations should be even more important in crisis situations since crisis resolution decisions usually define the company's future reputation. Not only are crisis decisions among the most significant made in terms of potential impact on reputation, opportunities may also be lost if ethical behavior is not a definite part of the crisis management process. For example: avoidance of crises may be easier if employees are ethically sensitized to stakeholder needs; phases of the crisis may be shortened if ethical behavior is expected of employees and/or damage to reputations may be minimized if the public expects ethical performance based on past corporate actions. Moreover, the degree of trust which ethical concern instils in a corporate culture will ensure that no information or option will be suppressed and not be given to the decision maker. Finally, constant concern for ethical principles should ensure that important issues are identified and the best alternatives canvassed to produce the optimal decision for the company.

Fundamental to the proper management of a crisis is an understanding of four phases of a crisis: pre-crisis, uncontrolled, controlled, and reputation restoration, which are outlined in Figure 6.3. The main goal of crisis management should be to avoid crises. If this is not possible, then the impacts should be minimized. This can be done by anticipating crisis or recognizing early warning signs as soon as possible, and responding to soften or minimize the impact and shorten the time during which the crisis is uncontrolled. These goals can best be achieved by proper advance planning, by continued monitoring, and by speedy, effective decision making during the crisis. Figure 6.3 shows two cost curves, where the lower one reflects the benefits of earlier control being applied, thus minimizing the overall cost and the ongoing damage to reputation.

FIGURE 6.3

PHASES OF A CRISIS

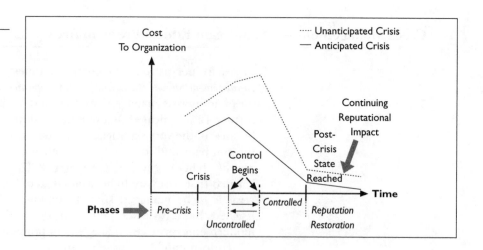

Advance planning for a crisis should be part of a modern enterprise risk assessment and contingency management program because of the growing recognition of the potential negative impact of an unanticipated crisis. It can be done effectively by brainstorming for potential problem areas, assessing those identified, and devising contingency plans for effective action. Second, red flags or warning indicators can be picked out which will identify what is developing so that the earliest action can be taken to minimize cost. In the 1997 survey noted above, 73% of the companies reporting had a senior level management and corporate level crisis management team that would focus on the crisis, and 76% had a crisis communication plan (questions 6, 50), which could include notification of the public, employees, government and the media.

The process of brainstorming to identify crises should consider problems that could arise of the seven types identified by Lerbinger (1997, pp.10–14):

1. Natural disasters
2. Technological disasters
3. Differences of expectations between individuals, groups and corporations leading to confrontations
4. Malevolent acts by terrorists, extremists, governments and individuals
5. Management values that do not keep pace with environmental and social requirements and obligations
6. Management deception
7. Management misconduct.

Managing the crisis effectively once it has happened is vital to the achievement of crisis management goals. Quick identification and assessment of a crisis can be instrumental in influencing the outcome efficiently and effectively. One of the key characteristics of a crisis is that it will degenerate if no action is taken (Hermann, 1963), so delay in identification and action can have serious consequences.

73% of the *Fortune* 1000 companies responding to the survey indicated that internal training was part of preparing for crisis awareness, identification and management, and 48% used outside contract trainers (Question 39). Major factors listed by respondents as needing improvement in crisis management included: internal awareness (51%), communication (46%), drills/training (38%), vulnerability/risk assessment (36%), information technology (33%), planning/coordinating (32%), and business continuity (25%) (Question 38).

Undivided attention to the crisis and avoidance of other problems which can befuddle decision makers will result in better decisions, just as will the making of plans on a contingency basis, and the integration of ethics into the decision making process.

One of the most important aspects to keep in mind during the assessment of crises, and how to avoid or minimize their impact, is the immediate and ongoing impact on the organization's reputation. By reflecting upon how the organization's response to the crisis will affect the perception by stakeholders of its trustworthiness, responsibility, reliability, and credibility, decision makers can make choices that benefit all stakeholders and often *enhance* the organization's reputational capital or shorten the period of diminishment.

Ethics can be integrated into the decision making process for crisis management in many ways. Specific instances involving prevention and warning, inclusion in an analytical approach, focussing a decision, and framing communications are outlined in Table 6.4.

TABLE 6.4

HOW TO INCORPORATE ETHICS
INTO CRISIS MANAGEMENT

Prevention and warning:
- Code of conduct: identify values, adopt, emphasize and make effective
- Identify potential ethics problems and warning indicators, and pre-plan responses, as part of an ongoing enterprise risk management and contingency planning program
- Ethical "red flags" or warning indicators:
  - Training to emphasize how to identify and what to do about them
  - Check as part of an ongoing enterprise risk management system
- Encourage by publicizing good examples, and awarding paper medals

Analytical approach:
- Apply a stakeholder-analysis framework as discussed in Chapter 5:
- External ethics consultant
- Checklist or specific time to consider:
  - ethics issues, alternatives & opportunities

Decision itself:
- Ethics/company's values: integrate into the decision making:
  - Consider how the crisis or its impact can be influenced ethically – timing, cost, mitigation?
  - Specific consideration of how to improve the organization's reputation drivers including – trustworthiness, responsibility, reliability, and credibility
  - Specific ethical communications objectives
  - Assign ethics watch-dog responsibility
  - Use a checklist or template with specific ethics objectives
  - Apply moral imagination as discussed in Chapter 5

Communications on ethical intent to:
- Media, employees, customers, government, public & other stakeholders

CONCLUSION

Modern corporations and other organizations are successful because they create, sustain, or inform upon value. Ultimately, success depends upon the support they engender from their stakeholders, and that depends upon the respect shown for stakeholder expectations. Appropriate or ethical behavior is therefore bounded by the expectations of stakeholders, and care is being shown for the creation of guidance and other means for encouraging employees to "do what is right."

In this new era of stakeholder accountability, organizations would do well to observe the six hypernorms: honesty, fairness, compassion, integrity, predictability, and responsibility. These values should be built into governance, risk management, strategy, operations, ethical decision making, disclosure, and crisis management. Reputation and success depend upon these values whether you are a director, executive, or professional accountant.

1. In what ways does ethics risk and opportunity management as described in this chapter go beyond the scope of traditional risk management?

2. If a corporation's governance process does not involve ethics risk management, what unfortunate consequences might befall a corporation?

3. How will the U.S. external auditor's mindset change in order to discharge the duties contemplated by SAS 99 on finding fraud?

4. How should a corporation keep abreast of the formulation of new alliances between stakeholders?

5. How could a corporation utilize stakeholder analysis to formulate strategies?

6. What would you list as the five most important ethical guidelines for dealing with North American employees?

7. Is trust really important—can't employees work effectively for someone they are afraid of, or at least where there is some "creative tension"?

8. Should a North American corporation operating abroad respect each foreign culture encountered, or insist that all employees and agents follow only one corporate culture?

9. What should a North American company do in a foreign country where women are regarded as secondary to men, and are not allowed to negotiate contracts or undertake senior coproate positions?

10. Descriptive commentary about corporate social performance is sometimes included in annual reports. Is this indicative of good performance, or is it just window dressing? How can the credibility of such commentary be enhanced?

11. Should professional accountants push for the development of a comprehensive framework for the reporting of corporate social performance? Why?

12. Do professional accountants have the expertise to audit corporate social performance reports?

13. Why should professional accountants be concerned that ethical decision making is incorporated into crisis management?

The cases provided to illuminate the issues developed in this chapter are surprisingly realistic and engage the reader quickly. The specific scenarios, with notation of the chapter section to which they primarily apply, are as follows:

Cases on Workplace Ethics

■ *Texaco's Jelly Beans* is the story of how Texaco's discrimination against black workers ended up costing a $300 million fine and lost respect. Why did it happen?

■ *Downsize or Bonus Allocation Decisions* confronts the reader with realistic, tough choices among staff, thus forcing decisions about what values the decision maker holds and which values ought to be communicated to the work team.

READINGS

The readings are intended to provide background on areas that will prove to be significant to future businesspeople and professional accountants. The drive to better manage corporate social performance will not subside, so articles by Roth et al., Donaldson, and Mitroff et al. should be essential reading. Appendices A and B on CSR/CEP programs and reporting provide useful benchmarks and frameworks.

REFERENCES

1997 Crisis Management Survey of Fortune 1000 Companies conducted by The George Washington University Institute for Crisis, Disaster, and Risk Management and The Corporate Response Group. The Survey had 105 respondents.

"Auditor's Responsibility for Fraud Detection," *Journal of Accountancy*, January 2003, 28–36.

Berenbeim, R. E., The Conference Board, Director, Working Group on Global Business Ethics Principles, 1999.

Brooks, L. J., "A Partial Preliminary Report on A Survey on the Effectiveness/Compliance of Corporate Codes of Conduct in Canada," unpublished manuscript, 1990.

_____, "Codes of Conduct, Trust, Innovation, Commitment, and Productivity: A Strategic-Cultural Perspective," Global Focus, Vol. 12, No. 2, 2000, 1–11.

Corporate Ethics Monitor, EthicScan Canada, Toronto, Canada.

Council on Economic Priorities, *SA8000: Guideline for Social Accountability*, New York, 1997.

De George, R. T., *Competing with Integrity in International Business*, Oxford University Press, Inc, New York, 1993.

Donaldson, T., *The Ethics of International Business*, Oxford University Press, Inc., New York, 1989.

_____, "Values in Tension: Ethics Away from Home," *Harvard Business Review*, September–October, 1996, 48–62.

Enterprise Risk Management: Trends and Emerging Practices, Tillinghast-Towers Perrin and the Institute of Internal Auditors Research Foundation, 2001.

Fombrun, C. J., *Reputation: Realizing Value from the Corporate Image*, Harvard Business School Press, Boston, 1996.

Gellerman, S. W., "Why Good Managers Make Bad Choices," *Harvard Business Review*, Vol. 64, Iss. 4(1986): 85–90.

Hermann, Charles F., "Some Consequences of Crisis Which Limit the Viability of Orgnizations," *Administrative Sciences Quarterly*, Vol. 8, No. 1 (1963), 62–82. Noted in Lerbinger, 1997, 7.

Lerbinger, Otto, *The Crisis Manager: Facing Risk and Responsibility*, Lawrence Erlbaum Associates, Inc., Mahwah, New Jersey, 1997.

Managing Risk in the New Economy, American Institute of Certified Public Accountants and the Canadian Institute of Chartered Accountants, 2001.

Maslow, A. H., *Motivation and Personality*, Harper and Row, 1954.

Mitchell, R. K., Agle, B. R., and Wood, D. J., "Toward a Theory of Stakeholder Identification and Salience: Defining the Principle of Who and What Really Counts," *Academy of Management Review*, Vol. 22, No. 4, 1997, 853–886.

Mitroff, I. I., Shrivastava, P., and Udwadia, F. E., "Effective Crisis Management," *Academy of Management Executive*, Vol. 1, No. 3, 1987, 283–292.

Nitkin, D., and Brooks, L. J., "Sustainability Auditing and Reporting: The Canadian Experience," *Journal of Business Ethics*, Vol. 17, 1998, 1499–1507.

Nudell, Mayer and Norman Antokol, *The Handbook for Effective Emergency and Crisis Management*, Lexington Books, 1988.

Pellizzari, P., *Conscious Consumption: Corporate Social Responsibility and Canada's Grocery Giants*, EthicScan Canada, 2002.

Roth, N. L., Hunt, T., Stravropoulos, M., and Babik, K., "Can't we all just get along: cultural variables in codes of ethics," *Public Relations Review*, Summer 1996, Vol. 22, No. 2, 15, 151–161.

Rowley, T., "Moving Beyond Dyadic Ties: A Network Theory of Stakeholder Influences," *Academy of Management Review*, Vol. 22, No. 4, 1997, 887–910.

"SAS 99," Official Releases column in the *Journal of Accountancy*, January 2003, 105–120.

Savage, G., "Strategies for Assessing and Managing Organizational Shareholders," *The Executive*, Vol. 3, No. 2, May 1991, 65.

Sethi, S. P., "Codes of Conduct for Global Business: Prospects and Challenges of Implementation," in *Principles of Stakeholder Management*, The Clarkson Centre for Business Ethics, 1999, 9–20.

Shopping for a Better World, Council on Economic Priorities, New York, 1994.

Shopping with a Conscience, by Achar, R., Nitkin, D., Otto, K., Pellzzari, P., and EthicScan Canda, John Wiley & Sons, Toronto, 1996.

Sustainability Reporting Guideline, CERES, Boston, Mass., 1999 (see http://brooks.swlearning.com).

Wartick, S. L. and Cochran, P. L., "The Evolution of the Corporate Social Performance Model," *Academy of Management Review*, 1985, Vol. 10, No. 4, 758–769.

Ethics case on workplace ethics

Texaco's Jelly Beans[1]

In March 1994, six African Americans employed at Texaco Inc. filed a class action lawsuit on behalf of 1,400 current and former African American employees. They alleged that Texaco had systematically discriminated against them in terms of promotions and had fostered a hostile corporate environment for minority employees.[2]

Richard Lundwall was the senior coordinator of personnel services in the Finance Department at Texaco's office in Harrison, New York. During an August 5, 1994, deposition,[3] he testified that he and other officials in Texaco's Finance Department retained records relating to the promotion of minority employees. He was asked to produce these documents. On August 14, 1994, Lundwall attended a meeting with other members of the Texaco Finance Department to discuss the production of these requested documents. Among the officers attending this meeting were Robert Ulrich, treasurer; David Keough, senior assistant treasurer; and various division heads such as Peter Meade, Brian Ashley, Pete Wissel, and Steve Carlson.[4] Prior to entering the meeting, Lundwall placed a small tape recorder in his pocket and turned it on. When later asked why he had taken such action, he stated that "over the years I've seen a number of people thrown to the wolves when something went wrong, and I didn't want to be fodder for the wolves."[5] On a more practical level, however, Lundwall was also in charge of taking minutes of the meeting and found that recording the meetings ensured the accuracy of the minutes.[6] He stated that after the meeting he placed the tapes in his desk and forgot about them.[7]

In the spring of 1996, Lundwall was informed that he was being downsized out of his job and had to leave Texaco by the end of August 1996. After thirty-one years of loyal service to Texaco, he expected more; he had seen other employees being pushed out when they reached fifty-five years of age and realized that the same thing was now happening to him.[8] It was not until he was in the hospital recovering from surgery in March 1996 that he remembered the tapes and had time to listen to them.[9] Lundwall maintains, on an interview on *60 Minutes,* that he had only to mention his possession of the tapes to a senior executive and his job would have been secure. When asked why he did not take such an action, he responded, "It's not the right thing to do. That's called extortion and that's illegal. And . . . the world's a crummy enough place without adding to it."[10]

By July 1996, Lundwall realized that there would be no job at Texaco. On his last day of work, he approached one of the employees who had launched

---

1. Prepared from a case submission by students: Sudha Kutty, Philip Malin, Yasmina Miller, Shelley Pancham-Candler, and David Wong.

2. *Roberts et al. v Texaco Inc.,* 94 Civ. 2015.

3. U.S. Attorney, Southern District of New York. Press release. November 19, 1996.

4. Affidavit of Cyrus Mehri, sworn October 28, 1996, citing deposition of R. Lundwall.

5. *60 Minutes* interview, p. 2 transcript.

6. Affidavit of Cyrus Mehri, p. 6.

7. *60 Minutes.*

8. Ibid.

9. Ibid., p. 3.

10. Ibid.

—*Continued*

Continued

the suit and informed her that "depending on how my situation turns out, you might have an ally."[11] Lundwall's reasoning was that, if a job did surface, then he would not have been able to come forward with the tapes, not for a while, anyway.[12] On August 1, 1996, Lundwall contacted Cyrus Mehri at the law firm of Cohen, Milstein, Hausfield, and Toll, lawyers for the plaintiffs. He informed Mehri that he had in his possession information that would be useful in the lawsuit against Texaco. In subsequent conversations, Lundwall informed Mehri that such information included tape recordings. On August 12, 1996, Lundwall met with Mehri and informed him that the tape recordings, created after the litigation began, revealed himself and other senior officials in the Finance Department discussing the destruction of documents relevant to the plaintiffs' case.[13] After this meeting, Lundwall retained a lawyer and in September 1996 handed over copies of two tapes to attorneys for the plaintiffs. On October 25, 1996, Lundwall met again with Mehri and listened to the tapes. He confirmed that the tapes were the same ones he

had provided to his counsel to hand over.[14] He admitted that one of the purposes for the meeting of August 14, 1994, was to review the materials requested by the plaintiffs after the deposition and to hide documents from the plaintiffs. He admitted that he and others had shredded portions of the requested evidence, that handwritten comments were deleted from certain documents, and that certain finance officials were told to say that they did not retain their own copies of such information.[15] In one part of the tape, the following was revealed:

> **Ulrich:** You know, there is no point in even keeping the restricted version any more. All it could do is to get us in trouble. That's the way I feel. I would not keep anything.
> **Lundwall:** Let me shred this thing and any other restricted version like it.

In another segment:

> **Keough:** They'll find it when they look through it.
> **Lundwall:** Not if I take it out they won't.

Matters did not end here. The tape recording of the August 14, 1994, meeting contained other interesting bits of conversation. The initial

transcript of the recordings which hit the *New York Times* on November 4, 1996, indicated the use of expletives and racist terms such as niggers and "black jelly beans." According to the *Times*, at one point in the tape the treasurer states, "It's this diversity thing. You know how black jelly beans agree . . . ," To which Lundwall responds, "That's funny. All the black jelly beans seem to be glued to the bottom of the bag." At another point in the tape, Lundwall states, "I'm still having trouble with Hanukkah. Now we have Kwanzaa. These f—ing niggers, they s— all over us with this."[16]

Texaco was quick to act over the revelation of these tapes. At a news conference held on November 4, 1996, Texaco chairman, Peter Bijur, apologized for the remarks on the tape, stating that such remarks represent not only a profound contempt for the law but also a contempt for Texaco's values and policies. Bijur indicated that the company was taking six steps to reinforce company policy and its code of conduct. Such measures included visits by senior executives to company locations to apologize to employees, the expansion of

---

11. Ibid.
12. Ibid.
13. Affidavit of Joseph Magan, special agent with the FBI, sworn November 19, 1996.

14. Ibid.
15. Ibid.

16. Court TV Library: Texaco Suit—Order to Show Cause, Transcript. Kwanzaa is an African American cultural festival.

—Continued

Continued

Texaco's "diversity learning experience," and a renewed emphasis on the company's core values. Two current employees were suspended with pay, and the benefits of Lundwall and former treasurer Robert Ulrich (who had retired in March 1995) were cut off. Texaco retained the services of Peter Armstrong, former Assistant U.S. Attorney for the Southern District of New York, to conduct an independent investigation into the matter. In his report released November 11, 1996, Mr. Armstrong notes that by using digital processing techniques, he was able to obtain a clearer version of the recording.[17] After listening to this version, he concluded that the word *nigger* was never used, as initially alleged in the plaintiffs' transcript. The relevant portion of the tape is actually

> **Ulrich:** "I've heard that diversity thing, we don't have black jelly beans or green . . ."
> **Lundwall:** ". . . that's funny, all the black jelly beans seem to be glued to the bottom of the bag."

Through his attorney, Mr. Ulrich indicated that the term *jelly bean* was not meant to be pejorative and actually was a reference from a speech given by a gentleman later identified

as Doctor R. Roosevelt Thomas Jr. who uses a jelly bean analogy as a means of describing diversity.[18]

Armstrong's conclusion was that the terms "f—ing nigger" were never used and that the references to jelly beans do not appear to have been intended as a racial slur. Bijur was quick to indicate that these preliminary findings merely correctly identified what words were actually spoken in the conversation but by no means changed the unacceptable context or tone of the conversation. The report's findings were published in the *New York Times* on November 11, 1996. Civil rights leaders interviewed on November 12, 1996, felt that the distinction in the transcript made little difference, as the tone of the conversation indicated a clear disdain for both Hanukkah and Kwanzaa and revealed intolerant overtures.[19] Bijur spent most of the day meeting with civil rights leaders, such as Kweisi Mfume of the National Association for the Advancement of Colored People and Reverend Jesse Jackson, many of whom called for a national boycott of Texaco.

On November 15, 1996, Texaco announced it had

reached an Agreement in Principle to settle the *Roberts et al. v Texaco* lawsuit. The terms of the settlement were as follows:

- Provide payment to the plaintiff class in the amount of $115 million, in addition to a one-time salary increase of approximately 11 percent for current employees of the plaintiff class effective January 1, 1997[20]
- Create an Equality and Tolerance Task Force, which will be charged with determining potential improvements to Texaco's human resources programs and monitor the progress of such programs
- Adopt and implement companywide diversity and sensitivity, mentoring and ombudsperson programs
- Consider nationwide job posting of more senior positions
- Monitor its performance on the programs and initiatives provided for in the settlement agreement

---

17. Interim report, p. 2.

18. Ibid.
19. "Civil Rights Leaders Issue Call for a National Boycott of Texaco." Kurt Eichenwald, November 13, 1996.

20. For the sake of accuracy, it should be noted that the plaintiff class had yet to be certified as a class and was to appear before the court on December 6, 1996, for a hearing regarding class certification. In the Agreement in Principle, the parties agree for the sake of the settlement to the certification of a class consisting of all African Americans employed in a salaried position in the United States by Texaco or its subsidiaries at any time from March 23, 1991, to November 16, 1996 [Agreement in Principle. November 15, 1996].

—Continued

Continued

The total cost of the agreement was said to be $176.1 million, making it the largest settlement for a race discrimination suit in history.[21] Texaco's problems, however, are far from over. On November 13, 1996, two Texaco shareholders launched a shareholder's derivative action lawsuit, stating that Texaco's directors and officers breached fiduciary duty and damaged Texaco's name.

Some would say that it was about time Texaco was finally caught. In 1991, Texaco paid a record $17.7 million in compensatory and punitive damages to an employee who sued for sex discrimination after the company denied her a promised promotion and gave her job to a man.[22] Others say that Texaco was forced to settle the case not on its legal merits but due to the inaccurate transcript published by the *New York Times*.[23] Some have argued that what the Texaco case proves is that "if you can create enough bad publicity, depicting a company as hopelessly racist, you can win without ever going to trial."[24] This may not be entirely correct. Had this matter gone to trial, damages in the Roberts action were estimated at $71 million in back pay and damages for each plaintiff in the amount of $300,000, resulting in a total liability of $491 million.[25] Furthermore, in June 1996, Spencer Lewis, Jr., a district director of the Equal Employment Opportunity Commission for the New York City District, found against Texaco for failing to promote blacks and pursuing a companywide pattern of racial bias.[26] Lewis held that Texaco used an evaluation system to promote employees that did not comply with EEOC guidelines. Questions about Texaco's corporate culture exist. In a company whose core values state that "Each person deserves to be treated with respect and dignity,"[27] and where it is within the corporate conduct guidelines to report known or suspected violations of company policy to supervisors, some say that such a conversation could not have arisen if it were not prevalent for such written policies to be undermined by the actions of senior executives.

When Lundwall was questioned as to why he turned over the tapes, he indicated that it was not to get back at Texaco but, rather, to maintain a job.[28] In retrospect, he admits that he was naive bordering on stupid to think that handing over the tapes would help his cause. If anything, handing over the tapes apparently hurt his cause. On November 19, 1996, Robert Lundwall was arrested and charged with obstruction of justice in that, from July 1994 to August 1994, he corruptibly destroyed, concealed, and withheld documents requested by attorneys for the plaintiffs. As of December 17, 1996, Lundwall was involved in discussions with the prosecuting attorneys to possibly resolve the charge without going to trial by either pleading to a lesser charge or offering help in exchange for immunity.[29] As a result of Lundwall's criminal subpoena before the grand jury, further questionable actions on the part of Texaco's executives have come to light. In addition to the documents pertaining to the promotion of minority employees, the grand jury records included a draft memo dated June 24, 1994, summarizing the results of an employee survey in Texaco's Finance Department. The results were distinctly unfavorable toward the criteria for promotions of employees.

21. *60 Minutes*, p. 1.
22. *Texaco's White Collar Bigots*, by Jack E. White.
23. Johon Leo, "Jelly Bean: The Sequel," *US News Online*.
24. Ibid.
25. Derivative Action Complaint filed November 13, 1996, p. 7.
26. "Texaco Discrimination Lawsuit Sparks National Dialog on Racism in Corporate America."
27. "Texaco Apologizes for Racist Remarks of Senior Executives but Questions About Culture Remain."
28. *60 Minutes*, p. 4.
29. "Ex-Texaco Exec May Avoid Trial," December 17, 1996.

—Continued

Continued

The draft results were forwarded by Lundwall to a lawyer in Texaco's Legal Department on June 30, 1994, requesting advice on publication of the survey results. A handwritten reply on Lundwall's covering memo from the lawyer dated July 26, 1994, advised delaying publication of the survey results to avoid its becoming part of the discovery process in the class action suit.[30] While Texaco lawyers state that this draft memorandum was not subject to discovery, the plaintiffs' lawyers claim that it did fall within the time frame.

When asked why it appears on certain portions of the tape that he took the initiative to shred documents, Lundwall would not comment.[31] His

attorney indicates that the transcripts of the tape make it clear that Lundwall was directed to shred and destroy the evidence.[32] When asked what he would do if he had to do it all over again, Lundwall stated that he would "slip quietly into the night with my benefits and let the system stay as screwed up as it is."[33]

Questions

1. In a company as progressive as Texaco, what permitted such discrimination to occur?

2. How could such discrimination have been prevented?

3. Is whistle-blowing ethical?

4. Could a protected whistle-blowing mechanism or

conscientious ombudsperson have helped?

SOURCES: Cohen, Milstein, Hausfeld, and Toll. *Texaco Discrimination Lawsuit Sparks National Dialog on Racism in Corporate America.* Internet Bulletin, (see *http://brooks.swlearning.com*), November 1996.

Court TV Library. *The Texaco Suit.* Internet Bulletin. See *http://brooks.swlearning.com*, 1996.

Eichenwald, K. *Texaco Lawyers Reportedly Tried to Conceal Damaging Documents.* Internet Bulletin. (See *http://brooks.swlearning.com*). November 15, 1996.

Leo, J. *Jelly Bean: The Sequel.* Internet Bulletin. (See *http://brooks.swlearning.com*)

Sixty Minutes. *The Texaco Tapes.* Livingston, NJ: Burrelle's Transcripts. April 13, 1997.

Stepshow, *Ex-Texaco Exec May Avoid Trial.* See *http://brooks.swlearning.com*, December 17, 1996.

White, J. B. *Texaco's White Collar Bigots.* Internet Bulletin, Volume 148. Number 123, November 18, 1996.

---

30. "Texaco Lawyers Reportedly Tried to Conceal Damaging Documents," Kurt Eichenwald, November 15, 1996.

31. *60 Minutes*, p. 5
32. Ibid.
33. Ibid., p. 6.

Ethics case on workplace ethics

Downsize or Bonus Allocation Decisions

Assume that you have just been placed in charge of the Claims Investigation Unit of a small insurance company based in Minneapolis. Your personnel department has provided the following details on your personnel. However, because your insurance company is in the midst of takeover discussions, you have been asked to decide whom you would terminate if you were called on to downsize by one person and, alternatively, how you would allocate a bonus of $20,000 if no one were to be dismissed. You really want your team to function well after the decision is made because your future depends on it.

Question

1. What would your answers be, and what would your reasoning be for each?

—*Continued*

Continued

PERSONNEL CHARACTERISTICS OF CLAIMS INVESTIGATION UNIT

NAME	SALARY	TITLE	YEARS OF SENIORITY	PERFORMANCE	PERSONAL
Carol	$84,000	Analyst	5	Acceptable, misses deadlines	Married, many dependents
Gord	$72,000	Analyst	2	Outstanding, pushy, suggestions	Single, no dependents
Jane	$68,000	Junior	8	Consistent, excellent, dependable	Married to successful architect
Ralph	$86,000	Senior	15	Acceptable, plodder	Married, two children in University
Hilary	$64,000	Junior	6	Acceptable, costly mistakes	Single, dependable, chronically ill mother

Ethics case on international operations

Jail and a German Sub-Contractor *(Names are fictitious)*

Harold Johns found himself in jail in Germany. He was a vice-president of Baranca Industries Inc., a U.S. firm that constructs and installs factory equipment. Unfortunately he was the highest-ranking Baranca official in Germany while he was in Germany overseeing the installation of some equipment. Much to his surprise, there was a problem with the way a sub-contractor paid his workers.

Apparently, the way the sub-contractor calculated the pay was illegal. In Germany, when a sub-contractor does something illegal, it is assumed that the company hiring the sub-contractor had knowledge and was also guilty. In addition, the highest-ranking officials with the sub-contractor and the firms who hired him are held legally responsible. Therefore Harold and the head of the sub-contractor were arrested — as well as the head of the enterprise that owned the factory.

Questions

1. Is this a fair law?
2. If you were Harold Johns, how would you ensure that Baranca executives and Baranca itself would never be vulnerable to such problems again?

AIDS Medication in South Africa

"South Africa and the drug companies have changed for ever, say David Pilling and Nicol degli Innocenti.[1]

South Africa is to the drug pharmaceutical industry what Vietnam was to the U.S. military. Nothing will be quite the same again.

That, at least, is the view of Oxfam, the U.K. charity that has mounted a campaign for affordable medicines in poor countries. With other activist groups, it has championed the cause of the South African government, which has been in a three-year legal tussle with the drug industry about national legislation making it easier to override patents.

Yesterday, the drug industry, exhausted by the vitriol that has been heaped upon it, through in the towel.

In return, they appear to have won certain assurances from the government that it will respect the World Trade

---

1. "A Crack in the Resolve of an Industry," *Financial Times*, April 19, 2001, 15.

Organization's Agreement on Trade Related Intellectual Property Rights (Trips), …[which they had earlier argued] allows the health minister to ignore patents without due process.

The threat of such wholesale disregard for patents—the lifeblood of the research-based drug industry—has prompted it to take some extraordinary steps. Several companies, …have offered to sell AIDS medicines to the developing world at manufacturing cost, slashing the price of triple therapy from at least $10,000 in the west for an annual supply to about $600.

[This differential price strategy] carries several risks. Drugs may flow back into western markets. The scheme also exposes the companies to political pressures in western markets, where consumers may start asking for similar discounts…[whereas the drug companies will]…"need some markets in which to recoup our development costs."

The article went on to raise questions about the way in which the government of South Africa was not waging an all-out war on AIDS, as follows. "The government doesn't have a good record with HIV, " says Glenda Gray, an HIV specialist in Soweto's enormous Barawanath hospital. "We have a president who questions whether HIV causes AIDS…and a program that raises awareness but can't get condoms to people. It's difficult to see how winning this court case would be translated into treatment."

Questions

1. Is it legal, moral, or ethical for South Africa to override AIDS medication patents?

2. Is it legal, moral, or ethical for drug patent holders to resist?

3. If you were a senior executive in an affected drug patent holder, what solution would you suggest?

The Exxon Valdez

Shortly after midnight on March 24, 1989, the oil tanker *Exxon Valdez* ran aground on Bligh Reef in Alaska's Prince William Sound, spilling

11 million gallons of crude oil. Ecological systems were threatened, and the lives and livelihood of area residents were severely disrupted. For the

tanker's owner, New York-based Exxon Corporation, the effects were profound.

How did such a tragedy occur? Opinions vary

—Continued

Continued

considerably. One oil company executive put it this way: "Its simple. A boat hit a rock." On the other hand, the evidence shows a much more complex picture of human and technical errors.

At the time of the grounding, the vessel had departed from normal shipping lanes to avoid ice in the water and had failed to make a corrective turn in time to avoid the submerged reef. The ship was piloted by third mate Gregory Cousins, who did not hold a required license; the captain, Joseph Hazelwood, was in his quarters. Hazelwood, whose driver's license was at the time suspended for driving while intoxicated, later failed a sobriety test. At the time, the pipeline was opened and strict traffic lanes were established in the sound to guarantee safe tanker passage. But, in recent years, disintegration of the Columbia Glacier had filled the lanes with ice. To avoid slowing down to dodge icebergs—thereby delaying the oil's delivery to market— tanker captains routinely moved out of the shipping lanes.

On shore, no one was keeping watch. Although the Coast Guard was charged with monitoring vessels through Prince William Sound, in fact, its outdated radar system did not reliably track vessels as far out as Bligh Reef. An earlier proposal to upgrade the radar system had been rejected as too expensive. And the Coast Guard's oversight, to say the least, was lax: at the time of the *Valdez* grounding, the only radar man on duty had stepped out for a cup of coffee.

Other corners had also been cut. The Coast Guard had reduced the use of specially trained harbor pilots to guide tankers out the sound and had withdrawn a proposal for tugboat escorts. Rules, such as those governing the number of crew members on the bridge, were not enforced.

The response to the accident was also fraught with difficulties. Alyeska, the consortium of oil companies that built and operate the Trans-Alaska pipeline, is responsible for cleaning up oil spills that occur in Prince William Sound. At the time of the accident, Alyeska's contingency plan promised to reach a stricken vessel within five and a half hours and to recover half of a 200,000-barrel spill within seventy-two hours, yet, when the event occurred, Alyeska's plan was revealed, as Alaska's Commissioner for Energy Conservation later put it, as "the greatest work of maritime fiction since *Moby Dick*." The clean-up crew had no instructions, the barge was in dry-dock for repairs, needed boom and skimmers were buried under tons of other equipment in a warehouse, and lightering supplies were lost under a snowdrift.

Alyeska did not even reach the *Valdez* until almost twelve hours after the accident and in the first three days was able to pick up only 3,000 barrels of oil—2 percent of what it had promised. Incredibly, a group of local fishermen, later dubbed the "mosquito fleet," managed to retrieve more oil with their fishing boats and five-gallon buckets than did Alyeska with all its money and equipment.

When Alyeska's cleanup collapsed, a response effort had to be hastily jury-rigged by Exxon and the federal and state governments. Federal law called for an interagency team effort in which Exxon was responsible for cleaning up the oil, and different federal agencies were responsible variously for providing scientific advice, protecting the parks, and safeguarding birds and animals. The U.S. Coast Guard and Alaska's Department of Environmental Conservation were supposed to supervise the whole effort, yet no established procedures existed for bringing these organizations together into a working crisis management team under unified leadership.

—Continued

Continued

The result was a response effort "paralyzed by indecision, a struggle over authority, and vastly different and conflicting expectations as to which measures would work."

The debate over the use of dispersants, detergent-like chemicals that break up oil into droplets that descend below the water's surface, illustrates the costs for this paralysis. Exxon wanted to use dispersants and immediately flew in planes and chemicals. But, under Alaskan guidelines, dispersants would be used in an oil spill only if less harmful to the environment than the crude itself. Since no one knew whether they were or not, the Coast Guard ordered tests, which were inconclusive. After two days of indecision, the government finally approved the dispersants—but that night the weather turned, and a spring blizzard whipped the oil into an impervious, frothy mousse. The opportunity had been lost.

The reaction of the public was predictable. A complete cleanup was demanded, which cost Exxon a reported $2 billion in 1989 and a further $200 million in 1990, with more out-of-pocket cost to come. More than 150 civil lawsuits were filed, not including those on behalf of the state and federal governments. The state and federal claims may be settled for a reported $1.2 billion.

Not surprisingly, Exxon's profits and stock price have remained flat since the accident. Shareholder groups have, however, been very active, particularly the institutional investors who as a group own 35 percent of Exxon's shares. With the support of the administrators of the New York City pension funds (which own 6 million Exxon shares) the Coalition for Environmentally Responsible Economies (CERES) brought pressure to bear on the company during 1990 to accept and endorse a code of conduct, known as The Valdez Principles (see next page), for dealing with the corporation's environmental behavior.

The company resisted accepting The Valdez Principles on several grounds, including that the principles were not sufficiently developed to be workable, that they went too far, and that further study was needed. In 1990 Exxon did, however, appoint an outside environmentalist to the board of directors and placed a senior officer in charge of environmental matters. The tanker was rechristened the *Exxon Mediterranean* and will operate henceforth in the Pacific Ocean. It was not refitted with a double hull that would have cost about $20 million. Observers have also reported that Exxon has bought back substantial amounts of its stock: a move possibly made to support the stock price and pressure investors.

Questions

1. Who was responsible for the accident?

2. What were the responsibilities of the company, the government authorities, and the employees of the company, which were not properly discharged?

3. Should Exxon abide by The Valdez Principles?

4. Could a better code of conduct have prevented this accident?

5. If Exxon had known, before the accident, about the captain's alcohol problem, what actions should have been taken, if any?

SOURCES: Barnard, J. W. "Exxon Collides with 'Valdez Principles.'" *Business & Society Review* (Fall 1990): 32–35.

Gehani, R. "Will Oil Spills Sink Exxon's Bottom Line." *Business & Society Review*, (Fall 1990): 80–83.

"Lawsuits Proliferate from Grounding of the Exxon Valdez." *Globe & Mail* (G&M), November 29, 1989, p. B2.

Lawrence, A. T. "An Accident Waiting to Happen." *Business & Society Review* (BSR) (Fall 1990): 93–95.

"Shareholders' suggestions get Exxon nod." *G&M*, May 12, 1989, p. B2.

"Exxon Looking at Offer to Settle Oil Spill Suits." *Financial Post*, February 8, 1991, p. 7.

—Continued

Continued

THE VALDEZ (CERES) PRINCIPLES

Leading environmental organizations—including the Sierra Club, National Audubon Society, and National Wildlife Federation—joined with the Social Investment Forum to form the Coalition for Environmentally Responsible Economics (CERES), whose first act was to draft the Valdez Principles for corporations to sign. The idea is to make the Valdez Principles a litmus test of corporate behavior. Companies are being pressured to abide by the following prescripts:

1. Protection of the Biosphere

We will minimize the release of any pollutant that may cause environmental damage to the air, water, or earth. We will safeguard habitats in rivers, lakes, wetlands, coastal zones, and oceans and will minimize contributing to the greenhouse effect, depletion of the ozone layer, acid rain, or smog.

2. Sustainable Use of Natural Resources

We will make sustainable use of renewable natural resources, such as water, soils and forests. We will conserve nonrenewable natural resources through efficient use and careful planning. We will protect wildlife habitat, open spaces, and wilderness, while preserving biodiversity.

3. Reduction and Disposal of Waste

We will minimize waste, especially hazardous waste, and wherever possible recycle materials. We will dispose of all wastes through safe and responsible methods.

4. Wise Use of Energy

We will make every effort to use environmentally safe and sustainable energy sources to meet our needs. We will invest in improved energy efficiency and conservation in our operations. We will maximize the energy efficiency of products we produce or sell.

5. Risk Reduction

We will minimize the environmental, health, and safety risks to our employees and the communities in which we operate by employing safe technologies and operating procedures and by being constantly prepared for emergencies.

6. Marketing of Safe Products and Services

We will sell products or services that minimize adverse environmental impacts and that are safe as consumers commonly use them. We will inform consumers of the environmental impacts of our products or services.

7. Damage Compensation

We will take responsibility for any harm we cause to the environment by making every effort to fully restore the environment and to compensate those persons who are adversely affected.

8. Disclosure

We will disclose to our employees and to the public incidents relating to our operations that cause environmental harm or pose health or safety hazards. We will disclose potential environmental, health, or safety hazards posed by our operations and we will not take any retaliatory personnel action against any employees who report on any condition that creates a danger to the environment or poses health or safety hazards.

9. Environmental Directors and Managers

At least one member of the board of directors will be a person qualified to represent environmental interests. We will commit management resources to implement these Principles, including the funding of an office of vice president for environmental affairs or an equivalent executive position, reporting directly to the CEO, to monitor and report on our implementation efforts.

10. Assessment and Annual Audit

We will conduct and make public an annual self-evaluation of our progress in implementing these Principles and in complying with all applicable laws and regulations throughout our worldwide operations. We will work toward the timely creation of independent environmental audit procedures which we will complete annually and make available to the public.

For more information, please visit *http://brooks.swlearning.com*

According to the Greenpeace webpage,

> On 16 February last year (1996), Greenpeace learned that the UK government had granted permission for Shell Oil to dump a huge, heavily contaminated oil installation, the 4,000 tonne Brent Spar, into the North Atlantic despite it being loaded with toxic and radioactive sludge. Dumping operations, just west of Ireland and Scotland, were expected to begin in May. Greenpeace went into action with plans to take over and occupy the rig to prevent the dumping. More than two dozen activists from six North Sea countries pulled operations together. Video and photo staff were called upon to document the Brent Spar platform and the occupation. The Moby Dick delivered activists to the platform (on April 30) and remained in the area to provide back up.
>
> . . . Greenpeace believes that if this platform were to be dumped at sea, with some 400 others at work in the North Sea alone, this would have set a dangerous precedent.

Without doubt, this act of piracy caused serious consternation at the headquarters of Shell UK, and at the parent company's head office in The Netherlands.

Shell UK had been studying options for decommissioning the oil storage and tanker loading platform since 1991, but no perfect option had emerged. The Brent Spar was 140 meters in length, with 109 below the water level, so tearing it apart would be likely to cause leakage of hazardous substances. Consequently, for reasons of cost as well as environmental safety, Shell had chosen to apply to the UK government for a permit to sink the platform in the deep ocean. This decision was based on extensive assessments of the following options:

- Horizontal dismantling (and onshore disposal)
- Vertical dismantling (and onshore disposal)
- In-field disposal
- Deep water disposal
- Refurbishment and re-use
- Continued maintenance

Deep water disposal (at roughly $60 million) was expected to be between 5 percent and 40 percent cheaper than other options, and, since the structure would not leak for 1,000 years, it was expected to be so buried by silt at that point as to be harmless.

The problem faced by Shell UK was what to do? The UK government was expected to issue a dumping permit momentarily. The Fourth North Sea Conference was scheduled to debate the issue of deep sea disposal on June 8–9, and rumor had it that eleven of the thirteen countries involved could call for a moratorium on such dumping.

The following events transpired on or just after April 30, 1995:

- April 30: Greenpeace charged that large amounts of hazardous and radioactive oil were stored on the Brent Spar.
- May 5: The UK government issued deep sea disposal permit.
- May 13: Shell failed to evict Greenpeace from oil platform.
- May 19: Shell failed to obtain court consent to evict Greenpeace.
- May 22: Shell failed to evict Greenpeace.
- May 23: Shell removed activists from Brent Spar.
- June 7: Greenpeace re-boarded and occupied tow tug.
- June 9: Greenpeace revealed leaked document about cheap land option.
- June 10: Greenpeace battled to prevent tow to dump site.
- June 11: Shell postponed tow due to bad weather, tangled wire.
- June 12: Shell begins tow.
- June 14: Protesters in Germany threatened to damage 200 Shell service stations—50 were subsequently damaged, two fire-bombed, and one raked with bullets—unrest continued until June 20.

—Continued

Continued

- June 15: Protesters in continental northern Europe strongly opposed — Chancellor Kohl protested deep water disposal at G7 Summit to 17th.
- June 16: Greenpeace re-occupied Brent Spar.
- June 20: Several governments opposed.
- June 20: Shell UK aborted deep water proposal and sought onshore disposal.

- June 21: Shell UK apologized to Prime Minister Major for any embarrassment.
- Late June: Support grew for Shell's early scientific approach.
- July 7: Permission granted to moor in Erford, Norway, temporarily.
- August 26: UK television executives admitted to lack of objectivity and balance in their coverage using dramatic film footage supplied by Greenpeace.

- September 5: Greenpeace apologizes to Shell UK for sampling errors and inaccurate claims that Spar contained 5,500 tonnes of oil in three of six tanks, and so on.

Questions

1. What would you have done if you were calling the shots at Shell UK? When?
2. What would you have done if you were calling the shots at the parent Shell head office?

http://brooks.
swlearning.com

STRUCTURE OF BRENT SPAR

Helideck

Accommodation

Overall height to turntable = 137 m

Column

Overall weight = 14,500 tonnes

Chain fenders

Buoyancy tanks

Anodes

Anchor chains

Oil storage tanks (Volume = 300,000 bbl)

Ballast

Main body diameter = 29 m

Crises at Wind River Energy Inc.

Lynn James was in the vortex of a set of crises. Lynn, an entrepreneur and the president, CEO, and 75 percent owner of Wind River Energy Inc., was one week away from closing a deal to secure much-needed financing for existing and new operations via an independent public offering (IPO) on NASDAQ under the sponsorship of prominent stockbrokers in New York and Toronto. All Lynn had worked for was in danger of going up in smoke, and there was grave risk to the lives of innocent workers and citizens. What on earth could and should Lynn do?

Over the last nine years, Lynn had been very successful. Initially Lynn had been intrigued by the possibility of developing small, freestanding energy installations that fed their power into regional electrical grids or provided power to small isolated towns. It had been possible to acquire and refurbish several small hydroelectric generating stations that had been mothballed by large north-eastern energy producers or the small cities that still owned them. Due to the rise in the cost of fossil and nuclear fuels, these waterfall plants made a rate of return on invested capital of roughly 22 percent. Over the years, Lynn and various associates had bought and refurbished five plants, sold two, and continued to operate three in Ontario and Vermont. Based on successful operations in the

east, Lynn had arranged for the incorporation of Wind River Energy Inc. into which energy holdings were transferred to provide collateral for bank loans and vendor mortgage financing.

During the last six years, Lynn became interested in the generation of energy using windmills. After visiting "wind farms" in California and off the shore of Denmark, Lynn realized that the wind conditions were exceptionally favorable just east of portions of the Rocky Mountains. He began to investigate providing energy needs to small isolated towns in that area. Four years ago, a ten-windmill installation was developed outside of Freeman, Alberta, which initially contributed to the town's energy needs. The town owned an old hydroelectric plant on the local river and had a back-up oil generator system for emergencies. Two years ago, Wind River acquired the town's energy generation systems and became the sole source of energy for Freeman. Four years ago, Freeman was a town of 2,000 homes that was using all the energy it could produce, so it welcomed the windmill installation. Since that time, 750 more homes were built to house the workers at two new mines in the area, and the town's hospital was enlarged. Further investment was now needed to provide additional generating capacity.

Based on favorable operations in Freeman, Wind River Energy had developed a reputation for reliability. The company took pride in keeping its commitments—a fact that attracted the attention of the mayor and leaders of West Fork, a neighboring town to Freeman. They approached Wind River, and Lynn signed a contract to provide energy to West Fork on the same basis as for Freeman. Part of the anticipated financing was to provide funds for the purchase of West Fork's electrical generating capacity.

Disaster struck during the last week. On Monday the Wind River manager in Freeman, Ben Trent, called Lynn in Toronto to say that something had gotten stuck in one of the water input pipes to the hydro station, and he wanted to know what to do. Summer was just starting, and air conditioning needs would go beyond Wind River's capacity. Wind River's chief engineer was away on holiday, but Lynn checked with his assistant who suggested that, if the input door could be closed, someone could enter the clean-out pipe that intersected the input pipe. When this was relayed to Ben, he said that he didn't think that the input door had ever been shut and might not work, nor had the clean-out pipe been used during the forty years the plant had been in service. He would check on them and call back.

—Continued

Continued

On Tuesday, Lynn received a notification from the Province of Ontario stipulating that Wind River's Ontario hydro station would have to be shut down no later than Thursday. The court order stated that the stagnant water at the edges of the pond where the water intake pipe was located was likely to allow the breeding of mosquitoes that would spread the West Nile Virus. The stagnant water situation would have to be remedied before the plant could restart, and Wind River would be liable to any persons from the local community who were diagnosed with West Nile Virus from Tuesday to five days after the stagnant water problem was remedied. When Lynn went to consult the chief engineer's assistant (the only other real engineer on staff), he found that the man had just gone home sick with a SARS-like attack of the flu. Unfortunately, the chief engineer was in the middle of a backpacking trip in the Rockies and would be unreachable unless he activated the satellite phone that Lynn had insisted he take.

Ben called back on Wednesday to say that they had finally closed the input door and had just sent a small, thin man into the clean-out pipe to crawl up the intake pipe and clear the obstruction. Because the fellow was so keen, Ben told him to crawl all the way up to the intake door and try to grease the hinges on the inside.

On Thursday morning Ben called to say that the fellow had done a great job of clearing the input pipe and had examined the hinges on the inside of the input door. He had just gone back in to try to remove the hinge pins, replace the bushings around the pins, and grease the bushings and pins. The mayor was pleased because the fellow was his brother-in-law who had never really done anything else very well.

At about noon on Thursday, Lynn's lawyer called to remind him of the meeting on the following Tuesday during which Lynn, the CFO, and the chief engineer would have to sign off documents attesting to the excellent status of the company so the IPO could go ahead. Any delay would jeopardize the financing deal. Lynn didn't know what to say. He just thanked his lawyer and hung up.

In the early afternoon, Ben called to say that the fellow had gotten out of the pipe all right, but had jammed one of the hinge pins when reinserting it and didn't think the input door would open to allow water into the generating equipment. Someone bigger and stronger would have to go into the pipe to fix the hinge. Ben didn't know what to do. He wasn't a real engineer, having been promoted to be manager on the basis of long service and personal connections with the city council, and he wanted Wind River's chief engineer to take responsibility and tell him what to do.

In addition, Ben said that the transformer station regulating the power from the company's windmills had been hit about a month ago by lightning and was operating only partially on an intermittent basis. The mayor of Freeman was getting calls about the intermittent "brown-outs" of electricity and was putting pressure on Ben. Ben was really fed up. He also had a call from the mayor of West Fork, but he hadn't returned it yet.

Questions

1. What would you do if you were Lynn?

Can't We All Just Get Along: Cultural Variables in Codes of Ethics

Nancy L. Roth, Todd Hunt, Maria Stavropoulos and Karen Babik

Ethical issues in the practice of public relations become increasingly complex when international borders are crossed. Differences in what "counts" as public relations as well as what "counts" as ethical practice abound. Rather than taking the position that a specific, "objective" code of ethics can be developed or arguing that cultural diversity makes ethical standards impossible, this paper argues that an international set of principles for practice is feasible. Such a set of principles can only be agreed upon if representatives of diverse organizations and cultural values will work together to understand each others' perspectives. This approach is consistent with the goal of "mutual understanding" that increasingly characterizes public relations practice. It is also consistent with recent theoretical work in ethics and postcolonialism. (Reprinted by permission of the publisher.)

Rodney King's plaintive plea "Can't we all just get along?"—voiced at a rally of his supporters after a notorious California trial that split Americans along cultural lines—may be a phrase with multiple utility. It is a question we should be asking at this point in the discussion about whether or not cultural variables make it impossible to construct a code of ethics that would govern the behaviors of public relations practitioners in global settings—people from countries with very diverse cultures. Are we really so different that we "can't all just get along?"

Arguing that such a code is possible, Hunt and Tirpok proposed that initial steps should be an attempt "to put forth a general code and let its interpretation and use suggest further refinements that will help adopt it to the nuances of the global community."(1) Kruckeberg seconded the motion, observing that "cultural relativism is not problematic for a universal ethics code" and that "globally . . . there is a plenitude of shared ethical values, and those which are within differing areas of moral 'taste' can be discussed, universally accepted or negotiated."(2) Wright dissented, noting that cultural differences cannot be accommodated by a code of ethics. According to Wright, "With or without professional codes of conduct most who practice public relations will choose to be ethical because they believe in themselves and want others to respect them," and thus an attempt at forging a universal ethics code is unnecessary.(3)

This paper extends the debate by exploring recent research about the meaning of "public relations" in cross-cultural settings, calling into question simplistic conceptions of cultural variability, and reviewing codes of ethics in use in global settings. We suggest ways that the door can be kept open to

discussion of a "universal" approach to ethical behavior that will be useful in the emerging era of Multi-National Enterprises (MNEs).(4) With increased globalization in all aspects of social life, it is essential for public relations practitioners to engage in ongoing discussions about ethical practice with international colleagues. While all may not agree to a specific ethics "code," there might be agreement to a set of principles that contain enough ambiguity to allow for differing interpretations and practices. Such a set of principles might move international public relations practice closer to the goal of "mutual understanding" that is the foundation for many of the "two-way" models of public relations currently in use.(5)

MULTICULTURAL MEANINGS OF PUBLIC RELATIONS

When questions of multicultural differences arise, it is easy to establish one type of practice or principles as the model against which all others are compared. In public relations, the United States model has played that role in the literature. In this section we will present examples of discussions of the public relations practices of "others" viewed from the perspective of United States practice. We will argue that it is dangerous to establish one mode of practice as the norm and thereby label all other practices as deviant. In the following section, an alternative perspective is proposed.

Over 25 years ago, a practical book called The Public Relations Man Abroad sketched out cultural differences in major trading partners of the United States, including Japan and Germany.(6) The Japanese, it was noted, say "yes" when they mean "no" out of politeness (p. 182). The Germans think it appropriate to serve champagne during a press conference, while Americans think drinking should wait until later (p. 97).

American companies are hyper-cautious about admitting any responsibility for causing a disaster, because company lawyers convince management that the courtroom is the only place to assess blame. The Japanese, however, are conditioned to ask forgiveness and even to express a willingness to resign . . . or even die. After a 1985 air crash, the company's president offered personal apologies to the families of the dead, made speedy financial reparations, and attended memorial services. A technician responsible for preparing the doomed plane for flight committed suicide to atone for his part in the disaster.(7) Indeed, a Japanese scholar studying in the United States suggests that the Japanese government's non-practice of public relations was responsible for a bungling of relationships with the international community following the Kobe earthquake. Unlike in America where

—Continued

Reprinted from *Public Relations Review*, Vol. 22, No. 2, Nancy L. Roth, et al., "Can't We All Just Get Along: Cultural Variables in Codes of Ethics", 1996, pp.151–161, with permission from Elsevier Science.

Continued

crisis communication plans are in place, in Japan it was days before the government appeared to be in control and before correct information was provided to key publics.(8)

On the other hand, American practices do not always serve well in foreign settings. One U.S. public relations agency lost an account in London because its budget for entertaining the media was too low, suggesting that the agency was not good at cozying up to the press and entertaining lavishly—practices frowned upon in America and specifically forbidden by the ethics codes of the Society of Professional Journalists and the Public Relations Society of America.(9)

As easygoing and casual as Americans are reputed to be both at home and abroad, Americans tend to think of business as just that—not to be confused with friendship or intimacy. Most other cultures are different. Culbertson notes that Confucian values emphasize personal relationships that govern business relationships to the point that "interpersonal relationships serve as the main basis for strong public relationships" (p. 38).(10)

In the Arab world, "public" is not even linked with "relations"; the preferred term is "general relations" or "general affairs" because the word "public" cannot be translated literally in Arabic. Al-Enad (p. 24) suggests that the semantic problem "may have contributed to the persistent vagueness of the nature, goals, roles, and functions of public relations" in the Arab countries.(11) In a similar vein, Signitzer suggests that "public diplomacy" may be a more palatable label for influence and persuasion in Europe, where "public relations" is seen as a tough-minded attempt to influence foreign attitudes through the use of rapid-fire media messages instead of slow debate.(12)

Americans often assume that media-use patterns are the same in other countries as they are in the U.S., and thus media relations can follow the same pattern. Even in neighboring Canada, there are far fewer "local" newspapers and several regional or national newspapers, so the concept of a "hometown news release" does not work as well north of the border as it does at home.(13)

A communications company executive in Hong Kong discovered that the colony, with approximately the same population as the Chicago area, is served by more than 40 newspapers and over 600 magazines, making media placement a nightmare.(14) "People tend to forget that Asia is even more complex than Europe because of the autonomous development of small geographies," said the executive. "Each has its own laws, business styles, ethics, history of business development. If you find anyone who really understands the media of Japan, China, India, Thailand, Vietnam, Malaysia . . . they are indeed a novelty" (p. 1–15).

The views expressed in this literature establish United States customs as the "norm" and those of practitioners in other countries as the "other." This approach leads to development of ethics codes that attempt to impose U.S. standards on practitioners from other countries and on U.S. nationals working elsewhere. Such an approach is problematic because U.S. standards are highly specific and legalistic and leave little room for cultural variation. It also establishes the U.S. method of conducting business as the most ethical without calling into question U.S. practices. For example, this literature might be viewed as suggesting not only that U.S. and Japanese practitioners might handle an airplane crash differently, but also that the U.S. tendency to protect the company name and wealth from lawsuits is more ethical than the Japanese desire to apologize and make restitution to affected families.

RETHINKING CULTURAL VARIABLES

Too often in the past, cultural variables were thought of as "quaint customs" that one merely had to "learn about" in order to succeed in foreign settings—don't show the bottom of your shoes to people in Arab lands, remember to bow when meeting the Japanese, take a gift when you are entertained in someone's home, and don't make this or that gesture that means something-or-other lewd in such-and-such country. The idea that knowledge about customs makes it possible for different cultures to overcome differences is simplistic. Recent writings by communication scholars—and, indeed, recent actions taken by companies and countries engaged in global commerce—indicate that cross-cultural sophistication is increasing.

Botan suggests that "what has been called international public relations may not actually be the two-way multicultural exercise that its name implies.(15) The practice of public relations across borders often . . . is controlled and directed from the home country based on assumptions inherent to the home country. As a result, business practice often may not really be international public relations but might better be called transborder public relations" (pp. 151–152). He proposes (p. 157) that overcoming ethnocentrism and viewing public relations "in different ways than many of us in developed countries have in the past" is the key to formulating a truly global approach.

L. Grunig suggests that too often what organizations try to perform on a global scale, public relations is equated with media relations.(16) She proposes (p. 129) that a new name might be in order—publics relations rather than public relations—to emphasize the "strategic constituencies" approach that is necessary when working on a global scale. In that way of thinking, the media would fall behind several other publics—most notably the local, regional and national governments of

—Continued

Continued

the host country—when laying plans for helping the MNE adjust to their many publics in a multinational setting.

Examples of how specific organizations are rethinking cultural variables abound:

- Wal-Mart, long accustomed to sending out English-only information in Canada, where it had little presence in the French-speaking areas, now has 22 Quebec stores operated entirely in French, including internal communications. The leader of Wal-Mart's transition team in Quebec was responsible for making the company "culturally correct" as well as legally correct.(17)

- Chubb, the American insurance company, is one of many firms that has learned how to cope with the routine expectation of bribes to public officials in many countries. The U.S., of course, forbids American companies from paying bribes to win international business. Chubb satisfied the Chinese expectation of "sweetening the pot" in order to do business there, and stayed within U.S. regulations, by agreeing to set up a $1 million program to teach insurance at a university in Shanghai. Disney flies people from other countries for free training at its Disney World educational facilities, a perk that includes lodging and entertainment at the theme parks. Another enticement: scholarships to American universities for the children of foreign officials.(18)

- European companies have long had difficulty understanding why American companies reveal so much about their condition and their plans on a quarterly basis. The norm in Europe is to keep silent about short-term decisions, because that is seen as impeding the flexibility of management decision-making. The norm is changing however, as European companies—eager to seek capital on the world stage—are moving toward the American system of full, open and frequent disclosure.(19)

These examples characterize a practice of public relations that takes into account local standards and values. Yet, rather than suggesting that differences among such standards mitigate against universal ethical standards, we argue that such a guideline is possible. In the following sections we review existing codes and suggest that their power lies in "authority" rather than "enforcement." We suggest that a universal set of principles based on authority with sufficient ambiguity to account for cross-cultural differences is feasible.

'AUTHORITY' UNDERLIES ASSOCIATION CODES

The two major ethics codes adopted by professional public relations associations in the U.S. are the "IABC Code of Ethics" that applies to all members of the International Association of Business Communicators and the "Code for Professional Standards for the Practice of Public Relations"

that applies to all members of the Public Relations Society of America. The codes also apply to the student groups affiliated with the professional associations. Since about one public relations professional in ten in the U.S. belongs to these associations, it is fair to say that only ten percent of American practitioners are bound by the codes and subject to penalty if they are charged with a violation.

Officers of the professional organizations have authority and responsibility to hold hearings, determine culpability, and expel from the association members who violate the code. In practice, very few violations are reported. In fact, when the president of one of the associations was charged publicly with a violation in the 1980s, he resigned his presidency and his membership, continuing the practice of public relations in the large regional firm that bears his name.

Thus it can be seen that while the power to expel members who violate their codes of ethics gives professional associations "authority" it really does not serve to give them control over the profession or its members. Indeed, ethics codes are not controllers of behavior, they are merely models for behavior. That raises the issue of whether they should even be called "codes," since a code usually implies enforcement, as in the military's codes of conduct or the code of laws enacted by governments. We are one step along the semantic trail of abandoning the term "ethics code."

Another problem with prescribing and proscribing through the use of a code is the need for completeness. The PRSA code is under 400 words long, and it highlights (literally, in boldface type) such overarching and generic concepts as public interest, honesty, integrity, deal fairly, accuracy, truth that it appears at first to be steering clear of cultural contexts. But the PRSA code does not stand alone. It is accompanied by a section called "Interpretations of the Code" that gets into very specific prohibitions on compensating or entertaining the media—rules that are counter to the norms in many countries. Other lengthy interpretative sections are provided for those who engage in the practice of political and financial public relations. In its attempt to account for all of the code violations that are likely to occur in specific settings, the PRSA code becomes increasingly ethnocentric, and increasingly difficult to apply to the work done by MNEs.

In the past two years, Russian public relations practitioners have moved to organize and to promote ethical behavior.(20) In 1994, a professional association was formed in Moscow, and on August 16, 1994, the St. Petersburg Association of Public Relations Specialists adopted a "Professional Code" that is remarkably similar to the IABC and PRSA codes. The St. Petersburg code calls for "protecting, preserving, and respecting freedom of speech, freedom of the press, and existing legislation." It states that public relations

—Continued

Continued

practitioners must provide "objective and reliable information," that they must not violate the fairness and objectivity of the mass media, that they must inform clients if there is a conflict of interest stemming from working for more than one client, and that they must report violations of the code to the Association.

In contrast, the Code of Athens—the International Code of Ethics that applies to members of the International Public Relations Association—is much more general, avoids interpretations, and bases its moral authority on the "Universal Declaration of Human Rights," which was adopted in 1948 by the United Nations General Assembly. In its simplicity, it probably is a much better starting place for understanding how we can "all get along" than are the ethics codes stamped "Made in America."

NEW THINKING ABOUT ETHICAL CONDUCT

In the past decade, analysis of the role of MNEs engaged in global communication has led to new thinking about how best to articulate basic expectations of ethical behavior.

Donaldson identified 10 "minimal" human rights that can be applied or honored by all international moral agents.(21) His list does not explicitly refer to any local culture:

1. The right to freedom of physical movement. 2. The right to ownership of property. 3. The right to freedom from torture. 4. The right to a fair trial. 5. The right to nondiscriminatory treatment (on the basis of race or sex). 6. The right to physical security. 7. The right to freedom of speech and association. 8. The right to minimal education. 9. The right to political participation. 10. The right to subsistence.

DeGeorge suggested that despite differences in culture and values among nations, there are moral norms that can be applied to multinational enterprises. He proposed seven principles to guide MNEs in ethical conduct:

1. MNEs should do no international direct harm.

2. MNEs should produce more good than bad for the host country.

3. MNEs should contribute by their activities to the host country's development.

4. MNEs should respect the human rights of their employees.

5. MNEs should pay their fair share of taxes.

6. To the extent that local culture does not violate moral norms, MNEs should respect the local culture and work with it, not against it.

7. MNEs should cooperate with the local government in the development and enforcement of just background institutions.(22)

Perhaps the first international code of ethics crafted by business leaders for business is the CAUX Round Table Principles, the result of a collaborative effort by business leaders from Japan, Europe, and the United States. The CAUX Round Table was established in 1986 in Caux-sur-Montreux, Switzerland, to bring together global business leaders to reduce trade tensions. The Principles reflect two ideals, Japan's concept of Kyosei—living and working together for the common good—and the Western concept of human dignity.(23) The Principles address the following concerns:

1. The responsibilities of businesses (which are further outlined in a lengthy section titled "Stakeholder Principles" that specifies behaviors toward customers, employees, owners/investors, suppliers, competitors, and communities).

2. The economic and social impact of business.

3. Business behavior that is based on trust.

4. Respect for rules.

5. Support for multilateral trade.

6. Respect for the environment.

7. Avoidance of illicit operations.

The CAUX Round Table Principles were based, in part, on the Minnesota Principles crafted by business leaders who are members of the Minnesota Center for Corporate Responsibility. Bob MacGregor, president of the Center, helped draft the CAUX Round Table Principles. MacGregor says acceptance of the Principles has been widespread and that "enlightened business leaders know that all stakeholders profit under a common set of values."

To reach the skeptics, however, MacGregor believes that business leaders who subscribe to the Principles will have to show how abiding by the precepts will open markets, increase productivity, and affect the bottom line of profits positively. The Principles do not explicitly acknowledge the need to respect the cultural diversity of each group of stakeholders— an issue MacGregor says was raised but not dealt with. With the addition of that perspective, the CAUX Round Table Principles would serve as a good model for a document of utility to MNEs as they pursue their global communications. The Principles also could and should be extended to include the ethical behavior of government, since business behaviors so often reflect compliance with the laws of home and host countries.(24)

CONCLUSION

The question of whether or not it is possible to develop a set of ethical principles that is meaningful across cultures in the

—Continued

Continued

current global business and political environment raises issues about objectivity. Do standards need to take into account cultural differences of what "counts" as "moral?" Does objectivity mean that cultural differences cannot be recognized?

Too often, as we noted in the introduction to this article, the debate about objectivity is reduced to a question of whether it is better to subscribe to a rigid, culturally specific value system that does not account for cultural difference ("weak objectivity") or to subscribe to a system of "judgmental relativism" where there are no standards. A third possibility, "strong objectivity," calls for an analysis of historically situated local beliefs—both those of "others" and those of the United States.(25) By looking at U.S. generated codes of ethics from the standpoint of "others" we might begin to understand and critique our own system of values, rather than trying to impose it uncritically on others.

From the perspective of "other," United States and other Western countries are seen as subscribing to an ethical position that values autonomy over most other principles. The individual has the privilege of ownership and autonomous action. In contrast, other cultures (including some women's cultures in the West) value connection. This might account for the differences mentioned above between the handling of air disasters in Japan and the U.S., for example. Neither of these ethical positions accounts for the relative differences in power wielded by different countries in the world economy.(26)

Recent post-colonial literature suggests that issues of relative power ought to be addressed as well. A universal set of ethical principles should take into account the differing power exerted by countries and organizations in the global economy.(27) Future work on international ethical principles should explore thoroughly the issue of power in the international practice of public relations.

Viewing Western values from the standpoint of others may lead to the ability to create or modify universal standards that account for cultural difference by using wording that allows for flexibility in interpretation,(28) but does not impose ethnocentric standards.(29) Such a move is consistent with the goal of "mutual understanding" that increasingly characterizes the practice of public relations in the global environment.(30)

American professional associations, particularly IABC and PRSA, should consider reviewing their codes of ethics from the standpoint of the "others" with whom practitioners are increasingly doing business. They should take into account differing cultural variations of autonomy and connectivity as well as differences in global power. Finally, they should consider the ramifications of carrying "codes" of "ethics" across national borders and consider instead the development of mutually agreed upon principles to guide global practice. Adoption of such practices is not only ethical, but it also might result in a move toward international cooperation—perhaps we can "get along."

Acknowledgment: The authors are indebted to Alexandre G. Nicolaev, a member of the board of directors of the Russian Public Communications Company, for providing a translation of the St. Petersburg Code. Mr. Nicolaev spent the 1995–1996 academic year as a visiting scholar at the Center for International Trade Development at Oklahoma State University. In a personal communication with the second author, he reported that while in the United States, he visited with Ray Gaulke and Elizabeth Allan, the top administrators of the PRSA and IABC respectively, and found "that there were more similarities than differences between us; we shared the same human values."

NOTES

1. Todd Hunt and Andrew Tirpok, "Universal Ethics Code: An Idea Whose Time Has Come," Public Relations Review 19 (1993), p. 141.

2. Dean Kruckeberg, "Universal Ethics Code: Both Possible and Feasible," Public Relations Review 19 (1993), pp. 21–31.

3. Donald K. Wright, "Enforcement Dilemma: Voluntary Nature of Public Relations Codes," Public Relations Review 19 (1993), pp. 13–20.

4. We have chosen MNEs rather than MNCs—Multi-National Corporations—because of our belief that non-profit groups and governmental groups face most of the issues that for-profit organizations must deal with in a global setting.

5. James Grunig and Todd Hunt, Managing Public Relations (New York: Harcourt, Brace, Jovanovich, 1984).

6. Geoffrey Kean, The Public Relations Man Abroad (New York: Praeger; 1968).

7. Marion K. Pinsdorf, "Flying Different Skies: How Cultures Respond to Airline Disasters," Public Relations Review 17 (1991), pp. 37–56.

8. Junko Taguchi, "Japanese Officials and PR Mentality," Public Relations Quarterly 40 (1995), pp. 31–37.

9. David M. Grant, "Cross-Cultural Crossed Signals," Public Relations Journal 44 (1988), p. 48.

10. Ni Chen and Hugh M. Culbertson, "Two Contrasting Approaches of Government Public Relations in Mainland China," Public Relations Quarterly 37 (1993), pp. 36–41.

11. Abdulrahman H. Al-Enad, "Public Relations' Roles in Developing Countries," Public Relations Quarterly 35 (1991), pp. 24–26.

—Continued

Continued

12. Benno H. Signitzer and Timothy Coombs, "Public Relations and Public Diplomacy: Conceptual Convergences" Public Relations Review 18 (1992), pp. 137–147.

13. Melvin L. Sharpe, "The Impact of Social and Cultural Conditioning on Global Public Relations," Public Relations Review 18 (1992), pp. 103–107.

14. Geoffrey L. Martin, "West Unraveling Mysteries of Culture," Advertising Age International (Oct. 16, 1995), pp. 115–116.

15. Carl Botan, "International Public Relations: Critique and Reformulation," Public Relations Review 18 (1992), pp. 149–159.

16. Larissa A. Grunig, "Strategic Public Relations Constituencies on a Global Scale," Public Relations Review 18 (1992), pp. 127–136.

17. Jon Kalina, "'Vive la Difference': Learning Trade North of 49th Parallel," Advertising Age International (Sept. 18, 1995), pp. 123, 130.

18. Dana Milbank and Marcus W. Brauchli, "Greasing Wheels: How U.S. Concerns Compete in Countries Where Bribes Flourish," The Wall Street Journal (Sept. 29, 1995), p. A1.

19. Editors, "Governance Goes Global," Inside PR V (1995), pp. 18–20.

20. Alexandre G. Nikolaev and A.G. Gorgin, "The Value of a PR Association to Russians," International Association of Business Communicators Communication World 12 (1995), pp. 7–9.

21. Thomas Donaldson, The Ethics of International Business (New York: Oxford University Press, 1989).

22. R.T. DeGeorge, "Ethical Dilemmas for Multinational Enterprises: A Philosophical Overview." In Hoffman, Lange and Fedo (Eds.) Ethics and the Multinational Enterprise: Proceedings of the Sixth National Conference on Business Ethics (New York: Oxford University Press, 1986), pp. 39–46.

23. Joe Skelly, "The Rise of International Ethics," Business Ethics, unnumbered reprint.

24. MacGregor was interviewed by one of the authors in August 1995.

25. Sandra Harding, Whose Science? Whose Knowledge? (Ithaca, New York: Cornell University Press, 1991).

26. Seyla Benhabib, Situating the Self: Gender, Community and Postmodernism in Contemporary Ethics (New York: Routledge, 1992).

27. Edward Said, Orientalism (New York: Routledge, 1978).

28. Eric Eisenberg, "Ambiguity as Strategic Organizational Communication," Communication Monographs 51 (1984), pp. 227–242.

29. Heddy R. Dexter, Kathy Drew, Jolanta A. Drzewiecka, Barbara M. Gayle, Dreama G. Moon, Sami Reist, Richard A. Rogers, Nancy L. Roth, Michelle T. Violanti, and Kathleen Wong, "Reconceptualizing Identity and Agency in Communication Theory," paper presented at the Speech Communications Association Annual Conference, San Antonio, TX, 1995.

30. James Grunig and Todd Hunt, op. cit.

Nancy L. Roth is Assistant Professor of Communication, Todd Hunt is Professor of Communication, Maria Stavropoulos is a Ph.D. student, and Karen Babik is completing her Masters Degree in the School of Communication, Information, and Library Studies at Rutgers University.

Readings

Values in Tension: Ethics Away from Home

by Thomas Donaldson

> **When is different just different and when is different wrong?**

When we leave home and cross our nation's boundaries, moral clarity often blurs. Without a backdrop of shared attitudes, and without familiar laws and judicial procedures that define standards of ethical conduct, certainty is elusive. Should a company invest in a foreign country where civil and political rights are violated? Should a company go along with a host country's discriminatory employment practices? If companies in developed countries shift facilities to developing nations that lack strict environmental and health regulations,

—Continued

Continued

or if those companies choose to fill management and other top-level positions in a host nation with people from the home country, whose standards should prevail?

Even the best-informed, best-intentioned executives must rethink their assumptions about business practice in foreign settings. What works in a company's home country can fail in a country with different standards of ethical conduct. Such difficulties are unavoidable for businesspeople who live and work abroad.

But how can managers resolve the problems? What are the principles that can help them work through the maze of cultural differences and establish codes of conduct for globally ethical business practice? How can companies answer the toughest question in global business ethics: What happens when a host country's ethical standards seem lower than the home country's?

COMPETING ANSWERS

One answer is as old as philosophical discourse. According to cultural relativism, no culture's ethics are better than any other's, therefore there are no international rights and wrongs. If the people of Indonesia tolerate the bribery of their public officials, so what? Their attitude is no better or worse than that of people in Denmark or Singapore who refuse to offer or accept bribes. Likewise, if Belgians fail to find insider trading morally repugnant, who cares? Not enforcing insider-trading laws is no more or less ethical than enforcing such laws.

The cultural relativist's creed—When in Rome, do as the Romans do—is tempting, especially when failing to do as the locals do means forfeiting business opportunities. The inadequacy of cultural relativism, however, becomes apparent when the practices in question are more damaging than petty bribery or insider trading.

In the late 1980s, some European tanneries and pharmaceutical companies were looking for cheap waste-dumping sites. They approached virtually every country on Africa's west coast from Morocco to the Congo. Nigeria agreed to take highly toxic polychlorinated biphenyls. Unprotected local workers, wearing thongs and shorts, unloaded barrels of PCBs and placed them near a residential area. Neither the residents nor the workers knew that the barrels contained toxic waste.

We may denounce governments that permit such abuses, but many countries are unable to police transnational corporations adequately even if they want to. And in many countries,

the combination of ineffective enforcement and inadequate regulations leads to behavior by unscrupulous companies that is clearly wrong. A few years ago, for example, a group of investors became interested in restoring the *SS United States*, once a luxurious ocean liner. Before the actual restoration could begin, the ship had to be stripped of its asbestos lining. A bid from a U.S. company, based on U.S. standards for asbestos removal, priced the job at more than $100 million. A company in the Ukranian city of Sevastopol offered to do the work for less than $2 million. In October 1993, the ship was towed to Sevastopol.

A cultural relativist would have no problem with that outcome, but I do. A country has the right to establish its own health and safety regulations, but in the case described above, the standards and the terms of the contract could not possibly have protected workers in Sevastopol from known health risks. Even if the contract met Ukranian standards, ethical businesspeople must object. Cultural relativism is morally blind. There are fundamental values that cross cultures, and companies must uphold them. [For an economic argument against cultural relativism, see the insert "The Culture and Ethics of Software Piracy."]

At the other end of the spectrum from cultural relativism is ethical imperialism, which directs people to do everywhere exactly as they do at home. Again, an understandably appealing approach but one that is clearly inadequate. Consider the large U.S. computer-products company that in 1993 introduced a course on sexual harassment in its Saudi Arabian facility. Under the banner of global consistency, instructors used the same approach to train Saudi Arabian managers that they had used with U.S. managers: the participants were asked to discuss a case in which a manager makes sexually explicit remarks to a new female employee over drinks in a bar. The instructors failed to consider how the exercise would work in a culture with strict conventions governing relationships between men and women. As a result, the training sessions were ludicrous. They baffled and offended the Saudi participants, and the message to avoid coercion and sexual discrimination was lost.

The theory behind ethical imperialism is absolutism, which is based on three problematic principles. Absolutists believe that there is a single list of truths, that they can be expressed only with one set of concepts, and that they call for exactly the same behavior around the world.

The first claim clashes with many people's belief that different cultural traditions must be respected. In some cultures, loyalty to a community—family, organization, or society—is the foundation of all ethical behavior. The Japanese, for example, define business ethics in terms of loyalty to their

—Continued

Continued

The Culture and Ethics of Software Piracy

Before jumping on the cultural relativism bandwagon, stop and consider the potential economic consequences of a when-in-Rome attitude toward business ethics. Take a look at the current statistics on software piracy: In the United States, pirated software is estimated to be 35% of the total software market, and industry losses are estimated at $2.3 billion per year. The piracy rate is 57% in Germany and 80% in Italy and Japan; the rates in most Asian countries are estimated to be nearly 100%.

There are similar laws against software piracy in those countries. What, then, accounts for the differences? Although a country's level of economic development plays a large part, culture, including ethical attitudes, may be a more crucial factor. The 1995 annual report of the Software Publishers Association connects software piracy directly to culture and attitude. It describes Italy and Hong Kong as having "'first world' per capita incomes, along with 'third world' rates of piracy." When asked whether one should use software without paying for it, most people, including people in Italy and Hong Kong, say no. But people in some countries regard the practice as less unethical than people in other countries do. Confucian culture, for example, stresses that individuals should share what they create with society. That may be, in part, what prompts the Chinese and other Asians to view the concept of intellectual property as a means for the West to monopolize its technological superiority.

What happens if ethical attitudes around the world permit large-scale software piracy? Software companies won't want to invest as much in developing new products, because they cannot expect any return on their investment in certain parts of the world. When ethics fail to support technological creativity, there are consequences that go beyond statistics—jobs are lost and livelihoods jeopardized.

Companies must do more than lobby foreign governments for tougher enforcement of piracy laws. They must cooperate with other companies and with local organizations to help citizens understand the consequences of piracy and to encourage the evolution of a different ethic toward the practice.

---

companies, their business networks, and their nation. Americans place a higher value on liberty than on loyalty, the U.S. tradition of rights emphasize equality, fairness, and individual freedom. It is hard to conclude that truth lies on one side or the other, but an absolutist would have us select just one.

The second problem with absolutism is the presumption that people must express moral truth using only one set of concepts. For instance, some absolutists insist that the language of basic rights provide the framework for any discussion of ethics. That means, though, that entire cultural traditions must be ignored. The notion of a right evolved with the rise of democracy in post-Renaissance Europe and the United States, but the term is not found in either Confucian or Buddhist traditions. We all learn ethics in the context of our particular cultures, and the power in the principles is deeply tied to the way in which they are expressed. Internationally accepted lists of moral principles, such as the United Nations' Universal Declaration of Human Rights, draw on many cultural and religious traditions. As philosopher Michael Walzer has noted, "There is no Esperanto of global ethics."

The third problem with absolutism is the belief in a global standard of ethical behavior. Context must shape ethical practice. Very low wages, for example, may be considered unethical in rich, advanced countries, but developing nations may be acting

WHAT DO THESE VALUES HAVE IN COMMON?

NON-WESTERN	WESTERN
Kyosei (Japanese): Living and working together for the common good.	Individual liberty
Dharma (Hindu): The fulfillment of inherited duty.	Egalitarianism
Santutthi (Buddhist): The importance of limited desires.	Political participation
Zakat (Muslim): The duty to give alms to the Muslim poor.	Human rights

ethically if they encourage investment and improve living standards by accepting low wages. Likewise, when people are malnourished or starving, a government may be wise to use more fertilizer in order to improve crop yields, even though that means settling for relatively high levels of thermal water pollution.

—Continued

Continued

When cultures have different standards of ethical behavior—and different ways of handling unethical behavior—a company that takes an absolutist approach may find itself making a disastrous mistake. When a manager at a large U.S. specialty-products company in China caught an employee stealing, she followed the company's practice and turned the employee over to the provincial authorities, who executed him. Managers cannot operate in another culture without being aware of that culture's attitudes toward ethics.

If companies can neither adopt a host country's ethics nor extend the home country's standards, what is the answer? Even the traditional litmus test—What would people think of your actions if they were written up on the front page of the newspaper?—is an unreliable guide, for there is no international consensus on standards of business conduct.

BALANCING THE EXTREMES: THREE GUIDING PRINCIPLES

Companies must help managers distinguish between practices that are merely different and those that are wrong. For relativists, nothing is sacred and nothing is wrong. For absolutists, many things that are different are wrong. Neither extreme illuminates the real world of business decision making. The answer lies somewhere in between.

When it comes to shaping ethical behavior, companies might be guided by three principles.

- Respect for core human values, which determine the absolute moral threshold for all business activities.

- Respect for local traditions.

- The belief that context matters when deciding what is right and what is wrong.

Consider those principles in action. In Japan, people doing business together often exchange gifts—sometimes expensive ones—in keeping with long-standing Japanese tradition. When U.S. and European companies started doing a lot of business in Japan, many Western businesspeople thought that the practice of gift giving might be wrong rather than simply different. To them, accepting a gift felt like accepting a bribe. As Western companies have become more familiar with Japanese traditions, however, most have come to tolerate the practice and to set different limits on gift giving in Japan than they do elsewhere.

Respecting differences is a crucial ethical practice. Research shows that management ethics differ among cultures; respecting those differences means recognizing that some cultures have obvious weaknesses—as well as hidden strengths. Managers in Hong Kong, for example, have a higher tolerance for some forms of bribery than their Western counterparts, but they have a much lower tolerance for the failure to acknowledge a subordinate's work. In some parts of the Far East, stealing credit from a subordinate is nearly an unpardonable sin.

People often equate respect for local traditions with cultural relativism. That is incorrect. Some practices are clearly wrong. Union Carbide's tragic experience in Bhopal, India, provides one example. The company's executives seriously underestimated how much on-site management involvement was needed at the Bhopal plant to compensate for the country's poor infrastructure and regulatory capabilities. In the aftermath of the disastrous gas leak, the lesson is clear: companies using sophisticated technology in a developing country must evaluate that country's ability to oversee its safe use. Since the incident at Bhopal, Union Carbide has become a leader in advising companies on using hazardous technologies safely in developing countries.

Some activities are wrong no matter where they take place. But some practices that are unethical in one setting may be acceptable in another. For instance, the chemical EDB, a soil fungicide, is banned for use in the United States. In hot climates, however, it quickly becomes harmless through exposure to intense solar radiation and high soil temperatures. As long as the chemical is monitored, companies may be able to use EDB ethically in certain parts of the world.

DEFINING THE ETHICAL THRESHOLD: CORE VALUES

Few ethical questions are easy for managers to answer. But there are some hard truths that must guide managers' actions, a set of what I call *core human values*, which define minimum ethical standards for all companies.[1] The right to good health and the right to economic advancement and an improved standard of living are two core human values. Another is what Westerners call the Golden Rule, which is recognizable in every major religious and ethical tradition around the world. In Book 15 of his *Analects*, for instance, Confucius counsels people to maintain reciprocity, or not to do to others what they do not want done to themselves.

Although no single list would satisfy every scholar, I believe it is possible to articulate three core values that incorporate the work of scores of theologians and philosophers around the world. To be broadly relevant, these values must include elements found in both Western and non-Western cultural

---

1. In other writings, Thomas W. Dunfee and I have used the term *hypernorm* instead of *core human value*.

—Continued

Continued

and religious traditions. Consider the examples of values in the insert "What Do These Values Have in Common?"

At first glance, the values expressed in the two lists seem quite different. Nonetheless, in the spirit of what philosopher John Rawls calls *overlapping consensus*, one can see that the seemingly divergent values converge at key points. Despite important differences between Western and non-Western cultural and religious traditions, both express shared attitudes about what it means to be human. First, individuals must not treat others simply as tools; in other words, they must recognize a person's value as a human being. Next, individuals and communities must treat people in ways that respect people's basic rights. Finally, members of a community must work together to support and improve the institutions on which the community depends. I call those three values *respect for human dignity*, *respect for basic rights*, and *good citizenship*.

Those values must be the starting point for all companies as they formulate and evaluate standards of ethical conduct at home and abroad. But they are only a starting point. Companies need much more specific guidelines, and the first step to developing those is to translate the core human values into core values for business. What does it mean, for example, for a company to respect human dignity? How can a company be a good citizen?

I believe that companies can respect human dignity by creating and sustaining a corporate culture in which employees, customers, and suppliers are treated not as means to an end but as people whose intrinsic value must be acknowledged, and by producing safe products and services in a safe workplace. Companies can respect basic rights by acting in ways that support and protect the individual rights of employees, customers, and surrounding communities, and by avoiding relationships that violate human beings' rights to health, education, safety, and an adequate standard of living. And companies can be good citizens by supporting essential social institutions, such as the economic system and the education system, and by working with host governments and other organizations to protect the environment.

> **Many companies don't do anything with their codes of conduct; they simply paste them on the wall.**

The core values establish a moral compass for business practice. They can help companies identify practices that are acceptable and those that are intolerable—even if the practices are compatible with a host country's norms and laws. Dumping pollutants near people's homes and accepting inadequate standards for handling hazardous materials are two examples of actions that violate core values.

Similarly, if employing children prevents them from receiving a basic education, the practice is intolerable. Lying

about product specifications in the act of selling may not affect human lives directly, but it too is intolerable because it violates the trust that is needed to sustain a corporate culture in which customers are respected.

Sometimes it is not a company's actions but those of a supplier or customer that pose problems. Take the case of the Tan family, a large supplier for Levi Strauss. The Tans were allegedly forcing 1,200 Chinese and Filipino women to work 74 hours per week in guarded compounds on the Mariana Islands. In 1992, after repeated warnings to the Tans, Levi Strauss broke off business relations with them.

CREATING AN ETHICAL CORPORATE CULTURE

The core values for business that I have enumerated can help companies begin to exercise ethical judgment and think about how to operate ethically in foreign cultures, but they are not specific enough to guide managers through actual ethical dilemmas. Levi Strauss relied on a written code of conduct when figuring out how to deal with the Tan family. The company's Global Sourcing and Operating Guidelines, formerly called the Business Partner Terms of Engagement, state that Levi Strauss will "seek to identify and utilize business partners who aspire as individuals and in the conduct of all their businesses to a set of ethical standards not incompatible with our own." Whenever intolerable business situations arise, managers should be guided by precise statements that spell out the behavior and operating practices that the company demands.

Ninety percent of all *Fortune 500* companies have codes of conduct, and 70% have statements of vision and values. In Europe and the Far East, the percentages are lower but are increasing rapidly. Does that mean that most companies have what they need? Hardly. Even though most large U.S. companies have both statements of values and codes of conduct, many might be better off if they didn't. Too many companies don't do anything with the documents; they simply paste them on the wall to impress employees, customers, suppliers, and the public. As a result, the senior managers who drafted the statements lose credibility by proclaiming values and not living up to them. Companies such as Johnson & Johnson, Levi Strauss, Motorola, Texas Instruments, and Lockheed Martin, however, do a great deal to make the words meaningful. Johnson & Johnson, for example, has become well known for its Credo Challenge sessions, in which managers discuss ethics in the context of their current business problems and are invited to criticize the company's credo and make suggestions for changes. The participants' ideas are passed on to the company's senior managers. Lockheed Martin has created an innovative site on the World Wide Web and on its local network that

—Continued

Continued

gives employees, customers, and suppliers access to the company's ethical code and the chance to voice complaints.

Codes of conduct must provide clear direction about ethical behavior when the temptation to behave unethically is strongest. The pronouncement in a code of conduct that bribery is unacceptable is useless unless accompanied by guidelines for gift giving, payments to get goods through customs, and "requests" from intermediaries who are hired to ask for bribes.

Motorola's values are stated very simply as "How we will always act: [with] constant respect for people [and] uncompromising integrity." The company's code of conduct, however, is explicit about actual business practice. With respect to bribery, for example, the code states that the "funds and assets of Motorola shall not be used, directly or indirectly, for illegal payments of any kind." It is unambiguous about what sort of payment is illegal: "the payment of a bribe to a public official or the kickback of funds to an employee of a customer. . . ." The code goes on to prescribe specific procedures for handling commissions to intermediaries, issuing sales invoices, and disclosing confidential information in a sales transaction—all situations in which employees might have an opportunity to accept or offer bribes.

> **Many activities are neither good nor bad but exist in moral free space.**

Codes of conduct must be explicit to be useful, but they must also leave room for a manager to use his or her judgment in situations requiring cultural sensitivity. Host-country employees shouldn't be forced to adopt all home-country values and renounce their own. Again, Motorola's code is exemplary. First, it gives clear direction: "Employees of Motorola will respect the laws, customs, and traditions of each country in which they operate, but will, at the same time, engage in no course of conduct which, even if legal, customary, and accepted in any such country, could be deemed to be in violation of the accepted business ethics of Motorola or the laws of the United States relating to business ethics." After laying down such absolutes, Motorola's code then makes clear when individual judgment will be necessary. For example, employees may sometimes accept certain kinds of small gifts "in rare circumstances, where the refusal to accept a gift" would injure Motorola's "legitimate business interests." Under certain circumstances, such gifts "may be accepted so long as the gift inures to the benefit of Motorola" and not "to the benefit of the Motorola employee."

Striking the appropriate balance between providing clear direction and leaving room for individual judgment makes crafting corporate values statements and ethics codes one of the hardest tasks that executives confront. The words are only a start. A company's leaders need to refer often to their organization's credo and code and must themselves be credible, committed, and consistent. If senior managers act as though ethics don't matter, the rest of the company's employees won't think they do, either.

CONFLICTS OF DEVELOPMENT AND CONFLICTS OF TRADITION

Managers living and working abroad who are not prepared to grapple with moral ambiguity and tension should pack their bags and come home. The view that all business practices can be categorized as either ethical or unethical is too simple. As Einstein is reported to have said, "Things should be as simple as possible—but no simpler." Many business practices that are considered unethical in one setting may be ethical in another. Such activities are neither black nor white but exist in what Thomas Dunfee and I have called *moral free space*.[2] In this gray zone, there are no tight prescriptions for a company's behavior. Managers must chart their own courses—as long as they do not violate core human values.

Consider the following example. Some successful Indian companies offer employees the opportunity for one of their children to gain a job with the company once the child has completed a certain level in school. The companies honor this commitment even when other applicants are more qualified than an employee's child. The perk is extremely valuable in a country where jobs are hard to find, and it reflects the Indian culture's belief that the West has gone too far in allowing economic opportunities to break up families. Not surprisingly, the perk is among the most cherished by employees, but in most Western countries, it would be branded unacceptable nepotism. In the United States, for example, the ethical principle of equal opportunity holds that jobs should go to the applicants with the best qualifications. If a U.S. company made such promises to its employees, it would violate regulations established by the Equal Employment Opportunity Commission. Given this difference in ethical attitudes, how should U.S. managers react to Indian nepotism? Should they condemn the Indian companies, refusing to accept them as partners or suppliers until they agree to clean up their act?

Despite the obvious tension between nepotism and principles of equal opportunity, I cannot condemn the practice for Indians. In a country, such as India, that emphasizes clan and family relationships and has catastrophic levels of unemployment, the practice must be viewed in moral free space. The

2. Thomas Donaldson and Thomas W. Dunfee, "Toward a Unified Conception of Business Ethics: Integrative Social Contracts Theory," *Academy of Management Review*, April 1994, and "Integrative Social Contracts Theory: A Communitarian Conception of Economic Ethics," *Economics and Philosophy*, spring 1995.

—Continued

Continued

decision to allow a special perk for employees and their children is not necessarily wrong—at least for members of that country.

How can managers discover the limits of moral free space? That is, how can they learn to distinguish a value in tension with their own from one that is intolerable? Helping managers develop good ethical judgment requires companies to be clear about their core values and codes of conduct. But even the most explicit set of guidelines cannot always provide answers. That is especially true in the thorniest ethical dilemmas, in which the host country's ethical standards not only are different but also seem lower than the home country's. Managers must recognize that when countries have different ethical standards, there are two types of conflict that commonly arise. Each type requires its own line of reasoning.

In the first type of conflict, which I call a *conflict of relative development*, ethical standards conflict because of the countries' different levels of economic development. As mentioned before, developing countries may accept wage rates that seem inhumane to more advanced countries in order to attract investment. As economic conditions in a developing country improve, the incidence of that sort of conflict usually decreases. The second type of conflict is a *conflict of cultural tradition*. For example, Saudi Arabia, unlike most countries, does not allow women to serve as corporate managers. Instead, women may work in only a few professions, such as education and health care. The prohibition stems from strongly held religious and cultural beliefs, any increase in the country's level of economic development, which is already quite high, is not likely to change the rules.

To resolve a conflict of relative development, a manager must ask the following question: Would the practice be acceptable at home if my country were in a similar stage of economic development? Consider the difference between wage and safety standards in the United States and in Angola, where citizens accept lower standards on both counts. If a U.S. oil company is hiring Angolans to work on an offshore Angolan oil rig, can the company pay them lower wages than it pays U.S. workers in the Gulf of Mexico? Reasonable people have to answer yes if the alternative for Angola is the loss of both the foreign investment and the jobs.

> **If a company declared all gift giving unethical, it wouldn't be able to do business in Japan.**

Consider, too, differences in regulatory environments. In the late 1980s, the government of India fought hard to be able to import Ciba-Ceigy's Entero Vioform, a drug known to be enormously effective in fighting dysentery but one that had been banned in the United States because some users experienced side effects. Although dysentery was not a big problem in the United States, in India, poor public sanitation was contributing to epidemic levels of the disease. Was it unethical to make the drug available in India after it had been banned in the United States? On the contrary, rational people should consider it unethical not to do so. Apply our test: Would the United States, at an earlier stage of development, have used this drug despite its side effects? The answer is clearly yes.

But there are many instances when the answer to similar questions is no. Sometimes a host country's standards are inadequate at any level of economic development. If a country's pollution standards are so low that working on an oil rig would considerably increase a person's risk of developing cancer, foreign oil companies must refuse to do business there. Likewise, if the dangerous side effects of a drug treatment outweigh its benefits, managers should not accept health standards that ignore the risks.

When relative economic conditions do not drive tensions, there is a more objective test for resolving ethical problems. Managers should deem a practice permissible only if they can answer no to both of the following questions: Is it possible to conduct business successfully in the host country without undertaking the practice? and Is the practice a violation of a core human value? Japanese gift giving is a perfect example of a conflict of cultural tradition. Most experienced businesspeople, Japanese and non-Japanese alike, would agree that doing business in Japan would be virtually impossible without adopting the practice. Does gift giving violate a core human value? I cannot identify one that it violates. As a result, gift giving may be permissible for foreign companies in Japan even if it conflicts with ethical attitudes at home. In fact, that conclusion is widely accepted, even by companies such as Texas Instruments and IBM, which are outspoken against bribery.

Does it follow that all nonmonetary gifts are acceptable or that bribes are generally acceptable in countries where they are common? Not at all. (See the insert "The Problem with Bribery.") What makes the routine practice of gift giving acceptable in Japan are the limits in its scope and intention. When gift giving moves outside those limits, it soon collides with core human values. For example, when Carl Kotchian, president of Lockheed in the 1970s, carried suitcases full of cash to Japanese politicians, he went beyond the norms established by Japanese tradition. That incident galvanized opinion in the United States Congress and helped lead to passage of the Foreign Corrupt Practices Act. Likewise, Roh Tae Woo went beyond the norms established by Korean cultural tradition when he accepted $635.4 million in bribes as president of the Republic of Korea between 1988 and 1993.

—Continued

Continued

GUIDELINES FOR ETHICAL LEADERSHIP

Learning to spot intolerable practices and to exercise good judgment when ethical conflicts arise requires practice. Creating a company culture that rewards ethical behavior is essential. The following guidelines for developing a global ethical perspective among managers can help.

Treat corporate values and formal standards of conduct as absolutes. Whatever ethical standards a company chooses, it cannot wave on its principles either at home or abroad. Consider what has become part of company lore at Motorola. Around 1950, a senior executive was negotiating with officials of a South American government on a $10 million sale that would have increased the company's annual net profits by nearly 25%. As the negotiations neared completion, however, the executive walked away from the deal because the officials were asking for $1 million for "fees." CEO Robert Galvin not only supported the executive's decision but also made it clear that Motorola would neither accept the sale on any terms nor do business with those government officials again. Retold over the decades, this story demonstrating Galvin's resolve has helped cement a culture of ethics for thousands of employees at Motorola.

Design and implement conditions of engagement for suppliers and customers. Will your company do business with any customer or supplier? What if a customer or supplier uses child labor? What if it has strong links with organized crime? What if it pressures your company to break a host country's laws? Such issues are best not left for spur-of-the-moment decisions. Some companies have realized that. Sears, for instance, has developed a policy of not contracting production to companies that use prison labor or infringe on workers' rights to health and safety. And BankAmerica has specified as a condition for many of its loans to developing countries that environmental standards and human rights must be observed.

Allow foreign business units to help formulate ethical standards and interpret ethical issues. The French pharmaceutical company Rhône-Poulenc Rorer has allowed foreign subsidiaries to augment lists of corporate ethical principles with their own suggestions. Texas Instruments has paid special attention to issues of international business ethics by creating the Global Business Practices Council, which is made up of managers from countries in which the company operates. With the overarching intent to create a "global ethics strategy, locally

---

The Problem with Bribery

Bribery is widespread and insidious. Managers in transnational companies routinely confront bribery even though most countries have laws against it. The fact is that officials in many developing countries wink at the practice, and the salaries of local bureaucrats are so low that many consider bribes a form of remuneration. The U.S. Foreign Corrupt Practices Act defines allowable limits on petty bribery in the form of routine payments required to move goods through customs. But demands for bribes often exceed those limits, and there is seldom a good solution.

Bribery disrupts distribution channels when goods languish on docks until local handlers are paid off, and it destroys incentives to compete on quality and cost when purchasing decisions are based on who pays what under the table. Refusing to acquiesce is often tantamount to giving business to unscrupulous companies.

I believe that even routine bribery is intolerable. Bribery undermines market efficiency and predictability, thus ultimately denying people their right to a minimal standard of living. Some degree of ethical commitment—some sense that everyone will play by the rules—is necessary for a sound economy. Without an ability to predict outcomes, who would be willing to invest?

There was a U.S. company whose shipping crates were regularly pilfered by handlers on the docks of Rio de Janeiro. The handlers would take about 10% of the contents of the crates, but the company was never sure which 10% it would be. In a partial solution, the company began sending two crates—the first with 90% of the merchandise, the second with 10%. The handlers learned to take the second crate and leave the first untouched. From the company's perspective, at least knowing which goods it would lose was an improvement.

Bribery does more than destroy predictability, it undermines essential social and economic systems. That truth is not lost on businesspeople in countries where the practice is woven into the social fabric. CEOs in India admit that their companies engage constantly in bribery, and they say that they have considerable disgust for the practice. They blame government policies in part, but Indian executives also know that their country's business practices perpetuate corrupt behavior. Anyone walking the streets of Calcutta, where it is clear that even a dramatic redistribution of wealth would still leave most of India's inhabitants in dire poverty, comes face-to-face with the devastating effects of corruption.

—Continued

Continued

deployed," the council's mandate is to provide ethics education and create local processes that will help managers in the company's foreign business units resolve ethical conflicts.

In host countries, support efforts to decrease institutional corruption. Individual managers will not be able to wipe out corruption in a host country, no matter how many bribes they turn down. When a host country's tax system, import and export procedures, and procurement practices favor unethical players, companies must take action.

Many companies have begun to participate in reforming host-country institutions. General Electric, for example, has taken a strong stand in India, using the media to make repeated condemnations of bribery in business and government. General Electric and others have found, however, that a single company usually cannot drive out entrenched corruption. Transparency International, an organization based in Germany, has been effective in helping coalitions of companies, government officials, and others work to reform bribery-ridden bureaucracies in Russia, Bangladesh, and elsewhere.

Exercise moral imagination. Using moral imagination means resolving tensions responsibly and creatively. Coca-Cola, for instance, has consistently turned down requests for bribes from Egyptian officials but has managed to gain political support and public trust by sponsoring a project to plant fruit trees. And take the example of Levi Strauss, which discovered in the early 1990s that two of its suppliers in Bangladesh were employing children under the age of 14—a practice that violated the company's principles but was tolerated in Bangladesh. Forcing the suppliers to fire the children would not have ensured that the children received an education, and it would have caused serious hardships for the families depending on the children's wages. In a creative arrangement, the suppliers agreed to pay the children's regular wages while they attended school and to offer each child a job at age 14. Levi Strauss, in turn, agreed to pay the children's tuition and provide books and uniforms. That arrangement allowed Levi Strauss to uphold its principles and provide long-term benefits to its host country.

Many people think of values as soft; to some they are usually unspoken. A South Seas island society uses the word *mokita*, which means, "the truth that everybody knows but nobody speaks." However difficult they are to articulate, values affect how we all behave. In a global business environment, values in tension are the rule rather than the exception. Without a company's commitment, statements of values and codes of ethics end up as empty platitudes that provide managers with no foundation for behaving ethically. Employees need and deserve more, and responsible members of the global business community can set examples for others to follow. The dark consequences of incidents such as Union Carbide's disaster in Bhopal remind us how high the stakes can be.

Thomas Donaldson is a professor at the Wharton School of the University of Pennsylvania in Philadelphia, where he teaches business ethics. He wrote The Ethics of International Business *(Oxford University Press, 1989), and is the coauthor, with Thomas W. Dunfee, of* Ties that Bind: A Social Contracts Approach to Business Ethics. *Harvard Business School Press (1999).*

SOURCE: Donaldson, T., "Values inTension: Ethics Away From Home", *Harvard Business Review*, Sept.–Oct., 1996, 48–62.

Effective Crisis Management

Ian I. Mitroff, *University of Southern California*
Paul Shrivastava, *New York University, Industrial Crisis Center*
Firdaus E. Udwadia, *University of Southern California*

Academy of Management Executive, 1987

Managers, consultants, and researchers have traditionally focused on problems of financial performance and growth, but have paid little heed to the effective management of corporate crisis. The negative effects of organizational and industrial activities have been treated as minor "externalities" of production. It can be argued that until recently, it was unnecessary to focus on such crises. Today, however, such crises as pollution, industrial accidents, and product defects have assumed greater magnitude. The consequences for many corporations—like Johns-Manville and A. H. Robins—have been near or actual bankruptcy.

Corporate crises are disasters precipitated by people, organizational structures, economics, and/or technology that cause extensive damage to human life and natural and social

—Continued

Continued

environments. They inevitably debilitate both the financial structure and the reputation of a large organization. Consider the following examples:

- In 1979, the Three Mile Island Nuclear Power Plant had an accident leading to the near meltdown of the plant's reactor core. The accident not only cost Metropolitan Edison—the company that owned the plant—billions of dollars; it altered the fate of the nuclear power industry in the United States.[1] The plant owners and operators paid $26 million in evacuation costs, financial losses, and medical surveillance; the estimated cost of repairs and the production of electricity via other means was $4 billion.

- In 1982 an unknown person or persons contaminated dozens of Tylenol capsules with cyanide, causing the deaths of eight people and a loss of $100 million in recalled packages for Johnson & Johnson. In 1986 a second poisoning incident forced J&J to withdraw all Tylenol capsules from the market at a loss of $150 million. The company abandoned the capsule form of medication and consequently had to redesign its production facility. The full cost of switching from the production of capsules to the production of other forms of medication was in the range of $500 million.

- In December 1984 the worst industrial accident in history occurred: Poisonous methyl isocyanate gas leaked from a storage tank at a Union Carbide plant in Bhopal, India, killing 2,000 people and injuring another 200,000. The accident caused unknown damage to flora and fauna in the area. Union Carbide was sued by victims for billions of dollars; compensation settlement is likely to be between $500 million and $1 billion. In addition, the company was forced to sell 20% of its most profitable assets to prevent a takeover attack mounted by GAF Corporation, which had acquired Carbide's undervalued stock after the accident.[2]

- In May and June 1985 deadly bacteria in Jalisco cheese caused the deaths of 84 people. The company that produced the product was forced into bankruptcy.

The list of recent corporate disasters is virtually unending. It includes executive kidnappings; hijackings, both in the air and at sea; hostile takeovers; and such acts of terrorism as the bombing of factories and warehouses. Most recently, slivers of glass have been found in Gerber's baby food. Contac—an over-the-counter cold remedy—has also been the object of product tampering.

Such incidents now happen on an ever-increasing basis. Further, the interval between major accidents is shrinking alarmingly.[3] The number of product-injury lawsuits terminating in million-dollar awards has increased dramatically in the past decade: In 1974 fewer than 2,000 product injury lawsuits were filed in U.S. courts; by 1984, the number had jumped to 10,000. In 1975, juries had awarded fewer than 50 compensation awards of greater than $1 million each; in 1985, there were more than 400 such awards. The costs of product- and production-related injury is one factor in the current liability insurance crisis. Many forms of liability insurance have simply vanished, and all forms of liability insurance have become so expensive, they are available only for small coverages.

The purpose of this article is to argue that while the situation is grave, it is far from hopeless for managers, researchers, and consultants who are prepared to confront the problem directly. While no one can prevent all disasters—let alone predict how, when, and where they will occur—organizations can adopt a systematic and comprehensive perspective for managing them more effectively. Anything less than such a perspective virtually guarantees that an organization will be less prepared to cope and recover effectively from a crisis.

THE ESSENTIAL PHASES OF CRISIS MANAGEMENT

Exhibit 1 presents a basic model of crisis management. It identifies as many of the phases necessary for effective crisis management as we have been able to discern through our research and consulting. The model, reflecting the variety of organizational patterns possible, can be entered at and exited from any point, and the action can proceed in any direction. We shall discuss this model by starting at the entry point labeled "detection" and proceeding clockwise.

The circle labeled "detection" stands for the organization's early warning systems. Those systems—including computerized process control systems, plant/equipment monitoring systems, management information systems, and environmental scanning systems—scan both the external and the internal environments for signals of impending crises.

We have placed "detection" before the sloping line labeled "prevention/preparation" to indicate that it is difficult, both systematically and comprehensively, to prevent or prepare for crises that one has not detected. For most people and most organizations, detection logically occurs before prevention. Although one may unintentionally prevent what one has not detected, prevention in such instances is based on luck and happenstance, not on deliberate organization intervention.

1. C. Perrow, *Normal Accidents*. New York: Basic Books, 1984.
2. P. Shrivastava, *Bhopal: Anatomy of a Disaster*. New York: Harper & Row, 1987.

3. B. A. Turner, *Man-made Disasters*. London: Wykeham Publications, 1978; Shrivastava, op. cit.

—Continued

Continued

EXHIBIT I

A MODEL OF CRISIS
MANAGEMENT

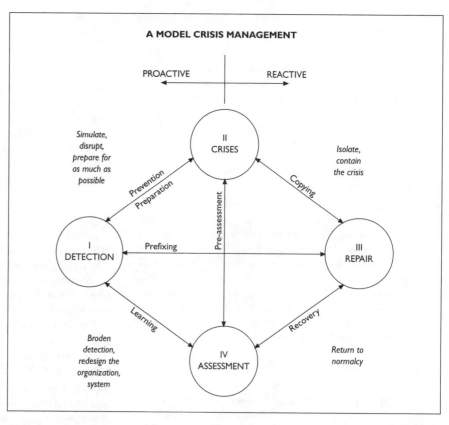

A MODEL CRISIS MANAGEMENT

Point II of the model indicates that no organization can prevent every crisis from occurring. Indeed, prevention of all crises is not the basic purpose of planning and crisis management. But constant testing and revision of plans should allow an organization to cope more effectively with crises that occur, because such efforts help it learn how to "roll with the punches." Prevention and preparation take the form of safety policies, maintenance, procedures, environmental-impact audits, crisis audits, emergency planning, and worker training.

Point III represents the major structures and mechanisms an organization has in place for guiding recovery. These include emergency plans, public relations plans, crisis management teams, etc. At Point IV, the organization asks itself what it has learned from its past crises and how it can use that knowledge in the future. It also assesses the effectiveness of its crisis handling strategies and identifies areas in which better crisis management capabilities need to be developed.

The more an organization denies its vulnerability, the more it will be focused on the right-hand side of Exhibit 1—the more it will respond *reactively* to crises it anticipates and the more potential crises it prepares for, the more it engages in *proactive* behavior.

The model allows us to draw some vital lessons for effective crisis management. First, and perhaps most important, is that most crises are preceded by a string of early warning signals. To prevent some major crisis, organizations need only learn to read these early warning signals and respond to them more effectively. For example, we have seen that for a year and a half before the Bhopal tragedy, messages repeatedly passed back and forth between Union Carbide's parent company in Danbury, Connecticut, Union Carbide Eastern in Hong Kong, a similar Union Carbide plant in West Virginia, and the Indian plant. The messages warned Bhopal plant management to fix potential problems that could cause a catastrophic explosion.[4] The signals were sent, but the system chose either to ignore them or not to act on them. This assessment holds even if, as Union Carbide contends, the catastrophe was caused by a deliberate act of on-site sabotage by a disgruntled employee.

The jury is still out, but Union Carbide may be legally accountable for the disaster unless it can show that it did everything humanly possible to read the early warning signs of internal sabotage and everything reasonable to lessen the chances

---

4. Shrivastava, op. cit.

—*Continued*

Continued

of sabotage—even if complete prevention was impossible. (Editor's note: Courts in India have subsequently decided that Union Carbide was guilty.) Indeed, because complete prevention may have been impossible, it will be all the more important for legal experts to assess what organizational mechanisms Union Carbide could have actually implemented (not just left on a shelf in paper form) to try to prevent a major disaster, cope with one, and help the company and its surrounding community recover in the event of a disaster.

Given today's extremely litigious environment and a news media that is more vigilant and aware of worldwide events than ever before, organizations can regard it as a virtual certainty that their plans for and performance on every phase of the model in Exhibit 1 will become available to the press.

The field of crisis management is still in its infancy, yet available data seem to indicate that the more potential crises an organization can anticipate and prepare for (regardless of whether it can completely prevent them or not), the more quickly and successfully it will recover from any crises that strike.[5] While planning cannot prevent every crisis, the process of planning teaches an organization how to cope more effectively with whatever does occur. In fact, a cardinal rule of crisis management is that no crisis ever unfolds exactly as it was envisioned or planned for. For this reason, effective crisis management is a never-ending process, not an event with a beginning and an end.

There is, in fact, a fundamental paradox connected with crisis management: The less vulnerable an organization thinks it is, the fewer crises it prepares for; as a result, the more vulnerable it becomes. Conversely, the *more* vulnerable an organization thinks it is, the more crises it prepares for; as a result, the less vulnerable it is likely to be. The tragic explosion of Space Shuttle Challenger should be enough to dispel any doubts about the validity of this paradox. The Presidential Commission's report painstakingly examined the contending, probable causes of the disaster and, one by one, ruled them out. Slowly but surely the true cause was revealed: the explosion was caused by the failure of two large, critical O-rings that were supposed to keep highly flammable rocket fuel from spilling over its incasement and igniting with the shuttle's main engines.

The real causes, however, had little to do with technology per se. Having located the technical cause of the disaster, the report then identifies the accompanying human and organizational causes. This part of the report graphically exposes how one of the nation's premier examples of a highly successful and respected organization—NASA—became accident prone through multiple organizational failures.

One of the most powerful aspects of the report is its well-stocked supply of pictures. The report not only recounts, frame by frame, the hundredths and thousandths of seconds leading up to the accident; it also contains detailed photographs of recovered parts from the ocean floor. Although there can be no doubt that the failure of O-rings led to the disaster, the most striking evidence pertains to faulty organization—the underlying cause of the accident. This evidence consists of a seemingly endless series of reproduced memos revealing the anguished cries from deep within NASA's flawed bureaucracy and the bureaucracy of one of its prime subcontractors, Morton Thiokol. If NASA had listened and attended to these early warning signals, in all likelihood it could have prevented the disaster. One of the most striking memos starts with the cry. "Help!" The memo goes on to say that if the shuttle continues to fly with the O-rings as they are designed, then NASA is almost guaranteed a disaster. The evidence shows an organization impervious to bad news. Instead of deliberately designing monitoring systems to pick up danger signals NASA designed, in effect, a management system that would intentionally tune out danger signals or downgrade their seriousness.

The early warning signals associated with crises are not only different for different types of organizations, but are seldom perfectly clear. Rarely, if ever, will a signal say, "The presence of such and such a defect automatically guarantees or invariably leads to disaster Y." Rather, signals will read, "It *appears* that there is a *good chance* that X will cause Y or is associated with its occurrence," or, "The numbers of Xs have been growing noticeably in recent months."

In addition, a big difference exists between warning signals external to an organization and its industry and those internal to them. Those internal to the organization and its industry are more likely to be taken seriously because they "fit in" with the business.

For these reasons, it should not be surprising to find that, based on what preliminary data we have, only 50% of *Fortune* 1000 organizations surveyed have any kind of contingency plan in place to cope with any kind of crisis.[6] Further, those organizations that are prepared have a narrow focus. They are preparing to "fight the last war" because they know how to read the signals and prepare for, cope with, and recover from those crises.

Yet this narrow focus stands in sharp contrast to what we have begun to learn about modern crises and disasters. Unlike previous crises and disasters, modern ones link up with one

---

5. S. Fink, *Crisis Management.* New York: AMACOM, 1986; and I. Mitroff and P. Shrivastava, "Strategic Management of Corporate Crises," *Columbia Journal of World Business*, Vol. 22, No. 1, Spring 1987, pp. 5–12.

6. Fink, op. cit.

—Continued

Continued

another and defy accepted truths. For instance, consider the recent finding of glass in Gerber's baby food. The food industry has long experienced such events, so they are historically well known to the industry. But what happened during the week that slivers of glass were found in Gerber's baby food was not part of the typical historic pattern. That week the Challenger exploded and Tylenol was poisoned for the second time. These events shattered the twin myths that "The worst can and won't happen twice to any organization" and "Lightening won't and can't strike twice in the same place."

As a consequence of these events, the media focused on Gerber's CEO as perhaps never before. Although he may have been right in not withdrawing his products—because withdrawing them may have encouraged "copycat killers"—he was wrong in another, more important sense. By being unwilling to withdraw the products, Gerber's CEO appeared callous toward the most fragile and most precious of all consumers—babies! Contrast this with the behavior of Johnson & Johnson's CEO, who unequivocally withdrew Tylenol from the shelves to demonstrate the company's long-standing commitment to the safety and well-being of its consumers.

AN EXPANDED TYPOLOGY OF CRISES

Clearly, every organization must attend not only to crises that are well known to it and its industry, but to the many disasters that can now happen to any organization and all industries. Such an expanded list of crises is presented in Exhibit 2.

Exhibit 2 differentiates between crises that arise within the organization and those that arise outside it. This distinction is critical because the warning signals will be different for each type of crisis. Exhibit 2 also differentiates between crises caused by technical/economic breakdowns and those caused by people/organizational/social breakdowns. This is because nearly every technical/economic breakdown is associated with a people/organizational/social breakdown, and vice versa. Thus, if we look at only one part of the chain, we miss valuable potential lessons for preparing and correcting the whole system.

Exhibit 3 shows various causes of each type of crisis listed in Exhibit 2. Finally, Exhibit 4 shows the wide variety of actions organizations can take to prepare for, cope with, reduce the effects of, and recover from the various kinds of crises we've identified.

Exhibit 4 shows that when it comes to taking action, we are faced with the problem of choosing between too many options, none of which can guarantee us prevention or complete containment. But then again, perfection is not an appropriate criterion for judging the success of crisis management.

Indeed, if an appropriate goal for crisis management is to learn to prepare for as many crises as possible, then a reasonable way of approaching this goal is to form a crisis portfolio based on Exhibits 2, 3, and 4. One way to do this is to select a minimum of one crisis from each of the cells in Exhibits 2 and 3. This way, organizations can avoid the tendency to prepare mainly for the crises listed in Cell 1 of these exhibits and can thus begin to broaden their perspective about potential crises. In the same way, organizations can form a portfolio of coping and recovery mechanisms based on a selection of at least one element from each of the cells in Exhibit 4.

CONCLUDING REMARKS

To manage crises effectively, organizations must first be aware of all the phases and steps involved in the entire process of crisis management. Next, they must be aware of the differences between the phases. For instance, the purpose of the "preparation and prevention phase" in Exhibit 1 is for organizations to ask themselves, "What can/cannot be prevented and/or prepared for?" The goal of this phase is to prepare for as many of the crises and causes of them listed in Exhibits 2 and 3 as possible.

Furthermore, because crises are becoming increasingly complex, a secondary step must be to prepare for the simultaneous occurrence of crises. Again, the purpose is to broaden the organization's outlook. Preparing for and attempting to prevent crises means constantly testing and simulating as many breakdowns as possible.

The breadth demanded in the prevention and preparation phase stands in sharp contrast to the narrow scope required in the "coping" phase. The goal of the "coping" phase is to draw a tight, narrow net around a crisis that has occurred. This will contain the crisis and prevent it from spreading either inside or outside the organization. To accomplish this, growing numbers of organizations have seen fit to establish special organizational units known as crisis management units or crisis teams. Their full-time responsibility is to prepare for and handle special, emerging situations. They are free to do this because they are buffered from the normal daily demands of the organization.

Finally, one of the many lessons emerging from the still new field of crisis management is worth stressing. For this lesson, consider an analogy with patients who have been informed that they have terminal cancer. It is believed that people go through four distinct phases upon being informed that their condition is terminal. The first is denial. When denial is no longer effective, one becomes angry at the universe, at God, for "letting this happen to me." At some point deep depression sets in. Most patients who live long enough to make it to the fourth and last stage: acceptance. This stage is accompanied by the feeling. "This may

—Continued

Continued

EXHIBIT 2

TYPES OF CORPORATE CRISES

	TECHNICAL/ECONOMIC	
Cell 1		**Cell 2**
• Product/service defects		• Widespread environmental destruction/industrial accidents
• Plant defects/industrial accidents		• Large-scale systems failure
• Computer breakdowns		• Natural disasters
• Defective, undisclosed information		• Hostile takeovers
• Bankruptcy		• Governmental crises
		• International crises
Internal		**External**
Cell 3		**Cell 4**
• Failure to adapt/change		• Symbolic projection
• Organizational breakdown		• Sabotage
• Miscommunication		• Terrorism
• Sabotage		• Executive kidnapping
• On-site product tampering		• Off-site product tampering
• Counterfeiting		• Counterfeiting
• Rumors, sick jokes, malicious slander		• False rumors, sick jokes malicious slander
• Illegal activities		• Labor strikes
• Sexual harassment		• Boycotts
• Occupational health diseases		
	PEOPLE/SOCIAL/ORGANIZATIONAL	

be it for me, but at least I can make a last, positive statement with my life and pass something of value on to others."

These steps also apply to organizations managing crises. Keep in mind that denial, anger, and depression are powerful human emotions that are difficult to manage, particularly during a crisis. For this reason, organizations are well advised to raise their anxiety levels when they prepare for the worst, so that they will be able to cope when a real crisis occurs.

No one should ever underestimate the emotional costs of a disaster. While the two Tylenol poisonings cost the company approximately half a billion dollars in total, there were the formidable emotional costs as well. Many executives associated with Tylenol still awake with nightmares on the anniversaries of the poisonings. Also, consider the fact that NASA had to set up special medical hotlines to help its personnel handle the

emotional trauma associated with the Challenger disaster. In addition to the explosion itself and the tragic loss of the seven astronauts' lives, more than one member of NASA couldn't handle the question posed by their own children: "Daddy (Mommy) were you responsible for killing the astronauts?"[7]

Is your organization prepared to handle the financial and emotional costs of a major disaster? For those who work in the field of crisis management it is no longer a question of whether a major disaster will strike any organization, but only a matter of *when, how, what form will it take, and who and how many will be affected.*

---

7. As reported to the first author in direct interviews with NASA officials.

—*Continued*

Continued

EXHIBIT 3

CAUSES AND SOURCES OF CORPORATE CRISES

TECHNICAL/ECONOMIC

Cell 1

- Undetected, unanalyzed, unsuspected product defects
- Undetected plant/manufacturing defects
- Faulty detection systems
- Faulty backup design/controls

Cell 2

- Unanticipated, unanalyzed environmental conditions
- Faulty technical monitoring systems
- Faulty strategic planning
- Poor societal planning
- Poor global monitoring

Internal   External

Cell 3

- Faulty organizational controls
- Poor company culture, information/communication structure, rewards
- Poor operator training
- Poor contingency planning
- Human operator failures/errors
- Internal saboteurs
- Faulty employee screening

Cell 4

- Failure to design and implement new societal institutions
- Faulty social monitoring of criminal stakeholders
  - Disgruntled ex-employees
  - Assassins
  - Kidnappers
  - Terrorists
  - External saboteurs
  - Copycat killers
  - Psychopaths

PEOPLE/SOCIAL/ORGANIZATIONAL

Because we started with a simple model (Exhibit 1) that stressed the positive steps organizations can take to blunt crises, we will close with a simple model (Exhibit 5) that shows the steps that almost guarantee an organization will experience a major crisis from which it will not recover. Every organization therefore has a fundamental choice: Practice insurance against disaster or follow almost a guaranteed design for disaster.

Ian I. Mitroff is the Harold Quinton Distinguished Professor of Business Policy and co-director of the Center for Crisis Management at the Graduate School of Business, University of Southern California. He received a B.S. in engineering physics, an M.S. in structural mechanics, and a Ph.D. in engineering science and the philosophy of social science, all from the University of California, Berkeley.

Professor Mitroff is a member of the American Association for the Advancement of Science, Academy of Management, American Psychological Association, *American Sociological Association, Philosophy of Science Association, and the Institute for Management Science. He has published over 200 papers and eight books in the areas of business policy, corporate culture, managerial psychology and psychiatry, strategic planning, and the philosophy and sociology of science, and has appeared on numerous radio and television programs. His most recent book is* Business Not As Usual: Rethinking Our Individual Corporate, and Industrial Strategies for Global Competition, *published by Jossey-Bass in 1987.*

Paul Shrivastava is associate professor in the Graduate School of Business Administration, New York University. He has a bachelor's degree in mechanical engineering and master's and Ph.D. degrees in management. His management research interests include the strategic management of organizations, crisis management, policy-making processes, design of information and learning systems for strategic decision making, and management and administrative problems of developing countries. He has spoken on these topics at

—Continued

Continued

EXHIBIT 4

PREVENTIVE ACTIONS FOR ORGANIZATIONS

TECHNICAL/ECONOMIC

One-Shot (Short Term)

- Preventive packaging
- Better detection
- Tighter system security
- Tighter internal operations
- Better operator/management controls
- Tighten design of plants/equipment
- Install chain of command
- Install crisis management units

Repeated (Long Term)

- Design expert monitoring systems, networks
- Hold "continental" planning workshops
- Bring in outside experts; form permanent networks
- Design stores of the future
- Install systems-wide monitoring
- Establish crises command centers
- Perform periodic, mandated reviews

TIME and SPACE

Immediate Environment (Limited Individual Parts)

- Ensure emotional preparation
- Provide psychological counseling for employees
- Provide security training for all employees
- Provide detection training
- Install social support groups
- Provide media training

Extended Environment (Systematic)

- Develop profiles of psychopaths, terrorists, copycats, etc.
- Establish preventive hot lines
- Sponsor community watch groups
- Provide consumer education
- Establish political action groups
- Sponsor mental-health programs
- Establish counseling groups
- Re-examine organizational culture
- Establish permanent crisis management units
- Perform organization redesign
- Appoint ombudsmen, whistle-blowers
- Establish outside auditing teams to inspect vulnerabilities
- Provide media programs/training for all executives
- Work with industry associations
- Work with research centers
- Establish programs on business ethics

PEOPLE/SOCIAL/ORGANIZATIONAL

—Continued

Continued

EXHIBIT 5

STEPS FOR CRISIS
MANAGEMENT

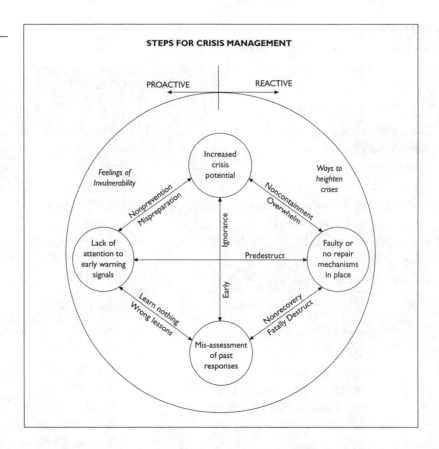

STEPS FOR CRISIS MANAGEMENT

national and international meetings and has published over three dozen articles on these topics in professional and scholarly journals.

Dr. Shrivastava has special expertise in managing decision-making processes in crises, and has chaired and conducted decision meetings and conference meetings in both corporate and professional environments. He was engaged in several major conflict resolution efforts that involved mediating conflicts between corporate, public, and government agencies. He now serves as executive director of the Industrial Crisis Institute, Inc., a nonprofit research organization devoted to resolving industrial crisis problems.

Dr. Shrivastava is the editor of Industrial Crisis Quarterly, *a coeditor (with Robert Lamb) of* Advances in Strategic Management, *and a contributing editor to the* Journal of Business Strategy. *He has received numerous awards and grants for his research from agencies such as the National Science Foundation, and is currently writing a book entitled* Bhopal: Anatomy of a Crisis, *to be published by Ballinger Publishing Company in 1987.*

Firdaus E. Udwadia received his M.S. and Ph.D. from the California Institute of Technology and his M.B.A. from the University of Southern California, where he is presently professor of business administration, civil engineering, and mechanical engineering. He is director of the Structural Identification Facility and co-director of the Center for Crisis Management at USC.

Professor Udwadia has received numerous awards, including the NASA Award for Outstanding Contributions to Technological Innovations, and has been a consultant to government and private industry in the areas of economic and engineering systems modeling, technology transfer, and project management and command, control and communications. His current research interest is in the area of crisis management.

SOURCE: Reprinted with the permission of the Academy of Management, PO Box 3020, Brior Cliff Manor, NY 10510–8020. *Effective Crisis Management*, Mitroff, I.I., et al., *Academy of Management Executive*, 1987, Vol. 1, No. 3. Reproduced by permission of the publisher via Copyright Clearance Center, Inc.

Appendix A

Corporate Ethical Performance Indicators Used in the Corporate Ethics Monitor Sept.–Oct. 1998

ETHICAL PERFORMANCE OF TELECOMMUNICATIONS COMPANIES

	BELL CANADA	BC TELECOM	BRUNCOR	MANITOBA	MT&T	QUÉBEC TEL	ROGERS CANTEL	SASKTEL	TELUS
Code of Ethics									
Existence	Yes	Yes	Yes	Yes	Yes	Yes	No	No	Yes
Date (Original/Most Recent Update)	1893, 1998	1980, 1992	No info, 1997	1979, 1998	1980, 1998	1988, 1996	Not applic	Not applic	1988, 1995
Reinforcement/Ethics Training	Yes	Yes	No	No	No info	Yes	No	No	Yes
Annual Sign-off	Yes	Yes	No	No	No info	No	Not applic	Not applic	Yes
Direct Job Creation									
Current Employment Canada	32,688	12,246	2,924	3,614	3,269	1,635	2,050	No info	8,972
Current Employment Worldwide	32,688	No info	2,924	3,614	3,269	1,635	No info	No info	No info
One Year Change (1998/97) Canada (%)	21.0%	No info	17.7%	Nil	8.4%	Nil	No info	No info	No info
Five Year Change (1998/93) Canada (%)	31.9%	(15%)	29.3%	18.0%	23.9%	4.3%	(35%)	No info	(15%)
Employment of Women									
Directors (#)	1 of 15	2 of 14	2 of 14	2 of 11	2 of 14	1 of 11	No info	2 of 7	2 of 13
Senior Management (%)	13%	12%	14%	No info	16%	17%	No info	No info	2%
Management (%)	47%	No info	No info	No info	28%	21%	No info	No info	24%
Workforce (%)	56%	No info	No info	No info	43%	43%	No info	No info	45%
Hiring and Promotion Programs									
Employment Equity	Yes	Yes	Yes	Yes	Yes	Yes	No info	Yes	Yes
Affirmative Action	Not applic	Yes	Yes	No	Yes	Yes	No info	Yes	Yes
Gender Programs & Policies	3	4	2	3	3	4	No info	1	3
Charitable Donations									
Total Amount 1997 ($)	$7.5 million	No info	No info	$600,000	No info	$220,541	No info	No info	$7.39 million
% Profit Before Taxes	0.5%	No info	No info	No info	1% +	0.4%	No info	No info	1% +
'Imagine Campaign' Pledge	Yes	No	No	Yes	Yes	No	No	No	Yes
Community Relations									
Scholarship Fund for Employees	No	No	No	No	Yes	No	No info	No	No
Scholarship Fund for Employees' Children	Yes	Yes	Yes	No	No	Yes	No info	No info	No
Matching Gift Program	Yes	Yes	No	Yes	Yes	No	No info	Yes	Yes
Sports/Athletic Support	Yes	Yes	Yes	Yes	Yes	Yes	No info	Yes	Yes
Health/Medical Support	Yes	Yes	Yes	Yes	Yes	Yes	No info	No info	Yes
Arts/Cultural Support	Yes	Yes	Yes	Yes	Yes	Yes	No info	Yes	Yes
Social/Welfare Support	Yes	Yes	Yes	Yes	Yes	Yes	No info	Yes	Yes
Progressive Staff Policies									
Corporate Sponsored Daycare (On-Site or Referral)	No	Yes, referral	No	No	Yes, referral	Yes, referral	No info	No	Yes, referral
Extended Maternity Leave	Yes	Yes	Yes	Yes	Yes	Yes	No info	Yes	Yes

	Co 1	Co 2	Co 3	Co 4	Co 5	Co 6	Co 7	Co 8	Co 9
Employee Assistance Program (EAP) (#)	4	4	1	3	4	4	No info	4	4
Health Program Plan (HPP) (#)	1	3	2	3	1	3	No info	2	3
Company Training Programs (1997) Amount $/Per Employee	$1,774	$1,800	$1,333	No info	$1,539	$43	No info	No info	No info
Tuition/Book Compensation	Yes (1)	100%	100%	100%	100%	100%	No info	100%	100%
Communications Programs (#)	5	3	5	3	2	4	No info	3	6
Retirement Counselling	Yes	Yes	Yes	Yes	Yes	Yes	No info	Yes	Yes
Same Sex Benefits	No info	Yes	No info	No	Yes	Yes	No info	No info	Yes
Gainsharing Programs									
ESOP - Yes/No/Employer Contribution	Yes, up to 6% of salary	Yes, 25% of share value	Yes, 25% of share value	Yes, 25% of share value	Yes, 25% of share value	Yes, 33% of share value	No info	No	Yes, 30% of share value
Stock Option Plan –Yes/No	Yes	Yes	Yes	Yes	Yes	Yes	No info	No	Yes
–Who Eligible	Officers	Senior managers	Key executives	Senior managers	Senior managers	Officers	No info	Not applic	Officers
Profit Sharing –Yes/No	Yes	No	Yes	No	Yes	No	No info	No	No
–Who Eligible	Senior management	Not applic	Non-unionized	Not applic	All	Not applic	No info	Not applic	Not applic
Labour Relations/Health and Safety									
Unionized (% of Workforce)	80%	70%	30%	95%	67%	93%	No info	80%	70%
Decertification Cases (#, Yr)	None	None	No info	None	None	None	No info	No info	None
Unjust Dismissals	No info	None	None	None	2	None	No info	No info	None
Strikes/Lockouts in Last 10 Years	1	3	Nil	No info	1	1	No info	2	Nil
Workplace Accidents and Injuries Data Supplied	Yes	Yes	No	Yes	Yes	No	No info	No	Yes
Lost Time Accidents (Per Million Hours Worked)	7.86	No info	No info	No info	12.43	No info	No info	No info	3.92 (2)
Occupational Health & Safety Cases (#, Fines)	None	No info	No info	No info	None	None	No info	No info	None
Occupational H&S Awards	None	Yes	No info	Yes	None	None	No info	No info	None
Environmental Management									
Formal Environmental Code Date (Original/Recent Update)	1990, 1993	1989, ongoing	1990, no info	1992, 1994	1990, 1994	No	No info	No	Yes, 1992, 1996
Undertaken Environmental Audits (Yes/No; Internal Staff/External Staff/Both)	Yes, both	Yes, internal	Yes, both	Yes, both	Yes, internal	Not applic	No info	Not applic	Yes, both
Frequency of Environmental Audits	2 year cycle	Not regular	Annual	No info	Yes	Not applic	No info	No info	Annual
Employees with Full Time Environmental Responsibility	14	29	Nil	2	1	Nil	No info	No info	4
Senior Position with Full Time Environmental Responsibility	Director	Director	None	Manager	Manager	None	No info	No info	Manager
Staff Environmental Committee	Yes	Yes	Yes	Yes	Yes	No	No info	No info	Yes
Environmental Committee of the Board of Directors	Yes	Yes	No	No	No	No	No info	No info	No
Environmental Reports to the Board of Directors (#/year)	2	2	2	Not regular	4	No	No info	No info	4
Issue Public Environmental Report (Yes/No; Frequency)	Yes	No	No	Yes (3)	No	No	No info	No	Yes
Charitable Giving to Environmental Organizations	Yes	Yes	No info	Yes	Yes	No	No info	No info	Yes

ETHICAL PERFORMANCE OF TELECOMMUNICATIONS COMPANIES—*CONTINUED*

	BELL CANADA	BC TELECOM	BRUNCOR	MANITOBA	MT&T	QUÉBEC TEL	ROGERS CANTEL	SASKTEL	TELUS
Environmental Management—continued									
Annual Report on Recycled Stock	Yes	Yes	Yes	Yes	Yes	No	No info	Yes	Yes
Environmental Section in Annual Report	No	No	No	No	No	No	No info	No info	No
Environmental Performance									
Environmental Prosecutions in Last 10 Years (#, Fines)	No info	None	None	None	None	No info	No info	No info	None
Environmental Awards	No info	10	No info	No info	1	None	No info	No info	1
Recycling Programs (#)	11	7	7	6	8	5	No info	2	7
Report Quantities Waste Recycled	Yes	Yes	Yes	Yes	Yes	No	No info	No info	Partial
Environmental Expenditures 1997 ($)	No info	$5–7 million	No info	$100,000	$60,000	No info	No info	No info	$924,000
Ethical Sourcing and Trading									
Commercial Relations with Repressive Regimes	China	China, Indonesia	No info	No	No	No	No info	No info	No
Candor Quotient (%)									
1998 Current Review	92%	85%	80%	88%	96%	95%	3%	49%	92%
1995 Previous Review	94%	96%	88%	87%	90%	100%	Not applic	66%	89%

Notes:
(1) Limit of $1,500 per year for tuition.
(2) Frequency of disabling injuries, accounting for hours of exposure.
(3) One report published in 1996.
Research Report filed by Jason Potts

Information for this comparison is drawn from the files of EthicScan Canada. Where the performance of a company is described as "No info," the company may have a salutary record, but the facts are not known to EthicScan researchers. The regular fact checking process involves corporate database reviews, interviews, and two requests that the company review, update and validate the major findings on file.

Ethics Audit Program Annual Audit Questions

Questions to Be Asked at Each Business Unit

Responsibility
- Is there a person at the business unit who is responsible for answering questions on and administering the *Code?* Who is this?
- Do the employees know of this person's responsibility with regard to the *Code?*

Awareness and Commitment
- Has the *Code* been distributed to all employees and managers?
- Have all managers signed the Representation Letter confirming that "during the past year, [they] and, to the best of their knowledge after due inquiry, [their] immediate subordinates who hold management responsibilities have complied with the *Code* and have taken appropriate actions to ensure compliance by other employees (who are [their] subordinates) and by contractors and consultants (who [they] have engaged or are responsible for)?
- Have all employees signed-off during the past year that they have observed the *Code* and will continue to do so, and that they know of no unreported breaches of the *Code?*
- Are all new employees signing-off when they join the company?
- Do all suppliers, contractors, and consultants receive a written notification that it is understood they will abide by the *Code* or specific provisions of it such as those on gifts or inducements, conflicts of interest, health and safety, or environmental protection?

Training
- Do new employees receive training on the *Code* when they join before they sign the *Code* sign-off?
- Have existing employees received training on the *Code* during the past year? What is the nature of this training?
- Do suppliers, contractors, and consultants receive a briefing on the *Code* and their need to observe it?

Commitment and Support Provided by Management
- Has management above the business unit shown personal commitment and support for the *Code* and the values on which it is based? How? (Speeches, memos, news articles, etc . . .)
- Has the management of the business unit shown personal commitment and support for the *Code* and the values on which it is based? How? (speeches, memos, use in screening merit and promotion decisions, etc.)
- Has there been reinforcing publicity in newsletters, or through publicity of good or bad examples of behavior?

Operations
Regarding the business unit's systems for answering ethics inquiries, bringing ethics concerns forward for investigation, and investigation and sanction:
- Do employees and managers have confidence in these systems?
  - Survey ten employees and five managers
- What are the annual usage statistics of each system?
- Were any significant ethical problems not handled appropriately?
- Were actions taken on a timely and appropriate basis?
- Do any items or issues require clarification to avoid further problems?
- Are there any suggestions for improvement of the *Code* or the processes involved?
- Do timely periodic reports to division management exist covering the activities of these systems?
- Are all items reported?

Questions to Be Asked of Each Division Operation, Assessment and Continuous Improvement
- Are there personnel assigned (specify who) and systems in place to monitor and ensure:
  - compliance with the *Code* in each business unit and at the division level?

—Continued

Continued

- effectiveness of the procedures for complying with the *Code* in such matters as training, sign-off, inquiry, investigation and sanction?
- assessment of operations and risks?
- reinforcement and support?
- Are necessary actions taken on timely and appropriate bases?
- Are timely reports prepared for and reviewed by division management?
- Are objectives related to the *Code* built into the divisional and business unit yearly operating objective statements?
- Are appropriate actions taken/reinforced by division management?

- Is there appropriate feed-forward reporting to head office to allow remedial action and solutions to be shared across the company?
- Does head office react and respond to feed-forward or requests for clarification?
- Has management above the division shown personal commitment and support for the *Code* and the values on which it is based? How? (speeches, memos, news articles, etc . . .)
- Are there any issues needing further clarification and/or suggestion?
- Are there any issues that should be reported to the board for information or action?